PARADISE LOST

AN AUTHORITATIVE TEXT

BACKGROUNDS AND SOURCES

CRITICISM

➤➤➤ A NORTON CRITICAL EDITION ◄◄◄

JOHN MILTON

PARADISE LOST

AN AUTHORITATIVE TEXT
BACKGROUNDS AND SOURCES
CRITICISM

➤➤➤◄◄◄

Edited by

SCOTT ELLEDGE

CORNELL UNIVERSITY

W · W · NORTON & COMPANY

New York · London

W. W. Norton & Company, Inc., 500 Fifth Avenue, New York, N.Y. 10110

Library of Congress Cataloging in Publication Data

Milton, John, 1608–1674.
  Paradise lost.

  (A Norton critical edition)
  Bibliography: p.
  I. Elledge, Scott. II. Title.
PR3560   1975   821'.4   75–12732

PRINTED IN THE UNITED STATES OF AMERICA

3 4 5 6 7 8 9 0

ISBN 0-393-04406-8 CL
ISBN 0-393-09230-5 PBK

Contents

Criticism

Preface

The text for this edition of *Paradise Lost* is a modernized version of the second of the two editions published under Milton's supervision. I have retained capital letters only where modern conventions call for them; I have put in Roman type the many proper nouns that are italicized in the original editions; and I have spelled all but a few of the words as they are now spelled. But with a very few exceptions I have retained Milton's punctuation because his periods, colons, semicolons, and commas are like rests of various lengths in a musical score, and to alter the punctuation in an effort to make the syntax clearer would be to change Milton's rhythmic notation.

My footnotes supply more information than do many school editions but not so much, I trust, as to overwhelm an intelligent but relatively uninitiated reader. I have not cited passages in the classical and Renaissance poems that Milton echoed, paraphrased, or otherwise alluded to in *Paradise Lost* because such notes do not enhance the poem for the readers I have in mind, who are likely to read Milton before they read Homer, Virgil, or Spenser. Many reasonably well-educated readers will not have read the Bible, either, but because even a piecemeal, *ad hoc* knowledge of the poem's principal source does make *Paradise Lost* more comprehensible and interesting, I have quoted the Scriptures liberally in my notes, and have included in the Backgrounds and Sources section a selection of the most relevant Biblical passages. And for readers equally uninformed about Christian theology I have also reprinted passages from Milton's *Christian Doctrine* which summarize some of the beliefs that Milton assumed his audience would be familiar with. In the footnotes I have supplied only the barest of explanations of geographical and mythological references in the poem, but I have been generous with notes on the meanings of words. Many words I have simply glossed by an obsolete meaning that comes closer to Milton's intention than any current connotation; of others I have given derivations that reveal a metaphorical vividness obscured by usage and unrecognizable to readers less conscious than Milton of root meanings.

One of the rewards of studying all Milton's poems is to discover how a knowledge of Milton's total achievement illuminates *Paradise Lost*. But notes and appendices are not adequate substitutes for such first-hand discoveries, and I have not, therefore, tried to do more by way of a background than to sketch in a biographical context in my Introduction, and to reprint in the Backgrounds and Sources section a few selections from Milton's prose.

The anthology of critical essays on the chief topics for a study of *Paradise Lost* is intended to help students discover new reasons for admiring and enjoying the poem rather than to introduce them to the work of critics who wish to show that Milton is, or has been overrated. Much of the anti-Milton criticism of the recent past now seems curiously out-of-date, and the most valuable essays on Milton today come largely from critics who are interested not so much in qualifying Milton's achievement as in examining it. Limits of space and the demands of my topical scheme prevented my including the criticism of several of the most interesting contemporary writers on Milton, but their works, along with those of many others, are listed in the Bibliography.

Among those who have helped me in the preparation of this edition, I should like to thank especially my colleagues Sanford Budick, Michael Colacurcio, Andrew Ettin, Charles Levy, Isaac Rabinowitz, and David Novarr. And among those who typed various parts of the manuscript I shall always remember most warmly Berniece Roske, Choosri Lohavicharn, and Marian Novick.

SCOTT ELLEDGE

Introduction

Samuel Johnson once implied that John Milton was vain enough to have created Adam in his own image. Milton, he noted, wore his hair shoulder-length, "according to the picture of Adam" in *Paradise Lost*. The implication of Johnson's sardonic remark is unfair, as Johnson himself might have admitted, but it is not entirely false, as Milton might have agreed. Milton was a good-looking man and may have been vain about his physical appearance, but more important, he was, in a good and ancient sense of the word, proud. He did not give Adam shoulder-length hair because he himself wore his hair that way, but he would have conceived of Adam as the embodiment of the ideal human virtues and attitudes that he himself hoped to exemplify in his own life.

In an autobiographical digression in one of his political pamphlets Milton admitted that he had "an honest haughtiness and self-esteem," and added that the envious could call that pride if they wished. He had been accused by another writer, in a rough and tumble debate, of frequenting bordellos and leading an otherwise dissolute life, and he may be excused for taking himself so seriously. But it was like Milton not only to refer to his pride without embarrassment, but to speak of the relationship between his virtue and his ambition. He had in his youth, he said, been convinced

> that he who would not be frustrate of his hope to write well hereafter in laudable things, ought himself to be a true poem, that is, a composition and pattern of the best and honorablest things—not presuming to sing high praises of heroic men or famous cities, unless he have in himself the experience and practice of all that which is praiseworthy.

Of his hope to "write well" he had already informed the readers of an earlier pamphlet. Explaining why he had temporarily abandoned his private studies to write propaganda, and why he had chosen a "manner of writing" inferior to his gifts as a poet, Milton had not hesitated to explain why his hope was in fact a confident ambition:

> [In my youth] it was found that [whatever I wrote] in English or other tongue, prosing or versing, but chiefly the latter, the style, by certain vital signs it had, was likely to live. But more latelier . . . I began thus far to assent to [the opinion of certain Italian men of letters] and divers of my friends here and at home, and not less to an inward prompting which now grew daily upon me, that by labor and intent study (which I take to be

my portion in this life), joined with a strong propensity of nature, I might perhaps leave something so written to aftertimes, as they should not willingly let it die.

He added that he had decided not to write this immortal work in Latin because in that language he could not hope to achieve better than second rank. He would write in English—would, in fact, try to "adorn" his "native tongue." Nor would he mind losing the international, Latin-reading audience (and presumably an international fame) if he could do for England "what the greatest and choicest wits of Athens, Rome, or modern Italy, and those Hebrews of old did for their country." His confident hope was simply to equal Moses, Sophocles, Virgil, and other great writers.

Milton must have known how hard it sometimes is to draw a line between the vice of pride or arrogance and the virtue of what he called *magnanimity*. Aristotle had used the Greek equivalent of the word to describe the "attitude of one who, rightly conscious of his own great merits, is indifferent to praise except from those whose approval is valuable [and who] regards the chances of fortune with equanimity" (*Oxford English Dictionary*). But Milton certainly knew the difference between magnanimity and pride, for in *Paradise Lost* he distinguished clearly between Satan's self-deceived sense of his own merit and Christ's magnanimity. And it was human magnanimity which he himself valued and which he ascribed to Adam. The angel Raphael, sent down by God to instruct Adam, who was worried about the inferiority he felt in the presence of Eve, told his pupil that "Oft times nothing profits more/Than self-esteem, grounded on just and right." Adam later forgot that advice, and his fall was in effect a lapse in magnanimity, a failure to remember who he was and what his powers, as well as his responsibilities, were. It was Aristotelian magnanimity, or high-mindedness, that allowed Milton to hope that his poem would find an audience worthy to judge it, would "fit audience find, though few."

The classical concept of magnanimity was, Milton thought, a good one under which to subsume various intellectual and ethical characteristics of the man God created "in his own image." For Aristotelian magnanimity included both "loftiness of thought" and "lofty courage." And when Milton gives us our first, stunning view of Adam and Eve in the Garden and says that the man and woman were not equal (meaning "not the same") in either sexual characteristics or in human responsibilities, he says that God created Adam "for contemplation and valor." These preeminent pagan virtues, wisdom (or prudence) and courage (or fortitude), were also among the seven Christian virtues; they were the secular heart of the Christian humanist's notion of the dignity and distinction of man, and they were essential to the ideal Renaissance man, who was both active and contemplative. It is not unreasonable to suppose that if Milton thought Adam was formed to live a life of contemplation and valor, he also thought his own life should exemplify those magnanimous ideals—as in fact it did.

Before the Fall, Adam's contemplation was a means of glorifying God and enjoying him, for to contemplate meant to observe God's works and to think about them. His intellect, or reason, made all the laws of nature intuitively available. But after the Fall, his intuitive powers were somewhat impaired. He was left with enough reason to enable him to be virtuous, but not enough to know God and all the laws of nature as fully as he had once known them. Consequently sons of Adam could only, in Milton's words, "repair the ruins of our first parents," by "labor and intent study."

No other English poet ever studied as much as Milton did, but *contemplation* means more than study. For Milton, it also meant what is implied in the Biblical admonition "be still and know that I am God." It meant maintaining a patient, receptive, listening attitude. It meant being alert to the voice of the heavenly spirit, who had once inspired the prophets, or to the voice of the Muse who could still put into the mouths of poets words whose truth might approach, though not attain, the Truth of divine revelation. Like meditation, contemplation was an exercise and a way of life, and a means of gaining the wisdom and the power needed for seeing visions and writing great poems. As Samuel Johnson said, Milton's "studies and meditations were an habitual prayer."

In "Il Penseroso" the thoughtful youth says he will be content to live with Melancholy if that goddess will bring with her

> Him that yon soars on golden wing,
> Guiding the fiery-wheeled throne,
> The cherub Contemplation,
> And the mute Silence hist along,
> 'Less Philomel will deign a song.

Here Contemplation is called a cherub to associate its powers with those of the cherubim in the vision of Ezekiel, the cherubim that ushered in the vision of God on his throne. Among the orders of angels, the cherubim were supposed to be distinguished by their ability to contemplate God. But this passage is revealing in another way to anyone who knows that from the age of twelve, in spite of weak eyes and frequent headaches, John Milton "hardly left [his] studies or went to bed before midnight," and that after he became blind and had begun to write *Paradise Lost*, he composed his poetry in the dark early hours of English winter mornings. In *Paradise Lost* (III.38), he compares the poetry his Muse inspired in him to the song of the "wakeful bird," the nightingale that "sings darkling."

Night, the time of "Silence" and freedom from the "noise of folly," was the time for contemplation, inspiration, and creativity.

In *Comus*, written when Milton was twenty-five, one of the characters says:

> Wisdom's self
> Oft seeks to sweet retired solitude,
> Where with her best nurse Contemplation,
> She plumes her feathers and lets grow her wings,
> That in the various bustle of resort
> Were all too-ruffled, and sometimes impaired.

Here the allusion is to a myth in Plato's *Phaedrus*, in which Socrates describes the long upward progress of the soul from an earthbound, body-imprisoned life towards heaven and a pure vision of ideal truth, goodness, and beauty. Like those of Ezekiel's vision, the details of Plato's myth are not perfectly comprehensible, but the idea is clear: as it begins to see the good, the beautiful, and the true in the world around it, the soul sprouts wings that may carry it eventually to heaven, though not before the wings have recovered from damage suffered in the soul's encounter with the physical world which it aspires to transcend. Perhaps another Greek myth was also in Milton's mind. Three years later he wrote a friend that he was beginning to sprout the wings of Pegasus, the winged horse who symbolized poetic inspiration.*

Though Milton was an activist during the revolutionary Civil War and the Commonwealth (1641–1660), vigorously debating with overwhelming learning and sometimes brutal rhetoric the issues involved in the struggle for religious and civil freedom, his life was predominantly contemplative. Even when he was writing on education, or freedom of the press, or the evils of the divorce laws, or the corruption of the clergy, or the tyranny of the monarchy, his life and style were those of a scholar. Milton was not unsociable. He was blessed with friends. He did not hate women (though his first marriage was not happy and his daughters brought him little joy). He loved life, he enjoyed walking and other physical exercise, and he had a strongly sensual nature (though he also loved and practiced temperance). He loved music and knew a great deal about it; he enjoyed singing ("he sang in his gout fits") and played the organ and bass viol. He read poetry (or had it read to him) every day of his life. Milton does not fit the ignorant stereotype of

---

* "[The] philosophical and religious system [of Marsilio Ficino, a Renaissance Platonist whose works Milton knew] leads to contemplation as the true end of man; and with this the arts are vitally linked, for he places their genesis in the contemplative experience. 'All those who have invented anything great in any of the nobler arts did so especially when they took refuge in the citadel of the Soul.' Poetry in particular is of this origin, for the poet is akin to the prophet, as being divinely inspired." Frances Yates, *The French Academies of the Sixteenth Century*, pp. 4–5.

the nay-saying Puritan. Still, his significant life, one suspects, was the solitary life of a man motivated by love of learning and art, by the desire to be a good man, and by an ambition to win fame as a poet. Learning all that was known in his day of history, science, philosophy, and religion, and reading essentially all of western literature was, like writing poetry, lonely work.

If Milton suffered an identity crisis, evidence of it has not survived. He seems always to have known who he was and what he would do. He was a poet, and he would prepare himself to write a poem that "aftertimes would not willingly let die." His father, a moderately well-to-do London business man and an accomplished musician, "destined [him] from a child to the pursuits of literature," and afforded him an expensive education consisting of about seven years of private tutoring, four years at St. Paul's School, seven years at Christ's College, Cambridge, six years of postgraduate private study, and fifteen months of travel, mainly in Italy. Until some time in his early twenties, Milton shared his father's assumption that he would become a minister, but neither of them would have thought such a calling at odds with an ambition to become a learned man and a distinguished poet (compare Donne, Herbert, and Herrick). There is evidence that the father at one point may have objected to his son's preoccupation with his own poetry, and no doubt he was disappointed when the young man decided he could not in good conscience enter the ministry of the Church of England. But the father's support of his son's ambition is evident in the fact that Milton never worked for pay except for a short time as a schoolmaster and a few years when employed by Parliament.

There was no identity crisis because the signs of who he was were so clear so early. He enjoyed learning languages because he enjoyed language itself and because he loved to read the books that his mastery of language made available to him. His first sign of genius was linguistic. His Latin was so good that as a young man he wrote Latin poems said to be the equal of any written after Latin became a "dead language." He loved Italian, and Dante and Petrarch, before he learned to love Italy. When he was twenty-one, eight years before he went abroad, he wrote sonnets in Italian so perfect that for two centuries biographers erroneously assumed they were written after he had spent a year speaking the language. His Greek opened Homer and Plato and the New Testament to him in their original language, and his Hebrew and Aramaic enabled him to read the Old Testament and the Jewish commentators like a scholar. In addition to French and Spanish, he may also have been able to read Anglo-Saxon. At the age of forty-three he studied Dutch with the help of Roger Williams, the Baptist founder of Rhode Island. It was his excellent ear, more perhaps than his extraordinary intellect and memory, that enabled him to be enchanted by the sound of English and Latin and Greek poetry—and by the songs of the Old Testament, which he maintained were the greatest of all lyric poetry. And it was his ear that made him so skillful in imitating those poets whose works kept him up reading by candle-light till midnight.

His early successes with his own verses, and the praise they prompted, fed his ambition. By the time he took his M.A. in 1632, at the age of twenty-three, he had written three masterpieces, "On the Morning of Christ's Nativity," "L'Allegro," and "Il Penseroso," and during the next six years, while he lived his contemplative life with his parents in the country (going up to London occasionally to buy books and "learn something new in mathematics or in music"), he wrote poems that alone would have assured his immortality—among them, *Comus* and "Lycidas." As far as we know, Milton had none of the painful problems associated with the insecurities of youth—or at least none that his faith in God and himself would not easily solve. During the first thirty years of his life he made himself one of England's most learned men and prepared himself to become one of her two or three finest poets. But if this period of studious, even laborious, leisure was a true poem, it was a pastoral poem: and to fit himself to write *Samson Agonistes*, *Paradise Lost*, and *Paradise Regained*, perhaps it was necessary that the next period of his life be another kind of poem. At any rate, his life did change, from passive to active, from pastoral to heroic, and the next twenty years furnished many challenges to his valor.

Valor is simply the self-confident strength of mind or spirit that enables a person to stand firm and endure. It is a quality that Milton, like Satan, showed more of than Adam did. Before he left for Italy (and the extended holiday that separated these two periods of his life) Milton was advised against arguing with his Catholic hosts about religion, but that advice, Milton says, he was unable to follow. Though he had decided against becoming an ordained minister, he did not intend to neglect what he took to be his Christian duty to be a witness to religious truth as he saw it. And that truth was, broadly speaking, Puritanism, which he may have been introduced to by a Puritan tutor, shortly before the Pilgrims landed at Plymouth Rock. His study of the Bible, as well as of the works of commentators, theologians, and historians, had led him to certain convictions different from those of the church of England. What most appealed to Milton in the Christian doctrine as he understood it was not Christ's promise of eternal life to all who believed in him, but the gospel of Grace, the gift of a New Testament, which by annulling the repressive laws of the Old Testament made men free. The Puritans believed that the Reformation had not gone far enough in freeing individuals from an ecclesiastical law that impaired Christian liberty. There was in the teaching of some Puritans a strong tendency toward a utopian (and anarchistic) state in which every person under God should be free to answer only to his own God-given conscience, or "right reason." The aim was not social disorder, of course, but rather a perfect social order (a congregation or commune) in which everyone disciplined himself without the aid of human authority. Christian liberty, as the Puritans conceived it, was therefore a threat not only to the hierarchical structure and authority of the Roman Catholic Church and the Church of England, but of civil governments whose power was maintained by the help of ecclesiastical power. Speaking out on these matters, in Italy or England, required courage.

When Milton returned home in 1639, England was already in the early stages of a revolution that was directed at both Church and State. Some years later Milton described his adjustment to the situation:

> As soon as I was able, I hired a spacious house in the city for myself and my books; where I again with rapture renewed my literary pursuits, and where I calmly awaited the issue of the contest, which I trusted to the wise conduct of Providence, and to the courage of the people. The vigor of Parliament had begun to humble the pride of the bishops. As long as the liberty of speech was no longer subject to control, all mouths began to be opened against the bishops; some complained of the vices of the individuals, others of those of the order. They said that it was unjust that they alone should differ from the model of other reformed churches; that the government of the church should be according to the pattern of other churches, and particularly the word of God. This awakened all my attention and my zeal. I saw that a way was opening for the establishment of real liberty; that the foundation was laying for the deliverance of man from the yoke of slavery and superstition; that the principles of religion, which were the first objects of our care, would exert a salutary influence on the manners and constitution of the republic; and as I had from my youth studied the distinctions between religious and civil rights, I perceived that if I ever wished to be of use, I ought at least not to be wanting to my country, to the church and to so many of my fellow-Christians, in a crisis of so much danger; I therefore determined to relinquish the other pursuits in which I was engaged, and to transfer the whole force of my talents and my industry to this one important object.

And so, at the age of thirty-two, in the prime of life and at what might have been the beginning of his most productive years, Milton published the first of many scholarly but polemical essays in support of Christian liberty as he understood its implications for various aspects of his society, and for twenty years he remained as much in the thick of revolution as a scholar and man of letters could be. He wrote first against the power of the bishops in an ecclesiastical hierarchy not authorized by the Scriptures. This illegal power had itself been corrupted by the bishops, who had extended the power of ecclesiastical courts. Like most revolutionaries, Milton was interested in the reform of education. In 1644 he published a description of a method and a curriculum designed to teach all young men to be both lovers of learning and national leaders. As for civil liberties, Milton defended the right of Parliament to depose Charles I on the ground that kings derive their power from the people, who may retrieve that power when it is exercised by tyrants. Milton was more liberal than many Puritans in that he dared express his fear of a people's collective power to tyrannize over individuals.

The clearest examples of the way Milton identified his own need for personal freedom with his notions of justice are *Areopagitica*, an essay on the freedom of the press, and his tracts on the laws governing divorce. In *Areopagitica* Milton argued against a law requiring that any piece of writing be approved by censors before publication; he did not deny the right of the state to prosecute writers *after* publication. This eloquent plea for a right basic to democracy is no less persuasive because it reflects Milton's indignation at the thought that the kind of person who would consent to be a censor should have the authority to pass on the truth or propriety of anything written by John Milton.

About the relationship between Milton's tracts on divorce and his own marriage, the facts are these. At the age of thirty-three, after a brief courtship, Milton married seventeen-year-old Mary Powell. Her father was a Royalist; he lived in Oxfordshire, where the King's support was strong; and he owed Milton money. A few months after the wedding, when the King's cause was prospering, Mary returned to the home of her parents. She had been quickly convinced of the impossibility of living happily with an anti-Royalist, a poet, and a scholar who had opened a small school for boys in his own home. She did not return to Milton till three years later, when the ultimate defeat of the Royalist army seemed imminent. The first of Milton's essays on divorce appeared within a year after his wife left him. His argument was essentially that adultery, the only legal cause for divorce, was not so offensive to the true purpose of marriage as the enforced cohabitation of incompatible people. It is foolish, Milton said, for a man to "prattle about liberty in assembly and marketplace who at home endures the slavery most unworthy of man, slavery to an inferior."

Milton's notions about religious, civil, and domestic liberty rested on his conviction that God gives people free will, for freedom from social tyranny would be meaningless if the actions of individuals were determined by a super-human agency, such as Fate, God, or

Nature. Predestination would not only remove purpose from life, it would remove character and identity from individuals, for it would prevent challenges that call for valor. Most of Milton's writings, prose and poetry, are affirmations of the kind of human dignity that is implied in the liberal concept of individual freedom and responsibility.

Milton's triumphs as a public figure were considerable. It was an honor to be sought out by the Parliament to serve as Latin secretary to the Council of State, and as chief apologist for the government. In public, international debate, conducted in Latin against the best scholars and writers the exiled monarchy could muster, Milton could rightly consider himself as a kind of heroic champion. In his old age he was often visited by foreigners who wished to meet the man who had written those great, fighting manifestos in "defense of the English people." But all during this period Milton's private life had few rewards, and he had need for a great deal of courageous patience. His career as a poet had been interrupted, and his contemplative life was disturbed by events in his domestic as well as his public life.

Within a year after she returned, Mary bore her first child, a crippled daughter with a speech defect. Her third child, a son named John was born five years later and died the following year, a month after his mother had died in bearing a third daughter. Milton was left a widower with three little girls. Four years later, at the age of forty-seven, after he had become totally blind and about the time he began to write *Paradise Lost*, he married Katharine Woodcock, who within a year bore a daughter. Mother and daughter died five months later.

The following year Cromwell died. But two years later, in 1660, when the failure of the Commonwealth was clear to everyone else and the return of Charles II from France to restore the monarchy was only a few months away, Milton's courage did not fail. He published one more appeal to his fellow countrymen, entitled optimistically "A Ready and Easy Way to Establish a Free Commonwealth." For a short time after the Restoration Milton faced the possibility of being hanged as the most widely read of those who had justified the beheading of Charles I, and he was forced to go into hiding until influential friends could intercede on his behalf. He lost a considerable amount of money when the new government annulled the bonds issued by the Commonwealth government.

From 1660 till his death in 1674, a period of great creativity, Milton was able to live a quiet life, domestically managed by a third wife. But there was no sudden change in his cheerfully disciplined life of creative contemplation. One evidence of this continuity is the fact that, between 1655 and 1661, working from a remarkable memory and with the help of people who read to him and took dictation from him, Milton completed his *De Doctrina Christiana*, a five-hundred-page exposition of Christian belief derived from his interpretation of the Bible. Excerpts from it in the Backgrounds and Sources section of this edition of *Paradise Lost* will illustrate Milton's methods and will suggest the thoroughness with which he tried to make clear for himself and others what the Bible means. The style of his Introduction suggests that Milton conceived of his function as similar to that of the first great Christian theologian, St. Paul; by writing in Latin and addressing all Christians everywhere, Milton may have thought he could speed an international union of protestants of all sects and the establishment of a universal Christian liberty that would free mankind from all forms of tyranny. Milton was still revising the work at the Restoration, however, and it was not published in his lifetime. Whatever he hoped or planned for the practical uses of the work, the *Christian Doctrine* was chiefly a labor of love conceived and executed by a man who would rather read and think and write about man and God than do anything else. It was a product of the same contemplation and valor that made possible the achievement of *Paradise Lost*.

II

Milton's decision to serve his God and his countrymen outside the establishment was consistent with his ambition to write immortal poems, tragic or epic, that would be "doctrinal and exemplary to a nation," that would "imbreed and cherish in a great people the seeds of virtue and public civility." And though *Paradise Lost* is not simply a didactic poem, one of its purposes was to persuade its readers to believe what Milton thought to be the truth. It is, therefore, in a special sense of the word, rhetorical, and as readers we are influenced by our perception of the man who is trying to persuade us. But Milton did not, as poets often do, try to create a character for his speaker. The "I" of *Paradise Lost* is not a persona or mask, as those terms are used in literary criticism. He intended that the "I" of the poem be no different from the historical John Milton, and he took pains to make the identification explicit in the introductions to Books III, VII, and IX—just as he had identified himself in extensive autobiographical sketches in three of his polemical pamphlets. In fact, in one of these pamphlets, written years before he began *Paradise Lost*, he said he thought that "a poet, soaring in the high region of his fancies with his garland and singing robes about him, might without apology speak more about himself" than the writer of a political speech might do.

Readers of *Paradise Lost* will not, therefore, understand the poem better or enjoy it more by trying to distinguish between John

Milton and the human bard who sings the epic. The garland and robe of his inspiration do not obscure the "human face divine" of the blind John Milton, nor does the epic tone of his song disguise the character of his voice. To be sure, what Milton chose to tell about himself in the autobiographical passages in the poem creates a recognizable character, and we may assume that his aim was to make his audience believe him to be a "reliable narrator," not only because his Muse is divine, but because his humanity is benevolent. Still, in the introductions to Books I, III, VII, and IX, where Milton most clearly distinguishes his own words from those "dictated" to him by his Muse, we are told some very personal things. He has been blinded by a *gutta serena* (translated literally in the line "So thick a *drop serene* hath quenched their orbs"), a disease which leaves the eyes clear and able to move normally—a fact he alludes to in "these eyes that roll in vain." His blindness has cut him off from one means of contemplation: he can no longer look at the glories of the Book of Nature or see intelligence, beauty, or love in human faces. But he hopes that his physical blindness is being compensated by spiritual vision, as it was in the case of Homer and certain men gifted with prophetic powers. In three of the passages he tells his readers how he composes. At night before he retires he "reads," and is nourished by, the poetry of the Bible and classical literature. Then during sleep and the very early hours of the dawn, his Muse voluntarily dictates to him his "unpremeditated, harmonious" verse. The poet has no sense of having himself willed the process in any way except by asking the Muse for aid. Milton tells of his ambition to excel all other epic poets by redefining the words *heroic* and *heroic poem*, to surpass the achievements of other Renaissance epic poets, including perhaps his own countryman Spenser. And he tells of his fears of failure: he may have waited too long to decide upon his subject and begin writing; it may be too late in the history of culture and taste for any epic poet to hope to succeed; he may be past the prime of his poetic power; the climate of England may be, as was commonly said, too cold to produce art equal to that of Greece and Rome; and before completing the epic, he has fallen on the evil and dangerous days of the Restoration.

If his success in the face of all these difficulties and doubts depended solely upon himself, Milton says, he would fail. For without the gift of inspiration he would be speechless or his words would not be equal to the task his subject imposed upon his language. Milton deliberately avoided identifying the Muse beyond tentatively calling her Urania. She is not one of the pagan muses; she is whoever inspired Moses, the historian, and David, the poet of the Psalms. She is heavenly, and though probably not specifically the Third Person of the Trinity, she is a holy spirit whose source is God. Milton does not claim the authenticity of the divinely inspired authors of the Bible. That he does not disclaim such authority proves nothing, of course. Like any poet, he simply knew that inspiration seems to come miraculously from outside oneself.

Most of *Paradise Lost* is narrated from the point of view of a Muse; and only a few of the authorial intrusions are clearly those of the human medium, John Milton. In many passages it is difficult to know whether Milton thought his readers would attribute the comment, judgment, or interpretation to the ethos of the poet or to a divine ethos speaking through him. Readers should keep that difficulty in mind as they judge the propriety or artistic effectiveness of the various ways in which the narrative mode of the epic admits the intrusion of the speaker. For Milton depended upon his audience's agreement to abide by the conventions of the epic genre, according to which the omniscient narrator does not deceive; the reader does not have to discover for himself the motives of the speaker or the other "characters"—he is simply told; nor is the reader expected to disagree with the explicit judgments of the narrator—mainly because the story in its broad outline is already known and the ethical character of the agents and their actions is already a matter of general agreement. Satan's motives were "envy and revenge"—period. When the good angel Uriel is deceived, it is the Muse who generalizes that

> neither man nor angel can discern
> Hypocrisy, the only evil that walks
> Invisible, except to God alone. (III.682)

But some generalizations, such as those predictions uttered by fallen Adam about the male unlucky in love, sound more like the opinions of the poet than those of the Muse:

> for either
> He shall never find out fit mate, but such
> As some misfortune brings him, or mistake,
> Or whom he wishes most shall seldom gain
> Through her perverseness, but shall see her gained
> By a far worse, or if she love, withheld
> By parents, or his happiest choice too late
> Shall meet, already linked and wedlock-bound
> To a fell adversary. (X.898)

Such instances are rare, and as here, are better considered lapses in the poet's control than intentional shifts in point of view.

There are, however, many intentional and effective interpolations, interjections, or asides spoken in the human voice by means of which the epic bard acts a little like the chorus of a Greek tragedy in addressing, and identifying with, the audience. In these intrusions we are made aware of our own fallen state by hearing the sound of the poet's humanity. One of Milton's simplest and most common devices for achieving this effect is the pronoun *our*. In the opening lines of the poem we may not notice the intent of *our* in "what cause/Moved our grand parents," but in Book IV, we are struck by the poet's awareness of our common destiny when, describing the Garden, he comes to the Tree of Life and then says,

> and next to Life
> Our death the Tree of Knowledge grew fast by. (220)

And we may be similarly startled a little later on by his saying, "So spake our general mother" (492). The means are somewhat different, calling for a more specifically historical comparison between Adam and Eve and us, between then and now, when Milton says that the naked couple entering the bridal bower were "eased the putting off/These troublesome disguises which we wear" (739).

Another rhetorical device is the interjection "O," which by calling attention to the bard's feeling reminds us that a fellow human being is addressing us. The first of these occurs in the opening description of Hell,

> O how unlike the place from which they fell,

where the poet, more than simply underlining the irony, helps us feel the pity and fear in our sympathy for Satan's tragedy. Understood properly, even the following apostrophe may seem less like preaching and more like a choral (human) lament:

> O shame to men! Devil with devil damned
> Firm concord holds, men only disagree
> Of creatures rational. (II.496)

Consider also the effect of the opening lines of Book IV, "O for that warning voice . . . ," where the poet expresses the wish of a sympathetic and involved audience that somehow an eloquent and inspired person could have warned our parents and thus prevented our suffering as well as theirs.

The utterances preceded by "O" are often apostrophes, rhetorical figures by which a speaker pretends to turn from his audience and address a person, thing, or idea, as in the opening line of "Lycidas": "Yet once more, O ye laurels," or later, "O Fountain Arethusa." In such turnings, a speaker may change his tone and pace, and in that way seem to intrude by calling attention to himself. In *Paradise Lost* the effect of Milton's apostrophes is to make the audience feel that though the poet is addressing some thing or idea, or some person not in the audience, he is in fact looking right at the audience and inviting them to share his thought and feeling. Almost without exception the attitude they express, though not inappropriate to an omniscient Muse, is that of ironic discovery. It is a

xxiv   ·   *Introduction*

common human form of simultaneous distancing and identifica-
tion, and a characteristically Miltonic form of discovery. Milton
and his readers (if they are fortunate) share appropriate tragic
feelings about not only the Fall but about each of the events that
constitute its story. In line three we *feel* the subject in the words *all
our woe,* and as soon as our eyes have become adjusted to the
visible darkness of hell, we can see and feel the fearful irony of
Satan's tragic catastrophe (the word means "overturning") :

> O how unlike the place from which they fell!

That is the prototypical response to the ironic content of tragic
reversal, or turning, or fall—the painful recognition of the contrast
between the happy "then" and the sad "now," the happy "there"
and the sad "here," the happy expectation and the sad event.

Our attitude towards the characters and their fate does not
change in the course of the poem as it might in a novel, and one
reason for this is that Milton keeps reminding us of our fallen
condition with apostrophic instructions:

> [Raphael:]   O fall
> From what high state of bliss into what woe! (V.542)
>
> O innocence/Deserving Paradise (V.445)
>
> O when meet now such pairs (VIII.57)
>
> O much deceived, much failing, hapless Eve (IX.404)
>
> O how unlike/To that naked glory! (IX.1114)
>
> [Adam:]   O fleeting joys
> Of paradise, dear bought with lasting woes! (X.741)
>
> [Michael:]   O that men
> (Canst thou believe?) should be so stupid grown. (XII.115)

Technically speaking not all these exclamations are apostrophic,
but their effect is essentially the same as other sad recognitions of
original irony expressed in true apostrophes:

>   honor dishonorable,
> Sin bred, how have ye troubled all mankind
> With shows instead, mere shows of seeming pure,
> And banished from man's life his happiest life,
> Simplicity and spotless innocence. (IV.315)
>
> Sleep on Blest pair (IV.773)
>
> How didst thou grieve then, Adam, to behold
> The end of all thy offspring (XI.754).

In the last of these Milton amplifies the irony by observing that the
vision of the destruction of man by the Flood made Adam weep
another flood of tears.

Finally, the most admired of Milton's intrusions are the similes, where the range of knowledge brought in to explain, interpret, or enhance seems to be more like the fruit of the poet's study of myth, poetry, history, science, and everyday human life than like the invention of the omniscient Muse. The similes tell us much about the poet, to be sure, but in the complexity of their analogies they tell us much more about the idea, image, or event they illuminate than do the similes of Homer or Virgil. Like all the other authorial interruptions in *Paradise Lost* they are part of a pattern of great integrity, and contribute to our sense of the authority of Milton's voice.

III

Milton's notion that his poetry should serve God, England, and his fellowmen was not revolutionary. Ancient ideas about the various uses of poetry were current in the Renaissance. Plato had disapproved of poetry not because it was useless, but because poets could not be trusted to use its power in the interests of truth. Aristotle had taught literary theorists to study the art of poetry by considering the affective powers of poetry, and had observed, without regard to morality, that tragedies seemed to have a healthful effect on audiences—to tone up their psyches, to free them from psychological debilitation. In *Areopagitica* Milton referred to the effectiveness of the moral teaching of Spenser's *Faerie Queene*, an unfinished Christian epic that Milton hoped to surpass, and said that he dared to let it be known that he considered "our sage and serious poet Spenser" to be "a better teacher than Scotus or Aquinas." But that was not a very daring revelation. The Presbyterians would not have thought highly of poets *or* Scholastics, and Catholics would have agreed that in a sense Dante was a better teacher than Aquinas.

Milton's understanding of the function of poetry was conventional and followed generic lines. Epics were particularly useful to *nations*; tragedies produced therapeutic purgings of pity and fear in *individuals*; and odes and hymns (i.e. lyrics), when they were songs of praise, served not only God himself but his worshippers as well. Milton wrote examples of all three genres—*Paradise Lost*, *Samson Agonistes*, and the "Nativity Ode," among others, and *Paradise Lost* contains all three genres. Poetry was a means, not an end. It made instruction and moral training and spiritual invigoration more attractive and more directly effective because as Milton said in *Of Education* poetry is "more simple, sensuous, and passionate" than the subtleties of the logic and rhetoric of prosaic philosophy or theology.

In his youth Milton considered writing a nationalistic epic that would remind his fellow Englishmen of their glorious heritage and incite them to greater glories. He had once thought that God might favor England by making it the leader in a reformation that would usher in the Millennium. His experience with the realities of revolution may have been the reason for his finally choosing a subject from the history of mankind rather than from the history of England, but a more important reason, probably, was his conviction that man's ultimate regaining of Paradise depended not upon the reformation of societies but on the perfection of individuals. Neither nations nor religious sects could accomplish what could be accomplished only privately by the contemplation and valor of men and women. He addressed his justification of God's ways not to "man," but to "men." And most important, perhaps, was his notion about the affective power of poetry. No doubt, its rhetorical powers could be used to teach virtue by example. But he may have thought its most telling effect was not intellectual but psychological. For some years, apparently, Milton planned to write *Paradise Lost* as a tragedy, and that early preference for the tragic rather than the epic genre is explained in his preface to *Samson Agonistes*. There he said that men had always thought classical tragedy "the most profitable of all other poems" because, as Aristotle had observed, it could "by raising pity and fear, or terror, purge the mind of those and suchlike passions, that is, temper and reduce them to just measure with a kind of delight, stirred up by reading or seeing those passions well-imitated." Certainly it is such affective and curative powers that are most available to modern readers of *Paradise Lost*—the powers, in Milton's words, "to allay the perturbations of the mind and set the affections [i.e., "the feeling aspects of consciousness"] in right tune."

IV

The word *event* in *Paradise Lost* almost always means "outcome," as its Latin derivation suggests. Milton uses its synonym *success* in a similarly literal way to mean simply "what followed," or "the consequence." *Paradise Lost* is a poem about "events" and "successes"—a story of causes and consequences. The central successes are failures: the success of Satan's revolt, the success of Satan's temptation of Eve, the success of Eve's persuading Adam to eat the apple—even the success of God's demand for full justice, full punishment, and death. The event of Satan's evil revolt was the creation of a perfect universe full of beautiful creatures, including an ideal human pair. The event of Satan's tempting Eve was the curse that her heel would crush the serpent's head. The success of Eve's persuading Adam to join her in eating was a separation from him. The success of God's demand for justice and death was mercy and life everlasting.

Tragedy and comedy are different ways of seeing and presenting ironic successes. When Satan, back in hell after his success on earth, bites into a beautiful apple and finds it full of ashes—when his last word in the poem, *bliss*, turns into a hiss—we recognize a grim joke. When Adam and Eve's grab for power and God-like wisdom produces weakness and clouded vision, we feel the pity and fear of tragedy. When Satan's effort to drag man to hell results in God's offer to man of a paradise within, happier far, fortunate readers feel that the human tragedy is part of a divine comedy.

The irony of events or successes in *Paradise Lost* informs or structures its plot as its verbal or rhetorical irony colors its style. The structural irony reflects an age-old view of history, or man's fate, fostered by Hebrew and Greek literature, but the stylistic irony reflects an element of Milton's character. Something in the man (and in some of his readers, at least) enjoys not only such discoveries as that when Satan is tempted he is tempted to be good, but also such discoveries as the implicit irony in the ambiguity of the word *fruit* in the first line. The heavily ironic rhetoric of Satan during the war in heaven represents a perversion (sarcastic) of the witty irony that Milton loved.

The verbal ambiguities that are scattered through the poem like land-mines are binary. *Or* is a favorite conjunction of Milton's. The logic, rhetoric, and diction of the poem are full of pairs of meanings. The argument has two sides, the ideas are antithetical, or paradoxical: justice and mercy; freedom and obedience; pride and love. Much of the poem consists of conversation between two people. The dramatic expression of temptation is dialectical. The conflicts in *Paradise Lost*, like those in all Milton's major poems, are debates. Naturally the poetry is rhetorical.

But critics who say they dislike Milton because his poetry is rhetorical object not so much to the persuasive speeches of the characters in the poem as to the artificiality of Milton's language—to the unnaturalness of its diction and syntax. Some, presumably, simply do not like elevated style (which of course is *not* always sublime) because it seems fake or pretentious. Taste is partly a matter of inheritance, perhaps; certainly it is a matter of conditioning. Some beginning readers of *Paradise Lost* may have to learn to enjoy Milton's style. But through all the revolutions in literary taste during the last three centuries, readers young and old, naive and sophisticated, have never ceased to be enchanted by Milton's language any more than listeners of a wide range of musical training have ceased to be ravished by Bach's fugues.

Another argument of those who object to Milton's rhetoric is that Milton has designs on his readers—is out to convert them—

and that his poetry is better called rhetoric, following the distinction made by Yeats when he said, "We make out of the quarrel with others, rhetoric, but of the quarrel with ourselves, poetry." But Milton's "great argument" is not a quarrel *with* the reader. The argument of *Paradise Lost* is the story. Here, as in so many places, seeing Milton's full meaning depends on a reader's knowledge of older meanings of the word. In Roman rhetoric the argument was that part of a forensic speech in which the speaker gave the facts— told the audience, judge or jury, what happened. It was in itself part of the proof. Obviously, the facts well presented may be more convincing than any amount of what today we could call argument —that is arguments constructed to support our conclusions logically. Milton's argument consisted of telling it the way it was, and when we consider that "it" was in effect everything, we understand why Milton spent fifty years of labor and study in preparation for his undertaking. The important thing to remember about Milton's designs on the reader is that *Paradise Lost* is not *De Doctrina Christiana* but a *poem*, based on what Milton and his audience believed to be history, revealing the kind of superior symbolic truth that poetry is capable of, and affecting its readers in such a way as to set their affections in right tune—that is, to produce a healthy psychic state, rather than, as in Satan's speeches to Eve, to induce a conversion that would lead to action.

The effect of the poem depends heavily on the tragic mode of the last four books. Books IX and X constitute the central tragic action: the catastrophe brought upon an almost perfect man and woman by a mistake of the head and heart, producing pity and fear in the audience. Books XI and XII constitute another kind of tragedy, something like that of *Oedipus at Colonus* or *Samson Agonistes*. It celebrates the "martyrdom," the "fortitude of patience," of heroic mankind. Such prototypical tragic actions require of the audience no special religious views. Still, the effect of the poem may be richer for those who see in Adam's experience in the last two books the pattern of the Christian concept of redemption. Michael takes Adam through the steps of regeneration that lead to salvation through faith. The preview of the history of the children of Adam, as Michael presents it, is a story of heroic agony, of conflict that leads to victory, and Milton has made that story of man's suffering struggle, as told in the Bible, a kind of objectification of Adam's own torture during the gradual unfolding of the universal meaning of his fall. Adam's last words, a summary of the lessons learned in that agony, are capped by the quiet, simple words of his acceptance of Christ, "whom I now/Acknowledge my Redeemer blest." Adam's last words mark the end of his fall and the beginning of his ascension. They are the crux of Adam's death and resurrection.

But old Adam does not have the last words. Michael's reply moves away from (or above, depending on your point of view) the specifically Christian mystery of grace through the death of Jesus, to that part of Christian teaching that has proved to be most ecumenical:

> This having learnt, thou hast attained the sum
> Of Wisdom; hope no higher, though all the stars
> Thou knew'st by name, and all th' ethereal powers,
> All secrets of the deep, all nature's works,
> Or works of God in heav'n, air, earth, or sea,
> And all riches of this world enjoyedst,
> And all the rule, one empire: only add
> Deeds to thy knowledge answerable, add faith,
> Add virtue, patience, temperance, add love,
> By name to come called charity, the soul
> Of all the rest: then wilt thou not be loth
> To leave this Paradise, but shalt possess
> A paradise within thee, happier far. (XII.575–87)

"Add love . . . the soul/Of all the rest," and you may regain an inner paradise, more valuable than any outer paradise, any environmental perfection or social utopia. Charity, not magnanimity, is the ultimate human duty and divine blessing.

Nor does Michael, the divine messenger, have the last word. In Milton's wise irony, that last word is given to the woman whose earlier "last" word before leaving Adam was followed by her withdrawing her hand from Adam's and going off, alone and liberated, to perform a work of supererogation. Now she speaks the last speech in the poem, just before she and Adam join hands and in their new union take their solitary way. The last words in her speech, to be sure, allude to a motherhood in which God will be her spouse, but this Christian element need not influence our secular response to her human love for Adam:

> With thee to go,
> Is to stay here; without thee here to stay
> Is to go hence unwilling; thou to me
> Art all things under heaven, all places thou. . . . (XII.615–19)

It is not only for Adam and Eve that we weep our "natural tears," but for ourselves, as well. And the weeping, in some miraculous way, makes us feel free and strong—sets our affections in right tune.

The Text of
Paradise Lost

A Note on the Footnotes

I have written these notes for people who will be reading *Paradise Lost* for the first time, and I have assumed that the most helpful notes for beginners are those which (1) call attention to obsolete or uncommon meanings of words, (2) supply illustrative citations to the Bible and to passages in Milton's *Christian Doctrine* that furnish answers to theological questions, and (3) explain allusions to myths, history, and geography. My aim in giving the derivations of words is not to suggest that Milton's English was more Latinate than that of other Renaissance English writers, but to uncover buried meanings of English words. Much of the metaphorical power of Milton's diction depends on the reader's knowing root meanings that Milton knew.

Like previous editors of *Paradise Lost*, I have made use of the work of my predecessors. I have not acknowledged specific debts to eighteenth, nineteenth, and early-twentieth-century editors, but I have at appropriate places given credit to the original contributions of the four men whose notes I consulted constantly. These are referred to unceremoniously as Hughes, Bush, Fowler, and Madsen. Their editions are as follows: *John Milton: Complete Poems and Major Prose*, ed. Merritt Y. Hughes (New York, The Odyssey Press, 1957); *The Complete Poetical Works of John Milton*, ed. Douglas Bush (Boston, Houghton Mifflin Co., 1965), *The Poems of John Milton*, ed. John Carey and Alastair Fowler (London, Longmans, Green and Co., Ltd., 1968), *Paradise Lost*, ed. William G. Madsen (New York, Random House, Inc., 1969).

I have not cited the sources for the derivations, synonyms, and definitions in my footnotes. Nor have I put quotation marks around brief definitions quoted verbatim. In almost all instances my source was *The Oxford English Dictionary* (OED).

The following abbreviations appear in the footnotes:

CD	Milton's *Christian Doctrine* (i.e., *De Doctrina Christiana*)
CE	The Columbia Edition of *The Works of John Milton*, ed. Frank Allen Patterson and others. 18 vols. New York, 1931–8.
D	Dutch
Fr	French
Gk	Greek
It	Italian
L	Latin
LL	Late Latin
ML	Mediaeval Latin
NEB	*The New English Bible, with the Apocrypha.* Oxford: The Oxford University Press, 1970. Biblical quotations not so indicated are from the Authorized King James Version.
OE	Old English
OED	*The Oxford English Dictionary*
OT	Old Testament
NT	New Testament
PL	*Paradise Lost*
PR	*Paradise Regained*

In references to passages in *Paradise Lost*, a line number without a Book number refers to a line in the same Book as the passage being annotated.

Paradise Loſt.
A
POEM
IN
TWELVE BOOKS.

The Author
JOHN MILTON.

The Second Edition
Reviſed and Augmented by the
ſame Author.

LONDON,
Printed by *S. Simmons* next door to the
Golden Lion in *Alderſgate-ſtreet,* 1674.

The Verse

The measure is English heroic verse without rhyme, as that of
Homer in Greek and of Virgil in Latin; rhyme being no necessary
adjunct or true ornament of poem or good verse, in longer works
especially, but the invention of a barbarous age, to set off wretched
matter and lame meter; graced indeed since by the use of some
famous modern poets, carried away by custom, but much to their
own vexation, hindrance, and constraint to express many things
otherwise, and for the most part worse than else they would have
expressed them. Not without cause therefore some both Italian and
Spanish poets of prime note have rejected rhyme both in longer and
shorter works, as have also long since our best English tragedies, as
a thing of itself, to all judicious ears, trivial and of no true musical
delight; which consists only in apt numbers, fit quantity of sylla-
bles, and the sense variously drawn out from one verse into an-
other, not in the jingling sound of like endings, a fault avoided by
the learned ancients both in poetry and all good oratory. This
neglect then of rhyme so little is to be taken for a defect, though it
may seem so perhaps to vulgar readers, that it rather is to be
esteemed an example set, the first in English, of ancient liberty
recovered to heroic poem from the troublesome and modern bond-
age of rhyming.

Book I

The Argument

This first book proposes, first in brief, the whole subject, man's disobedience, and the loss thereupon of Paradise wherein he was placed: then touches the prime cause of his fall, the Serpent, or rather Satan in the Serpent; who revolting from God, and drawing to his side many legions of angels, was by the command of God driven out of heaven with all his crew into the great deep. Which action passed over, the poem hastes into the midst of things, presenting Satan with his angels now fallen into hell, described here, not in the center (for heaven and earth may be supposed as yet not made, certainly not yet accursed) but in a place of utter darkness, fitliest called Chaos: here Satan with his angels lying on the burning lake, thunderstruck and astonished, after a certain space recovers, as from confusion, calls up him who next in order and dignity lay by him; they confer of their miserable fall. Satan awakens all his legions, who lay till then in the same manner confounded; they rise, their numbers, array of battle, their chief leaders named, according to the idols known afterwards in Canaan and the countries adjoining. To these Satan directs his speech, comforts them with hope yet of regaining heaven, but tells them lastly of a new world and new kind of creature to be created, according to an ancient prophecy or report in heaven; for that angels were long before this visible creation, was the opinion of many ancient Fathers. To find out the truth of this prophecy, and what to determine thereon he refers to a full council. What his associates thence attempt. Pandemonium the palace of Satan rises, suddenly built out of the deep: the infernal peers there sit in council.

> Of man's first disobedience, and the fruit
> Of that forbidden tree, whose mortal taste
> Brought death into the world, and all our woe,
> With loss of Eden, till one greater Man
> Restore us, and regain the blissful seat,   5

I. Argument. *the center:* i.e., of the earth. *heaven and earth:* the created universe. *yet not made.* I.e., chaos and hell existed before the Creation. *utter:* outer, extreme, complete. *Canaan:* Palestine. *Fathers:* early Christian theologians. Cf. *CD*, I.vii.E. (Passages in Milton's *Christian Doctrine* which, like this one, are cited without reference to the Columbia Edition of Milton's works (*CE*) can be found in the Backgrounds and Sources section, pp. 304–51. The capital letter in such citations refers to a passage which I have so marked for easy reference.)

1–5. This statement of subject is full of double meanings: the Hebrew name *Adam* means man; *first* may mean in time and in importance; *fruit* means profit or enjoyment and result or consequence, as well as apple; *mortal* means deadly as well as human. *Eden* means the garden of Eden, or Paradise, but it also means heavenly perfection. Being both man and god, Christ was *a greater Adam.*

Sing Heav'nly Muse, that on the secret top
Of Oreb, or of Sinai, didst inspire
That shepherd, who first taught the chosen seed,
In the beginning how the heav'ns and earth
Rose out of chaos: or if Sion hill   10
Delight thee more, and Siloa's brook that flowed
Fast by the oracle of God; I thence
Invoke thy aid to my advent'rous song,
That with no middle flight intends to soar
Above th' Aonian mount, while it pursues   15
Things unattempted yet in prose or rhyme.
And chiefly thou O Spirit, that dost prefer
Before all temples th' upright heart and pure,
Instruct me, for thou know'st; thou from the first
Wast present, and with mighty wings outspread   20
Dove-like sat'st brooding on the vast abyss
And mad'st it pregnant: what in me is dark

6. With the verb *sing* (meaning "sing through me") Milton invokes the aid of a superhuman inspiration, as did the epic poets before him; but Milton's Muse is not one of the nine pagan Muses—it is an abstraction of the wisdom and power of the Judeo-Christian divinity, identified here as the Muse that inspired Moses, who was then believed to have been the author of the first five books of the Bible. Milton's allusion conflates Moses the lawgiver, who received the ten commandments on Mount Horeb (Deut. 4.10) or on Mount Sinai (Exod. 19.20), with Moses the literal shepherd and figurative pastor, and with Moses as a kind of bard, or inspired singer, who may teach the past and reveal the future. See "Truth and Poetry," pp. 400–1.

10–15. By adding that the Muse may prefer to dwell on Mount Zion in Jerusalem, near *Siloa's brook*, Milton invites a comparison with the Greek Muses, who also favored mountains and their nearby fountains or streams. The oracle of Delphi was by the Castalian Spring on the side of Mount Parnassus, sacred to the Muses and to Apollo, the god of light, music, poetry, and prophecy; the *oracle of God* was near a spring (*Siloa's brook*) which was near Mount Zion (*Sion Hill*), where God spoke to his people through priests and prophets. Cf. Isa. 2.3: "Come ye, and let us go up to the mountain of the Lord . . . and he will teach us of his ways . . . for out of Zion shall go forth the law." In Greece the Muses were thought to live also near the spring Hippocrene, on the side of Mount Helicon (*th'Aonian mount*), a spring created by the hoof-stamp of Pegasus, a winged horse that symbolized poetic inspiration because he could fly to the top of Mount Olympus, the home of the gods. The earth, in Milton's time, was believed to be covered with three layers of atmo-

sphere, the second of which ("middle region") reached to the top of mountains. The highest heaven of the pagan gods, Mount Olympus, was in the *middle air* (see 514–7); and it is above this region that Milton's Pegasus must carry him on his *no middle flight*, since Milton intends to sing of true heaven, which is far above the universe. See "Universe," pp. 389–91. *pursues:* tries to accomplish.

16. This line is a translation of a line in Ariosto's Renaissance epic *Orlando Furioso*. Milton is not boasting; he is emphasizing the greatness and seriousness of his undertaking—a heroic poem that makes the ways of God seem just—a poem that makes man's fate seem reasonable and psychologically satisfying, an epic in which the hero is not an active warrior but patient, or suffering, mankind, including the first and second Adams.

17–22. *And chiefly thou O Spirit* may not refer to the same being as the Heavenly Muse, but the difference, if any, is slight. Here Milton emphasizes the creative power and wisdom needed for such great undertakings as creating the world and writing this definitive poem, and he calls, not upon the third person of the Trinity, but upon God. *Dove-like.* In the Gospels the Holy Spirit is said to have assumed the shape of a dove when it descended to earth. *sat'st.* The King James Version reads (Gen. 1.2) "moved," but the original Hebrew word means "hovered" or "brooded." *Abyss* (Gk *abyssos* without bottom) is a synonym for "the deep" of Gen. 1.2. *Vast* implies "waste" as well as "large," and helps to suggest the chaos out of which Milton says the world was made. *Brooding . . . mad'st it pregnant* is not, according to Fowler, a mixed metaphor, but "a deliberate allusion to the Hermetic doctrine that God is both masculine and feminine."

Illumine, what is low raise and support;
That to the highth of this great argument
I may assert Eternal Providence,   25
And justify the ways of God to men.
    Say first, for heav'n hides nothing from thy view
Nor the deep tract of hell, say first what cause
Moved our grand parents in that happy state,
Favored of Heav'n so highly, to fall off   30
From their Creator, and transgress his will
For one restraint, lords of the world besides?
Who first seduced them to that foul revolt?
Th' infernal Serpent; he it was, whose guile
Stirred up with envy and revenge, deceived   35
The mother of mankind, what time his pride
Had cast him out from heav'n, with all his host
Of rebel angels, by whose aid aspiring
To set himself in glory above his peers,
He trusted to have equaled the Most High,   40
If he opposed; and with ambitious aim
Against the throne and monarchy of God
Raised impious war in heav'n and battle proud
With vain attempt. Him the Almighty Power
Hurled headlong flaming from th' ethereal sky   45
With hideous ruin and combustion down
To bottomless perdition, there to dwell
In adamantine chains and penal fire,
Who durst defy th' Omnipotent to arms.
Nine times the space that measures day and night 50
To mortal men, he with his horrid crew
Lay vanquished, rolling in the fiery gulf
Confounded though immortal: but his doom
Reserved him to more wrath; for now the thought
Both of lost happiness and lasting pain   55

24. *to the highth of:* as far as is possible by means of. *argument:* L *argumentum* the part of a proof that rests on facts (as distinct from *ratio*, the part that depends on reason); a sign by which something is known. Though the word means also "theme" or "subject," Milton refers here to the narrative of the poem.
25. *assert:* (L *asserere* to put one's hand on the head of a slave to set him free or protect or defend him) take the part of, champion. *Eternal:* without beginning or end. *Providence:* (L *pro* before + *videre* to see; foresight) foreknowing, beneficent, and efficient concern. Cf. *CD*, I.viii.A, B, and C, and other uses of the word in the poem: I.162; II.559; XII.564, 647.
28. *what cause.* This opening question is an epic convention. Homer and Virgil both began by asking the Muse to tell which gods (or why a god) had caused the events of the story.
29. *grand:* supremely deserving of the title (equivalent to the prefix *arch*-).

32. *For:* because of. *besides:* otherwise.
34–49. Cf. Isa. 14.12–15, p. 375, and Rev. 20.1–2, p. 386.
43. *impious.* The L word means disrespectful of one's parents or one's country as well as of one's god.
45. *ethereal:* (Gk *aithein* to ignite, blaze) of the ether, the element supposed to fill the outer regions of the universe; not earth, air, fire, or water, it was not earthly but heavenly, and eternal.
46. This image of a meteorite is more distinct in the description of Satan's fall at 745 ("like a falling star"). *hideous:* Causing dread or horror. *ruin:* (L *ruere* to fall violently) ruins, rubble; fall, destruction. *combustion.* Cf. *combustible*, line 233.
53. *confounded:* (L *con* together + *fundere* to pour; *confundere* to mix up, confuse) ruined, routed; spoiled, corrupted.
53. *doom:* sentence of punishment.

Torments him; round he throws his baleful eyes
That witnessed huge affliction and dismay
Mixed with obdúrate pride and steadfast hate:
At once as far as angels ken he views
The dismal situation waste and wild,   60
A dungeon horrible, on all sides round
As one great furnace flamed, yet from those flames
No light, but rather darkness visible
Served only to discover sights of woe,
Regions of sorrow, doleful shades, where peace   65
And rest can never dwell, hope never comes
That comes to all; but torture without end
Still urges, and a fiery deluge, fed
With ever-burning sulphur unconsumed:
Such place Eternal Justice had prepared   70
For those rebellious, here their prison ordained
In utter darkness, and their portion set
As far removed from God and light of heav'n
As from the center thrice to th' utmost pole.
O how unlike the place from whence they fell!   75
There the companions of his fall, o'erwhelmed
With floods and whirlwinds of tempestuous fire,
He soon discerns, and welt'ring by his side
One next himself in power, and next in crime,
Long after known in Palestine, and named   80
Beëlzebub. To whom th' Arch-Enemy,
And thence in heav'n called Satan, with bold words
Breaking the horrid silence thus began.
    "If thou beest he; but O how fall'n! how changed

---

56. *baleful:* full of suffering; of pernicious influence.

57. *witnessed:* expressed, revealed.

60. *dismal:* calamitous, as well as depressingly dark.

63. *darkness visible.* Cf. Job 10.20–22: "Let me alone, that I may take comfort a little, before I go whence I shall not return, even to the land of darkness and the shadow of death; a land of darkness, as darkness itself; and of the shadow of death, without any order, and where the light is as darkness."

68. *Still:* constantly. *urges:* stimulates, excites, provokes. The idea is antithetical to that of *rest,* and the word was often used in a context of fire, as in "urge like fire."

70. *Such place.* The biblical authority for Milton's location and description of hell is cited in *CD,* I.xxxiii.D.

72. *utter darkness.* Speaking of the faith of some gentiles and the lack of faith among his own people, Christ said (Matt. 8.11–12): "Many shall come from the east and west and shall sit down with Abraham, and Isaac, and Jacob, in the kingdom of heaven. But the children [who were born to the kingdom—

(*NEB*)] shall be cast out into outer darkness [the place of wailing—(*NEB*)] and gnashing of teeth."

73–74. From hell to earth (*the center*) is twice as far as from earth to heaven, which lies just beyond the outer shell of the universe. *utmost pole:* the end of the axis of the universe. See "Universe," pp. 389–91.

78. *welt'ring:* rolling in the waves.

81. *Beëlzebub* is called "the prince of the devils" in Matt. 12.24, and the name may have been a synonym for Satan. Its meaning, "lord of the flies," suggests a mythical origin in the worship of a god who delivered men from insects or of one who was himself infested by flies (Hughes). But according to Fowler, Milton's portrayal of him "seems rather to be based on an allegorization invented by St. Jerome," in which the fly is a symbol of pertinacity. Beëlzebub "never ceases to infest the human race in every way."

82. *Satan:* the Hebrew word for adversary.

84. Cf. Isa. 14.12: "How art thou fallen from heaven, O Lucifer, son of the morning!"

From him, who in the happy realms of light   85
Clothed with transcendent brightness didst outshine
Myriads though bright: if he whom mutual league,
United thoughts and counsels, equal hope
And hazard in the glorious enterprise,
Joined with me once, now misery hath joined   90
In equal ruin: into what pit thou seest
From what highth fall'n, so much the stronger proved
He with his thunder: and till then who knew
The force of those dire arms? Yet not for those,
Nor what the potent victor in his rage   95
Can else inflict, do I repent or change,
Though changed in outward luster, that fixed mind
And high disdain, from sense of injured merit,
That with the mightiest raised me to contend,
And to the fierce contention brought along   100
Innumerable force of Spirits armed
That durst dislike his reign, and me preferring,
His utmost power with adverse power opposed
In dubious battle on the plains of heav'n,
And shook his throne. What though the field be lost?   105
All is not lost; the unconquerable will,
And study of revenge, immortal hate,
And courage never to submit or yield:
And what is else not to be overcome?
That glory never shall his wrath or might   110
Extort from me. To bow and sue for grace
With suppliant knee, and deify his power
Who from the terror of this arm so late
Doubted his empire, that were low indeed,
That were an ignominy and shame beneath   115
This downfall; since by fate the strength of gods
And this empyreal substance cannot fail,
Since through experience of this great event
In arms not worse, in foresight much advanced,
We may with more successful hope resolve   120
To wage by force or guile eternal war
Irreconcilable, to our grand foe,
Who now triúmphs, and in th' excess of joy
Sole reigning holds the tyranny of heav'n."
    So spake th' apostate angel, though in pain,   125
Vaunting aloud, but racked with deep despair:

98. *injured:* done an injustice to. *merit:* just claim to reward.
107. *study of:* application of thought to; zealous effort to achieve.
109. I.e.: What else does 'not being overcome' mean?
114. *Doubted:* feared for.
116. *fate. PL* is a Christian definition of fate as Providence, but Satan thinks of fate as a power greater than God. Cf. *CD,* I.ii.A, and other uses of the word in the poem: I.133; II.197, 232, 393, 550, 559, 560, 809; III.120; V.527; VI.869; IX.689, 885, 927; X.265, 480; XI.181. *Gods.* It is true that God refers to the angels as *gods* (III.341), but Satan's intent here may be to suggest that God is just another angel.
117. *empyreal:* (Gk *empyros* in fire, fiery) of the empyrean, the highest heaven; heavenly. See "Universe," pp. 389–91.

And him thus answered soon his bold compeer.
   "O Prince, O Chief of many thronèd Powers,
That led th' embattled Seraphim to war
Under thy conduct, and in dreadful deeds   130
Fearless, endangered heav'ns perpetual King;
And put to proof his high supremacy,
Whether upheld by strength, or chance, or fate;
Too well I see and rue the dire event,
That with sad overthrow and foul defeat   135
Hath lost us heav'n, and all this mighty host
In horrible destruction laid thus low,
As far as gods and heav'nly essences
Can perish: for the mind and spirit remains
Invincible, and vigor soon returns,   140
Though all our glory extinct, and happy state
Here swallowed up in endless misery.
But what if he our conqueror (whom I now
Of force believe almighty, since no less
Than such could have o'erpow'red such force as ours)   145
Have left us this our spirit and strength entire
Strongly to suffer and support our pains,
That we may so suffice his vengeful ire,
Or do him mightier service as his thralls
By right of war, whate'er his business be   150
Here in the heart of hell to work in fire,
Or do his errands in the gloomy deep;
What can it then avail though yet we feel
Strength undiminished, or eternal being
To undergo eternal punishment?"   155
Whereto with speedy words th' Arch-Fiend replied.
   "Fall'n Cherub, to be weak is miserable
Doing or suffering: but of this be sure,
To do aught good never will be our task,
But ever to do ill our sole delight,   160
As being the contrary to his high will
Whom we resist. If then his providence
Out of our evil seek to bring forth good,
Our labor must be to pervert that end,
And out of good still to find means of evil;   165
Which ofttimes may succeed, so as perhaps
Shall grieve him, if I fail not, and disturb
His inmost counsels from their destined aim.
But see the angry victor hath recalled
His ministers of vengeance and pursuit   170
Back to the gates of heav'n: the sulphurous hail

128–29. *Powers, Seraphim.* See "An-
gels," in p. 395.
  134. *event:* (L *e* out + *venire* come)
outcome.
  141. *extinct:* (be) put out.
  144. *of force.* May modify *believe* or

almighty.
  148. *suffice:* satisfy.
  149–52. Cf. *CD*, I.ix.**B**.
  157. *Cherub:* sing. of *cherubim.*
  167. *fail:* err.

Shot after us in storm, o'erblown hath laid
The fiery surge, that from the precipice
Of heav'n received us falling, and the thunder,
Winged with red lightning and impetuous rage,   175
Perhaps hath spent his shafts, and ceases now
To bellow through the vast and boundless deep.
Let us not slip th' occasion, whether scorn,
Or satiate fury yield it from our foe.
Seest thou yon dreary plain, forlorn and wild,   180
The seat of desolation, void of light,
Save what the glimmering of these livid flames
Casts pale and dreadful? Thither let us tend
From off the tossing of these fiery waves,
There rest, if any rest can harbor there,   185
And reassembling our afflicted powers,
Consult how we may henceforth most offend
Our enemy, our own loss how repair,
How overcome this dire calamity,
What reinforcement we may gain from hope,   190
If not what resolution from despair."
    Thus Satan talking to his nearest mate
With head uplift above the wave, and eyes
That sparkling blazed, his other parts besides
Prone on the flood, extended long and large   195
Lay floating many a rood, in bulk as huge
As whom the fables name of monstrous size,
Titanian, or Earth-born, that warred on Jove,
Briareos or Typhon, whom the den
By ancient Tarsus held, or that sea-beast   200
Leviathan, which God of all his works
Created hugest that swim th' ocean stream:
Him haply slumb'ring on the Norway foam
The pilot of some small night-foundered skiff,
Deeming some island, oft, as seamen tell,   205
With fixèd anchor in his scaly rind
Moors by his side under the lee, while night
Invests the sea, and wishèd morn delays:

172. *laid:* calmed.
178. *slip:* let pass by.
182. *livid:* blue, the color of burning sulphur.
186. *afflicted:* overthrown. *powers:* army.
187. *offend:* (L *offendere* to hit, strike, dash against) harm, wound, pain; vex, annoy, displease Cf. VIII.379.
195. *large:* broad.
196. *rood:* a quarter of an acre.
197–200. In pagan mythology the gods were attacked by the Titans (the twelve children of Heaven and Earth) and their offspring, the Giants (partly human monsters, whose feet were serpents). Briareos was a rebellious monster with 100 hands and Typhon was another, with 100 ser-

pent heads and fiery eyes. According to Hesiod *Jove* attacked Typhon with lightning, set him on fire, and hurled him into Tartarus (hell); according to Pindar Jove imprisoned him in a cave near *Tarsus* in Asia Minor. Christian mythographers moralized the revolt of Typhon as an analogy to the proud revolt of Satan.
200–8. *Leviathan* is an enemy of the Lord (Isa. 27.1) described as an amphibious behemoth, a huge crocodile-like dragon, in Job 40.15–41.34. He was identified by commentators with Satan, as was the whale. The story of the deceived sailor was common and had been moralized.
208. *Invests:* covers.

So stretched out huge in length the Arch-Fiend lay
Chained on the burning lake, nor ever thence   210
Had ris'n or heaved his head, but that the will
And high permission of all-ruling Heaven
Left him at large to his own dark designs,
That with reiterated crimes he might
Heap on himself damnation, while he sought   215
Evil to others, and enraged might see
How all his malice served but to bring forth
Infinite goodness, grace and mercy shown
On man by him seduced, but on himself
Treble confusion, wrath and vengeance poured.   220
Forthwith upright he rears from off the pool
His mighty stature; on each hand the flames
Driv'n backward slope their pointing spires, and rolled
In billows, leave i' th' midst a horrid vale.
Then with expanded wings he steers his flight   225
Aloft, incumbent on the dusky air
That felt unusual weight, till on dry land
He lights, if it were land that ever burned
With solid, as the lake with liquid fire,
And such appeared in hue; as when the force   230
Of subterranean wind transports a hill
Torn from Pelorus, or the shattered side
Of thund'ring Etna, whose combustible
And fueled entrails thence conceiving fire,
Sublimed with mineral fury, aid the winds,   235
And leave a singèd bottom all involved
With stench and smoke: such resting found the sole
Of unblest feet. Him followed his next mate,
Both glorying to have scaped the Stygian flood
As gods, and by their own recovered strength,   240
Not by the sufferance of supernal power.
    "Is this the region, this the soil, the clime,"
Said then the lost Archangel, "this the seat
That we must change for heav'n, this mournful gloom
For that celestial light? Be it so, since he   245

220. *confusion:* (L *confundere* to pour together) ruin, discomfiture, overthrow.
224. *horrid:* bristling (with the *spires* of flame).
226. *incumbent:* lying on.
229. As usual Milton's images are more factual than fanciful. The idea of the burning lake probably comes from accounts of the Dead Sea, on which floated a bituminous marl (see 296n), whose hydrocarbons furnished both an asphaltic mortar (as used in the Tower of Babel) and the "naphtha and asphaltus" that were burned for light in Pandemonium (see 728). The *solid* fire is explained in the note to line 296.
232. *Pelorus:* a promontory near Mount Etna in Sicily.

235. *Sublimed:* vaporized. *mineral fury:* deeply buried energy, violence. Sublimed sulphur is, in fact, produced by the spontaneous combustion of coal seams containing pyrites.
236. *involved:* enveloped.
237. *stench:* sulphur dioxide.
237–38. *sole Of unblest feet:* a good example of Milton's ironic humor. Is *sole* a pun? Certainly *unblest* means no longer blessed or enjoying the bliss of heaven.
239. *Stygian flood:* Styx-like gulf, lake, ocean.
243. *seat:* residence; abiding place (of departed souls).
244. *change:* exchange.

Who now is sovran can dispose and bid
What shall be right: farthest from him is best
Whom reason hath equaled, force hath made supreme
Above his equals. Farewell happy fields
Where joy for ever dwells: hail horrors, hail   250
Infernal world, and thou profoundest hell
Receive thy new possessor: one who brings
A mind not to be changed by place or time.
The mind is its own place, and in itself
Can make a heav'n of hell, a hell of heav'n.   255
What matter where, if I be still the same,
And what I should be, all but less than he
Whom thunder hath made greater? Here at least
We shall be free; th' Almighty hath not built
Here for his envy, will not drive us hence: 260
Here we may reign secure, and in my choice
To reign is worth ambition though in hell:
Better to reign in hell, than serve in heav'n.
But wherefore let we then our faithful friends,
Th' associates and copartners of our loss   265
Lie thus astonished on th' oblivious pool,
And call them not to share with us their part
In this unhappy mansion, or once more
With rallied arms to try what may be yet
Regained in heav'n, or what more lost in hell?"   270
   So Satan spake, and him Beëlzebub
Thus answered. "Leader of those armies bright,
Which but th' Omnipotent none could have foiled,
If once they hear that voice, their liveliest pledge
Of hope in fears and dangers, heard so oft   275
In worst extremes, and on the perilous edge
Of battle when it raged, in all assaults
Their surest signal, they will soon resume
New courage and revive, though now they lie
Groveling and prostrate on yon lake of fire,   280
As we erewhile, astounded and amazed,
No wonder, fall'n such a pernicious highth."
   He scarce had ceased when the superior Fiend
Was moving toward the shore; his ponderous shield
Ethereal temper, massy, large and round,   285
Behind him cast; the broad circumference
Hung on his shoulders like the moon, whose orb

257. *all but less than:* barely less than, all but equal to; but the *OED* gives no examples.

260. *for his envy:* out of envy; i.e., "because he liked the place."

261. *secure:* L *sine* without + *cura* care, anxiety.

262. *ambition:* L *ambitio* great exertion.

266. *astonished:* stunned. *oblivious*

pool: lake of forgetfulness.

268. *mansion:* dwelling place. Cf. John 14.2: "In my Father's house are many mansions: . . . I [Christ] go to prepare a place for you."

276. *edge:* a critical position or moment; front line of battle (like L *acies*).

282. *pernicious:* (L *per* + *nec-, nex* violent death) destructive.

285. *Ethereal.* See 45n.

Through optic glass the Tuscan artist views
At evening from the top of Fesole,
Or in Valdarno, to descry new lands,   290
Rivers or mountains in her spotty globe.
His spear, to equal which the tallest pine
Hewn on Norwegian hills, to be the mast
Of some great ammiral, were but a wand,
He walked with to support uneasy steps   295
Over the burning marl, not like those steps
On heaven's azure; and the torrid clime
Smote on him sore besides, vaulted with fire;
Nathless he so endured, till on the beach
Of that inflamèd sea, he stood and called   300
His legions, angel forms, who lay entranced
Thick as autumnal leaves that strow the brooks
In Vallombrosa, where th' Etrurian shades
High overarched embow'r; or scattered sedge
Afloat, when with fierce winds Orion armed   305
Hath vexed the Red Sea coast, whose waves o'erthrew
Busiris and his Memphian chivalry,
While with perfidious hatred they pursued
The sojourners of Goshen, who beheld
From the safe shore their floating carcasses   310
And broken chariot wheels. So thick bestrown
Abject and lost lay these, covering the flood,
Under amazement of their hideous change.
He called so loud, that all the hollow deep
Of hell resounded. "Princes, Potentates,   315
Warriors, the flow'r of heav'n, once yours, now lost,
If such astonishment as this can seize
Eternal Spirits: or have ye chos'n this place
After the toil of battle to repose
Your wearied virtue, for the ease you find   320

288–91. When Milton visited him in 1638 Galileo was living in Tuscany, near Florence, which is in the valley of the Arno River below the hills of Fiesole (*Fesole*). Galileo, an *artist* because he knew the art of astronomy, had published in 1610 his descriptions of the mountains on the moon as seen through a telescope.

292. *to equal:* compared with.

294. *ammiral:* admiral—a flagship.

296. *burning marl:* Milton's paraphrase of *brimstone* (ME *birnen* or *brinnen* to burn + *ston* stone), which is sulphur, an element commonly found in certain forms of calcium carbonates (or *marls*). From such sulphur-bearing marls the element is extracted by melting it in the intense heat generated by burning some of the sulphur itself. Cf. 350 and 562, below.

299. *Nathless:* nevertheless.

303. Homer, Virgil, and Dante had compared the numberless dead with fallen leaves. *Vallombrosa* (literally "shady valley," with pun on *shades* as "spirits"

or "souls") is a vale near Florence; Etruria was the classical name for the region that embraces modern Tuscany.

304–11. The Hebrew word for the Red Sea means "sedgy sea." *Orion*, a constellation configuring an armed man, was supposed to be a sign of stormy weather. When the Israelites (*sojourners of Goshen*) were fleeing from the Egyptians, God parted the waters of the Red Sea, let his people pass, and then let the waters flow together over the pursuing Egyptian army. See Exod. 14.5–31, pp. 364–65. Memphis was once the capital of Egypt. In Greek myth *Busiris*, son of Poseidon, was king of Egypt. Fowler notes that Christian mythographers had identified *Busiris* as the Pharaoh of Exod. 1. And early theologians had seen Pharaoh as a type of devil.

319. *repose:* (L *reponere* to replace) restore.

320. *virtue:* power inherent in supernatural beings; physical strength; valor.

To slumber here, as in the vales of heav'n?
Or in this abject posture have ye sworn
To adore the conqueror? who now beholds
Cherub and Seraph rolling in the flood
With scattered arms and ensigns, till anon   325
His swift pursuers from heav'n gates discern
Th' advantage, and descending tread us down
Thus drooping, or with linkèd thunderbolts
Transfix us to the bottom of this gulf.
Awake, arise, or be for ever fall'n."   330
   They heard, and were abashed, and up they sprung
Upon the wing, as when men wont to watch
On duty, sleeping found by whom they dread,
Rouse and bestir themselves ere well awake.
Nor did they not perceive the evil plight   335
In which they were, or the fierce pains not feel;
Yet to their general's voice they soon obeyed
Innumerable. As when the potent rod
Of Amram's son in Egypt's evil day
Waved round the coast, up called a pitchy cloud   340
Of locusts, warping on the eastern wind,
That o'er the realm of impious Pharaoh hung
Like night, and darkened all the land of Nile:
So numberless were those bad angels seen
Hovering on wing under the cope of hell   345
'Twixt upper, nether, and surrounding fires;
Till, as a signal giv'n, th' uplifted spear
Of their great Sultan waving to direct
Their course, in even balance down they light
On the firm brimstone, and fill all the plain;   350
A multitude, like which the populous North
Poured never from her frozen loins, to pass
Rhene or the Danaw, when her barbarous sons
Came like a deluge on the South, and spread
Beneath Gibraltar to the Libyan sands.   355
Forthwith from every squadron and each band
The heads and leaders thither haste where stood
Their great commander; godlike shapes and forms
Excelling human, princely dignities,
And powers that erst in heaven sat on thrones;   360

---

325. *ensigns:* military banners.
  339. *Amram:* Moses's father; the plague of locusts is described in Exòd. 10.12–15.
  340. *coast:* region.
  341. *warping:* (term from apiculture) swarming.
  345. *cope:* vaulted ceiling.
  351. The barbarian invasion of the civilized Roman Empire, which brought on the so-called Dark Ages, was something like the Flood (cf. *deluge*) of OT history. The Rhine and Danube rivers, which

freeze in winter, form two sides of a triangle that can be seen as an emblem of the part of the human body covered by a loin cloth (*loins* means generally the organs of reproduction). From this geographic region came the Vandals, who *poured* south into Italy and south-west through France and Spain to Gibraltar, then by sea to the coast of North Africa north of the Lybian desert. Cf. Job 38.29: "Out of whose womb came the ice? and the hoary frost of heaven, who hath gendered it?"

Though of their names in heav'nly records now
Be no memorial, blotted out and razed
By their rebellion, from the Books of Life.
Nor had they yet among the sons of Eve
Got them new names, till wand'ring o'er the earth,   365
Through God's high sufferance for the trial of man,
By falsities and lies the greatest part
Of mankind they corrupted to forsake
God their Creator, and th' invisible
Glory of him that made them, to transform   370
Oft to the image of a brute, adorned
With gay religions full of pomp and gold,
And devils to adore for deities:
Then were they known to men by various names,
And various idols through the heathen world.   375
Say, Muse, their names then known, who first, who last,
Roused from the slumber on that fiery couch,
At their great emperor's call, as next in worth
Came singly where he stood on the bare strand,
While the promiscuous crowd stood yet aloof.   380
The chief were those who from the pit of hell
Roaming to seek their prey on earth, durst fix
Their seats long after next the seat of God,
Their altars by his altar, gods adored
Among the nations round, and durst abide   385
Jehovah thund'ring out of Zion, throned
Between the Cherubim; yea, often placed
Within his sanctuary itself their shrines,
Abomination; and with cursèd things
His holy rites, and solemn feasts profaned,   390
And with their darkness durst affront his light.
First Moloch, horrid king besmeared with blood

362. *razed:* erased.

363. *Books of Life:* God's records of those who will escape damnation. Cf. Rev. 21.27, p. 388.

372. *gay religions:* showy, specious, (perhaps) immoral rites.

376–521. See "Angels," pp. 394–96. In adapting to his own purposes the epic device of listing names of famous warriors, Milton identifies certain fallen angels as spirits who later became the false gods of Israel's neighboring nations. Bush notes that the catalogue "recalls places where the enemies of God and Israel were overthrown [and] relates [Milton's] fable to the corrupted world of history."

380. *promiscuous:* of various kinds mixed together. *aloof:* (related to *luff*, "To stand aloof" meant to head into the wind and stand clear of the shore) at a distance.

383–87. *the seat of God:* generally, the court or residence of his power and presence; but *Jehovah* was specifically *throned* in his *sanctuary*, the Holy of Holies, within the Temple, on the "mercy-seat" (cf. XI.2n), the solid gold cover on the Ark of the Covenant, at opposite ends of which were golden *Cherubim* facing one another, their outspread wings above their heads forming a canopy.

387–91. For example, King Manasseh "did what was wrong in the eyes of the Lord. . . . He rebuilt the hill-shrines which his father Hezekiah had destroyed. . . . He built altars in the house of the Lord. . . . and the image he had made of the goddess Asherah he put in the house. . . ." [*NEB*] 2 Kings 21.2–7.

392–405. The brass idols of *Moloch* (whose name means "king") represented him with the head of a calf and arms outstretched to receive the *children* sacrificed to him. He was the god of the *Ammonites*, whose capital city, *Rabba*, was called the city of waters. He was

Of human sacrifice, and parents' tears,
Though for the noise of drums and timbrels loud
Their children's cries unheard, that passed through fire   395
To his grim idol. Him the Ammonite
Worshiped in Rabba and her wat'ry plain,
In Argob and in Basan, to the stream
Of utmost Arnon. Nor content with such
Audacious neighborhood, the wisest heart   400
Of Solomon he led by fraud to build
His temple right against the temple of God
On that opprobrious hill, and made his grove
The pleasant valley of Hinnom, Tophet thence
And black Gehenna called, the type of hell.   405
Next Chemos, th' obscene dread of Moab's sons,
From Aroer to Nebo, and the wild
Of southmost Abarim; in Hesebon
And Horonaim, Seon's realm, beyond
The flow'ry dale of Sibma clad with vines,   410
And Elealè to th' Asphaltic Pool.
Peor his other name, when he enticed
Israel in Sittim on their march from Nile
To do him wanton rites, which cost them woe.
Yet thence his lustful orgies he enlarged   415
Even to that hill of scandal, by the grove
Of Moloch homicide, lust hard by hate;

---

also worshipped in neighboring countries. *Gehenna*, meaning *valley of Hinnom*, became a synonym for hell. The place was also called *Tophet*, a word whose root is Hebrew *toph*, meaning "*drum*," perhaps in reference to the drums that were beaten to drown out the cries of the children being sacrificed. Cf. 1 Kings 11.1–7 [*NEB*]: "King Solomon was a lover of women, and besides Pharaoh's daughter he married many foreign women . . . from the nations with whom the Lord had forbidden the Israelites to intermarry, 'because,' he said, 'they will entice you to serve their gods.' But Solomon was devoted to them. . . . When he grew old, his wives turned his heart to follow other gods, and he did not remain wholly loyal to the Lord his God. . . . He built a hill-shrine for Kemosh, the loathsome god of Moab, on the height to the east of Jerusalem, and for Moloch, the loathsome god of the Ammonites." The Egyptian name for the planet Mars was *Moloch*, and Milton may have known of this association when he conceived of *Moloch* as warlike.

406–17. *Chemos* is the Kemosh for whom Solomon built a shrine beside the one for *Moloch*, on the *hill of scandal* (*opprobrious hill*), i.e., the Mount of Olives. A god of the Moabites (whose kingdom extended from the city of *Aroer* on the north, to *Nebo* on the east, to the mountains of *Abarim* on the south, to the Dead Sea, or *Asphaltic Pool* on the west), *Chemos* was thought by St. Jerome to be the same god as Priapus, the classical god of fertility represented as a grotesque figure with a prominent phallus. Cf. Num. 25.1–9 [*NEB*]: "When the Israelites were in Shittim [on their way from Egyptian captivity to the Promised Land], the people began to have intercourse with Moabite women, who invited them to the sacrifices offered to their gods; and they ate the sacrificial food and prostrated themselves before the Gods of Moab. The Israelites joined in the worship of the Baal of Peor. . . . One of the Israelites brought a Midianite woman into his family in open defiance of Moses and all the community of Israel, while they were weeping by the Tent of the Presence. Phinehas son of Eleazar, son of Aaron the priest, saw him. He stepped out from the crowd and took up a spear, and he went into the inner room after the Israelite and transfixed the two of them, the Israelite and the woman, pinning them together. Thus the plague, which had attacked the Israelites, was brought to a stop, but twenty-four thousand had already died."

Till good Josiah drove them thence to hell.
With these came they, who from the bord'ring flood
Of old Euphrates to the brook that parts   420
Egypt from Syrian ground, had general names
Of Baalim and Ashtaroth, those male,
These feminine. For Spirits when they please
Can either sex assume, or both; so soft
And uncompounded is their essence pure,   425
Not tied or manacled with joint or limb,
Nor founded on the brittle strength of bones,
Like cumbrous flesh; but in what shape they choose
Dilated or condensed, bright or obscure,
Can execute their airy purposes,   430
And works of love or enmity fulfill.
For those the race of Israel oft forsook
Their Living Strength, and unfrequented left
His righteous altar, bowing lowly down
To bestial gods; for which their heads as low   435
Bowed down in battle, sunk before the spear
Of despicable foes. With these in troop
Came Astoreth, whom the Phoenicians called
Astartè, queen of heav'n, with crescent horns;
To whose bright image nightly by the moon   440
Sidonian virgins paid their vows and songs,
In Sion also not unsung, where stood
Her temple on th' offensive mountain, built
By that uxorious king, whose heart though large,
Beguiled by fair idolatresses, fell   445
To idols foul. Thammuz came next behind,
Whose annual wound in Lebanon allured
The Syrian damsels to lament his fate
In amorous ditties all a summer's day,

418. *Josiah.* Cf. 2 Chron. 34.3 [*NEB*]: "In the eighth year of his reign, when he was still a boy, he began to seek guidance of the God of his forefather, David; and in the twelfth year he began to purge Judah and Jerusalem of the hill-shrines and the sacred poles, and the carved idols and the images of metal. He saw to it that the altars for the Baalim were destroyed."

422. *Baalim* (pl. of Baal) and *Ashtaroth* (pl. of Ashtoreth) were collective names for sun gods and moon goddesses of Phoenicia (Syria) and Palestine.

423–31. See "Angels," p. 394.

437–46. King Josiah also desecrated "on the east of Jerusalem, to the south of the Mount of Olives . . . the hill-shrines which Solomon the king of Israel had built for Ashtoreth the loathsome goddess of the Sidonians" (2 Kings 23.13, *NEB*). Sidon was a rich trading city of the Phoenicians on the coast of Syria. *Astarte*, a fertility goddess represented as a woman with the head of a bull whose horns resembled a crescent moon, was the Phoenician version of Aphrodite. *heart though large.* Cf. 1 Kings 4.29: "God gave Solomon . . . largeness of heart [the translators' word for the Hebrew word for intellect]."

446–57. Cf. Ezek. 8.12–14 [*NEB*]: " 'Man,' he said to me, 'do you see what the elders of Israel are doing in darkness, each at the shrine of his own carved image? . . . You will see,' he said, 'yet more monstrous abominations which they practise.' Then he brought me to that gateway of the Lord's house which faces north; and there I saw women sitting and wailing for Tammuz." *Thammuz* was the Phoenician name for Adonis, a very ancient god presiding over the cycle of death and rebirth of vegetation. He was the beloved of Aphrodite. Adonis was killed by a wild boar in Lebanon, where rises the river Adonis, whose waters, reddish from the soil they carried, the *Syrian damsels* believed to be colored by the blood of the god.

While smooth Adonis from his native rock   450
Ran purple to the sea, supposed with blood
Of Thammuz yearly wounded: the love-tale
Infected Sion's daughters with like heat,
Whose wanton passions in the sacred porch
Ezekiel saw, when by the vision led   455
His eye surveyed the dark idolatries
Of alienated Judah. Next came one
Who mourned in earnest, when the captive ark
Maimed his brute image, head and hands lopped off
In his own temple, on the grunsel edge,   460
Where he fell flat, and shamed his worshipers:
Dagon his name, sea monster, upward man
And downward fish: yet had his temple high
Reared in Azotus, dreaded through the coast
Of Palestine, in Gath and Ascalon   465
And Accaron and Gaza's frontier bounds.
Him followed Rimmon, whose delightful seat
Was fair Damascus, on the fertile banks
Of Abbana and Pharphar, lucid streams.
He also against the house of God was bold: 470
A leper once he lost and gained a king,
Ahaz his sottish conqueror, whom he drew
God's altar to disparage and displace
For one of Syrian mode, whereon to burn
His odious off'rings, and adore the gods   475
Whom he had vanquished. After these appeared

457–66. The mourning for *Thammuz* was insincere compared with *Dagon*'s mourning for his own fate. He was the god of the Israelites' enemy, the Philistines, whose chief cities were the five named in 464–66. Cf. 1 Sam. 5.1–5 [*NEB*]: "After the Philistines had captured the Ark of God, they brought it from Eben-ezer to Ashdod; and then they carried it into the temple of Dagon and set it beside Dagon himself. When the people of Ashdod rose next morning, there was Dagon fallen face downwards before the Ark of the Lord; so they took him and put him back in his place. Next morning when they rose, Dagon had again fallen face downwards before the Ark of the Lord, with his head and his two hands lying broken off beside his platform. This is why . . . the priests of Dagon . . . do not set foot on Dagon's platform." For *platform* the King James Version reads *threshold,* Milton's *grunsel.*

467–76. *Rimmon,* a Phoenician god, had a temple in the fabulously beautiful city of *Damascus.* When Naaman, a commander of the Syrian army, came to Israel in search of a cure for his leprosy, Elisha told him to wash in the river Jordan. Naaman at first indignantly refused: were not *Abbana* and *Pharphar*

"better than all the waters of Israel"? But he finally consented, was cured, and renounced his allegiance to *Rimmon* (2 Kings 5.1ff.). King Ahaz, the Israelite conqueror of Damascus, on the other hand, was much taken by an altar to *Rimmon,* sent sketches of it back home with orders to have it reproduced, and on his return worshipped the foreign god (2 Kings 16.10–18).

476–89. According to Ovid (*Metamorphoses* 5.319ff.), when the Giants invaded Olympus some of the gods fled in terror to Egypt, wandering there *disguised* as various animals. *Osiris,* in the image of a bull, and his wife, *Isis,* represented as a cow, were (among other things) fertility gods. *Orus* was their son. By killing in one night the firstborn of all the Egyptian people and of all their cattle (*bleating gods*), Jehovah forced the Giants to free the captive Israelites; but first he told the Israelites to "borrow" (*NEB*: "ask for") gold and silver jewelry from their "well-disposed" Egyptian neighbors. Later, on the journey home, while Moses was on Mount *Oreb* receiving God's word, the Israelites, impatient at his failure to return promptly, melted down their gold, made an image of a bull-calf, worshipped it, and "gave themselves up to revelry" [*NEB*]. Much

A crew who under names of old renown,
Osiris, Isis, Orus and their train
With monstrous shapes and sorceries abused
Fanatic Egypt and her priests, to seek   480
Their wand'ring gods disguised in brutish forms
Rather than human. Nor did Israel scape
Th' infection when their borrowed gold composed
The calf in Oreb: and the rebel king
Doubled that sin in Bethel and in Dan,   485
Lik'ning his Maker to the grazèd ox,
Jehovah, who in one night when he passed
From Egypt marching, equaled with one stroke
Both her first-born and all her bleating gods.
Belial came last, than whom a Spirit more lewd   490
Fell not from heaven, or more gross to love
Vice for itself: to him no temple stood
Or altar smoked; yet who more oft than he
In temples and at altars, when the priest
Turns atheist, as did Eli's sons, who filled   495
With lust and violence the house of God.
In courts and palaces he also reigns
And in luxurious cities, where the noise
Of riot ascends above their loftiest tow'rs,
And injury and outrage: and when night   500
Darkens the streets, then wander forth the sons
Of Belial, flown with insolence and wine.
Witness the streets of Sodom, and that night
In Gibeah, when the hospitable door
Exposed a matron to avoid worse rape.   505
These were the prime in order and in might;
The rest were long to tell, though far renowned,
Th' Ionian gods, of Javan's issue held
Gods, yet confessed later than Heav'n and Earth
Their boasted parents; Titan Heav'n's first-born   510

later in the history of the nation, King
Jeroboam, who had been in exile in
Egypt before he led a successful revolu-
tion, set up two golden calves in *Bethel*
and *Dan*, the two extremities of the
kingdom of Israel. Cf. Exod. 11, 12, 32
and 1 Kings 12. *abused:* deceived.
490–505. *Belial* in Hebrew means sim-
ply "wickedness," but the phrases "chil-
dren of belial" and "sons of belial," as
they are used in the OT led to personifi-
cation, as in Paul's second letter to the
Corinthians: "What concord hath Christ
with Belial?" (6.15), and Christians came
to think of "him" as a devil. Milton con-
ceived of *Belial* as a "sensualist . . . the
fleshliest incubus," "to vice industrious"
(*PR*, II.150–52. and *PL*, I.116). The sons
of Eli were priests who corrupted the
ceremony of sacrifice and "lay with the
women who were serving at the entrance
of the [Tabernacle]" (1 Sam. 2.12–25).

The reference to *Sodom* (Gen. 19) and
Gibeah (Judg. 19) identify homosexual
rapists as men of *Belial*.
502. *flown:* (archaic past participle of
flow) filled to excess; therefore, swollen—
as well as *flushed*, a word from the same
L stem as *flow*.
508–21. Biblical commentators had sug-
gested that the Greeks (*Ionians*) were
the descendants of the biblical *Javan*,
a grandson of Noah. Of the various ver-
sions available to him Milton chose the
story that *Saturn*, youngest of the *Titan*
sons of *Heaven* and *Earth*, overthrew his
oldest brother to seize the throne, and
that he in turn was overthrown by his
own son *Jove*, who reigned on Mount
Ida in *Crete*, then in various other places
in Greece till he had to flee over the
Adriatic to Italy, France, and Great Brit-
ain (*the utmost isles*).

With his enormous brood, and birthright seized
By younger Saturn, he from mightier Jove
His own and Rhea's son like measure found;
So Jove usurping reigned: these first in Crete
And Ida known, thence on the snowy top   515
Of cold Olympus ruled the middle air
Their highest heav'n; or on the Delphian cliff,
Or in Dodona, and through all the bounds
Of Doric land; or who with Saturn old
Fled over Adria to th' Hesperian fields,   520
And o'er the Celtic roamed the utmost isles.
All these and more came flocking; but with looks
Downcast and damp, yet such wherein appeared
Obscure some glimpse of joy, to have found their chief
Not in despair, to have found themselves not lost   525
In loss itself; which on his count'nance cast
Like doubtful hue: but he his wonted pride
Soon recollecting, with high words, that bore
Semblance of worth, not substance, gently raised
Their fainting courage, and dispelled their fears.   530
Then straight commands that at the warlike sound
Of trumpets loud and clarions be upreared
His mighty standard; that proud honor claimed
Azazel as his right, a Cherub tall:
Who forthwith from the glittering staff unfurled   535
Th' imperial ensign, which full high advanced
Shone like a meteor streaming to the wind
With gems and golden luster rich emblazed,
Seraphic arms and trophies: all the while
Sonorous metal blowing martial sounds: 540
At which the universal host upsent
A shout that tore hell's concave, and beyond
Frighted the reign of Chaos and old Night.
All in a moment through the gloom were seen
Ten thousand banners rise into the air   545
With orient colors waving: with them rose
A forest huge of spears: and thronging helms
Appeared, and serried shields in thick array
Of depth immeasurable: anon they move
In perfect phalanx to the Dorian mood   550
Of flutes and soft recorders; such as raised

516. *middle air.* See 10–15n.
523. *damp:* stupefied.
528. *recollecting:* recovering, rallying.
532. *clarions:* shrill trumpets used in war.
534. *Azazel.* See "Angels," p. 395.
535–39. This flag of the empire of hell contained the coats of arms of the various orders of the fallen angels as well as devices memorializing the battles they had fought.
542. *concave:* commonly meant "the

vault of heaven," as Fowler notes.
546. *orient:* sparkling.
548. *serried:* pressed close together.
550. *perfect phalanx:* "a square battle formation common in Milton's time" (Fowler). *Dorian mood:* one of the three musical modes in ancient Greece (the others: Phrygian and Lydian). It was distinguished for its manly and grave style. To such music the Spartans marched to battle.

To highth of noblest temper heroes old
Arming to battle, and instead of rage
Deliberate valor breathed, firm and unmoved
With dread of death to flight or foul retreat,   555
Nor wanting power to mitigate and swage
With solemn touches, troubled thoughts, and chase
Anguish and doubt and fear and sorrow and pain
From mortal or immortal minds. Thus they
Breathing united force with fixèd thought   560
Moved on in silence to soft pipes that charmed
Their painful steps o'er the burnt soil; and now
Advanced in view they stand, a horrid front
Of dreadful length and dazzling arms, in guise
Of warriors old with ordered spear and shield,   565
Awaiting what command their mighty chief
Had to impose: he through the armèd files
Darts his experienced eye, and soon traverse
The whole battalion views, their order due,
Their visages and stature as of gods,   570
Their number last he sums. And now his heart
Distends with pride, and hard'ning in his strength
Glories: for never since created man,
Met such embodied force, as named with these
Could merit more than that small infantry   575
Warred on by cranes: though all the giant brood
Of Phlegra with th' heroic race were joined
That fought at Thebes and Ilium, on each side
Mixed with auxiliar gods; and what resounds
In fable or romance of Uther's son   580
Begirt with British and Armoric knights;
And all who since, baptized or infidel
Jousted in Aspramont or Montalban,
Damasco, or Marocco, or Trebisond,
Or whom Biserta sent from Afric shore   585
When Charlemain with all his peerage fell
By Fontarabbia. Thus far these beyond

563. *horrid:* bristling.
567–69. Satan reviews the troops rank (*traverse*) and *file.*
575. *small infantry:* the Pygmies referred to by Homer (*Iliad* III.6) and described by Pliny as little people (note Milton's pun on *infant*) living in India. Hughes cites Wm. Cunningham's *Cosmographical Glasse* (London, 1559), where they are said to be about eighteen inches high and to ride on goats in battle against cranes.
577. *Phlegra:* a place in Thessaly where, in Greek myth, the Giants battled the gods. But Milton may allude to the Phlegraean plains near Mt. Vesuvius, where in Roman myth Jupiter fought the Giants with thunderbolts that left the region a volcanic desert, like hell.

578. *Thebes and Ilium.* Milton refers to the great epic stories of the war between the sons of Oedipus at Thebes and the war between the Greeks and the Trojans at Troy, in which various gods assisted certain of the heroes.
579–87. *Uther's son:* King Arthur. *Armoric:* from Brittany. *Aspramont* and *Montalban* are castles in Ariosto's *Orlando Furioso.* Damascus and *Trebisond* were scenes of tournaments in the wars between the Christians and the Saracens. *Biserta* in Tunis was a Saracen city. In the *Song of Roland* Roland (not *Charlemain*) died at Roncevalles, not far from *Fontarabbia.*

Compare of mortal prowess, yet observed
Their dread commander: he above the rest
In shape and gesture proudly eminent   590
Stood like a tow'r; his form had yet not lost
All her original brightness, nor appeared
Less than Archangel ruined, and th' excess
Of glory obscured: as when the sun ris'n
Looks through the horizontal misty air   595
Shorn of his beams, or from behind the moon
In dim eclipse disastrous twilight sheds
On half the nations, and with fear of change
Perplexes monarchs. Darkened so, yet shone
Above them all th' Archangel: but his face   600
Deep scars of thunder had intrenched, and care
Sat on his faded cheek, but under brows
Of dauntless courage, and considerate pride
Waiting revenge: cruel his eye, but cast
Signs of remorse and passion to behold   605
The fellows of his crime, the followers rather
(Far other once beheld in bliss) condemned
For ever now to have their lot in pain,
Millions of Spirits for his fault amerced
Of heav'n, and from eternal splendors flung   610
For his revolt, yet faithful how they stood,
Their glory withered: as when heaven's fire
Hath scathed the forest oaks, or mountain pines,
With singèd top their stately growth though bare
Stands on the blasted heath. He now prepared   615
To speak; whereat their doubled ranks they bend
From wing to wing, and half enclose him round
With all his peers: attention held them mute.
Thrice he assayed, and thrice in spite of scorn,
Tears such as angels weep, burst forth: at last   620
Words interwove with sighs found out their way.
     "O myriads of immortal Spirits, O Powers
Matchless, but with th' Almighty, and that strife
Was not inglorious, though th' event was dire,
As this place testifies, and this dire change   625
Hateful to utter: but what power of mind
Foreseeing or presaging, from the depth
Of knowledge past or present, could have feared,
How such united force of gods, how such

---

588. *observed:* acknowledged the authority, superiority, of.
592. *her.* L *forma* (feminine) means shape, appearance, beauty, pattern, nature— cf. Gk *idea.* See VII.557n.
594. *glory:* splendor. *obscured:* darkened.
597. *disastrous:* (L *dis* + *astrum* star) astrologically unfavorable.
603. *considerate:* (L *considerare*, liter-

ally, to observe the stars) circumspect, wary.
605. *remorse:* (L *remordere* to bite again) pangs of conscience. *passion:* suffering. The emphasis is on Satan's pain, not his love.
609. *amerced:* fined; i.e., punished by being deprived.
624. *event:* outcome.

As stood like these, could ever know repulse?   630
For who can yet believe, though after loss,
That all these puissant legions, whose exile
Hath emptied heav'n, shall fail to reascend
Self-raised, and repossess their native seat?
For me, be witness all the host of heav'n,   635
If counsels different, or danger shunned
By me, have lost our hopes. But he who reigns
Monarch in heav'n, till then as one secure
Sat on his throne, upheld by old repute,
Consent or custom, and his regal state   640
Put forth at full, but still his strength concealed,
Which tempted our attempt, and wrought our fall.
Henceforth his might we know, and know our own
So as not either to provoke, or dread
New war, provoked; our better part remains   645
To work in close design, by fraud or guile
What force effected not: that he no less
At length from us may find, who overcomes
By force, hath overcome but half his foe.
Space may produce new worlds; whereof so rife   650
There went a fame in heav'n that he ere long
Intended to create, and therein plant
A generation, whom his choice regard
Should favor equal to the sons of heaven:
Thither, if but to pry, shall be perhaps   655
Our first eruption, thither or elsewhere:
For this infernal pit shall never hold
Celestial Spirits in bondage, not th' abyss
Long under darkness cover. But these thoughts
Full counsel must mature: peace is despaired,   660
For who can think submission? War then, war
Open or understood must be resolved."
    He spake: and to confirm his words, out flew
Millions of flaming swords, drawn from the thighs
Of mighty Cherubim; the sudden blaze   665
Far round illumined hell: highly they raged
Against the Highest, and fierce with graspèd arms
Clashed on their sounding shields the din of war,
Hurling defiance toward the vault of heav'n.
    There stood a hill not far whose grisly top   670
Belched fire and rolling smoke; the rest entire

---

636. *different:* differing.
646. *close:* concealed.
650–54. Milton does not say how the rumor got started. In VII.150–61, God implies that the creation of man was a consequence of the revolt of the angels. See *CD,* I.vii.
653. *generation:* (L *genus* stock, race) family, breed, race. *choice:* discriminative.
656. *eruption:* (L *erumpere* to break out, burst forth) sallying forth (as of soldiers from a fort), escape (as from a prison); outbreak (as of a disease or a volcano).
662. *understood:* undeclared.

Shone with a glossy scurf, undoubted sign
That in his womb was hid metallic ore,
The work of sulphur. Thither winged with speed
A numerous brigade hastened. As when bands   675
Of pioneers with spade and pickax armed
Forerun the royal camp, to trench a field,
Or cast a rampart. Mammon led them on,
Mammon, the least erected Spirit that fell
From heav'n, for ev'n in heav'n his looks and thoughts   680
Were always downward bent, admiring more
The riches of heav'n's pavement, trodden gold,
Than aught divine or holy else enjoyed
In vision beatific: by him first
Men also, and by his suggestion taught,   685
Ransacked the center, and with impious hands
Rifled the bowels of their mother earth
For treasures better hid. Soon had his crew
Opened into the hill a spacious wound
And digged out ribs of gold. Let none admire   690
That riches grow in hell; that soil may best
Deserve the precious bane. And here let those
Who boast in mortal things, and wond'ring tell
Of Babel, and the works of Memphian kings,
Learn how their greatest monuments of fame,   695
And strength and art are easily outdone
By Spirits reprobate, and in an hour
What in an age they with incessant toil
And hands innumerable scarce perform.
Nigh on the plain in many cells prepared,   700
That underneath had veins of liquid fire
Sluiced from the lake, a second multitude
With wondrous art founded the massy ore,
Severing each kind, and scummed the bullion dross:
A third as soon had formed within the ground   705
A various mold, and from the boiling cells
By strange conveyance filled each hollow nook,

672–74. *scurf:* a hard crust made of a volcanic mixture of hydrocarbons and sulphur. Alchemists believed that sulphur was the "father" of all metals.

676. *pioneers:* military engineers.

679. The word *mammon,* meaning "riches," appears in Matt. 6.24: "Ye cannot serve God and mammon." Commentators identified the "prince of this world" (John 12.31) as Mammon, and this personification became a kind of Christian equivalent of Plutus. The angelologists made him prince of the lowest order of angels.

682. *gold.* Cf. Rev. 21.21, p. 388.

684. *vision beatific:* a theological term meaning the mystical experience of see-
ing God in the glory of heaven.

690. *ribs:* the solid parts of a vein of ore (technical term). *admire:* wonder.

692. *bane:* (OE *bana* murderer) what destroys life, deadly poison, ruin, cause of ruin.

694. The tower of *Babel* is described in Gen. 11.1–9, p. 362. *works:* i.e., the Pyramids.

697. *reprobate:* (L *reprobare* to disapprove, from *re* + *probare* to test, prove) condemned.

703–4. *founded:* melted. *massy:* of high specific gravity. *Severing:* separating. *bullion:* (L to be in bubbling motion) of unrefined gold. *dross:* scum produced by boiling impure metals.

As in an organ from one blast of wind
To many a row of pipes the soundboard breathes.
Anon out of the earth a fabric huge   710
Rose like an exhalation, with the sound
Of dulcet symphonies and voices sweet,
Built like a temple, where pilasters round
Were set, and Doric pillars overlaid
With golden architrave; nor did there want   715
Cornice or frieze, with bossy sculptures grav'n;
The roof was fretted gold. Not Babylon,
Nor great Alcairo such magnificence
Equaled in all their glories, to enshrine
Belus or Serapis their gods, or seat   720
Their kings, when Egypt with Assyria strove
In wealth and luxury. Th' ascending pile
Stood fixed her stately highth, and straight the doors
Opening their brazen folds discover wide
Within, her ample spaces, o'er the smooth   725
And level pavement: from the archèd roof
Pendent by subtle magic many a row
Of starry lamps and blazing cressets fed
With naphtha and asphaltus yielded light
As from a sky. The hasty multitude   730
Admiring entered, and the work some praise
And some the architect: his hand was known
In heav'n by many a towered structure high,

710–30. The exterior of a classical temple in the Doric style (like the Parthenon—or the Pantheon, in Rome, which fits Milton's description in detail) consisted of a row of fluted columns supporting (*overlaid With*) an entablature of three layers of stone: the *architrave*, sometimes covered with gold leaf; the *frieze*, a row of figures carved (embossed, *bossy*) in relief; and the *cornice*, a thin band of stone, sculptured or otherwise ornamented. Within this outer row of columns was an inner wall whose surface was interrupted by *pilasters*, rectangular columns partially projecting from the wall surface. *Pandemonium* (756) is a building (*fabric*) of monumental architecture for political congresses, and in the Argument Milton calls it the Palace of Satan; but by describing it in terms of a classical temple and contrasting it with Assyrian and Egyptian shrines, Milton suggests its religious as well as political functions. This mixture of worldly and spiritual powers might remind Milton's readers of St. Peter's in Rome. And though the pure Doric style of Pandemonium may have been more to Milton's taste than the art of *Babylon* and Memphis (*Alcairo*), still the emphasis on its magnificence would have made it seem sinful to Puritans, who believed, with Milton, that God preferred "Before all

temples th' upright heart and pure" (8). *fretted:* richly ornamented. *Belus or Serapis:* alternate names for Baal and Osiris. *cressets:* iron baskets holding coal or pitched rope burnt for illumination. Among the arts incorporated in this description of the building of Pandemonium are two Milton may have observed. One is that of casting large ornamental iron or bronze gates, doors, railings, etc. Milton imagines the temple as one gigantic casting made by pouring molten metal into an intricate mold dug out of the earth. The other is stagecraft: when the building rose out of the earth it did so as buildings were made, by means of elaborate machinery, to rise out of the stage in masques designed by Inigo Jones for great court performances.

732–51. *Mulciber*, meaning "one who refines ore by melting it and pouring it into a mould," was another name for Vulcan, a Roman fire god, or god of smiths, identified with the Greek god of fire and arts, Hephaestus, the son of Hera, who is said to have thrown him out of heaven because he was born lame, and Zeus (*Jove*), who in another version is said to have thrown him out because in a quarrel between his parents he took his mother's side. Homer (*Iliad* I.590) says the fall lasted a day and ended on Lemnos. *Ausonian land:* Italy.

Where sceptered angels held their residence,
And sat as princes, whom the Súpreme King   735
Exalted to such power, and gave to rule,
Each in his hierarchy, the orders bright.
Nor was his name unheard or unadored
In ancient Greece; and in Ausonian land
Men called him Mulciber; and how he fell   740
From heav'n, they fabled, thrown by angry Jove
Sheer o'er the crystal battlements: from morn
To noon he fell, from noon to dewy eve,
A summer's day; and with the setting sun
Dropped from the zenith like a falling star,   745
On Lemnos th' Aégean isle: thus they relate,
Erring; for he with this rebellious rout
Fell long before; nor aught availed him now
To have built in heav'n high tow'rs; nor did he scape
By all his engines, but was headlong sent   750
With his industrious crew to build in hell.
Meanwhile the wingèd heralds by command
Of sovran power, with awful ceremony
And trumpet's sound throughout the host proclaim
A solemn council forthwith to be held   755
At Pandemonium, the high capitol
Of Satan and his peers: their summons called
From every band and squarèd regiment
By place or choice the worthiest; they anon
With hunderds and with thousands trooping came   760
Attended: all access was thronged, the gates
And porches wide, but chief the spacious hall
(Though like a covered field, where champions bold
Wont ride in armed, and at the Soldan's chair
Defied the best of paynim chivalry   765
To mortal combat or career with lance)
Thick swarmed, both on the ground and in the air,
Brushed with the hiss of rustling wings. As bees

746–47. The poet's Muse, or Milton as bard, comments. On Milton's Christian views of the truth of pagan myths see "Truth and Poetry," pp. 400–1.

750. *engines.* Vulcan was a man of ingenuity—inventor of things as well as of tricks.

756. *Pandemonium.* Milton invents a Gk name from *pan* all + *daimonion* (evil) spirits, demons—analogous with *pantheion* temple of all the gods. *capitol.* In the ms. of Bk. I *Capitoll* was corrected to *Capitall,* as it appears in the first and second editions. But, as Helen Darbishire pointed out, Milton probably meant *capitol,* which comes from L *capitolium,* the temple of Jupiter on the Capitoline Hill, and means a building in which a legislative body meets.

759. *By place or choice:* ex officio or by election. *worthiest:* highest-ranking.

760. *hunderds.* Milton called for this spelling in the list of *errata* added to a later printing of the first edition.

764. *Wont:* were wont to. *Soldan's:* Sultan's.

765. *paynim:* pagan.

768–88. Bee similes were commonplace in the epic tradition from Homer through the Renaissance. Milton characteristically enriched the significance of his version with meaningful detail. Instead of wild bees (as in Homer and others) Milton refers to a domestic swarm, housed in a man-made work of art—a hive of woven straw set on a plank which the beekeeper has made glassy smooth with the same kind of balsam gum bees themselves use to smooth any rough place on which they congregate. The dome of St. Peter's is shaped like a hive; St. Peter's Square is like the plank; when Milton was in

In springtime, when the sun with Taurus rides,
Pour forth their populous youth about the hive   77◀
In clusters; they among fresh dews and flowers
Fly to and fro, or on the smoothèd plank,
The suburb of their straw-built citadel,
New rubbed with balm, expatiate and confer
Their state affairs. So thick the aery crowd   77
Swarmed and were straitened; till the signal giv'n,
Behold a wonder! they but now who seemed
In bigness to surpass Earth's giant sons
Now less than smallest dwarfs, in narrow room
Throng numberless, like that Pygmean race   78◀
Beyond the Indian mount, or fairy elves,
Whose midnight revels, by a forest side
Or fountain some belated peasant sees,
Or dreams he sees, while overhead the moon
Sits arbitress, and nearer to the earth   78
Wheels her pale course: they on their mirth and dance
Intent, with jocund music charm his ear;
At once with joy and fear his heart rebounds.
Thus incorporeal Spirits to smallest forms
Reduced their shapes immense, and were at large,   79◀
Though without number still amidst the hall
Of that infernal court. But far within
And in their own dimensions like themselves
The great Seraphic Lords and Cherubim
In close recess and secret conclave sat   79
A thousand demi-gods on golden seats,
Frequent and full. After short silence then
And summons read, the great consult began.

Rome, the Pope's personal insignia was a bee and his followers were called "bees." The grand irony is perhaps in God as beekeeper, but the strawbuilt citadel and the smooth, balm-rubbed plank are typical of Milton's sardonic humor. *with Taurus rides:* is in the sign of Taurus. *expatiate:* walk about (suggesting "to expatiate upon"). *confer:* discuss. *Earth's giant sons:* the Titans of Greek mythology. *Pygmean race.* See I.575n. *arbitress:* presiding authority (over the fairy revels).

795. *close recess:* secret place. *conclave:* L word meaning "a room that can be locked." The meeting of Cardinals at which the Pope is elected is called conclave.

797. *Frequent and full:* (an idiom) crowded together in great numbers.

798. *consult:* a meeting for consultation; in the seventeenth century, often secret, seditious meeting.

Book II

The Argument

The consultation begun, Satan debates whether another battle be to be hazarded for the recovery of heaven: some advise it, others dissuade: a third proposal is preferred, mentioned before by Satan, to search the truth of that prophecy or tradition in heaven concerning another world, and another kind of creature equal or not much inferior to themselves, about this time to be created: their doubt who shall be sent on this difficult search: Satan their chief undertakes alone the voyage, is honored and applauded. The council thus ended, the rest betake them several ways and to several employments, as their inclinations lead them, to entertain the time till Satan return. He passes on his journey to hell gates, finds them shut, and who sat there to guard them, by whom at length they are opened, and discover to him the great gulf between hell and heaven; with what difficulty he passes through, directed by Chaos, the power of that place, to the sight of this new world which he sought.

High on a throne of royal state, which far
Outshone the wealth of Ormus and of Ind,
Or where the gorgeous East with richest hand
Show'rs on her kings barbaric pearl and gold,
Satan exalted sat, by merit raised   5
To that bad eminence; and from despair
Thus high uplifted beyond hope, aspires
Beyond thus high, insatiate to pursue
Vain war with Heav'n, and by success untaught
His proud imaginations thus displayed.   10
    "Powers and Dominions, deities of heaven,
For since no deep within her gulf can hold
Immortal vigor, though oppressed and fall'n,
I give not heav'n for lost. From this descent
Celestial Virtues rising, will appear   15
More glorious and more dread than from no fall,
And trust themselves to fear no second fate:
Me though just right, and the fixed laws of heav'n
Did first create your leader, next, free choice,
With what besides, in counsel or in fight,   20
Hath been achieved of merit, yet this loss

II.2. *Ormus:* Hormuz, trading town on the Persian Gulf, then famous for spices, drugs, diamonds, and pearls. *Ind:* India.
    5. *merit:* that for which a person deserves reward or punishment. Cf. I.98; II.21; III.309.
    6. *eminence:* (L *eminere* to project) height, rank.
    9. *success:* (L *succedere* to follow

after) outcome. But, as with *merit*, the normally positive connotation produces Milton's characteristic irony.
    10. *imaginations:* schemes, plots.
    11. *Dominions:* synonym for *Dominations*, one of the angelic orders. See "Angels," p. 395.
    15. *Virtues:* another angelic order.

29

Thus far at least recovered, hath much more
Established in a safe unenvied throne
Yielded with full consent. The happier state
In heaven, which follows dignity, might draw   25
Envy from each inferior; but who here
Will envy whom the highest place exposes
Foremost to stand against the thunderer's aim
Your bulwark, and condemns to greatest share
Of endless pain? Where there is then no good   30
For which to strive, no strife can grow up there
From faction; for none sure will claim in hell
Precédence, none, whose portion is so small
Of present pain, that with ambitious mind
Will covet more. With this advantage then   35
To union, and firm faith, and firm accord,
More than can be in heav'n, we now return
To claim our just inheritance of old,
Surer to prosper than prosperity
Could have assured us; and by what best way,   40
Whether of open war or covert guile,
We now debate; who can advise, may speak."
   He ceas'd, and next him Moloch, sceptered king
Stood up, the strongest and the fiercest Spirit
That fought in heav'n; now fiercer by despair: 45
His trust was with th' Eternal to be deemed
Equal in strength, and rather than be less
Cared not to be at all; with that care lost
Went all his fear: of God, or hell, or worse
He recked not, and these words thereafter spake.   50
   "My sentence is for open war: of wiles,
More unexpert, I boast not: them let those
Contrive who need, or when they need, not now.
For while they sit contriving, shall the rest,
Millions that stand in arms, and longing wait   55
The signal to ascend, sit lingering here
Heav'n's fugitives, and for their dwelling-place
Accept this dark opprobrious den of shame,
The prison of his tyranny who reigns
By our delay? No, let us rather choose   60
Armed with hell flames and fury all at once
O'er heav'n's high tow'rs to force resistless way,
Turning our tortures into horrid arms
Against the torturer; when to meet the noise
Of his almighty engine he shall hear   65
Infernal thunder, and for lightning see
Black fire and horror shot with equal rage

---

50. *recked:* took heed. *thereafter:* ac-
cordingly.
51. *sentence:* opinion.
52. *unexpert:* inexperienced.

63. *horrid:* bristling.
65. *engine:* machine of war; i.e., thun-
der.

Among his angels; and his throne itself
Mixed with Tartarean sulfur, and strange fire,
His own invented torments. But perhaps   70
The way seems difficult and steep to scale
With upright wing against a higher foe.
Let such bethink them, if the sleepy drench
Of that forgetful lake benumb not still,
That in our proper motion we ascend   75
Up to our native seat: descent and fall
To us is adverse. Who but felt of late
When the fierce foe hung on our broken rear
Insulting, and pursued us through the deep,
With what compulsion and laborious flight   80
We sunk thus low? Th' ascent is easy then;
Th' event is feared; should we again provoke
Our stronger, some worse way his wrath may find
To our destruction: if there be in hell
Fear to be worse destroyed: what can be worse   85
Than to dwell here, driven out from bliss, condemned
In this abhorrèd deep to utter woe;
Where pain of unextinguishable fire
Must exercise us without hope of end
The vassals of his anger, when the scourge   90
Inexorably, and the torturing hour
Calls us to penance? More destroyed than thus
We should be quite abolished and expire.
What fear we then? What doubt we to incense
His utmost ire? which to the highth enraged,   95
Will either quite consume us, and reduce
To nothing this essential, happier far
Than miserable to have eternal being:
Or if our substance be indeed divine,
And cannot cease to be, we are at worst   100
On this side nothing; and by proof we feel
Our power sufficient to disturb his heav'n,
And with perpetual inroads to alarm,
Though inaccessible, his fatal throne:
Which if not victory is yet revenge."   105
    He ended frowning, and his look denounced

68–69. The throne of God was "like the fiery flame" (Dan. 7.9), a pure fire that Moloch proposes to adulterate with fires of hell.

69. *Tartarean:* of Tartarus, a region of Hades (the "lower world" of classical myth) where the most guilty were punished. *strange fire.* Cf. Lev. 10.1–2: ". . . the sons of Aaron . . . offered strange fire before the Lord, which he commanded them not. And there went out fire from the Lord, and devoured them. . . ."

73. *drench:* potion; large draught.

74. *forgetful lake.* Cf. "oblivious pool,"

I.266.

75. I.e.: it is our nature to ascend.

77. *adverse:* contrary to our nature.

79. *Insulting:* (L *insultare* to spring upon) triumphantly scorning.

82. *event:* outcome.

89. *exercise:* L *exerceo* to vex or plague, as in the baiting of wild beasts.

90. *vassals:* slaves.

94. *doubt we:* makes us hesitate.

97. *essential:* essence.

104. *fatal:* established by fate; also, deadly.

106. *denounced:* portended.

Desperate revenge, and battle dangerous
To less than gods. On th' other side up rose
Belial, in act more graceful and humane;
A fairer person lost not heav'n; he seemed   110
For dignity composed and high exploit:
But all was false and hollow; though his tongue
Dropped manna, and could make the worse appear
The better reason, to perplex and dash
Maturest counsels: for his thoughts were low;   115
To vice industrious, but to nobler deeds
Timorous and slothful: yet he pleased the ear,
And with persuasive accent thus began.
   "I should be much for open war, O Peers,
As not behind in hate; if what was urged   120
Main reason to persuade immediate war,
Did not dissuade me most, and seem to cast
Ominous conjecture on the whole success:
When he who most excells in fact of arms,
In what he counsels and in what excels   125
Mistrustful, grounds his courage on despair
And utter dissolution, as the scope
Of all his aim, after some dire revenge.
First, what revenge? The tow'rs of heav'n are filled
With armèd watch, that render all access   130
Impregnable; oft on the bordering deep
Encamp their legions, or with óbscure wing
Scout far and wide into the realm of Night,
Scorning surprise. Or could we break our way
By force, and at our heels all hell should rise   135
With blackest insurrection, to confound
Heav'n's purest light, yet our great enemy
All incorruptible would on his throne
Sit unpolluted, and th' ethereal mold
Incapable of stain would soon expel   140
Her mischief, and purge off the baser fire
Victorious. Thus repulsed, our final hope
Is flat despair: we must exasperate
Th' almighty victor to spend all his rage,
And that must end us, that must be our cure,   145
To be no more; sad cure; for who would lose,
Though full of pain, this intellectual being,
Those thoughts that wander through eternity,
To perish rather, swallowed up and lost
In the wide womb of uncreated night,   150
Devoid of sense and motion? And who knows,

---

109. *Belial.* See I.490–505n above and
"Angels," p. 395. *humane:* civil, polite.
  113. *manna:* sweetness.
  114. *reason:* argument.
  124. *fact:* feat.

127. *scope:* target, range, extent.
  139. *mold:* substance.
  148. *wander.* Milton may have wanted
to make Belial unintentionally ironic with
a word that also means to stray, or err.

Let this be good, whether our angry foe
Can give it, or will ever? How he can
Is doubtful; that he never will is sure.
Will he, so wise, let loose at once his ire,   155
Belike through impotence, or unaware,
To give his enemies their wish, and end
Them in his anger, whom his anger saves
To punish endless? 'Wherefore cease we then?'
Say they who counsel war, 'We are decreed,   160
Reserved and destined to eternal woe;
Whatever doing, what can we suffer more,
What can we suffer worse?' Is this then worst,
Thus sitting, thus consulting, thus in arms?
What when we fled amain, pursued and strook   165
With Heav'n's afflicting thunder, and besought
The deep to shelter us? This hell then seemed
A refuge from those wounds: or when we lay
Chained on the burning lake? That sure was worse.
What if the breath that kindled those grim fires   170
Awaked should blow them into sevenfold rage
And plunge us in the flames? Or from above
Should intermitted vengeance arm again
His red right hand to plague us? What if all
Her stores were opened, and this firmament   175
Of hell should spout her cataracts of fire,
Impendent horrors, threat'ning hideous fall
One day upon our heads; while we perhaps
Designing or exhorting glorious war,
Caught in a fiery tempest shall be hurled   180
Each on his rock transfixed, the sport and prey
Of racking whirlwinds, or for ever sunk
Under yon boiling ocean, wrapped in chains;
There to converse with everlasting groans,
Unrespited, unpitied, unreprieved,   185
Ages of hopeless end; this would be worse.
War therefore, open or concealed, alike
My voice dissuades; for what can force or guile
With him, or who deceive his mind, whose eye
Views all things at one view? He from heav'n's highth   190
All these our motions vain, sees and derides;
Not more almighty to resist our might
Than wise to frustrate all our plots and wiles.
Shall we then live thus vile, the race of heav'n

---

156. *Belike:* probably (ironic).
161. *reserved.* Cf. *CD*, I.ix.B.
165. *amain:* with full speed.
170. Cf. Isa. 30.33: "The breath of the Lord, like a stream of brimstone, doth kindle [the fire of Tophet]." Cf. I.404–5.
173. *intermitted:* suspended.
174. *red right hand.* Horace refers to Jupiter, the hurler of thunderbolts, as having a red right hand.
176. *cataracts:* waterspouts.
182. *racking:* pulling, straining, torturing.
190–91. Cf. Ps. 2.4: "He that sitteth in the heavens shall laugh; the Lord shall have them in derision." Cf. *CD*, I.ii.B.
191. *motions:* proposals.

Thus trampled, thus expelled to suffer here   195
Chains and these torments? Better these than worse
By my advice; since fate inevitable
Subdues us, and omnipotent decree,
The victor's will. To suffer, as to do,
Our strength is equal, nor the law unjust   200
That so ordains: this was at first resolved,
If we were wise, against so great a foe
Contending, and so doubtful what might fall.
I laugh, when those who at the spear are bold
And vent'rous, if that fail them, shrink and fear   205
What yet they know must follow, to endure
Exile, or ignominy, or bonds, or pain,
The sentence of their conqueror: This is now
Our doom; which if we can sustain and bear,
Our Súpreme foe in time may much remit   210
His anger, and perhaps thus far removed
Not mind us not offending, satisfied
With what is punished; whence these raging fires
Will slacken, if his breath stir not their flames.
Our purer essence then will overcome   215
Their noxious vapor, or inured not feel,
Or changed at length, and to the place conformed
In temper and in nature, will receive
Familiar the fierce heat, and void of pain;
This horror will grow mild, this darkness light,   220
Besides what hope the never-ending flight
Of future days may bring, what chance, what change
Worth waiting, since our present lot appears
For happy though but ill, but ill not worst,
If we procure not to ourselves more woe."   225
    Thus Belial with words clothed in reason's garb
Counseled ignoble ease, and peaceful sloth,
Not peace: and after him thus Mammon spake.
    "Either to disenthrone the King of heav'n
We war, if war be best, or to regain   230
Our own right lost: him to unthrone we then
May hope when everlasting fate shall yield
To fickle chance, and Chaos judge the strife:
The former vain to hope argues as vain
The latter: for what place can be for us   235
Within heav'n's bound, unless heav'n's Lord supreme
We overpower? Suppose he should relent
And publish grace to all, on promise made
Of new subjection; with what eyes could we

199–203. I.e.: We are able to take as much punishment as we are able to inflict (and the natural law that makes that true is not unfair). If we were wise, we agreed upon that before we undertook to contend against so great a foe, since we were so uncertain of the outcome.

212–13. *what is punished:* (L syntax) the punishment.
216. *inured:* accustomed to.
223–24. I.e.: Though our present lot, considered for its happiness, seems an ill one, when considered as an ill lot, it seems not the worst.

Stand in his presence humble, and receive   240
Strict laws imposed, to celebrate his throne
With warbled hymns, and to his Godhead sing
Forced hallelujahs; while he lordly sits
Our envied Sovran, and his altar breathes
Ambrosial odors and ambrosial flowers,   245
Our servile offerings. This must be our task
In heav'n, this our delight; how wearisome
Eternity so spent in worship paid
To whom we hate. Let us not then pursue
By force impossible, by leave obtained   250
Unácceptable, though in heav'n, our state
Of splendid vassalage, but rather seek
Our own good from ourselves, and from our own
Live to ourselves, though in this vast recess,
Free, and to none accountable, preferring   255
Hard liberty before the easy yoke
Of servile pomp. Our greatness will appear
Then most conspicuous, when great things of small,
Useful of hurtful, prosperous of adverse
We can create, and in what place soe'er   260
Thrive under evil, and work ease out of pain
Through labor and endurance. This deep world
Of darkness do we dread? How oft amidst
Thick clouds and dark doth heav'n's all-ruling Sire
Choose to reside, his glory unobscured,   265
And with the majesty of darkness round
Covers his throne; from whence deep thunders roar
Must'ring their rage, and heav'n resembles hell?
As he our darkness, cannot we his light
Imitate when we please? This desert soil   270
Wants not her hidden luster, gems and gold;
Nor want we skill or art, from whence to raise
Magnificence; and what can heav'n show more?
Our torments also may in length of time
Become our elements, these piercing fires   275
As soft as now severe, our temper changed
Into their temper; which must needs remove
The sensible of pain. All things invite
To peaceful counsels, and the settled state
Of order, how in safety best we may   280
Compose our present evils, with regard

---

243. *hallelujahs:* songs of praise. The
Hebrew word means: Praise ye the Lord
(i.e., *Jah,* or *Jehovah*).
245. *Ambrosial:* (Gk *ambrosia* immor-
tality; elixir of life) of the fragrance (or
flavor) of a food (or drink) worthy of
the gods; divinely fragrant.
263–67. Cf. Ps. 18.11: "He made dark-
ness his secret place; his pavilion round

about him were dark waters and thick
clouds. . . ."
271. *Wants:* lacks.
276. *temper:* (L *temperare* to mix) na-
ture, constitution; see theory of humors
in "Physiology and Psychology," p. 391.
278. *sensible:* physical part.
281. *Compose:* come to terms with.
evils: misfortunes.

Of what we are and where, dismissing quite
All thoughts of war: ye have what I advise."
    He scarce had finished, when such murmur filled
Th' assembly, as when hollow rocks retain   285
The sound of blust'ring winds, which all night long
Had roused the sea, now with hoarse cadence lull
Seafaring men o'erwatched, whose bark by chance
Or pinnace anchors in a craggy bay
After the tempest: such applause was heard   290
As Mammon ended, and his sentence pleased,
Advising peace: for such another field
They dreaded worse than hell: so much the fear
Of thunder and the sword of Michaël
Wrought still within them; and no less desire   295
To found this nether empire, which might rise
By policy, and long process of time,
In emulation opposite to heav'n.
Which then Beëlzebub perceived, than whom,
Satan except, none higher sat, with grave   300
Aspect he rose, and in his rising seemed
A pillar of state; deep on his front engraven
Deliberation sat and public care;
And princely counsel in his face yet shone,
Majestic though in ruin: sage he stood   305
With Atlantean shoulders fit to bear
The weight of mightiest monarchies; his look
Drew audience and attention still as night
Or summer's noontide air, while thus he spake.
    "Thrones and imperial Powers, offspring of heav'n,   310
Ethereal Virtues; or these titles now
Must we renounce, and changing style be called
Princes of hell? for so the popular vote
Inclines, here to continue, and build up here
A growing empire; doubtless; while we dream,   315
And know not that the King of heav'n hath doomed
This place our dungeon, not our safe retreat
Beyond his potent arm, to live exempt
From Heav'n's high jurisdiction, in new league
Banded against his throne, but to remain   320
In strictest bondage, though thus far removed,
Under th' inevitable curb, reserved
His captive multitude: for he, be sure,
In highth or depth, still first and last will reign

288–89. *bark:* ship. *pinnace:* boat.
292. *field:* battle.
294. *Michael.* See "Angels," p. 395.
297. *policy:* statecraft.
302. *front:* forehead, face.
306. *Atlantean.* When with other Titans, Atlas unsuccessfully revolted against the gods, he was punished by being forced to hold up the heavens on his shoulders.
312. *style:* official titles.
324–25. Cf. Rev. 22.13: "I am Alpha and Omega, the beginning and the end, the first and the last."

Sole king, and of his kingdom lose no part   325
By our revolt, but over hell extend
His empire, and with iron scepter rule
Us here, as with his golden those in heav'n.
What sit we then projecting peace and war?
War hath determined us, and foiled with loss   330
Irreparable; terms of peace yet none
Voutsafed or sought; for what peace will be giv'n
To us enslaved, but custody severe,
And stripes, and arbitrary punishment
Inflicted? And what peace can we return,   335
But to our power hostility and hate,
Untamed reluctance, and revenge though slow,
Yet ever plotting how the conqueror least
May reap his conquest, and may least rejoice
In doing what we most in suffering feel?   340
Nor will occasion want, nor shall we need
With dangerous expedition to invade
Heav'n, whose high walls fear no assault or siege,
Or ambush from the deep. What if we find
Some easier enterprise? There is a place   345
(If ancient and prophetic fame in heav'n
Err not) another world, the happy seat
Of some new race called Man, about this time
To be created like to us, though less
In power and excellence, but favored more   350
Of him who rules above; so was his will
Pronounced among the gods, and by an oath,
That shook heav'n's whole circumference, confirmed.
Thither let us bend all our thoughts, to learn
What creatures there inhabit, of what mold,   355
Or substance, how endued, and what their power,
And where their weakness, how attempted best,
By force or subtlety: though heav'n be shut,
And heav'n's high arbitrator sit secure
In his own strength, this place may lie exposed   360
The utmost border of his kingdom, left
To their defense who hold it: here perhaps
Some advantageous act may be achieved
By sudden onset, either with hell fire
To waste his whole creation, or possess   365
All as our own, and drive as we were driven,
The puny habitants, or if not drive,

327–28. Cf. Ps. 2.9: "Thou shalt break
them with a rod of iron; thou shalt dash
them in pieces, like a potter's vessel."
  330. *determined:* (L to enclose within
boundaries) put an end or limit to.
  332. *Voutsafed:* vouchsafed, granted.
  336. *to:* to the limit of.
  337. *reluctance:* L *reluctare* to struggle
against.

346. *fame:* rumor. Cf. I.650–54n.
  349–51. Cf. Ps. 8.5 "For thou [O Lord]
hast made him [man] a little lower than
the angels, and hast crowned him with
glory and honor."
  357. *attempted:* tempted; seduced; as-
saulted.
  367. *puny:* Fr *puis né* born since.

Seduce them to our party, that their God
May prove their foe, and with repenting hand
Abolish his own works. This would surpass   370
Common revenge, and interrupt his joy
In our confusion, and our joy upraise
In his disturbance; when his darling sons
Hurled headlong to partake with us, shall curse
Their frail original, and faded bliss,   375
Faded so soon. Advise if this be worth
Attempting, or to sit in darkness here
Hatching vain empires." Thus Beëlzebub
Pleaded his devilish counsel, first devised
By Satan, and in part proposed: for whence,   380
But from the author of all ill could spring
So deep a malice, to confound the race
Of mankind in one root, and earth with hell
To mingle and involve, done all to spite
The great Creator? But their spite still serves   385
His glory to augment. The bold design
Pleased highly those infernal States, and joy
Sparkled in all their eyes; with full assent
They vote: whereat his speech he thus renews.
    "Well have ye judged, well ended long debate,   390
Synod of gods, and like to what ye are,
Great things resolved, which from the lowest deep
Will once more lift us up, in spite of fate,
Nearer our ancient seat; perhaps in view
Of those bright confines, whence with neighboring arms   395
And opportune excursion we may chance
Re-enter heav'n; or else in some mild zone
Dwell not unvisited of heav'n's fair light
Secure, and at the bright'ning orient beam
Purge off this gloom; the soft delicious air,   400
To heal the scar of these corrosive fires
Shall breathe her balm. But first whom shall we send
In search of this new world, whom shall we find
Sufficient? Who shall tempt with wand'ring feet
The dark unbottomed infinite abyss   405
And through the palpable obscure find out
His uncouth way, or spread his aery flight
Upborne with indefatigable wings

368–70. Cf. Gen. 6.7 "And the Lord said, I will destroy man whom I have created from the face of the earth . . . for it repenteth me that I have made [him and all the other creatures]."

374. *partake:* share.

376. *Advise:* consider.

379–80. See I.650–56.

382. *confound:* (L *confundere* to pour together, confuse—see *mingle* and *involve* two lines below) ruin.

387. *States:* statesmen; representatives of the ruling classes met in political assembly.

404. *tempt:* try; risk the perils of.

406. *palpable obscure.* Cf. Exod. 10.21: "And the Lord said unto Moses, Stretch out thine hand toward heaven, that there may be darkness over the land of Egypt, even darkness which may be felt."

407. *uncouth:* unknown.

Over the vast abrupt, ere he arrive
The happy isle; what strength, what art can then   410
Suffice, or what evasion bear him safe
Through the strict senteries and stations thick
Of angels watching round? Here he had need
All circumspection, and we now no less
Choice in our suffrage; for on whom we send,   415
The weight of all and our last hope relies."
    This said, he sat; and expectation held
His look suspense, awaiting who appeared
To second, or oppose, or undertake
The perilous attempt: but all sat mute,   420
Pondering the danger with deep thoughts; and each
In other's count'nance read his own dismay
Astonished: none among the choice and prime
Of those heav'n-warring champions could be found
So hardy as to proffer or accept   425
Alone the dreadful voyage; till at last
Satan, whom now transcendent glory raised
Above his fellows, with monarchal pride
Conscious of highest worth, unmoved thus spake.
    "O progeny of heav'n, empyreal Thrones,   430
With reason hath deep silence and demur
Seized us, though undismayed: long is the way
And hard, that out of hell leads up to light;
Our prison strong, this huge convex of fire,
Outrageous to devour, immures us round   435
Ninefold, and gates of burning adamant
Barred over us prohibit all egress.
These passed, if any pass, the void profound
Of unessential night receives him next
Wide gaping, and with utter loss of being   440
Threatens him, plunged in that abortive gulf.
If thence he scape into whatever world,
Or unknown region, what remains him less
Than unknown dangers and as hard escape?
But I should ill become this throne, O Peers,   445
And this imperial sovranty, adorned
With spendor, armed with power, if aught proposed
And judged of public moment, in the shape
Of difficulty or danger could deter

---

409. *abrupt:* L *abrumpere* to break off.
Milton uses the adjective for a noun, as
with *obscure,* line 406.
    410. *The happy isle.* In early Greek
mythology the Islands of the Blest, where
the gods sent those whom they wished to
reward with immortality, were located in
the West, in Oceanus, a river thought to
encircle the flat continent of the world.
The irony, of course, is Milton's not
Beëlzebub's.

415. *Choice:* discrimination. *suffrage:*
vote.
    423. *Astonished:* struck with fear.
    431. *demur:* hesitation.
    438–41. *the void profound* is literally
the bottomless emptiness of a night that
has no essence or being. Such a *gulf*
would be an *abortive* womb because it
could not hold anything. *unessential:*
having no real substance.

Me from attempting. Wherefore do I assume   450
These royalties, and not refuse to reign,
Refusing to accept as great a share
Of hazard as of honor, due alike
To him who reigns, and so much to him due
Of hazard more, as he above the rest   455
High honored sits? Go therefore mighty Powers,
Terror of heav'n, though fall'n; intend at home,
While here shall be our home, what best may ease
The present misery, and render hell
More tolerable; if there be cure or charm   460
To respite or deceive, or slack the pain
Of this ill mansion: intermit no watch
Against a wakeful foe, while I abroad
Through all the coasts of dark destruction seek
Deliverance for us all: this enterprise   465
None shall partake with me." Thus saying rose
The monarch, and prevented all reply,
Prudent, lest from his resolution raised
Others among the chief might offer now
(Certain to be refused) what erst they feared;   470
And so refused might in opinion stand
His rivals, winning cheap the high repute
Which he through hazard huge must earn. But they
Dreaded not more th' adventure than his voice
Forbidding; and at once with him they rose;   475
Their rising all at once was as the sound
Of thunder heard remote. Towards him they bend
With awful reverence prone; and as a god
Extol him equal to the Highest in heav'n:
Nor failed they to express how much they praised,   480
That for the general safety he despised
His own: for neither do the Spirits damned
Lose all their virtue; lest bad men should boast
Their specious deeds on earth, which glory excites,
Or close ambition varnished o'er with zeal.   485
Thus they their doubtful consultations dark
Ended rejoicing in their matchless chief:
As when from mountain tops the dusky clouds
Ascending, while the north wind sleeps, o'erspread
Heav'n's cheerful face, the louring element   490
Scowls o'er the darkened lantskip snow, or show'r;
If chance the radiant sun with farewell sweet
Extend his evening beam, the fields revive,
The birds their notes renew, and bleating herds

451. *royalties:* royal prerogatives (*splendor, power,* line 447).
452. *Refusing:* if I refuse.
457. *intend at:* turn (your) thoughts to.
461. *respite:* relieve. *deceive:* beguile.
478. *awful:* full of awe.
483–85. I.e.: Lest bad men take pride
in virtuous deeds performed for selfish motives, [God ordained that] even the devils in hell retain *that* kind of virtue.
485. *close:* hidden.
490. *element:* sky.
491. *lantskip:* landscape.

Attest their joy, that hill and valley rings.   495
O shame to men! Devil with devil damned
Firm concord holds, men only disagree
Of creatures rational, though under hope
Of heavenly grace: and God proclaiming peace,
Yet live in hatred, enmity, and strife   500
Among themselves, and levy cruel wars,
Wasting the earth, each other to destroy:
As if (which might induce us to accord)
Man had not hellish foes enow besides,
That day and night for his destruction wait.   505
    The Stygian council thus dissolved; and forth
In order came the grand infernal peers:
Midst came their mighty paramount, and seemed
Alone th' antagonist of Heav'n, nor less
Than hell's dread emperor with pomp supreme,   510
And god-like imitated state; him round
A globe of fiery Seraphim enclosed
With bright emblazonry and horrent arms.
Then of their session ended they bid cry
With trumpet's regal sound the great result: 515
Toward the four winds four speedy Cherubim
Put to their mouths the sounding alchemy
By herald's voice explained; the hollow abyss
Heard far and wide, and all the host of hell
With deaf'ning shout, returned them loud acclaim.   520
Thence more at ease their minds and somewhat raised
By false presumptuous hope, the rangèd powers
Disband, and wand'ring, each his several way
Pursues, as inclination or sad choice
Leads him perplexed, where he may likeliest find   525
Truce to his restless thoughts, and entertain
The irksome hours, till his great chief return.
Part on the plain, or in the air sublime
Upon the wing, or in swift race contend,
As at th' Olympian games or Pythian fields;   530
Part curb their fiery steeds, or shun the goal

496. *O shame to men!* This speech of the bard on the ways of men is like the lament of an OT prophet, but more like the bardic asides that became conventional after Virgil.
504. *enow:* enough.
508. *paramount:* supreme ruler.
511. *state:* magnificence.
512. *globe:* perhaps literally three-dimensional, though the L word also meant a compact body of persons, a crowd.
513. *emblazonry:* the brightly colored coats of arms that were painted on shields; here, the armor itself. *horrent:* bristling.
516–18. When Christ told his disciples about his second coming, he said (Matt. 24.30–31): "And then shall appear the sign of the Son of man in heaven: and

then shall all the tribes of the earth mourn, and they shall see the Son of man coming in the clouds of heaven with power and great glory. And he shall send his angels with a great sound of a trumpet, and they shall gather together his elect from the four winds, from one end of heaven to the other." *alchemy:* gold-like metal; brass. Heralds *explained* the meaning of the trumpets' *sound.*
526. *entertain:* while away.
528. *sublime:* borne aloft; on high.
530. *Pythian fields.* The Pythian games, held at Delphi, were like the ancient Olympic games.
531. *Shun the goal:* Come close but not hit the pole around which a charioteer had to turn in a race.

With rapid wheels, or fronted brígades form.
As when to warn proud cities war appears
Waged in the troubled sky, and armies rush
To battle in the clouds, before each van   535
Prick forth the aery knights, and couch their spears
Till thickest legions close; with feats of arms
From either end of heav'n the welkin burns.
Others with vast Typhoean rage more fell
Rend up both rocks and hills, and ride the air   540
In whirlwind; hell scarce holds the wild uproar.
As when Alcides from Oechalia crowned
With conquest, felt th' envenomed robe, and tore
Through pain up by the roots Thessalian pines,
And Lichas from the top of Oeta threw   545
Into th' Euboic sea. Others more mild,
Retreated in a silent valley, sing
With notes angelical to many a harp
Their own heroic deeds and hapless fall
By doom of battle; and complain that fate   550
Free virtue should enthrall to force or chance.
Their song was partial, but the harmony
(What could it less when Spirits immortal sing?)
Suspended hell, and took with ravishment
The thronging audience. In discourse more sweet   555
(For eloquence the soul, song charms the sense)
Others apart sat on a hill retired,
In thoughts more elevate, and reasoned high
Of providence, foreknowledge, will, and fate,
Fixed fate, free will, foreknowledge absolute,   560
And found no end, in wand'ring mazes lost.
Of good and evil much they argued then,
Of happiness and final misery,
Passion and apathy, and glory and shame,
Vain wisdom all, and false philosophy: 565

536. The language of chivalric tourna-
ments. *prick:* advance on horseback.
538. *welkin:* vault of heaven.
539. *Typhoean rage.* See I.199n.
542–46. When Hercules (*Alcides*) de-
feated the king of *Oechalia*, and prepared
to sacrifice the king's daughter, Hercules'
wife mistook his intention and sent him,
by his friend *Lichas*, a sacrificial robe
smeared with the blood of a centaur
(whom Hercules had killed some time be-
fore), thinking it would work like a love
potion and insure her husband's con-
stancy. Instead, it was a burning poison
and stuck to him so firmly that he could
not remove it. In his torment he seized
Lichas and threw him into the sea *from
the top of Oeta*, a mountain in Thessaly.
550. *doom:* decision.
552. *partial:* prejudiced; possibly a pun
on "in parts," or "polyphonic."
554. *took. Ravish, rapture,* and *rape*

all come from L *rapere* take, seize, rob.
555–65. As God in the OT holds his
enemies in derision, so the poet's irony
mocks the philosophers of hell—making
their discussions sound like a parody of
high talk by ignorant men on popular
theological and philosophical topics. *Pas-
sion and apathy* may be an allusion to
the stoic belief that men should try to
avoid all feeling, and *glory and shame*
to an opposing pagan philosophy of he-
roic action. *PL* is in part a definition of
Christian patience and Christian heroism.
559. *foreknowledge.* See *CD,* I.iii.A;
other uses of the word in the poem:
III.116, 118, and IX.768; and "God,"
p. 396.
560. *free will:* God-given, autonomous
faculty by which one chooses and pro-
poses. Cf. *CD,* I.iii.A and I.xii.B, and
other uses of the phrase in the poem:
IV.66; V.236; VIII.636; IX.1174; X.9, 46.

Yet with a pleasing sorcery could charm
Pain for a while or anguish, and excite
Fallacious hope, or arm th' obdurèd breast
With stubborn patience as with triple steel.
Another part in squadrons and gross bands,   570
On bold adventure to discover wide
That dismal world, if any clime perhaps
Might yield them easier habitation, bend
Four ways their flying march, along the banks
Of four infernal rivers that disgorge   575
Into the burning lake their baleful streams:
Abhorrèd Styx the flood of deadly hate,
Sad Acheron of sorrow, black and deep;
Cocytus, named of lamentation loud
Heard on the rueful stream; fierce Phlegethon   580
Whose waves of torrent fire inflame with rage.
Far off from these a slow and silent stream,
Lethe the river of oblivion rolls
Her wat'ry labyrinth, whereof who drinks,
Forthwith his former state and being forgets,   585
Forgets both joy and grief, pleasure and pain.
Beyond this flood a frozen continent
Lies dark and wild, beat with perpetual storms
Of whirlwind and dire hail, which on firm land
Thaws not, but gathers heap, and ruin seems   590
Of ancient pile; all else deep snow and ice,
A gulf profound as that Serbonian bog
Betwixt Damiata and Mount Casius old,
Where armies whole have sunk: the parching air
Burns frore, and cold performs th' effect of fire.   595
Thither by harpy-footed Furies haled,
At certain revolutions all the damned
Are brought: and feel by turns the bitter change
Of fierce extremes, extremes by change more fierce,
From beds of raging fire to starve in ice   600
Their soft ethereal warmth, and there to pine
Immovable, infixed, and frozen round,

568. *obdured:* hardened. An example of prolepsis, a figure in which the adjective describes the state yet to be produced by the action signified by the verb.

570. *gross:* compact.

575–86. A *burning lake* is mentioned in Rev. 20.10, p. 386. The five rivers are classical, but their confluence into a lake is Milton's idea. Each of the descriptions of the rivers is a translation of their Greek names. In Dante's *Inferno*, Lethe is said to be *far off* from the other rivers. *baleful:* of deadly influence.

586–95. The notion that hell provides both cold and hot tortures "goes back to OT apocryphal writings" (Fowler).

591. *pile:* building.

592–94. Lake Serbonis, near the city of Damiata, on one of the eastern mouths of the Nile, was surrounded by high dunes, whose sand, blown to the shore, formed quicksand.

595. *frore:* frozen.

596. In Greek mythology *harpies* were bird-like creatures with faces of women, thought to be spirits of the dead who returned to earth to carry off the living. The *Furies*, or Eumenides, were winged women, born of Uranus, whose function it was to avenge crimes. *haled:* hauled, pulled.

597. *revolutions:* recurrent periods of time.

600. *starve:* to kill or make numb with cold.

Periods of time, thence hurried back to fire.
They ferry over this Lethean sound
Both to and fro, their sorrow to augment,   605
And wish and struggle, as they pass, to reach
The tempting stream, with one small drop to lose
In sweet forgetfulness all pain and woe,
All in one moment, and so near the brink;
But fate withstands, and to oppose th' attempt   610
Medusa with Gorgonian terror guards
The ford, and of itself the water flies
All taste of living wight, as once it fled
The lip of Tantalus. Thus roving on
In cónfused march forlorn, th' advent'rous bands   615
With shudd'ring horror pale, and eyes aghast
Viewed first their lamentable lot, and found
No rest: through many a dark and dreary vale
They passed, and many a region dolorous,
O'er many a frozen, many a fiery alp,   620
Rocks, caves, lakes, fens, bogs, dens, and shades of death,
A universe of death, which God by curse
Created evil, for evil only good,
Where all life dies, death lives, and nature breeds,
Perverse, all monstrous, all prodigious things,   625
Abominable, inutterable, and worse
Than fables yet have feigned, or fear conceived,
Gorgons and Hydras, and Chimeras dire.
     Meanwhile the Adversary of God and man,
Satan with thoughts inflamed of highest design,   630
Puts on swift wings, and towards the gates of hell
Explores his solitary flight; sometimes
He scours the right-hand coast, sometimes the left,
Now shaves with level wing the deep, then soars
Up to the fiery concave tow'ring high.   635
As when far off at sea a fleet descried

611–14. *Medusa:* one of three Gorgons, the snaky-haired children of the goddess Ge (Earth) who could turn to stone anyone who looked them in the eye.

614. *Tantalus:* a mythological character condemned eternally to fail in his effort to drink from the pool in which he was set.

617–18. Cf. Matt. 12.43: "When the unclean spirit is gone out of a man, [it] walketh through dry places, seeking rest, and findeth none."

624. *nature.* See *CD*, I.ii.A and I.x.B. and other uses of this word in the sense of a creative and ordering power (as distinct from the sense of the products of that power): III.49, 455; IV.207, 242, 314; V.24, 45, 181, 294, 318; VII.482; VIII.26, 459, 534, 541, 561; IX.624; X.805; XI.49, 602; XII.29, 578.

628. *Hydras:* poisonous water snakes whose multiple heads were regenerative.

A *Chimera* had the head of a lion, the body of a goat, and the tail of a dragon.

629. *Adversary.* See I.82n.

632. *Explores his solitary flight:* (L *explorare*, to spy out, reconnoiter) searches out, pioneers, his solitary journey. Cf., *took their solitary way,* XII.649.

633. *scours:* passes rapidly along in search of something.

636–42. *discried:* seen from far off. *Hangs:* seems suspended. *equinoctial:* in the region on either side of the equator, where the trade winds blow in a general direction towards the equator. *trading flood:* the sea where the trade winds blow: here the Indian Ocean (*Ethiopian*). *Close sailing* ("close hauled"), *ply* ("steer" and "work to windward"), and *stemming* ("making headway against the wind") emphasize Satan's struggle and are true to the facts of the simile, for in

Hangs on the clouds, by equinoctial winds
Close sailing from Bengala, or the isles
Of Ternate and Tidore, whence merchants bring
Their spicy drugs: they on the trading flood   640
Through the wide Ethiopian to the Cape
Ply stemming nightly toward the pole. So seemed
Far off the flying Fiend: at last appear
Hell bounds high reaching to the horrid roof,
And thrice threefold the gates; three folds were brass,   645
Three iron, three of adamantine rock,
Impenetrable, impaled with circling fire,
Yet unconsumed. Before the gates there sat
On either side a formidable shape;
The one seemed woman to the waist, and fair,   650
But ended foul in many a scaly fold
Voluminous and vast, a serpent armed
With mortal sting: about her middle round
A cry of hell-hounds never ceasing barked
With wide Cerberean mouths full loud, and rung   655
A hideous peal: yet, when they list, would creep,
If aught disturbed their noise, into her womb,
And kennel there, yet there still barked and howled,
Within unseen. Far less abhorred than these
Vexed Scylla bathing in the sea that parts   660
Calabria from the hoarse Trinacrian shore:
Nor uglier follow the night-hag, when called
In secret, riding through the air she comes
Lured with the smell of infant blood, to dance
With Lapland witches, while the laboring moon   665
Eclipses at their charms. The other shape,
If shape it might be called that shape had none
Distinguishable in member, joint, or limb,
Or substance might be called that shadow seemed,
For each seemed either; black it stood as night,   670
Fierce as ten Furies, terrible as hell,
And shook a dreadful dart; what seemed his head
The likeness of a kingly crown had on.
Satan was now at hand, and from his seat

---

the south Indian Ocean, ships sailing SW towards the *Cape* (of Good Hope) would, from April to September, when nights in the southern hemisphere are long (*nightly*), be sailing into the prevailing SW monsoons. *Bengala:* Bengal. *Tirnate, Tidore:* islands in the Moluccas, or Spice Islands.

647. *impaled:* enclosed, as with stakes.

648–66. At the doors of the hell Aeneas visited in Virgil's poem there were "stalled" horrible beasts, including "double-shaped Scyllas." *Scylla,* the daughter of *Hecate,* goddess of night and the lower world (the *night-hag* of 662), was turned into a monster with a waist of dogs' heads, above which she had the body of a young woman, and below, the tail of a dolphin. From her cave on the Straits of Messina (between *Calabria* and the *Trinacrian shore*) opposite the whirlpool of Charybdis, she preyed on sailors passing through that dangerous channel. Cerberus was the multiheaded watchdog of Hades. *voluminous:* many-coiled. *Lapland* was famous for witchcraft. *laboring:* L *laborare* to be in distress, difficulty (said of a moon in eclipse because it suffers from the loss of the sun's light).

654. *cry:* pack.

662–63. *called/In secret:* conjured.

The monster moving onward came as fast   675
With horrid strides, hell trembled as he strode.
Th' undaunted Fiend what this might be admired,
Admired, not feared; God and his Son except,
Created thing naught values he nor shunned;
And with disdainful look thus first began.   680
    "Whence and what art thou, execrable shape,
That dar'st, though grim and terrible, advance
Thy miscreated front athwart my way
To yonder gates? Through them I mean to pass,
That be assured, without leave asked of thee: 685
Retire, or taste thy folly, and learn by proof,
Hell-born, not to contend with Spirits of heav'n."
    To whom the goblin full of wrath replied:
"Art thou that traitor angel, art thou he,
Who first broke peace in heav'n and faith, till then   690
Unbroken, and in proud rebellious arms
Drew after him the third part of heav'n's sons
Conjured against the Highest, for which both thou
And they outcast from God, are here condemned
To waste eternal days in woe and pain?   695
And reckon'st thou thyself with Spirits of heav'n,
Hell-doomed, and breath'st defiance here and scorn,
Where I reign king, and to enrage thee more,
Thy king and lord? Back to thy punishment,
False fugitive, and to thy speed add wings,   700
Lest with a whip of scorpions I pursue
Thy ling'ring, or with one stroke of this dart
Strange horror seize thee, and pangs unfelt before."
    So spake the grisly terror, and in shape,
So speaking and so threat'ning, grew tenfold   705
More dreadful and deform: on th' other side
Incensed with indignation Satan stood
Unterrified, and like a comet burned,
That fires the length of Ophiuchus huge
In th' arctic sky, and from his horrid hair   710
Shakes pestilence and war. Each at the head
Leveled his deadly aim; their fatal hands
No second stroke intend, and such a frown
Each cast at th' other, as when two black clouds
With heav'n's artillery fraught, come rattling on   715

677. *admired*: wondered.

686. *taste*. This important word in *PL* meant in Milton's time, "to learn by proof, test, or experience," as well as "to try, examine, or explore by touch," "to handle," and "to have carnal knowledge of." It also meant "to perceive by the sense of taste or smell."

692. *the third part*. Cf. Rev. 12.4, p. 385.

693. *Conjured*: (L *con* together + *jurare* swear) conspired; perhaps also be-

witched (see 662–63n).

701. Cf. 1 Kings 12.11: ". . . my father hath chastened you with whips, but I will chastise you with scorpions [whips with metal studs]."

709. *Ophiuchus*: "the serpent-bearer," a large constellation.

710. *horrid hair*. *Comet* comes from Gk *komētēs* long-haired. Comets portended horrible events. *Horrid* comes from L *horrere* to bristle.

Over the Caspian, then stand front to front
Hov'ring a space, till winds the signal blow
To join their dark encounter in mid-air:
So frowned the mighty combatants, that hell
Grew darker at their frown, so matched they stood;   720
For never but once more was either like
To meet so great a foe: and now great deeds
Had been achieved, whereof all hell had rung,
Had not the snaky sorceress that sat
Fast by hell gate, and kept the fatal key,   725
Ris'n, and with hideous outcry rushed between.
    "O father, what intends thy hand," she cried,
"Against thy only son? What fury O son,
Possesses thee to bend that mortal dart
Against thy father's head? And know'st for whom;   730
For him who sits above and laughs the while
At thee ordained his drudge, to execute
Whate'er his wrath, which he calls justice, bids,
His wrath which one day will destroy ye both."
    She spake, and at her words the hellish pest   735
Forbore, then these to her Satan returned.
    "So strange thy outcry, and thy words so strange
Thou interposest, that my sudden hand
Prevented spares to tell thee yet by deeds
What it intends; till first I know of thee,   740
What thing thou art, thus double-formed, and why
In this infernal vale first met thou call'st
Me father, and that phantasm call'st my son?
I know thee not, nor ever saw till now
Sight more detestable than him and thee."   745
    T' whom thus the portress of hell gate replied:
"Hast thou forgot me then, and do I seem
Now in thine eye so foul, once deemed so fair
In heav'n, when at th' assembly, and in sight
Of all the Seraphim with thee combined   750
In bold conspiracy against heav'n's King,
All on a sudden miserable pain
Surprised thee, dim thine eyes, and dizzy swum
In darkness, while thy head flames thick and fast
Threw forth, till on the left side op'ning wide,   755
Likest to thee in shape and count'nance bright,
Then shining heav'nly fair, a goddess armed
Out of thy head I sprung: amazement seized
All th' host of heav'n; back they recoiled afraid

718. *mid-air*. See "Universe," pp. 390–91.
721–22. Christ would finally destroy them.
739. *Prevented:* held back.
749–61. Zeus swallowed his wife fearing she would give birth to a son greater than he, but a daughter—Athena, goddess of wisdom—sprang full grown from his head. The story of the birth of Eve furnishes an even greater ironic contrast to that of Sin. Milton's genealogy of Sin and Death comes ultimately from James 1.15: "Then when lust hath conceived, it bringeth forth sin; and sin, when it is finished, bringeth forth death."

At first, and called me Sin, and for a sign   760
Portentous held me; but familiar grown,
I pleased, and with attractive graces won
The most averse, thee chiefly, who full oft
Thyself in me thy perfect image viewing
Becam'st enamored, and such joy thou took'st   765
With me in secret, that my womb conceived
A growing burden. Meanwhile war arose,
And fields were fought in heav'n; wherein remained
(For what could else) to our almighty foe
Clear victory, to our part loss and rout   770
Through all the empyrean: down they fell
Driv'n headlong from the pitch of heaven, down
Into this deep, and in the general fall
I also; at which time this powerful key
Into my hand was giv'n, with charge to keep   775
These gates for ever shut, which none can pass
Without my op'ning. Pensive here I sat
Alone, but long I sat not, till my womb
Pregnant by thee, and now excessive grown
Prodigious motion felt and rueful throes.   780
At last this odious offspring whom thou seest
Thine own begotten, breaking violent way
Tore through my entrails, that with fear and pain
Distorted, all my nether shape thus grew
Transformed: but he my inbred enemy   785
Forth issued, brandishing his fatal dart
Made to destroy: I fled, and cried out 'Death';
Hell trembled at the hideous name, and sighed
From all her caves, and back resounded 'Death.'
I fled, but he pursued (though more, it seems,   790
Inflamed with lust than rage) and swifter far,
Me overtook his mother all dismayed,
And in embraces forcible and foul
Engend'ring with me, of that rape begot
These yelling monsters that with ceaseless cry   795
Surround me, as thou saw'st, hourly conceived
And hourly born, with sorrow infinite
To me, for when they list, into the womb
That bred them they return, and howl and gnaw
My bowels, their repast; then bursting forth   800
Afresh with conscious terrors vex me round,
That rest or intermission none I find.
Before mine eyes in opposition sits
Grim Death my son and foe, who sets them on,
And me his parent would full soon devour   805

---

772. *pitch*: zenith.
782. *Thine own begotten*: an ironic echo of "For God so loved the world that he gave his only begotten son . . ." (John 3.16). Cf. 728: *thy only son*.

795ff. Milton's allegory is not specific, but the consequences of Sin's second incest, or act of perversion, are torments that may include disease, as well as the guilt and fear that Fowler suggests.

For want of other prey, but that he knows
His end with mine involved; and knows that I
Should prove a bitter morsel, and his bane,
Whenever that shall be; so fate pronounced.
But thou O father, I forewarn thee, shun   810
His deadly arrow; neither vainly hope
To be invulnerable in those bright arms,
Though tempered heav'nly, for that mortal dint,
Save he who reigns above, none can resist."
 She finished, and the subtle Fiend his lore   815
Soon learned, now milder, and thus answered smooth.
"Dear daughter, since thou claim'st me for thy sire,
And my fair son here show'st me, the dear pledge
Of dalliance had with thee in heav'n, and joys
Then sweet, now sad to mention, through dire change   820
Befall'n us unforeseen, unthought of, know
I come no enemy, but to set free
From out this dark and dismal house of pain,
Both him and thee, and all the heav'nly host
Of Spirits that in our just pretenses armed   825
Fell with us from on high: from them I go
This uncouth errand sole, and one for all
Myself expose, with lonely steps to tread
Th' unfounded deep, and through the void immense
To search with wand'ring quest a place foretold   830
Should be, and, by concurring signs, ere now
Created vast and round, a place of bliss
In the purlieus of heav'n, and therein placed
A race of upstart creatures, to supply
Perhaps our vacant room, though more removed,   835
Lest heav'n surcharged with potent multitude
Might hap to move new broils: be this or aught
Than this more secret now designed, I haste
To know, and this once known, shall soon return,
And bring ye to the place where thou and Death   840
Shall dwell at ease, and up and down unseen
Wing silently the buxom air, embalmed
With odors; there ye shall be fed and filled
Immeasurably, all things shall be your prey."
He ceased, for both seemed highly pleased, and Death   845
Grinned horrible a ghastly smile, to hear
His famine should be filled, and blessed his maw
Destined to that good hour: no less rejoiced
His mother bad, and thus bespake her sire.

---

813. *dint:* blow; stroke of thunder.
815. *lore:* lesson.
825. *pretenses:* claims.
 826ff. A parody of Christ's *errand* on
earth, where his *sole* self-sacrifice was
made *for all* men, where his career end-
ing on the cross was a *lonely* one, and
where he promised men that on his re-
turn to heaven he would prepare a *place*
for those who believed in him.
 833. *purlieus:* environs.
 836. *surcharged:* overstocked.
 842. *buxom:* pliable. See V.270n. *em-
balmed:* made fragrant and soothing, as
with a balm.
 847. *famine:* ravenous appetite.

"The key of this infernal pit by due,   850
And by command of heav'n's all-powerful King
I keep, by him forbidden to unlock
These adamantine gates; against all force
Death ready stands to interpose his dart,
Fearless to be o'ermatched by living might.   855
But what owe I to his commands above
Who hates me, and hath hither thrust me down
Into this gloom of Tartarus profound,
To sit in hateful office here confined,
Inhabitant of heav'n, and heav'nly-born,   860
Here in perpetual agony and pain,
With terrors and with clamors compassed round
Of mine own brood, that on my bowels feed:
Thou art my father, thou my author, thou
My being gav'st me; whom should I obey   865
But thee, whom follow? Thou wilt bring me soon
To that new world of light and bliss, among
The gods who live at ease, where I shall reign
At thy right hand voluptuous, as beseems
Thy daughter and thy darling, without end."   870
    Thus saying, from her side the fatal key,
Sad instrument of all our woe, she took;
And towards the gate rolling her bestial train,
Forthwith the huge portcullis high up drew,
Which but herself not all the Stygian powers   875
Could once have moved; then in the key-hole turns
Th' intrícate wards, and every bolt and bar
Of massy iron or solid rock with ease
Unfastens: on a sudden open fly
With impetuous recoil and jarring sound   880
Th' infernal doors, and on their hinges grate
Harsh thunder, that the lowest bottom shook
Of Erebus. She opened, but to shut
Excelled her power; the gates wide open stood,
That with extended wings a bannered host   885
Under spread ensigns marching might pass through
With horse and chariots ranked in loose array;
So wide they stood, and like a furnace mouth
Cast forth redounding smoke and ruddy flame.

850. *due:* right.
865. *obey:* L *oboedire, ob* towards + *oedire* (akin to *audire* to hear). This, the first occurrence of a word and idea central to the plot, is a clue to the meaning of *obedience,* i.e., an attitude and behavior of a creature towards its creator, of children to parents. See *CD,* I.x.A, and cf. other uses of *obey, obedient,* and *obedience:* III.95, 107, 190, 191, 269; IV.428, 520, 636; V.501, 514, 522, 537, 551, 806; VI.185, 740, 741, 902; VII.48, 159, 498; VIII. 240, 325, 634; IX.368, 570, 701; X.14, 145; XI.112;

XII.126, 397, 403, 408, 561.
868–70. Cf. the Nicene creed: "We believe in . . . one Lord Jesus Christ . . . who . . . sitteth on the right hand of the Father, and . . . of whose kingdom there shall be no end."
875. *powers:* army.
877. *wards:* the matching grooves and notches on keys and in locks.
883. *Erebus:* primeval Darkness, son of Chaos and brother of *Night* (894); hell.
889. *redounding:* billowing.

Before their eyes in sudden view appear 890
The secrets of the hoary deep, a dark
Illimitable ocean without bound,
Without dimension, where length, breadth, and highth,
And time and place are lost; where eldest Night
And Chaos, ancestors of Nature, hold 895
Eternal anarchy, amidst the noise
Of endless wars, and by confusion stand.
For Hot, Cold, Moist, and Dry, four champions fierce
Strive here for maistry, and to battle bring
Their embryon atoms; they around the flag 900
Of each his faction, in their several clans,
Light-armed or heavy, sharp, smooth, swift or slow,
Swarm populous, unnumbered as the sands
Of Barca or Cyrene's torrid soil,
Levied to side with warring winds, and poise 905
Their lighter wings. To whom these most adhere,
He rules a moment; Chaos umpire sits,
And by decision more embroils the fray
By which he reigns: next him high arbiter
Chance governs all. Into this wild abyss, 910
The womb of Nature and perhaps her grave,
Of neither sea, nor shore, nor air, nor fire,
But all these in their pregnant causes mixed
Confus'dly, and which thus must ever fight,
Unless th' Almighty Maker them ordain 915
His dark materials to create more worlds,
Into this wild abyss the wary Fiend
Stood on the brink of hell and looked a while,
Pondering his voyage; for no narrow frith
He had to cross. Nor was his ear less pealed 920
With noises loud and ruinous (to compare
Great things with small) than when Bellona storms,
With all her battering engines bent to raze
Some capital city; or less than if this frame
Of heav'n were falling, and these elements 925
In mutiny had from her axle torn
The steadfast earth. At last his sail-broad vans
He spreads for flight, and in the surging smoke

---

891. *hoary deep:* greyish white ocean. Cf. the description of the wake of the leviathan in Job 41.32: "one would think the deep to be hoary" or (*NEB*) "like white hair."

898–906. In the simile, countless atoms are enlisted to serve the four warring elements of fire, earth, water, and air, just as countless particles of sand are enlisted by the warring winds of the desert to serve them by lending weight (*poise*) or force to the warring winds. *Barca, Cyrene:* cities in North Africa. *embryon:* undeveloped.

912. Not the four elements, but what they came from.

919. *frith:* firth, an estuary, where the meeting of a river current and an ocean tide makes the waters turbulent and dangerous (cf. *boiling gulf,* 1027). Chaos was like a firth, but not narrow.

920. *pealed:* assailed, dinned.

922. *Bellona:* goddess of war.

924. *frame:* structure, fabric; also order, plan, scheme, system. A common synonym for universe.

927. *vans:* (L *vannus* fan for winnowing grain) fans. The sails of windmills were called "vans" or "vanes."

Uplifted spurns the ground, thence many a league
As in a cloudy chair ascending rides   930
Audacious, but that seat soon failing, meets
A vast vacuity: all unawares
Flutt'ring his pennons vain plumb down he drops
Ten thousand fadom deep, and to this hour
Down had been falling, had not by ill chance   935
The strong rebuff of some tumultuous cloud
Instinct with fire and niter hurried him
As many miles aloft: that fury stayed,
Quenched in a boggy Syrtis, neither sea,
Nor good dry land: nigh foundered on he fares,   940
Treading the crude consistence, half on foot,
Half flying; behoves him now both oar and sail.
As when a gryphon through the wilderness
With wingèd course o'er hill or moory dale,
Pursues the Arimaspian, who by stealth   945
Had from his wakeful custody purloined
The guarded gold: so eagerly the Fiend
O'er bog or steep, through strait, rough, dense, or rare,
With head, hands, wings, or feet pursues his way,
And swims or sinks, or wades, or creeps, or flies: 950
At length a universal hubbub wild
Of stunning sounds and voices all confused
Borne through the hollow dark assaults his ear
With loudest vehemence: thither he plies,
Undaunted to meet there whatever Power   955
Or Spirit of the nethermost abyss
Might in that noise reside, of whom to ask
Which way the nearest coast of darkness lies
Bordering on light; when straight behold the throne
Of Chaos, and his dark pavilion spread   960
Wide on the wasteful deep; with him enthroned
Sat sable-vested Night, eldest of things,
The consort of his reign; and by them stood
Orcus and Ades, and the dreaded name
Of Demogorgon; Rumor next and Chance,   965
And Tumult and Confusion all embroiled,
And Discord with a thousand various mouths.
    T' whom Satan turning boldly, thus. "Ye Powers
And Spirits of this nethermost abyss,

936. *rebuff:* (It. *ri* + *buffo* puff) counter blast. *tumultuous:* (L *tumere* to swell) exploding.
937. *instinct with:* impelled by. *fire:* sulphur, which is mixed with saltpeter to make gunpowder. Lava was also called "fire;" and the "fire" of thunder and lightning was considered sulphurous. Milton's imagery is both volcanic and meteorological.
939. The Syrtes were tidal marshes on the shore of North Africa.

943–47. According to a legend told by Herodotus, one-eyed creatures called Arimaspi stole gold guarded by griffons, who were half eagle and half lion.
964. *Orcus:* another name for *Ades* (Hades) or Pluto, king of hell.
965. *Demogorgon.* Not a god of classical mythology. Milton elsewhere identified him with Chaos, and during the Renaissance *Night*, *Ades*, *Rumor*, etc., were sometimes represented as his children. In Chaos even genealogy is confused.

Chaos and ancient Night, I come no spy,   970
With purpose to explore or to disturb
The secrets of your realm, but by constraint
Wand'ring this darksome desert, as my way
Lies through your spacious empire up to light,
Alone, and without guide, half lost, I seek   975
What readiest path leads where your gloomy bounds
Confine with heav'n; or if some other place
From your dominion won, th' Ethereal King
Possesses lately, thither to arrive
I travel this profound; direct my course;   980
Directed, no mean recompense it brings
To your behoof, if I that region lost,
All usurpation thence expelled, reduce
To her original darkness and your sway
(Which is my present journey) and once more   985
Erect the standard there of ancient Night;
Yours be th' advantage all, mine the revenge."
    Thus Satan; and him thus the anarch old
With falt'ring speech and visage incomposed
Answered. "I know thee, stranger, who thou art,   990
That mighty leading angel, who of late
Made head against heav'n's King, though overthrown.
I saw and heard, for such a numerous host
Fled not in silence through the frighted deep
With ruin upon ruin, rout on rout,   995
Confusion worse confounded; and heav'n gates
Poured out by millions her victorious bands
Pursuing. I upon my frontiers here
Keep residence; if all I can will serve,
That little which is left so to defend,   1000
Encroached on still through our intestine broils
Weak'ning the scepter of old Night: first hell
Your dungeon stretching far and wide beneath;
Now lately heaven and earth, another world
Hung o'er my realm, linked in a golden chain   1005
To that side heav'n from whence your legions fell:
If that way be your walk, you have not far;
So much the nearer danger; go and speed;
Havoc and spoil and ruin are my gain."
    He ceased; and Satan stayed not to reply,   1010
But glad that now his sea should find a shore,
With fresh alacrity and force renewed

---

977. *Confine with:* border on.
980. *profound:* L *pro* prior to + *fundus* bottom.
982. *behoof:* advantage.
988. *anarch.* The "ruler" of an anarchy ("no ruler") must be a non-ruler.
989. *incomposed:* disordered, disturbed.
990. A man possessed of the spirit of an unclean devil addressed Christ in the same words: "I know thee who thou art" (Mark 1.24).
1001. *still:* constantly. *intestine broils:* civil wars.
1004. *heaven:* the universe around the earth.
1009. *Havoc:* destruction. *spoil:* plunder. *ruin:* what remains after destruction.

Springs upward like a pyramid of fire
Into the wild expanse, and through the shock
Of fighting elements, on all sides round   1015
Environed wins his way; harder beset
And more endangered, than when Argo passed
Through Bosporus betwixt the justling rocks:
Or when Ulysses on the larboard shunned
Charybdis, and by th' other whirlpool steered.   1020
So he with difficulty and labor hard
Moved on, with difficulty and labor he;
But he once passed, soon after when man fell,
Strange alteration! Sin and Death amain
Following his track, such was the will of Heav'n,   1025
Paved after him a broad and beaten way
Over the dark abyss, whose boiling gulf
Tamely endured a bridge of wondrous length
From hell continued reaching th' utmost orb
Of this frail world; by which the Spirits perverse   1030
With easy intercourse pass to and fro
To tempt or punish mortals, except whom
God and good angels guard by special grace.
But now at last the sacred influence
Of light appears, and from the walls of heav'n   1035
Shoots far into the bosom of dim Night
A glimmering dawn; here Nature first begins
Her farthest verge, and Chaos to retire
As from her outmost works a broken foe
With tumult less and with less hostile din,   1040
That Satan with less toil, and now with ease
Wafts on the calmer wave by dubious light
And like a weather-beaten vessel holds
Gladly the port, though shrouds and tackle torn;
Or in the emptier waste, resembling air,   1045
Weighs his spread wings, at leisure to behold
Far off th' empyreal heav'n, extended wide

1013. *pyramid:* (Milton probably thought Gk *pyr* fire its root) spire.
1016–17. The Argonauts, in quest of the Golden Fleece, sailed their ship the *Argo* between two floating stone cliffs that crushed ships in the trap-like straits.
1018–20. See II.648–66n.
1024. *amain:* with all (their) might.
1029. *utmost orb:* outermost sphere of the universe.
1032–33. *tempt:* L *temptare* to feel, try, tempt; akin to L *tendere* to stretch. For Milton on "temptation," see *CD*, I.viii.C. Cf. other uses of *tempt* and temptation: IV.65; V.846; VI.908; VIII.643; IX.281, 296, 299, 328, 364, 531, 736; X.14. See "Angels," pp. 394–96.
1033. Cf. *CD*, I.ix.A.
1034. *influence:* (L *influere* to flow

into) an astrological term for the effective virtue, power, force (an "etherial fluid") emitted by the stars and the heavens, and acting upon the earth and its creatures; here, a kind of metaphor, since the *sacred* light naturalizes chaos.
1036. *bosom:* (root meaning, "the space embraced by two arms") womb, stomach; here, the interior.
1037. *Nature:* order; the antithesis of Chaos.
1039–40. A military simile. *works:* fortifications.
1043. *holds:* makes for.
1046. *Weighs:* balances (like the arms of a pair of scales), keeps steady.
1047. *empyreal heav'n:* as distinct from the heavens of the universe. See I.117n.

In circuit, undetermined square or round,
With opal tow'rs and battlements adorned
Of living sapphire, once his native seat;   1050
And fast by hanging in a golden chain
This pendent world, in bigness as a star
Of smallest magnitude close by the moon.
Thither full fraught with mischievous revenge,
Accursed, and in a curséd hour, he hies.   1055

1048. *undetermined:* not authoritatively decided, undeterminable; or (because of its size) beyond Satan's power to tell.

1050. *living:* in its native state. *sapphire.* Cf. Rev. 21.19, p. 387.

1051. *golden chain.* In a note to his translation of one of Milton's academic exercises (*Prolusion II*), Merritt Y. Hughes says: "Homer's story (*II* 8.18–29) of the challenge of Zeus to the other gods to drag him from heaven by a golden chain, and of his boast that he would be able to lift them all up to heaven with it, passed through many allegorical interpretations, from that of Plato's *Thaeatetus*, 153c, to Bacon's in *The Advancement of Learning* I.i.3: 'The highest link of nature's chain must needs be tied to the foot of Jupiter's chain.' " The passage in Milton's exercise reads: "and that universal interaction of all things, that lovely concord among them, which Pythagoras poetically symbolized as harmony, was splendidly and aptly represented by Homer's figure of the golden chain which Jove suspended from heaven" (trans. Hughes). See "Scale of Nature," pp. 392–93.

1052. *pendent world:* the universe.

Book III

The Argument

God sitting on his throne sees Satan flying towards this world, then newly created; shows him to the Son who sat at his right hand; foretells the success of Satan in perverting mankind; clears his own justice and wisdom from all imputation, having created man free and able enough to have withstood his tempter; yet declares his purpose of grace towards him, in regard he fell not of his own malice, as did Satan, but by him seduced. The Son of God renders praises to his Father for the manifestation of his gracious purpose towards man; but God again declares, that grace cannot be extended towards man without the satisfaction of divine justice; man hath offended the majesty of God by aspiring to Godhead, and therefore with all his progeny devoted to death must die, unless someone can be found sufficient to answer for his offense, and undergo his punishment. The Son of God freely offers himself a ransom for man: the Father accepts him, ordains his incarnation, pronounces his exaltation above all names in heaven and earth; commands all the angels to adore him; they obey, and hymning to their harps in full choir, celebrate the Father and the Son. Meanwhile Satan alights upon the bare convex of this world's outermost orb; where wandering he first finds a place since called the Limbo of Vanity; what persons and things fly up thither; thence comes to the gate of heaven, described ascending by stairs, and the waters above the firmament that flow about it: his passage thence to the orb of the sun; he finds there Uriel the regent of that orb, but first changes himself into the shape of a meaner angel; and pretending a zealous desire to behold the new creation and man whom God had placed there, inquires of him the place of his habitation, and is directed; alights first on Mount Niphates.

> Hail holy Light, offspring of Heav'n first-born,
> Or of th' Eternal coeternal beam

III.1–55. To move from hell to heaven is to move from darkness to light, and Milton marks this change by a second invocation, this one to holy Light, God himself, who is light and dwells in fire, flame, dazzling brightness. Milton's speculations include common theological questions: If God is light and God is eternal, isn't light also without beginning? But God's first words in Gen. 1 are, "Let there be light." Perhaps God was not creating light but only calling upon light to *invest/ The rising world,* the heaven and earth he had just begun to create, cf. Gen. 1.1–3, p. 352. The poet's invocation is not, however, a theological or a scientific discussion. *Light* may carry suggestions of God, Christ ("I am the light of the world"), wisdom, and inspiration of the Holy Spirit, at the same time that it means the physical light by which men see nature—if they are not, like John Milton, totally blind. The invocation is a hymn and a prayer, uttered by Milton, the bard, the *vates,* the seer, the prophetic maker of this poem, who, like Homer, could see only with his memory and his inward eye.

1. *first-born.* In an oration written as an undergraduate (*Prolusion I*) Milton argued that "Day is more ancient than Night; that this world, recently emerged from Chaos, was illuminated by diffused light before Night had begun her alternations" (*CE,* XII.135).

May I express thee unblamed? Since God is light,
And never but in unapproachèd light
Dwelt from eternity, dwelt then in thee,   5
Bright effluence of bright essence increate.
Or hear'st thou rather pure ethereal stream,
Whose fountain who shall tell? Before the sun,
Before the heavens thou wert, and at the voice
Of God, as with a mantle didst invest   10
The rising world of waters dark and deep,
Won from the void and formless infinite.
Thee I revisit now with bolder wing,
Escaped the Stygian pool, though long detained
In that obscure sojourn, while in my flight   15
Through utter and through middle darkness borne
With other notes than to th' Orphéan lyre
I sung of Chaos and eternal Night,
Taught by the Heav'nly Muse to venture down
The dark descent, and up to reascend,   20
Though hard and rare: thee I revisit safe,
And feel thy sovran vital lamp; but thou
Revisit'st not these eyes, that roll in vain
To find thy piercing ray, and find no dawn;
So thick a drop serene hath quenched their orbs,   25
Or dim suffusion veiled. Yet not the more
Cease I to wander where the Muses haunt
Clear spring, or shady grove, or sunny hill,
Smit with the love of sacred song; but chief

3. *God is light*. Cf. 1 John 1.5: "This then is the message which we have heard of him, and declare unto you, that God is light, and in him is no darkness at all." *express:* describe. *unblamed:* without being guilty of improper speculation.

4–5. Cf. 1 Tim. 6.16: "[God] only hath immortality, dwelling in the light which no man can approach unto. . . ."

6. *effluence:* L *ex* out + *fluere* to flow. *increate:* uncreated.

10. *invest:* (L *in* + *vestis* garment) envelop. Cf. Ps. 104.1–2 "O Lord my God . . . who coverest thyself with light as with a garment."

16. The *utter* (outer, beyond limits) *darkness* is hell; the *middle*, chaos.

17. *Orphean.* In Greek myth Orpheus, whose music could spellbind wild beasts, descended into hell in a vain effort to charm Pluto and Persephone by song into letting him regain his wife Eurydice. Milton's *notes* are epic, whereas those of Orpheus's hymn "To Night" were lyric.

25. *drop serene: gutta serena,* the medical term for Milton's blindness.

26. *dim suffusion: suffusio nigra,* medical term for a cataract.

26–32. "He rendered his studies and various works more easy and pleasant by alloting them their several portions of the day. Of these the time friendly to the Muses fell to his poetry; and he, waking early (as is the use of temperate men), had commonly a good stack of verses ready against his amanuensis came; which if it happened to be later than ordinary, he would complain that 'he wanted to be milked.' The evenings he likewise spent in reading some choice poets, by way of refreshment after the day's toil, and to store his fancy against morning. Besides his ordinary lectures [i.e., readings] out of the Bible and the best commentators on the week day, that was his sole subject on Sunday." From the anonymous *Life of Milton.* In his essay *Of Education* Milton recommended that the students in his ideal boarding school occupy themselves between dinner and bedtime with "the easy grounds of religion and the story of scriptures."

29–32. I.e., the poetry of the Bible, which Milton read in Hebrew, Aramaic, and Greek, as well as in Latin and English translations. Here he refers chiefly to "those frequent songs [i.e., odes and hymns] throughout the law and prophets [which are] beyond all [pagan examples], not in their divine argument alone, but in the very critical art of composition, [and which] may be easily made appear over all the kinds of lyric poesy to be incomparable." *The Reason of Church*

Thee Sion and the flow'ry brooks beneath   30
That wash thy hallowed feet, and warbling flow,
Nightly I visit: nor sometimes forget
Those other two equaled with me in fate,
So were I equaled with them in renown,
Blind Thamyris and blind Maeonides,   35
And Tiresias and Phineus prophets old.
Then feed on thoughts, that voluntary move
Harmonious numbers; as the wakeful bird
Sings darkling, and in shadiest covert hid
Tunes her nocturnal note. Thus with the year   40
Seasons return, but not to me returns
Day, or the sweet approach of ev'n or morn,
Or sight of vernal bloom, or summer's rose,
Or flocks, or herds, or human face divine;
But cloud instead, and ever-during dark   45
Surrounds me, from the cheerful ways of men
Cut off, and for the book of knowledge fair
Presented with a universal blank
Of nature's works to me expunged and razed,
And wisdom at one entrance quite shut out.   50
So much the rather thou celestial Light
Shine inward, and the mind through all her powers
Irradiate, there plant eyes, all mist from thence
Purge and disperse, that I may see and tell
Of things invisible to mortal sight.   55
    Now had the Almighty Father from above,
From the pure empyrean where he sits
High throned above all highth, bent down his eye,
His own works and their works at once to view:
About him all the sanctities of heaven   60
Stood thick as stars, and from his sight received
Beatitude past utterance; on his right
The radiant image of his glory sat,
His only Son; on earth he first beheld

Government, p. 293. *Sion . . . brooks.*
Cf. I.10–11. *nightly:* in the night. Cf.
darkling at 39.

35–36. *Thamyris:* a blind poet alluded
to in the *Iliad* II.594–600. *Maeonides:*
Homer. *Tiresias* was the blind old man in
Oedipus and *Antigone* whose prophecies
proved to be true. *Phineus:* another myth-
ical blind prophet.

37–38. "The thoughts, as if by their
own power, produce the lines of poetry."
In an early work (*An Apology for Smec-
tymnuus*), speaking of his own experience
in writing prose, Milton gave a similar
description of the "voluntary" nature of
composition: "For me, readers, although
I cannot say that I am utterly untrained
in those rules which best rhetoricians
have given, or unacquainted with those
examples which the prime authors of elo-

quence have written in any learned
tongue; yet true eloquence I find to be
none, but the serious and hearty love of
truth: and that whose mind soever is
fully possessed with a fervent desire to
know good things, and with the dearest
charity to infuse the knowledge of them
into others, when such a man would
speak, his words (by what I can express)
like so many nimble and airy servitors,
trip about him at command, and in well-
ordered files, as he would wish, fall aptly
into their own places."

38. *numbers:* verses. *wakeful bird.*
nightingale.

39. *darkling:* in the dark.

57. *pure empyrean:* (Gk *pyr* fire) re-
gion of pure light.

60. *sanctities:* angels.

Our two first parents, yet the only two   65
Of mankind, in the happy garden placed,
Reaping immortal fruits of joy and love,
Uninterrupted joy, unrivaled love
In blissful solitude; he then surveyed
Hell and the gulf between, and Satan there   70
Coasting the wall of heav'n on this side Night
In the dun air sublime, and ready now
To stoop with wearied wings, and willing feet
On the bare outside of this world, that seemed
Firm land embosomed without firmament,   75
Uncertain which, in ocean or in air.
Him God beholding from his prospect high,
Wherein past, present, future he beholds,
Thus to his only Son foreseeing spake.
   "Only begotten Son, seest thou what rage   80
Transports our Adversary, whom no bounds
Prescribed, no bars of hell, nor all the chains
Heaped on him there, nor yet the main abyss
Wide interrupt can hold; so bent he seems
On desperate revenge, that shall redound   85
Upon his own rebellious head. And now
Through all restraint broke loose he wings his way
Not far off heav'n, in the precincts of light,
Directly towards the new-created world,
And man there placed, with purpose to assay   90
If him by force he can destroy, or worse,
By some false guile pervert; and shall pervert;
For man will hearken to his glozing lies,
And easily transgress the sole command,
Sole pledge of his obedience: so will fall   95
He and his faithless progeny: whose fault?
Whose but his own? Ingrate, he had of me
All he could have; I made him just and right,
Sufficient to have stood, though free to fall.
Such I created all th' ethereal Powers   100

71. *Coasting:* sailing along the shore of.
72. *dun:* dusky. *sublime:* above.
73. *stoop:* descend; (of a heavenly body) to begin to descend; (of a bird of prey) to swoop down on.
74. *world:* the sphere which enclosed all the smaller spheres constituting the universe.
75. *firmament:* the atmosphere, which exists only *within* the universe.
81. The God of the OT could be derisive, and Milton's natural ironic bent led easily to the pun on *Transports*, meaning "enraptures" as well as "carries across."
83. *main:* vast, as in "the ocean main," or (VII.279) *main ocean.*
84. *interrupt:* (a past participle) forming a *wide interval* (between hell and the

world).
92–134. See "God," p. 396, "Reason," p. 392, "Freedom," p. 397, and *CD*, I.iii. Cf. VIII.325ff.
93. *glozing:* flattering.
95. *sole pledge.* The only token, sign, proof, evidence of Adam's obedience was his not eating the fruit. His only "act" of obedience was not eating—as God's only law, only command, was not to eat. Milton uses *pledge* elsewhere in the sense of "child," a token of its parents' love. Adam's abstaining was a child of his obedience. In *CD*, I.x.A, Milton called the Tree "a pledge, as it were, and memorial of obedience"—here the word means a concrete "outward sign." Similarly Samson's hair was a *pledge*, as was his not cutting it.

And Spirits, both them who stood and them who failed;
Freely they stood who stood, and fell who fell.
Not free, what proof could they have giv'n sincere
Of true allegiance, constant faith or love,
Where only what they needs must do, appeared, 105
Not what they would? What praise could they receive?
What pleasure I from such obedience paid,
When will and reason (reason also is choice)
Useless and vain, of freedom both despoiled,
Made passive both, had served necessity, 110
Not me. They therefore as to right belonged,
So were created, nor can justly accuse
Their Maker, or their making, or their fate,
As if predestination overruled
Their will, disposed by absolute decree 115
Or high foreknowledge; they themselves decreed
Their own revolt, not I: if I foreknew,
Foreknowledge had no influence on their fault,
Which had no less proved certain unforeknown.
So without least impulse or shadow of fate, 120
Or aught by me immutably foreseen,
They trespass, authors to themselves in all
Both what they judge and what they choose; for so
I formed them free, and free they must remain,
Till they enthrall themselves: I else must change 125
Their nature, and revoke the high decree
Unchangeable, eternal, which ordained
Their freedom, they themselves ordained their fall.
The first sort by their own suggestion fell,
Self-tempted, self-depraved: man falls deceived 130
By the other first: man therefore shall find grace,
The other none: in mercy and justice both,
Through heav'n and earth, so shall my glory excel,
But mercy first and last shall brightest shine."
Thus while God spake, ambrosial fragrance filled 135
All heav'n, and in the blessèd Spirits elect
Sense of new joy ineffable diffused:
Beyond compare the Son of God was seen
Most glorious, in him all his Father shone
Substantially expressed, and in his face 140
Divine compassion visibly appeared,
Love without end, and without measure grace,

108. *reason:* the power of judging rightly, of distinguishing true from false and right from wrong. See *CD*, I.ii.B, I.x.B, and I.xii.A. Cf. other related uses of the word: V.102, 106, 487; VI.41, 42, 125, 126; VIII.554, 591; IX.352, 360, 654, 1130; XII.84, 86, 89, 92, 98.
117. *if:* granted that.
129. *The first sort:* the fallen angels. *suggestion:* temptation.

136. *Spirits elect:* the angels who did not revolt. See "Angels," pp. 394–96.
140. *Substantially:* in essence. But the term had a special meaning in theological discussions about the nature of the Trinity, the subtleties of which Milton avoided in *PL*.
142. *grace.* See "The Fortunate Fall," pp. 398–99.

Which uttering thus he to his Father spake.
"O Father, gracious was that word which closed
Thy sovran sentence, that man should find grace;   145
For which both heav'n and earth shall high extol
Thy praises, with th' innumerable sound
Of hymns and sacred songs, wherewith thy throne
Encompassed shall resound thee ever blessed.
For should man finally be lost, should man   150
Thy creature late so loved, thy youngest son
Fall circumvented thus by fraud, though joined
With his own folly? That be from thee far,
That far be from thee, Father, who art judge
Of all things made, and judgest only right.   155
Or shall the Adversary thus obtain
His end, and frustrate thine, shall he fulfill
His malice, and thy goodness bring to naught,
Or proud return though to his heavier doom,
Yet with revenge accomplished, and to hell   160
Draw after him the whole race of mankind,
By him corrupted? Or wilt thou thyself
Abolish thy creation, and unmake,
For him, what for thy glory thou hast made?
So should thy goodness and thy greatness both   165
Be questioned and blasphemed without defense."
      To whom the great Creator thus replied.
"O Son, in whom my soul hath chief delight,
Son of my bosom, Son who art alone
My Word, my wisdom, and effectual might,   170
All hast thou spoken as my thoughts are, all
As my eternal purpose hath decreed:
Man shall not quite be lost, but saved who will,
Yet not of will in him, but grace in me
Freely voutsafed; once more I will renew   175
His lapsèd powers, though forfeit and enthralled
By sin to foul exorbitant desires;
Upheld by me, yet once more he shall stand
On even ground against his mortal foe,
By me upheld, that he may know how frail   180
His fall'n condition is, and to me owe

153. See the words Abraham used in pleading with the Lord, Gen. 18.25: "That be far from thee to do after this manner, to slay the righteous with the wicked: and that the righteous should be as the wicked, that be far from thee: Shall not the Judge of all the earth do right?"
156. *Adversary:* meaning of the Hebrew word *Satan.*
159. *doom:* condemnation.
169. *Son of my bosom.* Cf. John 1.18: "the only begotten Son, which is in the bosom of the Father . . ."
170. *My Word.* Cf. *CD,* I.v (*CE,* XIV.181), "the Son existed in the beginning, under the name of the logos or word, and was the first of the whole creation, by whom afterwards all other things were made both in heaven and earth. John 1.1–3: 'in the beginning was the Word, and the Word was with God, and the Word was God'. . . ." *my wisdom:* 1 Cor. 1.24: "Christ the power of God, and the wisdom of God."
180–81. Cf. Ps. 39.4: "Lord, make me to know mine end, and the measure of my days, what it is; that I may know how frail I am."

All his deliv'rance, and to none but me.
Some I have chosen of peculiar grace
Elect above the rest; so is my will:
The rest shall hear me call, and oft be warned   185
Their sinful state, and to appease betimes
Th' incensèd Deity, while offered grace
Invites; for I will clear their senses dark,
What may suffice, and soften stony hearts
To pray, repent, and bring obedience due.   190
To prayer, repentance, and obedience due,
Though but endeavored with sincere intent,
Mine ear shall not be slow, mine eye not shut.
And I will place within them as a guide
My umpire conscience, whom if they will hear,   195
Light after light well used they shall attain,
And to the end persisting, safe arrive.
This my long sufferance and my day of grace
They who neglect and scorn, shall never taste;
But hard be hardened, blind be blinded more,   200
That they may stumble on, and deeper fall;
And none but such from mercy I exclude.
But yet all is not done; man disobeying,
Disloyal breaks his fealty, and sins
Against the high supremacy of Heav'n,   205
Affecting Godhead, and so losing all,
To expiate his treason hath naught left,
But to destruction sacred and devote,
He with his whole posterity must die,
Die he or justice must; unless for him   210
Some other able, and as willing, pay
The rigid satisfaction, death for death.
Say heav'nly Powers, where shall we find such love,
Which of ye will be mortal to redeem
Man's mortal crime, and just th' unjust to save,   215
Dwells in all heaven charity so dear?''

184. *Elect.* Milton rejected the Calvin-ist doctrine that God had from the be-ginning predestined the damnation or salvation of each individual soul. Rather, he thought that only the general reward of salvation to all who "believed" was predestined: no soul was damned before it was, so to speak, born. But Milton agreed with St. Augustine that for rea-sons not revealed to men certain human beings and all unfallen angels were elected in that they were predestined to be exemplarily holy. These were the *blessed Spirits elect* (136) and the sons of Adam here referred to as *of peculiar* [i.e., special or individual] *grace*—that is, holy men, or saints. But at line 330 *saints* means the elect of both sorts—those who were elected from the beginning and those who by their own choice contributed to their own salvation. Cf. *CD*, I, iv (*CE*,

XIV.125): "God . . . has elected who-ever believes and continues in the faith."
189. Cf. Ezek. 11.19: "I will take the stony heart out of their flesh, and will give them an heart of flesh."
195. *conscience.* See *CD*, I.ii.A; also "Reason," p. 392, and cf. other uses of the word: IV.23; X.842, 849; XII.297, 522, 529.
200. See *CD*, I.viii.B.
203–16. See "The Fortunate Fall," pp. 398–99.
206. *Affecting:* aspiring to.
208. *sacred and devote:* synonyms for *consecrated,* meaning "set apart for some holy purpose," such as sacrifice.
215. Cf. 1 Pet. 3.18: "For Christ also hath once suffered for sins, the just for the unjust, that he might bring us to God."
216. *charity:* LL *caritas* Christian love.

He asked, but all the heav'nly quire stood mute,
And silence was in heav'n; on man's behalf
Patron or intercessor none appeared,
Much less that durst upon his own head draw   220
The deadly forfeiture, and ransom set.
And now without redemption all mankind
Must have been lost, adjudged to death and hell
By doom severe, had not the Son of God,
In whom the fullness dwells of love divine,   225
His dearest mediation thus renewed.
   "Father, thy word is passed, man shall find grace;
And shall grace not find means, that finds her way,
The speediest of thy wingèd messengers,
To visit all thy creatures, and to all   230
Comes unprevented, unimplored, unsought,
Happy for man, so coming; he her aid
Can never seek, once dead in sins and lost;
Atonement for himself or offering meet,
Indebted and undone, hath none to bring: 235
Behold me then, me for him, life for life
I offer, on me let thine anger fall;
Account me man; I for his sake will leave
Thy bosom, and this glory next to thee
Freely put off, and for him lastly die   240
Well pleased, on me let Death wreck all his rage;
Under his gloomy power I shall not long
Lie vanquished; thou hast giv'n me to possess
Life in myself forever, by thee I live,
Though now to Death I yield, and am his due   245
All that of me can die, yet that debt paid,
Thou wilt not leave me in the loathsome grave
His prey, nor suffer my unspotted soul
Forever with corruption there to dwell;
But I shall rise victorious, and subdue   250

217–18. Cf. Rev. 8.1: "And when he had opened the seventh seal, there was silence in heaven about the space of half an hour."
219. *Patron:* an advocate, such as a patron saint. Cf. 1 John 2.1: "My little children, these things write I unto you, that ye sin not. And if any man sin, we have an advocate with the Father, Jesus Christ the righteous."
224. *doom:* judgment.
225. Cf. Col. 2.9: "In him dwelleth all the fulness of the Godhead bodily."
227. *passed:* pledged.
231. *unprevented:* unanticipated.
233. Cf. Eph. 2.4–5: "But God, who is rich in mercy, for his great love wherewith he loved us, even when we were dead in sins, hath quickened us together with Christ (by grace ye are saved)."
243–44. Cf. John 5.26 "For as the Father hath life in himself; so hath he

given to the Son to have life in himself."
247–49. Cf. Ps. 16.10: "For thou wilt not leave my soul in hell; neither wilt thou suffer thine Holy One to see corruption."
250–59. Cf. 1 Cor. 15.26, 51–55: "The last enemy that shall be destroyed is death. . . . Behold, I shew you a mystery; We shall not all sleep, but we shall all be changed, In a moment, in the twinkling of an eye, at the last trump: for the trumpet shall sound, and the dead shall be raised incorruptible, and we shall be changed. For this corruptible must put on incorruption, and this mortal must put on immortality. So when this corruptible shall have put on incorruption, and this mortal shall have put on immortality, then shall be brought to pass the saying that is written, Death is swallowed up in victory. O death, where is thy sting? O grave, where is thy victory?" Col. 2.15:

My vanquisher, spoiled of his vaunted spoil;
Death his death's wound shall then receive, and stoop
Inglorious, of his mortal sting disarmed.
I through the ample air in triumph high
Shall lead hell captive maugre hell, and show   255
The powers of darkness bound. Thou at the sight
Pleased, out of heaven shalt look down and smile,
While by thee raised I ruin all my foes,
Death last, and with his carcass glut the grave:
Then with the multitude of my redeemed   260
Shall enter heaven long absent, and return,
Father, to see thy face, wherein no cloud
Of anger shall remain, but peace assured,
And reconcilement; wrath shall be no more
Thenceforth, but in thy presence joy entire."   265
    His words here ended, but his meek aspéct
Silent yet spake, and breathed immortal love
To mortal men, above which only shone
Filial obedience: as a sacrifice
Glad to be offered, he attends the will   270
Of his great Father. Admiration seized
All heav'n, what this might mean, and wither tend
Wond'ring; but soon th' Almighty thus replied:
    "O thou in heav'n and earth the only peace
Found out for mankind under wrath, O thou   275
My sole complacence! well thou know'st how dear
To me are all my works, nor man the least
Though last created, that for him I spare
Thee from my bosom and right hand, to save,
By losing thee a while, the whole race lost.   280
Thou therefore whom thou only canst redeem,
Their nature also to thy nature join;
And be thyself man among men on earth,
Made flesh, when time shall be, of virgin seed,
By wondrous birth: be thou in Adam's room   285
The head of all mankind, though Adam's son.
As in him perish all men, so in thee
As from a second root shall be restored,

"And having spoiled principalities and powers, he made a shew of them openly, triumphing over them in it." Col. 1.12–13: "Giving thanks unto the Father, . . . Who hath delivered us from the power of darkness."

254–65. Having predicted his triumphant resurrection after the crucifixion (250–53), Christ skips forward to the time of the Last Judgment, at the end of his 1,000 years' reign on earth (the Millennium).

255. Cf. Eph. 4.8: "When he ascended up on high, he led captivity captive."

maugre: in spite of.

258. *ruin:* L *ruere* hurl to the ground.
270. *attends:* awaits.
271. *Admiration:* astonishment.
276. *complacence:* source of pleasure.
285–86. Cf. 1 Cor. 11.3 "The head of every man is Christ." *room:* place. *Adam's son:* Jesus, son of man.
287. Cf. 1 Cor. 15.22 "As in Adam all die, even so in Christ shall all be made alive." See "The Fortunate Fall," pp 398–99.
288. Cf. Rev. 22.16: "I am the root and the offspring of David."

As many as are restored, without thee none.
His crime makes guilty all his sons, thy merit 290
Imputed shall absolve them who renounce
Their own both righteous and unrighteous deeds,
And live in thee transplanted, and from thee
Receive new life. So man, as is most just,
Shall satisfy for man, be judged and die, 295
And dying rise, and rising with him raise
His brethren, ransomed with his own dear life.
So heav'nly love shall outdo hellish hate,
Giving to death, and dying to redeem,
So dearly to redeem what hellish hate 300
So easily destroyed, and still destroys
In those who, when they may, accept not grace.
Nor shalt thou by descending to assume
Man's nature, lessen or degrade thine own.
Because thou hast, though throned in highest bliss 305
Equal to God, and equally enjoying
God-like fruition, quitted all to save
A world from utter loss, and hast been found
By merit more than birthright Son of God,
Found worthiest to be so by being good, 310
Far more than great or high; because in thee
Love hath abounded more than glory abounds,
Therefore thy humiliation shall exalt
With thee thy manhood also to this throne;
Here shalt thou sit incarnate, here shalt reign 315
Both God and man, Son both of God and man,
Anointed universal King; all power
I give thee, reign forever, and assume
Thy merits; under thee as Head Supreme
Thrones, Princedoms, Powers, Dominions I reduce: 320
All knees to thee shall bow, of them that bide
In heaven, or earth, or under earth in hell;

290–94. Cf. Rom. 5.15–19 [*NEB*]: "But God's act of grace is out of all proportion to Adam's wrongdoing. For if the wrongdoing of that one man brought death upon so many, its effect is vastly exceeded by the grace of God and the gift that came to so many by the grace of the one man, Jesus Christ. And again, the gift of God is not to be compared in its effect with that one man's sin; for the judicial action, following upon the one offence, issued in a verdict of condemnation, but the act of grace, following upon so many misdeeds, issued in a verdict of acquittal. For if by the wrongdoing of that one man death established its reign, through a single sinner, much more shall those who receive in far greater measure God's grace, and his gift of righteousness, live and reign through the one man, Jesus Christ." *Imputed:* credited by

transferal (to *them who* etc.). See *CD*, I.xxii.A and **B**.
297. *ransomed.* Cf. Matt. 20.28: "Even as the Son of man came not to be ministered unto, but to minister, and to give his life a ransom for many."
307. *fruition:* pleasure of possession. *quitted:* given up.
317. *Anointed:* meaning of the Hebrew word *mashiah.* Cf. Matt. 28.18: "And Jesus came and spake unto them, saying, All power is given unto me in heaven and in earth."
320. *Princedoms:* Principalities. See "Angels," p. 394. *reduce:* bring back, restore.
321–22. Cf. Phil. 2.10 "That at the name of Jesus every knee should bow, of things in heaven, and things in earth, and things under the earth."

When thou attended gloriously from heav'n
Shalt in the sky appear, and from thee send
The summoning Archangels to proclaim   325
Thy dread tribunal: forthwith from all winds
The living, and forthwith the cited dead
Of all past ages to the general doom
Shall hasten, such a peal shall rouse their sleep.
Then all thy saints assembled, thou shalt judge   330
Bad men and angels, they arraigned shall sink
Beneath thy sentence; hell, her numbers full,
Thenceforth shall be forever shut. Meanwhile
The world shall burn, and from her ashes spring
New heav'n and earth, wherein the just shall dwell,   335
And after all their tribulations long
See golden days, fruitful of golden deeds,
With joy and love triumphing, and fair truth.
Then thou thy regal scepter shalt lay by,
For regal scepter then no more shall need,   340
God shall be all in all. But all ye gods,
Adore him, who to compass all this dies,
Adore the Son, and honor him as me."
      No sooner had th' Almighty ceased, but all
The multitude of angels with a shout   345
Loud as from numbers without number, sweet
As from blest voices, uttering joy, heav'n rung
With jubilee, and loud hosannas filled
Th' eternal regions: lowly reverent
Towards either throne they bow, and to the ground   350
With solemn adoration down they cast
Their crowns inwove with amarant and gold,

323–41. Milton's description of the Last Judgment echoes several biblical accounts, including the prophecies of Christ himself: Matt. 24.30–31: "And then shall appear the sign of the Son of man in heaven: and then shall all the tribes of the earth mourn, and they shall see the Son of man coming in the clouds of heaven with power and great glory. And he shall send his angels with a great sound of a trumpet, and they shall gather together his elect from the four winds, from one end of heaven to the other." Matt. 25.31–32 "When the Son of man shall come in his glory, and all the holy angels with him, then shall he sit upon the throne of his glory: And before him shall be gathered all nations: and he shall separate them one from another, as a shepherd divideth his sheep from the goats." For descriptions by others, see 2 Pet. 3.12–13: ". . . the day of God, wherein the heavens being on fire shall be dissolved, and the elements shall melt with fervent heat[.] Nevertheless we, according to his promise, look for new heavens and a new earth, wherein dwelleth righteousness." Cf. also Rev. 21.1, p. 387, and 1 Cor. 15.28, p. 384 and 51–52, p. 384, and see *CD*, I.xxxiii.A., B., and C. *cited:* summoned to appear before a court. *general doom:* universal judgment. *saints:* the elect, mentioned in Matt. 24.31, above. *gods:* angels.

347. *rung:* made ring.

348. *jubilee:* (a Hebrew word for a ram's horn) the joyful noise of celebration. *hosannas:* a Hebrew word from Ps. 118.25 meaning "pray, save [us]!" used liturgically in prayers for deliverance and in praise of God.

349–71. For the source of some of the details in this passage see Rev. 4.4–10, p. 384, and 21.11, p. 387. Cf. also Rev. 22.1–2: "And he shewed me a pure river of water of life, clear as crystal, proceeding out of the throne of God and of the Lamb. In the midst of the street of it . . . was there the tree of life . . . and the leaves of the tree were for the healing of the nations."

352. *amarant:* amaranth (Gk *amarantos* unwithering), an imaginary, immortal flower, as well as a real, purple one. Cf. 1 Pet. 5.4: "Ye shall receive a crown of glory that fadeth not away."

Immortal amarant, a flow'r which once
In Paradise, fast by the Tree of Life
Began to bloom, but soon for man's offense   355
To heav'n removed where first it grew, there grows,
And flow'rs aloft shading the fount of life,
And where the river of bliss through midst of heav'n
Rolls o'er Elysian flow'rs her amber stream;
With these that never fade the Spirits elect   360
Bind their resplendent locks inwreathed with beams,
Now in loose garlands thick thrown off, the bright
Pavement that like a sea of jasper shone
Impurpled with celestial roses smiled.
Then crowned again their golden harps they took,   365
Harps ever tuned, that glittering by their side
Like quivers hung, and with preamble sweet
Of charming symphony they introduce
Their sacred song, and waken raptures high;
No voice exempt, no voice but well could join   370
Melodious part, such concord is in heav'n.
  Thee Father first they sung omnipotent,
Immutable, immortal, infinite,
Eternal King; thee Author of all being,
Fountain of light, thyself invisible   375
Amidst the glorious brightness where thou sitt'st
Throned inaccessible, but when thou shad'st
The full blaze of thy beams, and through a cloud
Drawn round about thee like a radiant shrine,
Dark with excessive bright thy skirts appear,   380
Yet dazzle heav'n, that brightest Seraphim
Approach not, but with both wings veil their eyes.
Thee next they sang of all creation first,
Begotten Son, Divine Similitude,
In whose conspicuous count'nance, without cloud   385
Made visible, th' Almighty Father shines,
Whom else no creature can behold; on thee
Impressed th' effulgence of his glory abides,
Transfused on thee his ample spirit rests.
He heav'n of heavens and all the Powers therein   390
By thee created, and by thee threw down

359. *Elysian:* like those of Elysium, heaven in Gk mythology. *amber:* clear, pure.
370. *exempt:* excluded from participation.
372–82. Cf. Exod. 24.16–17, p. 368, and Isa. 6.1–2, p. 373. Also 1 Tim. 6.15–16: ". . . the King of kings, and Lord of lords; Who only hath immortality, dwelling in the light which no man can approach unto; whom no man hath seen, nor can see . . ."
377. *but:* except.
383. *of all creation first.* See 170n, and *CD*, I.v. Milton believed that the ortho-

dox Trinitarian doctrine of the co-eternity of the Father and Son could not be supported by the Scriptures, which in several places refer to Christ as the first-born of God.
384. *Begotten Son.* Cf. John 3.16: "For God so loved the world, that he gave his only begotten son."
385–87. Cf. John 1.18 [*NEB*]: "No one has ever seen God; but God's only Son, he who is nearest to the Father's heart, he has made him known." John 14.9: "He that hath seen me hath seen the Father."

Th' aspiring Dominations: thou that day
Thy Father's dreadful thunder didst not spare,
Nor stop thy flaming chariot wheels, that shook
Heav'n's everlasting frame, while o'er the necks   395
Thou drov'st of warring angels disarrayed.
Back from pursuit thy Powers with loud acclaim
Thee only extolled, Son of thy Father's might,
To execute fierce vengeance on his foes,
Not so on man; him through their malice fall'n,   400
Father of mercy and grace, thou didst not doom
So strictly, but much more to pity incline:
No sooner did thy dear and only Son
Perceive thee purposed not to doom frail man
So strictly, but much more to pity inclined,   405
He to appease thy wrath, and end the strife
Of mercy and justice in thy face discerned,
Regardless of the bliss wherein he sat
Second to thee, offered himself to die
For man's offense. O unexampled love,   410
Love nowhere to be found less than divine!
Hail Son of God, Saviour of men, thy name
Shall be the copious matter of my song
Henceforth, and never shall my harp thy praise
Forget, nor from thy Father's praise disjoin.   415
  Thus they in heav'n, above the starry sphere,
Their happy hours in joy and hymning spent.
Meanwhile upon the firm opacous globe
Of this round world, whose first convex divides
The luminous inferior orbs, enclosed   420
From Chaos and th' inroad of Darkness old,
Satan alighted walks: a globe far off
It seemed, now seems a boundless continent
Dark, waste, and wild, under the frown of Night
Starless exposed, and ever-threatening storms   425
Of chaos blust'ring round, inclement sky;
Save on that side which from the wall of heav'n
Though distant far some small reflection gains
Of glimmering air less vexed with tempest loud:
Here walked the Fiend at large in spacious field.   430
As when a vulture on Imaus bred,
Whose snowy ridge the roving Tartar bounds,
Dislodging from a region scarce of prey

392. *Dominations.* See "Angels," p. 395.
401. *doom:* pronounce judgment.
403–10. I.e.: No sooner did . . . [than] He, to appease. . . .
416–30. See "Universe," pp. 389–91.
429. *vexed:* L *vexare* to shake.
431–39. *Imaus:* a range of mountains running roughly NE from Afghanistan to the Arctic Ocean and separating Tartary (roughly Sibera) from Mongolia and the Gobi desert. *Sericana:* a region in NW China. Satan's flight from hell to Paradise is like a flight from a most barbarous and physically rugged country to Eden-like Kashmir, where the *Hydaspes* (modern Jhelum) River rises. Folklore had it that vultures could smell their prey clear across a continent. *yeanling:* new born.

To gorge the flesh of lambs or yeanling kids
On hills where flocks are fed, flies toward the springs   435
Of Ganges or Hydaspes, Indian streams;
But in his way lights on the barren plains
Of Sericana, where Chineses drive
With sails and wind their cany wagons light:
So on this windy sea of land, the Fiend   440
Walked up and down alone bent on his prey,
Alone, for other creature in this place
Living or lifeless to be found was none,
None yet, but store hereafter from the earth
Up hither like aërial vapors flew   445
Of all things transitory and vain, when sin
With vanity had filled the works of men:
Both all things vain, and all who in vain things
Built their fond hopes of glory or lasting fame,
Or happiness in this or th' other life;   450
All who have their reward on earth, the fruits
Of painful superstition and blind zeal,
Naught seeking but the praise of men, here find
Fit retribution, empty as their deeds;
All th' unaccomplished works of nature's hand,   455
Abortive, monstrous, or unkindly mixed,
Dissolved on earth, fleet hither, and in vain,
Till final dissolution, wander here,
Not in the neighboring moon, as some have dreamed;
Those argent fields more likely habitants,   460
Translated saints, or middle Spirits hold
Betwixt th' angelical and human kind:
Hither of ill-joined sons and daughters born
First from the ancient world those giants came
With many a vain exploit, though then renowned: 465
The builders next of Babel on the plain
Of Sennaär, and still with vain design
New Babels, had they wherewithal, would build:
Others came single; he who to be deemed
A god, leaped fondly into Etna flames,   470
Empedocles, and he who to enjoy
Plato's Elysium, leaped into the sea,

440–41. Cf. Job 1.7: "And the Lord said unto Satan, Whence comest thou? Then Satan answered the Lord, and said, From going to and fro in the earth, and from walking up and down in it."
449. *fond:* foolish.
452. *painful:* painstaking.
455–57. *unaccomplished:* incomplete, imperfect. *Abortive:* prematurely born. *monstrous:* L *monstrum*, evil omen, prodigy; abnormal. *unkindly:* (OE *gecynde* nature) unnaturally. *mixed:* conceived by sexual intercourse. *fleet:* OE *fleotan* to float or drift (as refuse floated on the Fleet river, in London).

459. *some:* Ariosto and others.
461. *Translated saints:* holy men, Enoch (Gen. 5.24) and Elijah (2 Kings 2.11), whom God removed from earth.
463–65. Cf. Gen. 6, pp. 357–58.
467. *Sennaär:* Shinar, in Babylonia. See Gen. 11, p. 362, and XII.38–62 for the story of the Tower of Babel.
471. *Empedocles:* a philosopher who secretly threw himself into Etna hoping that having disappeared without leaving a trace he would be thought by his students to have been a god. The volcano belched out the metal soles of his shoes and his folly was thereby discovered.

Cleombrotus, and many more too long,
Embryos and idiots, eremites and friars
White, black, and gray, with all their trumpery.   475
Here pilgrims roam, that strayed so far to seek
In Golgotha him dead, who lives in heav'n;
And they who to be sure of paradise
Dying put on the weeds of Dominic,
Or in Franciscan think to pass disguised;   480
They pass the planets seven, and pass the fixed,
And that crystálline sphere whose balance weighs
The trepidation talked, and that first moved;
And now Saint Peter at heav'n's wicket seems
To wait them with his keys, and now at foot   485
Of heav'n's ascent they lift their feet, when lo
A violent crosswind from either coast
Blows them transverse ten thousand leagues awry
Into the devious air, then might ye see
Cowls, hoods and habits with their wearers tossed   490
And fluttered into rags; then relics, beads,
Indulgences, dispenses, pardons, bulls,
The sport of winds: all these upwhirled aloft
Fly o'er the backside of the world far off
Into a limbo large and broad, since called   495
The Paradise of Fools, to few unknown
Long after, now unpeopled, and untrod;
All this dark globe the Fiend found as he passed,
And long he wandered, till at last a gleam
Of dawning light turned thitherward in haste   500
His traveled steps; far distant he descries
Ascending by degrees magnificent
Up to the wall of heaven a structure high,
At top whereof, but far more rich appeared
The work as of a kingly palace gate   505
With frontispiece of diamond and gold
Embellished; thick with sparkling orient gems

---

473. *Cleombrotus:* a youth so enamored by Plato's description of the life beyond that he committed suicide.

474. *eremites:* hermits.

475. *White, black, and gray:* the Carmelite, Dominican, and Franciscan orders.

477. *Golgotha:* where Christ was crucified. Cf. Luke 24.5–6: "Why seek ye the living among the dead? He is not here, but is risen."

481–83. See "Universe," pp. 389–91.

485. Cf. Matt. 16.19: "And I [Jesus] will give unto thee [Peter] the keys of the kingdom of heaven."

490. *Cowls, hoods, habits:* the dress of monks.

491. *relics:* holy objects associated with a saint, assumed by some Catholics to have miraculous powers. *beads* (ME

bede prayer) as in a rosary.

492. *Indulgences, dispenses, pardons:* various ecclesiastical pardons for sin, which Protestants believed to be fraudulent and a cause of corruption in the clergy. *bulls:* Papal decrees.

494. *backside:* under side, back part, rump.

495. *limbo:* (ML, ablative of *limbus* border) a region, according to Catholic doctrine, bordering on hell, where dwelt the souls of good people who died before the Christian era, as well as those of unbaptized infants. Milton rejects this notion and invents another limbo.

501. *traveled:* (OF *travaillier* to travail, toil) weary.

502. *degrees:* steps.

507. *orient:* lustrous, like the most lustrous of pearls, those from the east.

The portal shone, inimitable on earth.
By model, or by shading pencil drawn.
The stairs were such as whereon Jacob saw   510
Angels ascending and descending, bands
Of guardians bright, when he from Esau fled
To Padan-Aram in the field of Luz,
Dreaming by night under the open sky,
And waking cried, "This is the gate of heav'n."   515
Each stair mysteriously was meant, nor stood
There always, but drawn up to heav'n sometimes
Viewless, and underneath a bright sea flowed
Of jasper, or of liquid pearl, whereon
Who after came from earth, sailing arrived,   520
Wafted by angels, or flew o'er the lake
Rapt in a chariot drawn by fiery steeds.
The stairs were then let down, whether to dare
The Fiend by easy ascent, or aggravate
His sad exclusion from the doors of bliss.   525
Direct against which opened from beneath,
Just o'er the blissful seat of Paradise,
A passage down to th' earth, a passage wide,
Wider by far than that of aftertimes
Over Mount Zion, and, though that were large,   530
Over the Promised Land to God so dear,
By which, to visit oft those happy tribes,
On high behests his angels to and fro
Passed frequent, and his eye with choice regard
From Paneas the fount of Jordan's flood   535
To Beërsaba, where the Holy Land
Borders on Egypt and the Arabian shore;
So wide the op'ning seemed, where bounds were set
To darkness, such as bound the ocean wave.
Satan from hence now on the lower stair   540

508. *The portal shone*. Cf. Rev. 21.21, p. 387.

515. Cf. Gen. 28.12–17 "And he dreamed, and behold a ladder set up on the earth, and the top of it reached to heaven: and behold the angels of God ascending and descending on it. And, behold, the Lord stood above it, and said, I am the Lord God of Abraham thy father, and the God of Isaac: the land whereon thou liest, to thee I will give it, and to thy seed; . . . And Jacob awaked out of his sleep, and he said, Surely the Lord is in this place; and I knew it not. And he was afraid, and said, How dreadful is this place! this in none other but the house of God, and this is the gate of heaven."

516. *mysteriously was meant*. A mystery is a meaning available only to the initiated. The rungs in Jacob's ladder, and the stairs to heaven, could symbolize the great ascending chain of being.

518. *a bright sea*. See "Universe," p. 389.

520–22. In one of Christ's parables (Luke 16.19–22), when the beggar Lazarus died, he was "carried by the angels" into heaven. Cf. 2 Kings 2.11: "As [Elijah and Elisha] . . . talked . . . there appeared a chariot of fire, and horses of fire, and parted them both asunder; and Elijah went up by a whirlwind into heaven."

526–27. The axis of the earth is here conceived as parallel to the floor of heaven.

534. *choice regard*: discriminative look.

535. *Paneas*: a later name for Dan, the northernmost city of Palestine as well as for the mountain near which a spring (*fount*) served as one of the sources of the *Jordan* River (*flood*).

536. *Beërsaba*: Beersheba, southernmost city of Palestine.

That scaled by steps of gold to heaven gate
Looks down with wonder at the sudden view
Of all this world at once. As when a scout
Through dark and desert ways with peril gone
All night; at last by break of cheerful dawn   545
Obtains the brow of some high-climbing hill,
Which to his eye discovers unaware
The goodly prospect of some foreign land
First seen, or some renowned metropolis
With glistering spires and pinnacles adorned,   550
Which now the rising sun gilds with his beams.
Such wonder seized, though after heaven seen,
The Spirit malign, but much more envy seized
At sight of all this world beheld so fair.
Round he surveys, and well might, where he stood   555
So high above the circling canopy
Of night's extended shade; from eastern point
Of Libra to the fleecy star that bears
Andromeda far off Atlantic seas
Beyond th' horizon; then from pole to pole   560
He views in breadth, and without longer pause
Down right into the world's first region throws
His flight precipitant, and winds with ease
Through the pure marble air his oblique way
Amongst innumerable stars, that shone   565
Stars distant, but nigh hand seemed other worlds,
Or other worlds they seemed, or happy isles,
Like those Hesperian gardens famed of old,
Fortunate fields, and groves and flow'ry vales,
Thrice happy isles, but who dwelt happy there   570
He stayed not to inquire: above them all
The golden sun in splendor likest heaven
Allured his eye: thither his course he bends
Through the calm firmament; but up or down
By center, or eccentric, hard to tell,   575
Or longitude, where the great luminary

546. *Obtains:* gains.
556. *circling canopy.* The earth was between Satan and the sun; therefore Satan looked directly down on the conical shadow presumed to be cast by the earth. It was midnight in Eden, as Fowler points out.
558. *fleecy star:* the constellation of Aries, the Ram; in the Zodiac, the sign opposite Libra.
559. *Andromeda:* a constellation near that of Aries.
562. *first region:* the part of the universe between the outer shell and the sphere of the moon. See "Universe," p. 390.
563–64. *precipitant:* falling headlong, descending vertically. *oblique:* inclined; devious.
564. *marble:* Gk *marmareos* sparkling, gleaming.
566. *other worlds.* The possibility of other inhabited worlds in the universe was recognized by the ancients and was much discussed in Milton's time.
567. See II.410n.
568. *Hesperian gardens:* another classical mythological version of paradise. Here Jupiter placed the daughters of Hesperus to guard a tree on which hung three golden apples.
575. *hard to tell.* I.e., it is hard for the poet to describe Satan's navigation in his three-dimensional flight; much would depend on the observer's position.

Aloof the vulgar constellations thick,
That from his lordly eye keep distance due,
Dispenses light from far; they as they move
Their starry dance in numbers that compute   580
Days, months, and years, towards his all-cheering lamp
Turn swift their various motions, or are turned
By his magnetic beam, that gently warms
The universe, and to each inward part
With gentle penetration, though unseen,   585
Shoots invisible virtue even to the deep:
So wondrously was set his station bright.
There lands the Fiend, a spot like which perhaps
Astronomer in the sun's lucent orb
Through his glazed optic tube yet never saw.   590
The place he found beyond expression bright,
Compared with aught on earth, metal or stone;
Not all parts like, but all alike informed
With radiant light, as glowing iron with fire;
If metal, part seemed gold, part silver clear;   595
If stone, carbuncle most or chrysolite,
Ruby or topaz, to the twelve that shone
In Aaron's breastplate, and a stone besides
Imagined rather oft than elsewhere seen,
That stone, or like to that which here below   600
Philosophers in vain so long have sought,
In vain, though by their powerful art they bind
Volátile Hermes, and call up unbound
In various shapes old Proteus from the sea,
Drained through a limbec to his native form.   605
What wonder then if fields and regions here
Breathe forth elixir pure, and rivers run
Potable gold, when with one virtuous touch
Th' arch-chemic sun so far from us remote

580. *Their starry dance.* In Plato's *Timaeus* the stars are said to dance as a chorus and thus to mark out the divisions of time. *numbers that compute:* rhythms that count out.

582–83. *turned/By his magnetic beam.* Kepler's theory that the planets are moved round the sun by the power of the sun's magnetism had been published in 1609.

586. *virtue:* power, influence.

588–90. Galileo first telescopically observed sun-spots in 1609.

591–612. The brightness of the sun is compared with the brightest, most sought after metals (*silver* and *gold*) and precious stones (*carbuncle, chrysolite, ruby, topaz*) because these metals and stones were believed by the alchemists to receive their power to shine from the sun; indeed, the stones were believed to shine in the dark. The hypothetical *philoso-* *phers'* (i.e., scientists') *stone*, which if it could be found would turn base metals into gold, was also thought to be a product of the sun. In its powdered form (literal meaning of *elixir*) the stone would, like colloidal gold (*potable gold*), be medicinal, prolonging life. In Exodus 28.15–20 *Aaron's breastplate* is described as decorated with twelve different gems, of which Milton lists the first four. Lines 602–5 describe the efforts of alchemists to imitate the processes of the sun, who was *arch-chemic* because he was the supreme chemist. To *bind Volatile Hermes* was to remove the "air" from a compound of mercury, which could be extracted from primal matter, i.e., *old Proteus*, who took many forms. *humor:* moisture.

605. *limbec:* alembic; any device for refining or transmuting as if by distillation.

Produces with terrestrial humor mixed 610
Here in the dark so many precious things
Of color glorious and effect so rare?
Here matter new to gaze the Devil met
Undazzled, far and wide his eye commands,
For sight no obstacle found here, nor shade, 615
But all sunshine, as when his beams at noon
Culminate from th' equator, as they now
Shot upward still direct, whence no way round
Shadow from body opaque can fall, and the air,
Nowhere so clear, sharpened his visual ray 620
To objects distant far, whereby he soon
Saw within ken a glorious angel stand,
The same whom John saw also in the sun:
His back was turned, but not his brightness hid;
Of beaming sunny rays, a golden tiar 625
Circled his head, nor less his locks behind
Illustrious on his shoulders fledge with wings
Lay waving round; on some great charge employed
He seemed, or fixed in cogitation deep.
Glad was the Spirit impure; as now in hope 630
To find who might direct his wand'ring flight
To Paradise the happy seat of man,
His journey's end and our beginning woe.
But first he casts to change his proper shape,
Which else might work him danger or delay: 635
And now a stripling Cherub he appears,
Not of the prime, yet such as in his face
Youth smiled celestial, and to every limb
Suitable grace diffused, so well he feigned;
Under a coronet his flowing hair 640
In curls on either cheek played, wings he wore
Of many a colored plume sprinkled with gold,
His habit fit for speed succinct, and held
Before his decent steps a silver wand.
He drew not nigh unheard; the angel bright, 645
Ere he drew nigh, his radiant visage turned,
Admonished by his ear, and straight was known
Th' Archangel Uriel, one of the sev'n
Who in God's presence, nearest to his throne
Stand ready at command, and are his eyes 650
That run through all the heav'ns, or down to th' earth

---

617. *Culminate:* reach their zenith. Before the Fall (and consequent tipping of the earth's axis) the sun at noon, on the equator, never cast a shadow.
623. *whom John saw.* Cf. Rev. 19:17: "I saw an angel standing in the sun."
625. *tiar:* tiara, crown, halo.
627. *Illustrious:* (L *lustrare* to purify,

make bright) shining.
634. *casts:* considers how; contrives; determines.
643. *succinct:* (L *sub* under + *cingere* to tuck) close-fitting.
644. *decent:* handsome.
648. *Uriel.* See "Angels," pp. 395–96.

Bear his swift errands over moist and dry,
O'er sea and land: him Satan thus accosts.
    "Uriel, for thou of those sev'n Spirits that stand
In sight of God's high throne, gloriously bright,   655
The first art wont his great authentic will
Interpreter through highest heav'n to bring,
Where all his sons thy embassy attend;
And here art likeliest by supreme decree
Like honor to obtain, and as his eye   660
To visit oft this new creation round;
Unspeakable desire to see, and know
All these his wondrous works, but chiefly man,
His chief delight and favor, him for whom
All these his works so wondrous he ordained,   665
Hath brought me from the choirs of Cherubim
Alone thus wand'ring. Brightest Seraph tell
In which of all these shining orbs hath man
His fixèd seat, or fixèd seat hath none,
But all these shining orbs his choice to dwell;   670
That I may find him, and with secret gaze,
Or open admiration him behold
On whom the great Creator hath bestowed
Worlds, and on whom hath all these graces poured;
That both in him and all things, as is meet,   675
The Universal Maker we may praise;
Who justly hath driv'n out his rebel foes
To deepest hell, and to repair that loss
Created this new happy race of men
To serve him better: wise are all his ways."   680
    So spake the false dissembler unperceived;
For neither man nor angel can discern
Hypocrisy, the only evil that walks
Invisible, except to God alone,
By his permissive will, through heav'n and earth: 685
And oft though wisdom wake, suspicion sleeps
At wisdom's gate, and to simplicity
Resigns her charge, while goodness thinks no ill
Where no ill seems: which now for once beguiled
Uriel, though regent of the sun, and held   690
The sharpest-sighted Spirit of all in heav'n;
Who to the fraudulent impostor foul
In his uprightness answer thus returned.
"Fair angel, thy desire which tends to know
The works of God, thereby to glorify   695
The great Work-maister, leads to no excess
That reaches blame, but rather merits praise

694–701. See "Knowledge," p. 398.

The more it seems excess, that led thee hither
From thy empyreal mansion thus alone,
To witness with thine eyes what some perhaps   700
Contented with report hear only in heav'n:
For wonderful indeed are all his works,
Pleasant to know, and worthiest to be all
Had in remembrance always with delight;
But what created mind can comprehend   705
Their number, or the wisdom infinite
That brought them forth, but hid their causes deep.
I saw when at his word the formless mass,
This world's material mold, came to a heap:
Confusion heard his voice, and wild uproar   710
Stood ruled, stood vast infinitude confined;
Till at his second bidding darkness fled,
Light shone, and order from disorder sprung:
Swift to their several quarters hasted then
The cumbrous elements, earth, flood, air, fire,   715
And this ethereal quíntessence of heav'n
Flew upward, spirited with various forms,
That rolled orbicular, and turned to stars
Numberless, as thou seest, and how they move;
Each had his place appointed, each his course,   720
The rest in circuit walls this universe.
Look downward on that globe whose hither side
With light from hence, though but reflected, shines;
That place is earth the seat of man, that light
His day, which else as th' other hemisphere   725
Night would invade, but there the neighboring moon
(So call that opposite fair star) her aid
Timely interposes, and her monthly round
Still ending, still renewing through mid-heav'n,
With borrowed light her countenance triform   730
Hence fills and empties to enlighten th' earth,
And in her pale dominion checks the night.

702–4. Cf. Ps. 111.2–4: "The works of the Lord are great, sought out of all them that have pleasure therein. . . . He hath made his wonderful works to be remembered."

705–7. See *CD*, I.ix.B.

706–7. Cf. Prov. 3.19: "The Lord by wisdom hath founded the earth." Prov. 8.1–27: "Doth not wisdom cry? and understanding put forth her voice? . . . She crieth at the gates, at the entry of the city. . . . Unto you, O men, I call. . . . The Lord possessed me in the beginning of his way, before his works of old. I was set up from everlasting, from the beginning, or ever the earth was. When there were no depths, I was brought forth; when there were no fountains abounding with water. Before the moun-

tains were settled, before the hills was I brought forth. . . . When he prepared the heavens, I was there: when he set a compass upon the face of the depth. . . ."

709. *material mold:* (OE *molde* earth, ground, soil) here, the constituent matter of the universe.

715–21. See "Universe," pp. 389–91. *This ethereal quintessence.* The sun, on which the angels are standing, and other heavenly bodies were supposed to be composed of a fifth element, ether, not the same as air.

717. *spirited with various forms:* presided over, inhabited by, spirits or souls of various forms, as in Plato's *Timaeus*.

740. *ecliptic:* course described by the movement of the sun.

That spot to which I point is Paradise,
Adam's abode, those lofty shades his bow'r.
Thy way thou canst not miss, me mine requires."   735
    Thus said, he turned, and Satan bowing low,
As to superior Spirits is wont in heav'n,
Where honor due and reverence none neglects,
Took leave, and toward the coast of earth beneath,
Down from th' ecliptic, sped with hoped success,   740
Throws his steep flight in many an airy wheel,
Nor stayed, till on Niphates' top he lights.

742. *Niphates:* a mountain in Assyria, to the north of Eden.

Book IV

The Argument

Satan now in prospect of Eden, and nigh the place where he must now attempt the bold enterprise which he undertook alone against God and man, falls into many doubts with himself, and many passions, fear, envy, and despair; but at length confirms himself in evil, journeys on to Paradise, whose outward prospect and situation is described, overleaps the bounds, sits in the shape of a cormorant on the Tree of Life, as highest in the Garden to look about him. The Garden described; Satan's first sight of Adam and Eve; his wonder at their excellent form and happy state, but with resolution to work their fall; overhears their discourse, thence gathers that the Tree of Knowledge was forbidden them to eat of, under penalty of death; and thereon intends to found his temptation, by seducing them to transgress: then leaves them a while, to know furder of their state by some other means. Meanwhile Uriel descending on a sunbeam warns Gabriel, who had in charge the gate of Paradise, that some evil Spirit had escaped the deep, and passed at noon by his sphere in the shape of a good angel down to Paradise, discovered after by his furious gestures in the mount. Gabriel promises to find him ere morning. Night coming on, Adam and Eve discourse of going to their rest: their bower described; their evening worship. Gabriel drawing forth his bands of nightwatch to walk the round of Paradise, appoints two strong angels to Adam's bower, lest the evil Spirit should be there doing some harm to Adam or Eve sleeping; there they find him at the ear of Eve, tempting her in a dream, and bring him, though unwilling, to Gabriel; by whom questioned, he scornfully answers, prepares resistance, but hindered by a sign from heaven, flies out of Paradise.

> O for that warning voice, which he who saw
> Th' Apocalypse, heard cry in heaven aloud,
> Then when the Dragon, put to second rout,
> Came furious down to be revenged on men,
> "Woe to the inhabitants on earth!" that now,　　　　5
> While time was, our first parents had been warned
> The coming of their secret foe, and scaped
> Haply so scaped his mortal snare; for now
> Satan, now first inflamed with rage, came down,
> The tempter ere th' accuser of mankind,　　　　10
> To wreck on innocent frail man his loss
> Of that first battle, and his flight to hell:
> Yet not rejoicing in his speed, though bold,
> Far off and fearless, nor with cause to boast,

IV.1–5. Cf. Rev. 12.7–12, p. 386.　　　11. *wreck:* avenge.
10. *accuser:* betrayer.

78

Begins his dire attempt, which nigh the birth   15
Now rolling, boils in his tumultuous breast,
And like a devilish engine back recoils
Upon himself; horror and doubt distract
His troubled thoughts, and from the bottom stir
The hell within him, for within him hell   20
He brings, and round about him, nor from hell
One step no more than from himself can fly
By change of place: now conscience wakes despair
That slumbered, wakes the bitter memory
Of what he was, what is, and what must be   25
Worse; of worse deeds worse sufferings must ensue.
Sometimes towards Eden which now in his view
Lay pleasant, his grieved look he fixes sad,
Sometimes towards heav'n and the full-blazing sun,
Which now sat high in his meridian tow'r: 30
Then much revolving, thus in sighs began.
      "O thou that with surpassing glory crowned,
Look'st from thy sole dominion like the god
Of this new world; at whose sight all the stars
Hide their diminished heads; to thee I call,   35
But with no friendly voice, and add thy name
O sun, to tell thee how I hate thy beams
That bring to my remembrance from what state
I fell, how glorious once above thy sphere;
Till pride and worse ambition threw me down   40
Warring in heav'n against heav'n's matchless King:
Ah wherefore! he deserved no such return
From me, whom he created what I was
In that bright eminence, and with his good
Upbraided none; nor was his service hard.   45
What could be less than to afford him praise,
The easiest recompense, and pay him thanks,
How due! yet all his good proved ill in me,
And wrought but malice; lifted up so high
I sdained subjection, and thought one step higher   50
Would set me highest, and in a moment quit

17. *engine:* L *ingenium*, the faculty of invention; here an engine of war, the cannon, invented by Satan (see VI.470).

18. *distract:* L *distrahere*, to draw asunder; agitate.

31. *revolving:* meditating.

32–41. Milton's nephew Edward Phillips, in his *Life of Milton*, said he saw these lines "several years before the poem was begun." They were, he said, to be the opening lines of a tragedy. See "Four Outlines for Tragedies," pp. 288–90.

35. *diminished:* reduced in authority or dignity.

37. Cf. John 3.20: "For every one that doeth evil hateth the light, neither cometh to the light, lest his deeds should be reproved."

38–39. Cf. Rev. 2.5 "Remember therefore from whence thou art fallen . . ."

43–45. Cf. Ezek. 28.15–17: "Thou wast perfect in thy ways from the day that thou wast created, till iniquity was found in thee. . . . Thine heart was lifted up because of thy beauty, thou hast corrupted thy wisdom by reason of thy brightness: I will cast thee to the ground, I will lay thee before kings, that they may behold thee." James 1.5: "If any of you lack wisdom [to resist temptation], let him ask of God, that giveth to all men liberally, and upbraideth not; and it shall be given him."

50. *sdained:* disdained.

51. *quit:* pay.

The debt immense of endless gratitude,
So burthensome still paying, still to owe;
Forgetful what from him I still received,
And understood not that a grateful mind   55
By owing owes not, but still pays, at once
Indebted and discharged; what burden then?
O had his powerful destiny ordained
Me some inferior angel, I had stood
Then happy; no unbounded hope had raised   60
Ambition. Yet why not? some other Power
As great might have aspired, and me though mean
Drawn to his part; but other Powers as great
Fell not, but stand unshaken, from within
Or from without, to all temptations armed.   65
Hadst thou the same free will and power to stand?
Thou hadst: whom hast thou then or what to accuse,
But heav'n's free love dealt equally to all?
Be then his love accursed, since love or hate,
To me alike, it deals eternal woe.   70
Nay cursed be thou; since against his thy will
Chose freely what it now so justly rues.
Me miserable! which way shall I fly
Infinite wrath, and infinite despair?
Which way I fly is hell; myself am hell;   75
And in the lowest deep a lower deep
Still threat'ning to devour me opens wide,
To which the hell I suffer seems a heav'n.
O then at last relent: is there no place
Left for repentance, none for pardon left?   80
None left but by submission; and that word
Disdain forbids me, and my dread of shame
Among the Spirits beneath, whom I seduced
With other promises and other vaunts
Than to submit, boasting I could subdue   85
Th' Omnipotent. Ay me, they little know
How dearly I abide that boast so vain,
Under what torments inwardly I groan:
While they adore me on the throne of hell,
With diadem and scepter high advanced   90
The lower still I fall, only supreme
In misery; such joy ambition finds.
But say I could repent and could obtain
By act of grace my former state; how soon

---

53. *still:* always.
56. *owing:* both owing a debt and own-
ing (admitting) a debt. The old form of
the past tense of *owe* was *ought. Owe*
comes from ME *owen,* to have, to own,
to have (to do), hence, to owe.
79–80. Cf. Heb. 12.17 "For ye know
how that afterward, when he [Esau]
would have inherited the blessing, he was
rejected: for he found no place of repent-
ance, though he sought it carefully with
tears."
87. *abide:* (in the sixteenth and seven-
teenth centuries erroneously used for
abye) pay the penalty for, atone for,
suffer for, endure.
94. *act of grace:* suspension of sen-
tence.

Would highth recall high thoughts, how soon unsay 95
What feigned submission swore: ease would recant
Vows made in pain, as violent and void.
For never can true reconcilement grow
Where wounds of deadly hate have pierced so deep:
Which would but lead me to a worse relapse, 100
And heavier fall: so should I purchase dear
Short intermission bought with double smart.
This knows my punisher; therefore as far
From granting he, as I from begging peace:
All hope excluded thus, behold instead 105
Of us outcast, exiled, his new delight,
Mankind created, and for him this world.
So farewell hope, and with hope farewell fear,
Farewell remorse: all good to me is lost;
Evil be thou my good; by thee at least 110
Divided empire with heav'n's King I hold
By thee, and more than half perhaps will reign;
As man ere long, and this new world shall know."
    Thus while he spake, each passion dimmed his face
Thrice changed with pale, ire, envy and despair, 115
Which marred his borrowed visage, and betrayed
Him counterfeit, if any eye beheld.
For heav'nly minds from such distempers foul
Are ever clear. Whereof he soon aware,
Each perturbation smoothed with outward calm, 120
Artificer of fraud; and was the first
That practiced falsehood under saintly show,
Deep malice to conceal, couched with revenge:
Yet not enough had practiced to deceive
Uriel once warned; whose eye pursued him down 125
The way he went, and on th' Assyrian mount
Saw him disfigured, more than could befall
Spirit of happy sort: his gestures fierce
He marked and mad demeanor, then alone,
As he supposed, all unobserved, unseen. 130
So on he fares, and to the border comes
Of Eden, where delicious Paradise,
Now nearer, crowns with her enclosure green,

---

109. *remorse:* L *remordere* to bite
again.
110. Cf. Isa. 5.20 "Woe unto them that
call evil good, and good evil; that put
darkness for light, and light for dark-
ness; that put bitter for sweet, and sweet
for bitter!"
115. *changed with pale:* paled (from
cherubic red).
118. *distempers:* disorders of body or
mind from improper mixture of the
humors. See "Physiology and Psychol-
ogy," pp. 391–92.

123. *couched:* which lay hidden.
126. *Assyrian mount:* Mt. Niphates
(III.742).
131–71. See "Paradise," pp. 399–400,
and VIII.302ff.
132. *Eden:* (a Hebrew word meaning
"delight" or "place of pleasure") the
region in which Paradise was located.
delicious: L *deliciae*, delight. *Paradise:*
paradeisos, the Gk form of an Oriental
word (Sanscrit *paradesa*; Arabic *firdaus;*
Hebrew *pardes*) meaning "park" or
"pleasure ground."

As with a rural mound the champaign head
Of a steep wilderness, whose hairy sides   135
With thicket overgrown, grotesque and wild,
Access denied; and overhead up grew
Insuperable highth of loftiest shade,
Cedar, and pine, and fir, and branching palm,
A sylvan scene, and as the ranks ascend   140
Shade above shade, a woody theater
Of stateliest view. Yet higher than their tops
The verdurous wall of Paradise up sprung:
Which to our general sire gave prospect large
Into his nether empire neighboring round.   145
And higher than that wall a circling row
Of goodliest trees loaden with fairest fruit,
Blossoms and fruits at once of golden hue
Appeared, with gay enameled colors mixed:
On which the sun more glad impressed his beams   150
Than in fair evening cloud, or humid bow,
When God hath show'red the earth; so lovely seemed
That lantskip: and of pure now purer air
Meets his approach, and to the heart inspires
Vernal delight and joy, able to drive   155
All sadness but despair: now gentle gales
Fanning their odoriferous wings dispense
Native perfumes, and whisper whence they stole
Those balmy spoils. As when to them who sail
Beyond the Cape of Hope, and now are past   160
Mozambic, off at sea northeast winds blow
Sabean odors from the spicy shore
Of Araby the Blest, with such delay
Well pleased they slack their course, and many a league
Cheered with the graceful smell old Ocean smiles.   165
So entertained those odorous sweets the Fiend
Who came their bane, though with them better pleased
Than Asmodeus with the fishy fume,
That drove him, though enamored, from the spouse
Of Tobit's son, and with a vengeance sent   170
From Media post to Egypt, there fast bound.

134. *rural:* as in open fields. *mound:* hedge or other fence bounding a field or garden; a hedgerow.
136. *grotesque:* in Milton's time a relatively new word, used in various ways. Milton meant "characterized by interwoven, tangled vines and branches, as in painted and carved decoration." *Bosky* was a synonym.
144. *general:* L *genus* race.
149. *enameled:* variegated.
155. *drive:* force to flee.
157. *odoriferous:* L *odorifer* bearing fragrance.
161. *Mozambic:* the channel between Madagascar and the SE coast of Africa— a trade route.

162. *Sabean:* of Sheba, an ancient country in south west Arabia, or *Araby the Blest.*
166–71. According to the Apocryphal Book of Tobit, an evil spirit, Ashmodeus (Satan?) killed on their wedding nights the seven men who, in succession, had been married to Sarah. But the eighth, Tobias, was advised by the angel Raphael to burn the heart and liver of a fish in the bridal chamber, and the odor drove the daemon lover all the way to Egypt. Raphael thus saved Tobias and his wife from the designs of Satan, though he failed to save Adam and Eve. Cf. Asmadai, VI.365.

Now to th'ascent of that steep savage hill
Satan had journeyed on, pensive and slow;
But further way found none, so thick entwined,
As one continued brake, the undergrowth   175
Of shrubs and tangling bushes had perplexed
All path of man or beast that passed that way:
One gate there only was, and that looked east
On th' other side: which when th' arch-felon saw
Due entrance he disdained, and in contempt,   180
At one slight bound high overleaped all bound
Of hill or highest wall, and sheer within
Lights on his feet. As when a prowling wolf,
Whom hunger drives to seek new haunt for prey,
Watching where shepherds pen their flocks at eve   185
In hurdled cotes amid the field secure,
Leaps o'er the fence with ease into the fold:
Or as a thief bent to unhoard the cash
Of some rich burgher, whose substantial doors,
Cross-barred and bolted fast, fear no assault,   190
In at the window climbs, or o'er the tiles;
So clomb this first grand thief into God's fold:
So since into his church lewd hirelings climb.
Thence up he flew, and on the Tree of Life,
The middle tree and highest there that grew,   195
Sat like a cormorant; yet not true life
Thereby regained, but sat devising death
To them who lived; nor on the virtue thought
Of that life-giving plant, but only used
For prospect, what well used had been the pledge   200
Of immortality. So little knows
Any, but God alone, to value right
The good before him, but perverts best things
To worst abuse, or to their meanest use.
Beneath him with new wonder now he views   205
To all delight of human sense exposed
In narrow room nature's whole wealth, yea more,
A heav'n on earth: for blissful Paradise
Of God the garden was, by him in the east

---

172. *savage:* L *silvaticus* woody, wild.
176. *perplexed:* L *plectare* to plait or braid.
182. *sheer:* perpendicularly.
183–93. Cf. John 10.1–11: "Verily, verily, I say unto you, He that entereth not by the door into the sheepfold, but climbeth up some other way, the same is a thief and a robber. . . . The thief cometh not, but for to steal, and to kill, and to destroy: I [Christ] am come that they might have life, and that they might have it more abundantly. I am the good shepherd."
186. *hurdled:* formed by hurdles, sectional fencing made of plaited branches.

cotes: folds. *secure:* (L *sine* without + *cura* care) free from anxiety.
192. *grand thief:* "thief of thieves" (as in "King of kings"); cf. I.29n.
193. *lewd:* ME *lewd*, lay, ignorant, vile, OE *lœwede* laical. *hirelings:* those who work only for money—here, paid clergymen, in contrast to unpaid ministers in some of the Puritan sects. Cf. John 10.11–12: "The good shepherd giveth his life for the sheep. But he that is an hireling, and not the shepherd, whose own the sheep are not, seeth the wolf coming . . . and fleeth."
194. *Tree of Life.* See Gen. 2.9, p. 354.

Of Eden planted; Eden stretched her line   210
From Auran eastward to the royal tow'rs
Of great Seleucia, built by Grecian kings,
Or where the sons of Eden long before
Dwelt in Telassar: in this pleasant soil
His far more pleasant garden God ordained;   215
Out of the fertile ground he caused to grow
All trees of noblest kind for sight, smell, taste;
And all amid them stood the Tree of Life,
High eminent, blooming ambrosial fruit
Of vegetable gold; and next to life   220
Our death the Tree of Knowledge grew fast by,
Knowledge of good bought dear by knowing ill.
Southward through Eden went a river large,
Nor changed his course, but through the shaggy hill
Passed underneath engulfed, for God had thrown   225
That mountain as his garden mold high raised
Upon the rapid current, which through veins
Of porous earth with kindly thirst up drawn,
Rose a fresh fountain, and with many a rill
Watered the garden; thence united fell   230
Down the steep glade, and met the nether flood,
Which from his darksome passage now appears,
And now divided into four main streams,
Runs diverse, wand'ring many a famous realm
And country whereof here needs no account,   235
But rather to tell how, if art could tell,
How from that sapphire fount the crispèd brooks,
Rolling on orient pearl and sands of gold,
With mazy error under pendent shades
Ran nectar, visiting each plant, and fed   240
Flow'rs worthy of Paradise which not nice art
In beds and curious knots, but nature boon
Poured forth profuse on hill and dale and plain,
Both where the morning sun first warmly smote
The open field, and where the unpierced shade   245
Embrowned the noontide bow'rs: thus was this place,
A happy rural seat of various view;

211. *Auran:* probably the province of Hauran on the eastern border of Israel, and the Harran that God told Abram to leave in favor of Canaan.
212. *Seleucia:* a city on the Tigris river, built by one of Alexander's generals, near modern Baghdad.
214. *Telassar:* a city in Eden.
219. *blooming:* bearing. *ambrosial:* See II.245n; here the primary meaning may be "giving immortality"—Fowler cites Gen. 3.22, where God fears lest Adam "put forth his hand, and take also of the tree of life, and eat, and live for ever."
220. *vegetable:* living, growing, like a plant.
222. See selection from *Areopagitica,*

p. 290, and *CD,* I.x.A.
226. *mold:* earth good for gardening, rich and crumbly.
228. *kindly:* (OE *cynd* nature) natural.
237. *crisped:* L *crispus,* curly.
238. *orient:* shining, pearl-like.
239. *error:* (L *errare* to go astray) wandering.
242. *curious:* (L *cura* care) carefully, neatly, or exquisitely made. *knots:* patterned flower beds. *boon:* bounteous, opposite of *nice* (241).
246. *Embrowned:* darkened.
247. *seat:* (as in "country-seat," estate) residence. *of various view:* with a variety of prospects.

Groves whose rich trees wept odorous gums and balm,
Others whose fruit burnished with golden rind
Hung amiable, Hesperian fables true,   250
If true, here only, and of delicious taste:
Betwixt them lawns, or level downs, and flocks
Grazing the tender herb, were interposed,
Or palmy hillock, or the flow'ry lap
Of some irriguous valley spread her store,   255
Flow'rs of all hue, and without thorn the rose:
Another side, umbrageous grots and caves
Of cool recess, o'er which the mantling vine
Lays forth her purple grape, and gently creeps
Luxuriant; meanwhile murmuring waters fall   260
Down the slope hills, dispersed, or in a lake,
That to the fringèd bank with myrtle crowned,
Her crystal mirror holds, unite their streams.
The birds their choir apply; airs, vernal airs,
Breathing the smell of field and grove, attune   265
The trembling leaves, while universal Pan
Knit with the Graces and the Hours in dance
Led on th' eternal spring. Not that fair field
Of Enna, where Proserpine gathering flow'rs
Herself a fairer flow'r by gloomy Dis   270
Was gathered, which cost Ceres all that pain
To seek her through the world; nor that sweet grove
Of Daphne by Orontes, and th' inspired
Castalian spring, might with this Paradise
Of Eden strive; nor that Nyseian isle   275

250. *amiable:* lovely. *Hesperian fables.* See III.568n.
252. *lawns:* pastures. *downs:* (OE *dun*) here tracts of open upland.
255. *irriguous:* well-watered.
257. *umbrageous:* shady.
258–63. Fowler's note is illuminating: "That the *myrtle* is intended as Venus' tree is made clear by the immediately succeeding image of the mirror, another of her iconographical attributes. . . . Venus is present not only in her capacity as goddess of gardens, but also as the form-giver, presiding over the generative cycle unfolded in the Graces and the Hours. Paradises were commonly portrayed as gardens of Venus; see, e.g., Spenser, *Faerie Queene* III vi and IV x. The vine at 258–60 falls in with the same complex of associations; see Ovid, *Ars amatoria* i 244 (*Venus in vinis, ignis in igne fuit*). . . . [The ancients believed] that wine contains *pneuma,* the stuff of life."
264. *apply:* devote their energies to. *airs:* both breezes and melodies.
266–75. *Pan.* Though Pan probably got his name from the Gk word for shepherd, Milton may here allude to the notion that the name came from the Gk word for "all"— hence *universal Pan.* Fowler notes

that Renaissance mythographers interpreted Pan "as a symbol of 'universal nature.' " *Knit:* clasping hands. *Graces:* (L *gratus* beloved) the sister goddesses Euphrosyne (mirth), Aglaia (splendor), and Thalia (bloom), who danced attendance on (*Led on*) Venus. *Hours:* (Gk *hōra* season) goddesses of the seasons. Before the Fall there was only one season—eternal spring. Cf. Milton's *Comus* 983–85. "Along the crisped shades and bow'rs/ Revels the spruce and jocund Spring,/ The Graces and the rosy-bosom'd Hours." *Enna:* a grove of eternal spring in Sicily. *Proserpine:* daughter of the goddess of agriculture, *Ceres. Dis:* Pluto, god of the underworld, who abducted Proserpine. Zeus agreed to free Proserpine if she had not eaten anything while in Hades, but she [cf. Eve] had eaten a pomegranate [cf. apple], and for that was allowed only six months a year on earth. *Daphne:* a famous grove on the *Orontes* R. near Antioch, sacred to Apollo, consecrated to voluptuousness and luxury, and (according to Fowler) containing "an Apolline oracle (hence *inspired*) and a stream named after the famous *Castalian spring* of Parnassus."
275–79. According to one ancient historian, *Ammon* (the name of the Jove

Girt with the river Triton, where old Cham,
Whom Gentiles Ammon call and Libyan Jove,
Hid Amalthea and her florid son
Young Bacchus from his stepdame Rhea's eye;
Nor where Abassin kings their issue guard,   280
Mount Amara, though this by some supposed
True Paradise under the Ethiop line
By Nilus' head, enclosed with shining rock,
A whole day's journey high, but wide remote
From this Assyrian garden, where the Fiend   285
Saw undelighted all delight, all kind
Of living creatures new to sight and strange:
Two of far nobler shape erect and tall,
God-like erect, with native honor clad
In naked majesty seemed lords of all,   290
And worthy seemed, for in their looks divine
The image of their glorious Maker shone,
Truth, wisdom, sanctitude severe and pure,
Severe but in true filial freedom placed;
Whence true authority in men; though both   295
Not equal, as their sex not equal seemed;
For contemplation he and valor formed,
For softness she and sweet attractive grace,
He for God only, she for God in him:
His fair large front and eye sublime declared   300
Absolute rule; and hyacinthine locks
Round from his parted forelock manly hung
Clust'ring, but not beneath his shoulders broad:
She as a veil down to the slender waist
Her unadorned golden tresses wore   305
Disheveled, but in wanton ringlets waved
As the vine curls her tendrils, which implied
Subjection, but required with gentle sway,
And by her yielded, by him best received,
Yielded with coy submission, modest pride,   310
And sweet reluctant amorous delay.

---

worshipped in N. Africa), king of Libya and husband of *Rhea*, hid *Bacchus*, his son by the nymph *Amalthea*, on the fabulously beautiful island *Nysa* (whence the name Dio*nysus*). *Ammon* (or Hammon) was thought in Milton's time to have been Noah's son Ham (or *Cham*). *florid:* (L *floridus* blooming), healthy, beautiful, rosy-complexioned.

280–84. *Abassin:* Abyssinian. *Ethiop line:* the equator. *Nilus' head:* head of the Nile.

300. *large front:* broad forehead. *sublime:* not downcast.

301–11. Cf. 1 Cor. 11.7–15: "For a man indeed ought not to cover his head, forasmuch as he is the image and glory of God: but the woman is the glory of the man. For the man is not of the woman; but the woman of the man. . . . Judge in yourselves: is it comely that a woman pray unto God uncovered? Doth not even nature . . . teach you, that, if a man have long hair, it is a shame unto him? But if a woman have long hair, it is a glory to her: for her hair is given her for a covering." *hyacinthine:* curled in the form of hyacinth petals—as in some classical sculpture; an epithet from Homer. *Disheveled:* let down. *wanton:* luxuriant, unrestrained. *required:* asked for by right of authority (sway). *sway:* controlling influence. *coy:* (L *quietus* quiet) modest. *reluctant:* L *reluctare* to struggle against.

Nor those mysterious parts were then concealed,
Then was not guilty shame, dishonest shame
Of nature's works, honor dishonorable,
Sin-bred, how have ye troubled all mankind   315
With shows instead, mere shows of seeming pure,
And banished from man's life his happiest life,
Simplicity and spotless innocence.
So passed they naked on, nor shunned the sight
Of God or angel, for they thought no ill: 320
So hand in hand they passed, the loveliest pair
That ever since in love's embraces met,
Adam the goodliest man of men since born
His sons, the fairest of her daughters Eve.
Under a tuft of shade that on a green   325
Stood whispering soft, by a fresh fountain side
They sat them down, and after no more toil
Of their sweet gard'ning labor than sufficed
To recommend cool Zephyr, and made ease
More easy, wholesome thirst and appetite   330
More grateful, to their supper fruits they fell,
Nectarine fruits which the compliant boughs
Yielded them, sidelong as they sat recline
On the soft downy bank damasked with flow'rs:
The savory pulp they chew, and in the rind   335
Still as they thirsted scoop the brimming stream;
Nor gentle purpose, nor endearing smiles
Wanted, nor youthful dalliance as beseems
Fair couple, linked in happy nuptial league,
Alone as they. About them frisking played   340
All beasts of th' earth, since wild, and of all chase
In wood or wilderness, forest or den;
Sporting the lion ramped, and in his paw
Dandled the kid; bears, tigers, ounces, pards
Gamboled before them; th' unwieldy elephant   345
To make them mirth used all his might, and wreathed
His lithe proboscis; close the serpent sly
Insinuating, wove with Gordian twine
His braided train, and of his fatal guile
Gave proof unheeded; others on the grass   350
Couched, and now filled with pasture gazing sat,

312. *mysterious.* Cf. 743, and see 750n.
313. *dishonest:* unchaste.
329. *recommend:* make attractive. *Zephyr:* west wind, the wind of spring and fecundity.
330. *easy:* comfortable.
332. *Nectarine:* Gk *nektar,* the drink of the gods. *compliant:* L *plicare* to bend.
334. *damasked:* ornamental in variegated patterns.
337. *gentle:* OF *gentil* well-born, polite, refined. *purpose:* conversation.

338. *Wanted:* were lacking. *dalliance:* amorous play.
341. *chase:* literally, a tract of unenclosed land used as a game preserve; here, a place where animals live.
343. *ramped:* stood rampant—on his hind legs.
344. *ounces:* lynxes. *pards:* leopards.
348. *Insinuating:* (L *insinuare* to bend, curve) worming his way. *Gordian twine:* a twining, twisting motion as intricate and subtle as the Gordian knot.

Or bedward ruminating: for the sun
Declined was hasting now with prone career
To th' Ocean Isles, and in th' ascending scale
Of heav'n the stars that usher evening rose: 355
When Satan still in gaze, as first he stood,
Scarce thus at length failed speech recovered sad.
    "O hell! what do mine eyes with grief behold,
Into our room of bliss thus high advanced
Creatures of other mold, earth-born perhaps,   360
Not Spirits, yet to heav'nly Spirits bright
Little inferior; whom my thoughts pursue
With wonder, and could love, so lively shines
In them divine resemblance, and such grace
The hand that formed them on their shape hath poured.   365
Ah gentle pair, ye little think how nigh
Your change approaches, when all these delights
Will vanish and deliver ye to woe,
More woe, the more your taste is now of joy;
Happy, but for so happy ill secured   370
Long to continue, and this high seat your heav'n
Ill fenced for Heav'n to keep out such a foe
As now is entered; yet no purposed foe
To you whom I could pity thus forlorn
Though I unpitied: league with you I seek,   375
And mutual amity so strait, so close,
That I with you must dwell, or you with me
Henceforth; my dwelling haply may not please
Like this fair Paradise, your sense, yet such
Accept your Maker's work; he gave it me,   380
Which I as freely give; hell shall unfold,
To entertain you two, her widest gates,
And send forth all her kings; there will be room,
Not like these narrow limits, to receive
Your numerous offspring; if no better place,   385
Thank him who puts me loath to this revenge
On you who wrong me not for him who wronged.
And should I at your harmless innocence
Melt, as I do, yet public reason just,
Honor and empire with revenge enlarged,   390

352. *ruminating:* chewing the cud.
353. *prone:* L *pronus* sinking; also, flying swiftly. *career:* swift course.
354. *Ocean Isles:* the Azores. *scale:* ladder, staircase; but Fowler notes that in the zodiac the *stars that usher evening* "rise in Libra, the Scales, the portion of the sky . . . opposite" Aries, where the sun is setting.
359. *room:* place (left vacant by our fall).
361–62. Cf. Ps. 8.5: "For thou hast made him a little lower than the angels, and hast crowned him with glory and honor."
370. *for so happy:* for people so happy as you.
376. *strait:* L *strictus* drawn together.
381–83. Cf. Matt. 10.8 "Heal the sick, cleanse the lepers, raise the dead, cast out the devils: freely ye have received, freely give." Isa. 14.9: "Hell from beneath is moved for thee to meet thee at thy coming: it stirreth up the dead for thee, even all the chief ones of the earth; it hath raised up from their thrones all the kings of the nations."
386. *puts:* OE *putian* to push, thrust.
387. *for:* in place of.

By conquering this new world, compels me now
To do what else though damned I should abhor."
      So spake the Fiend, and with necessity,
The tyrant's plea, excused his devilish deeds.
Then from his lofty stand on that high tree   395
Down he alights among the sportful herd
Of those four-footed kinds, himself now one,
Now other, as their shape served best his end
Nearer to view his prey, and unespied
To mark what of their state he more might learn   400
By word or action marked: about them round
A lion now he stalks with fiery glare,
Then as a tiger, who by chance hath spied
In some purlieu two gentle fawns at play,
Straight couches close, then rising changes oft   405
His couchant watch, as one who chose his ground
Whence rushing he might surest seize them both
Gripped in each paw: when Adam first of men
To first of women Eve thus moving speech
Turned him all ear to hear new utterance flow.   410
      "Sole partner and sole part of all these joys,
Dearer thyself than all; needs must the Power
That made us, and for us this ample world
Be infinitely good, and of his good
As liberal and free as infinite,   415
That raised us from the dust and placed us here
In all this happiness, who at his hand
Have nothing merited, nor can perform
Aught whereof he hath need, he who requires
From us no other service than to keep   420
This one, this easy charge, of all the trees
In Paradise that bear delicious fruit
So various, not to taste that only Tree
Of Knowledge, planted by the Tree of Life,
So near grows death to life, whate'er death is,   425
Some dreadful thing no doubt; for well thou know'st
God hath pronounced it death to taste that Tree,
The only sign of our obedience left
Among so many signs of power and rule
Conferred upon us, and dominion giv'n   430
Over all other creatures that possess
Earth, air, and sea. Then let us not think hard
One easy prohibition, who enjoy

---

402. Cf. 1 Pet. 5.8: "Be sober, be vig-
ilant; because your adversary the devil,
as a roaring lion, walketh about, seeking
whom he may devour."
      404. *purlieu:* outskirts of a forest.
      408–10. A difficult passage. Perhaps
"new utterance" means a kind of speech
new to Satan, and *him* refers to Satan.
      411. I.e.: Only partner in and a unique

part of. . . .
      418–19. Cf. Acts 17.24–25: "God that
made the world and all things therein
. . . [is not] worshipped with men's
hands, as though he needed any thing,
seeing he giveth to all life, and breath,
and all things."
      433. *easy:* not oppressive.

Free leave so large to all things else, and choice
Unlimited of manifold delights: 435
But let us ever praise him, and extol
His bounty, following our delightful task
To prune these growing plants, and tend these flow'rs,
Which were it toilsome, yet with thee were sweet."
    To whom thus Eve replied. "O thou for whom   440
And from whom I was formed flesh of thy flesh,
And without whom am to no end, my guide
And head, what thou hast said is just and right.
For we to him indeed all praises owe,
And daily thanks, I chiefly who enjoy   445
So far the happier lot, enjoying thee
Preeminent by so much odds, while thou
Like consort to thyself canst nowhere find.
That day I oft remember, when from sleep
I first awaked, and found myself reposed   450
Under a shade on flowers, much wond'ring where
And what I was, whence thither brought, and how.
Not distant far from thence a murmuring sound
Of waters issued from a cave and spread
Into a liquid plain, then stood unmoved   455
Pure as th' expanse of heav'n; I thither went
With unexperienced thought, and laid me down
On the green bank, to look into the clear
Smooth lake, that to me seemed another sky.
As I bent down to look, just opposite,   460
A shape within the wat'ry gleam appeared
Bending to look on me, I started back,
It started back, but pleased I soon returned,
Pleased it returned as soon with answering looks
Of sympathy and love; there I had fixed   465
Mine eyes till now, and pined with vain desire,
Had not a voice thus warned me, 'What thou seest,
What there thou seest fair creature is thyself,
With thee it came and goes: but follow me,
And I will bring thee where no shadow stays   470
Thy coming, and thy soft embraces, he
Whose image thou art, him thou shalt enjoy
Inseparably thine, to him shalt bear
Multitudes like thyself, and thence be called
Mother of human race:' what could I do,   475
But follow straight, invisibly thus led?
Till I espied thee, fair indeed and tall,

---

440. *Eve.* Cf. Gen. 3.20: "And Adam called his wife's name Eve; because she was the mother of all living." The root of the Hebrew word means "to live."
441. Cf. Gen. 2.23, p. 354.
443. Cf. 1 Cor. 11.3: "The head of every man is Christ; and the head of the woman is the man; and the head of Christ is God."
447. *so much odds:* such a great amount in excess.
450. *reposed:* reclining, resting.
470. *stays:* awaits.
476. *straight:* at once.

Under a platan, yet methought less fair,
Less winning soft, less amiably mild,
Than that smooth wat'ry image; back I turned,   490
Thou following cried'st aloud, 'Return fair Eve,
Whom fli'st thou? Whom thou fli'st, of him thou art,
His flesh, his bone; to give thee being I lent
Out of my side to thee, nearest my heart
Substantial life, to have thee by my side   485
Henceforth an individual solace dear;
Part of my soul I seek thee, and thee claim
My other half: with that thy gentle hand
Seized mine, I yielded, and from that time see
How beauty is excelled by manly grace   490
And wisdom, which alone is truly fair."
    So spake our general mother, and with eyes
Of conjugal attraction unreproved,
And meek surrender, half embracing leaned
On our first father, half her swelling breast   495
Naked met his under the flowing gold
Of her loose tresses hid: he in delight
Both of her beauty and submissive charms
Smiled with superior love, as Jupiter
On Juno smiles, when he impregns the clouds   500
That shed May flowers; and pressed her matron lip
With kisses pure: aside the Devil turned
For envy, yet with jealous leer malign
Eyed them askance, and to himself thus plained.
    "Sight hateful, sight tormenting! thus these two   505
Imparadised in one another's arms
The happier Eden, shall enjoy their fill
Of bliss on bliss, while I to hell am thrust,
Where neither joy nor love, but fierce desire,
Among our other torments not the least,   510
Still unfulfilled with pain of longing pines;
Yet let me not forget what I have gained
From their own mouths; all is not theirs it seems:
One fatal tree there stands of Knowledge called,
Forbidden them to taste: Knowledge forbidden?   515
Suspicious, reasonless. Why should their Lord
Envy them that? Can it be sin to know,
Can it be death? And do they only stand
By ignorance, is that their happy state,
The proof of their obedience and their faith?   520
O fair foundation laid whereon to build
Their ruin! Hence I will excite their minds
With more desire to know, and to reject

---

478. *platan:* plane tree.   501. *matron:* here an adjective; wifely.
486. *individual:* inseparable.   503. *jealous:* lustful; covetous.
492. *general.* Cf. *our general sire,* 144. 511. *Still:* always. *pines:* is consumed
493. *unreproved:* unreprovable.   (the metaphor of Tantalus).
500. *impregns:* impregnates.   517. *Envy:* begrudge.

Envious commands, invented with design
To keep them low whom knowledge might exalt   525
Equal with gods; aspiring to be such,
They taste and die: what likelier can ensue?
But first with narrow search I must walk round
This garden, and no corner leave unspied;
A chance but chance may lead where I may meet   530
Some wand'ring Spirit of heav'n, by fountain side,
Or in thick shade retired, from him to draw
What further would be learnt. Live while ye may,
Yet happy pair; enjoy, till I return,
Short pleasures, for long woes are to succeed."   535
    So saying, his proud step he scornful turned,
But with sly circumspection, and began
Through wood, through waste, o'er hill, o'er dale his roam.
Meanwhile in utmost longitude, where heav'n
With earth and ocean meets, the setting sun   540
Slowly descended, and with right aspéct
Against the eastern gate of Paradise
Leveled his evening rays: it was a rock
Of alablaster, piled up to the clouds,
Conspicuous far, winding with one ascent   545
Accessible from earth, one entrance high;
The rest was craggy cliff, that overhung
Still as it rose, impossible to climb.
Betwixt these rocky pillars Gabriel sat
Chief of th' angelic guards, awaiting night;   550
About him exercised heroic games
Th' unarmèd youth of heav'n, but nigh at hand
Celestial armory, shields, helms, and spears
Hung high with diamond flaming, and with gold.
Thither came Uriel, gliding through the even   555
On a sunbeam, swift as a shooting star
In autumn thwarts the night, when vapors fired
Impress the air, and shows the mariner
From what point of his compass to beware
Impetuous winds: he thus began in haste.   560
    "Gabriel, to thee thy course by lot hath giv'n
Charge and strict watch that to this happy place
No evil thing approach or enter in;
This day at highth of noon came to my sphere
A Spirit, zealous, as he seemed, to know   565
More of th' Almighty's works, and chiefly man
God's latest image: I described his way
Bent all on speed, and marked his airy gait;

530. *A chance but chance:* there is a chance that luck. . . .
541. *with right aspect:* at right angles to.
544. *alablaster:* alabaster; a white, translucent marble, veined with colors.
549. *Gabriel.* See "Angels," p. 395.

557. *thwarts:* passes across.
558. *Impress:* exert pressure upon.
567. *described:* descried, observed. *way:* course.
568. *gait:* variation of *gate* path (archaic).

But in the mount that lies from Eden north,
Where he first lighted, soon discerned his looks   570
Alien from heav'n, with passions foul obscured:
Mine eye pursued him still, but under shade
Lost sight of him; one of the banished crew
I fear, hath ventured from the deep, to raise
New troubles; him thy care must be to find."   575
   To whom the wingèd warrior thus returned:
"Uriel, no wonder if thy perfet sight,
Amid the sun's bright circle where thou sitt'st,
See far and wide: in at this gate none pass
The vigilance here placed, but such as come   580
Well known from heav'n; and since meridian hour
No creature thence: if Spirit of other sort,
So minded, have o'erleaped these earthy bounds
On purpose, hard thou know'st it to exclude
Spiritual substance with corporeal bar.   585
But if within the circuit of these walks,
In whatsoever shape he lurk, of whom
Thou tell'st, by morrow dawning I shall know."
   So promised he, and Uriel to his charge
Returned on that bright beam, whose point now raised   590
Bore him slope downward to the sun now fall'n
Beneath th' Azorès; whether the prime orb,
Incredible how swift, had thither rolled
Diurnal, or this less volúble earth
By shorter flight to th' east, had left him there   595
Arraying with reflected purple and gold
The clouds that on his western throne attend:
Now came still evening on, and twilight gray
Had in her sober livery all things clad;
Silence accompanied, for beast and bird,   600
They to their grassy couch, these to their nests
Were slunk, all but the wakeful nightingale;
She all night long her amorous descant sung;
Silence was pleased: now glowed the firmament
With living sapphires: Hesperus that led   605
The starry host, rode brightest, till the moon
Rising in clouded majesty, at length
Apparent queen unveiled her peerless light,
And o'er the dark her silver mantle threw.
   When Adam thus to Eve: "Fair consort, th' hour   610
Of night, and all things now retired to rest
Mind us of like repose, since God hath set
Labor and rest, as day and night to men
Successive, and the timely dew of sleep

---

572. *shade:* trees forming shade.
  592. *prime orb: primum mobile*; see
"Universe," p. 390.
  594. *Diurnal:* daily. *voluble:* able to
move quickly.
  603. *descant:* a strain of melody, sung
by a soprano voice.
  605. *Hesperus:* the Evening Star.

Now falling with soft slumbrous weight inclines   615
Our eyelids; other creatures all day long
Rove idle unemployed, and less need rest;
Man hath his daily work of body or mind
Appointed, which declares his dignity,
And the regard of Heav'n on all his ways;   620
While other animals unactive range,
And of their doings God takes no account.
To morrow ere fresh morning streak the east
With first approach of light, we must be ris'n,
And at our pleasant labor, to reform   625
Yon flow'ry arbors, yonder alleys green,
Our walk at noon, with branches overgrown,
That mock our scant manuring, and require
More hands than ours to lop their wanton growth:
Those blossoms also, and those dropping gums,   630
That lie bestrown unsightly and unsmooth,
Ask riddance, if we mean to tread with ease;
Meanwhile, as nature wills, night bids us rest."
    To whom thus Eve with perfet beauty adorned.
"My author and disposer, what thou bidd'st   635
Unargued I obey; so God ordains,
God is thy law, thou mine: to know no more
Is woman's happiest knowledge and her praise.
With thee conversing I forget all time,
All seasons and their change, all please alike.   640
Sweet is the breath of morn, her rising sweet,
With charm of earliest birds; pleasant the sun
When first on this delightful land he spreads
His orient beams, on herb, tree, fruit, and flow'r,
Glist'ring with dew; fragrant the fertile earth   645
After soft showers; and sweet the coming on
Of grateful evening mild, then silent night
With this her solemn bird and this fair moon,
And these the gems of heav'n, her starry train:
But neither breath of morn when she ascends   650
With charm of earliest birds, nor rising sun
On this delightful land, nor herb, fruit, flow'r,
Glist'ring with dew, nor fragrance after showers,
Nor grateful evening mild, nor silent night
With this her solemn bird, nor walk by moon,   655
Or glittering starlight without thee is sweet.
But wherefore all night long shine these, for whom
This glorious sight, when sleep hath shut all eyes?"
    To whom our general ancestor replied.

628. *manuring:* OF *manouvrer* to culti-
vate by manual (L *manus* hand) labor.
635. *disposer:* regulator, manager, em-
ployer.
640. *seasons:* times, occasions.
642. *charm:* (OE *cirman* to cry out,

make a noise, esp. as of birds) "the
blended singing or noise of many birds"
OED.
    648. *solemn:* inspiring awe, devotion,
or reverence.

"Daughter of God and man, accomplished Eve,   660
Those have their course to finish, round the earth,
By morrow evening, and from land to land
In order, though to nations yet unborn,
Minist'ring light prepared, they set and rise;
Lest total darkness should by night regain   665
Her old possession, and extinguish life
In nature and all things, which these soft fires
Not only enlighten, but with kindly heat
Of various influence foment and warm,
Temper or nourish, or in part shed down   670
Their stellar virtue on all kinds that grow
On earth, made hereby apter to receive
Perfection from the sun's more potent ray.
These then, though unbeheld in deep of night,
Shine not in vain, nor think, though men were none,   675
That heav'n would want spectators, God want praise;
Millions of spiritual creatures walk the earth
Unseen, both when we wake, and when we sleep:
All these with ceaseless praise his works behold
Both day and night: how often from the steep   680
Of echoing hill or thicket have we heard
Celestial voices to the midnight air,
Sole, or responsive each to other's note
Singing their great Creator: oft in bands
While they keep watch, or nightly rounding walk,   685
With heav'nly touch of instrumental sounds
In full harmonic number joined, their songs
Divide the night, and lift our thoughts to heaven."
    Thus talking hand in hand alone they passed
On to their blissful bower; it was a place   690
Chos'n by the sovran Planter, when he framed
All things to man's delightful use; the roof
Of thickest covert was inwoven shade
Laurel and myrtle, and what higher grew
Of firm and fragrant leaf; on either side   695
Acanthus, and each odorous bushy shrub
Fenced up the verdant wall; each beauteous flow'r,
Iris all hues, roses, and jessamine
Reared high their flourished heads between, and wrought
Mosaic; underfoot the violet,   700

---

660. *accomplished:* "complete, perfect; esp. in acquirements, or as a result of training," *OED*.

664. *prepared.* Cf. Ps. 74.16: "The day is thine, the night also is thine: thou hast prepared the light and the sun."

667. *soft:* agreeable.

668. *kindly.* Kind originally meant "natural" and "innate"; later, "benevolent."

669. *influence:* (L *in* + *fluere* flow) originally an astrological term for the

flowing of "ethereal fluid" from stars to earth. *foment:* to stimulate by application of warm liquid.

688. *divide.* The L military phrase *dividere noctem* meant to mark the watches of the night, but as Fowler notes, "perhaps there is also a play on the musical sense of *divide* (*OED* 11 a, perform with 'divisions'—florid melodic passages or descants)."

691. *framed:* fashioned.

699. *flourished:* L *flos, floris* flower.

Crocus, and hyacinth with rich inlay
Broidered the ground, more colored than with stone
Of costliest emblem: other creature here
Beast, bird, insect, or worm durst enter none;
Such was their awe of man. In shadier bower   705
More sacred and sequestered, though but feigned,
Pan or Silvanus never slept, nor nymph,
Nor Faunus haunted. Here in close recess
With flowers, garlands, and sweet-smelling herbs
Espousèd Eve decked first her nuptial bed,   710
And heav'nly quires the hymenean sung,
What day the genial angel to our sire
Brought her in naked beauty more adorned,
More lovely than Pandora, whom the gods
Endowed with all their gifts, and O too like   715
In sad event, when to the unwiser son
Of Japhet brought by Hermes, she ensnared
Mankind with her fair looks, to be avenged
On him who had stole Jove's authentic fire.
    Thus at their shady lodge arrived, both stood,   720
Both turned, and under open sky adored
The God that made both sky, air, earth and heav'n
Which they beheld, the moon's resplendent globe
And starry pole: "Thou also mad'st the night,
Maker Omnipotent, and thou the day,   725
Which we in our appointed work employed
Have finished happy in our mutual help
And mutual love, the crown of all our bliss
Ordained by thee, and this delicious place
For us too large, where thy abundance wants   730
Partakers, and uncropped falls to the ground.
But thou hast promised from us two a race
To fill the earth, who shall with us extol
Thy goodness infinite, both when we wake,
And when we seek, as now, thy gift of sleep."   735
    This said unanimous, and other rites
Observing none, but adoration pure
Which God likes best, into their inmost bow'r
Handed they went; and eased the putting off
These troublesome disguises which we wear,   740

703. *emblem:* mosaic.
704. *worm:* a class including snakes.
706. *feigned:* existing in fiction.
707–8. *Pan, Silvanus,* and *Faunus* were fauns associated with sacred, sequestered, rural places and with generation. *close:* secluded.
711. *hymenean:* wedding hymn; *Hymen,* god of marriage.
712. *genial:* L *genialis,* from *gignere* to beget.
714–19. After Prometheus, the wise son of Iapetus (identified by Christian mythologists with Iapet, i.e., *Japhet,* son of Noah) had stolen fire from heaven, angry *Jove* avenged himself on all mankind by means of *Pandora,* whom Prometheus' brother fell in love with and married. To marriage Pandora brought a treasure chest which, when her unwary husband opened it, turned out to hold all the evils and woes that have since afflicted mankind. *authentic:* Gk *authentēs* one who does anything with his own hand.
724. *pole:* sky.
739. *Handed:* hand in hand.

Straight side by side were laid, nor turned I ween
Adam from his fair spouse, nor Eve the rites
Mysterious of connubial love refused:
Whatever hypocrites austerely talk
Of purity and place and innocence,   745
Defaming as impure what God declares
Pure, and commands to some, leaves free to all.
Our Maker bids increase, who bids abstain
But our destroyer, foe to God and man?
Hail wedded Love, mysterious law, true source   750
Of human offspring, sole propriety
In Paradise of all things common else.
By thee adulterous lust was driv'n from men
Among the bestial herds to range, by thee
Founded in reason, loyal, just, and pure,   755
Relations dear, and all the charities
Of father, son, and brother first were known.
Far be it, that I should write thee sin or blame,
Or think thee unbefitting holiest place,
Perpetual fountain of domestic sweets,   760
Whose bed is undefiled and chaste pronounced,
Present, or past, as saints and patriarchs used.
Here Love his golden shafts employs, here lights
His constant lamp, and waves his purple wings,
Reigns here and revels; not in the bought smile   765
Of harlots, loveless, joyless, unendeared,
Casual fruition, nor in court amours,
Mixed dance, or wanton masque, or midnight ball,
Or serenate, which the starved lover sings
To his proud fair, best quitted with disdain.   770
These lulled by nightingales embracing slept,
And on their naked limbs the flow'ry roof
Show'red roses, which the morn repaired. Sleep on,
Blest pair; and O yet happiest if ye seek
No happier state, and know to know no more.   775

---

742. *rites:* those things which are proper for, or incumbent on, one to do.
743. *Mysterious:* beyond explanation.
744–48. Cf. 1 Tim. 4.1–3: "Now the Spirit speaketh expressly, that in the latter times some shall depart from the faith, giving heed to seducing spirits, and doctrines of devils; Speaking lies in hypocrisy; having their conscience seared with a hot iron; Forbidding to marry, and commanding to abstain from meats, which God hath created to be received with thanksgiving of them which believe and know the truth."
747. Cf. 1 Cor. 7.1–2: "It is good for a man not to touch a woman. Nevertheless, to avoid fornication, let every man have his own wife."
750. Cf. Eph. 5.31–32: "For this cause shall a man leave his father and mother, and shall be joined unto his wife, and they two shall be one flesh. This is a great mystery: but I speak concerning Christ and the church."
751. *propriety:* (OF *proprieté*, L *proprius* one's own) private property.
756. *charities:* loves.
761. Cf. Heb. 13.4: "Marriage is honourable in all, and the bed undefiled: but whoremongers and adulterers God will judge."
763. *Love:* Eros or Cupid, whose gold-tipped arrows inspired love—his lead-tipped, hate.
768. *masque:* masquerade.
769. *serenate:* Italian form of *serenade.*
773. *repaired:* restored by replacing.
774–75. See "Knowledge," p. 398.

Now had night measured with her shadowy cone
Half way up hill this vast sublunar vault,
And from their ivory port the Cherubim
Forth issuing at th' accustomed hour stood armed
To their night-watches in warlike parade,   780
When Gabriel to his next in power thus spake.
    "Uzziel, half these draw off, and coast the south
With strictest watch; these other wheel the north,
Our circuit meets full west." As flame they part
Half wheeling to the shield, half to the spear.   785
From these, two strong and subtle Spirits he called
That near him stood, and gave them thus in charge.
    "Ithuriel and Zephon, with winged speed
Search through this garden, leave unsearched no nook,
But chiefly where those two fair creatures lodge,   790
Now laid perhaps asleep secure of harm.
This evening from the sun's decline arrived
Who tells of some infernal Spirit seen
Hitherward bent (who could have thought?) escaped
The bars of hell, on errand bad no doubt: 795
Such where ye find, seize fast, and hither bring."
    So saying, on he led his radiant files,
Dazzling the moon; these to the bower direct
In search of whom they sought: him there they found
Squat like a toad, close at the ear of Eve;   800
Assaying by his devilish art to reach
The organs of her fancy, and with them forge
Illusions as he list, phantasms and dreams;
Or if, inspiring venom, he might taint
Th' animal spirits that from pure blood arise   805
Like gentle breaths from rivers pure, thence raise
At least distempered, discontented thoughts,
Vain hopes, vain aims, inordinate desires
Blown up with high conceits engend'ring pride.
Him thus intent Ithuriel with his spear   810
Touched lightly; for no falsehood can endure
Touch of celestial temper, but returns
Of force to its own likeness: up he starts
Discovered and surprised. As when a spark
Lights on a heap of nitrous powder, laid   815
Fit for the tun some magazine to store

776–77. The imagined conical shadow
cast by the earth in the light of the sun
has moved half way up to its zenith; it
is 9 P.M., the end of the first three-hour
watch.
782. *coast:* follow the coastline of.
782,788. See "Angels," pp. 396–97.
783. *wheel:* (military term) turn to.
785. *shield:* left. *spear:* right.
791. *secure of:* unconcerned about.
793. *Who:* one who. *infernal:* L *in-
fernus* that lies beneath.

804. *inspiring:* L *in* + *spirare* to
breathe.
805. *animal spirits.* See "Physiology
and Psychology," p. 391.
807. *distempered:* unbalanced; disor-
dered.
809. *conceits:* ideas.
812. *celestial temper:* anything, like
the spear, made (tempered) in heaven.
816. I.e.: Ready to be put in barrels to
supply an ammunition dump.

Against a rumored war, the smutty grain
With sudden blaze diffused, inflames the air:
So started up in his own shape the Fiend.
Back stepped those two fair angels half amazed   820
So sudden to behold the grisly king;
Yet thus, unmoved with fear, accost him soon.
 "Which of those rebel Spirits adjudged to hell
Com'st thou, escaped thy prison; and transformed,
Why sat'st thou like an enemy in wait   825
Here watching at the head of these that sleep?"
 "Know ye not then" said Satan, filled with scorn,
"Know ye not me? Ye knew me once no mate
For you, there sitting where ye durst not soar;
Not to know me argues yourselves unknown,   830
The lowest of your throng; or if ye know,
Why ask ye, and superfluous begin
Your message, like to end as much in vain?"
To whom thus Zephon, answering scorn with scorn.
 "Think not, revolted Spirit, thy shape the same,   835
Or undiminished brightness, to be known
As when thou stood'st in heav'n upright and pure;
That glory then, when thou no more wast good,
Departed from thee, and thou resembl'st now
Thy sin and place of doom obscure and foul.   840
But come, for thou, be sure, shalt give account
To him who sent us, whose charge is to keep
This place inviolable, and these from harm."
 So spake the Cherub, and his grave rebuke
Severe in youthful beauty, added grace   845
Invincible: abashed the Devil stood,
And felt how awful goodness is, and saw
Virtue in her shape how lovely, saw, and pined
His loss; but chiefly to find here observed
His luster visibly impaired; yet seemed   850
Undaunted. "If I must contend," said he,
"Best with the best, the sender not the sent,
Or all at once; more glory will be won,
Or less be lost." "Thy fear," said Zephon bold,
"Will save us trial what the least can do   855
Single against thee wicked, and thence weak."
 The Fiend replied not, overcome with rage;
But like a proud steed reined, went haughty on,
Champing his iron curb: to strive or fly
He held it vain; awe from above had quelled   860
His heart, not else dismayed. Now drew they nigh
The western point, where those half-rounding guards

---

817. *Against:* in anticipation of. *smutty grain:* seed-shaped particles that blacken the touch.
830. *argues:* proves.

840. *obscure:* (L *obscurus* covered) dark.
848. *pined:* suffered for.

Just met, and closing stood in squadron joined
Awaiting next command. To whom their chief
Gabriel from the front thus called aloud.   865
    "O friends, I hear the tread of nimble feet
Hasting this way, and now by glimpse discern
Ithuriel and Zephon through the shade,
And with them comes a third of regal port,
But faded splendor wan; who by his gait   870
And fierce demeanor seems the Prince of Hell,
Not likely to part hence without contést;
Stand firm, for in his look defiance lours."
    He scarce had ended, when those two approached
And brief related whom they brought, where found,   875
How busied, in what form and posture couched.
    To whom with stern regard thus Gabriel spake.
"Why hast thou, Satan, broke the bounds prescribed
To thy transgressions, and disturbed the charge
Of others, who approve not to transgress   880
By thy example, but have power and right
To question thy bold entrance on this place;
Employed it seems to violate sleep, and those
Whose dwelling God hath planted here in bliss?"
    To whom thus Satan, with contemptuous brow.   885
"Gabriel, thou hadst in heav'n th' esteem of wise,
And such I held thee; but this question asked
Puts me in doubt. Lives there who loves his pain?
Who would not, finding way, break loose from hell,
Though thither doomed? Thou wouldst thyself, no doubt,   890
And boldly venture to whatever place
Farthest from pain, where thou mightst hope to change
Torment with ease, and soonest recompense
Dole with delight, which in this place I sought;
To thee no reason; who know'st only good,   895
But evil hast not tried: and wilt object
His will who bound us? Let him surer bar
His iron gates, if he intends our stay
In that dark durance: thus much what was asked.
The rest is true, they found me where they say;   900
But that implies not violence or harm."
    Thus he in scorn. The warlike angel moved,
Disdainfully half smiling thus replied.
"O loss of one in heav'n to judge of wise,
Since Satan fell, whom folly overthrew,   905
And now returns him from his prison scaped,
Gravely in doubt whether to hold them wise
Or not, who ask what boldness brought him hither

---

868. *shade:* shade trees.
870. *wan:* dark, faint, sickly.
879. *the charge Of:* those under the protection of.
886. *esteem of:* reputation of being.

894. *Dole:* L *dolor* pain, distress, grief, sorrow.
896. *wilt object:* wilt thou produce as an argument (against my escape).
899. *durance:* confinement.

Unlicensed from his bounds in hell prescribed;
So wise he judges it to fly from pain   910
However, and to scape his punishment.
So judge thou still, presumptuous, till the wrath,
Which thou incurr'st by flying, meet thy flight
Sevenfold, and scourge that wisdom back to hell,
Which taught thee yet no better, that no pain   915
Can equal anger infinite provoked.
But wherefore thou alone? Wherefore with thee
Came not all hell broke loose? Is pain to them
Less pain, less to be fled, or thou than they
Less hardy to endure? Courageous chief,   920
The first in flight from pain, hadst thou alleged
To thy deserted host this cause of flight,
Thou surely hadst not come sole fugitive."
      To which the Fiend thus answered frowning stern.
"Not that I less endure, or shrink from pain,   925
Insulting angel, well thou know'st I stood
Thy fiercest, when in battle to thy aid
The blasting volleyed thunder made all speed
And seconded thy else not dreaded spear.
But still thy words at random, as before,   930
Argue thy inexperience what behoves
From hard assays and ill successes past
A faithful leader, not to hazard all
Through ways of danger by himself untried.
I therefore, I alone first undertook   935
To wing the desolate abyss, and spy
This new-created world, whereof in hell
Fame is not silent, here in hope to find
Better abode, and my afflicted powers
To settle here on earth, or in mid-air;   940
Though for possession put to try once more
What thou and thy gay legions dare against;
Whose easier business were to serve their Lord
High up in heav'n, with songs to hymn his throne,
And practiced distances to cringe, not fight."   945
      To whom the warrior angel soon replied.
"To say and straight unsay, pretending first
Wise to fly pain, professing next the spy,
Argues no leader, but a liar traced,
Satan, and couldst thou faithful add? O name,   950
O sacred name of faithfulness profaned!
Faithful to whom? To thy rebellious crew?

---

911. *However:* howsoever.
926. *stood:* withstood.
932. *From:* after. *assays:* attempts; or (military) attacks. *successes:* outcomes.
938. *Fame:* rumor.
939. *afflicted:* (L *affligere* to throw down) downcast, depressed. *powers:* army.

940. *mid-air.* See "Universe," pp. 390–91.
941. *put:* forced. *try:* test.
942. *gay:* in dress and behavior like courtiers.
945. *distances:* attitudes of deference. *cringe:* bow or kneel in humility or fear.
949. *traced:* found out.

Army of fiends, fit body to fit head;
Was this your discipline and faith engaged,
Your military obedience, to dissolve   955
Allegiance to th' acknowledged Power Supreme?
And thou sly hypocrite, who now wouldst seem
Patron of liberty, who more than thou
Once fawned, and cringed, and serviley adored
Heav'n's awful Monarch? Wherefore but in hope   960
To dispossess him, and thyself to reign?
But mark what I areed thee now, avaunt;
Fly thither whence thou fledd'st: if from this hour
Within these hallowed limits thou appear,
Back to th' infernal pit I drag thee chained,   965
And seal thee so, as henceforth not to scorn
The facile gates of hell too slightly barred."
    So threatened he, but Satan to no threats
Gave heed, but waxing more in rage replied.
    "Then when I am thy captive talk of chains,   970
Proud limitary Cherub, but ere then
Far heavier load thyself expect to feel
From my prevailing arm, though heaven's King
Ride on thy wings, and thou with thy compeers,
Used to the yoke, draw'st his triumphant wheels   975
In progress through the road of heav'n star-paved."
    While thus he spake, th' angelic squadron bright
Turned fiery red, sharp'ning in moonèd horns
Their phalanx, and began to hem him round
With ported spears, as thick as when a field   980
Of Ceres ripe for harvest waving bends
Her bearded grove of ears, which way the wind
Sways them; the careful ploughman doubting stands
Lest on the threshing-floor his hopeful sheaves
Prove chaff. On th' other side Satan alarmed   985
Collecting all his might dilated stood,
Like Teneriffe or Atlas unremoved:
His stature reached the sky, and on his crest
Sat Horror plumed; nor wanted in his grasp
What seemed both spear and shield: now dreadful deeds   990
Might have ensued, nor only Paradise
In this commotion, but the starry cope
Of heav'n perhaps, or all the elements
At least had gone to wrack, disturbed and torn
With violence of this conflict, and not soon   995

962. *areed:* advise.
966. Cf. Rev. 20.3, p. 386.
967. *facile:* easily moved.
971. *limitary:* frontier guard; also, one of limited authority.
974. Cf. Ps. 18.10: "And he rode upon a cherub, and did fly: yea, he did fly upon the wings of the wind."
978. *mooned horns:* a crescent-shaped

military formation.
980. *ported:* held slantwise, in front.
981. *Ceres:* Roman goddess of grain; here the grain itself.
983. *careful:* anxious.
987. *Teneriffe* is a mountain in the Canary Islands; *Atlas*, in Morocco. *unremoved:* unremovable.
992. *cope:* vault-like canopy.

Th' Eternal to prevent such horrid fray
Hung forth in heav'n his golden scales, yet seen
Betwixt Astraea and the Scorpion sign,
Wherein all things created first he weighed,
The pendulous round earth with balanced air   1000
In counterpoise, now ponders all events,
Battles and realms: in these he put two weights
The sequel each of parting and of fight;
The latter quick up flew, and kicked the beam;
Which Gabriel spying, thus bespake the Fiend.   1005
    "Satan, I know thy strength, and thou know'st mine,
Neither our own but giv'n; what folly then
To boast what arms can do, since thine no more
Than Heav'n permits, nor mine, though doubled now
To trample thee as mire: for proof look up,   1010
And read thy lot in yon celestial sign
Where thou art weighed, and shown how light, how weak,
If thou resist." The Fiend looked up and knew
His mounted scale aloft: nor more; but fled
Murmuring, and with him fled the shades of night.   1015

997–1013. In the classical epic simile which Milton here imitates, the gods weigh the fates of opposing heroes before battle (Hector and Achilles in the *Iliad*, Turnus and Aeneas in the *Aeneid*), but Milton adds to this conventional meaning (i.e., the fate of Satan) God's *pondering*, or weighing the consequences (*sequel*) of allowing Satan and Gabriel to fight and the consequences of preventing the fight. The second "weighed" more —was more desirable. Milton also enriched the conventional figure by identifying the scales with Libra, the sign in the Zodiac, and by alluding to Biblical metaphors of weighing: Isa. 40.12: "Who hath measured the waters in the hollow of his hand, and meted out heaven with the span, and comprehended the dust of the earth in a measure, and weighed the mountains in scales, and the hills in a balance?" 1 Sam. 2.3: "Talk no more so exceeding proudly; let not arrogancy come out of your mouth: for the Lord is a God of knowledge, and by him actions are weighed." Dan. 5.27 "Tekel; Thou art weighed in the balances, and art found wanting."

Book V

The Argument

Morning approached, Eve relates to Adam her troublesome dream; he likes it not, yet comforts her: they come forth to their day labors: their morning hymn at the door of their bower. God to render man inexcusable sends Raphael to admonish him of his obedience, of his free estate, of his enemy near at hand; who he is, and why his enemy, and whatever else may avail Adam to know. Raphael comes down to Paradise, his appearance described, his coming discerned by Adam afar off sitting at the door of his bower; he goes out to meet him, brings him to his lodge, entertains him with the choicest fruits of Paradise got together by Eve; their discourse at table: Raphael performs his message, minds Adam of his state and of his enemy; relates at Adam's request who that enemy is, and how he came to be so, beginning from his first revolt in heaven, and the occasion thereof; how he drew his legions after him to the parts of the north, and there incited them to rebel with him, persuading all but only Abdiel a Seraph, who in argument dissuades and opposes him, then forsakes him.

> Now Morn her rosy steps in th' eastern clime
> Advancing, sowed the earth with orient pearl,
> When Adam waked, so customed, for his sleep
> Was aery light, from pure digestion bred,
> And temperate vapors bland, which th' only sound   5
> Of leaves and fuming rills, Aurora's fan,
> Lightly dispersed, and the shrill matin song
> Of birds on every bough; so much the more

V. *The Argument. admonish:* (L *admonere* to remind) warn. *avail:* profit. *message:* a messenger's errand.

1–8. The imagery in this fine passage is complex. Sleep was suposed to be induced by vapors generated in the stomach, according to the same physiology expressed in the lines about Satan's hope that by breathing poison into Eve's ear he might "taint / The animal spirits that from pure blood arise / Like gentle breaths from rivers pure" (IV.804–6). Adam's sleep was *aery light* because the elements in his vapors were mixed in perfect proportion (*temperate*)—and because Satan had not poisoned them. These sleep-producing vapors were *dispersed* by the *sound* of *leaves, rills,* and bird *songs.* But associated with all three were vapors of various sorts that acted upon the vapors of sleep: there was the morning breeze that rustled the leaves; there was the mist rising from the stream; and there were, in a pun, the "airs, vernal airs" (cf. IV.264) of the

bird songs. Dawn, *Morn, Aurora* is personified first by her *rosy steps* and her *sowing the earth with orient pearl,* and then by her *fan* (the trees), and finally by the mist, which is her veil. For if we remember that Milton later (IX.425) described Eve as "Veiled in a cloud of fragrance," we may realize that *fume* here has the then common meaning of fragrant exhalation or incense, and that the fragrant cloud of fresh, rural morning mist was the goddess's veil. The harmony of rustling leaves, singing birds, and rippling brooks was a literary cliché, as Fowler points out in his note to IV.263–66. But Milton's synesthetic association, here and elsewhere, of sounds, fragrances, and other non-visual sensations of morning came from deep within his own experience. According to Milton's history of man the first line of the first love lyric ever sung was Eve's "Sweet is the breath of morn, her rising sweet" (IV.641).

104

His wonder was to find unwakened Eve
With tresses discomposed, and glowing cheek,　　10
As through unquiet rest: he on his side
Leaning half-raised, with looks of cordial love
Hung over her enamored, and beheld
Beauty, which whether waking or asleep,
Shot forth peculiar graces; then with voice　　15
Mild, as when Zephyrus on Flora breathes,
Her hand soft touching, whispered thus. "Awake
My fairest, my espoused, my latest found,
Heav'n's last best gift, my ever new delight,
Awake, the morning shines, and the fresh field　　20
Calls us, we lose the prime, to mark how spring
Our tended plants, how blows the citron grove,
What drops the myrrh, and what the balmy reed,
How nature paints her colors, how the bee
Sits on the bloom extracting liquid sweet."　　25
　Such whispering waked her, but with startled eye
On Adam, whom embracing, thus she spake.
　"O sole in whom my thoughts find all repose,
My glory, my perfection, glad I see
Thy face, and morn returned, for I this night,　　30
Such night till this I never passed, have dreamed,
If dreamed, not as I oft am wont, of thee,
Works of day past, or morrow's next design,
But of offense and trouble, which my mind
Knew never till this irksome night; methought　　35
Close at mine ear one called me forth to walk
With gentle voice, I thought it thine; it said,
'Why sleep'st thou Eve? now is the pleasant time,
The cool, the silent, save where silence yields
To the night-warbling bird, that now awake　　40
Tunes sweetest his love-labored song; now reigns
Full-orbed the moon, and with more pleasing light
Shadowy sets off the face of things; in vain,
If none regard; heav'n wakes with all his eyes,
Whom to behold but thee, nature's desire,　　45
In whose sight all things joy, with ravishment
Attracted by thy beauty still to gaze.'
I rose as at thy call, but found thee not;
To find thee I directed then my walk;
And on, me thought, alone I passed through ways　　50
That brought me on a sudden to the tree
Of interdicted knowledge: fair it seemed,

12. *cordial:* (L *cordis* heart) reviving.
15. *peculiar:* (L *peculium* private property) its own.
16. *Zephyrus:* the western wind. *Flora:* goddess of flowers.
17–25. Cf. Song of Solomon 2.10: "My beloved spake, and said unto me / Rise up, my love, my fair one, and come away."
21. *prime:* the first hour of the day.
22. *blows:* blossoms.
23. *myrrh* and balm are odoriferous resins.
34. *offense:* L *offendere* to stumble, commit a fault.

Much fairer to my fancy than by day:
And as I wond'ring looked, beside it stood
One shaped and winged like one of those from heav'n   55
By us oft seen; his dewy locks distilled
Ambrosia; on that tree he also gazed;
And 'O fair plant,' said he, 'with fruit surcharged,
Deigns none to ease thy load and taste thy sweet,
Nor god, nor man; is knowledge so despised?   60
Or envy, or what reserve forbids to taste?
Forbid who will, none shall from me withhold
Longer thy offered good, why else set here?'
This said he paused not, but with vent'rous arm
He plucked, he tasted; me damp horror chilled   65
At such bold words vouched with a deed so bold:
But he thus overjoyed, 'O fruit divine,
Sweet of thyself, but much more sweet thus cropped,
Forbidden here, it seems, as only fit
For gods, yet able to make gods of men: 70
And why not gods of men, since good, the more
Communicated, more abundant grows,
The author not impaired, but honored more?
Here, happy creature, fair angelic Eve,
Partake thou also; happy though thou art,   75
Happier thou may'st be, worthier canst not be:
Taste this, and be henceforth among the gods
Thyself a goddess, not to earth confined,
But sometimes in the air, as we, sometimes
Ascend to heav'n, by merit thine, and see   80
What life the gods live there, and such live thou.'
So saying, he drew nigh, and to me held,
Even to my mouth of that same fruit held part
Which he had plucked; the pleasant savory smell
So quickened appetite, that I, me thought,   85
Could not but taste. Forthwith up to the clouds
With him I flew, and underneath beheld
The earth outstretched immense, a prospect wide
And various: wond'ring at my flight and change
To this high exaltation; suddenly   90
My guide was gone, and I, methought, sunk down,
And fell asleep; but O how glad I waked
To find this but a dream!" Thus Eve her night
Related, and thus Adam answered sad.
   "Best image of myself and dearer half,   95
The trouble of thy thoughts this night in sleep
Affects me equally; nor can I like
This uncouth dream, of evil sprung I fear;

57. *Ambrosia:* heavenly perfume.
60. *god:* angel.
61. I.e.: Whose envy or what restriction forbids your being tasted?
73. *impaired:* (L *pejorare* to make worse) injured, diminished.
94. *sad:* soberly.
98. *uncouth:* strange; unpleasant, improper.

Yet evil whence? in thee can harbor none,
Created pure. But know that in the soul   100
Are many lesser faculties that serve
Reason as chief; among these fancy next
Her office holds; of all external things,
Which the five watchful senses represent,
She forms imaginations, aery shapes,   105
Which reason joining or disjoining, frames
All what we affirm or what deny, and call
Our knowledge or opinion; then retires
Into her private cell when nature rests.
Oft in her absence mimic fancy wakes   110
To imitate her; but misjoining shapes,
Wild work produces oft, and most in dreams,
Ill matching words and deeds long past or late.
Some such resemblances methinks I find
Of our last evening's talk, in this thy dream,   115
But with addition strange; yet be not sad.
Evil into the mind of god or man
May come and go, so unapproved, and leave
No spot or blame behind: which gives me hope
That what in sleep thou didst abhor to dream,   120
Waking thou never wilt consent to do.
Be not disheartened then, nor cloud those looks
That wont to be more cheerful and serene
Than when fair morning first smiles on the world,
And let us to our fresh employments rise   125
Among the groves, the fountains, and the flow'rs
That open now their choicest bosomed smells
Reserved from night, and kept for thee in store."
    So cheered he his fair spouse, and she was cheered,
But silently a gentle tear let fall   130
From either eye, and wiped them with her hair;
Two other precious drops that ready stood,
Each in their crystal sluice, he ere they fell
Kissed as the gracious signs of sweet remorse
And pious awe, that feared to have offended.   135
    So all was cleared, and to the field they haste.
But first from under shady arborous roof,
Soon as they forth were come to open sight
Of day-spring, and the sun, who scarce up risen
With wheels yet hov'ring o'er the ocean brim,   140

100–113. Fowler quotes Burton, *Anat-
omy of Melancholy* (1621) I.1.2.vii:
"Phantasy, or imagination . . . is an in-
ner sense which doth more fully examine
the species perceived by common sense,
of things present or absent. . . . In time
of sleep this faculty is free, and many
times conceives strange, stupend, absurd
shapes. . . . In men it is subject and gov-
erned by reason, or at least should be."
See "Physiology and Psychology," p.

392.
  104. *represent:* present to the mind.
  105. *imaginations:* images.
  117. *god:* angel.
  118. *so unapproved:* so long as it is
(1) not approved or (2) not experienced
or put to proof.
  125. *fresh:* refreshing.
  127. *bosomed:* enclosed.
  135. *pious:* devoted, as becoming to a
spouse. *awe:* veneration.

Shot parallel to the earth his dewy ray,
Discovering in wide lantskip all the east
Of Paradise and Eden's happy plains,
Lowly they bowed adoring, and began
Their orisons, each morning duly paid   145
In various style, for neither various style
Nor holy rapture wanted they to praise
Their Maker, in fit strains pronounced or sung
Unmeditated, such prompt eloquence
Flowed from their lips, in prose or numerous verse, 150
More tuneable than needed lute or harp
To add more sweetness, and they thus began.
 "These are thy glorious works, Parent of good,
Almighty, thine this universal frame,
Thus wondrous fair; thyself how wondrous then! 155
Unspeakable, who sitt'st above these heavens,
To us invisible or dimly seen
In these thy lowest works, yet these declare
Thy goodness beyond thought, and power divine:
Speak ye who best can tell, ye sons of light, 160
Angels, for ye behold him, and with songs
And choral symphonies, day without night,
Circle his throne rejoicing, ye in heav'n,
On earth join all ye creatures to extol
Him first, him last, him midst, and without end. 165
Fairest of stars, last in the train of night,
If better thou belong not to the dawn,
Sure pledge of day, that crown'st the smiling morn
With thy bright circlet, praise him in thy sphere
While day arises, that sweet hour of prime. 170
Thou sun, of this great world both eye and soul,
Acknowledge him thy greater, sound his praise
In thy eternal course, both when thou climb'st,
And when high noon hast gained, and when thou fall'st.
Moon, that now meet'st the orient sun, now fli'st 175
With the fixed stars, fixed in their orb that flies,
And ye five other wand'ring fires that move
In mystic dance not without song, resound
His praise, who out of darkness called up light.
Air, and ye elements the eldest birth   180

144–52. Milton reflects a puritan disdain for elaborate liturgical worship. *numerous:* metrical.

153–208. Cf. Ps. 104, pp. 370–72, and 148, pp. 372–73.

165. Cf. Rev. 22.13: "I am Alpha and Omega, the beginning and the end, the first and the last."

166. *Fairest of stars:* Venus, the morning star and the evening star.

176. *their orb:* the sphere of the fixed stars, which if it turned about the earth would do so at incredible speed.

177. Since Venus has already been mentioned, Fowler suggests Milton may be counting earth. The planets (Gk *planētēs* wandering), unlike the fixed stars, change their relative positions.

178. *not without song.* From Pythagoras, Plato took the notion that on the sphere of each of the planets there was a siren who sang a note which in combination with the notes sung by the others produced a harmony of the spheres inaudible to impure, mortal man.

180. *eldest.* Earth, water, and fire (light) were the first "elements" mentioned in Genesis.

Of nature's womb, that in quaternion run
Perpetual circle, multiform, and mix
And nourish all things, let your ceaseless change
Vary to our great Maker still new praise.
Ye mists and exhalations that now rise   185
From hill or steaming lake, dusky or gray,
Till the sun paint your fleecy skirts with gold,
In honor to the world's great Author rise,
Whether to deck with clouds the uncolored sky,
Or wet the thirsty earth with falling showers,   190
Rising or falling still advance his praise.
His praise ye winds, that from four quarters blow,
Breathe soft or loud; and wave your tops, ye pines,
With every plant, in sign of worship wave.
Fountains and ye, that warble, as ye flow,   195
Melodious murmurs, warbling tune his praise.
Join voices all ye living souls: ye birds,
That singing up to heaven gate ascend,
Bear on your wings and in your notes his praise;
Ye that in waters glide, and ye that walk   200
The earth, and stately tread, or lowly creep;
Witness if I be silent, morn or even,
To hill, or valley, fountain, or fresh shade
Made vocal by my song, and taught his praise.
Hail universal Lord, be bounteous still   205
To give us only good; and if the night
Have gathered aught of evil or concealed,
Disperse it, as now light dispels the dark."
    So prayed they innocent, and to their thoughts
Firm peace recovered soon and wonted calm.   210
On to their morning's rural work they haste
Among sweet dews and flow'rs; where any row
Of fruit trees over-woody reached too far
Their pampered boughs, and needed hands to check
Fruitless embraces: or they led the vine   215
To wed her elm; she spoused about him twines
Her marriageable arms, and with her brings
Her dow'r th' adopted clusters, to adorn
His barren leaves. Them thus employed beheld
With pity heav'n's high King, and to him called   220
Raphael, the sociable Spirit, that deigned
To travel with Tobias, and secured
His marriage with the seven-times-wedded maid.
    "Raphael," said he, "thou hear'st what stir on earth
Satan from hell scaped through the darksome gulf   225
Hath raised in Paradise, and how disturbed

181. *quaternion:* a fourfold changing relationship; i.e., one produces another, or one feeds on another, or two or more combine in various ways, then disinte-grate. Cf. 415–17.
205. *still:* always.
221. *Raphael.* See "Angels," p. 395.
222. *Tobias.* Cf. IV.166–71n.

This night the human pair, how he designs
In them at once to ruin all mankind.
Go therefore, half this day as friend with friend
Converse with Adam, in what bow'r or shade   230
Thou find'st him from the heat of noon retired,
To respite his day-labor with repast,
Or with repose; and such discourse bring on,
As may advise him of his happy state,
Happiness in his power left free to will,   235
Left to his own free will, his will though free,
Yet mutable; whence warn him to beware
He swerve not too secure: tell him withal
His danger, and from whom, what enemy
Late fall'n himself from heav'n, is plotting now   240
The fall of others from like state of bliss;
By violence, no, for that shall be withstood,
But by deceit and lies; this let him know,
Lest wilfully transgressing he pretend
Surprisal, unadmonished, unforewarned."   245
     So spake th' Eternal Father, and fulfilled
All justice: nor delayed the wingèd saint
After his charge received; but from among
Thousand celestial ardors, where he stood
Veiled with his gorgeous wings, up springing light   250
Flew through the midst of heav'n; th' angelic quires
On each hand parting, to his speed gave way
Through all th' empyreal road; till at the gate
Of heav'n arrived, the gate self-opened wide
On golden hinges turning, as by work   255
Divine the sovran Architect had framed.
From hence, no cloud, or, to obstruct his sight,
Star interposed, however small he sees,
Not unconform to other shining globes,
Earth and the gard'n of God, with cedars crowned   260
Above all hills. As when by night the glass
Of Galileo, less assured, observes
Imagined lands and regions in the moon:
Or pilot from amidst the Cyclades
Delos or Samos first appearing kens   265
A cloudy spot. Down thither prone in flight
He speeds, and through the vast ethereal sky
Sails between worlds and worlds, with steady wing
Now on the polar wings, then with quick fan

---

229. Cf. Exod. 33.11: "And the Lord spake unto Moses face to face, as a man speaketh unto his friend."
247. *saint:* angel (as the word is used in the Bible).
249. *ardors:* (L *ardere* to burn) bright or effulgent spirits. The Hebrew *saraph* means "to burn."
255. *work:* works, mechanism.

261–63. Cf. I.288–91n.
264–65. *Delos,* one of the islands forming the *Cyclades,* was the birthplace of Apollo and Diana. On *Samos,* another island in the Aegean, Juno was born and was married to Jupiter.
266. *prone:* L *pronus* bent forward.
269. *fan:* L *vannus* fan, fan for winnowing.

Winnows the buxom air; till within soar   270
Of tow'ring eagles, to all the fowls he seems
A phoenix, gazed by all, as that sole bird
When to enshrine his relics in the sun's
Bright temple, to Egyptian Thebes he flies.
At once on th' eastern cliff of Paradise   275
He lights, and to his proper shape returns
A Seraph winged; six wings he wore, to shade
His lineaments divine; the pair that clad
Each shoulder broad, came mantling o'er his breast
With regal ornament; the middle pair   280
Girt like a starry zone his waist, and round
Skirted his loins and thighs with downy gold
And colors dipped in heav'n; the third his feet
Shadowed from either heel with feathered mail
Sky-tinctured grain. Like Maia's son he stood,   285
And shook his plumes, that heav'nly fragrance filled
The circuit wide. Straight knew him all the bands
Of angels under watch; and to his state,
And to his message high in honor rise;
For on some message high they guessed him bound.   290
Their glittering tents he passed, and now is come
Into the blissful field, through groves of myrrh,
And flow'ring odors, cassia, nard, and balm;
A wilderness of sweets; for nature here
Wantoned as in her prime, and played at will   295
Her virgin fancies, pouring forth more sweet,
Wild above rule or art; enormous bliss.
Him through the spicy forest onward come
Adam discerned, as in the door he sat
Of his cool bow'r, while now the mounted sun   300
Shot down direct his fervid rays, to warm
Earth's inmost womb, more warmth than Adam needs;
And Eve within, due at her hour prepared
For dinner savory fruits, of taste to please
True appetite, and not disrelish thirst   305
Of nectarous draughts between, from milky stream,

270. *buxom:* ME *buxum* pliable, from OE *būgan* to bend.
272–74. *phoenix:* the mythical, unique bird who every 500 years, after it had burned itself up and had been reborn from its own ashes, flew the ashes to a shrine in Heliopolis, the city of the sun, which Milton refers to as *Egyptian Thebes.* Christians saw it as a symbol of immortality.
277–85. Cf. Isa. 6.2, p. 373. Bush notes that the feathers of the phoenix were traditionally purple, gold, and blue. *lineaments:* parts of the body. *zone:* L *zona* belt. *mail:* armor made of pieces of metal arranged like fish scales. *grain:* color. *Maia's son:* Mercury, messenger of the gods, who also had wings on his heels.

288. *state:* status.
289. *message:* mission.
293. *odors:* substances (bark, roots, or gums) that emit spicy fragrances. *cassia:* cinnamon. *nard:* spikenard. *balm:* balsam. All were used to make perfumed ointments associated with religious rituals, and are mentioned in the Bible.
295. *played:* acted out.
297. *enormous:* L *e* out + *norma* rule.
299. Cf. Gen. 18.1: "And the Lord appeared unto him [Abraham] in the plains of Mamre: and he sat in the tent door in the heat of the day."
303. *due:* duly, fittingly.
306. *milky:* pleasant and nourishing.

Berry or grape: to whom thus Adam called.
   "Haste hither Eve, and worth thy sight behold
Eastward among those trees, what glorious shape
Comes this way moving; seems another morn   310
Ris'n on mid-noon; some great behest from Heav'n
To us perhaps he brings, and will voutsafe
This day to be our guest. But go with speed,
And what thy stores contain, bring forth and pour
Abundance, fit to honor and receive   315
Our heav'nly stranger; well we may afford
Our givers their own gifts, and large bestow
From large bestowed, where nature multiplies
Her fertile growth, and by disburd'ning grows
More fruitful, which instructs us not to spare."   320
   To whom thus Eve. "Adam, earth's hallowed mold,
Of God inspired, small store will serve, where store,
All seasons, ripe for use hangs on the stalk;
Save what by frugal storing firmness gains
To nourish, and superfluous moist consumes: 325
But I will haste and from each bough and brake,
Each plant and juiciest gourd will pluck such choice
To entertain our angel guest, as he
Beholding shall confess that here on earth
God hath dispensed his bounties as in heav'n."   330
   So saying, with dispatchful looks in haste
She turns, on hospitable thoughts intent
What choice to chose for delicacy best,
What order, so contrived as not to mix
Tastes, not well joined, inelegant, but bring   335
Taste after taste upheld with kindliest change,
Bestirs her then, and from each tender stalk
Whatever earth all-bearing mother yields
In India east or west, or middle short
In Pontus or the Punic coast, or where   340
Alcinous reigned, fruit of all kinds, in coat,
Rough, or smooth-rined, or bearded husk, or shell
She gathers, tribute large, and on the board
Heaps with unsparing hand; for drink the grape
She crushes, inoffensive must, and meaths   345
From many a berry, and from sweet kernels pressed
She tempers dulcet creams, nor these to hold
Wants her fit vessels pure, then strews the ground
With rose and odors from the shrub unfumed.

---

317. *large:* liberally.
322. *small store:* few stored foods. *store:* a great quantity.
324. *frugal:* L *frugalis* virtuous, *frugal*, from *frux* fruit.
336. *upheld:* maintained, provided with sustenance. *kindliest:* most natural.
340. *Pontus:* south shore of the Black Sea. *Punic:* Tunisian.
341. *Alcinous:* a king whose everbear-

ing gardens are described in the *Odyssey*.
345. *must:* unfermented fruit juice. *meaths:* meads, drinks sweetened with honey.
347. *tempers:* blends.
349. *rose and odors:* roses and other fragrant substances; cf. 22–23n, and 293n. *unfumed:* not artificially vaporized, as in burning incense.

Meanwhile our primitive great sire, to meet   350
His godlike guest, walks forth, without more train
Accompanied than with his own complete
Perfections, in himself was all his state,
More solemn than the tedious pomp that waits
On princes, when their rich retínue long   355
Of horses led, and grooms besmeared with gold
Dazzles the crowd, and sets them all agape.
Nearer his presence Adam though not awed,
Yet with submiss approach and reverence meek,
As to a superior nature, bowing low,   360
   Thus said. "Native of heav'n, for other place
None can than heav'n such glorious shape contain;
Since by descending from the thrones above,
Those happy places thou hast deigned a while
To want, and honor these, voutsafe with us   365
Two only, who yet by sovran gift possess
This spacious ground, in yonder shady bow'r
To rest, and what the garden choicest bears
To sit and taste, till this meridian heat
Be over, and the sun more cool decline."   370
   Whom thus the angelic Virtue answered mild.
"Adam, I therefore came, nor art thou such
Created, or such place hast here to dwell,
As may not oft invite, though Spirits of heav'n
To visit thee; lead on then where thy bow'r   375
O'ershades; for these mid-hours, till evening rise
I have at will." So to the sylvan lodge
They came, that like Pomona's arbor smiled
With flow'rets decked and fragrant smells; but Eve
Undecked, save with herself more lovely fair   380
Than wood-nymph, or the fairest goddess feigned
Of three that in Mount Ida naked strove,
Stood to entertain her guest from heav'n; no veil
She needed, virtue-proof, no thought infirm
Altered her cheek. On whom the angel "Hail"   385
Bestowed, the holy salutation used
Long after to blest Mary, second Eve.
   "Hail mother of mankind, whose fruitful womb
Shall fill the world more numerous with thy sons
Than with these various fruits the trees of God   390
Have heaped this table." Raised of grassy turf

353. *state: pomp that waits On princes,*
354–55.
354. *solemn:* awe-inspiring, ceremonial.
365. *want:* be without.
378. *Pomona:* (L *pomum* fruit; later, an apple) a wood nymph, goddess of fruit trees.
379. *decked:* D *dekken* to cover.
381–82. *feigned:* (L *fingere* to invent) imagined, i.e., by the maker of the myth about the judgment of Paris, who awarded the apple of strife to Venus rather than to Juno or Minerva, in a famous beauty contest that led, as Fowler notes, to the rape of Helen and the fall of Troy (the subject of the *Iliad*). Fowler also notes that in pictorial representations of the judgment wing-footed Mercury is often one of the figures.
384. *infirm:* weak, irresolute.
385–87. Cf. Luke 1.28–31, p. 381.

Their table was, and mossy seats had round,
And on her ample square from side to side
All autumn piled, though spring and autumn here
Danced hand in hand. A while discourse they hold;   395
No fear lest dinner cool; when thus began
Our author. "Heav'nly stranger, please to taste
These bounties which our Nourisher, from whom
All perfet good unmeasured out, descends,
To us for food and for delight hath caused   400
The earth to yield; unsavory food perhaps
To spiritual natures; only this I know,
That one Celestial Father gives to all."
    To whom the angel. "Therefore what he gives
(Whose praise be ever sung) to man in part   405
Spiritual, may of purest Spirits be found
No ingrateful food: and food alike those pure
Intelligential substances require
As doth your rational; and both contain
Within them every lower faculty   410
Of sense, whereby they hear, see, smell, touch, taste,
Tasting concoct, digest, assimilate,
And corporeal to incorporeal turn.
For know, whatever was created, needs
To be sustained and fed; of elements   415
The grosser feeds the purer, earth the sea,
Earth and the sea feed air, the air those fires
Ethereal, and as lowest first the moon;
Whence in her visage round those spots, unpurged
Vapors not yet into her substance turned.   420
Nor doth the moon no nourishment exhale
From her moist continent to higher orbs.
The sun that light imparts to all, receives
From all his alimental recompense
In humid exhalations, and at even   425
Sups with the ocean: though in heav'n the trees
Of life ambrosial fruitage bear, and vines
Yield nectar, though from off the boughs each morn
We brush mellifluous dews, and find the ground
Covered with pearly grain; yet God hath here   430
Varied his bounty so with new delights,
As may compare with heaven; and to taste
Think not I shall be nice." So down they sat,

404–33. See *CD*, I.vii.C, and "Angels,"
p. 394.
    412. *concoct:* L *concoquere* to cook to-
gether, digest.
    419. *unpurged:* still containing grosser
elements from earth.
    424. *alimental:* L *alere* to nourish.
    427. *ambrosial.* See II.245n; cf. III.135
and V.57.

429. *mellifluous:* L *mellis* honey +
fluere to flow.
    430. *pearly grain.* Fowler notes that
manna is called "the corn of heaven"
and "angel's food" in Ps. 78.24–25, and
described as "a small round thing, as
small as the hoar frost on the ground" in
Exod. 16.14.
    433. *nice:* fastidious.

And to their viands fell, nor seemingly
The angel, nor in mist, the common gloss ·   435
Of theologians, but with keen dispatch
Of real hunger, and concoctive heat
To transubstantiate; what redounds, transpires
Through Spirits with ease; nor wonder; if by fire
Of sooty coal the empiric alchemist   440
Can turn, or holds it possible to turn
Metals of drossiest ore to perfet gold
As from the mine. Meanwhile at table Eve
Ministered naked, and their flowing cups
With pleasant liquors crowned: O innocence   445
Deserving Paradise! if ever, then,
Then had the Sons of God excuse to have been
Enamored at that sight; but in those hearts
Love unlibidinous reigned, nor jealousy
Was understood, the injured lover's hell.   450
     Thus when with meats and drinks they had sufficed,
Not burdened nature, sudden mind arose
In Adam, not to let th' occasion pass
Given him by this great conference to know
Of things above his world, and of their being   455
Who dwell in heav'n, whose excellence he saw
Transcend his own so far, whose radiant forms
Divine effulgence, whose high power so far
Exceeded human, and his wary speech
Thus to th' empyreal minister he framed.   460
     "Inhabitant with God, now know I well
Thy favor, in this honor done to man,
Under whose lowly roof thou hast voutsafed
To enter, and these earthly fruits to taste,
Food not of angels, yet accepted so,   465
As that more willingly thou couldst not seem
At heav'n's high feasts to have fed: yet what compare?"
     To whom the wingèd Hierarch replied.
     "O Adam, one Almighty is, from whom
All things proceed, and up to him return,   470

---

434. *nor seemingly:* not just seemed to.
435. *gloss:* explanation.
438. *transubstantiate:* change into another substance. *redounds:* is not digested. *transpires:* passes out as vapor through pores, evaporates.
440. *empiric:* working by trial and error, not by theory.
445. *crowned:* filled to overflowing.
446–48. Cf. Gen. 6.1–4, pp. 357–58.
458. *effulgence:* (L *effulgare* to shine forth) the diffusing of intense light. As in *radiant* in the line above, the word emphasizes the energy and dynamism of heavenly beauty.
468. *Hierarch:* member of the hierarchy of angels (see "Angels," pp. 394–

95), or one of the angelic leaders; from Gk *hieros* sacred + *archos* leader, ruler.
469–90. See *CD*, I.vii.C, and "Scale of Nature," pp. 392–93. *consummate:* (L *consummare* to sum up, finish) perfect. *scale:* L *scala* staircase, ladder. *vital spirits.* In Milton's physiology spirits were conceived of as liquids produced by the heart and essential to life. *Animal* spirits, also a fluid, produced in the brain, fed the nervous system (sensation, thought, and action). *Reason.* See "Reason," p. 392. *discursive:* (like *discourse*, L *discurrere* to run to and fro) deliberative. *intuitive:* L *intueri* to look upon) knowing directly, without reasoning.

If not depraved from good, created all
Such to perfection, one first matter all,
Endued with various forms, various degrees
Of substance, and in things that live, of life;
But more refined, more spiritous, and pure,   475
As nearer to him placed or nearer tending
Each in their several active spheres assigned,
Till body up to spirit work, in bounds
Proportioned to each kind. So from the root
Springs lighter the green stalk, from thence the leaves   480
More airy, last the bright consummate flow'r
Spirits odórous breathes: flow'rs and their fruit
Man's nourishment, by gradual scale sublimed
To vital spirits aspire, to animal,
To intellectual, give both life and sense,   485
Fancy and understanding, whence the soul
Reason receives, and reason is her being,
Discursive, or intuitive; discourse
Is oftest yours, the latter most is ours,
Differing but in degree, of kind the same.   490
Wonder not then, what God for you saw good
If I refuse not, but convert, as you,
To proper substance; time may come when men
With angels may participate, and find
No inconvenient diet, nor too light fare: 495
And from these corporal nutriments perhaps
Your bodies may at last turn all to spirit,
Improved by tract of time, and winged ascend
Ethereal, as we, or may at choice
Here or in heav'nly paradises dwell;   500
If ye be found obedient, and retain
Unalterably firm his love entire
Whose progeny you are. Meanwhile enjoy
Your fill what happiness this happy state
Can comprehend, incapable of more."   505
     To whom the patriarch of mankind replied.
"O favorable Spirit, propitious guest,
Well hast thou taught the way that might direct
Our knowledge, and the scale of nature set
From center to circumference, whereon   510
In contemplation of created things
By steps we may ascend to God. But say,
What meant that caution joined, 'If ye be found
Obedient'? Can we want obedience then
To him, or possibly his love desert   515
Who formed us from the dust, and placed us here

493. *proper:* suitable.
498. *tract:* continued duration.
505. *incapable:* L *in* not + *capere* to
contain.

507. *propitious:* favorable; kind, gra-
cious.
509–12. See "Scale of Nature," pp.
392–93.

Full to the utmost measure of what bliss
Human desires can seek or apprehend?"
    To whom the angel. "Son of heav'n and earth,
Attend: that thou art happy, owe to God;   520
That thou continu'st such, owe to thyself,
That is, to thy obedience; therein stand.
This was that caution giv'n thee; be advised.
God made thee perfet, not immutable;
And good he made thee, but to persevere   525
He left it in thy power, ordained thy will
By nature free, not overruled by fate
Inextricable, or strict necessity;
Our voluntary service he requires,
Not our necessitated, such with him   530
Finds no acceptance, nor can find, for how
Can hearts, not free, be tried whether they serve
Willing or no, who will but what they must
By destiny, and can no other choose?
Myself and all th' angelic host that stand   535
In sight of God enthroned, our happy state
Hold, as you yours, while our obedience holds;
On other surety none; freely we serve,
Because we freely love, as in our will
To love or not; in this we stand or fall: 540
And some are fall'n, to disobedience fall'n,
And so from heav'n to deepest hell; O fall
From what high state of bliss into what woe!"
    To whom our great progenitor. "Thy words
Attentive, and with more delighted ear,   545
Divine instructor, I have heard, than when
Cherubic songs by night from neighboring hills
Aerial music send: nor knew I not
To be both will and deed created free;
Yet that we never shall forget to love   550
Our Maker, and obey him whose command
Single, is yet so just, my constant thoughts
Assured me, and still assure: though what thou tell'st
Hath passed in heav'n, some doubt within me move,
But more desire to hear, if thou consent,   555
The full relation, which must needs be strange,
Worthy of sacred silence to be heard;
And we have yet large day, for scarce the sun
Hath finished half his journey, and scarce begins
His other half in the great zone of heav'n."   560
    Thus Adam made request, and Raphael
After short pause assenting, thus began.
    "High matter thou enjoin'st me. O prime of men,

---

521. *owe:* attribute.

Sad task and hard, for how shall I relate
To human sense th' invisible exploits   565
Of warring Spirits; how without remorse
The ruin of so many glorious once
And perfet while they stood; how last unfold
The secrets of another world, perhaps
Not lawful to reveal? Yet for thy good   570
This is dispensed, and what surmounts the reach
Of human sense, I shall delineate so,
By lik'ning spiritual to corporal forms,
As may express them best, though what if earth
Be but the shadow of heav'n, and things therein   575
Each to other like, more than on earth is thought?
    "As yet this world was not, and Chaos wild
Reigned where these heav'ns now roll, where earth now rests
Upon her center poised, when on a day
(For time, though in eternity, applied   580
To motion, measures all things durable
By present, past, and future) on such day
As heav'n's great year brings forth, th' empyreal host
Of angels by imperial summons called,
Innumerable before th' Almighty's throne   585
Forthwith from all the ends of heav'n appeared
Under their hierarchs in orders bright.
Ten thousand thousand ensigns high advanced,
Standards, and gonfalons 'twixt van and rear
Stream in the air, and for distinction serve   590

564–76. Milton himself faced two of the three difficulties referred to by this angel, who was, in a way, the first epic poet: how to describe events in heaven to human beings, whose experience is limited to earth, and how to tell the story of Satan's fall without arousing sympathy in his audience or, perhaps, in himself. As for the third, since he was unable to reveal what God had not chosen to reveal to men in the Bible, he could not unlawfully reveal anything. But by means of Raphael's speech to Adam, Milton was about to give an imagined elaboration of a story that was only hinted at, or given in barest outline, in the Bible, and Milton's justification for doing so, is essentially that of Raphael and all other poets, who believe that truth may be revealed by metaphor and fiction. So, to the spare Biblical account of Adam's life Milton added this imagined account of Raphael's visit, as well as the details of Raphael's own account of the revolt in heaven and the creation of the universe, and thus made Raphael's "poem" part of his own larger poem. Milton's task was harder than Raphael's, who had only to find the language to express the facts, whereas Milton had also to do what

Aristotle said was the poet's essential task—that is, to invent the plot (or at least the episodes). The Platonic notion that all earthly things are imitations (shadows) of heavenly ideas or realities had been the basis of the chief apology for poetry from Aristotle on down: poetry tells a truth beyond that of history—or history is itself the vehicle of a metaphysical metaphor. Theologians had relied on a similar assumption in their theories about typology and "accommodation" and the meaning of myth. See "Truth and Poetry," pp. 400–1.
580–82. *time* and *motion*. See *CD*, I.vii.E.
583. *heav'n's great year.* The point in time when, according to a myth of Plato, a celestial cycle is completed and all stars and planets are back in the same position as they were at the beginning of the cycle. Fowler notes that the range of allusion may include the myth that the great year also marked the end of a cycle of uniformity and the beginning of one of dissimilarity or disintegration. So the great year here may mark the beginning of the period that would end only with the millennium.
589. *gonfalons:* flags of princes or states, fastened to crosspieces or frames.

Of hierarchies, of orders, and degrees;
Or in their glittering tissues bear emblazed
Holy memorials, acts of zeal and love
Recorded eminent. Thus when in orbs
Of circuit inexpressible they stood,   595
Orb within orb, the Father Infinite,
By whom in bliss embosomed sat the Son,
Amidst as from a flaming mount, whose top
Brightness had made invisible, thus spake.
    " 'Hear all ye angels, progeny of Light,   600
Thrones, Dominations, Princedoms, Virtues, Powers,
Hear my decree, which unrevoked shall stand.
This day I have begot whom I declare
My only Son, and on this holy hill
Him have anointed, whom ye now behold   605
At my right hand; your head I him appoint;
And by my Self have sworn to him shall bow
All knees in heav'n, and shall confess him Lord:
Under his great vicegerent reign abide
United as one individual soul   610
Forever happy: him who disobeys
Me disobeys, breaks union, and that day
Cast out from God and blessèd vision, falls
Into utter darkness, deep engulfed, his place
Ordained without redemption, without end.'   615
    "So spake th' Omnipotent, and with his words
All seemed well pleased, all seemed, but were not all.
That day, as other solemn days, they spent
In song and dance about the sacred hill,
Mystical dance, which yonder starry sphere   620
Of planets and of fixed in all her wheels
Resembles nearest, mazes intricate,
Eccentric, interinvolved, yet regular
Then most, when most irregular they seem:
And in their motions harmony divine   625
So smooths her charming tones, that God's own ear
Listens delighted. Evening now approached
(For we have also our evening and our morn,
We ours for change delectable, not need)
Forthwith from dance to sweet repast they turn   630
Desirous; all in circles as they stood,
Tables are set, and on a sudden piled

---

591. *degrees.* Though there was no
rank in Paradise (see IX.883), the an-
gelic society was highly hierarchical. See
CD, I.xxxiii.E; and lines 707, 750, 792,
838; VIII.176.
593. Unlike the military blazonry of
the fallen angels in I.539, as Fowler
notes.
595. *circuit:* circumference.
614. *utter.* Cf. I.72n.

618. *solemn days:* holy days.
625–26. The movements of the angels
in their dance, like those of the planets
in the Pythagorean theory of music of
the spheres (see 178n), produced har-
mony. Fowler notes that "the intervals
between the planetary spheres were an-
alysed as musical proportions by astron-
omers as late as Kepler." *charming:*
enchanting, spell-binding.

With angels' food, and rubied nectar flows
In pearl, in diamond, and massy gold,
Fruit of delicious vines, the growth of heav'n.   635
Of flow'rs reposed, and with fresh flow'rets crowned,
They eat, they drink, and in communion sweet
Quaff immortality and joy, secure
Of surfeit where full measure only bounds
Excess, before th' all-bounteous King, who show'red   640
With copious hand, rejoicing in their joy.
Now when ambrosial night with clouds exhaled
From that high mount of God, whence light and shade
Spring both, the face of brightest heav'n had changed
To grateful twilight (for night comes not there   645
In darker veil) and roseate dews disposed
All but the unsleeping eyes of God to rest,
Wide over all the plain, and wider far
Than all this globous earth in plain outspread,
(Such are the courts of God) th' angelic throng   650
Dispersed in bands and files their camp extend
By living streams among the trees of life,
Pavilions numberless, and sudden reared,
Celestial tabernacles, where they slept
Fanned with cool winds, save those who in their course   655
Melodious hymns about the sovran throne
Alternate all night long: but not so waked
Satan, so call him now, his former name
Is heard no more in heav'n; he of the first,
If not the first Archangel, great in power,   660
In favor and pre-eminence, yet fraught
With envy against the Son of God, that day
Honored by his great Father, and proclaimed
Messiah King anointed, could not bear
Through pride that sight, and thought himself impaired.   665
Deep malice thence conceiving and disdain,
Soon as midnight brought on the dusky hour
Friendliest to sleep and silence, he resolved
With all his legions to dislodge, and leave
Unworshiped, unobeyed the throne supreme   670
Contemptuous, and his next subordinate
Awak'ning, thus to him in secret spake.
    " 'Sleep'st thou companion dear, what sleep can close

637–40. Cf. Ps. 36.8–9: "They shall be abundantly satisfied with the fatness of thy house; and thou shalt make them drink of the river of thy pleasures. For with thee is the fountain of life: in thy light shall we see light."
645–46. Cf. Rev. 21.25: "And the gates of it shall not be shut at all by day: for there shall be no night there."
647. Cf. Ps. 121.4: "Behold, he that keepeth Israel shall neither slumber nor sleep."

651. *files*: detachments.
652. Cf. Rev. 22.1–2: "And he shewed me a pure river of water of life, clear as crystal, proceeding out of the throne of God and of the Lamb. In the midst of the street of it, and on either side of the river, was there the tree of life."
664. *Messiah*: the Gk form of the Hebrew *mashiah* anointed.
665. *impaired*. See 73n.
669. *dislodge*: (military term) leave camp.

Thy eyelids? and remember'st what decree
Of yesterday, so late hath passed the lips   675
Of heav'n's Almighty. Thou to me thy thoughts
Wast wont, I mine to thee was wont to impart;
Both waking we were one; how then can now
Thy sleep dissent? New laws thou seest imposed;
New laws from him who reigns, new minds may raise   680
In us who serve, new counsels, to debate
What doubtful may ensue, more in this place
To utter is not safe. Assemble thou
Of all those myriads which we lead the chief;
Tell them that by command, ere yet dim night   685
Her shadowy cloud withdraws, I am to haste,
And all who under me their banners wave,
Homeward with flying march where we possess
The quarters of the north, there to prepare
Fit entertainment to receive our King   690
The great Messiah, and his new commands,
Who speedily through all the hierarchies
Intends to pass triumphant, and give laws.'
    "So spake the false Archangel, and infused
Bad influence into th' unwary breast   695
Of his associate; he together calls,
Or several one by one, the regent powers,
Under him regent, tells, as he was taught,
That the Most High commanding, now ere night,
Now ere dim night had disencumbered heav'n,   700
The great hierarchal standard was to move;
Tells the suggested cause, and casts between
Ambiguous words and jealousies, to sound
Or taint integrity; but all obeyed
The wonted signal, and superior voice   705
Of their great potentate; for great indeed
His name, and high was his degree in heav'n;
His count'nance, as the morning star that guides
The starry flock, allured them, and with lies
Drew after him the third part of heav'n's host: 710
Meanwhile th' Eternal eye, whose sight discerns
Abstrusest thoughts, from forth his holy mount
And from within the golden lamps that burn
Nightly before him, saw without their light
Rebellion rising, saw in whom, how spread   715
Among the sons of morn, what multitudes
Were banded to oppose his high decree;

689. Cf. Isa. 14.13, p. 375.
700. *dim night:* the agency that pro-
duces night; cf. 642–45. *disencumbered:*
(LL *in + combrus* barricade) i.e., re-
moved the clouds (cf. 642) that barri-
caded the "sky" of heaven.
702. *suggested:* (L *sub* under + *gerere*

to put) insinuating or prompting to evil.
casts: contrives, schemes.
703. *jealousies:* fears, suspicions, re-
sentments. *sound:* measure.
708. Cf. Isa. 14.12, p. 375.
713. Cf. Rev. 4.5, p. 384.

And smiling to his only Son thus said.
  " 'Son, thou in whom my glory I behold
In full resplendence, heir of all my might,   720
Nearly it now concerns us to be sure
Of our omnipotence, and with what arms
We mean to hold what anciently we claim
Of deity or empire, such a foe
Is rising, who intends to erect his throne   725
Equal to ours, throughout the spacious north;
Nor so content, hath in his thought to try
In battle, what our power is, or our right.
Let us advise, and to this hazard draw
With speed what force is left, and all employ   730
In our defense, lest unawares we lose
This our high place, our sanctuary, our hill.'
  "To whom the Son with calm aspect and clear
Lightning divine, ineffable, serene,
Made answer. 'Mighty Father, thou thy foes   735
Justly hast in derision, and secure
Laugh'st at their vain designs and tumults vain,
Matter to me of glory, whom their hate
Illustrates, when they see all regal power
Giv'n me to quell their pride, and in event   740
Know whether I be dextrous to subdue
Thy rebels, or be found the worst in heav'n.'
  "So spake the Son, but Satan with his powers
Far was advanced on wingèd speed, an host
Innumerable as the stars of night,   745
Or stars of morning, dewdrops, which the sun
Impearls on every leaf and every flower.
Regions they passed, the mighty regencies
Of Seraphim and Potentates and Thrones
In their triple degrees, regions to which   750
All thy dominion, Adam, is no more
Than what this garden is to all the earth,
And all the sea, from one entire globose
Stretched into longitude; which having passed
At length into the limits of the north   755
They came, and Satan to his royal seat
High on a hill, far blazing, as a mount
Raised on a mount, with pyramids and tow'rs
From diamond quarries hewn, and rocks of gold,

---

734. *Lightning.* In his vision Daniel saw a man whose face was "as the appearance of lightning, and his eyes as lamps of fire" (Dan. 10.6).
  736. Cf. Ps. 59.8: "But thou, O Lord, shalt laugh at them; thou shalt have all the heathen in derision."
  739. *Illustrates:* illuminates, makes illustrious or luminous.
  740. *event:* L *e* out + *venire* to come.

741. *dextrous:* L *dexter* on the right hand. A pun.
  743. *powers:* armies.
  750. *triple degrees.* See "Angels," p. 395.
  753. *globose:* globe.
  754. *Stretched into longitude:* spread out flat.
  755. *limits:* regions.

The palace of great Lucifer, (so call   760
That structure in the dialect of men
Interpreted) which not long after, he
Affecting all equality with God,
In imitation of that mount whereon
Messiah was declared in sight of heav'n,   765
The Mountain of the Congregation called;
For thither he assembled all his train,
Pretending so commanded to consult
About the great reception of their King,
Thither to come, and with calumnious art   770
Of counterfeited truth thus held their ears.
    " 'Thrones, Dominations, Princedoms, Virtues, Powers,
If these magnific titles yet remain
Not merely titular, since by decree
Another now hath to himself engrossed   775
All power, and us eclipsed under the name
Of King anointed, for whom all this haste
Of midnight march, and hurried meeting here,
This only to consult how we may best
With what may be devised of honors new   780
Receive him coming to receive from us
Knee-tribute yet unpaid, prostration vile,
Too much to one, but double how endured,
To one and to his image now proclaimed?
But what if better counsels might erect   785
Our minds and teach us to cast off this yoke?
Will ye submit your necks, and choose to bend
The supple knee? Ye will not, if I trust
To know ye right, or if ye know yourselves
Natives and sons of heav'n possessed before   790
By none, and if not equal all, yet free,
Equally free; for orders and degrees
Jar not with liberty, but well consist.
Who can in reason then or right assume
Monarchy over such as live by right   795
His equals, if in power and splendor less,
In freedom equal? or can introduce
Law and edíct on us, who without law
Err not, much less for this to be our Lord,
And look for adoration to th' abuse   800
Of those imperial titles which assert
Our being ordained to govern, not to serve?'
    "Thus far his bold discourse without control
Had audience, when among the Seraphim
Abdiel, than whom none with more zeal adored   805

763. *Affecting:* aspiring to, assuming, arrogating.
764–65. Cf. 603.
766. See 689n.

777. *King anointed.* Cf. 664n.
790. *possessed:* (modifies *heav'n*) owned, claimed.
805. *Abdiel.* See "Angels," p. 395.

The Deity, and divine commands obeyed,
Stood up, and in a flame of zeal severe
The current of his fury thus opposed.
    " 'O argument blasphémous, false and proud!
Words which no ear ever to hear in heav'n   810
Expected, least of all from thee, ingrate,
In place thyself so high above thy peers.
Canst thou with impious obloquy condemn
The just decree of God, pronounced and sworn,
That to his only Son by right endued   815
With regal scepter, every soul in heav'n
Shall bend the knee, and in that honor due
Confess him rightful King? Unjust thou says't,
Flatly unjust, to bind with laws the free,
And equal over equals to let reign,   820
One over all with unsucceeded power.
Shalt thou give law to God, shalt thou dispute
With him the points of liberty, who made
Thee what thou art, and formed the pow'rs of heav'n
Such as he pleased, and circumscribed their being?   825
Yet by experience taught we know how good,
And of our good, and of our dignity
How provident he is, how far from thought
To make us less, bent rather to exalt
Our happy state under one head more near   830
United. But to grant it thee unjust,
That equal over equals monarch reign:
Thyself though great and glorious dost thou count,
Or all angelic nature joined in one,
Equal to him begotten Son, by whom   835
As by his Word the mighty Father made
All things, ev'n thee, and all the Spirits of heav'n
By him created in their bright degrees,

813. *impious:* disloyal. *obloquy:* (L *ob* against + *loqui* to speak) calumny.

816–18. Cf. Phil. 2.10–11: "At the name of Jesus every knee should bow, of things in heaven, and things in earth, and things under the earth; And . . . every tongue should confess that Jesus Christ is Lord."

821. *unsucceeded:* without successor.

822–25. Cf. Rom. 9.20: "Nay but, O man, who art thou that repliest against God? Shall the thing formed say to him that formed it, Why hast thou made me thus?"

827. *dignity:* high status.

828. *provident:* careful in preparing for future exigencies.

831–45. The awkward and precipitous syntax of Abdiel's speech reflects his unartful zeal. The argument goes like this: "Granted that it would be unjust for an equal to reign as monarch over his equals; but do you, though great and powerful—though, indeed, a complete and perfect angel—do you count yourself equal to Christ, by whom God made all things (including you) by whom God created all the angels in their bright degrees, crowned them with glory, and named them to their glory Thrones, Dominations, etc., and by putting Christ above them as ruler did not obscure that glory, but rather made it more glorious since in taking this assignment as head of us he becomes one of us [as Jesus was later to become man], his laws become our laws, and all honor done to him is done to all of us." *the Word.* See III.170n. Cf. Col. 1.16–18: "For by him [Christ] were all things created, that are in heaven, and that are in earth, visible and invisible, whether they be thrones, or dominions, or principalities, or powers: all things were created by him, and for him: And he is before all things, and by him all things consist. And he is the head of the body, the church." *bright:* illustrious, glorious.

Crowned them with glory, and to their glory named
Thrones, Dominations, Princedoms, Virtues, Powers,   840
Essential Powers, nor by his reign obscured,
But more illustrious made, since he the head
One of our number thus reduced becomes,
His laws our laws, all honor to him done
Returns our own. Cease then this impious rage,   845
And tempt not these; but hasten to appease
Th' incensèd Father and th' incensèd Son,
While pardon may be found in time besought.'
    "So spake the fervent angel, but his zeal
None seconded, as out of season judged,   850
Or singular and rash, whereat rejoiced
Th' Apostate, and more haughty thus replied.
'That we were formed then say'st thou? and the work
Of secondary hands, by task transferred
From Father to his Son? Strange point and new!   855
Doctrine which we would know whence learnt: who saw
When this creation was? Remember'st thou
Thy making, while the Maker gave thee being?
We know no time when we were not as now;
Know none before us, self-begot, self-raised   860
By our own quick'ning power, when fatal course
Had circled his full orb, the birth mature
Of this our native heav'n, ethereal sons.
Our puissance is our own, our own right hand
Shall teach us highest deeds, by proof to try   865
Who is our equal: then thou shalt behold
Whether by supplication we intend
Address, and to begirt th' Almighty throne
Beseeching or besieging. This report,
These tidings carry to th' anointed King;   870
And fly, ere evil intercept thy flight.'
    "He said, and as the sound of waters deep
Hoarse murmur echoed to his words applause
Through the infinite host, nor less for that
The flaming Seraph fearless, though alone   875
Encompassed round with foes, thus answered bold.
    " 'O alienate from God, O Spirit accurst,
Forsaken of all good; I see thy fall
Determined, and thy hapless crew involved
In this perfidious fraud, contagion spread   880
Both of thy crime and punishment: henceforth
No more be troubled how to quit the yoke

---

861. *fatal course:* the course of fate.
864–65. Cf. Ps. 45.4: "And in thy majesty ride prosperously because of truth and meekness and righteousness; and thy right hand shall teach thee terrible things."
872. Cf. Rev. 19.6 "And I heard as it were the voice of a great multitude, and as the voice of many waters, and as the voice of mighty thunderings, saying, Alleluia: for the Lord God omnipotent reigneth."
882–83. Cf. Matt. 11.30: "For my [Christ's] yoke is easy, and my burden is light."

Of God's Messiah; those indulgent laws
Will not be now voutsafed, other decrees
Against thee are gone forth without recall;   885
That golden scepter which thou didst reject
Is now an iron rod to bruise and break
Thy disobedience. Well thou didst advise,
Yet not for thy advice or threats I fly
These wicked tents devoted, lest the wrath   890
Impendent, raging into sudden flame
Distinguish not: for soon expect to feel
His thunder on thy head, devouring fire.
Then who created thee lamenting learn,
When who can uncreate thee thou shalt know.'   895
    "So spake the Seraph Abdiel faithful found,
Among the faithless, faithful only he;
Among innumerable false, unmoved,
Unshaken, unseduced, unterrified
His loyalty he kept, his love, his zeal;   900
Nor number, nor example with him wrought
To swerve from truth, or change his constant mind
Though single. From amidst them forth he passed,
Long way through hostile scorn, which he sustained
Superior, nor of violence feared aught;   905
And with retorted scorn his back he turned
On those proud tow'rs to swift destruction doomed."

890. Cf. Num. 16.26: "And he spake unto the congregation, saying, Depart, I pray you, from the tents of these wicked men, and touch nothing of theirs, lest ye be consumed in all their sins." Ps. 84.10: "For a day in thy courts is better than a thousand. I had rather be a doorkeeper in the house of my God, than to dwell in the tents of wickedness." *devoted*: doomed.

906. *retorted*: (L *re* back + *torquere* to turn, twist) retaliated.
907. Cf. 2 Pet. 2.1: "But there were false prophets also among the people, even as there shall be false teachers among you, who privily shall bring in damnable heresies, even denying the Lord that bought them, and bring upon themselves swift destruction."

Book VI

The Argument

Raphael continues to relate how Michael and Gabriel were sent forth to battle against Satan and his angels. The first fight described: Satan and his powers retire under night: he calls a council, invents devilish engines, which in the second day's fight put Michael and his angels to some disorder; but they at length pulling up mountains overwhelmed both the force and machines of Satan: yet the tumult not so ending, God on the third day sends Messiah his Son, for whom he had reserved the glory of that victory: he in the power of his Father coming to the place, and causing all his legions to stand still on either side, with his chariot and thunder driving into the midst of his enemies, pursues them unable to resist towards the wall of heaven; which opening, they leap down with horror and confusion into the place of punishment prepared for them in the deep: Messiah returns with triumph to his Father.

"All night the dreadless angel unpursued
Through heav'n's wide champaign held his way, till Morn,
Waked by the circling Hours, with rosy hand
Unbarred the gates of light. There is a cave
Within the mount of God, fast by his throne,   5
Where light and darkness in perpetual round
Lodge and dislodge by turns, which makes through heav'n
Grateful vicissitude, like day and night;
Light issues forth, and at the other door
Obsequious darkness enters, till her hour   10
To veil the heav'n, though darkness there might well
Seem twilight here; and now went forth the Morn
Such as in highest heav'n, arrayed in gold
Empyreal; from before her vanished night,
Shot through with orient beams: when all the plain   15
Covered with thick embattled squadrons bright,
Chariots and flaming arms, and fiery steeds
Reflecting blaze on blaze, first met his view:
War he perceived, war in procinct, and found
Already known what he for news had thought   20
To have reported: gladly then he mixed
Among those friendly Powers who him received
With joy and acclamations loud, that one
That of so many myriads fall'n, yet one
Returned not lost: on to the sacred hill   25
They led him high applauded, and present

VI.8. *vicissitude:* (L *vicissim* in turn, *vicis* change, alternation) alternating succession of contrasting things.
10. *Obsequious:* (L *ob* towards + *sequi* to follow) compliant.

14. *Empyreal:* (Gk *pyr* fire) heavenly.
16. *embattled:* drawn up in battle array.
19. *in procinct:* prepared.

Before the seat supreme; from whence a voice
From midst a golden cloud thus mild was heard.
  " 'Servant of God, well done, well hast thou fought
The better fight, who single hast maintained   30
Against revolted multitudes the cause
Of truth, in word mightier than they in arms;
And for the testimony of truth hast borne
Universal reproach, far worse to bear
Than violence: for this was all thy care   35
To stand approved in sight of God, though worlds
Judged thee perverse: the easier conquest now
Remains thee, aided by this host of friends,
Back on thy foes more glorious to return
Than scorned thou didst depart, and to subdue   40
By force, who reason for their law refuse,
Right reason for their law, and for their King
Messiah, who by right of merit reigns.
Go Michael of celestial armies prince,
And thou in military prowess next   45
Gabriel, lead forth to battle these my sons
Invincible, lead forth my armèd saints
By thousands and by millions ranged for fight;
Equal in number to that godless crew
Rebellious, them with fire and hostile arms   50
Fearless assault, and to the brow of heav'n
Pursuing drive them out from God and bliss,
Into their place of punishment, the gulf
Of Tartarus, which ready opens wide
His fiery chaos to receive their fall.'   55
  "So spake the Sovran Voice, and clouds began
To darken all the hill, and smoke to roll
In dusky wreaths reluctant flames, the sign
Of wrath awaked: nor with less dread the loud
Ethereal trumpet from on high gan blow: 60
At which command the powers militant,
That stood for heav'n, in mighty quadrate joined
Of union irresistible, moved on
In silence their bright legions, to the sound
Of instrumental harmony that breathed   65
Heroic ardor to advent'rous deeds
Under their godlike leaders, in the cause

---

29. *Servant of God:* the literal meaning of the Hebrew word *abdiel.* Cf. Matt. 25.21: "His lord said unto him, Well done, thou good and faithful servant." 2 Tim. 4.7: "I have fought a good fight, I have finished my course, I have kept the faith."

33–34. Cf. Ps. 69.7: "Because for thy sake I have borne reproach."

36. Cf. 2 Tim. 2.15: "Study to show thyself approved unto God."

42. *Right reason.* See "Reason," p. 392.

44ff. For the biblical authority for the war in heaven see Isa. 14.1–21, Rev. 12.4–9, pp. 374 and 385, and *CD*, I.ix.B.

44–46. See "Angels," p. 395.

47. *saints:* angels.

56–59. Cf. Exod. 19.16, 18, p. 366.

58. *reluctant:* L *re* back + *luctari* to struggle.

62. *quadrate:* a square military formation in close order.

Of God and his Messiah. On they move
Indíssolubly firm; nor obvious hill,
Nor strait'ning vale, nor wood, nor stream divides   70
Their perfet ranks; for high above the ground
Their march was, and the passive air upbore
Their nimble tread; as when the total kind
Of birds in orderly array on wing
Came summoned over Eden to receive   75
Their names of thee; so over many a tract
Of heav'n they marched, and many a province wide
Tenfold the length of this terrene: at last
Far in th' horizon to the north appeared
From skirt to skirt a fiery region, stretched   80
In battailous aspéct, and nearer view
Bristled with upright beams innumerable
Of rigid spears, and helmets thronged, and shields
Various, with boastful argument portrayed,
The banded powers of Satan hasting on   85
With furious expedition; for they weened
That selfsame day by fight, or by surprise
To win the mount of God, and on his throne
To set the envier of his state, the proud
Aspirer, but their thoughts proved fond and vain   90
In the mid-way: though strange to us it seemed
At first, that angel should with angel war,
And in fierce hosting meet, who wont to meet
So oft in festivals of joy and love
Unanimous, as sons of one great Sire   95
Hymning th' Eternal Father: but the shout
Of battle now began, and rushing sound
Of onset ended soon each milder thought.
High in the midst exalted as a god
Th' Apostate in his sun-bright chariot sat   100
Idol of majesty divine, enclosed
With flaming Cherubim, and golden shields;
Then lighted from his gorgeous throne, for now
'Twixt host and host but narrow space was left,
A dreadful interval, and front to front   105
Presented stood in terrible array
Of hideous length: before the cloudy van,
On the rough edge of battle ere it joined,
Satan with vast and haughty strides advanced,
Came tow'ring, armed in adamant and gold;   110
Abdiel that sight endured not, where he stood
Among the mightiest, bent on highest deeds,

---

69. *obvious:* standing in the way of.
78. *terrene:* (an adjective used as a noun) terrain.
81. *battailous:* warlike.
83–84. On the shields were drawn heraldic emblems with their mottoes.
86. *furious:* (L *furia* rage) rushing.

expedition: speed.
90. *fond* (ME *fon* fool) foolish. *vain:* L *vanus* empty.
93. *hosting:* hostile encounter.
100. *Apostate:* Gk *apo* out from, against + *stēnai* to stand.

And thus his own undaunted heart explores.
   " 'O heav'n! that such resemblance of the Highest
Should yet remain, where faith and realty   115
Remain not; wherefore should not strength and might
There fail where virtue fails, or weakest prove
Where boldest; though to sight unconquerable?
His puissance, trusting in th' Almighty's aid,
I mean to try, whose reason I have tried   120
Unsound and false; nor is it aught but just,
That he who in debate of truth hath won,
Should win in arms, in both disputes alike
Victor; though brutish that contést and foul,
When reason hath to deal with force, yet so   125
Most reason is that reason overcome.'
   "So pondering, and from his armèd peers
Forth stepping opposite, half-way he met
His daring foe, at this prevention more
Incensed, and thus securely him defied.   130
   " 'Proud, art thou met? Thy hope was to have reached
The highth of thy aspiring unopposed,
The throne of God unguarded, and his side
Abandoned at the terror of thy power
Or potent tongue; fool, not to think how vain   135
Against th' Omnipotent to rise in arms;
Who out of smallest things could without end
Have raised incessant armies to defeat
Thy folly; or with solitary hand
Reaching beyond all limit at one blow   140
Unaided could have finished thee, and whelmed
Thy legions under darkness; but thou seest
All are not of thy train; there be who faith
Prefer, and piety to God, though then
To thee not visible, when I alone   145
Seemed in thy world erroneous to dissent
From all: my sect thou seest, now learn too late
How few sometimes may know, when thousands err.'
   "Whom the grand Foe with scornful eye askance
Thus answered. 'Ill for thee, but in wished hour   150
Of my revenge, first sought for thou return'st
From flight, seditious angel, to receive
Thy merited reward, the first assay
Of this right hand provoked, since first that tongue
Inspired with contradiction durst oppose   155
A third part of the gods, in synod met
Their deities to assert, who while they feel
Vigor divine within them, can allow
Omnipotence to none. But well thou com'st

---

115. *realty:* sincerity.
120. *tried:* (OF *trier* to sift, cull, pick
out) proved.
129. *prevention:* the act of forestalling.

130. *securely:* confidently.
144. *piety:* loyalty.
147. *sect:* kind (of person).
156. *third.* See II.692n.

Before thy fellows, ambitious to win   160
From me some plume, that thy success may show
Destruction to the rest: this pause between
(Unanswered lest thou boast) to let thee know;
At first I thought that liberty and heav'n
To heav'nly souls had been all one; but now   165
I see that most through sloth had rather serve,
Minist'ring Spirits, trained up in feast and song;
Such hast thou armed, the minstrelsy of heav'n,
Servility with freedom to contend,
As both their deeds compared this day shall prove.'   170
    "To whom in brief thus Abdiel stern replied.
'Apostate, still thou err'st, nor end wilt find
Of erring, from the path of truth remote:
Unjustly thou deprav'st it with the name
Of servitude to serve whom God ordains,   175
Or nature; God and nature bid the same,
When he who rules is worthiest, and excels
Them whom he governs. This is servitude,
To serve th' unwise, or him who hath rebelled
Against his worthier, as thine now serve thee,   180
Thyself not free, but to thyself enthralled;
Yet lewdly dar'st our minist'ring upbraid.
Reign thou in hell thy kingdom, let me serve
In heav'n God ever blest, and his divine
Behests obey, worthiest to be obeyed;   185
Yet chains in hell, not realms expect: meanwhile
From me returned, as erst thou saidst, from flight,
This greeting on thy impious crest receive.'
    "So saying, a noble stroke he lifted high,
Which hung not, but so swift with tempest fell   190
On the proud crest of Satan, that no sight,
Nor motion of swift thought, less could his shield
Such ruin intercept: ten paces huge
He back recoiled; the tenth on bended knee
His massy spear upstayed; as if on earth   195
Winds under ground or waters forcing way
Sidelong, had pushed a mountain from his seat
Half sunk with all his pines. Amazement seized
The rebel Thrones, but greater rage to see
Thus foiled their mightiest: ours joy filled, and shout,   200
Presage of victory and fierce desire

---

161. *thy success:* the outcome of your action.
163. I.e.: Lest thou boast that I did not answer your argument.
174. *deprav'st:* malignest.
176. See "Reason," p. 392.
182. *lewdly:* ignorantly and basely.
193. *ruin:* L *ruere* to fall.
198–202. *Amazement* and *rage seized* the rebellious angels; *joy* and *shout*(ing)

and *desire* filled *ours.* Fowler notes: "The *shout* is *Presage* of the final *victory* over Satan; when 'The Lord himself shall descend from heaven with a shout, with the voice of the archangel, and with the trump of God: and the dead in Christ shall rise' (I Thess. 4.16)."
    199. Here as elsewhere, Milton uses the name of one of the angelic orders to mean all angels.

Of battle: whereat Michaël bid sound
Th' Archangel trumpet; through the vast of heav'n
It sounded, and the faithful armies rung
Hosanna to the Highest: nor stood at gaze   205
The adverse legions, nor less hideous joined
The horrid shock: now storming fury rose,
And clamor such as heard in heav'n till now
Was never, arms on armor clashing brayed
Horrible discord, and the madding wheels   210
Of brazen chariots raged; dire was the noise
Of conflict; overhead the dismal hiss
Of fiery darts in flaming volleys flew,
And flying vaulted either host with fire.
So under fiery cope together rushed   215
Both battles main, with ruinous assault
And inextinguishable rage; all heav'n
Resounded, and had earth been then, all earth
Had to her center shook. What wonder? when
Millions of fierce encount'ring angels fought   220
On either side, the least of whom could wield
These elements, and arm him with the force
Of all their regions: how much more of power
Army against army numberless to raise
Dreadful combustion warring, and disturb,   225
Though not destroy, their happy native seat;
Had not th' Eternal King Omnipotent
From his stronghold of heav'n high overruled
And limited their might; though numbered such
As each divided legion might have seemed   230
A numerous host, in strength each armèd hand
A legion; led in fight, yet leader seemed
Each warrior single as in chief, expert
When to advance, or stand, or turn the sway
Of battle, open when, and when to close   235
The ridges of grim war; no thought of flight,
None of retreat, no unbecoming deed
That argued fear; each on himself relied,
As only in his arm the moment lay
Of victory; deeds of eternal fame   240
Were done, but infinite: for wide was spread
That war and various; sometimes on firm ground
A standing fight, then soaring on main wing
Tormented all the air; all air seemed then

205. *Hosanna.* See III.348.
212. *dismal:* (L *dies mali,* evil days)
sinister, dreadful.
216. *battles main:* (military term) the
principal, central body of an army (as
distinguished from the van, rear, and
wings) in full array. See 654n.
223. *their regions:* the regions of the
four *elements* of the earth. Cf. *quarters*

in III.714, and see "Universe," pp. 390–
91.
225. *combustion:* violent commotion.
236. *ridges:* ranks.
239. *moment:* the force or weight that
will tip the scales.
243. *main:* powerful.
244. *Tormented:* agitated, stirred up.

Conflicting fire: long time in even scale   245
The battle hung; till Satan, who that day
Prodigious power had shown, and met in arms
No equal, ranging through the dire attack
Of fighting Seraphim confused, at length
Saw where the sword of Michael smote, and felled   250
Squadrons at once; with huge two-handed sway
Brandished aloft the horrid edge came down
Wide-wasting; such destruction to withstand
He hasted, and opposed the rocky orb
Of tenfold adamant, his ample shield   255
A vast circumference: at his approach
The great Archangel from his warlike toil
Surceased, and glad as hoping here to end
Intestine war in heav'n, the Arch-Foe subdued
Or captive dragged in chains, with hostile frown   260
And visage all inflamed first thus began.
     " 'Author of evil, unknown till thy revolt,
Unnamed in heav'n, now plenteous, as thou seest
These acts of hateful strife, hateful to all,
Though heaviest by just measure on thyself   265
And thy adherents: how hast thou disturbed
Heav'n's blessèd peace, and into nature brought
Misery, uncreated till the crime
Of thy rebellion! how hast thou instilled
Thy malice into thousands, once upright   270
And faithful, now proved false! But think not here
To trouble holy rest; heav'n casts thee out
From all her confines. Heav'n the seat of bliss
Brooks not the works of violence and war.
Hence then, and evil go with thee along   275
Thy offspring, to the place of evil, hell,
Thou and thy wicked crew; there mingle broils,
Ere this avenging sword begin thy doom,
Or some more sudden vengeance winged from God
Precipitate thee with augmented pain.'   280
     "So spake the Prince of Angels; to whom thus
The Adversary. 'Nor think thou with wind
Of airy threats to awe whom yet with deeds
Thou canst not. Hast thou turned the least of these
To flight, or if to fall, but that they rise   285
Unvanquished, easier to transact with me
That thou shouldst hope, imperious, and with threats
To chase me hence? Err not that so shall end
The strife which thou call'st evil, but we style

267. *nature*. Cf. 176. In the form of
God or order nature existed from the be-
ginning—even before the creation of the
universe.
     277. *mingle*: concoct. *broils*: (Fr
brouiller to disorder) quarrels.
     282. *Adversary*. See I.82n.

284–88. I.e.: Hast thou turned the
weakest of my host to flight, made any
fall who have not risen again, that thou
shouldst hope it would be easier to ne-
gotiate with me imperiously and to chase
me hence with threats?

The strife of glory: which we mean to win,   290
Or turn this heav'n itself into the hell
Thou fablest, here however to dwell free,
If not to reign: meanwhile thy utmost force,
And join him named Almighty to thy aid,
I fly not, but have sought thee far and nigh.'   295
    "They ended parle, and both addressed for fight
Unspeakable; for who, though with the tongue
Of angels, can relate, or to what things
Liken on earth conspicuous, that may lift
Human imagination to such highth   300
Of godlike power: for likest gods they seemed,
Stood they or moved, in stature, motion, arms
Fit to decide the empire of great heav'n.
Now waved their fiery swords, and in the air
Made horrid circles; two broad suns their shields   305
Blazed opposite, while expectation stood
In horror; from each hand with speed retired
Where erst was thickest fight, th' angelic throng,
And left large field, unsafe within the wind
Of such commotion, such as to set forth   310
Great things by small, if nature's concord broke,
Among the constellations war were sprung,
Two planets rushing from aspéct malign
Of fiercest opposition in mid sky,
Should combat, and their jarring spheres confound.   315
Together both with next to almighty arm,
Uplifted imminent one stroke they aimed
That might determine, and not need repeat,
As not of power, at once; nor odds appeared
In might or swift prevention; but the sword   320
Of Michael from the armory of God
Was giv'n him tempered so, that neither keen
Nor solid might resist that edge: it met
The sword of Satan with steep force to smite
Descending, and in half cut sheer, nor stayed,   325
But with swift wheel reverse, deep ent'ring shared
All his right side; then Satan first knew pain,

---

296. *parle:* parley. *addressed:* (OF *a* + *drecier* to straighten, arrange) prepared.
299. *conspicuous:* L *conspicere* to get sight of, perceive.
302. *Stood they or moved:* standing or moving.
310–13. I.e.: Such commotion as if (*to set forth . . . small*), nature's concord having been broken, war were to spring up among the constellations [and] two diametrically opposed planets should combat, etc. *aspect malign.* Astrologists believe that when two planets are diametrically opposed in the heavens (in *malign aspect*), their conflicting rays are harmful to men.

315. *confound:* (L *confundere* to pour together) destroy.
317. *imminent:* L *imminere*, to project, threaten.
318. *determine:* (L *de* + *terminare* to limit) to bring to an end. *repeat:* repetition.
319. *As not of power.* I.e.: since they would not have the power (to repeat the blow). *odds:* inequality.
320. *prevention:* power to forestall, to strike the first blow.
321. Cf. Jer. 50.25: "The Lord hath opened his armoury, and hath brought forth the weapons of his indignation."
326. *shared:* OE *sceran* to shear.

And writhed him to and fro convolved; so sore
The griding sword with discontinuous wound
Passed through him, but th' ethereal substance closed   330
Not long divisible, and from the gash
A stream of nectarous humor issuing flowed
Sanguine, such as celestial Spirits may bleed,
And all his armor stained erewhile so bright.
Forthwith on all sides to his aid was run   335
By angels many and strong, who interposed
Defense, while others bore him on their shields
Back to his chariot, where it stood retired
From off the files of war; there they him laid
Gnashing for anguish and despite and shame   340
To find himself not matchless, and his pride
Humbled by such rebuke, so far beneath
His confidence to equal God in power.
Yet soon he healed; for Spirits that live throughout
Vital in every part, not as frail man   345
In entrails, heart or head, liver or reins,
Cannot but by annihilating die;
Nor in their liquid texture mortal wound
Receive, no more than can the fluid air:
All heart they live, all head, all eye, all ear,   350
All intellect, all sense, and as they please,
They limb themselves, and color, shape, or size
Assume, as likes them best, condense or rare.
      "Meanwhile in other parts like deeds deserved
Memorial, where the might of Gabriel fought,   355
And with fierce ensigns pierced the deep array
Of Moloch furious king, who him defied,
And at his chariot wheels to drag him bound
Threatened, nor from the Holy One of heav'n
Refrained his tongue blasphémous; but anon   360
Down clov'n to the waist, with shattered arms
And uncouth pain fled bellowing. On each wing
Uriel and Raphael his vaunting foe,
Though huge, and in a rock of diamond armed,
Vanquished Adramelech, and Asmadai,   365
Two potent Thrones, that to be less than gods
Disdained, but meaner thoughts learned in their flight,
Mangled with ghastly wounds through plate and mail.
Nor stood unmindful Abdiel to annoy

---

328. *convolved* L *con* together + *vol-*
vere to roll. *sore:* painfully.
  329. *griding:* (ME *gird* to strike, to
smite) piercing through so as to cause
intense, rasping pain. *discontinous:* gap-
ing.
  335–36. *to his aid was run / By angels:*
(L syntax. Cf. II.213 and IX.253) angels
ran aid to him.

344–53. See "Angels," p. 394.
  356. *array:* troops in formation.
  359–60. Cf. 2 Kings 19.22: "Whom hast
thou reproached and blasphemed? and
against whom hast thou exalted thy voice,
and lifted up thine eyes on high? even
against the Holy One of Israel."
  362. *uncouth:* (hitherto) unknown.
  365, 371–72. See "Angels," p. 395.

The atheist crew, but with redoubled blow   370
Ariel and Arioch, and the violence
Of Ramiel scorched and blasted overthrew.
I might relate of thousands, and their names
Eternize here on earth; but those elect
Angels contented with their fame in heav'n   375
Seek not the praise of men: the other sort
In might though wondrous and in acts of war,
Nor of renown less eager, yet by doom
Cancelled from heav'n and sacred memory,
Nameless in dark oblivion let them dwell.   380
For strength from truth divided and from just,
Illaudable, naught merits but dispraise
And ignominy, yet to glory aspires
Vainglorious, and through infamy seeks fame:
Therefore eternal silence be their doom.   385
    "And now their mightiest quelled, the battle swerved,
With many an inroad gored; deformèd rout
Entered, and foul disorder; all the ground
With shivered armor strown, and on a heap
Chariot and charioteer lay overturned   390
And fiery foaming steeds; what stood, recoiled
O'erwearied, through the faint Satanic host
Defensive scarce, or with pale fear surprised,
Then first with fear surprised and sense of pain
Fled ignominious, to such evil brought   395
By sin of disobedience, till that hour
Not liable to fear or flight or pain.
Far otherwise th' inviolable saints
In cubic phalanx firm advanced entire,
Invulnerable, impenetrably armed: 400
Such high advantages their innocence
Gave them above their foes, not to have sinned,
Not to have disobeyed; in fight they stood
Unwearied, unobnoxious to be pained
By wound, though from their place by violence moved.   405
    "Now night her course began, and over heav'n
Inducing darkness, grateful truce imposed,
And silence on the odious din of war:
Under her cloudy covert both retired,
Victor and vanquished: on the foughten field   410
Michaël and his angels prevalent
Encamping, placed in guard their watches round,
Cherubic waving fires: on th' other part
Satan with his rebellious disappeared,
Far in the dark dislodged, and void of rest,   415

370. *atheist:* godless.
393. *Defensive scarce:* scarcely defend-
ing themselves. *surprised:* (L *super* over
+ *prendere* to take) overcome, seized
unexpectedly.

404. *unobnoxious:* (L *ob* open to +
noxa harm) not liable.
411. *prevalent:* victorious.
415. *dislodged:* (military term) shifted
his quarters.

His potentates to council called by night;
And in the midst thus undismayed began.
   " 'O now in danger tried, now known in arms
Not to be overpowered, companions dear,
Found worthy not of liberty alone,   420
Too mean pretense, but what we more affect,
Honor, dominion, glory, and renown,
Who have sustained one day in doubtful fight,
(And if one day, why not eternal days?)
What heaven's Lord had powerfullest to send   425
Against us from about his throne, and judged
Sufficient to subdue us to his will,
But proves not so: then fallible, it seems,
Of future we may deem him, though till now
Omniscient thought. True is, less firmly armed,   430
Some disadvantage we endured and pain,
Till now not known, but known as soon contemned,
Since now we find this our empyreal form
Incapable of mortal injury
Imperishable, and though pierced with wound,   435
Soon closing, and by native vigor healed.
Of evil then so small as easy think
The remedy; perhaps more valid arms,
Weapons more violent, when next we meet,
May serve to better us, and worse our foes,   440
Or equal what between us made the odds,
In nature none: if other hidden cause
Left them superior, while we can preserve
Unhurt our minds, and understanding sound,
Due search and consultation will disclose.'   445
   "He sat; and in th' assembly next upstood
Nisroch, of Principalities the prime;
As one he stood escaped from cruel fight,
Sore toiled, his riven arms to havoc hewn,
And cloudy in aspéct thus answering spake.   450
'Deliverer from new lords, leader to free
Enjoyment of our right as gods; yet hard
For gods, and too unequal work we find
Against unequal arms to fight in pain,
Against unpained, impassive; from which evil   455
Ruin must needs ensue; for what avails
Valor or strength, though matchless, quelled with pain
Which all subdues, and makes remiss the hands
Of mightiest. Sense of pleasure we may well

421. *mean:* low. *pretense:* aim. *affect:* aspire to.
423. *doubtful:* indecisive.
429. *Of future:* about what will happen in the future.
432. *known as soon contemned:* despised as soon as known.
438. *valid:* L *validus* strong.

439. *violent:* powerful.
447. *Nisroch.* See "Angels," p. 395.
449. *to havoc hewn:* cut to pieces.
455. *impassive:* (L *passus,* from *pati* to suffer) insensitive.
458. *remiss:* L *remittere, remissum,* to relax.

Spare out of life perhaps, and not repine,   460
But live content, which is the calmest life:
But pain is perfet misery, the worst
Of evils, and excessive, overturns
All patience. He who therefore can invent
With what more forcible we may offend   465
Our yet unwounded enemies, or arm
Ourselves with like defense, to me deserves
No less than for deliverance what we owe.'
    "Whereto with look composed Satan replied.
'Not uninvented that, which thou aright   470
Believ'st so main to our success, I bring;
Which of us who beholds the bright surfáce
Of this ethereous mold whereon we stand,
This continent of spacious heav'n, adorned
With plant, fruit, flow'r ambrosial, gems and gold,   475
Whose eye so superficially surveys
These things, as not to mind from whence they grow
Deep under ground, materials dark and crude,
Of spiritous and fiery spume, till touched
With heav'n's ray, and tempered they shoot forth   480
So beauteous, op'ning to the ambient light.
These in their dark nativity the deep
Shall yield us, pregnant with infernal flame,
Which into hollow engines long and round
Thick-rammed, at th' other bore with touch of fire   485
Dilated and infuriate shall send forth
From far with thund'ring noise among our foes
Such implements of mischief as shall dash
To pieces, and o'erwhelm whatever stands
Adverse, that they shall fear we have disarmed   490
The thunderer of his only dreaded bolt.
Nor long shall be our labor, yet ere dawn,
Effect shall end our wish. Meanwhile revive;
Abandon fear; to strength and counsel joined
Think nothing hard, much less to be despaired.'   495
He ended, and his words their drooping cheer
Enlightened, and their languished hope revived.
Th' invention all admired, and each, how he
To be th' inventor missed, so easy it seemed
Once found, which yet unfound most would have thought   500
Impossible: yet haply of thy race

---

465. *offend:* (L *offendere* to strike against) attack.
468. I.e.: No less than what we owe [Satan] for [our] deliverance.
471. *main:* essential.
479. *spume.* See 512n.
481. *ambient:* circumfused, enveloping.
483. *infernal:* L *infernus* that which lies beneath.
485. *Thick:* compactly. *other bore:* the touchhole, drilled into the barrel of a cannon, into which fine powder was poured to serve as a fuse for the charge.
494. *counsel:* judgment, wisdom, prudence.
496. *cheer:* (OF *chiere, chere,* face) state of mind.
498. *admired:* wondered at.
501. *haply:* by chance.

In future days, if malice should abound,
Some one intent on mischief, or inspired
With dev'lish machination might devise
Like instrument to plague the sons of men   505
For sin, on war and mutual slaughter bent.
Forthwith from council to the work they flew,
None arguing stood, innumerable hands
Were ready, in a moment up they turned
Wide the celestial soil, and saw beneath   510
Th' originals of nature in their crude
Conception; sulphurous and nitrous foam
They found, they mingled, and with subtle art,
Concocted and adusted they reduced
To blackest grain, and into store conveyed: 515
Part hidden veins digged up (nor hath this earth
Entrails unlike) of mineral and stone,
Whereof to found their engines and their balls
Of missive ruin; part incentive reed
Provide, pernicious with one touch to fire.   520
So all ere day-spring, under conscious night
Secret they finished, and in order set,
With silent circumspection unespied.
Now when fair morn orient in heav'n appeared
Up rose the victor angels, and to arms   525
The matin trumpet sung: in arms they stood
Of golden panoply, refulgent host,
Soon banded; others from the dawning hills
Looked round, and scouts each coast light-armèd scour,
Each quarter, to descry the distant foe,   530
Where lodged, or whither fled, or if for fight,
In motion or in alt: him soon they met
Under spread ensigns moving nigh, in slow
But firm battalion; back with speediest sail
Zophiel, of Cherubim the swiftest wing,   535
Came flying, and in mid-air aloud thus cried.
  " 'Arm, warriors, arm for fight, the foe at hand,
Whom fled we thought, will save us long pursuit
This day, fear not his flight; so thick a cloud
He comes, and settled in his face I see   540
Sad resolution and secure: let each

---

512. *foam:* like *spume* (479), a word for the chemical compound called a "salt." Potassium nitrate and sulphur are components of gunpowder.
514. *concocted:* refined by mixing and cooking. *adusted:* dried by heating.
515. *grain:* granules.
518. *found:* (L *fundere* to pour) to form or cast, as in a foundry.
519. *missive:* capable of being projected. *incentive:* kindling (a pun involving *incendiary*, L *incendium* a fire, and

incentive, L *incinere* to strike up a tune, from *in* + *canere* to sing). *incentive reed:* both matchstick and musical instrument.
520. *pernicious:* (L *pernix* nimble) quick; and (L *per* + *nex* violent death) destructive.
521. *conscious:* guiltily aware (of what they were doing).
532. *alt:* halt.
535. *Zophiel:* See "Angels," p. 396.
541. *Sad:* firm. *secure:* confident.

His adamantine coat gird well, and each
Fit well his helm, gripe fast his orbèd shield,
Borne ev'n or high, for this day will pour down,
If I conjecture aught, no drizzling shower,   545
But rattling storm of arrows barbed with fire.'
So warned he them aware themselves, and soon
In order, quit of all impediment;
Instant without disturb they took alarm,
And onward move embattled; when behold   550
Not distant far with heavy pace the foe
Approaching gross and huge; in hollow cube
Training his devilish enginry, impaled
On every side with shadowing squadrons deep,
To hide the fraud. At interview both stood   555
A while, but suddenly at head appeared
Satan: and thus was heard commanding loud.
    " 'Vanguard, to right and left the front unfold;
That all may see who hate us, how we seek
Peace and composure, and with open breast   560
Stand ready to receive them, if they like
Our overture, and turn not back perverse;
But that I doubt, however witness heaven,
Heav'n witness thou anon, while we discharge
Freely our part: ye who appointed stand   565
Do as you have in charge, and briefly touch
What we propound, and loud that all may hear.'
    "So scoffing in ambiguous words, he scarce
Had ended; when to right and left the front
Divided, and to either flank retired.   570
Which to our eyes discovered new and strange,
A triple-mounted row of pillars laid
On wheels (for like to pillars most they seemed
Or hollowed bodies made of oak or fir
With branches lopped, in wood or mountain felled)   575
Brass, iron, stony mold, had not their mouths
With hideous orifice gaped on us wide,
Portending hollow truce; at each behind
A Seraph stood, and in his hand a reed
Stood waving tipped with fire; while we suspense,   580

544. *ev'n:* straight out in front of the body.
547–48. *aware themselves:* already wary, cautious of danger. *Aware* and *warn* both come from OE *wær* wary. *and soon* [they were] *In order:* battle order. *quit:* free. *impediment:* equipment not needed in battle.
549. I.e.: Instantly without disorder they obeyed the call to arms.
550. *embattled:* in battle formation.
552. *gross:* compact. Cf. II.570.
553. *Training:* (OF *traîner* to draw) pulling. *impaled:* fenced in.
555. *At interview:* in view of one an-other.
560. *composure:* agreement. *breast:* front ranks; also heart.
562. *overture:* (L *apertura* opening, hole) offer to negotiate; opening of the ranks concealing the cannon—or the muzzle of the cannon.
564. *discharge:* another pun.
566–67. *charge, touch, propound, loud:* all puns.
572. *triple-mounted:* in three rows. Cf. 605 and 650.
576. *mold:* matter.
580. *suspense:* undecided where to turn.

Collected stood within our thoughts amused,
Not long, for sudden all at once their reeds
Put forth, and to a narrow vent applied
With nicest touch. Immediate in a flame,
But soon obscured with smoke, all heav'n appeared,   585
From those deep-throated engines belched, whose roar
Emboweled with outrageous noise the air,
And all her entails tore, disgorging foul
Their devilish glut, chained thunderbolts and hail
Of iron globes, which on the victor host   590
Leveled, with such impetuous fury smote,
That whom they hit, none on their feet might stand,
Though standing else as rocks, but down they fell
By thousands, Angel on Archangel rolled,
The sooner for their arms; unarmed they might   595
Have easily as Spirits evaded swift
By quick contraction or remove; but now
Foul dissipation followed and forced rout;
Nor served it to relax their serried files.
What should they do? If on they rushed, repulse   600
Repeated, and indecent overthrow
Doubled, would render them yet more despised,
And to their foes a laughter; for in view
Stood ranked of Seraphim another row
In posture to displode their second tire   605
Of thunder: back defeated to return
They worse abhorred. Satan beheld their plight,
And to his mates thus in derision called.
   " 'O friends, why come not on these victors proud?
Erewhile they fierce were coming, and when we,   610
To entertain them fair with open front
And breast, (what could we more?) propounded terms
Of composition, straight they changed their minds,
Flew off, and into strange vagaries fell,
As they would dance, yet for a dance they seemed   615
Somewhat extravagant and wild, perhaps
For joy of offering peace: but I suppose
If our proposals once again were heard
We should compel them to a quick result.'
   "To whom thus Belial in like gamesome mood.   620
'Leader, the terms we sent were terms of weight,
Of hard contents, and full of force urged home,

---

581. *amused:* preoccupied; or (in the military sense) with attention diverted from the enemy's intention.

587. *Emboweled:* disemboweled.

598. *Foul dissipation:* dishonorable rout.

599. *served it:* did it do any good. *relax:* loosen up, make less compact. *serried files:* rows pressed together in close order.

601. *indecent.* Like *foul* in 598, *indecent* implies obscene, offensive to good taste, not to be looked at, not to be countenanced; hence, disgraceful.

605. *displode:* explode. *tire:* volley.

611–19. *front* (face), *breast* (heart), *propounded, composition, Flew off, result* (L *re* back + *saltare* to leap): all puns.

614. *vagaries:* eccentric motions.

Such as we might perceive amused them all,
And stumbled many: who receives them right,
Had need from head to foot well understand;   625
Not understood, this gift they have besides,
They show us when our foes walk not upright.'
    "So they among themselves in pleasant vein
Stood scoffing, highthened in their thoughts beyond
All doubt of victory, Eternal Might   630
To match with their inventions they presumed
So easy, and of his thunder made a scorn,
And all his host derided, while they stood
A while in trouble; but they stood not long,
Rage prompted them at length, and found them arms   635
Against such hellish mischief fit to oppose.
Forthwith (behold the excellence, the power,
Which God hath in his mighty angels placed)
Their arms away they threw, and to the hills
(For earth hath this variety from heav'n   640
Of pleasure situate in hill and dale)
Light as the lightning glimpse they ran, they flew,
From their foundations loos'ning to and fro
They plucked the seated hills with all their load,
Rocks, waters, woods, and by the shaggy tops   645
Uplifting bore them in their hands: amaze,
Be sure, and terror seized the rebel host,
When coming towards them so dread they saw
The bottom of the mountains upward turned,
Till on those cursèd engines' triple-row   650
They saw them whelmed, and all their confidence
Under the weight of mountains buried deep,
Themselves invaded next, and on their heads
Main promontories flung, which in the air
Came shadowing, and oppressed whole legions armed,   655
Their armor helped their harm, crushed in and bruised
Into their substance pent, which wrought them pain
Implacable, and many a dolorous groan,
Long struggling underneath, ere they could wind
Out of such prison, though Spirits of purest light,   660
Purest at first, now gross by sinning grown.
The rest in imitation to like arms
Betook them, and the neighboring hills uptore;
So hills amid the air encountered hills
Hurled to and fro with jaculation dire,   665
That underground they fought in dismal shade;

623. *amused:* held their attention; be-
wildered them (pun). Cf. 581.
624. *stumbled:* perplexed (pun).
625. *understand:* another pun.
633. *they:* the rebels' enemies.
653. *invaded:* attacked.
654. *Main:* (OE *magan* to be able)
(when used of an army) numerous and
fully equipped; (of things) great in bulk
or strength; (of earth or rock) forming
the principal or entire mass; as in "with
might and main." *promontories:* L *pro-
munturium* a mountain ridge, a headland.
    665. *jaculation:* L *jacere* to throw;
jaculum a dart.

Infernal noise; war seemed a civil game
To this uproar; horrid confusion heaped
Upon confusion rose: and now all heav'n
Had gone to wrack, with ruin overspread,   670
Had not th' Almighty Father where he sits
Shrined in his sanctuary of heav'n secure,
Consulting on the sum of things, foreseen
This tumult, and permitted all, advised:
That his great purpose he might so fulfill,   675
To honor his anointed Son avenged
Upon his enemies, and to declare
All power on him transferred: whence to his Son
Th' assessor of his throne he thus began.
    " 'Effulgence of my glory, Son beloved,   680
Son in whose face invisible is beheld
Visibly, what by Deity I am,
And in whose hand what by decree I do,
Second Omnipotence, two days are passed,
Two days, as we compute the days of heav'n,   685
Since Michael and his powers went forth to tame
These disobedient; sore hath been their fight,
As likeliest was, when two such foes met armed;
For to themselves I left them, and thou know'st,
Equal in their creation they were formed,   690
Save what sin hath impaired, which yet hath wrought
Insensibly, for I suspend their doom;
Whence in perpetual fight they needs must last
Endless, and no solution will be found:
War wearied hath performed what war can do,   695
And to disordered rage let loose the reins,
With mountains as with weapons armed, which makes
Wild work in heav'n, and dangerous to the main.
Two days are therefore passed, the third is thine;
For thee I have ordained it, and thus far   700
Have suffered, that the glory may be thine
Of ending this great war, since none but thou
Can end it. Into thee such virtue and grace
Immense I have transfused, that all may know
In heav'n and hell thy power above compare,   705
And this perverse commotion governed thus,

673. *Consulting on:* considering. *the sum of things.* Fowler notes that the phrase is a translation of L *summa rerum*, "highest public interest," and that by *sum* Milton may intend the meaning of "goal."
674. *advised:* advisedly, having advised himself. L *ad* towards + *visum*, from *videre* to see. Milton plays a variation on *foreseen* in the line above, and *providence*, which is his theme.
679. *assessor:* (L *assessor*, one who sits beside) associate.
681–82. Cf. Col. 1.15: "Who is the image of the invisible God . . ."
692. *Insensibly:* imperceptibly.
695. *War wearied:* war, itself worn out.
698. *main:* i.e., "continent" of heaven.
699. *therefore:* in that way. *the third is thine.* Fowler notes that "Typologically, the reference would be to Christ's rising on the third day . . . : Messiah's defeat of Satan here foreshadows the later victory of the resurrection." See XII.232–33n.
701. *suffered:* permitted.

To manifest thee worthiest to be Heir
Of all things, to be Heir and to be King
By sacred unction, thy deservèd right.
Go then thou mightiest in thy Father's might,   710
Ascend my chariot, guide the rapid wheels
That shake heav'n's basis, bring forth all my war,
My bow and thunder, my almighty arms
Gird on, and sword upon thy puissant thigh;
Pursue these sons of darkness, drive them out   715
From all heav'n's bounds into the utter deep:
There let them learn, as likes them, to despise
God and Messiah his anointed King.'
 "He said, and on his Son with rays direct
Shone full, he all his Father full expressed   720
Ineffably into his face received,
And thus the Filial Godhead answering spake:
 " 'O Father, O Supreme of heav'nly Thrones,
First, highest, holiest, best, thou always seek'st
To glorify thy Son, I always thee,   725
As is most just; this I my glory account,
My exaltation, and my whole delight,
That thou in me well pleased, declar'st thy will
Fulfilled, which to fulfill is all my bliss.
Scepter and power, thy giving, I assume,   730
And gladlier shall resign, when in the end
Thou shalt be all in all, and I in thee
For ever, and in me all whom thou lov'st:
But whom thou hat'st, I hate, and can put on
Thy terrors, as I put thy mildness on,   735
Image of thee in all things; and shall soon,
Armed with thy might, rid heav'n of these rebelled,
To their prepared ill mansion driven down
To chains of darkness, and th' undying worm,

712. *war:* instrument of war.
714. Cf. Ps. 45.3: "Gird thy sword upon thy thigh, O most mighty, with thy glory and thy majesty."
716. *utter:* outer.
720–21. Cf. 2 Cor. 4.6: "For God, who commanded the light to shine out of darkness, hath shined in our hearts, to give the light of the knowledge of the glory of God in the face of Jesus Christ." *ineffably:* unutterably.
725. Cf. John 17.1: "These words spake Jesus, and lifted up his eyes to heaven, and said, Father, the hour is come; glorify thy Son, that thy Son also may glorify thee."
728. Cf. Matt. 3.17: "And lo a voice from heaven, saying, This is my beloved Son, in whom I am well pleased."
731–32. Cf. 1 Cor. 15.24,28: "Then cometh the end when he shall have delivered up the kingdom to God, even the Father; when he shall have put down all rule and all authority and power. . . .

And when all things shall be subdued unto him, then shall the Son also himself be subject unto him that put all things under him, that God may be all in all."
734. Cf. Ps. 139.21: "Do not I hate them, O Lord, that hate thee? and am not I grieved with those that rise up against thee?"
738. Cf. John 14.2: "In my Father's house are many mansions: if it were not so, I [Christ] would have told you. I go to prepare a place for you." *ill:* evil, painful, unwholesome. *mansion:* (L *manere* to dwell) abode.
739. Cf. 2 Pet. 2.4: ". . . God spared not the angels that sinned, but cast them down to hell, and delivered them into chains of darkness, to be reserved unto judgement." Jude 6: "And the angels which kept not the first estate, but left their own habitation, he hath reserved in everlasting chains under darkness unto the judgement of the great day." Isa. 66.24: "And they shall go forth, and look

That from thy just obedience could revolt,   740
Whom to obey is happiness entire.
Then shall thy saints unmixed, and from th' impure
Far separate, circling thy holy mount
Unfeignèd hallelujahs to thee sing,
Hymns of high praise, and I among them chief.'   745
So said, he o'er his scepter bowing, rose
From the right hand of Glory where he sat,
And the third sacred morn began to shine
Dawning through heav'n: forth rushed with whirlwind sound
The chariot of Paternal Deity,   750
Flashing thick flames, wheel within wheel undrawn,
Itself instinct with spirit, but convoyed
By four Cherubic shapes, four faces each
Had wondrous, as with stars their bodies all
And wings were set with eyes, with eyes the wheels   755
Of beryl, and careering fires between;
Over their heads a crystal firmament,
Whereon a sapphire throne, inlaid with pure
Amber, and colors of the show'ry arch.
He in celestial panoply all armed   760
Of radiant Urim, work divinely wrought,
Ascended, at his right hand Victory
Sat eagle-winged, beside him hung his bow
And quiver with three-bolted thunder stored,
And from about him fierce effusion rolled   765
Of smoke and bickering flame, and sparkles dire;
Attended with ten thousand thousand saints,
He onward came, far off his coming shone,
And twenty thousand (I their number heard)
Chariots of God, half on each hand were seen: 770
He on the wings of Cherub rode sublime
On the crystálline sky, in sapphire throned,

upon the carcases of the men that have transgressed against me: for their worm shall not die, neither shall their fire be quenched; and they shall be an abhorring unto all flesh." Mark 9.44: "Where their worm dieth not, and the fire is not quenched."

749–59. See Ezekiel 1, pp. 378–79.

752. *instinct with:* (L *in* + *stinguere* to prick, to stick) impelled by.

755. Cf. Ezek. 10.12: "And their whole body, and their backs, and their hands, and their wings, and the wheels, were full of eyes round about, even the wheels that they four had."

759. *show'ry arch:* rainbow.

761. *Urim.* When God instructed Moses to make his brother Aaron a priest, he gave instructions about the holy garments Aaron was to wear. These included a "breastplate of judgement," into which was to be put "Urim and Thummim" (Exod. 28.30). *Urim* would

seem to be a symbol, or a jewel or jewels. Fowler notes that "many alchemical theorists" thought *Urim* was the philosopher's stone. Cf. III.596–605.

763. *eagle-winged.* The eagle was the symbol of Jupiter, the hurler of thunderbolts.

766. *bickering:* flickering.

767. Cf. Rev. 5.11: "And I beheld, and I heard the voice of many angels round the throne and the beasts and the elders: and the number of them was ten thousand times ten thousand, and thousands of thousands."

769–70. Cf. Ps. 68.17: "The chariots of God are twenty thousand, even thousands of angels: the Lord is among them, as in Sinai, in the holy place."

771. Cf. Sam. 22.11: "And he rode upon a cherub, and did fly: and he was seen upon the wings of the wind." *sublime:* raised up.

Illustrious far and wide, but by his own
First seen: them unexpected joy surprised,
When the great ensign of Messiah blazed   775
Aloft by angels borne, his sign in heav'n:
Under whose conduct Michael soon reduced
His army, circumfused on either wing,
Under their Head embodied all in one.
Before him Power Divine his way prepared;   780
At his command the uprooted hills retired
Each to his place, they heard his voice and went
Obsequious, heav'n his wonted face renewed,
And with fresh flow'rets hill and valley smiled.
This saw his hapless foes but stood obdured,   785
And to rebellious fight rallied their powers
Insensate, hope conceiving from despair.
In heav'nly Spirits could such perverseness dwell?
But to convince the proud what signs avail,
Or wonders move th' obdúrate to relent?   790
They hardened more by what might most reclaim,
Grieving to see his glory, at the sight
Took envy, and aspiring to his highth,
Stood re-embattled fierce, by force or fraud
Weening to prosper, and at length prevail   795
Against God and Messiah, or to fall
In universal ruin last, and now
To final battle drew, disdaining flight,
Or faint retreat; when the great Son of God
To all his host on either hand thus spake.   800
    " 'Stand still in bright array ye saints, here stand
Ye angels armed, this day from battle rest;
Faithful hath been your warfare, and of God
Accepted, fearless in his righteous cause,
And as ye have received, so have ye done   805
Invincibly; but of this cursèd crew
The punishment to other hand belongs,
Vengeance is his, or whose he sole appoints;
Number to this day's work is not ordained
Nor multitude, stand only and behold   810
God's indignation on these godless poured
By me, not you but me they have despised,
Yet envied; against me is all their rage,
Because the Father, t' whom in heav'n supreme

---

776. Cf. Matt. 24.30: "And then shall appear the sign of the Son of man in heaven: and then shall all the tribes of the earth . . . see the Son of man coming in the clouds of heaven with power and great glory."

777. *reduced:* L *re* back + *ducere* to lead.

778. *circumfused:* L *circum* around + *fundere* to pour.

785. *obdured:* hardened. Cf. III.200n.

791. *what might most reclaim.* I.e., the sight of Christ.

801. Cf. Exod. 14.13, p. 364.

808. Cf. Rom. 12.19: "Dearly beloved, avenge not yourselves, but rather give place unto wrath: for it is written, Vengeance is mine; I will repay, saith the Lord."

Kingdom and power and glory appertains,   815
Hath honored me according to his will.
Therefore to me their doom he hath assigned;
That they may have their wish, to try with me
In battle which the stronger proves, they all,
Or I alone against them, since by strength   820
They measure all, of other excellence
Not emulous, nor care who them excels;
Nor other strife with them do I voutsafe.'
      "So spake the Son, and into terror changed
His count'nance too severe to be beheld   825
And full of wrath bent on his enemies.
At once the Four spread out their starry wings
With dreadful shade contiguous, and the orbs
Of his fierce chariot rolled, as with the sound
Of torrent floods, or of a numerous host.   830
He on his impious foes right onward drove,
Gloomy as night; under his burning wheels
The steadfast empyrean shook throughout,
All but the throne itself of God. Full soon
Among them he arrived; in his right hand   835
Grasping ten thousand thunders, which he sent
Before him, such as in their souls infixed
Plagues; they astonished all resistance lost,
All courage; down their idle weapons dropped;
O'er shields and helms, and helmèd heads he rode   840
Of Thrones and mighty Seraphim prostráte,
That wished the mountains now might be again
Thrown on them as a shelter from his ire.
Nor less on either side tempestuous fell
His arrows, from the fourfold-visaged Four,   845
Distinct with eyes, and from the living wheels,
Distinct alike with multitude of eyes;
One spirit in them ruled, and every eye
Glared lightning, and shot forth pernicious fire
Among th' accursed, that withered all their strength, 850
And of their wonted vigor left them drained,
Exhausted, spiritless, afflicted, fall'n.
Yet half his strength he put not forth, but checked
His thunder in mid-volley, for he meant
Not to destroy, but root them out of heav'n: 855

827. *the Four:* Ezekiel's *four Cherubic shapes* of line 753.
833. Cf. 2 Sam. 22.8: "Then the earth shook and trembled; the foundations of heaven moved and shook, because he was wroth."
836–38. Cf. Ps. 18.13–14: "The Lord also thundered in the heavens, and the Highest gave his voice; hail stones and coals of fire. Yea, he sent out his arrows, and scattered them; and he shot out lightnings, and discomfited them."

838. *Plagues:* L *plaga* a blow. *astonished:* (L *ex* out + *tonare* to thunder) struck with fear.
842–43. Cf. Hos. 10.8: "The high places also of Aven, the sin of Israel, shall be destroyed: . . . and they shall say to the mountains, Cover us; and to the hills, Fall on us." Cf. also the vision of the Last Judgment, in Rev. 6.15–17, p. 385.

846. *Distinct:* decorated.
849. *pernicious:* deadly. Cf. 520.

The overthrown he raised, and as a herd
Of goats or timorous flock together thronged
Drove them before him thunderstruck, pursued
With terrors and with furies to the bounds
And crystal wall of heav'n, which op'ning wide,   860
Rolled inward, and a spacious gap disclosed
Into the wasteful deep; the monstrous sight
Strook them with horror backward, but far worse
Urged them behind; headlong themselves they threw
Down from the verge of heav'n, eternal wrath   865
Burnt after them to the bottomless pit.
    "Hell heard th' unsufferable noise, hell saw
Heav'n ruining from heav'n, and would have fled
Affrighted; but strict fate had cast too deep
Her dark foundations, and too fast had bound.   870
Nine days they fell; confounded Chaos roared,
And felt tenfold confusion in their fall
Through his wild anarchy, so huge a rout
Encumbered him with ruin: hell at last
Yawning received them whole, and on them closed,   875
Hell their fit habitation fraught with fire
Unquenchable, the house of woe and pain.
Disburdened heav'n rejoiced, and soon repaired
Her mural breach, returning whence it rolled.
Sole victor from th' expulsion of his foes   880
Messiah his triumphal chariot turned:
To meet him all his saints, who silent stood
Eye-witnesses of his almighty acts,
With jubilee advanced; and as they went,
Shaded with branching palm, each order bright   885
Sung triumph, and him sung victorious King,
Son, Heir, and Lord, to him dominion giv'n,
Worthiest to reign: he celebrated rode
Triumphant through mid-heav'n, into the courts
And temple of his mighty Father throned   890
On high: who into glory him received,
    Where now he sits at the right hand of bliss.
    "Thus measuring things in heav'n by things on earth

857. *goats.* Cf. Matt. 25.31–41: "When the Son of man shall come in his glory . . . then shall he sit upon the throne of his glory: and before him shall be gathered all nations: and he shall separate them one from another, as a shepherd divideth his sheep from the goats: and he shall set the sheep on his right hand, but the goats on the left. . . . Then shall he say also unto them on the left hand, Depart from me, ye cursed, into everlasting fire, prepared for the devil and his angels."
862. *wasteful:* full of emptiness. *monstrous:* unnatural.
868. *ruining:* (L *ruina* a falling) tumbling down.

871. *confounded* (L *con* together + *fundere, fusum,* to pour) confused.
874–75. Cf. Isa. 5.14: "Therefore hell hath enlarged herself, and opened her mouth without measure: and their glory, and their multitude, and their pomp, and he that rejoiceth, shall descend into it."
884. *jubilee:* joyful shouting.
892. Cf. Heb. 1.3: "Who [Christ, after his crucifixion and resurrection] being the brightness of his [God's] glory, and the express image of his person, and upholding all things by the word of his power, when he had by himself purged our sins, sat down on the right hand of the majesty on high. . . ."

At thy request, and that thou may'st beware
By what is past, to thee I have revealed   895
What might have else to human race been hid;
The discord which befell, and war in heav'n
Among th' angelic powers, and the deep fall
Of those too high aspiring, who rebelled
With Satan, he who envies now thy state,   900
Who now is plotting how he may seduce
Thee also from obedience, that with him
Bereaved of happiness thou may'st partake
His punishment, eternal misery;
Which would be all his solace and revenge,   905
As a despite done against the Most High,
Thee once to gain companion of his woe.
But listen not to his temptations, warn
Thy weaker; let it profit thee to have heard
By terrible example the reward   910
Of disobedience; firm they might have stood,
Yet fell; remember, and fear to transgress."

909. *Thy weaker:* Cf. 1 Pet. 3.7: "Likewise, ye husbands, dwell with them according to knowledge, giving honour unto the wife, as unto the weaker vessel, and as being heirs together of the grace of life; that your prayers be not hindered."

Book VII

The Argument

Raphael at the request of Adam relates how and wherefore this world was first created; that God, after the expelling of Satan and his angels out of heaven, declared his pleasure to create another world and other creatures to dwell therein; sends his Son with glory and attendance of angels to perform the work of creation in six days: the angels celebrate with hymns the performance thereof, and his reascension into heaven.

> Descend from heav'n Urania, by that name
> If rightly thou art called, whose voice divine
> Following, above th' Olympian hill I soar,
> Above the flight of Pegasean wing.
> The meaning, not the name I call: for thou   5
> Nor of the muses nine, nor on the top
> Of old Olympus dwell'st, but heav'nly born,
> Before the hills appeared, or fountain flowed,
> Thou with eternal Wisdom didst converse,
> Wisdom thy sister, and with her didst play   10
> In presence of th' Almighty Father, pleased
> With thy celestial song. Up led by thee
> Into the heav'n of heav'ns I have presumed,
> An earthly guest, and drawn empyreal air,
> Thy temp'ring; with like safety guided down   15
> Return me to my native element:

VII.1. *Urania:* (Gk *Ourania* the heavenly one) the Muse of astronomy.

2–3. Cf. I.14–15. In Greek mythology, Mount Olympus was the dwelling place of the gods, and *Pegasus* was a winged horse, representing poetic inspiration, who dwelt in the heavens. See 17–20n, below.

5–12. Cf. the speech of Wisdom in Prov. 8.22–30, where she says "The Lord possessed me in the beginning of his way [*NEB:* "created me the beginning of his works"], before his works of old. I was set up from everlasting, from the beginning, or ever the earth was. When there were no depths, I was brought forth; when there were no fountains abounding with water. Before the mountains were settled, before the hills was I brought forth: While as yet he had not made the earth, nor the fields, nor the highest part of the dust of the world. When he prepared the heavens, I was there: when he set a compass upon the face of the depth: When he established the clouds above: when he strengthened the fountains of the deep: When he gave to the sea his decree, that the waters should not pass his commandment: when

he appointed the foundations of the earth: Then I was by him, as one brought up with him: and I was daily his delight, rejoicing always before him." Since Christ in the form of the Logos, or Word, was the only other agency or power said to have been present with God at the Creation, Wisdom's sibling would seem to be Christ. But Milton clearly does not pray for Christ's assistance. His Muse defies personification or deification; she is, we must think, the holy spirit that inspired Moses and other religious poets and prophets in the Judeo-Christian tradition. Nor may we doubt that Milton believed literally in her being or powers of performance. Milton called her Urania for want of a more appropriate or lovelier word.

9. *converse:* (L *con* with + *vertere* to turn about; *conversaria* to live, keep company with) associate, live.

15. *Thy temp'ring:* made suitable (for a mortal) by thee. The "air" of the empyrean was ethereal, not like the air of the earth's four elements. See "Universe," pp. 390–91.

16. *native element:* the earth.

Lest from this flying steed unreined (as once
Bellerophon, though from a lower clime)
Dismounted, on th' Aleian field I fall
Erroneous there to wander and forlorn.   20
Half yet remains unsung, but narrower bound
Within the visible diurnal sphere;
Standing on earth, not rapt above the pole,
More safe I sing with mortal voice, unchanged
To hoarse or mute, though fall'n on evil days,   25
On evil days though fall'n, and evil tongues;
In darkness, and with dangers compassed round,
And solitude; yet not alone, while thou
Visit'st my slumbers nightly, or when morn
Purples the east: still govern thou my song,   30
Urania, and fit audience find, though few.
But drive far off the barbarous dissonance
Of Bacchus and his revelers, the race
Of that wild rout that tore the Thracian bard
In Rhodope, where woods and rocks had ears   35
To rapture, till the savage clamor drowned
Both harp and voice; nor could the Muse defend
Her son. So fail not thou, who thee implores:
For thou art heav'nly, she an empty dream.
    Say goddess, what ensued when Raphael,   40
The affable Archangel, had forewarned
Adam by dire example to beware
Apostasy, by what befell in heaven
To those apostates, lest the like befall
In Paradise to Adam or his race,   45
Charged not to touch the interdicted tree,
If they transgress, and slight that sole command,
So easily obeyed amid the choice
Of all tastes else to please their appetite,

17–20. Pegasus *unreined* may be too dangerous a vehicle for any human being, but in the case of *Bellerophon*, Jupiter made Pegasus throw his rider. Milton alludes to *Bellerophon's* presumption in trying to gain forbidden knowledge as well as to the consequences, one of which, Hughes notes, was said to have been blindness. *Aleian:* (Gk wandering) the field on which *Bellerophon* fell, and was doomed to wander the rest of his life. *Erroneous:* wandering.

22. *diurnal sphere:* the universe, which is *diurnal* because from earth it all seems to revolve daily.

23. *rapt:* transported. *pole:* zenith of the universe; i.e., above the universe.

25–28. If Milton here refers to his personal life right after the Restoration, when he went into hiding for fear of arrest, *hoarse or mute* may mean the rejected options of speaking out polemi-

cally or not speaking at all. He has chosen to continue to "speak" as a poet, and now to speak more safely of earthly things, not heavenly. See Introduction for these matters as well as for his habits of composition referred to in line 29, as well as in III.32 and IX.22.

32–38. In Greek mythology, the music of Orpheus, the *Thracian bard*, son of the *Muse* Calliope, charmed even the *woods and rocks*, but he and his mother were unable to prevent his being murdered by a *wild rout* of Bacchanalian *revelers*, who threw his dismembered body in the Hebrus river, which rises in the *Rhodope* mountains, sacred to Bacchus. The *barbarous dissonance* is, perhaps, that of Restoration society.

43. *Apostasy:* (Gk *apo* away from + *stēnai* to stand) defection.

46. *touch.* Cf. Gen. 3.2,3, p. 355.

Though wand'ring. He with his consorted Eve   50
The·story heard attentive, and was filled
With admiration, and deep muse to hear
Of things so high and strange, things to their thought
So unimaginable as hate in heav'n,
And war so near the peace of God in bliss   55
With such confusion: but the evil soon
Driv'n back redounded as a flood on those
From whom it sprung, impossible to mix
With blessedness. Whence Adam soon repealed
The doubts that in his heart arose: and now   60
Led on, yet sinless, with desire to know
What nearer might concern him, how this world
Of heav'n and earth conspicuous first began,
When, and whereof created, for what cause,
What within Eden or without was done   65
Before his memory, as one whose drouth
Yet scarce allayed still eyes the current stream,
Whose liquid murmur heard new thirst excites,
Proceeded thus to ask his heav'nly guest.
    "Great things, and full of wonder in our ears,   70
Far differing from this world, thou hast revealed
Divine interpreter, by favor sent
Down from the empyrean to forewarn
Us timely of what might else have been our loss,
Unknown, which human knowledge could not reach: 75
For which to the Infinitely Good we owe
Immortal thanks, and his admonishment
Receive with solemn purpose to observe
Immutably his sovran will, the end
Of what we are. But since thou hast voutsafed   80
Gently for our instruction to impart
Things above earthly thought, which yet concerned
Our knowing, as to Highest Wisdom seemed,
Deign to descend now lower, and relate
What may no less perhaps avail us known,   85
How first began this heav'n which we behold
Distant so high, with moving fires adorned
Innumerable, and this which yields or fills
All space, the ambient air wide interfused
Embracing round this florid earth, what cause   90
Moved the Creator in his holy rest
Through all eternity so late to build
In chaos, and the work begun, how soon
Absolved, if unforbid thou may'st unfold

---

50. *consorted:* (L *con* with, together + *sors* lot, fate, share) wedded.
52. *admiration:* wonder, astonishment. *muse:* meditation.
57. *redounded:* L *re* back + *undare* to rise in waves.
59. *repealed:* gave up.

63. *conspicuous:* visible.
67. *current:* flowing.
79. *end:* purpose (i.e., to observe . . . his will).
90. *florid:* L *flos, floris* flower.
94. *Absolved:* finished.

What we, not to explore the secrets ask   95
Of his eternal empire, but the more
To magnify his works, the more we know.
And the great light of day yet wants to run
Much of his race though steep, suspense in heav'n
Held by thy voice, thy potent voice he hears,   100
And longer will delay to hear thee tell
His generation, and the rising birth
Of nature from the unapparent deep:
Or if the star of evening and the moon
Haste to thy audience, night with her will bring   105
Silence, and sleep list'ning to thee will watch,
Or we can bid his absence, till thy song
End, and dismiss thee ere the morning shine."
    Thus Adam his illustrious guest besought:
    And thus the godlike angel answered mild.   110
"This also thy request with caution asked
Obtain: though to recount almighty works
What words or tongue of Seraph can suffice,
Or heart of man suffice to comprehend?
Yet what thou canst attain, which best may serve   115
To glorify the Maker, and infer
Thee also happier, shall not be withheld
Thy hearing, such commission from above
I have received, to answer thy desire
Of knowledge within bounds; beyond abstain   120
To ask, nor let thine own inventions hope
Things not revealed, which th' invisible King,
Only omniscient, hath suppressed in night,
To none communicable in earth or heaven:
Enough is left besides to search and know.   125
But knowledge is as food, and needs no less
Her temperance over appetite, to know
In measure what the mind may well contain,
Oppresses else with surfeit, and soon turns
Wisdom to folly, as nourishment to wind.   130
    "Know then, that after Lucifer from heav'n
(So call him, brighter once amidst the host
Of angels, than that star the stars among)
Fell with his flaming legions through the deep
Into his place, and the great Son returned   135
Victorious with his saints, th' Omnipotent
Eternal Father from his throne beheld

97. Cf. Job 36.24: "Remember that thou magnify his work, which men behold."
99. *suspense:* attentive; also, hanging.
103. *unapparent deep:* chaos, invisible because without form.
106. *watch:* stay awake.
116. *infer:* (L *inferre* to bring about) make.

121. *inventions:* powers of discovery, as well as discoveries. Eccles. 7.29: "God hath made man upright; but they have sought out many inventions [i.e., subtleties, falsehoods]."
122–23. Cf. 1 Tim. 1.17: ". . . the King eternal, immortal, invisible, the only wise God. . . ."

Their multitude, and to his Son thus spake.
   " 'At least our envious foe hath failed, who thought
All like himself rebellious, by whose aid   140
This inaccessible high strength, the seat
Of Deity supreme, us dispossessed,
He trusted to have seized, and into fraud
Drew many, whom their place knows here no more;
Yet far the greater part have kept, I see,   145
Their station, heav'n yet populous retains
Number sufficient to possess her realms
Though wide, and this high temple to frequent
With ministeries due and solemn rites:
But lest his heart exalt him in the harm   150
Already done, to have dispeopled heav'n,
My damage fondly deemed, I can repair
That detriment, if such it be to lose
Self-lost, and in a moment will create
Another world, out of one man a race   155
Of men innumerable, there to dwell,
Not here, till by degrees of merit raised
They open to themselves at length the way
Up hither, under long obedience tried,
And earth be changed to heav'n, and heav'n to earth, 160
One kingdom, joy and union without end.
Meanwhile inhabit lax, ye Powers of heav'n;
And thou my Word, begotten Son, by thee
This I perform, speak thou, and be it done:
My overshadowing Spirit and might with thee 165
I send along, ride forth, and bid the deep
Within appointed bounds be heav'n and earth,
Boundless the deep, because I am who fill
Infinitude, nor vacuous the space.
Though I uncircumscribed myself retire,   170
And put not forth my goodness, which is free

139. *At least:* a misprint for "at last"?
142. *us dispossessed:* we having been dispossessed.
143. *fraud:* deception, error.
144. Cf. Job 7.10: "He shall return no more to his house, neither shall his place know him any more."
152. *fondly:* foolishly.
154–61. Cf. St. Augustine, *City of God*, XXII.i (trans. by Marcus Dods): "[God] at the same time foresaw what good He Himself would bring out of the evil, and how from this mortal race, deservedly and justly condemned, He would by this grace collect, as now He does, a people so numerous, that He thus fills up and repairs the blank made by the fallen angels, and that thus that . . . heavenly city is not defrauded of the full number of its citizens, but perhaps may even rejoice in a still more overflowing population."

162. *inhabit lax:* dwell loose, i.e., spread out and fill the vacancies left by the fallen angels.
163. Cf. III.170n. and John 1.1–4, p. 381.
165. Cf. Luke 1.35: "And the angel answered and said unto her, The Holy Ghost shall come upon thee, and the power of the Highest shall overshadow thee: therefore also that holy thing which shall be born of thee shall be called the Son of God."
168–73. If God fills *infinitude*, the universe could not have been created out of nothing. And even if God had *retired* from Chaos, or was not making his influence felt there, that did not mean that *fate* or *chance* ruled there. Nor was God forced by necessity to make the universe. Creation was an act of his free will. See *CD*, I.ii.A and I.vii.A.

To act or not, necessity and chance
Approach not me, and what I will is fate.'
    "So spake th' Almighty, and to what he spake
His Word, the Filial Godhead, gave effect.   175
Immediate are the acts of God, more swift
Than time or motion, but to human ears
Cannot without process of speech be told,
So told as earthly notion can receive.
Great triumph and rejoicing was in heav'n   180
When such was heard declared the Almighty's will;
Glory they sung to the Most High, good will
To future men, and in their dwellings peace:
Glory to him whose just avenging ire
Had driven out th' ungodly from his sight   185
And th' habitations of the just; to him
Glory and praise, whose wisdom had ordained
Good out of evil to create, instead
Of Spirits malign a better race to bring
Into their vacant room, and thence diffuse   190
His good to worlds and ages infinite.
So sang the hierarchies: meanwhile the Son
On his great expedition now appeared,
Girt with omnipotence, with radiance crowned
Of majesty divine, sapience and love   195
Immense, and all his Father in him shone.
About his chariot numberless were poured
Cherub and Seraph, Potentates and Thrones,
And Virtues, winged Spirits, and chariots winged,
From the armory of God, where stand of old   200
Myriads between two brazen mountains lodged
Against a solemn day, harnessed at hand,
Celestial equipage; and now came forth
Spontaneous, for within them spirit lived,
Attendant on their Lord: heav'n opened wide   205
Her ever-during gates, harmonious sound
On golden hinges moving, to let forth
The King of Glory in his powerful Word
And Spirit coming to create new worlds.
On heav'nly ground they stood, and from the shore   210
They viewed the vast immeasurable abyss
Outrageous as a sea, dark, wasteful, wild,
Up from the bottom turned by furious winds

---

179. *notion:* intellect.
182–83. Cf. Luke 2.13–14: "And suddenly there was with the angel a multitude of the heavenly host praising God, and saying, 'Glory to God in the highest, and on earth peace, good will toward men.' "
194. Cf. Ps. 18.39: "For thou hast girded me with strength unto the battle."
201. Cf. Zech. 6.1: "And I turned, and lifted up mine eyes, and looked, and, be-

hold, there came four chariots out from between two mountains; and the mountains were mountains of brass."
202. *Against:* in preparation for. *solemn:* appointed, festive, holy, important.
204. Cf. Ezek. 1.20, p. 379.
206–8. *during:* lasting. Cf. Ps. 24.9: "Lift up your heads, O ye gates; even lift them up, ye everlasting doors; and the King of glory shall come in."
212. *Outrageous:* violent.

And surging waves, as mountains to assault
Heav'n's highth, and with the center mix the pole.   215
    " 'Silence, ye troubled waves, and thou deep, peace,'
Said then th' Omnific Word, 'your discord end:'
    "Nor stayed, but on the wings of Cherubim
Uplifted, in paternal glory rode
Far into chaos, and the world unborn;   220
For chaos heard his voice: him all his train
Followed in bright procession to behold
Creation, and the wonders of his might.
Then stayed the fervid wheels, and in his hand
He took the golden compasses, prepared   225
In God's eternal store, to circumscribe
This universe, and all created things:
One foot he centered, and the other turned
Round through the vast profundity obscure,
And said, 'Thus far extend, thus far thy bounds,   230
This be thy just circumference, O world.'
Thus God the heav'n created, thus the earth,
Matter unformed and void: darkness profound
Covered th' abyss: but on the wat'ry calm
His brooding wings the Spirit of God outspread,   235
And vital virtue infused, and vital warmth
Throughout the fluid mass, but downward purged
The black tartareous cold infernal dregs
Adverse to life: then founded, then conglobed
Like things to like, the rest to several place   240
Disparted, and between spun out the air,
And earth self-balanced on her center hung.
    " 'Let there be light,' said God, and forthwith light
Ethereal, first of things, quintessence pure
Sprung from the deep, and from her native east   245
To journey through the airy gloom began,
Sphered in a radiant cloud, for yet the sun
Was not; she in a cloudy tabernacle
Sojourned the while. God saw the light was good;
And light from darkness by the hemisphere   250
Divided: light the day, and darkness night

216. Cf. Mark 4.39: "And he arose, and rebuked the wind, and said unto the sea, Peace, be still. And the wind ceased, and there was a great calm."
217. *Omnific:* all-creating.
224. *fervid:* burning.
225. Cf. Prov. 8.27.
232. From here on the account of creation follows that in Genesis; pp. 352–54.
233. *profound:* L *pro* out of + *fundus* bottom.
235. *brooding wings.* The Hebrew word translated in the King James version as "moved" also means "brood" or "hover." Cf. I.20–22 and note.
236. *virtue:* power.

238. *tartareous:* pertaining to Tartarus, in Greek myth the *infernal* region below Hades. The *dregs* are stuff other than the elements that constitute the universe.
239. *founded:* (L *fundere* to pour, melt, fuse) mixed together. *conglobed:* rolled into a ball.
242. Cf. Job 26.7: "He stretcheth out the north over the empty place, and hangeth the earth upon nothing."
244. *quintessence:* the fifth element, of which heavenly things are made. See "Universe," p. 390.
248. Cf. Ps. 19.4: "Their line is gone out through all the earth, and their words to the end of the world. In them hath he set a tabernacle for the sun."

He named. Thus was the first day ev'n and morn:
Nor passed uncelebrated, nor unsung
By the celestial choirs, when orient light
Exhaling first from darkness they beheld;   255
Birthday of heav'n and earth; with joy and shout
The hollow universal orb they filled,
And touched their golden harps, and hymning praised
God and his works, Creator him they sung,
Both when first evening was, and when first morn.   260
    "Again, God said, 'Let there be firmament
Amid the waters, and let it divide
The waters from the waters': and God made
The firmament, expanse of liquid, pure,
Transparent, elemental air, diffused   265
In circuit to the uttermost convex
Of this great round: partition firm and sure,
The waters underneath from those above
Dividing: for as earth, so he the world
Built on circumfluous waters calm, in wide   270
Crystálline ocean, and the loud misrule
Of Chaos far removed, lest fierce extremes
Contiguous might distemper the whole frame:
And heav'n he named the firmament: so ev'n
And morning chorus sung the second day.   275
    "The earth was formed, but in the womb as yet
Of waters, embryon immature involved,
Appeared not: over all the face of earth
Main ocean flowed, not idle, but with warm
Prolific humor soft'ning all her globe,   280
Fermented the great mother to conceive,
Satiate with genial moisture, when God said,
'Be gathered now ye waters under heav'n
Into one place, and let dry land appear.'
Immediately the mountains huge appear   285
Emergent, and their broad bare backs upheave
Into the clouds, their tops ascend the sky:
So high as heaved the tumid hills, so low
Down sunk a hollow bottom broad and deep,
Capacious bed of waters: thither they   290

252. *ev'n and morn:* night and day, or one twenty-four–hour period measured, as the Jews measure, from sundown to sundown. Cf. Gen. 1.5, p. 352.
253–4. See Job 38.6–7, p. 369.
261. *firmament.* See "Universe," p. 389.
264. *liquid:* clear, transparent, bright.
267. *this great round:* the universe.
269–70. Cf. Ps. 24.2: "For he [the Lord] hath founded it [the world] upon the seas, and established it upon the floods."
271. *Crystalline ocean:* not the crystal-line sphere. See "Universe," p. 389.
273. *distemper:* disturb the order and mixture of the elements. *frame.* See II.924n.
274. *heav'n:* the sky.
277. *involved:* enfolded.
279. *Main:* (as in "mainland," or "the ocean main") of great expanse.
280. *humor:* moisture.
282. *genial:* (L *genialis,* from *gignere* to beget) generative; cf. *Prolific humor* two lines above.
288. *tumid:* swollen.
290–306. Cf. Ps. 104, pp. 370–71.

Hasted with glad precipitance, uprolled
As drops on dust conglobing from the dry;
Part rise in crystal wall, or ridge direct,
For haste; such flight the great command impressed
On the swift floods: as armies at the call   295
Of trumpet (for of armies thou hast heard)
Troop to their standard, so the wat'ry throng,
Wave rolling after wave, where way they found,
If steep, with torrent rapture, if through plain,
Soft-ebbing; nor withstood them rock or hill,   300
But they, or under ground, or circuit wide
With serpent error wand'ring, found their way,
And on the washy ooze deep channels wore;
Easy, ere God had bid the ground be dry,
All but within those banks, where rivers now   305
Stream, and perpetual draw their humid train.
The dry land, earth, and the great receptacle
Of congregated waters he called seas:
And saw that it was good, and said, 'Let th' earth
Put forth the verdant grass, herb yielding seed,   310
And fruit-tree yielding fruit after her kind;
Whose seed is in herself upon the earth.'
He scarce had said, when the bare earth, till then
Desert and bare, unsightly, unadorned,
Brought forth the tender grass, whose verdure clad   315
Her universal face with pleasant green,
Then herbs of every leaf, that sudden flow'red
Op'ning their various colors, and made gay
Her bosom smelling sweet: and these scarce blown,
Forth flourished thick the clust'ring vine, forth crept   320
The swelling gourd, up stood the corny reed
Embattled in her field: add the humbled shrub,
And bush with frizzled hair implicit: last
Rose as in dance the stately trees, and spread
Their branches hung with copious fruit; or gemmed   325
Their blossoms: with high woods the hills were crowned,
With tufts the valleys and each fountain side,
With borders long the rivers. That earth now
Seemed like to heav'n, a seat where gods might dwell,
Or wander with delight, and love to haunt   330
Her sacred shades: though God had yet not rained
Upon the earth, and man to till the ground
None was, but from the earth a dewy mist
Went up and watered all the ground, and each
Plant of the field, which ere it was in the earth   335

299. *rapture:* L *repere* to sweep away.
302. Cf. *mazy error*, IV.239.
303. *washy ooze:* mud like that of a wash, or land alternately covered and exposed by the movement of the sea.
319. *blown:* blossomed.
321. *corny:* (L *cornus* horn) hard as horn. *reed:* cane, bamboo.
322. *humbled:* low-growing.
323. *implicit:* (L *implicare* to infold) tangled.
325. *gemmed:* L *gemmare* to put forth buds.

God made, and every herb, before it grew
On the green stem; God saw that it was good:
So ev'n and morn recorded the third day.
 "Again th' Almighty spake: 'Let there be lights
High in th' expanse of heaven to divide   340
The day from night; and let them be for signs,
For seasons, and for days, and circling years,
And let them be for lights as I ordain
Their office in the firmament of heav'n
To give light on the earth'; and it was so.   345
And God made two great lights, great for their use
To man, the greater to have rule by day,
The less by night altern: and made the stars,
And set them in the firmament of heav'n
To illuminate the earth, and rule the day   350
In their vicissitude, and rule the night,
And light from darkness to divide. God saw,
Surveying his great work, that it was good:
For of celestial bodies first the sun
A mighty sphere he framed, unlightsome first,   355
Though of ethereal mold: then formed the moon
Globose, and every magnitude of stars,
And sowed with stars the heav'n thick as a field:
Of light by far the greater part he took,
Transplanted from her cloudy shrine, and placed 360
In the sun's orb, made porous to receive
And drink the liquid light, firm to retain
Her gathered beams, great palace now of light.
Hither as to their fountain other stars
Repairing, in their golden urns draw light,   365
And hence the morning planet gilds her horns;
By tincture or reflection they augment
Their small peculiar, though from human sight
So far remote, with dimunition seen.
First in his east the glorious lamp was seen,   370
Regent of day, and all th' horizon round
Invested with bright rays, jocund to run
His longitude through heav'n's high road: the gray
Dawn, and the Pleiades before him danced
Shedding sweet influence: less bright the moon, 375
But opposite in leveled west was set
His mirror, with full face borrowing her light
From him, for other light she needed none

338. *recorded:* bore witness to.
351. *vicissitude:* regular alternation.
356. *mold:* stuff.
360. *cloudy shrine.* Cf. 248.
366. Through his telescope Galileo had discovered that Venus has phases, like the moon. In her first quarter her image was crescent-shaped.
367. *tincture:* absorption, as in dyeing.

368. *peculiar:* (L *peculium* private property) own (light).
371. *horizon:* rim of the image of the sun.
373. *longitude:* distance from east to west.
374. Cf. Job 38.31: "Canst thou bind the sweet influences of Pleiades, or loose the bands of Orion?"

In that aspéct, and still that distance keeps
Till night, then in the east her turn she shines,   380
Revolved on heav'n's great axle, and her reign
With thousand lesser lights dividual holds,
With thousand thousand stars, that then appeared
Spangling the hemisphere: then first adorned
With their bright luminaries that set and rose,   385
Glad evening and glad morn crowned the fourth day.
    And God said, 'Let the waters generate
Reptile with spawn abundant, living soul:
And let fowl fly above the earth, with wings
Displayed on the op'n firmament of heav'n.'   390
And God created the great whales, and each
Soul living, each that crept, which plenteously
The waters generated by their kinds,
And every bird of wing after his kind;
And saw that it was good, and blessed them, saying,   395
'Be fruitful, multiply, and in the seas
And lakes and running streams the waters fill;
And let the fowl be multiplied on the earth.'
Forthwith the sounds and seas, each creek and bay
With fry innumerable swarm, and shoals   400
Of fish that with their fins and shining scales
Glide under the green wave, in sculls that oft
Bank the mid-sea: part single or with mate
Graze the seaweed their pasture, and through groves
Of coral stray, or sporting with quick glance   405
Show to the sun their waved coats dropped with gold,
Or in their pearly shells at ease, attend
Moist nutriment, or under rocks their food
In jointed armor watch: on smooth the seal,
And bended dolphins play: part huge of bulk   410
Wallowing unwieldy, enormous in their gait
Tempest the ocean: there leviathan
Hugest of living creatures, on the deep
Stretched like a promontory sleeps or swims,
And seems a moving land, and at his gills   415
Draws in, and at his trunk spouts out a sea.
Meanwhile the tepid caves, and fens and shores
Their brood as numerous hatch, from th' egg that soon
Bursting with kindly rupture forth disclosed
Their callow young, but feathered soon and fledge   420

---

379. *In that aspect:* i.e., when full.
382. *dividual:* divided.
386. *Glad:* (OE *glæd* bright, glad)
bright, gay, beautiful.
388. *Reptile:* (L *repere* to creep)
snakes, lizards, etc.
390. *Displayed* (L *displicare* to un-
fold) spread out.
400. *shoals.* Like "schools" and per-

haps *sculls,* two lines below, *shoals* is
related to OE *scolu, sceolu,* a company,
crowd.
407. *attend:* (L *attendere* to stretch)
await or watch for.
412. *leviathan.* Cf. I.200–8n.
419. *kindly:* natural.
420. *callow:* without feathers. *fledge:*
fit to fly.

They summed their pens, and soaring th' air sublime
With clang despised the ground, under a cloud
In prospect; there the eagle and the stork
On cliffs and cedar tops their eyries build:
Part loosely wing the region, part more wise   425
In common, ranged in figure wedge their way,
Intelligent of seasons, and set forth
Their aery caravan high over seas
Flying, and over lands with mutual wing
Easing their flight; so steers the prudent crane   430
Her annual voyage, borne on winds; the air
Floats, as they pass, fanned with unnumbered plumes:
From branch to branch the smaller birds with song
Solaced the woods, and spread their painted wings
Till ev'n, nor then the solemn nightingale   435
Ceased warbling, but all night tuned her soft lays:
Others on silver lakes and rivers bathed
Their downy breast; the swan, with archèd neck
Between her white wings mantling proudly, rows
Her state with oary feet: yet oft they quit   440
The dank, and rising on stiff pennons, tow'r
The mid-aerial sky: others on ground
Walked firm; the crested cock whose clarion sounds
The silent hours, and th' other whose gay train
Adorns him, colored with the florid hue   445
Of rainbows and starry eyes. The waters thus
With fish replenished, and the air with fowl,
Evening and morn solemnized the fifth day.
    "The sixth, and the creation last arose
With evening harps and matin, when God said,   450
'Let th' earth bring forth soul living in her kind,
Cattle and creeping things, and beast of the earth,
Each in their kind.' The earth obeyed, and straight
Op'ning her fertile womb teemed at a birth
Innumerous living creatures, perfet forms,   455
Limbed and full grown: out of the ground up rose
As from his lair the wild beast where he wons

421. *summed their pens:* brought their feathers to full growth.
422–23. *clang:* cry, like that of cranes or geese. *despised:* literally, looked down upon (*the ground,* which seemed [*In prospect*] to be *under a cloud* of birds).
425. *loosely:* separately. *region:* the middle air; see 442 and note. See "Universe," pp. 390–91.
426. *In common:* in a convoy.
429–30. Ancient lore was that cranes rested in flight by placing their necks on the backs of birds in front of them. But Fowler notes St. Basil's belief that storks in flight "used their wings to support [those of] their ancient parents."
432. *Floats:* moves in waves.
434. *painted:* colored.

439. I.e.: proudly mantling herself between her white wings, or wearing her wings like a cloak. Cf. V.279.
440. *state:* a person of high rank: i.e., she rows her ladyship, as lords and ladies were rowed on the Thames.
441. *dank:* pond, lake, pool. *tow'r:* to fly high into.
442. *mid-aerial sky:* mid-air, the region of clouds and cold. Cf. *two black clouds . . . encounter in mid-air,* II.714–718.
444. *th' other:* the peacock.
447. *replenished:* (L *plenus* full) fully supplied, perfected, stocks. Cf. VIII.371n.
450. *matin:* morning.
454. *teemed:* bore, brought forth.
457. *wons:* dwells.

In forest wild, in thicket, brake, or den;
Among the trees in pairs they rose, they walked:
The cattle in the fields and meadows green: 460
Those rare and solitary, these in flocks
Pasturing at once, and in broad herds upsprung.
The grassy clods now calved, now half appeared
The tawny lion, pawing to get free
His hinder parts, then springs as broke from bonds,   465
And rampant shakes his brinded mane; the ounce,
The libbard, and the tiger, as the mole
Rising, the crumbled earth above them threw
In hillocks; the swift stag from under ground
Bore up his branching head: scarce from his mold   470
Behemoth biggest born of earth upheaved
His vastness: fleeced the flocks and bleating rose,
As plants: ambiguous between sea and land
The river-horse and scaly crocodile.
At once came forth whatever creeps the ground,   475
Insect or worm; those waved their limber fans
For wings, and smallest lineaments exact
In all the liveries decked of summer's pride
With spots of gold and purple, azure and green:
These as a line their long dimension drew,   480
Streaking the ground with sinuous trace; not all
Minims of nature; some of serpent kind
Wondrous in length and corpulence involved
Their snaky folds, and added wings. First crept
The parsimonious emmet, provident   485
Of future, in small room large heart enclosed,
Pattern of just equality perhaps
Hereafter, joined in her popular tribes
Of commonalty: swarming next appeared
The female bee that feeds her husband drone   490
Deliciously, and builds her waxen cells
With honey stored: the rest are numberless,
And thou their natures know'st, and gav'st them names,
Needless to thee repeated; nor unknown
The serpent subtlest beast of all the field,   495
Of huge extent sometimes, with brazen eyes
And hairy mane terrific, though to thee

461. *rare:* dispersed.
466. *brinded:* brindled.
467. *libbard:* leopard.
471. *Behemoth:* the name given by the translator of the King James version to the dragon-crocodile-hippopotamus-like amphibian described in Job 40.15–41.34, and also called leviathan. Commentators had identified the beast as an elephant, and as Fowler notes, line 474 suggests that Milton here was thinking of a land animal.
476. *worm:* any animal that worms its way.

478. *pride:* glory.
482. *Minims:* smallest animals.
483. *corpulence:* bulk. *involved:* coiled.
484. Cf. Isa. 30.6: ". . . the land of trouble and anguish, from whence come the young and old lion, the viper and fiery flying serpent."
485. *parsimonious:* (L *parcere* to spare) thrifty. *emmet:* ant.
486. *large heart:* great wisdom. See I.437–46n.
488–89. I.e., united in self-governing groups of common people.

Not noxious, but obedient at thy call.
Now heav'n in all her glory shone, and rolled
Her motions, as the great First Mover's hand   500
First wheeled their course; earth in her rich attire
Consummate lovely smiled; air, water, earth,
By fowl, fish, beast, was flown, was swum, was walked
Frequent; and of the sixth day yet remained;
There wanted yet the master work, the end   505
Of all yet done; a creature who not prone
And brute as other creatures, but endued
With sanctity of reason, might erect
His stature, and upright with front serene
Govern the rest, self-knowing, and from thence   510
Magnanimous to correspond with heav'n,
But grateful to acknowledge whence his good
Descends, thither with heart and voice and eyes
Directed in devotion, to adore
And worship God supreme, who made him chief   515
Of all his works: therefore th' Omnipotent
Eternal Father (for where is not he
Present) thus to his Son audibly spake.
   " 'Let us make now man in our image, man
In our similitude, and let them rule   520
Over the fish and fowl of sea and air,
Beast of the field, and over all the earth,
And every creeping thing that creeps the ground.'
This said, he formed thee, Adam, thee O man
Dust of the ground, and in thy nostrils breathed   525
The breath of life; in his own image he
Created thee, in the image of God
Express, and thou becam'st a living soul.
Male he created thee, but thy consórt
Female for race; then blessed mankind, and said,   530
'Be fruitful, multiply, and fill the earth,
Subdue it, and throughout dominion hold
Over fish of the sea, and fowl of the air,
And every living thing that moves on the earth.'
Wherever thus created, for no place   535
Is yet distinct by name, thence, as thou know'st
He brought thee into this delicious grove,

502. *Consummate.* See V.481n.
504. *Frequent:* (L *frequens* crowded) in throngs.
505–16. The syntax of this sentence is elliptical: There wanted yet . . . a creature who . . . might erect . . . and . . . govern . . . and from these virtues might be sufficiently magnanimous to correspond with heaven yet sufficiently grateful to acknowledge whence his good descends and (consequently?), with his heart . . . directed in devotion thither (i.e., whence his good descends), to adore, etc. *end:*

purpose. *sanctity:* the virtue or blessing of holiness which sets the sanctified apart. *front:* face. *Magnanimous:* great-souled, noble, high-minded, self-respecting. *correspond:* confer, consult, converse. The notion that man's erect stance is a sign of his superiority over all other animals is ancient.
528. *Express:* exact. Cf. Heb. 1.1–3: "God . . . hath . . . spoken to us by his Son, Who being . . . the express image of his person, etc."
537. *delicious.* See IV.132n.

This garden, planted with the trees of God,
Delectable both to behold and taste;
And freely all their pleasant fruit for food   540
Gave thee, all sorts are here that all th' earth yields,
Variety without end; but of the tree
Which tasted works knowledge of good and evil,
Thou may'st not; in the day thou eat'st, thou di'st;
Death is the penalty imposed, beware,   545
And govern well thy appetite, lest Sin
Surprise thee, and her black attendant Death.
Here finished he, and all that he had made
Viewed, and behold all was entirely good;
So ev'n and morn accomplished the sixth day: 550
Yet not till the Creator from his work
Desisting, though unwearied, up returned
Up to the heav'n of heav'ns his high abode,
Thence to behold his new-created world
Th' addition of his empire, how it showed   555
In prospct from his throne, how good, how fair,
Answering his great idea. Up he rode
Followed with acclamation and the sound
Symphonious of ten thousand harps that tuned
Angelic harmonies: the earth, the air   560
Resounded (thou remember'st, for thou heard'st),
The heav'ns and all the constellations rung,
The planets in their stations list'ning stood,
While the bright pomp ascended jubilant.
'Open, ye everlasting gates,' they sung,   565
'Open, ye heav'ns, your living doors; let in
The great Creator from his work returned
Magnificent, his six days' work, a world;
Open, and henceforth oft; for God will deign
To visit oft the dwellings of just men   570
Delighted, and with frequent intercourse
Thither will send his wingèd messengers
On errands of supernal grace.' So sung
The glorious train ascending: he through heav'n,
That opened wide her blazing portals, led   575
To God's eternal house direct the way,
A broad and ample road, whose dust is gold
And pavement stars, as stars to thee appear,
Seen in the Galaxy, that Milky Way
Which nightly as a circling zone thou seest   580
Powdered with stars. And now on earth the seventh
Evening arose in Eden, for the sun
Was set, and twilight from the east came on,

557. *idea:* (Gk *idein* to see) eternal
archetype or pattern, as in Plato; image
or concept (in the mind of God).
559. *Symphonious:* harmonious.
564. *pomp:* procession. *jubilant:* (L

jubilum a wild cry, shout) making a joy-
ful noise.
565–66. Cf. 206–8n.
575. *blazing:* effulgent, radiant.
580. *zone:* belt.

Forerunning night; when at the holy mount
Of heav'n's high-seated top, th' imperial throne   585
Of Godhead, fixed forever firm and sure,
The Filial Power arrived, and sat him down
With his great Father, for he also went
Invisible, yet stayed (such privilege
Hath Omnipresence) and the work ordained,   590
Author and end of all things, and from work
Now resting, blessed and hallowed the sev'nth day,
As resting on that day from all his work,
But not in silence holy kept; the harp
Had work and rested not, the solemn pipe,   595
And dulcimer, all organs of sweet stop,
All sounds on fret by string or golden wire
Tempered soft tunings, intermixed with voice
Choral or unison: of incense clouds
Fuming from golden censers hid the mount.   600
Creation and the six days' acts they sung:
'Great are thy works, Jehovah, infinite
Thy power; what thought can measure thee or tongue
Relate thee; greater now in thy return
Than from the giant angels; thee that day   605
Thy thunders magnified; but to create
Is greater than created to destroy.
Who can impair thee, mighty king, or bound
Thy empire? Easily the proud attempt
Of Spirits apostate and their counsels vain   610
Thou hast repelled, while impiously they thought
Thee to diminish, and from thee withdraw
The number of thy worshipers. Who seeks
To lessen thee, against his purpose serves
To manifest the more thy might: his evil   615
Thou usest, and from thence creat'st more good.
Witness this new-made world, another heav'n
From heaven gate not far, founded in view
On the clear hyaline, the glassy sea;
Of amplitude almost immense, with stars   620
Numerous, and every star perhaps a world
Of destined habitation; but thou know'st

588–90. *he:* the Father. *went Invisible.*
Cf. 165 and 196. *ordained:* ordered, en-
acted.
596. *dulcimer.* Fowler notes that "the
dulcimer is here not the stringed instru-
ment usually called by that name, but
the Hebrew 'bagpipe' (Gk *symphonia*)."
organs: wind instruments.
598. *Tempered:* brought into harmony.
tunings: musical sounds.
599–600. Cf. Rev. 8.3: "And another
angel came and stood at the altar, having
a golden censer; and there was given unto

him much incense, that he should offer
it with the prayers of all saints upon
the golden altar which was before the
throne."
599. *Choral:* in parts.
608. *impair:* (LL *impejorare* to make
worse) diminish, lessen.
619. See "Universe," p. 389. *hy-*
aline. From the word for glass used in
the Greek of Rev. 4.6, p. 384.
620. *immense:* (L *im* not + *mensus*
measured) immeasurable.
621–22. See III.566n.

Their seasons: among these the seat of men,
Earth with her nether ocean circumfused,
Their pleasant dwelling-place. Thrice happy men,   625
And sons of men, whom God hath thus advanced,
Created in his image, there to dwell
And worship him, and in reward to rule
Over his works, on earth, in sea, or air,
And multiply a race of worshipers   630
Holy and just: thrice happy if they know
Their happiness, and persevere upright.'
    "So sung they, and the empyrean rung,
With hallelujahs: thus was Sabbath kept.
And thy request think now fulfilled, that asked   635
How first this world and face of things began,
And what before thy memory was done
From the beginning, that posterity
Informed by thee might know; if else thou seek'st
Aught, not surpassing human measure, say."   640

623. *seasons.* As in Acts 1.6–7: "They asked of [Christ] . . . wilt thou at this time restore again the kingdom of Israel? And he said . . . it is not for you to know the times or the seasons, which the Father hath put in his own power."

624. *nether ocean:* the waters below the firmament. Cf. 261–73.

632. *persevere.* In theology perseverance means "continuance in a state of grace until it is succeeded by a state of glory."

634. *hallelujahs.* See II.243n.

Book VIII

The Argument

Adam inquires concerning celestial motions, is doubtfully answered, and exhorted to search rather things more worthy of knowledge: Adam assents, and still desirous to detain Raphael, relates to him what he remembered since his own creation, his placing in Paradise, his talk with God concerning solitude and fit society, his first meeting and nuptials with Eve, his discourse with the angel thereupon; who after admonitions repeated departs.

The angel ended, and in Adam's ear
So charming left his voice, that he a while
Thought him still speaking, still stood fixed to hear;
Then as new-waked thus gratefully replied.
"What thanks sufficient, or what recompense   5
Equal have I to render thee, divine
Historian, who thus largely hast allayed
The thirst I had of knowledge, and voutsafed
This friendly condescension to relate
Things else by me unsearchable, now heard   10
With wonder, but delight, and, as is due,
With glory attribúted to the high
Creator; something yet of doubt remains,
Which only thy solution can resolve.
When I behold this goodly frame, this world   15
Of heav'n and earth consisting, and compute
Their magnitudes, this earth a spot, a grain,
An atom, with the firmament compared
And all her numbered stars, that seem to roll
Spaces incomprehensible (for such   20
Their distance argues and their swift return
Diurnal) merely to officiate light
Round this opacous earth, this punctual spot,
One day and night; in all their vast survey
Useless besides; reasoning I oft admire,   25
How nature wise and frugal could commit
Such disproportions, with superfluous hand
So many nobler bodies to create,
Greater so manifold, to this one use,

VIII.1–4. When he divided Book VII of the first, ten-book edition into Books VII and VIII of the present, twelve-book edition, Milton replaced a line reading "To whom thus Adam gratefully replied" with these introductory lines.

2. *charming*: (L *canere* to sing, as in English *chant*) spell-binding.

11. *but*. This conjunction suggests that *wonder* implies some puzzlement or effort to understand.

14. *solution*: (L *solvere* to loosen) ex-

planation.

15. *frame*. See II.924n.

16. *compute*: (L *com* + *putare* to reckon, think). take account of, consider.

19. *numbered*: numerous.

22. *officiate*: supply.

23. *opacous*: L *opacus* shady, dark. *punctual*: (L *punctus* point) as small as a point.

25. *admire*: wonder.

29. *Greater so manifold:* so many times greater.

167

For aught appears, and on their orbs impose   30
Such restless revolution day by day
Repeated, while the sedentary earth,
That better might with far less compass move,
Served by more noble than herself, attains
Her end without least motion, and receives,   35
As tribute such a sumless journey brought
Of incorporeal speed, her warmth and light;
Speed, to describe whose swiftness number fails."
    So spake our sire, and by his count'nance seemed
Ent'ring on studious thoughts abstruse, which Eve   40
Perceiving where she sat retired in sight,
With lowliness majestic from her seat,
And grace that won who saw to wish her stay,
Rose, and went forth among her fruits and flow'rs,
To visit how they prospered, bud and bloom,   45
Her nursery; they at her coming sprung
And touched by her fair tendance gladlier grew.
Yet went she not as not with such discourse
Delighted, or not capable her ear
Of what was high: such pleasure she reserved,   50
Adam relating, she sole auditress;
Her husband the relater she preferred
Before the angel, and of him to ask
Chose rather; he, she knew would intermix
Grateful digressions, and solve high dispute   55
With conjugal caresses, from his lip
Not words alone pleased her. O when meet now
Such pairs, in love and mutual honor joined?
With goddess-like demeanor forth she went;
Not unattended, for on her as queen   60
A pomp of winning Graces waited still,
And from about her shot darts of desire
Into all eyes to wish her still in sight.
And Raphael now to Adam's doubt proposed
Benevolent and facile thus replied.   65
    "To ask or search I blame thee not, for heav'n
Is as the book of God before thee set,
Wherein to read his wondrous works, and learn
His seasons, hours, or days, or months, or years:
This to attain, whether heav'n move or earth,   70
Imports not, if thou reckon right; the rest
From man or angel the great Architect
Did wisely to conceal, and not divulge
His secrets to be scanned by them who ought

---

30. *For aught appears:* as far as can
be seen.
36. *sumless journey:* immeasurable dis-
tance.
45. *visit:* (L *videre* to see) to go to see.
46. *Her nursery:* the objects of her
nursing.
55. *high dispute:* profound debate.
61. *pomp.* See V.353n. *Graces.* See
IV.267n.
65. *facile:* easy and mild in manner.
74. *scanned:* judged critically.

Rather admire; or if they list to try   75
Conjecture, he his fabric of the heav'ns
Hath left to their disputes, perhaps to move
His laughter at their quaint opinions wide
Hereafter, when they come to model heav'n
And calculate the stars, how they will wield   80
The mighty frame, how build, unbuild, contrive
To save appearances, how gird the sphere
With centric and eccentric scribbled o'er,
Cycle and epicycle, orb in orb:
Already by thy reasoning this I guess,   85
Who art to lead thy offspring, and supposest
That bodies bright and greater should not serve
The less not bright, nor heav'n such journeys run,
Earth sitting still, when she alone receives
The benefit: consider first, that great   90
Or bright infers not excellence: the earth
Though, in comparison of heav'n, so small,
Nor glistering, may of solid good contain
More plenty than the sun that barren shines,
Whose virtue on itself works no effect,   95
But in the fruitful earth; there first received
His beams, unactive else, their vigor find.
Yet not to earth are those bright luminaries
Officious, but to thee earth's habitant.
And for the heav'n's wide circuit, let it speak   100
The Maker's high magnificence, who built
So spacious, and his line stretched out so far;
That man may know he dwells not in his own;
An edifice too large for him to fill,
Lodged in a small partition, and the rest   105
Ordained for uses to his Lord best known.
The swiftness of those circles áttribute,
Though numberless, to his omnipotence,
That to corporeal substances could add
Speed almost spiritual; me thou think'st not slow,   110
Who since the morning hour set out from heav'n
Where God resides, and ere mid-day arrived
In Eden, distance inexpressible

75. *admire:* marvel.
76. *fabric:* structural plan, design.
78. *wide:* as in "wide of the mark."
80. *calculate:* arrange, design; or, anticipate movements mathematically. *wield:* manage, deal with.
81–82. *contrive/To save appearances:* try to find explanations for the apparent inadequacies of their hypotheses.
83–84. Both Ptolemaic and Copernican astronomies resorted to complicated theories to explain variations (apparent irregularities) in the motions of the planets.
91. *infers:* implies, brings about.

96–97. The sun's beams perform no function until the earth has *received* them.
99. *Officious.* Cf. *officiate*, line 22.
100. *speak:* bespeak.
102. Cf. Job 38.5: "Who hath laid the measures thereof, if thou knowest? or who hath stretched the line upon it?"
107. *attribute:* pay tribute.
108. *numberless.* Probably modifies swiftness, as Fowler notes. Cf. 36n.
110. *Speed almost spiritual:* almost the speed of thought. Cf. *incorporeal speed*, line 37.

By numbers that have name. But this I urge,
Admitting motion in the heav'ns, to show   115
Invalid that which thee to doubt it moved;
Not that I so affirm, though so it seem
To thee who hast thy dwelling here on earth.
God to remove his ways from human sense,
Placed heav'n from earth so far, that earthly sight,   120
If it presume, might err in things too high,
And no advantage gain. What if the sun
Be center to the world, and other stars
By his attractive virtue and their own
Incited, dance about him various rounds?   125
Their wand'ring course now high, now low, then hid,
Progressive, retrograde, or standing still,
In six thou seest, and what if sev'nth to these
The planet earth, so steadfast though she seem,
Insensibly three different motions move?   130
Which else to several spheres thou must ascribe,
Moved contrary with thwart obliquities,
Or save the sun his labor, and that swift
Nocturnal and diurnal rhomb supposed,
Invisible else above all stars, the wheel   135
Of day and night; which needs not thy belief,
If earth industrious of herself fetch day
Traveling east, and with her part averse
From the sun's beam meet night, her other part
Still luminous by his ray. What if that light   140
Sent from her through the wide transpicuous air,

115–18. Raphael carefully does not grant Adam's assumption that because the planets seem to revolve about the earth, they in fact do.

122–40. For background, see "Universe," pp. 389–90. Raphael simply raises the possibility that what appears to Adam as movements in the heavens are largely the result of movements of the earth as it spins on its axis and, like the "other" planets, orbits the sun. Such an hypothesis should relieve Adam of his doubts about the "disproportions" (line 27) he had found in nature's design, for it would (1) place the tiny earth elsewhere than the center of the universe, (2) eliminate the need to imagine the speed (*labor*, line 133) of the sun in his daily orbit of the earth, and (3) dispense with the *supposed* device of the *primum mobile* (*that swift nocturnal and diurnal rhomb*), which was, after all, *invisible*. Milton, we may assume, was here more interested in the nature of scientific speculation and the limits of knowledge than in the details of the contemporary scientific debate, which would not, in any event, have been relevant to a dialogue between an angel and prelapsarian man, whose world, incidentally, moved differently from that of postlapsarian man.

Newton was about twenty when Milton wrote these lines, but Kepler had already suggested that the *attractive virtue* (power) of the sun moved the planets. See III.582–83n. *rounds:* circular dances. *wand'ring.* The Greek word *planētēs* means wanderer. *Progressive:* moving in the direction of the general planetary course; *retrograde* is the opposite. *three motions.* About the third, editors disagree. Adam could not have observed precession of the equinoxes (a phenomenon with a cycle of nearly 26,000 years) because before the Fall there were no equinoxes by which to measure precession—the earth's axis then being perpendicular to the plane of its orbit. Fowler, citing J. L. E. Dreyer, *A History of Astronomy from Thales to Kepler* (1953), p. 328, notes that Copernicus's third motion was not the tilt of the earth's axis (which causes the semiannual equinoxes) but an incorrectly hypothecated swivel of the axis which would account for a phenomenon which Adam might have observed (inaccurately, as it turned out): "that the axis of the earth . . . always points to the same spot in the celestial sphere." *rhomb:* (Gk *rombos* a top, spinning motion, magic wheel) the *primum mobile*.

To the terrestrial moon be as a star
Enlight'ning her by day, as she by night
This earth? Reciprocal, if land be there,
Fields and inhabitants: her spots thou seest   145
As clouds, and clouds may rain, and rain produce
Fruits in her softened soil, for some to eat
Allotted there; and other suns perhaps
With their attendant moons thou wilt descry
Communicating male and female light,   150
Which two great sexes animate the world,
Stored in each orb perhaps with some that live.
For such vast room in nature unpossessed
By living soul, desert and desolate,
Only to shine, yet scarce to cóntribute   155
Each orb a glimpse of light, conveyed so far
Down to this habitable, which returns
Light back to them, is obvious to dispute.
But whether thus these things, or whether not,
Whether the sun predominant in heav'n   160
Rise on the earth, or earth rise on the sun,
He from the east his flaming road begin,
Or she from west her silent course advance
With inoffensive pace that spinning sleeps
On her soft axle, while she paces ev'n,   165
And bears thee soft with the smooth air along,
Solicit not thy thoughts with matters hid,
Leave them to God above, him serve and fear;
Of other creatures, as him pleases best,
Wherever placed, let him dispose: joy thou   170
In what he gives to thee, this Paradise
And thy fair Eve; heav'n is for thee too high
To know what passes there; be lowly wise:
Think only what concerns thee and thy being;
Dream not of other worlds, what creatures there   175
Live, in what state, condition, or degree,
Contented that thus far hath been revealed
Not of earth only but of highest heav'n."
　　To whom thus Adam cleared of doubt, replied.
"How fully hast thou satisfied me, pure   180
Intelligence of heav'n, angel serene,
And freed from intricacies, taught to live
The easiest way, nor with perplexing thoughts
To interrupt the sweet of life, from which
God hath bid dwell far off all anxious cares,   185
And not molest us, unless we ourselves
Seek them with wand'ring thoughts, and notions vain.

153–58. I.e.: For whether such vast
room in nature is unpossessed . . . is
open to question.
　164. *inoffensive:* (L *offendare* to strike
against, stumble, injure; Engl. *to offend*

to stumble) without stumbling.
　167. *Solicit:* disturb.
　181. *Intelligence:* intelligent or rational
being, spirit. *serene:* pure, clear, bright,
calm, steady.

But apt the mind or fancy is to rove
Unchecked, and of her roving is no end;
Till warned, or by experience taught, she learn,   190
That not to know at large of things remote
From use, obscure and subtle, but to know
That which before us lies in daily life,
Is the prime wisdom; what is more, is fume,
Or emptiness, or fond impertinence,   195
And renders us in things that most concern
Unpracticed, unprepared, and still to seek.
Therefore from this high pitch let us descend
A lower flight, and speak of things at hand
Useful, whence haply mention may arise   200
Of something not unseasonable to ask
By sufferance, and thy wonted favor deigned.
Thee I have heard relating what was done
Ere my remembrance: now hear me relate
My story, which perhaps thou hast not heard;   205
And day is yet not spent; till then thou seest
How subtly to detain thee I devise,
Inviting thee to hear while I relate,
Fond, were it not in hope of thy reply:
For while I sit with thee, I seem in heav'n,   210
And sweeter thy discourse is to my ear
Than fruits of palm-tree pleasantest to thirst
And hunger both, from labor, at the hour
Of sweet repast; they satiate, and soon fill,
Though pleasant, but thy words with grace divine   215
Imbued, bring to their sweetness no satiety."
      To whom thus Raphael answered heav'nly meek.
"Nor are thy lips ungraceful, sire of men,
Nor tongue ineloquent; for God on thee
Abundantly his gifts hath also poured   220
Inward and outward both, his image fair:
Speaking or mute all comeliness and grace
Attends thee, and each word, each motion forms.
Nor less think we in heav'n of thee on earth
Than of our fellow-servant, and inquire   225
Gladly into the ways of God with man:
For God we see hath honored thee, and set
On man his equal love: say therefore on;
For I that day was absent, as befell,
Bound on a voyage uncouth and obscure,   230
Far on excursion toward the gates of hell;
Squared in full legion (such command we had)

---

194. *fume:* vapor; something unsub-
stantial; something that "goes to the
head" and clouds the reason.
195. *fond impertinence:* foolish irrele-
vance.
197. *still to seek:* always lacking.

198. *pitch:* summit.
218. Cf. Ps. 45.2: "Grace is poured
into thy lips: therefore God hath blessed
thee for ever."
230. *uncouth:* strange.

To see that none thence issued forth a spy,
Or enemy, while God was in his work,
Lest he incensed at such eruption bold,   235
Destruction with creation might have mixed.
Not that they durst without his leave attempt,
But us he sends upon his high behests
For state, as sovran King, and to inure
Our prompt obedience. Fast we found, fast shut   240
The dismal gates, and barricadoed strong;
But long ere our approaching heard within
Noise, other than the sound of dance or song,
Torment, and loud lament, and furious rage.
Glad we returned up to the coasts of light   245
Ere Sabbath evening: so we had in charge.
But thy relation now; for I attend,
Pleased with thy words no less than thou with mine."
    So spake the godlike Power, and thus our sire.
"For man to tell how human life began   250
Is hard; for who himself beginning knew?
Desire with thee still longer to converse
Induced me. As new-waked from soundest sleep
Soft on the flow'ry herb I found me laid
In balmy sweat, which with his beams the sun   255
Soon dried, and on the reeking moisture fed.
Straight toward heav'n my wond'ring eyes I turned,
And gazed a while the ample sky, till raised
By quick instinctive motion up I sprung,
As thitherward endeavoring, and upright   260
Stood on my feet; about me round I saw
Hill, dale, and shady woods, and sunny plains,
And liquid lapse of murmuring streams; by these,
Creatures that lived, and moved, and walked, or flew,
Birds on the branches warbling; all things smiled,   265
With fragrance and with joy my heart o'erflowed.
Myself I then perused, and limb by limb
Surveyed, and sometimes went, and sometimes ran
With supple joints, as lively vigor led:
But who I was, or where, or from what cause,   270
Knew not; to speak I tried, and forthwith spake,
My tongue obeyed and readily could name
Whate'er I saw. 'Thou sun,' said I, 'fair light,
And thou enlightened earth, so fresh and gay,
Ye hills and dales, ye rivers, woods, and plains,   275
And ye that live and move, fair creatures, tell,
Tell, if ye saw, how came I thus, how here?
Not of myself; by some great Maker then,
In goodness and in power preeminent;

239. *For state:* as expressions of his power and glory. *inure:* strengthen by exercise.
246. *Sabbath evening:* eve of the Seventh Day.
256. *reeking moisture:* vapor.
263. *lapse:* (L *labi* to slip, slide) flow.
268. *went:* walked.

Tell me, how may I know him, how adore,   280
From whom I have that thus I move and live,
And feel that I am happier than I know.'
While thus I called, and strayed I knew not wither,
From where I first drew air, and first beheld
This happy light, when answer none returned,   285
On a green shady bank profuse of flow'rs
Pensive I sat me down; there gentle sleep
First found me, and with soft oppression seized
My drowsèd sense, untroubled, though I thought
I then was passing to my former state   290
Insensible, and forthwith to dissolve:
When suddenly stood at my head a dream,
Whose inward apparition gently moved
My fancy to believe I yet had being,
And lived: one came, methought, of shape divine,   295
And said, 'Thy mansion wants thee, Adam, rise,
First man, of men innumerable ordained
First father, called by thee I come thy guide
To the garden of bliss, thy seat prepared.'
So saying, by the hand he took me raised,   300
And over fields and waters, as in air
Smooth sliding without step, last led me up
A woody mountain; whose high top was plain,
A circuit wide, enclosed, with goodliest trees
Planted, with walks, and bowers, that what I saw   305
Of earth before scarce pleasant seemed. Each tree
Load'n with fairest fruit, that hung to the eye
Tempting, stirred in me sudden appetite
To pluck and eat; whereat I waked, and found
Before mine eyes all real, as the dream   310
Had lively shadowed: here had new begun
My wand'ring, had not he who was my guide
Up hither, from among the trees appeared,
Presence Divine. Rejoicing, but with awe
In adoration at his feet I fell   315
Submiss: he reared me, and 'Whom thou sought'st I am,'
Said mildly, 'Author of all this thou seest
Above, or round about thee or beneath.
This paradise I give thee, count it thine
To till and keep, and of the fruit to eat: 320
Of every tree that in the garden grows
Eat freely with glad heart; fear here no dearth:
But of the tree whose operation brings

281. Cf. Acts 17.28: [St. Paul preach-
ing in Athens said] "For in him we live,
and move, and have our being; as cer-
tain also of your own poets have said,
For we are also his offspring."
    296. *mansion:* dwelling place. *wants:*
lacks.

299. *seat:* residence.
311. *lively:* vividly.
316. *Submiss:* submissive.
320. *keep:* care for.
323. *operation:* (L *operari* to work)
action.

Knowledge of good and ill, which I have set
The pledge of thy obedience and thy faith,   325
Amid the garden by the Tree of Life,
Remember what I warn thee, shun to taste,
And shun the bitter consequence: for know,
The day thou eat'st thereof, my sole command
Transgressed, inevitably thou shalt die;   330
From that day mortal, and this happy state
Shalt lose, expelled from hence into a world
Of woe and sorrow.' Sternly he pronounced
The rigid interdiction, which resounds
Yet dreadful in mine ear, though in my choice   335
Not to incur; but soon his clear aspéct
Returned and gracious purpose thus renewed.
'Not only these fair bounds, but all the earth
To thee and to thy race I give; as lords
Possess it, and all things that therein live,   340
Or live in sea, or air, beast, fish, and fowl.
In sign whereof each bird and beast behold
After their kinds; I bring them to receive
From thee their names, and pay thee fealty
With low subjection; understand the same   345
Of fish within their wat'ry residence,
Not hither summoned, since they cannot change
Their element to draw the thinner air.'
As thus he spake, each bird and beast behold
Approaching two and two, these cow'ring low   350
With blandishment, each bird stooped on his wing.
I named them, as they passed, and understood
Their nature, with such knowledge God endued
My sudden apprehension: but in these
I found not what methought I wanted still;   355
And to the heav'nly Vision thus presumed.
    " 'O by what name, for thou above all these,
Above mankind, or aught than mankind higher,
Surpassest far my naming, how may I
Adore thee, Author of this universe,   360
And all this good to man, for whose well-being
So amply, and with hands so liberal
Thou hast provided all things: but with me
I see not who partakes. In solitude
What happiness, who can enjoy alone,   365

325. *pledge.* See III.95 and note; also
IV.428.
329–31. Milton followed the language
of Genesis: "in the day that thou eatest
thereof thou shalt surely die." But since
Adam did not die on that day, Milton
followed the commentators who inter-
preted *die* to mean *From that day mortal*,
i.e., subject to death. See *CD*, I.xii.A.
335–36. I.e.: Though it is within my
power to choose not to incur this doom.

337. *purpose:* speech.
343–44. See *CD*, I.vii.F.
350. *cow'ring:* stooping.
351. *blandishment:* flattering gesture.
stooped: (a participle, like *cow'ring*)
swooped down, like a bird of prey (a
term from falconry). But Milton is think-
ing of another term from falconry, cow-
ering, which meant, "The quivering of
young hawks, who shake their wings, in
sign of obedience to the old ones."

Or all enjoying, what contentment find?'
Thus I presumptuous; and the Vision bright,
As with a smile more brightened, thus replied.
    " 'What call'st thou solitude? Is not the earth
With various living creatures, and the air   370
Replenished, and all these at thy command
To come and play before thee? Know'st thou not
Their language and their ways? They also know,
And reason not contemptibly; with these
Find pastime, and bear rule; thy realm is large.'   375
So spake the Universal Lord, and seemed
So ordering. I with leave of speech implored,
And humble deprecation thus replied.
    " 'Let not my words offend thee, Heav'nly Power,
My Maker, be propitious while I speak.   380
Hast thou not made me here thy substitute,
And these inferior far beneath me set?
Among unequals what society
Can sort, what harmony or true delight?
Which must be mutual, in proportion due   385
Giv'n and received; but in disparity
The one intense, the other still remiss
Cannot well suit with either, but soon prove
Tedious alike: of fellowship I speak
Such as I seek, fit to participate   390
All rational delight, wherein the brute
Cannot be human consort; they rejoice
Each with their kind, lion with lioness;
So fitly them in pairs thou hast combined;
Much less can bird with beast, or fish with fowl   395
So well converse, nor with the ox the ape;
Worse then can man with beast, and least of all.'
    "Whereto th' Almighty answered, not displeased.
'A nice and subtle happiness I see
Thou to thyself proposest, in the choice   400
Of thy associates, Adam, and wilt taste
No pleasure, though in pleasure, solitary.
What think'st thou then of me, and this my state,
Seem I to thee sufficiently possessed
Of happiness, or not? who am alone   405
From all eternity, for none I know
Second to me or like, equal much less.
How have I then with whom to hold converse
Save with the creatures which I made, and those
To me inferior, infinite descents   410

371. *Replenished:* fully stocked.
373. *know:* have knowledge and understanding.
384. *sort:* consort, meet as equals.
387. *intense:* (L *intendere* to stretch out) high-strung in a musical sense; therefore of one pitch (high). *remiss:* (L *remittere* to send back, relax) low strung, of low pitch.
390. *participate:* partake of.
396. *converse:* L *conversari* to keep company with.
399. *nice:* discriminating.

Beneath what other creatures are to thee?'
"He ceased, I lowly answered. 'To attain
The highth and depth of thy eternal ways
All human thoughts come short, Supreme of things;
Thou in thyself art perfet, and in thee   415
Is no deficience found; not so is man,
But in degree, the cause of his desire
By conversation with his like to help,
Or solace his defects. No need that thou
Shouldst propagate, already infinite;   420
And through all numbers absolute, though One;
But man by number is to manifest
His single imperfection, and beget
Like of his like, his image multiplied,
In unity defective, which requires   425
Collateral love, and dearest amity.
Thou in thy secrecy although alone,
Best with thyself accompanied, seek'st not
Social communication, yet so pleased,
Canst raise thy creature to what highth thou wilt   430
Of union or communion, deified;
I by conversing cannot these erect
From prone, nor in their ways complacence find.'
Thus I emboldened spake, and freedom used
Permissive, and acceptance found, which gained   435
This answer from the gracious Voice Divine.
    " 'Thus far to try thee, Adam, I was pleased,
And find thee knowing not of beasts alone,
Which thou hast rightly named, but of thyself,
Expressing well the spirit within thee free,   440
My image, not imparted to the brute,
Whose fellowship therefore unmeet for thee
Good reason was thou freely shouldst dislike,
And be so minded still; I, ere thou spak'st,
Knew it not good for man to be alone,   445
And no such company as then thou saw'st
Intended thee, for trial only brought,
To see how thou couldst judge of fit and meet:
What next I bring shall please thee, be assured,
Thy likeness, thy fit help, thy other self,   450

416–26. Compared with God, a human being is imperfect because in its unity, or singleness, it does not contain all—is not divinely infinite and self-sufficient. It seeks to remedy (*help*, as in "help meet") or compensate for (*solace*) this imperfection by companionship with another human being. A human being's desire to procreate or multiply itself is a sign of the same imperfection—a lack of God's self-contained infinity of numbers. Singleness (unity) in God is perfection; in human beings it is an imperfection. *ab-solute:* complete, perfect. *Collateral:* (L *latus* side) side by side; mutual, equal.

431. Fowler notes that "it is difficult not to see [in *union or communion*] references to mystical union and Holy Communion" (i.e., "identity" and "fellowship").

433. *complacence:* pleasure, delight.

435. *Permissive:* permitted (modifies *freedom*).

450. *fit help:* help meet, as in Genesis, "I will make him an help meet."

Thy wish, exactly to thy heart's desire.'
   "He ended, or I heard no more, for now
My earthly by his heav'nly overpowered,
Which it had long stood under, strained to the highth
In that celestial colloquy sublime,   455
As with an object that excels the sense,
Dazzled and spent, sunk down, and sought repair
Of sleep, which instantly fell on me, called
By nature as in aid, and closed mine eyes.
Mine eyes he closed, but open left the cell   460
Of fancy my internal sight, by which
Abstract as in a trance methought I saw,
Though sleeping, where I lay, and saw the shape
Still glorious before whom awake I stood;
Who stooping opened my left side, and took   465
From thence a rib, with cordial spirits warm,
And life-blood streaming fresh; wide was the wound,
But suddenly with flesh filled up and healed:
The rib he formed and fashioned with his hands;
Under his forming hands a creature grew,   470
Man-like, but different sex, so lovely fair,
That what seemed fair in all the world, seemed now
Mean, or in her summed up, in her contained
And in her looks, which from that time infused
Sweetness into my heart, unfelt before,   475
And into all things from her air inspired
The spirit of love and amorous delight.
She disappeared, and left me dark, I waked
To find her, or for ever to deplore
Her loss, and other pleasures all abjure: 480
When out of hope, behold her, not far off,
Such as I saw her in my dream, adorned
With what all earth or heaven could bestow
To make her amiable: on she came,
Led by her heav'nly Maker, though unseen,   485
And guided by his voice, nor uniformed
Of nuptial sanctity and marriage rites:
Grace was in all her steps, heav'n in her eye,
In every gesture dignity and love.
I overjoyed could not forbear aloud.   490
   " 'This turn hath made amends; thou hast fulfilled
Thy words, Creator bounteous and benign,
Giver of all things fair, but fairest this
Of all thy gifts, nor enviest. I now see
Bone of my bone, flesh of my flesh, my self   495
Before me; woman is her name, of man

462. *Abstract:* (L *ab* from + *trahere* to draw) mentally withdrawn.
466. *cordial:* (L *cor* heart) vital.
476–77. *air:* breath, as well as looks. *inspired:* breathed into, as well as prompted. *spirit:* breath, as well as life.
484. *amiable:* lovable.
494. *nor enviest:* nor dost thou begrudge me it.
495. Cf. Gen. 2.23–24, p. 354.

Extracted; for this cause he shall forgo
Father and mother, and to his wife adhere;
And they shall be one flesh, one heart, one soul.'
    "She heard me thus, and though divinely brought,   500
Yet innocence and virgin modesty,
Her virtue and the conscience of her worth,
That would be wooed, and not unsought be won,
Not obvious, not obtrusive, but retired,
The more desirable, or to say all,   505
Nature herself, though pure of sinful thought,
Wrought in her so, that seeing me, she turned;
I followed her, she what was honor knew,
And with obsequious majesty approved
My pleaded reason. To the nuptial bow'r   510
I led her blushing like the morn: all heav'n,
And happy constellations on that hour
Shed their selectest influence; the earth
Gave sign of gratulation, and each hill;
Joyous the birds; fresh gales and gentle airs   515
Whispered it to the woods, and from their wings
Flung rose, flung odors from the spicy shrub,
Disporting, till the amorous bird of night
Sung spousal, and bid haste the evening star
On his hill top, to light the bridal lamp.   520
Thus I have told thee all my state, and brought
My story to the sum of earthly bliss
Which I enjoy, and must confess to find
In all things else delight indeed, but such
As used or not, works in the mind no change,   525
Nor vehement desire, these delicacies
I mean of taste, sight, smell, herbs, fruits, and flow'rs,
Walks, and the melody of birds; but here
Far otherwise, transported I behold,
Transported touch; here passion first I felt,   530
Commotion strange, in all enjoyments else
Superior and unmoved, here only weak
Against the charm of beauty's powerful glance.
Or nature failed in me, and left some part
Not proof enough such object to sustain,   535
Or from my side subducting, took perhaps
More than enough; at least on her bestowed
Too much of ornament, in outward show

---

502. *conscience:* consciousness.
504. *obvious:* L *obvius* easy of access, outgoing.
508. Cf. Heb. 13.4: "Marriage is honourable in all, and the bed undefiled; but whoremongers and adulterers God will judge."
509. *obsequious:* compliant, devoted.
514. *gratulation:* rejoicing.
517. *rose . . . odors.* Cf. V.293n and
349.
518. *Disporting:* Frolicking.
519. *evening star:* Venus.
526. *vehement:* L *vehe* lacking + *mens* mind. Cf. use of *vehemence* in Argument to IX.
531. *Commotion:* mental agitation.
535. *proof:* resistant. *sustain:* withstand.

Elaborate, of inward less exact.
For well I understand in the prime end   540
Of nature her th' inferior, in the mind
And inward faculties, which most excel,
In outward also her resembling less
His image who made both, and less expressing
The character of that dominion giv'n   545
O'er other creatures; yet when I approach
Her loveliness, so absolute she seems
And in herself complete, so well to know
Her own, that what she wills to do or say,
Seems wisest, virtuousest, discreetest, best;   550
All higher knowledge in her presence falls
Degraded, wisdom in discourse with her
Loses discount'nanced, and like folly shows;
Authority and reason on her wait,
As one intended first, not after made   555
Occasionally; and to consúmmate all,
Greatness of mind and nobleness their seat
Build in her loveliest, and create an awe
About her, as a guard angelic placed."
To whom the angel with contracted brow.   560
    "Accuse not nature, she hath done her part;
Do thou but thine, and be not diffident
Of wisdom, she deserts thee not, if thou
Dismiss not her, when most thou need'st her nigh,
By áttributing overmuch to things   565
Less excellent, as thou thyself perceiv'st.
For what admir'st thou, what transports thee so,
An outside? Fair no doubt, and worthy well
Thy cherishing, thy honoring, and thy love,
Not thy subjection: weigh with her thyself;   570
Then value: ofttimes nothing profits more
Than self-esteem, grounded on just and right
Well managed; of that skill the more thou know'st,
The more she will acknowledge thee her head,
And to realities yield all her shows: 575
Made so adorn for thy delight the more,
So awful, that with honor thou may'st love
Thy mate, who sees when thou art seen least wise.
But if the sense of touch whereby mankind
Is propagated seem such dear delight   580

---

539. *Elaborate:* highly finished, worked out in detail. *exact:* (L *exigere* to demand, to weigh accurately, to bring to perfection) perfect, finished, highly wrought, elaborate, well-designed.
547. *absolute*. Cf. 421 and note.
553. *discount'nanced:* disconcerted, made to lose its self-confidence, abashed.
556. *Occasionally:* incidentally.
557. *greatness of mind:* magnanimity.

Cf. VII.511, and Introduction, p. xii.
562. *diffident:* (L *dis* + *fidere* to trust) distrustful.
573. *skill:* understanding; reason for doing something.
574. Cf. 1 Cor. 11.3: "The head of every man is Christ; and the head of the woman is the man; and the head of Christ is God."
577. *awful:* awe-inspiring.

Beyond all other, think the same voutsafed
To cattle and each beast; which would not be
To them made common and divulged, if aught
Therein enjoyed were worthy to subdue
The soul of man, or passion in him move.   585
What higher in her society thou find'st
Attractive, human, rational, love still;
In loving thou dost well, in passion not,
Wherein true love consists not; love refines
The thoughts, and heart enlarges, hath his seat   590
In reason, and is judicious, is the scale
By which to heav'nly love thou may'st ascend,
Not sunk in carnal pleasure, for which cause
Among the beasts no mate for thee was found."
    To whom thus half abashed Adam replied.   595
"Neither her outside formed so fair, nor aught
In procreation common to all kinds
(Though higher of the genial bed by far,
And with mysterious reverence I deem)
So much delights me, as those graceful acts,   600
Those thousand decencies that daily flow
From all her words and actions, mixed with love
And sweet compliance, which declare unfeigned
Union of mind, or in us both one soul;
Harmony to behold in wedded pair   605
More grateful than harmonious sound to the ear.
Yet these subject not; I to thee disclose
What inward thence I feel, not therefore foiled,
Who meet with various objects, from the sense
Variously representing; yet still free   610
Approve the best, and follow what I approve.
To love thou blam'st me not, for love thou say'st
Leads up to heav'n, is both the way and guide;
Bear with me then, if lawful what I ask;
Love not the heav'nly Spirits, and how their love   615
Express they, by looks only, or do they mix
Irradiance, virtual or immediate touch?"
    To whom the angel with a smile that glowed
Celestial rosy red, love's proper hue,
Answered. "Let it suffice thee that thou know'st   620
Us happy, and without love no happiness.
Whatever pure thou in the body enjoy'st

590. *heart enlarges:* make the intellect capacious; cf. VII.486 and I.437–46n.
591. *scale:* ladder.
595. Cf. *discount'nanced,* 553 and note.
598. *genial:* of or pertaining to marriage or generation. Cf. VII.282.
599. *mysterious.* See IV.750n.
601. *decencies:* fitting, becoming, or appropriate acts.
608. *therefore foiled:* thereby defiled, dishonored (by *these,* in line above). Cf.

Mark 7.18: "And [Christ] saith unto them . . . Do you not perceive, that whatsoever thing from without entereth into the man, it cannot defile him."
616–17. Expression of love *by looks* would be virtually the same as *touch; immediate,* or real, *touch* would produce an interpenetration of emitted radiances of light, spirit, intelligence.
620ff. See "Angels," p. 394.

(And pure thou wert created) we enjoy
In eminence, and obstacle find none
Of membrane, joint, or limb, exclusive bars: 625
Easier than air with air, if Spirits embrace,
Total they mix, union of pure with pure
Desiring; nor restrained conveyance need
As flesh to mix with flesh, or soul with soul.
But I can now no more; the parting sun 630
Beyond the earth's green cape and verdant isles
Hesperian sets, my signal to depart.
Be strong, live happy, and love, but first of all
Him whom to love is to obey, and keep
His great command; take heed lest passion sway 635
Thy judgment to do aught, which else free will
Would not admit; thine and of all thy sons
The weal or woe in thee is placed; beware.
I in thy persevering shall rejoice,
And all the blest: stand fast; to stand or fall 640
Free in thine own arbitrament it lies.
Perfet within, no outward aid require;
And all temptation to transgress repel."
    So saying, he arose; whom Adam thus
Followed with benediction. "Since to part, 645
Go heavenly guest, ethereal messenger,
Sent from whose sovran goodness I adore.
Gentle to me and affable hath been
Thy condescension, and shall be honored ever
With grateful memory: thou to mankind 650
Be good and friendly still, and oft return."
    So parted they, the angel up to heav'n
From the thick shade, and Adam to his bow'r.

---

628. *conveyance:* mode of expression.
630–32. *Hesperian* means "western," but Raphael alludes to the gardens of Hesperus, thought to be, like the Isles of the Blest, in the eastern Atlantic (cf. III.568)—perhaps the Azores or, as here, the Cape Verde Islands. Adam knew at least as much geography as Milton, it seems.

634–35. Cf. 1 John 5.3: "For this is the love of God, that we keep his commandments."
639. *persevering.* See VII.632n.
641. *arbitrament:* power to decide.
642. *require:* request.

Book IX

The Argument

Satan having compassed the earth, with meditated guile returns as a mist by night into Paradise, enters into the serpent sleeping. Adam and Eve in the morning go forth to their labors, which Eve proposes to divide in several places, each laboring apart: Adam consents not, alleging the danger, lest that enemy, of whom they were forewarned, should attempt her found alone: Eve loath to be thought not circumspect or firm enough, urges her going apart, the rather desirous to make trial of her strength; Adam at last yields: the Serpent finds her alone; his subtle approach, first gazing, then speaking, with much flattery extolling Eve above all other creatures. Eve wondering to hear the Serpent speak, asks how he attained to human speech and such understanding not till now; the Serpent answers, that by tasting of a certain tree in the garden he attained both to speech and reason, till then void of both: Eve requires him to bring her to that tree, and finds it to be the Tree of Knowledge forbidden: the Serpent now grown bolder, with many wiles and arguments induces her at length to eat; she pleased with the taste deliberates a while whether to impart thereof to Adam or not, at last brings him of the fruit, relates what persuaded her to eat thereof: Adam at first amazed, but perceiving her lost, resolves through vehemence of love to perish with her; and extenuating the trespass, eats also of the fruit: the effects thereof in them both; they seek to cover their nakedness; then fall to variance and accusation of one another.

No more of talk where God or angel guest
With man, as with his friend, familiar used
To sit indulgent, and with him partake
Rural repast, permitting him the while
Venial discourse unblamed: I now must change   5
Those notes to tragic; foul distrust, and breach
Disloyal on the part of man, revolt,
And disobedience: on the part of heav'n
Now alienated, distance and distaste,
Anger and just rebuke, and judgment giv'n,   10
That brought into this world a world of woe,
Sin and her shadow Death, and misery
Death's harbinger: sad task, yet argument

IX.3. *indulgent:* L *indulgere* to grant as a favor. *partake:* share.
5. *Venial:* (L *venia* grace, favor) un- objectionable, allowable.
6. *breach:* disagreement, quarrel; breaking of a law, duty, or promise.

Not less but more heroic than the wrath
Of stern Achilles on his foe pursued   15
Thrice fugitive about Troy wall; or rage
Of Turnus for Lavinia disespoused,
Or Neptune's ire or Juno's, that so long
Perplexed the Greek and Cytherea's son;
If answerable style I can obtain   20
Of my celestial patroness, who deigns
Her nightly visitation unimplored,
And dictates to me slumb'ring, or inspires
Easy my unpremeditated verse:
Since first this subject for heroic song   25
Pleased me long choosing, and beginning late;
Not sedulous by nature to indite
Wars, hitherto the only argument
Heroic deemed, chief maistry to dissect
With long and tedious havoc fabled knights   30
In battles feigned; the better fortitude
Of patience and heroic martyrdom
Unsung; or to describe races and games,
Or tilting furniture, emblazoned shields,
Impresses quaint, caparisons and steeds;   35
Bases and tinsel trappings, gorgeous knights
At joust and tournament; then marshaled feast.
Served up in hall with sewers, and seneschals;
The skill of artifice or office mean,
Not that which justly gives heroic name   40
To person or to poem. Me of these
Nor skilled nor studious, higher argument
Remains, sufficient of itself to raise
That name, unless an age too late, or cold
Climate, or years damp my intended wing   45
Depressed, and much they may, if all be mine,
Not hers who brings it nightly to my ear.
    The sun was sunk, and after him the star
Of Hesperus, whose office is to bring

14–19. The themes of the *Iliad*, the *Aeneid*, and the *Odyssey*. *heroic:* appropriate to heroes, as well as to epic poetry; cf. *heroic song* (25) and *heroic name* (40). *his foe:* Hector. *Lavinia* was betrothed by her father to Aeneas. *Neptune* made life hard for (*perplexed*) Odysseus (*the Greek*); and *Juno* for Aeneas, son of Venus (*Cytherea*). Man's odyssey would be more heroic than that of Odysseus or Aeneas.
20. *answerable:* capable of meeting requirements; corresponding, suitable.
21. *patroness:* Urania. See VII.1.
23–24. See Introduction, and III.37ff. and n.
28. *argument:* subject; narrative.
29. *maistry:* mastery, skill.
31. *feigned:* represented in fiction.

34–38. Milton alludes to medieval romances such as Malory's *Morte d'Arthur* and such Renaissance epics as those of Tasso and Spenser. *tilting furniture:* equipment for jousting. *Impresses quaint:* skillfully wrought coats of arms. *caparisons:* rich trappings for horses (and people). *Bases:* mantles worn from waist to knee by knights on horseback. *sewers and seneschals:* household officers in charge of banquets.
44–45. Milton wonders whether (1) society has not lost its taste for true Christian heroism or for epic poems, or (2) the climate (Gk *klima* inclination, latitude) of England is not inimical to the production of works of genius, or (3) he is himself not too old for such an undertaking. *damp:* depress, check. *wing.* Cf. I.14–15; III.13; VII.3–4.

Twilight upon the earth, short arbiter   50
'Twixt day and night, and now from end to end
Night's hemisphere had veiled the horizon round:
When Satan who late fled before the threats
Of Gabriel out of Eden, now improved
In meditated fraud and malice, bent   55
On man's destruction, maugre what might hap
Of heavier on himself, fearless returned.
By night he fled, and at midnight returned
From compassing the earth, cautious of day,
Since Uriel regent of the sun descried   60
His entrance, and forewarned the Cherubim
That kept their watch; thence full of anguish driv'n,
The space of seven continued nights he rode
With darkness, thrice the equinoctial line
He circled, four times crossed the car of Night   65
From pole to pole, traversing each colure;
On the eighth returned, and on the coast averse
From entrance or Cherubic watch, by stealth
Found unsuspected way. There was a place,
Now not, though sin, not time, first wrought the change,   70
Where Tigris at the foot of Paradise
Into a gulf shot under ground, till part
Rose up a fountain by the Tree of Life;
In with the river sunk, and with it rose
Satan involved in rising mist, then sought   75
Where to lie hid; sea he had searched and land
From Eden over Pontus, and the pool
Maeotis, up beyond the river Ob;
Downward as far antarctic; and in length
West from Orontes to the ocean barred   80
At Darien, thence to the land where flows
Ganges and Indus: thus the orb he roamed
With narrow search; and with inspection deep
Considered every creature, which of all
Most opportune might serve his wiles, and found   85
The serpent subtlest beast of all the field.
Him after long debate, irresolute

54. *improved:* increased.
56. *maugre:* in spite of.
59. Cf. Job 1.7: "And the Lord said unto Satan, Whence comest thou? Then Satan answered the Lord, and said, From going to and fro in the earth, and from walking up and down in it."
63–66. Before the earth was tilted on its axis at the time of the Fall, there were no *colures,* the two circles that run perpendicular to the circle of the earth's annual orbit around the sun and that intersect that circle at the two points of the equinoxes and the two points of the solstices. Whatever his reason for referring to them, Milton intended to picture Satan keeping the earth between him and the sun, first by following the equator for three days and then (for four) so timing his transpolar flights as to achieve the same effect. *equinoctial line:* in the Ptolemaic system of astronomy the circle of the sun around the earth, in the same plane, before the Fall, with that of the earth's equator.
77–81. *Pontus:* the Black Sea. *Maeotis:* the Sea of Azov in Russia. *Ob:* in Siberia, runs into the Arctic Ocean. *Orontes:* a river in N. Syria. *Darien:* the Isthmus of Panama.
87–88. *irresolute/Of thoughts revolved:* undecided after meditating. *sentence:* judgment.

Of thoughts revolved, his final sentence chose
Fit vessel, fittest imp of fraud, in whom
To enter, and his dark suggestions hide   90
From sharpest sight: for in the wily snake,
Whatever sleights none would suspicious mark,
As from his wit and native subtlety
Proceeding, which in other beasts observed
Doubt might beget of diabolic pow'r   95
Active within beyond the sense of brute.
Thus he resolved, but first from inward grief
His bursting passion into plaints thus poured:
    "O earth, how like to heav'n, if not preferred
More justly, seat worthier of gods, as built   100
With second thoughts, reforming what was old!
For what God after better worse would build?
Terrestrial heav'n, danced round by other heav'ns
That shine, yet bear their bright officious lamps,
Light above light, for thee alone, as seems,   105
In thee concentring all their precious beams
Of sacred influence: as God in heav'n
Is center, yet extends to all, so thou
Centring receiv'st from all those orbs; in thee,
Not in themselves, all their known virtue appears   110
Productive in herb, plant, and nobler birth
Of creatures animate with gradual life
Of growth, sense, reason, all summed up in man.
With what delight could I have walked thee round,
If I could joy in aught, sweet interchange   115
Of hill and valley, rivers, woods and plains,
Now land, now sea, and shores with forest crowned,
Rocks, dens, and caves; but I in none of these
Find place or refuge; and the more I see
Pleasures about me, so much more I feel   120
Torment within me, as from the hateful siege
Of contraries; all good to me becomes
Bane, and in heav'n much worse would be my state.
But neither here seek I, no nor in heav'n
To dwell, unless by maistring heav'n's Supreme;   125
Nor hope to be myself less miserable
By what I seek, but others to make such
As I, though thereby worse to me redound:
For only in destroying I find ease

89. *imp:* offshoot; child.
90. *suggestions:* temptations.
92. *sleights:* deceitful artifices.
95. *Doubt:* suspicion.
103–7. Satan joins Eve (IV.657) and Adam (VIII.15ff) in this observation. *danced.* Cf. III.580n; V.178, 620–27; VII.374; VIII.125. *officious:* helpful, ministering.
112–13. *gradual:* progressive, from, as

Fowler notes, vegetable (*growth*) to animal (*sense*) to rational (*reason*) souls. Cf. V.469–90; and see "Physiology and Psychology," pp. 391–92.
121. The pain (*Torment*) within Satan is in conflict with, is besieged by, *pleasures* from without. *siege:* persistent attack; also, seat, throne.
123. *Bane:* poison; cause of ruin or woe. Cf. I.692.

To my relentless thoughts; and him destroyed,   130
Or won to what may work his utter loss,
For whom all this was made, all this will soon
Follow, as to him linked in weal or woe:
In woe then; that destruction wide may range:
To me shall be the glory sole among   135
The infernal Powers, in one day to have ...arred
What he Almighty styled, six nights and days
Continued making, and who knows how long
Before had been contriving, though perhaps
Not longer than since I in one night freed   140
From servitude inglorious well-nigh half
Th' angelic name, and thinner left the throng
Of his adorers: he to be avenged,
And to repair his numbers thus impaired,
Whether such virtue spent of old now failed   145
More angels to create, if they at least
Are his created, or to spite us more,
Determined to advance into our room
A creature formed of earth, and him endow,
Exalted from so base original,   150
With heav'nly spoils, our spoils: what he decreed
He effected; man he made, and for him built
Magnificent this world, and earth his seat,
Him lord pronounced, and, O indignity!
Subjected to his service angel wings,   155
And flaming ministers to watch and tend
Their earthy charge: of these the vigilance
I dread, and to elude, thus wrapped in mist
Of midnight vapor glide obscure, and pry
In every bush and brake, where hap may find   160
The serpent sleeping, in whose mazy folds
To hide me, and the dark intent I bring.
O foul descent! that I who erst contended
With gods to sit the highest, am now constrained
Into a beast, and mixed with bestial slime,   165
This essence to incarnate and imbrute,
That to the highth of deity aspired;
But what will not ambition and revenge
Descend to? Who aspires must down as low
As high he soared, obnoxious first or last   170
To basest things. Revenge, at first though sweet,
Bitter ere long back on itself recoils;
Let it; I reck not, so it light well aimed,
Since higher I fall short, on him who next

---

145. *virtue:* power.
150. *base original:* common origin (i.e., *earth*).
155–57. Cf. Ps. 104.4: "Who maketh his angels spirits; his ministers a flaming fire." Ps. 91.11: "For he shall give his angels charge over thee, to keep thee in all thy ways."
160. *hap:* luck.
170. *obnoxious:* (L *ob* facing + *noxa* harm) vulnerable; (with *to*) dependent on, subject to the power of.

Provokes my envy, this new favorite   175
Of Heav'n, this man of clay, son of despite,
Whom us the more to spite his Maker raised
From dust: spite then with spite is best repaid."
     So saying, through each thicket dank or dry,
Like a black mist low creeping, he held on   180
His midnight search, where soonest he might find
The serpent: him fast sleeping soon he found
In labyrinth of many a round self-rolled,
His head the midst, well stored with subtle wiles:
Not yet in horrid shade or dismal den,   185
Nor nocent yet, but on the grassy herb
Fearless unfeared he slept: in at his mouth
The Devil entered, and his brutal sense,
In heart or head, possessing soon inspired
With act intelligential; but his sleep   190
Disturbed not, waiting close th' approach of morn.
Now whenas sacred light began to dawn
In Eden on the humid flow'rs, that breathed
Their morning incense, when all things that breathe,
From th' earth's great altar send up silent praise   195
To the Creator, and his nostrils fill
With grateful smell, forth came the human pair
And joined their vocal worship to the choir
Of creatures wanting voice; that done, partake
The season, prime for sweetest scents and airs: 200
Then cómmune how that day they best may ply
Their growing work; for much their work outgrew
The hands' dispatch of two gard'ning so wide.
And Eve first to her husband thus began.
     "Adam, well may we labor still to dress   205
This garden, still to tend plant, herb and flow'r,
Our pleasant task enjoined, but till more hands
Aid us, the work under our labor grows,
Luxurious by restraint; what we by day
Lop overgrown, or prune, or prop, or bind,   210
One night or two with wanton growth derides,
Tending to wild. Thou therefore now advise
Or hear what to my mind first thoughts present,
Let us divide our labors, thou where choice
Leads thee, or where most needs, whether to wind   215
The woodbine round this arbor, or direct
The clasping ivy where to climb, while I

---

186. *nocent:* harmful; guilty of crime.
191. *close:* hidden.
192. *whenas:* when. *sacred light.* Cf.
III.1–6; IX.107.
196–97. Cf. Gen. 8.21: "And [after the
Flood] the Lord smelled a sweet savour;
and the Lord said in his heart, I will not
again curse the ground any more for
man's sake."

198. *choir:* Gk *chorus* dance, company
of dancers.
199–200. *wanting:* lacking. *partake/The
season:* Bush suggests "enjoy the morn-
ing." *prime:* the best. But the word also
means the first hour of the day, and a
set time for morning prayers.
201. *ply:* apply [themselves] to.

In yonder spring of roses intermixed
With myrtle, find what to redress till noon:
For while so near each other thus all day   220
Our task we choose, what wonder if so near
Looks intervene and smiles, or object new
Casual discourse draw on, which intermits
Our day's work brought to little, though begun
Early, and th' hour of supper comes unearned."   225
    To whom mild answer Adam thus returned.
"Sole Eve, associate sole, to me beyond
Compare above all living creatures dear,
Well hast thou motioned, well thy thoughts employed
How we might best fulfill the work which here   230
God hath assigned us, nor of me shalt pass
Unpraised: for nothing lovelier can be found
In woman, than to study household good,
And good works in her husband to promote.
Yet not so strictly hath our Lord imposed   235
Labor, as to debar us when we need
Refreshment, whether food, or talk between,
Food of the mind, or this sweet intercourse
Of looks and smiles, for smiles from reason flow,
To brute denied, and are of love the food,   240
Love not the lowest end of human life.
For not to irksome toil, but to delight
He made us, and delight to reason joined.
These paths and bowers doubt not but our joint hands
Will keep from wilderness with ease, as wide   245
As we need walk, till younger hands ere long
Assist us: but if much convérse perhaps
Thee satiate, to short absence I could yield.
For solitude sometimes is best society,
And short retirement urges sweet return.   250
But other doubt possesses me, lest harm
Befall thee severed from me; for thou know'st
What hath been warned us, what malicious foe
Envying our happiness, and of his own
Despairing, seeks to work us woe and shame   255
By sly assault; and somewhere nigh at hand
Watches, no doubt, with greedy hope to find
His wish and best advantage, us asunder,
Hopeless to circumvent us joined, where each
To other speedy aid might lend at need;   260
Whether his first design be to withdraw
Our fealty from God, or to disturb
Conjugal love, than which perhaps no bliss
Enjoyed by us excites his envy more;

---

218. *spring:* thicket.
219. *redress:* set upright again.
229. *motioned:* proposed.

232–34. For the biblical authority for
Milton's ideas of the mutual duties of
husband and wife see *CD*, II.xv.

Or this, or worse, leave not the faithful side 265
That gave thee being, still shades thee and protects.
The wife, where danger or dishonor lurks,
Safest and seemliest by her husband stays,
Who guards her, or with her the worst endures."
    To whom the virgin majesty of Eve, 270
As one who loves, and some unkindness meets,
With sweet austere composure thus replied.
    "Offspring of heav'n and earth, and all earth's lord,
That such an enemy we have, who seeks
Our ruin, both by thee informed I learn, 275
And from the parting angel overheard
As in a shady nook I stood behind,
Just then returned at shut of evening flow'rs.
But that thou shouldst my firmness therefore doubt
To God or thee, because we have a foe 280
May tempt it, I expected not to hear.
His violence thou fear'st not, being such,
As we, not capable of death or pain,
Can either not receive, or can repel.
His fraud is then thy fear, which plain infers 285
Thy equal fear that my firm faith and love
Can by his fraud be shaken or seduced;
Thoughts, which how found they harbor in thy breast,
Adam, misthought of her to thee so dear?"
    To whom with healing words Adam replied. 290
"Daughter of God and man, immortal Eve,
For such thou art, from sin and blame entire:
Not diffident of thee do I dissuade
Thy absence from my sight, but to avoid
Th' attempt itself, intended by our foe. 295
For he who tempts, though in vain, at least asperses
The tempted with dishonor foul, supposed
Not incorruptible of faith, not proof
Against temptation: thou thyself with scorn
And anger wouldst resent the offered wrong, 300
Though ineffectual found; misdeem not then,
If such affront I labor to avert
From thee alone, which on us both at once
The enemy, though bold, will hardly dare,
Or daring, first on me th' assault shall light. 305
Nor thou his malice and false guile contemn;
Subtle he needs must be, who could seduce
Angels, nor think superfluous others' aid.

265. *Of this:* whether (his *design,* 261) be this.
270. *virgin majesty:* maidenly dignity.
272. *austere:* (GK *austēros* making the tongue dry and rough) uniting astringency with sourness; stern.
292. *entire:* (L *integer* untouched) free.
293. *diffident:* (L *dis* + *fidere* to trust) distrustful.
296–99. I.e.: Who tempts another, even unsuccessfully, dishonors him by implying that the tempted is capable of being tempted. Cf. 327–33. *asperses:* (L *ad* + *spargere* to scatter) bespatters. *faith:* loyalty.
306. *contemn:* view with contempt.

I from the influence of thy looks receive
Access in every virtue, in thy sight   310
More wise, more watchful, stronger, if need were
Of outward strength; while shame, thou looking on,
Shame to be overcome or overreached
Would utmost vigor raise, and raised unite.
Why shouldst not thou like sense within thee feel   315
When I am present, and thy trial choose
With me, best witness of thy virtue tried."
    So spake domestic Adam in his care
And matrimonial love; but Eve, who thought
Less attribúted to her faith sincere,   320
Thus her reply with accent sweet renewed.
    "If this be our condition, thus to dewll
In narrow circuit straitened by a foe,
Subtle or violent, we not endued
Single with like defense, wherever met,   325
How are we happy, still in fear of harm?
But harm precedes not sin: only our foe
Tempting affronts us with his foul esteem
Of our integrity: his foul esteem
Sticks no dishonor on our front, but turns   330
Foul on himself; then wherefore shunned or feared
By us? who rather double honor gain
From his surmise proved false, find peace within,
Favor from Heav'n, our witness from th' event.
And what is faith, love, virtue unassayed   335
Alone, without exterior help sustained?
Let us not then suspect our happy state
Left so imperfect by the Maker wise,
As not secure to single or combined.
Frail is our happiness, if this be so,   340
And Eden were no Eden thus exposed."
    To whom thus Adam fervently replied.
"O woman, best are all things as the will
Of God ordained them, his creating hand
Nothing imperfect or deficient left   345
Of all that he created, much less man,
Or aught that might his happy state secure,
Secure from outward force; within himself
The danger lies, yet lies within his power:
Against his will he can receive no harm.   350
But God left free the will, for what obeys
Reason, is free, and reason he made right,

---

310. *Access:* increase.
320. *sincere:* whole, unadulterated.
323. *straitened:* confined.
327–28. I.e.: In tempting us our foe
only confronts (also insults) us. . . .
330. *front:* countenance.
334. *event:* (L *e* out + *venire* to come)

outcome.
335–36. Cf. *Areopagitica*, pp. 290–91.
339. I.e.: As not to be safe for us,
whether alone or together.
341. *Eden*. See IV.132n.
352. See "Reason," p. 392.

But bid her well beware, and still erect,
Lest by some fair appearing good surprised
She dictate false, and misinform the will   355
To do what God expressly hath forbid.
Not then mistrust, but tender love enjoins,
That I should mind thee oft, and mind thou me.
Firm we subsist, yet possible to swerve,
Since reason not impossibly may meet   360
Some specious object by the foe suborned,
And fall into deception unaware,
Not keeping strictest watch, as she was warned.
Seek not temptation then, which to avoid
Were better, and most likely if from me   365
Thou sever not: trial will come unsought.
Wouldst thou approve thy constancy, approve
First thy obedience; th' other who can know,
Not seeing thee attempted, who attest?
But if thou think, trial unsought may find   370
Us both securer than thus warned thou seem'st,
Go; for thy stay, not free, absents thee more;
Go in thy native innocence, rely
On what thou hast of virtue, summon all,
For God towards thee hath done his part, do thine." 375
    So spake the patriarch of mankind, but Eve
Persisted, yet submiss, though last, replied.
    "With thy permission then, and thus forewarned
Chiefly by what thy own last reasoning words
Touched only, that our trial, when least sought,   380
May find us both perhaps far less prepared,
The willinger I go, nor much expect
A foe so proud will first the weaker seek;
So bent, the more shall shame him his repulse."
Thus saying, from her husband's hand her hand   385
Soft she withdrew, and like a wood-nymph light
Oread or Dryad, or of Delia's train,
Betook her to the groves, but Delia's self
In gait surpassed and goddess-like deport,
Though not as she with bow and quiver armed,   390
But with such gardening tools as art yet rude,
Guiltless of fire had formed, or angels brought.

---

353. I.e.: But he bid reason to be very careful and always alert.
358. *mind:* remind.
361. *suborned:* (L *sub* secretly + *ornare* to equip) secretly procured or enlisted to commit a crime.
367. *approve:* prove.
371. *securer:* more careless, less on guard. Cf. 380–81.
377. *submiss:* submissive.
386. *light:* light-footed. Cf. 452.
387. *Oread:* a mountain nymph. *Dryad:*

a wood nymph. *Delia:* Diana, goddess of the wood, who hunted with a *train* of nymphs.
389. *deport:* bearing.
392. *Guiltless of fire.* In pastoral Paradise there was no need for swords or ploughshares—hence no need for metal, smelting or fire. Milton may allude to the guilt of Prometheus, who stole fire from heaven, according to a Greek myth that accounted for the introduction of evil into the world.

To Pales, or Pomona, thus adorned,
Likest she seemed, Pomona when she fled
Vertumnus, or to Ceres in her prime,   395
Yet virgin of Proserpina from Jove.
Her long with ardent look his eye pursued
Delighted, but desiring more her stay.
Oft he to her his charge of quick return
Repeated, she to him as oft engaged   400
To be returned by noon amid the bow'r,
And all things in best order to invite
Noontide repast, or afternoon's repose.
O much deceived, much failing, hapless Eve,
Of thy presumed return! event perverse!   405
Thou never from that hour in Paradise
Found'st either sweet repast, or sound repose;
Such ambush hid among sweet flow'rs and shades
Waited with hellish rancor imminent
To intercept thy way, or send thee back   410
Despoiled of innocence, of faith, of bliss.
For now, and since first break of dawn the Fiend,
Mere serpent in appearance, forth was come,
And on his quest, where likeliest he might find
The only two of mankind, but in them   415
The whole included race, his purposed prey.
In bow'r and field he sought, where any tuft
Of grove or garden-plot more pleasant lay,
Their tendance or plantation for delight,
By fountain or by shady rivulet   420
He sought them both, but wished his hap might find
Eve separate, he wished, but not with hope
Of what so seldom chanced, when to his wish,
Beyond his hope, Eve separate he spies,
Veiled in a cloud of fragrance, where she stood,   425
Half spied, so thick the roses bushing round
About her glowed, oft stooping to support
Each flow'r of slender stalk, whose head though gay
Carnation, purple, azure, or specked with gold,
Hung drooping unsustained, them she upstays   430
Gently with myrtle band, mindless the while,
Herself, though fairest unsupported flow'r,
From her best prop so far, and storm so nigh.
Nearer he drew, and many a walk traversed

393–96. *Pales* was a goddess of animal husbandry; *Pomona*, of horticulture; *Ceres*, of agriculture (esp. of grain crops). *Vertumnus* wooed Pomona in many disguises before she accepted him. *Jove* made Ceres pregnant with *Proserpina*.
404. *failing*: mistaking, erring, at fault. *hapless*: unlucky.
405. *event*: outcome. *perverse*: (L *perversus* turned the wrong way) adverse, unpropitious, turned from right to wrong. Cf. I.164.
409. *imminent*: intent.
413. *Mere*: pure, nothing more or less than.
419. I.e.: Which they had cultivated or planted for their pleasure.
431. *mindless the while*: not mindful for the moment (that she was so far . . .). *myrtle band*: ties of myrtle vine.

Of stateliest covert, cedar, pine, or palm,   435
Then voluble and bold, now hid, now seen
Among thick-woven arborets and flow'rs
Embordered on each bank, the hand of Eve:
Spot more delicious than those gardens feigned
Or of revived Adonis, or renowned   440
Alcinous, host of old Laertes' son,
Or that, not mystic, where the sapient king
Held dalliance with his fair Egyptian spouse.
Much he the place admired, the person more.
As one who long in populous city pent,   445
Where houses thick and sewers annoy the air,
Forth issuing on a summer's morn to breathe
Among the pleasant villages and farms
Adjoined, from each thing met conceives delight,
The smell of grain, or tedded grass, or kine,   450
Or dairy, each rural sight, each rural sound;
If chance with nymph-like step fair virgin pass,
What pleasing seemed, for her now pleases more,
She most, and in her look sums all delight.
Such pleasure took the Serpent to behold   455
This flow'ry plat, the sweet recess of Eve
Thus early, thus alone; her heav'nly form
Angelic, but more soft, and feminine,
Her graceful innocence, her every air
Of gesture or least action overawed   460
His malice, and with rapine sweet bereaved
His fierceness of the fierce intent it brought:
That space the Evil One abstracted stood
From his own evil, and for the time remained
Stupidly good, of enmity disarmed,   465
Of guile, of hate, of envy, of revenge;
But the hot hell that always in him burns,
Though in mid-heav'n, soon ended his delight,
And tortures him now more, the more he sees
Of pleasure not for him ordained: then soon   470

436. *voluble:* undulating; moving easily or quickly.
437. *arborets:* groves, arbors.
438. *hand:* handiwork.
439–43. After his death, the beautiful youth *Adonis*, at the pleading of enamored Aphrodite, was *revived* by Zeus. The gardens of Adonis were beds of beautiful, rapidly-withering plants set around images of him by worshiping maidens. See I.446–57n. Odysseus (*Laertes' son*) was entertained in the gardens of *Alcinous*. Unlike these mythological (*mystic*) gardens was the real, or historical, garden where Solomon (*the sapient king*) entertained his bride, a Pharaoh's daughter. It was thought to be the garden alluded to in the Song of Solomon. *sapient:* L *sapere* to taste, be

wise. Fowler calls it a "heavily thematic word" in *PL* and refers to *sapience* in line 1018, where *taste* and *savor* (L *sapere*) are part of the context.
446. *annoy:* (etymologically related to noisome) make offensive to the smell (though the *OED* does not list that meaning).
450. *tedded grass:* hay spread out to dry. *kine:* cattle.
453. *for:* because of.
456. *plat:* plot. *recess:* retreat.
459. *air:* manner.
461. *rapine:* like *rapture*, L *rapere* to seize and carry off.
463. *abstracted:* mentally withdrawn.
465. *stupidly good:* good because stupified, or impotent.

Fierce hate he recollects, and all his thoughts
Of mischief, gratulating, thus excites.
   "Thoughts, whither have ye led me, with what sweet
Compulsion thus transported to forget
What hither brought us, hate, not love, nor hope   475
Of Paradise for hell, hope here to taste
Of pleasure, but all pleasure to destroy,
Save what is in destroying, other joy
To me is lost. Then let me not let pass
Occasion which now smiles, behold alone   480
The woman, opportune to all attempts,
Her husband, for I view far round, not nigh,
Whose higher intellectual more I shun,
And strength, of courage haughty, and of limb
Heroic built, though of terrestrial mold,   485
Foe not informidable, exempt from wound,
I not; so much hath hell debased, and pain
Enfeebled me, to what I was in heav'n.
She fair, divinely fair, fit love for gods,
Not terrible, though terror be in love   490
And beauty, not approached by stronger hate,
Hate stronger, under show of love well feigned,
The way which to her ruin now I tend."
   So spake the Enemy of mankind, enclosed
In serpent, inmate bad, and toward Eve   495
Addressed his way, not with indented wave,
Prone on the ground, as since, but on his rear,
Circular base of rising folds, that tow'red
Fold above fold a surging maze, his head
Crested aloft, and carbuncle his eyes;   500
With burnished neck of verdant gold, erect
Amidst his circling spires, that on the grass
Floated redundant: pleasing was his shape,
And lovely, never since of serpent kind
Lovelier, not those that in Illyria changed   505
Hermione and Cadmus, or the god
In Epidaurus; nor to which transformed
Ammonian Jove, or Capitoline was seen,

472–73. I.e.: And thus calls out (*excites*) all his thoughts of mischief, hailing and welcoming (*gratulating*) them.

481. *opportune to:* (L *ob* facing + *portus* port, harbor) ready for, open to, liable to.

484. *courage:* mind, spirit, disposition. *haughty:* noble, exalted.

485. *of terrestrial mold:* made of earthly material.

486–87. Cf. 283 and VI.327.

490. *terrible:* terrifying.

491. *not:* unless.

496. *indented:* zigzag.

500. *carbuncle:* red.

502. *spires:* coils.

503. *redundant:* (L *re* back + *undare*

to rise in waves) undulating; overflowing.

504–10. *Cadmus,* founder of Thebes, thinking himself cursed for slaying a serpent, asked to be changed into a snake; then his wife, *Hermione,* made and was granted the same wish. Aesculapius, the god of healing, was brought to Rome, from *Epidaurus,* in Greece, in the form of a snake, to rid the city of a plague. The *Jove* worshipped in Libya and called Ammon (cf. IV.277n) made love to *Olympias* (mother of Alexander the Great) in the form of a snake. *Capitoline Jove* (worshipped in Rome), similarly disguised, sired *Scipio* Africanus. *tract:* course, route.

He with Olympias, this with her who bore
Scipio, the highth of Rome. With tract oblique 510
At first, as one who sought accéss, but feared
To interrupt, sidelong he works his way.
As when a ship by skilful steersman wrought
Nigh river's mouth or foreland, where the wind
Veers oft, as oft so steers, and shifts her sail; 515
So varied he, and of his tortuous train
Curled many a wanton wreath in sight of Eve,
To lure her eye; she busied heard the sound
Of rustling leaves, but minded not, as used
To such disport before her through the field, 520
From every beast, more duteous at her call,
Than at Circean call the herd disguised.
He bolder now, uncalled before her stood;
But as in gaze admiring: oft he bowed
His turret crest, and sleek enameled neck, 525
Fawning, and licked the ground whereon she trod.
His gentle dumb expression turned at length
The eye of Eve to mark his play; he glad
Of her attention gained, with serpent tongue
Organic, or impulse of vocal air, 530
His fraudulent temptation thus began.
　　"Wonder not, sovran mistress, if perhaps
Thou canst, who art sole wonder, much less arm
Thy looks, the heav'n of mildness, with disdain,
Displeased that I approach thee thus, and gaze 535
Insatiate, I thus single, nor have feared
Thy awful brow, more awful thus retired.
Fairest resemblance of thy Maker fair,
Thee all things living gaze on, all things thine
By gift, and thy celestial beauty adore 540
With ravishment beheld, there best beheld
Where universally admired; but here
In this enclosure wild, these beasts among,
Beholders rude, and shallow to discern
Half what in thee is fair, one man except, 545
Who sees thee? (and what is one?) who shouldst be seen
A goddess among gods, adored and served
By angels numberless, thy daily train."
　　So glozed the Tempter, and his proem tuned;
Into the heart of Eve his words made way, 550
Though at the voice much marveling; at length
Not unamazed she thus in answer spake.
　　"What may this mean? Language of man pronounced
By tongue of brute, and human sense expressed?

513–15. Cf. *opportune*, 481 and n.
517. *wanton:* unruly, gay, luxuriant, provocative.
522. Circe cast spells over men and changed them into various kinds of ani-
mals.
525. *enameled:* of various colors.
530. *Organic:* instrumental, used as a tool. *impulse:* surge.
549. *glozed:* flattered. *proem:* prelude.

The first at least of these I thought denied   555
To beasts, whom God on their creation-day
Created mute to all articulate sound;
The latter I demur, for in their looks
Much reason, and in their actions oft appears.
Thee, serpent, subtlest beast of all the field   560
I knew, but not with human voice endued;
Redouble then this miracle, and say,
How cam'st thou speakable of mute, and how
To me so friendly grown above the rest
Of brutal kind, that daily are in sight?   565
Say, for such wonder claims attention due."
    To whom the guileful Tempter thus replied.
"Empress of this fair world, resplendent Eve,
Easy to me it is to tell thee all
What thou command'st, and right thou shouldst be obeyed: 570
I was at first as other beasts that graze
The trodden herb, of abject thoughts and low,
As was my food, nor aught but food discerned
Or sex, and apprehended nothing high:
Till on a day roving the field, I chanced   575
A goodly tree far distant to behold
Loaden with fruit of fairest colors mixed,
Ruddy and gold: I nearer drew to gaze;
When from the boughs a savory odor blown,
Grateful to appetite, more pleased my sense   580
Than smell of sweetest fennel, or the teats
Of ewe or goat dropping with milk at ev'n,
Unsucked of lamb or kid, that tend their play.
To satisfy the sharp desire I had
Of tasting those fair apples, I resolved   585
Not to defer; hunger and thirst at once,
Powerful persuaders, quickened at the scent
Of that alluring fruit, urged me so keen.
About the mossy trunk I wound me soon,
For high from ground the branches would require   590
Thy utmost reach or Adam's: round the tree
All other beasts that saw, with like desire
Longing and envying stood, but could not reach.
Amid the tree now got, where plenty hung
Tempting so nigh, to pluck and eat my fill   595
I spared not, for such pleasure till that hour
At feed or fountain never had I found.
Sated at length, ere long I might perceive
Strange alteration in me, to degree

---

558. *demur:* (L *demorari* to linger, to delay) hesitate about, take exception to.
572. *abject:* mean-spirited, servile.
579. *savory.* See 442n and 1018–19n. *Savor* (L *sapere* to taste, to have good taste) meant both "physical taste" and "intellectual discernment."
581–82. According to Pliny *fennel* aids snakes in shedding their skin and sharpens their eyesight. More recent folklore held that snakes sucked the *teats* of sheep.

Of reason in my inward powers, and speech   600
Wanted not long, though to this shape retained.
Thenceforth to speculations high or deep
I turned my thoughts, and with capacious mind
Considered all things visible in heav'n,
Or earth, or middle, all things fair and good;   605
But all that fair and good in thy divine
Semblance, and in thy beauty's heav'nly ray
United I beheld; no fair to thine
Equivalent or second, which compelled
Me thus, though importune perhaps, to come   610
And gaze, and worship thee of right declared
Sovran of creatures, universal dame.''
    So talked the spirited sly snake; and Eve
Yet more amazed unwary thus replied.
    "Serpent, thy overpraising leaves in doubt   615
The virtue of that fruit, in thee first proved:
But say, where grows the tree, from hence how far?
For many are the trees of God that grow
In Paradise, and various, yet unknown
To us, in such abundance lies our choice,   620
As leaves a greater store of fruit untouched,
Still hanging incorruptible, till men
Grow up to their provision, and more hands
Help to disburden nature of her bearth.''
    To whom the wily adder, blithe and glad.   625
"Empress, the way is ready, and not long,
Beyond a row of myrtles, on a flat,
Fast by a fountain, one small thicket past
Of blowing myrrh and balm; if thou accept
My conduct, I can bring thee thither soon.''   630
    "Lead then,'' said Eve. He leading swiftly rolled
In tangles, and made intricate seem straight,
To mischief swift. Hope elevates, and joy
Brightens his crest, as when a wand'ring fire,
Compact of unctuous vapor, which the night   635
Condenses, and the cold environs round,
Kindled through agitation to a flame,
Which oft, they say, some evil spirit attends,
Hovering and blazing with delusive light,
Misleads th' amazed night-wanderer from his way   640

605. *middle:* the regions between.
608. *fair:* beauty.
610. *importune:* inopportunely.
612. *universal dame:* mistress of the universe.
613. *spirited:* inspired by (and possessed by) the spirit Satan.
616. *virtue:* power. *proved:* tested.
623. *Grow up to their provision:* increase to a number where the demand equals the supply (which has been provided by the providence of God).

624. *bearth:* (Milton's apparently deliberate spelling) what she bears.
629. *blowing myrrh and balm:* blossoming trees that exude the aromatic gums called myrrh and balm (or balsam) frequently mentioned in the Bible.
634. *wand'ring fire: ignis fatuus,* or will-o'-the-wisp.
635. *Compact:* composed. *unctuous:* oily.
640. *amazed:* perplexed, as in a maze. Cf. Eve's amazement, line 614.

To bogs and mires, and oft through pond or pool,
There swallowed up and lost, from succor far.
So glistered the dire snake, and into fraud
Led Eve our credulous mother, to the tree
Of prohibition, root of all our woe;   645
Which when she saw, thus to her guide she spake.
    "Serpent, we might have spared our coming hither,
Fruitless to me, though fruit be here to excess,
The credit of whose virtue rest with thee,
Wondrous indeed, if cause of such effects.   650
But of this tree we may not taste nor touch;
God so commanded, and left that command
Sole daughter of his voice; the rest, we live
Law to ourselves, our reason is our law."
    To whom the Tempter guilefully replied.   655
"Indeed? hath God then said that of the fruit
Of all these garden trees ye shall not eat,
Yet lords declared of all in earth or air?"
    To whom thus Eve yet sinless. "Of the fruit
Of each tree in the garden we may eat,   660
But of the fruit of this fair tree amidst
The garden, God hath said, 'Ye shall not eat
Thereof, nor shall ye touch it, lest ye die.' "
    She scarce had said, though brief, when now more bold
The Tempter, but with show of zeal and love   665
To man, and indignation at his wrong,
New part puts on, and as to passion moved,
Fluctuates disturbed, yet comely, and in act
Raised, as of some great matter to begin.
As when of old some orator renowned   670
In Athens or free Rome, where eloquence
Flourished, since mute, to some great cause addressed,
Stood in himself collected, while each part,
Motion, each act won audience ere the tongue,

649. I.e.: Let the belief in (or reason for believing in, or the custody of) whose powers remain with thee.

653. *Sole daughter of his voice:* God's only commandment. In Hebrew *Bath Kol*, "daughter of a voice," means a voice from heaven.

654. Cf. Rom. 2.14: "For when the Gentiles, which have not the law, do by nature the things contained in the law, these, having not the law, are a law unto themselves."

667. *New part puts on.* Satan's rhetorical task has changed because the argument has changed: now the topic is philosophical, religious, and political, and his speech will be like one of those great, ancient deliberative (or political) orations advising the audience on the best course of action. In his new role he will urge man to exercise his "right to know."

668. *Fluctuates:* (L *fluctuare* to undu-

late) Milton may ironically glance at Satan's snake-like motion, but the primary senses of the word are to pace back and forth and to express vacillation of mental attitude. *disturbed:* disordered, discomposed. *act:* in Latin rhetoric *actio* meant the exterior air or bearing of an orator.

669. *Raised:* drawn up to full dignity.

672. *to some great cause .addressed:* prepared to speak on some great question of debate or case before a court.

673–74. *Stood in himself collected.* Cf. *in act Raised* (668). *each part, Motion, each act:* never satisfactorily explained (why each?). Thinking of accounts of classical orators as versatile actors able to move their audiences simply by pantomime, Milton may see the silent serpent Satan *fluctuating* (668) in role, gesture, and physical bearing or attitude. *audience:* attention.

Sometimes in highth began, as no delay   675
Of preface brooking through his zeal of right.
So standing, moving, or to highth upgrown
The Tempter all impassioned thus began.
    "O sacred, wise, and wisdom-giving plant,
Mother of science, now I feel thy power   680
Within me clear, not only to discern
Things in their causes, but to trace the ways
Of highest agents, deemed however wise.
Queen of this universe, do not believe
Those rigid threats of death; ye shall not die: 685
How should ye? By the fruit? It gives you life
To knowledge. By the Threat'ner? Look on me,
Me who have touched and tasted, yet both live,
And life more perfet have attained than fate
Meant me, by vent'ring higher than my lot.   690
Shall that be shut to man, which to the beast
Is open? Or will God incense his ire
For such a petty trespass, and not praise
Rather your dauntless virtue, whom the pain
Of death denounced, whatever thing death be,   695
Deterred not from achieving what might lead
To happier life, knowledge of good and evil;
Of good, how just? Of evil, if what is evil
Be real, why not known, since easier shunned?
God therefore cannot hurt ye, and be just;   700
Not just, not God; not feared then, nor obeyed:
Your fear itself of death removes the fear.
Why then was this forbid? Why but to awe,
Why but to keep ye low and ignorant,
His worshipers; he knows that in the day   705
Ye eat thereof, your eyes that seem so clear,
Yet are but dim, shall perfetly be then
Opened and cleared, and ye shall be as gods,
Knowing both good and evil as they know.
That ye should be as gods, since I as man,   710
Internal man, is but proportion meet,
I of brute human, ye of human gods.
So ye shall die perhaps, by putting off
Human, to put on gods, death to be wished,
Though threatened, which no worse than this can bring.   715
And what are gods that man may not become

675. *in highth*: in the kind of impassioned style orators usually do not work up to until well into their oration.
677. *standing, moving*. Cf. 673, 674, and VI.301–3. *to highth upgrown*. Cf. *in act Raised* (668), *act* (674), and *highth* (675).
680. *science*: knowledge.
687. *To*: in addition to.
692. *incense*: L *incendere* to set on fire.
694–95. *virtue*: courage, manliness; but perhaps also, goodness. *the pain/Of death denounced*: the announcement of the punishment of death.
711. *Internal man*. Cf. *my inward powers* (600).
713–14. An ironic parody of phrases used to describe the process of salvation; cf. 1 Cor. 15.53: "For this corruptible must put on incorruption, and this mortal must put on immortality."

As they, participating godlike food?
The gods are first, and that advantage use
On our belief, that all from them proceeds;
I question it, for this fair earth I see,   720
Warmed by the sun, producing every kind,
Them nothing: if they all things, who enclosed
Knowledge of good and evil in this tree,
That whoso eats thereof, forthwith attains
Wisdom without their leave? And wherein lies   725
Th' offense, that man should thus attain to know?
What can your knowledge hurt him, or this tree
Impart against his will if all be his?
Or is it envy, and can envy dwell
In heav'nly breasts? These, these and many more   730
Causes import your need of this fair fruit.
Goddess humane, reach then, and freely taste."
    He ended, and his words replete with guile
Into her heart too easy entrance won:
Fixed on the fruit she gazed, which to behold   735
Might tempt alone, and in her ears the sound
Yet rung of his persuasive words, impregned
With reason, to her seeming, and with truth;
Meanwhile the hour of noon drew on, and waked
An eager appetite, raised by the smell   740
So savory of that fruit, which with desire,
Inclinable now grown to touch or taste,
Solicited her longing eye; yet first
Pausing a while, thus to herself she mused:
    "Great are thy virtues, doubtless, best of fruits,   745
Though kept from man, and worthy to be admired,
Whose taste, too long forborne, at first assay
Gave elocution to the mute, and taught
The tongue not made for speech to speak thy praise:
Thy praise he also who forbids thy use,   750
Conceals not from us, naming thee the Tree
Of Knowledge, knowledge both of good and evil;
Forbids us then to taste, but his forbidding
Commends thee more, while it infers the good
By thee communicated, and our want: 755
For good unknown, sure is not had, or had
And yet unknown, is as not had at all.
In plain then, what forbids he but to know,
Forbids us good, forbids us to be wise?
Such prohibitions bind not. But if death   760

717. *participating:* sharing, partaking of.
722. I.e.: If they [produced] all things.
731. *Causes:* reasons. *import:* indicate, prove.
732. *humane:* a common spelling for *human* in the seventeenth century, but in the only other instances of this spelling in Milton's poetry the word means kind, gentle, or gracious.
741. *savory.* See 579n.
745. *virtues:* powers.
755. *want:* lack.
758. *In plain:* plainly.

Bind us with after-bands, what profits then
Our inward freedom? In the day we eat
Of this fair fruit, our doom is, we shall die.
How dies the serpent? He hath eat'n and lives,
And knows, and speaks, and reasons, and discerns,   765
Irrational till then. For us alone
Was death invented? Or to us denied
This intellectual food, for beasts reserved?
For beasts it seems: yet that one beast which first
Hath tasted, envies not, but brings with joy   770
The good befall'n him, author unsuspect,
Friendly to man, far from deceit or guile.
What fear I then, rather what know to fear
Under this ignorance of good and evil,
Of God or death, of law or penalty?   775
Here grows the cure of all, this fruit divine,
Fair to the eye, inviting to the taste,
Of virtue to make wise: what hinders then
To reach, and feed at once both body and mind?"
       So saying, her rash hand in evil hour   780
Forth reaching to the fruit, she plucked, she eat:
Earth felt the wound, and nature from her seat
Sighing through all her works gave signs of woe,
That all was lost. Back to the thicket slunk
The guilty serpent, and well might, for Eve   785
Intent now wholly on her taste, naught else
Regarded, such delight till then, as seemed,
In fruit she never tasted, whether true
Or fancied so, through expectation high
Of knowledge, nor was Godhead from her thought.   790
Greedily she engorged without restraint,
And knew not eating death: satiate at length,
And highthened as with wine, jocund and boon,
Thus to herself she pleasingly began.
       "O sovran, virtuous, precious of all trees   795
In Paradise, of operation blest
To sapience, hitherto obscured, infamed,
And thy fair fruit let hang, as to no end
Created; but henceforth my early care,
Not without song, each morning, and due praise   800
Shall tend thee, and the fertile burden ease
Of thy full branches offered free to all;
Till dieted by thee I grow mature

---

763. *doom:* irrevocable destiny.
770. *envies:* begrudges.
771. *author:* authority, informant. *un-suspect:* beyond suspicion.
781. *eat:* past tense.
782. *her seat:* where she holds court.
792. *knew not* [that she was] *eating.*
793. *jocund and boon:* merry and (in a jovial bacchanalian sense) jolly, con-

vivial.
795. *virtuous, precious:* most powerful and valuable.
796–97. *of operation blest/To:* endowed with the power to give. *sapience:* wisdom. Cf. *science* (knowledge) in 680, as Madsen suggests, and 442n. *obscured:* imperfectly understood. *infamed:* defamed.

In knowledge, as the gods who all things know;
Though others envy what they cannot give; 805
For had the gift been theirs, it had not here
Thus grown. Experience, next to thee I owe,
Best guide; not following thee, I had remained
In ignorance, thou open'st wisdom's way,
And giv'st accéss, though secret she retire. 810
And I perhaps am secret; Heav'n is high,
High and remote to see from thence distinct
Each thing on earth; and other care perhaps
May have diverted from continual watch
Our great Forbidder, safe with all his spies 815
About him. But to Adam in what sort
Shall I appear? shall I to him make known
As yet my change, and give him to partake
Full happiness with me, or rather not,
But keep the odds of knowledge in my power 820
Without copartner? so to add what wants
In female sex, the more to draw his love,
And render me more equal, and perhaps,
A thing not undesirable, sometime
Superior; for inferior who is free? 825
This may be well: but what if God have seen,
And death ensue? Then I shall be no more,
And Adam wedded to another Eve,
Shall live with her enjoying, I extinct;
A death to think. Confirmed then I resolve, 830
Adam shall share with me in bliss or woe:
So dear I love him, that with him all deaths
I could endure, without him live no life."
    So saying, from the tree her step she turned,
But first low reverence done, as to the power 835
That dwelt within, whose presence had infused
Into the plant sciential sap, derived
From nectar, drink of gods. Adam the while
Waiting desirous her return, had wove
Of choicest flow'rs a garland to adorn 840
Her tresses, and her rural labors crown,
As reapers oft are wont their harvest queen.
Great joy he promised to his thoughts, and new
Solace in her return, so long delayed;
Yet oft his heart, divine of something ill, 845
Misgave him; he the falt'ring measure felt;
And forth to meet her went, the way she took
That morn when first they parted; by the Tree

---

805. I.e.: Though they [the gods] be-
grudge to others what they have no
power to give.
811. *secret:* hidden, unseen.
815. *safe:* not likely to come out, inter-
vene, or do hurt.

816. *sort:* manner.
820. *odds:* advantage.
837. *sciential:* knowledge-producing.
845. *divine:* prophetic.
846. *falt'ring measure:* irregular [heart]
beat.

Of Knowledge he must pass; there he her met,
Scarce from the tree returning; in her hand   850
A bough of fairest fruit that downy smiled,
New gathered, and ambrosial smell diffused.
To him she hasted, in her face excuse
Came prologue, and apology to prompt,
Which with bland words at will she thus addressed.   855
    "Hast thou not wondered, Adam, at my stay?
Thee I have missed, and thought it long, deprived
Thy presence, agony of love till now
Not felt, nor shall be twice, for never more
Mean I to try, what rash untried I sought,   860
The pain of absence from thy sight. But strange
Hath been the cause, and wonderful to hear:
This tree is not as we are told, a tree
Of danger tasted, nor to evil unknown
Op'ning the way, but of divine effect   865
To open eyes, and make them gods who taste;
And hath been tasted such: the serpent wise,
Or not restrained as we, or not obeying,
Hath eaten of the fruit, and is become,
Not dead, as we are threatened, but thenceforth   870
Endued with human voice and human sense,
Reasoning to admiration, and with me
Persuasively hath so prevailed, that I
Have also tasted, and have also found
Th' effects to correspond, opener mine eyes,   875
Dim erst, dilated spirits, ampler heart,
And growing up to godhead; which for thee
Chiefly I sought, without thee can despise.
For bliss, as thou hast part, to me is bliss,
Tedious, unshared with thee, and odious soon.   880
Thou therefore also taste, that equal lot
May join us, equal joy, as equal love;
Lest thou not tasting, different degree
Disjoin us, and I then too late renounce
Deity for thee, when fate will not permit."   885
    Thus Eve with count'nance blithe her story told;
But in her cheek distemper flushing glowed.
On th' other side, Adam, soon as he heard
The fatal trespass done by Eve, amazed,
Astonied stood and blank, while horror chill   890

853–55. I.e.: Excuse came like the pro-
logue in a play, and apology served as a
prompter, as Eve recited her speech of
self-defense, which she dressed, or
adorned, in the following way with
soothing words chosen without regard to
anything but her own purpose.
860–85. In reading this passage re-
member that *try, taste, test,* and *tempt*
can be synonymous.
860. *rash:* modifies *I; untried* modifies

what.
    872. *to admiration:* so as to cause won-
der and delight.
    881. *equal lot.* Cf. *consort,* 954n.
    887. *distemper:* physical disorder; in-
toxication.
    889. *amazed:* stupefied; confused; ter-
ror-stricken.
    890. *Astonied:* (L *ex* + *tonare* to
thunder) stunned. *blank:* pale, con-
founded.

Ran through his veins, and all his joints relaxed;
From his slack hand the garland wreathed for Eve
Down dropped, and all the faded roses shed:
Speechless he stood and pale, till thus at length
First to himself he inward silence broke.   895
  "O fairest of creation, last and best
Of all God's works, creature in whom excelled
Whatever can to sight or thought be formed,
Holy, divine, good, amiable, or sweet!
How art thou lost, how on a sudden lost,   900
Defaced, deflow'red, and now to death devote?
Rather how hast thou yielded to transgress
The strict forbiddance, how to violate
The sacred fruit forbidd'n! some cursèd fraud
Of enemy hath beguiled thee, yet unknown,   905
And me with thee hath ruined, for with thee
Certain my resolution is to die;
How can I live without thee, how forgo
Thy sweet converse and love so dearly joined,
To live again in these wild woods forlorn?   910
Should God create another Eve, and I
Another rib afford, yet loss of thee
Would never from my heart; no no, I feel
The link of nature draw me: flesh of flesh,
Bone of my bone thou art, and from thy state   915
Mine never shall be parted, bliss or woe."
  So having said, as one from sad dismay
Recomforted, and after thoughts disturbed
Submitting to what seemed remédiless,
Thus in calm mood his words to Eve he turned.   920
  "Bold deed thou hast presumed, advent'rous Eve,
And peril great provoked, who thus hast dared
Had it been only coveting to eye
That sacred fruit, sacred to abstinence,
Much more to taste it under ban to touch.   925
But past who can recall, or done undo?
Not God omnipotent, nor fate; yet so
Perhaps thou shalt not die, perhaps the fact
Is not so heinous now, foretasted fruit,
Profaned first by the serpent, by him first   930
Made common and unhallowed ere our taste;
Nor yet on him found deadly, he yet lives,
Lives, as thou saidst, and gains to live as man
Higher degree of life, inducement strong

901. *devote:* devoted, doomed.
904. *sacred:* consecrated, set apart.
906–7. I.e.: My resolution to die with
thee is fixed, unalterable. Cf. *fixed*, 952.
  914–15. *flesh of flesh,/Bone of my
bone.* Cf. Gen. 2.23–24, p. 354.
918. *Recomforted:* comforted, refreshed.
925. *touch.* Cf. VII.46 and IX.651 and

663, where the command not to touch the
fruit (Gen. 3.2, 3, p. 355) is alluded
to. Adam says it was dangerous even to
look at the fruit and certainly more dan-
gerous to eat what they had been told not
even to touch.
  928. *fact:* crime, deed.

To us, as likely tasting to attain   935
Proportional ascent, which cannot be
But to be gods, or angels demi-gods.
Nor can I think that God, Creator wise,
Though threat'ning, will in earnest so destroy
Us his prime creatures, dignified so high,   940
Set over all his works, which in our fall,
For us created, needs with us must fail,
Dependent made; so God shall uncreate,
Be frustrate, do, undo, and labor lose,
Not well conceived of God, who though his power   945
Creation could repeat, yet would be loath
Us to abolish, lest the Adversary
Triumph and say; 'Fickle their state whom God
Most favors, who can please him long? Me first
He ruined, now mankind; whom will he next?'   950
Matter of scorn, not to be given the Foe.
However I with thee have fixed my lot,
Certain to undergo like doom; if death
Consort with thee, death is to me as life;
So forcible within my heart I feel   955
The bond of nature draw me to my own,
My own in thee, for what thou art is mine;
Our state cannot be severed, we are one,
One flesh; to lose thee were to lose myself."
    So Adam, and thus Eve to him replied.   960
"O glorious trial of exceeding love,
Illustrious evidence, example high!
Engaging me to emulate, but short
Of thy perfection, how shall I attain,
Adam, from whose dear side I boast me sprung,   965
And gladly of our union hear thee speak,
One heart, one soul in both; whereof good proof
This day affords, declaring thee resolved,
Rather than death or aught than death more dread
Shall separate us, linked in love so dear,   970
To undergo with me one guilt, one crime,
If any be, of tasting this fair fruit,
Whose virtue, for of good still good proceeds,
Direct, or by occasion hath presented
This happy trial of thy love, which else   975
So eminently never had been known.

---

944. *frustrate:* frustrated, defined by "do, undo."

953. *Certain:* resolved. Cf. 907. *doom:* sentence of punishment.

954. *Consort:* keep company, associate. Since the noun *consort* (L *con* with + *sortis* lot, fate; *consors* partner, fellow, one having a common lot or fate with another) is used several times in refer-ence to Eve's married relationship with Adam, Milton's choice of the verb here, in the context of *lot* and *like doom* barely avoids the suggestion that Adam would be jealous of death, as Eve earlier feared that Adam would find a second Eve.

974. *Direct, or by occasion:* as the real, fundamental cause, or as the immediate, circumstantial cause.

Were it I thought death menaced would ensue
This my attempt, I would sustain alone
The worst, and not persuade thee, rather die
Deserted, than oblige thee with a fact   980
Pernicious to thy peace, chiefly assured
Remarkably so late of thy so true,
So faithful love unequaled; but I feel
Far otherwise th' event, not death, but life
Augmented, opened eyes, new hopes, new joys,   985
Taste so divine, that what of sweet before
Hath touched my sense, flat seems to this, and harsh.
Of my experience, Adam, freely taste,
And fear of death deliver to the winds."
   So saying, she embraced him, and for joy   990
Tenderly wept, much won that he his love
Had so ennobled, as of choice to incur
Divine displeasure for her sake, or death.
In recompense (for such compliance bad
Such recompense best merits) from the bough   995
She gave him of that fair enticing fruit
With liberal hand: he scrupled not to eat
Against his better knowledge, not deceived,
But fondly overcome with female charm.
Earth trembled from her entrails, as again   1000
In pangs, and nature gave a second groan;
Sky loured, and muttering thunder, some sad drops
Wept at completing of the mortal sin
Original; while Adam took no thought,
Eating his fill, nor Eve to iterate   1005
Her former trespass feared, the more to soothe
Him with her loved society, that now
As with new wine intoxicated both
They swim in mirth, and fancy that they feel
Divinity within them breeding wings   1010
Wherewith to scorn the earth: but that false fruit
Far other operation first displayed,
Carnal desire inflaming, he on Eve
Began to cast lascivious eyes, she him
As wantonly repaid; in lust they burn: 1015
Till Adam thus 'gan Eve to dalliance move.
   "Eve, now I see thou art exact of taste,

---

977. *menaced:* threatened.
980. *oblige:* (L *obligare* to bind one in a criminal plot) make guilty, liable to penalty. *fact:* deed, crime.
981–82. I.e.: Particularly since I have so recently been notably assured of, etc.
984. *event:* consequence.
998–99. Cf. 1 Tim. 2.14: "And Adam was not deceived, but the woman being deceived was in the transgression." Cf. St. Augustine, *The City of God*, XIV.xi (trans. by Marcus Dods): "We cannot

believe that Adam was deceived, and supposed the devil's word to be truth, and therefore transgressed God's law, but that he by the drawings of kindred yielded to the woman, the husband to the wife, the one human being to the only other human being."
1003–4. *mortal sin/Original.* Cf. *CD*, I.xi.C.
1005. *iterate:* repeat.
1012. *operation.* Cf. VIII.323n.
1017. *exact:* L *exigere* to demand.

And elegant, of sapience no small part,
Since to each meaning savor we apply,
And palate call judicious; I the praise   1020
Yield thee, so well this day thou hast purveyed.
Much pleasure we have lost, while we abstained
From this delightful fruit, nor known till now
True relish, tasting; if such pleasure be
In things to us forbidden, it might be wished,   1025
For this one tree had been forbidden ten.
But come, so well refreshed, now let us play,
As meet is, after such delicious fare;
For never did thy beauty since the day
I saw thee first and wedded thee, adorned   1030
With all perfections, so inflame my sense
With ardor to enjoy thee, fairer now
Than ever, bounty of this virtuous tree."
    So said he, and forbore not glance or toy
Of amorous intent, well understood   1035
Of Eve, whose eye darted contagious fire.
Her hand he seized, and to a shady bank,
Thick overhead with verdant roof embow'red
He led her nothing loath; flow'rs were the couch,
Pansies, and violets, and asphodel,   1040
And hyacinth, earth's freshest softest lap.
There they their fill of love and love's disport
Took largely, of their mutual guilt the seal,
The solace of their sin, till dewy sleep
Oppressed them, wearied with their amorous play.   1045
Soon as the force of that fallacious fruit,
That with exhilarating vapor bland
About their spirits had played, and inmost powers
Made err, was now exhaled, and grosser sleep
Bred of unkindly fumes, with conscious dreams   1050
Encumbered, now had left them, up they rose
As from unrest, and each the other viewing,
Soon found their eyes how opened, and their minds
How darkened; innocence, that as a veil
Had shadowed them from knowing ill, was gone,   1055

1018–19. *elegant:* L *eligere* to select.
sapience: L *sapere*, to taste, have sense,
know. Adam says that we use the word
savor to mean both the ability to taste
or enjoy (*taste*) and the ability to know
or discriminate (*sapience*). Cf. 442, 579,
741.
    1021. *purveyed:* provided.
    1027–28. Cf. Exod. 32.6: "And they
rose up early on the morrow, and offered
burnt offerings, and brought peace offer-
ings; and the people sat down to eat and
drink, and rose up to play." 1 Cor. 10.7:
"Neither be ye idolaters, as were some of
them; as it is written, The people sat
down to eat and drink, and rose up to

play. Neither let us commit fornication,
as some of them committed. . . ."
    1034. *toy:* caress.
    1042–44. *fill of love . . . took . . . sol-
ace:* In Prov. 7.18 a harlot says, "Come,
let us take our fill of love until the
morning: let us solace ourselves with
loves."
    1047. *bland:* flattering, seductive, sen-
suously pleasing.
    1050. *unkindly:* unnatural. *fumes:* nox-
ious exhalations rising to the brain from
the stomach. *conscious:* self-knowing,
guilty.
    1051. *Encumbered:* oppressed.
    1054–58. Cf. *CD*, I.xii.A.

Just confidence, and native righteousness,
And honor from about them, naked left
To guilty Shame: he covered, but his robe
Uncovered more. So rose the Danite strong
Hercúlean Samson from the harlot-lap   1060
Of Philistéan Dálilah, and waked
Shorn of his strength, they destitute and bare
Of all their virtue: silent, and in face
Confounded long they sat, as strucken mute,
Till Adam, though not less than Eve abashed,   1065
At length gave utterance to these words constrained.
    "O Eve, in evil hour thou didst give ear
To that false worm, of whomsoever taught
To counterfeit man's voice, true in our fall,
False in our promised rising; since our eyes   1070
Opened we find indeed, and find we know
Both good and evil, good lost and evil got,
Bad fruit of knowledge, if this be to know,
Which leaves us naked thus, of honor void,
Of innocence, of faith, of purity,   1075
Our wonted ornaments now soiled and stained,
And in our faces evident the signs
Of foul concupiscence; whence evil store;
Even shame, the last of evils; of the first
Be sure then. How shall I behold the face   1080
Henceforth of God or angel, erst with joy
And rapture so oft beheld? Those heav'nly shapes
Will dazzle now this earthly, with their blaze
Insufferably bright. O might I here
In solitude live savage, in some glade   1085
Obscured, where highest woods impenetrable
To star or sunlight, spread their umbrage broad,
And brown as evening: cover me ye pines,
Ye cedars, with innumerable boughs
Hide me, where I may never see them more.   1090
But let us now, as in bad plight, devise
What best may for the present serve to hide
The parts of each from other, that seem most
To shame obnoxious, and unseemliest seen,

1058. *Shame* is personified. Cf. 1097.
he covered: i.e., Shame covered them.
    1059–62. *Samson* (of the tribe of
Dan) told *Dalilah* (of the Philistines,
enemies of Israel) that his strength was
due to his not cutting his hair. She
sheared it off while he slept, and he was
no longer strong as Hercules. See Judg.
16.
    1063–64. *in face/Confounded:* with an
expression of dismay, confusion, shame.
Cf. *confound* in II.382.
    1066. *constrained:* strained, forced, un-
natural.
    1078. *evil store:* an abundance of evil.

    1079. *the last . . . the first:* perhaps:
Be sure that if the signs of shame are
evident in our faces, signs of the evils
that caused it are also evident.
    1080–84. Cf. VII.506–11, where Adam
was promised the privilege to *correspond
with Heaven.*
    1088. *brown:* dark.
    1090. Cf. Rev. 6.16: "And said to the
mountains and rocks, Fall on us, and
hide us from the face of him that sitteth
on the throne, and from the wrath of the
Lamb:"
    1094. *obnoxious:* exposed, subject.

Some tree whose broad smooth leaves together sewed,   1095
And girded on our loins, may cover round
Those middle parts, that this newcomer, Shame,
There sit not, and reproach us as unclean."
    So counseled he, and both together went
Into the thickest wood, there soon they chose   1100
The figtree, not that kind for fruit renowned,
But such as at this day to Indians known
In Malabar or Deccan spreads her arms
Branching so broad and long, that in the ground
The bended twigs take root, and daughters grow   1105
About the mother tree, a pillared shade
High overarched, and echoing walks between;
There oft the Indian herdsman shunning heat
Shelters in cool, and tends his pasturing herds
At loopholes cut through thickest shade: those leaves   1110
They gathered, broad as Amazonian targe,
And with what skill they had, together sewed,
To gird their waist, vain covering if to hide
Their guilt and dreaded shame; O how unlike
To that first naked glory. Such of late   1115
Columbus found th' American so girt
With feathered cincture, naked else and wild,
Among the trees on isles and woody shores.
Thus fenced, and as they thought, their shame in part
Covered, but not at rest or ease of mind,   1120
They sat them down to weep, nor only tears
Rained at their eyes, but high winds worse within
Began to rise, high passions, anger, hate,
Mistrust, suspicion, discord, and shook sore
Their inward state of mind, calm region once   1125
And full of peace, now tossed and turbulent:
For understanding ruled not, and the will
Heard not her lore, both in subjection now
To sensual appetite, who from beneath
Usurping over sovran reason claimed   1130
Superior sway: from thus distempered breast,
Adam, estranged in look and altered style,
Speech intermitted thus to Eve renewed.
    "Would thou hadst hearkened to my words, and stayed
With me, as I besought thee, when that strange   1135
Desire of wand'ring this unhappy morn,

1101–10. Milton's description follows in detail that of the "arched Indian Figtree" in Gerard's *Herball* (1597) and others. Milton did not know that the banyan, which fits the description in other respects, has small leaves. *Malabar or Deccan*: in India.

1111. *Amazonian targe*: the shields of Amazons.

1117. *cincture*: belt.

1121. Cf. Ps. 137.1: "By the rivers of Babylon, there we [the Israelites in exile] sat down, yea, we wept, when we remembered Zion."

1127–31. See "Physiology and Psychology," p. 392.

1132. *estranged*: unlike himself.

I know not whence possessed thee; we had then
Remained still happy, not as now, despoiled
Of all our good, shamed, naked, miserable.
Let none henceforth seek needless cause to approve   1140
The faith they owe; when earnestly they seek
Such proof, conclude, they then begin to fail."
    To whom soon moved with touch of blame thus Eve.
"What words have passed thy lips, Adam severe,
Imput'st thou that to my default, or will   1145
Of wand'ring, as thou call'st it, which who knows
But might as ill have happened thou being by,
Or to thyself perhaps: hadst thou been there,
Or here th' attempt, thou couldst not have discerned
Fraud in the serpent, speaking as he spake;   1150
No ground of enmity between us known,
Why he should mean me ill, or seek to harm.
Was I to have never parted from thy side?
As good have grown there still a lifeless rib.
Being as I am, why didst not thou the head   1155
Command me absolutely not to go,
Going into such danger as thou saidst?
Too facile then thou didst not much gainsay,
Nay didst permit, approve, and fair dismiss.
Hadst thou been firm and fixed in thy dissent,   1160
Neither had I transgressed, nor thou with me."
    To whom then first incensed Adam replied.
"Is this the love, is this the recompense
Of mine to thee, ingrateful Eve, expressed
Immutable when thou wert lost, not I,   1165
Who might have lived and joyed immortal bliss,
Yet willingly chose rather death with thee:
And am I now upbraided, as the cause
Of thy transgressing? not enough severe,
It seems, in thy restraint: what could I more?   1170
I warned thee, I admonished thee, foretold
The danger, and the lurking Enemy
That lay in wait; beyond this had been force,
And force upon free will hath here no place.
But confidence then bore thee on, secure   1175
Either to meet no danger, or to find
Matter of glorious trial; and perhaps
I also erred in overmuch admiring
What seemed in thee so perfet, that I thought
No evil durst attempt thee, but I rue   1180
That error now, which is become my crime,

1140. *approve:* prove.
1141. *owe:* own.
1155. *head.* Cf. 1 Cor. 11.3: "the head of the woman is the man."
1158. *facile:* easily persuaded; mild

mannered.
1164–65. *expressed/Immutable:* demonstrated to be unchangeable.
1175. *secure:* sure, self-assured.
1177. *Matter of:* occasion for.

And thou th' accuser. Thus it shall befall
Him who to worth in women overtrusting
Lets her will rule; restraint she will not brook,
And left to herself, if evil thence ensue,   1185
She first his weak indulgence will accuse."
    Thus they in mutual accusation spent
The fruitless hours, but neither self-condemning,
And of their vain contést appeared no end.

Book X

Man's transgression known, the guardian angels forsake Paradise, and return up to heaven to approve their vigilance, and are approved, God declaring that the entrance of Satan could not be by them prevented. He sends his Son to judge the transgressors, who descends and gives sentence accordingly; then in pity clothes them both, and reascends. Sin and Death, sitting till then at the gates of hell, by wondrous sympathy feeling the success of Satan in this new world, and the sin by man there committed, resolve to sit no longer confined in hell, but to follow Satan their sire up to the place of man: to make the way easier from hell to this world to and fro, they pave a broad highway or bridge over chaos, according to the track that Satan first made; then preparing for earth, they meet him proud of his success returning to hell; their mutual gratulation. Satan arrives at Pandemonium, in full assembly relates with boasting his success against man; instead of applause is entertained with a general hiss by all his audience, transformed with himself also suddenly into serpents, according to his doom given in Paradise; then deluded with a show of the Forbidden Tree springing up before them, they greedily reaching to take of the fruit, chew dust and bitter ashes. The proceedings of Sin and Death; God foretells the final victory of his Son over them, and the renewing of all things; but for the present commands his angels to make several alterations in the heavens and elements. Adam more and more perceiving his fallen condition, heavily bewails, rejects the condolement of Eve; she persists and at length appeases him: then to evade the curse likely to fall on their offspring, proposes to Adam violent ways which he approves not, but conceiving better hope, puts her in mind of the late promise made them, that her seed should be revenged on the Serpent, and exhorts her with him to seek peace of the offended Deity, by repentance and supplication.

Meanwhile the heinous and despiteful act
Of Satan done in Paradise, and how
He in the serpent had perverted Eve,
Her husband she, to taste the fatal fruit,
Was known in heav'n; for what can scape the eye   5
Of God all-seeing, or deceive his heart
Omniscient, who in all things wise and just,
Hindered not Satan to attempt the mind
Of man, with strength entire, and free will armed,
Complete to have discovered and repulsed   10
Whatever wiles of foe or seeming friend.

X.10. *Complete:* perfectly equipped.

213

For still they knew, and ought to have still remembered
The high injunction not to taste that fruit,
Whoever tempted; which they not obeying,
Incurred, what could they less, the penalty,   15
And manifold in sin, deserved to fall.
Up into heav'n from Paradise in haste
Th' angelic guards ascended, mute and sad
For man, for of his state by this they knew,
Much wond'ring how the subtle Fiend had stol'n   20
Entrance unseen. Soon as th' unwelcome news
From earth arrived at heaven gate, displeased
All were who heard, dim sadness did not spare
That time celestial visages, yet mixed
With pity, violated not their bliss.   25
About the new-arrived, in multitudes
Th' ethereal people ran, to hear and know
How all befell: they towards the throne supreme
Accountable made haste to make appear
With righteous plea, their utmost vigilance,   30
And easily approved; when the Most High
Eternal Father from his secret cloud,
Amidst in thunder uttered thus his voice.
    "Assembled Angels, and ye Powers returned
From unsuccessful charge, be not dismayed,   35
Nor troubled at these tidings from the earth,
Which your sincerest care could not prevent,
Foretold so lately what would come to pass,
When first this Tempter crossed the gulf from hell.
I told ye then he should prevail and speed   40
On his bad errand, man should be seduced
And flattered out of all, believing lies
Against his Maker; no decree of mine
Concurring to necessitate his fall,
Or touch with lightest moment of impulse   45
His free will, to her own inclining left
In even scale. But fall'n he is, and now
What rests, but that the mortal sentence pass
On his transgression, death denounced that day,
Which he presumes already vain and void,   50
Because not yet inflicted, as he feared,
By some immediate stroke; but soon shall find
Forbearance no acquittance ere day end.
Justice shall not return as bounty scorned.

---

12. *still:* always.
16. *manifold in sin.* See *CD*, I.xi.A.
28–31. I.e.: Responsible for their actions, they hastened towards the supreme throne to make plain their utmost vigilance with a righteous plea, and easily gained approval.
33. Cf. Rev. 4.5, p. 384.

40. *speed:* succeed.
44. *Concurring:* cooperating.
45. *moment:* the smallest weight that will tip a balance (scale).
48. *rests:* remains.
53. *Forbearance:* abstinence from enforcing the payment of a debt. *acquittance:* discharge from a debt.

But whom send I to judge them? Whom but thee   55
Vicegerent Son, to thee I have transferred
All judgment, whether in heav'n, or earth, or hell.
Easy it may be seen that I intend
Mercy colleague with justice, sending thee
Man's friend, his mediator, his designed   60
Both ransom and redeemer voluntary,
And destined man himself to judge man fall'n."
  So spake the Father, and unfolding bright
Toward the right hand his glory, on the Son
Blazed forth unclouded deity; he full   65
Resplendent all his Father manifest
Expressed, and thus divinely answered mild.
  "Father Eternal, thine is to decree,
Mine both in heav'n and earth to do thy will
Supreme, that thou in me thy Son beloved   70
May'st ever rest well pleased. I go to judge
On earth these thy transgressors; but thou know'st,
Whoever judged, the worst on me must light,
When time shall be, for so I undertook
Before thee; and not repenting, this obtain   75
Of right, that I may mitigate their doom
On me derived, yet I shall temper so
Justice with mercy, as may illustrate most
Them fully satisfied, and thee appease.
Attendance none shall need, nor train, where none   80
Are to behold the judgment, but the judged,
Those two; the third best absent is condemned,
Convict by flight, and rebel to all law:
Conviction to the Serpent none belongs."
  Thus saying, from his radiant seat he rose   85
Of high collateral glory: him Thrones and Powers,
Princedoms, and Dominations ministrant
Accompanied to heaven gate, from whence
Eden and all the coast in prospect lay.
Down he descended straight; the speed of gods   90
Time counts not, though with swiftest minutes winged.
Now was the sun in western cadence low
From noon, and gentle airs due at their hour
To fan the earth now waked, and usher in
The evening cool, when he from wrath more cool   95
Came the mild judge and intercessor both
To sentence man: the voice of God they heard

55–57. Cf. John 5.22: "For the Father judgeth no man, but hath committed all judgment unto the Son."
77–79. I.e.: I shall temper justice with mercy in such a way that, though their demands are fully satisfied, they adorn (make bright) one another—and I shall [still] appease you.
77. *derived:* (L *de* from + *rivus* stream) channelled, diverted, brought down.
83. *Convict:* convicted.
84. The serpent has no right to trial by law.
86. *collateral:* placed side by side.
89. *coast:* (L *costa* side) surrounding territory.
92. *cadence:* L *cadere* to fall.

Now walking in the garden, by soft winds
Brought to their ears, while day declined; they heard,
And from his presence hid themselves among   100
The thickest trees, both man and wife, till God
Approaching, thus to Adam called aloud.
    "Where art thou Adam, wont with joy to meet
My coming seen far off? I miss thee here,
Not pleased, thus entertained with solitude,   105
Where obvious duty erewhile appeared unsought:
Or come I less conspicuous, or what change
Absents thee, or what chance detains? Come forth."
He came, and with him Eve, more loth, though first
To offend, discount'nanced both, and discomposed;   110
Love was not in their looks, either to God
Or to each other, but apparent guilt,
And shame, and perturbation, and despair,
Anger, and obstinacy, and hate, and guile.
Whence Adam falt'ring long, thus answered brief.   115
    "I heard thee in the garden, and of thy voice
Afraid, being naked, hid myself." To whom
The gracious Judge without revile replied.
    "My voice thou oft hast heard, and hast not feared,
But still rejoiced, how is it now become   120
So dreadful to thee? That thou art naked, who
Hath told thee? Hast thou eaten of the tree
Whereof I gave thee charge thou shouldst not eat?"
    To whom thus Adam sore beset replied.
"O heav'n! in evil strait this day I stand   125
Before my Judge, either to undergo
Myself the total crime, or to accuse
My other self, the partner of my life;
Whose failing, while her faith to me remains,
I should conceal, and not expose to blame   130
By my complaint; but strict necessity
Subdues me, and calamitous constraint,
Lest on my head both sin and punishment,
However insupportable, be all
Devolved; though should I hold my peace, yet thou   135
Wouldst easily detect what I conceal.
This woman whom thou mad'st to be my help,
And gav'st me as thy perfet gift, so good,
So fit, so acceptáble, so divine,
That from her hand I could suspect no ill,   140
And what she did, whatever in itself,
Her doing seemed to justify the deed;
She gave me of the Tree, and I did eat."
    To whom the Sovran Presence thus replied.

101. *God:* Christ.
106. *obvious duty:* your social obliga-
tion to greet me (L *obvius* in the way, so
as to meet, meeting; affable, courteous).

112. *apparent:* easily seen.
118. *revile:* reviling, abusive attack.
131. *necessity.* Cf. IV.393.
135. *Devolved:* passed down.

"Was she thy God, that her thou didst obey   145
Before his voice, or was she made thy guide,
Superior, or but equal, that to her
Thou didst resign thy manhood, and the place
Wherein God set thee above her made of thee,
And for thee, whose perfection far excelled   150
Hers in all real dignity: adorned
She was indeed, and lovely to attract
Thy love, not thy subjection, and her gifts
Were such as under government well seemed,
Unseemly to bear rule, which was thy part   155
And person, hadst thou known thyself aright."
    So having said, he thus to Eve in few:
"Say woman, what is this which thou hast done?"
    To whom sad Eve with shame nigh overwhelmed,
Confessing soon, yet not before her Judge   160
Bold or loquacious, thus abashed replied.
    "The serpent me beguiled and I did eat."
    Which when the Lord God heard, without delay
To judgment he proceeded on th' accused
Serpent though brute, unable to transfer   165
The guilt on him who made him instrument
Of mischief, and polluted from the end
Of his creation; justly then accursed,
As vitiated in nature: more to know
Concerned not man (since he no further knew)   170
Nor altered his offense; yet God at last
To Satan first in sin his doom applied,
Though in mysterious terms, judged as then best:
And on the serpent thus his curse let fall.
    "Because thou hast done this, thou art accursed   175
Above all cattle, each beast of the field;
Upon thy belly groveling thou shalt go,
And dust shalt eat all the days of thy life.
Between thee and the woman I will put
Enmity, and between thine and her seed;   180
Her seed shall bruise thy head, thou bruise his heel."
    So spake this oracle, then verified
When Jesus son of Mary second Eve,
Saw Satan fall like lightning down from heav'n,
Prince of the air; then rising from his grave   185

149–50. Cf. 1 Cor. 11.8–9: "For the man is not of the woman; but the woman of the man. Neither was the man created for the woman; but the woman for the man."
155–56. *part/And person:* role and character (persona as in L *persona* mask).
167. *end:* purpose.
173. *mysterious:* having a hidden meaning.
175–81. Cf. Gen. 3.14–15, p. 355.
184. Cf. Luke 10.17–18: "And the sev-

enty returned again with joy, saying, Lord, even the devils are subject unto us through thy name. And he said unto them, I beheld Satan as lightning fall from heaven."
185–90. Cf. Eph. 2.2: "Wherein in time past ye walked according to the course of this world, according to the prince of the power of the air, the spirit that now worketh in the children of disobedience." Col. 2.15: "And having spoiled principalities and powers, he

Spoiled Principalities and Powers, triumphed
In open show, and with ascension bright
Captivity led captive through the air,
The realm itself of Satan long usurped,
Whom he shall tread at last under our feet;   190
Ev'n he who now foretold his fatal bruise,
And to the woman thus his sentence turned.
　　"Thy sorrow I will greatly multiply
By thy conception; children thou shalt bring
In sorrow forth, and to thy husband's will   195
Thine shall submit, he over thee shall rule."
　　On Adam last thus judgment he pronounced.
"Because thou hast hearkened to the voice of thy wife,
And eaten of the tree concerning which
I charged thee, saying: Thou shalt not eat thereof,   200
Cursed is the ground for thy sake, thou in sorrow
Shalt eat thereof all the days of thy life;
Thorns also and thistles it shall bring thee forth
Unbid, and thou shalt eat th' herb of the field,
In the sweat of thy face shalt thou eat bread,   205
Till thou return unto the ground, for thou
Out of the ground wast taken: know thy birth,
For dust thou art, and shalt to dust return."
　　So judged he man, both judge and saviour sent,
And th' instant stroke of death denounced that day   210
Removed far off; then pitying how they stood
Before him naked to the air, that now
Must suffer change, disdained not to begin
Thenceforth the form of servant to assume,
As when he washed his servants' feet, so now   215
As father of his family he clad
Their nakedness with skins of beasts, or slain,
Or as the snake with youthful coat repaid;
And thought not much to clothe his enemies:
Nor he their outward only with the skins   220
Of beasts, but inward nakedness, much more
Opprobrious, with his robe of righteousness,

---

made a shew of them openly, triumphing over them in it." Ps. 68.18: "Thou hast ascended on high, thou hast led captivity captive: thou hast received gifts for men; yea, for the rebellious also, that the Lord God might dwell among them." Rom. 16.20: "And the God of peace shall bruise Satan under your feet shortly. The grace of our Lord Jesus Christ be with you. Amen."
210. *denounced:* proclaimed, gave warning of.
213–17. Cf. Phil. 2.7: "But [Christ] made himself of no reputation, and took upon him the form of a servant, and was made in the likeness of men." John 13.5: "After that he poureth water into a basin, and began to wash the disciples' feet, and to wipe them with the towel wherewith he was girded."
217–18. *or slain,/Or:* either of beasts slain for their hides or of others, like the snake, that shed their skins.
219. *thought not much:* thought it not too much.
222. Cf. Isa. 61.10: "I will greatly rejoice in the Lord, my soul shall be joyful in my God; for he hath clothed me with the garments of salvation, he hath covered me with the robe of righteousness, as a bridegroom decketh himself with ornaments, and as a bride adorneth herself with her jewels."

Arraying covered from his Father's sight.
To him with swift ascent he up returned,
Into his blissful bosom reassumed   225
In glory as of old, to him appeased
All, though all-knowing, what had passed with man
Recounted, mixing intercession sweet.
Meanwhile ere thus was sinned and judged on earth,
Within the gates of hell sat Sin and Death,   230
In counterview within the gates, that now
Stood open wide, belching outrageous flame
Far into chaos, since the Fiend passed through,
Sin opening, who thus now to Death began.
    "O son, why sit we here each other viewing   235
Idly, while Satan our great author thrives
In other worlds, and happier seat provides
For us his offspring dear? It cannot be
But that success attends him; if mishap,
Ere this he had returned, with fury driv'n   240
By his avengers, since no place like this
Can fit his punishment, or their revenge.
Methinks I feel new strength within me rise,
Wings growing, and dominion giv'n me large
Beyond this deep; whatever draws me on,   245
Or sympathy, or some connatural force
Powerful at greatest distance to unite
With secret amity things of like kind
By secretest conveyance. Thou my shade
Inseparable must with me along: 250
For Death from Sin no power can separate.
But lest the difficulty of passing back
Stay his return perhaps over this gulf
Impassable, impervious, let us try
Advent'rous work, yet to thy power and mine   255
Not unagreeable, to found a path
Over this main from hell to that new world
Where Satan now prevails, a monument
Of merit high to all th' infernal host,
Easing their passage hence, for intercourse,   260
Or transmigration, as their lot shall lead.
Nor can I miss the way, so strongly drawn
By this new-felt attraction and instínct."

232. *outrageous:* unrestrained, fierce.
235. Cf. 2 Kings 7.3: "And there were four leprous men at the entering in of the gate: and they said one to another, Why sit we here until we die?" Matt. 20.6: "And about the eleventh hour he went out, and found others standing idle, and saith unto them, Why stand ye here all the day idle?"
236. *author:* father. Cf. II.864.
241. *like this.* Modifies *fit.*
246. *sympathy:* an attraction between

opposite (or complementary) natures or between similar natures. *connatural:* innate.
249. *conveyance:* communication.
254. *impervious:* (L *im* not + *per* through + *via* way) affording no passage.
256. *found:* establish, lay the foundation for.
260–61. *intercourse,/Or transmigration:* going back and forth, or emigrating to earth.

Whom thus the meager shadow answered soon.
"Go whither fate and inclination strong   265
Leads thee, I shall not lag behind, nor err
The way, thou leading, such a scent I draw
Of carnage, prey innumerable, and taste
The savor of death from all things there that live:
Nor shall I to the work thou enterprisest   270
Be wanting, but afford thee equal aid."
    So saying, with delight he snuffed the smell
Of mortal change on earth. As when a flock
Of ravenous fowl, though many a league remote,
Against the day of battle, to a field,   275
Where armies lie encamped, come flying, lured
With scent of living carcasses designed
For death, the following day, in bloody fight.
So scented the grim feature, and upturned
His nostril wide into the murky air,   280
Sagacious of his quarry from so far.
Then both from out hell gates into the waste
Wide anarchy of chaos damp and dark
Flew diverse, and with power (their power was great)
Hovering upon the waters, what they met   285
Solid or slimy, as in raging sea
Tossed up and down, together crowded drove
From each side shoaling towards the mouth of hell.
As when two polar winds blowing adverse
Upon the Cronian Sea, together drive   290
Mountains of ice, that stop th' imagined way
Beyond Petsora eastward, to the rich
Cathaian coast. The aggregated soil
Death with his mace petrific, cold and dry,
As with a trident smote, and fixed as firm   295
As Delos floating once; the rest his look
Bound with Gorgonian rigor not to move,
And with asphaltic slime; broad as the gate,

264. *meager:* having no or little flesh.
279. *feature:* (L *facere* to make) a creature, sometimes used as a term of contempt.
281. *Sagacious:* keen in sense perception, especially in scenting.
284. *diverse:* in different directions.
285–304. The engineers, Sin and Death, first built a *mole* (300), or *gathered beach* (299), extending like a pier or breakwater from the mouth of hell out into the *waters* (285) of chaos. On this they built the first pier of the bridge, which Milton describes (313) as a *ridge* (i.e., a long reef) *of pendent* (i.e., supported by arches) *rock.* The other end of the bridge was fastened by *pins* and *chains* to the outer shell of the universe (302–3, 318). Later (415) Milton called the whole thing a *causey,* a word some-

times used to refer to both a bridge and its causeway-like approaches.
288. *shoaling:* forming a shoal.
290–93. A sea passage in the Arctic Ocean (*Cronian Sea*) between a bay in Siberia (Pechora) and the north China (*Cathay*) coast was only an *imagined* (by Hudson) *way* because it was blocked by ice.
293–98. Death's *mace* petrified the *cold and dry* elements of the collected matter and made the other (hot and liquid) elements into a kind of mortar, using asphalt and the magic power of his look, which, like that of Medusa, a Gorgon, turned what was looked at into stone. Neptune was said to have *fixed* the *floating* island of *Delos* (in the Aegean) by a stroke of his *trident.*

Deep to the roots of hell the gathered beach
They fastened, and the mole immense wrought on   300
Over the foaming deep high-arched, a bridge
Of length prodigious joining to the wall
Immovable of this now fenceless world
Forfeit to Death; from hence a passage broad,
Smooth, easy, inoffensive down to hell.   305
So, if great things to small may be compared,
Xerxes, the liberty of Greece to yoke,
From Susa his Memnonian palace high
Came to the sea, and over Hellespont
Bridging his way, Europe with Asia joined,   310
And scourged with many a stroke th' indignant waves.
Now had they brought the work by wondrous art
Pontifical, a ridge of pendent rock
Over the vexed abyss, following the track
Of Satan, to the selfsame place where he   315
First lighted from his wing, and landed safe
From out of chaos to the outside bare
Of this round world: with pins of adamant
And chains they made all fast, too fast they made
And durable; and now in little space   320
The confines met of empyrean heav'n
And of this world, and on the left hand hell
With long reach interposed; three sev'ral ways
In sight, to each of these three places led.
And now their way to earth they had descried,   325
To Paradise first tending, when behold
Satan in likeness of an angel bright
Betwixt the Centaur and the Scorpion steering
His zenith, while the sun in Aries rose:
Disguised he came, but those his children dear   330
Their parent soon discerned, though in disguise.
He, after Eve seduced, unminded slunk
Into the wood fast by, and changing shape
To observe the sequel, saw his guileful act

305. *inoffensive:* free from obstacles.
306–11. *Xerxes,* the powerful Persian king who invaded *Greece* in 480 B.C., ordered that the sea be whipped for having destroyed the bridge of boats he built over the *Hellespont. Susa,* the winter residence of Xerxes, was founded by the son of Memnon.
313. *Pontifical.* L *pontifex* was thought to have come from *pons, pontis* bridge + *facere* to make, and Milton could not resist making a punning allusion to the papacy or any episcopacy—or the chance to reinforce the pun by the word *rock* and its allusion to the doctrine that Peter (L *petrus* rock) was the first pope: "Thou art Peter, and upon this rock I will build my church"; Matt. 16.18.
314. *vexed:* (L *vexare* to shake, agitate) stirred up.

320–24. See "Universe," pp. 389–91.
322. Cf. Matt. 25.33: "And he shall set the sheep on his right hand, but the goats on the left."
328–29. Fowler notes: "The . . . reason for steering *betwixt the Centaur* (Sagittarius) *and the Scorpion* is . . . that the only constellation noticeably spread over these two signs is Anguis [L for snake], the serpent held by Ophiuchus [Gk for serpent-bearer]. . . . Anguis has its head in Libra, and extends through Scorpio into Sagittarius. Accordingly Satan enters the world in Libra [III.551–61], but leaves it between Scorpio and Sagittarius."
332. *after Eve seduced:* Eve having been seduced. *unminded:* unnoticed.
334. *sequel:* consequence.

By Eve, though all unweeting, seconded   335
Upon her husband, saw their shame that sought
Vain covertures; but when he saw descend
The Son of God to judge them, terrified
He fled, not hoping to escape, but shun
The present, fearing guilty what his wrath   340
Might suddenly inflict; that past, returned
By night, and list'ning where the hapless pair
Sat in their sad discourse, and various plaint,
Thence gathered his own doom, which understood
Not instant, but of future time. With joy   345
And tidings fraught, to hell he now returned,
And at the brink of chaos, near the foot
Of this new wondrous pontifice, unhoped
Met who to meet him came, his offspring dear.
Great joy was at their meeting, and at sight   350
Of that stupendious bridge his joy increased.
Long he admiring stood, till Sin, his fair
Enchanting daughter, thus the silence broke.
    "O Parent, these are thy magnific deeds,
Thy trophies, which thou view'st as not thine own,   355
Thou art their author and prime architect:
For I no sooner in my heart divined,
My heart, which by a secret harmony
Still moves with thine, joined in connection sweet,
That thou on earth hadst prospered, which thy looks   360
Now also evidence, but straight I felt
Though distant from thee worlds between, yet felt
That I must after thee with this thy son;
Such fatal consequence unites us three:
Hell could no longer hold us in her bounds,   365
Nor this unvoyageable gulf obscure
Detain from following thy illustrious track.
Thou hast achieved our liberty, confined
Within hell gates till now, thou us empow'red
To fortify thus far, and overlay   370
With this portentous bridge the dark abyss.
Thine now is all this world, thy virtue hath won
What thy hands builded not, thy wisdom gained
With odds what war hath lost, and fully avenged
Our foil in heav'n; here thou shalt monarch reign,   375
There didst not; there let him still victor sway,
As battle hath adjudged, from this new world
Retiring, by his own doom alienated,
And henceforth monarchy with thee divide
Of all things parted by th' empyreal bounds,   380

335. *unweeting:* unaware.
364. *consequence:* connection of cause to effect.
370. *fortify:* erect fortifications.
371. *portentous:* marvelous (as well as ominous).
372. *virtue:* power, courage, manliness.
373–75. I.e.: thy wisdom regained all that was lost—and then some. *foil:* defeat.

His quadrature, from thy orbicular world,
Or try thee now more dangerous to his throne."
    Whom thus the Prince of Darkness answered glad.
"Fair daughter, and thou son and grandchild both,
High proof ye now have giv'n to be the race   385
Of Satan (for I glory in the name,
Antagonist of heav'n's Almighty King)
Amply have merited of me, of all
Th' infernal empire, that so near heav'n's door
Triumphal with triumphal act have met,   390
Mine with this glorious work, and made one realm
Hell and this world, one realm, one continent
Of easy thoroughfare. Therefore while I
Descend through darkness, on your road with ease
To my associate Powers, them to acquaint   395
With these successes, and with them rejoice,
You two this way, among those numerous orbs
All yours, right down to Paradise descend;
There dwell and reign in bliss, thence on the earth
Dominion exercise and in the air,   400
Chiefly on man, sole lord of all declared,
Him first make sure your thrall, and lastly kill.
My substitutes I send ye, and create
Plenipotent on earth, of matchless might
Issuing from me: on your joint vigor now   405
My hold of this new kingdom all depends,
Through Sin to Death exposed by my exploit.
If your joint power prevail, th' affairs of hell
No detriment need fear, go and be strong."
    So saying he dismissed them, they with speed   410
Their course through thickest constellations held
Spreading their bane; the blasted stars looked wan,
And planets, planet-strook, real eclipse
Then suffered. Th' other way Satan went down
The causey to hell gate; on either side   415
Disparted chaos over-built exclaimed,
And with rebounding surge the bars assailed,
That scorned his indignation: through the gate,
Wide open and unguarded, Satan passed,
And all about found desolate; for those   420
Appointed to sit there, had left their charge,
Flown to the upper world; the rest were all
Far to the inland retired, about the walls
Of Pandemonium, city and proud seat

---

381. Cf. Rev. 21.16: "And the city [of God] lieth four-square, and the length is as large as the breadth."
382. *try:* prove.
403–4. *create/Plenipotent:* give [them] full power.
412. *bane:* poison, death, ruin, woe.

blasted: injured, as by a harmful wind. *wan:* dark, dusky.
413. *planet-strook:* injured by the astrological influence of a planet. Planets in *eclipse* seem to lose their light; here they really did so.
415. *causey:* causeway.

Of Lucifer, so by allusion called,   425
Of that bright star to Satan paragoned.
There kept their watch the legions, while the grand
In council sat, solicitous what chance
Might intercept their Emperor sent, so he
Departing gave command, and they observed.   430
As when the Tartar from his Russian foe
By Astracan over the snowy plains
Retires, or Bactrian Sophi from the horns
Of Turkish crescent, leaves all waste beyond
The realm of Aladule, in his retreat   435
To Tauris or Casbeen: so these the late
Heav'n-banished host, left desert utmost hell
Many a dark league, reduced in careful watch
Round their metropolis, and now expecting
Each hour their great adventurer from the search   440
Of foreign worlds: he through the midst unmarked,
In show plebeian angel militant
Of lowest order, passed; and from the door
Of that Plutonian hall, invisible
Ascended his high throne, which under state   445
Of richest texture spread, at th' upper end
Was placed in regal luster. Down a while
He sat, and round about him saw unseen:
At last as from a cloud his fulgent head
And shape star-bright appeared, or brighter, clad   450
With what permissive glory since his fall
Was left him, or false glitter: all amazed
At that so sudden blaze the Stygian throng
Bent their aspéct, and whom they wished beheld,
Their mighty chief returned: loud was th' acclaim: 455
Forth rushed in haste the great consulting peers,

---

425. *Lucifer:* the morning star. Commentators had taken "Lucifer" in Isa. 14.12 (see I.84n) to mean Satan. Cf. V.708–10. *allusion:* metaphor.

426. *paragoned:* compared.

427. *the grand: the great consulting peers* of 456. See I.794ff.

431–36. *Astracan* was a region west of the Caspian Sea inhabited by Tatars but conquered by Russia in the sixteenth century. In his *Brief History of Moscovia* Milton described its chief city (modern Astrakhan) as "situate in an island [at the mouth of the Volga River] . . . walled with earth, but the castle with earth and timber; the houses . . . poor and simple; the ground utterly barren, and without wood: they live there on fish . . . which hanging up to dry in the streets and houses brings swarms of flies, and infection to the air, and oft great pestilence. This island . . . is the Russian limit toward the Caspian, which he keeps with a strong garrison [against the Turks

to the south and the Tartars beyond the steppes (*snowy plains*) to the east]." Milton remembered a particular siege of the city of 70,000 "Turkes and Tartars," which was raised "by reason of the winter approached" and because the Russians sent a relief expedition. The other retreating pagan army in this simile was Persian. *Aladule*, a region now divided between Turkey and Iran, once called Armenia, was the farthest western reach of the Persian empire. From this wild and mountainous country Anadule, a Persian king (*Bactrian Sophi*), was forced to retreat eastward from the Turks, first to Tabriz (*Tauris*) and later to Kazvin (*Casbeen*). The simile emphasizes the physical hardships of life in such rugged, uncivilized outposts, as well as the religion of the infidel Tatars, Turks, and Persians.

438. *reduced:* drawn together.

445. *state:* canopy.

451. *permissive:* permitted.

Raised from their dark divan, and with like joy
Congratulant approached him, who with hand
Silence, and with these words attention won.
   "Thrones, Dominations, Princedoms, Virtues, Powers,   460
For in possession such, not only of right,
I call ye and declare ye now, returned
Successful beyond hope, to lead ye forth
Triumphant out of this infernal pit
Abominable, accurst, the house of woe,   465
And dungeon of our tyrant: now possess,
As lords, a spacious world, to our native heaven
Little inferior, by my adventure hard
With peril great achieved. Long were to tell
What I have done, what suffered, with what pain   470
Voyaged th' unreal, vast, unbounded deep
Of horrible confusion, over which
By Sin and Death a broad way now is paved
To expedite your glorious march; but I
Toiled out my uncouth passage, forced to ride   475
Th' untractable abyss, plunged in the womb
Of unoriginal Night and Chaos wild,
That jealous of their secrets fiercely opposed
My journey strange, with clamorous uproar
Protesting fate supreme; thence how I found   480
The new-created world, which fame in heav'n
Long had foretold, a fabric wonderful
Of absolute perfection, therein man
Placed in a paradise, by our exile
Made happy: him by fraud I have seduced   485
From his Creator, and the more to increase
Your wonder, with an apple; he thereat
Offended, worth your laughter, hath giv'n up
Both his beloved man and all his world,
To Sin and Death a prey, and so to us,   490
Without our hazard, labor, or alarm,
To range in, and to dwell, and over man
To rule, as over all he should have ruled.
True is, me also he hath judged, or rather
Me not, but the brute serpent in whose shape   495
Man I deceived; that which to me belongs,
Is enmity, which he will put between
Me and mankind; I am to bruise his heel;
His seed, when is not set, shall bruise my head:
A world who would not purchase with a bruise,   500

---

457. *Raised:* adjourned. *divan:* (a Persian word) council of state.
  461. The titles are no longer only claims to heavenly ranks now that the fallen angels possess the earth.
  471. *unreal.* According to Plato, only ideas (that is, forms) are real; chaos was "without form."
  475. *uncouth:* unknown; strange, unpleasant; wild, desolate.
  477. *unoriginal:* having no origin or beginning.
  480. *Protesting:* calling as a witness, appealing to.

Or much more grievous pain? Ye have th' account
Of my performance: what remains, ye gods,
But up and enter now into full bliss."
    So having said, a while he stood, expecting
Their universal shout and high applause   505
To fill his ear, when contrary he hears
On all sides, from innumerable tongues
A dismal universal hiss, the sound
Of public scorn; he wondered, but not long
Had leisure, wond'ring at himself now more;   510
His visage drawn he felt to sharp and spare,
His arms clung to his ribs, his legs entwining
Each other, till supplanted down he fell
A monstrous serpent on his belly prone,
Reluctant, but in vain, a greater power   515
Now ruled him, punished in the shape he sinned,
According to his doom: he would have spoke,
But hiss for hiss returned with forkèd tongue
To forkèd tongue, for now were all transformed
Alike, to serpents all as accessóries   520
To his bold riot: dreadful was the din
Of hissing through the hall, thick swarming now
With complicated monsters, head and tail,
Scorpion and asp, and amphisbaena dire,
Cerastes horned, hydrus, and ellops drear,   525
And dipsas (not so thick swarmed once the soil
Bedropped with blood of Gorgon, or the isle
Ophiusa) but still greatest he the midst,
Now dragon grown, larger than whom the sun
Engendered in the Pythian vale on slime,   530
Huge Python, and his power no less he seemed
Above the rest still to retain; they all
Him followed issuing forth to th' open field,
Where all yet left of that revolted rout
Heav'n-fall'n, in station stood or just array,   535
Sublime with expectation when to see
In triumph issuing forth their glorious chief;
They saw, but other sight instead, a crowd

---

508. *dismal* (L *dies mali* evil days) sinister, dreadful, gloomy.

512. *clung:* (participle) stuck fast.

513. *supplanted:* (L *supplantare* to overthrow by tripping up, from *sub* under + *planta* sole of the foot) tripped up; made to fall (as Satan supplanted Eve).

515. *Reluctant:* L *re* + *luctare* to struggle.

523. *complicated:* (L *cum* together + *plicare* to fold) tangled.

524–32. *Scorpion:* an arachnid with a venomous sting at the tip of its tail. *asp:* a small viper of Egypt. *Cerastes:* a kind of asp with horny processes over each eye. The *hydrus* (a sea-snake), *ellops,* and *dipsas* (whose bite was supposed to produce mortal thirst) were fabulous serpents, as was the *amphisbaena,* which had a head at each end. *Gorgon:* Medusa, the drops of blood from whose severed head turned into snakes. *Ophiusa:* (Gk "island of serpents") modern Formentara, off the E coast of Spain. *Python:* a fabulous serpent who guarded a shrine at Delphi which Apollo appropriated after slaying the serpent. Apollo was considered a type of Christ.

535. *in station:* at [their] stations. *just array:* close, or full, formation.

536. *Sublime:* raised up.

Of ugly serpents; horror on them fell,
And horrid sympathy; for what they saw,   540
They felt themselves now changing; down their arms,
Down fell both spear and shield, down they as fast,
And the dire hiss renewed, and the dire form
Catched by contagion, like in punishment,
As in their crime. Thus was th' applause they meant,   545
Turned to exploding hiss, triumph to shame
Cast on themselves from their own mouths. There stood
A grove hard by, sprung up with this change,
His will who reigns above, to aggravate
Their penance, laden with fair fruit, like that   550
Which grew in Paradise, the bait of Eve
Used by the Tempter: on that prospect strange
Their earnest eyes they fixed, imagining
For one forbidden tree a multitude
Now ris'n, to work them further woe or shame;   555
Yet parched with scalding thirst and hunger fierce,
Though to delude them sent, could not abstain,
But on they rolled in heaps, and up the trees
Climbing, sat thicker than the snaky locks
That curled Megaera: greedily they plucked   560
The fruitage fair to sight, like that which grew
Near that bituminous lake where Sodom flamed;
This more delusive, not the touch, but taste
Deceived; they fondly thinking to allay
Their appetite with gust, instead of fruit   565
Chewed bitter ashes, which th' offended taste
With spattering noise rejected: oft they assayed,
Hunger and thirst constraining, drugged as oft,
With hatefulest disrelish writhed their jaws
With soot and cinders filled; so oft they fell   570
Into the same illusion, not as man
Whom they triumphed once lapsed. Thus were they plagued

546. *exploding:* L *explodere* to drive out a player by clapping, from *ex* out + *plaudere, plodere* to clap. *Applause* is derived from *ad* towards + *plaudere*.
547–72. The biblical passages on which this episode is grounded are Deut. 32.32–33: "For their vine is of the vine of Sodom, and of the fields of Gomorrah: their grapes are grapes of gall, their clusters are bitter: Their wine is the poison of dragons, and the cruel venom of asps," and Gen. 19.24: "Then the Lord rained upon Sodom and upon Gomorrah brimstone and fire from the Lord out of heaven." But Milton got the idea for the ironic apples from the well-known Jewish historian Josephus, who claimed such fruit grew by the Dead Sea (*bituminous lake,* cf. I.411), and from the myth of Tantalus, whose punishment consisted of enduring a thirst which he could not quench because when he stooped to drink the stream receded and when he reached for luscious fruit it too eluded him. The trees are an ironic metamorphosis of the Tree of Knowledge, and the image of the snakes in the tree may have come, as Fowler points out, from a late Latin poet's account of "a dreadful grove hung with Jupiter's spoils" from the war against the Giants, one of whom was Ophion (581), which means "serpent." *Megaera:* one of the mythical snaky-haired Erinys, or avenging spirits. *gust:* (L *gustus* taste) relish, gusto. *drugged:* nauseated. *triumphed:* triumphed over.
572–84. The fallen angels were *permitted* by God to resume their original *shape* except during the annual repetition of the ironic serpentine metamorphosis. Among the heathen whom they later seduced they spread (*dispersed*) the story (*tradition*) that Satan and Eve were the original rulers of heaven. Milton followed

And worn with famine, long and ceaseless hiss,
Till their lost shape, permitted, they resumed,
Yearly enjoined, some say, to undergo   575
This annual humbling certain numbered days,
To dash their pride, and joy for man seduced.
However some tradition they dispersed
Among the heathen of their purchase got,
And fabled how the serpent, whom they called   580
Ophion with Eurynome, the wide-
Encroaching Eve perhaps, had first the rule
Of high Olympus, thence by Saturn driv'n
And Ops, ere yet Dictaean Jove was born.
Meanwhile in Paradise the hellish pair   585
Too soon arrived, Sin there in power before,
Once actual, now in body, and to dwell
Habitual habitant; behind her Death
Close following pace for pace, not mounted yet
On his pale horse: to whom Sin thus began.   590
    "Second of Satan sprung, all-conquering Death,
What think'st thou of our empire now, though earned
With travail difficult, not better far
Than still at hell's dark threshold to have sat watch,
Unnamed, undreaded, and thyself half-starved?"   595
    Whom thus the Sin-born monster answered soon.
"To me, who with eternal famine pine,
Alike is hell, or Paradise, or heaven,
There best, where most with ravin I may meet;
Which here, though plenteous, all too little seems   600
To stuff this maw, this vast unhidebound corpse."
    To whom th' incestuous mother thus replied.
"Thou therefore on these herbs, and fruits, and flow'rs
Feed first, on each beast next, and fish, and fowl,
No homely morsels, and whatever thing   605
The scythe of Time mows down, devour unspared,
Till I in man residing through the race,
His thoughts, his looks, words, actions all infect,
And season him thy last and sweetest prey."
    This said, they both betook them several ways,   610
Both to destroy, or unimmortal make
All kinds, and for destruction to mature

---

a common Christian interpretation of the myth in identifying *Ophion* as Satan, but he seems to have invented the suggestion that *Eurynome* could have been falsely interpreted as Eve because the Gk word *Eurynome* could mean wide-encroaching and could be an epithet for Eve. *Saturn* and Rhea (*Ops*) overthrew (in this version of the story) *Ophion* and *Eurynome*, but they were in turn overthrown by Jupiter (*Jove*, who lived on the mountain Dicte) whom Christians interpreted as God. *purchase:* prey.

585–90. *Sin* (586) and *Death* (588) are in syntactical apposition with *hellish pair*. Before the Fall sin was present in Paradise only potentially (*in power*), but *once* it had become *actual* in the act of Adam and Eve, it could be said to be totally (*in body* as well as spirit) in Paradise. The word play in *dwell Habitual habitant* is enriched by the derivation of *habit*, L *habere* to have, possess.
   590. Cf. Rev. 6.8, p. 385.
   601. *unhidebound:* literally not bound by its hide, which is infinitely expansible.

Sooner or later; which th' Almighty seeing,
From his transcendent seat the saints among,
To those bright orders uttered thus his voice.   615
   "See with what heat these dogs of hell advance
To waste and havoc yonder world, which I
So fair and good created, and had still
Kept in that state, had not the folly of man
Let in these wasteful furies, who impute   620
Folly to me, so doth the Prince of Hell
And his adherents, that with so much ease
I suffer them to enter and possess
A place so heav'nly, and conniving seem
To gratify my scornful enemies,   625
That laugh, as if transported with some fit
Of passion, I to them had quitted all,
At random yielded up to their misrule;
And know not that I called and drew them thither
My hell-hounds, to lick up the draff and filth   630
Which man's polluting sin with taint hath shed
On what was pure, till crammed and gorged, nigh burst
With sucked and glutted offal, at one sling
Of thy victorious arm, well-pleasing Son,
Both Sin, and Death, and yawning grave at last   635
Through chaos hurled, obstruct the mouth of hell
For ever, and seal up his ravenous jaws.
Then heav'n and earth renewed shall be made pure
To sanctity that shall receive no stain:
Till then the curse pronounced on both precedes."   640
   He ended, and the heav'nly audience loud
Sung halleluiah, as the sound of seas,
Through multitude that sung: "Just are thy ways,
Righteous are thy decrees on all thy works;
Who can extenuate thee? Next, to the Son,   645
Destined restorer of mankind, by whom
New heav'n and earth shall to the ages rise,
Or down from heav'n descend." Such was their song,
While the Creator calling forth by name
His mighty angels gave them several charge,   650
As sorted best with present things. The sun

617. *havoc:* plunder.
624. *conniving:* (L *connivere* to shut the eyes) feigning ignorance.
626–27. *as if . . . passion.* Modifies *I.* *quitted:* surrendered.
630. *draff:* refuse, swill.
633. Cf. 1 Sam. 25.29: ". . . the souls of thine enemies, them shall he sling out, as out of the middle of a sling."
640. *precedes:* has precedence.
641–43. Cf. Rev. 19.6: "And I heard as it were the voice of a great multitude, and as the voice of many waters, and the voice of many thunderings, saying, Alleluia: for the Lord God omnipotent reigneth."
643–44. Cf. Rev. 15.3: "And they sing the song of Moses the servant of God, and the song of the Lamb, saying, Great and marvellous are thy works, Lord God Almighty; just and true are thy ways, thou King of saints." Rev. 16.7: "And I heard another out of the altar say, Even so, Lord God Almighty, true and righteous are thy judgments."
645. *extenuate:* weaken, underestimate, disparage.
647. *ages:* the Millennium.
647–48. Cf. Rev. 21.1–2, p. 387.
651. *sorted . . . with:* suited.

Had first his precept so to move, so shine,
As might affect the earth with cold and heat
Scarce tolerable, and from the north to call
Decrepit winter, from the south to bring   655
Solstitial summer's heat. To the blank moon
Her office they prescribed, to th' other five
Their planetary motions and aspécts
In sextile, square, and trine, and opposite,
Of noxious efficacy, and when to join   660
In synod unbenign, and taught the fixed
Their influence malignant when to show'r,
Which of them rising with the sun, or falling,
Should prove tempestuous: to the winds they set
Their corners, when with bluster to confound   665
Sea, air, and shore, the thunder when to roll
With terror through the dark aerial hall.
Some say he bid his angels turn askance
The poles of earth twice ten degrees and more
From the sun's axle; they with labor pushed   670
Oblique the centric globe: some say the sun
Was bid turn reins from th' equinoctial road
Like distant breadth to Taurus with the sev'n
Atlantic Sisters, and the Spartan Twins
Up to the Tropic Crab; thence down amain   675
By Leo and the Virgin and the Scales,
As deep as Capricorn, to bring in change
Of seasons to each clime; else had the spring
Perpetual smiled on earth with vernant flow'rs,
Equal in days and nights, except to those   680
Beyond the polar circles; to them day
Had unbenighted shone, while the low sun
To recompense his distance, in their sight
Had rounded still th' horizon, and not known
Or east or west, which had forbid the snow   685
From cold Estotiland, and south as far
Beneath Magellan. At that tasted fruit
The sun, as from Thyestean banquet, turned
His course intended; else how had the world
Inhabited, though sinless, more than now,   690
Avoided pinching cold and scorching heat?
These changes in the heav'ns, though slow, produced

---

656. *blank:* white, pale.
657–706. See "Universe," p. 391.
659. *sextile, square, trine,* and *opposite* are astrological terms describing the relative positions of planets as angles of 60, 90, 120, and 180 degrees.
661. *synod:* conjunction. *fixed:* fixed stars.
673–77. All but *Atlantic Sisters* (the Pleiades) are constellations in the zodiac.
679. *vernant:* vernal.

684. *still:* always.
686. *Estotiland:* fabulous island near the NE coast of N. America; perhaps the NE coast of Labrador.
687. *Magellan:* the region of the Straits of Magellan.
688–89. When Atreus invited his brother Thyestes to a banquet where he served the flesh of Thyestes' son, the sun to avoid the sight changed his course.

Like change on sea and land, sideral blast,
Vapor, and mist, and exhalation hot,
Corrupt and pestilent: now from the north   695
Of Norumbega, and the Samoed shore
Bursting their brazen dungeon, armed with ice
And snow and hail and stormy gust and flaw,
Boreas and Caecias and Argestes loud
And Thrascias rend the woods and seas upturn;   700
With adverse blast upturns them from the south
Notus and Afer black with thund'rous clouds
From Serraliona; thwart of these as fierce
Forth rush the Levant and the ponent winds
Eurus and Zephyr with their lateral noise,   705
Sirocco and Libecchio. Thus began
Outrage from lifeless things; but Discord first
Daughter of Sin, among th' irrational,
Death introduced through fierce antipathy:
Beast now with beast gan war, and fowl with fowl,   710
And fish with fish; to graze the herb all leaving,
Devour'd each other; nor stood much in awe
Of man, but fled him, or with count'nance grim
Glared on him passing: these were from without
The growing miseries, which Adam saw   715
Already in part, though hid in gloomiest shade,
To sorrow abandoned, but worse felt within,
And in a troubled sea of passion tossed,
Thus to disburden sought with sad complaint.
    "O miserable of happy! Is this the end   720
Of this new glorious world, and me so late
The glory of that glory, who now become
Accurst of blessèd, hide me from the face
Of God, whom to behold was then my highth
Of happiness: yet well, if here would end   725
The misery, I deserved it, and would bear
My own deservings; but this will not serve;
All that I eat or drink, or shall beget,
Is propagated curse. O voice once heard
Delightfully, 'Increase and multiply,'   730
Now death to hear! For what can I increase
Or multiply, but curses on my head?
Who of all ages to succeed, but feeling
The evil on him brought by me, will curse
My head, 'Ill fare our ancestor impure,   735

693. *sideral blast:* blight or ruin caused by the malign influence of the stars. See *bane* in 412 and n.
695–706. *Norumbega:* northeastern North America, including New England. *Samoed:* Siberian. *brazen dungeon:* the cave in which Aeolus imprisoned the winds. *flaw:* squall. *Boreas, Caecius, Argestes, Thrascias:* winds that blow from the N, NE, and NW. *Notus, Afer:* winds that blow from the S and SW (Africa). *Serraliona:* Sierra Leone, on the W coast of Africa. *thwart:* diagonally. *Levant:* from the east. *ponent:* from the west. *Eurus:* the east wind. *Zephyr:* the west wind. *Sirocco, Libecchio:* winds from the SE and SW.

For this we may thank Adam'; but his thanks
Shall be the execration; so besides
Mine own that bide upon me, all from me
Shall with a fierce reflux on me redound,
On me as on their natural center light   740
Heavy, though in their place. O fleeting joys
Of Paradise, dear bought with lasting woes!
Did I request thee, Maker, from my clay
To mold me man, did I solicit thee
From darkness to promote me, or here place   745
In this delicious garden? As my will
Concurred not to my being, it were but right
And equal to reduce me to my dust,
Desirous to resign, and render back
All I received, unable to perform   750
Thy terms too hard, by which I was to hold
The good I sought not. To the loss of that,
Sufficient penalty, why hast thou added
The sense of endless woes? Inexplicable
Thy justice seems; yet to say truth, too late   755
I thus contest; then should have been refused
Those terms whatever, when they were proposed:
Thou didst accept them; wilt thou enjoy the good,
Then cavil the conditions? And though God
Made thee without thy leave, what if thy son   760
Prove disobedient, and reproved, retort,
'Wherefore didst thou beget me? I sought it not:'
Wouldst thou admit for his contempt of thee
That proud excuse? Yet him not thy election,
But natural necessity begot.   765
God made thee of choice his own, and of his own
To serve him, thy reward was of his grace,
Thy punishment then justly is at his will.
Be it so, for I submit, his doom is fair,
That dust I am, and shall to dust return: 770
O welcome hour whenever! Why delays
His hand to execute what his decree
Fixed on this day? Why do I overlive,
Why am I mocked with death, and lengthened out
To deathless pain? How gladly would I meet   775
Mortality my sentence, and be earth
Insensible, how glad would lay me down
As in my mother's lap! There I should rest

---

740. *On me . . . light:* fall upon me, be my lot.

741. *Heavy, though in their place.* Having found *their natural center* (740), the curses should, by Adam's law of gravitation, be weightless.

743–44. Cf. Isa. 45.9: "Woe unto him that striveth with his Maker! Let the potsherd strive with the potsherds of the earth. Shall the clay say to him that fashioneth it, What makest thou? or thy work, He hath no hands?"

748. *equal:* fair, just.

762. Cf. Isa. 45.10: "Woe unto him that saith unto his father, What begettest thou? or to the woman, What hast thou brought forth?"

764. *election:* choice.

And sleep secure; his dreadful voice no more
Would thunder in my ears, no fear of worse   780
To me and to my offspring would torment me
With cruel expectation. Yet one doubt
Pursues me still, lest all I cannot die,
Lest that pure breath of life, the spirit of man
Which God inspired, cannot together perish   785
With this corporeal clod; then in the grave,
Or in some other dismal place, who knows
But I shall die a living death? O thought
Horrid, if true! Yet why? It was but breath
Of life that sinned; what dies but what had life   790
And sin? The body properly hath neither.
All of me then shall die: let this appease
The doubt, since human reach no further knows.
For though the Lord of all be infinite,
Is his wrath also? Be it, man is not so,   795
But mortal doomed. How can he exercise
Wrath without end on man whom death must end?
Can he make deathless death? That were to make
Strange contradiction, which to God himself
Impossible is held, as argument   800
Of weakness, not of power. Will he draw out,
For anger's sake, finite to infinite
In punished man, to satisfy his rigor
Satisfied never; that were to extend
His sentence beyond dust and nature's law,   805
By which all causes else according still
To the reception of their matter act,
Not to th' extent of their own sphere. But say
That death be not one stroke, as I supposed,
Bereaving sense, but endless misery   810
From this day onward, which I feel begun
Both in me, and without me, and so last
To perpetuity; ay me, that fear
Comes thund'ring back with dreadful revolution
On my defenseless head; both Death and I   815
Am found eternal, and incorporate both,
Nor I on my part single, in me all
Posterity stands cursed: fair patrimony
That I must leave ye, sons; O were I able
To waste it all myself, and leave ye none!   820
So disinherited how would ye bless
Me now your curse! Ah, why should all mankind
For one man's fault thus guiltless be condemned,

782–93. Milton believed that the soul
dies with the body. See *CD*, I.xiii (*CE*,
XV.215–33). *all I:* all of me.
801–8. Adam argues that *finite* (802)
matter (807) cannot suffer *infinite* pun-
ishment because according to *nature's
law* the efficacy of all *causes* (forces) is

limited by the nature of the things they
act upon. The notion is as old as Aris-
totle.
810. *Bereaving:* taking away. *endless
misery.* Cf. *CD*, I.xxxiii.C.
814. *revolution:* recurrence.
816. *incorporate:* united in one body.

If guiltless? But from me what can proceed,
But all corrupt, both mind and will depraved,   825
Not to do only, but to will the same
With me? How can they then acquitted stand
In sight of God? Him after all disputes
Forced I absolve: all my evasions vain
And reasonings, though through mazes, lead me still   830
But to my own conviction: first and last
On me, me only, as the source and spring
Of all corruption, all the blame lights due;
So might the wrath. Fond wish! Couldst thou support
That burden heavier than the earth to bear,   835
Than all the world much heavier, though divided
With that bad woman? Thus what thou desir'st,
And what thou fear'st, alike destroys all hope
Of refuge, and concludes thee miserable
Beyond all past example and future,   840
To Satan only like both crime and doom.
O conscience, into what abyss of fears
And horrors hast thou driv'n me; out of which
I find no way, from deep to deeper plunged!"
    Thus Adam to himself lamented loud   845
Through the still night, not now, as ere man fell,
Wholesome and cool, and mild, but with black air
Accompanied, with damps and dreadful gloom,
Which to his evil conscience represented
All things with double terror: on the ground   850
Outstretched he lay, on the cold ground, and oft
Cursed his creation, Death as oft accused
Of tardy execution, since denounced
The day of his offense. "Why comes not Death,"
Said he, "with one thrice-ácceptáble stroke   855
To end me? Shall Truth fail to keep her word,
Justice divine not hasten to be just?
But Death comes not at call, Justice divine
Mends not her slowest pace for prayers or cries.
O woods, O fountains, hillocks, dales and bow'rs,   860
With other echo late I taught your shades
To answer, and resound far other song."
Whom thus afflicted when sad Eve beheld,
Desolate where she sat, approaching nigh,
Soft words to his fierce passion she assayed: 865
But her with stern regard he thus repelled.
    "Out of my sight, thou serpent, that name best

825. *mind and will depraved.* Cf. *CD*, I.xi.C.
828–34. Cf. *CD*, I.xix, where Milton says that "conviction of sin" is the first of four steps towards regeneration of a sinner. *Fond:* foolish.
848. *damps:* noxious vapors.

853. *since denounced:* inasmuch as it was announced as coming on the day of the crime. Cf. 962.
867. *thou serpent.* Bush notes that "In patristic etymologizing, 'Heva,' Eve's name aspirated, meant 'serpent.'"

Befits thee with him leagued, thyself as false
And hateful; nothing wants, but that thy shape,
Like his, and color serpentine may show   870
Thy inward fraud, to warn all creatures from thee
Henceforth; lest that too heav'nly form, pretended
To hellish falsehood, snare them. But for thee
I had persisted happy, had not thy pride
And wand'ring vanity, when least was safe,   875
Rejected my forewarning, and disdained
Not to be trusted, longing to be seen
Though by the Devil himself, him overweening
To overreach, but with the serpent meeting
Fooled and beguiled, by him thou, I by thee,   880
To trust thee from my side, imagined wise,
Constant, mature, proof against all assaults,
And understood not all was but a show
Rather than solid virtue, all but a rib
Crooked by nature, bent, as now appears,   885
More to the part sinister from me drawn,
Well if thrown out, as supernumerary
To my just number found. O why did God,
Creator wise, that peopled highest heav'n
With Spirits masculine, create at last   890
This novelty on earth, this fair defect
Of nature, and not fill the world at once
With men as angels without feminine,
Or find some other way to generate
Mankind? This mischief had not then befall'n,   895
And more that shall befall, innumerable
Disturbances on earth through female snares,
And strait conjunction with this sex: for either
He never shall find out fit mate, but such
As some misfortune brings him, or mistake,   900
Or whom he wishes most shall seldom gain
Through her perverseness, but shall see her gained
By a far worse, or if she love, withheld
By parents, or his happiest choice too late
Shall meet, already linked and wedlock-bound   905
To a fell adversary, his hate or shame:
Which infinite calamity shall cause

872–73. *pretended/To:* (L *prae* before + *tendere* stretch) held before, as a disguise.
878. *overweening:* overconfident. *him overweening/To overreach:* i.e., being overconfident that you could get the better of him.
884–88. One sign of Adam's fallen condition is this expression of misogyny. It is a composite of myths well known in Milton's time: that woman was morally crooked because the rib she was made of was defective; that the rib was taken from Adam's left side (the Bible does not specify), not because that was nearest Adam's heart, but because the left, or *sinister*, side is the evil side; and that Adam originally had thirteen ribs on his left side, so that the removal of one left him perfect.
891–92. *defect/Of nature.* Fowler notes that "Aristotle had said . . . that the female is a defective male."
898. *strait:* close; also, distressful.
906. *fell:* cruel, terrible.

To human life, and household peace confound."
He added not, and from her turned, but Eve
Not so repulsed, with tears that ceased not flowing,   910
And tresses all disordered, at his feet
Fell humble, and embracing them, besought
His peace, and thus proceeded in her plaint.
    "Forsake me not thus, Adam, witness Heav'n
What love sincere, and reverence in my heart   915
I bear thee, and unweeting have offended,
Unhappily deceived; thy suppliant
I beg, and clasp thy knees; bereave me not,
Whereon I live, thy gentle looks, thy aid,
Thy counsel in this uttermost distress,   920
My only strength and stay: forlorn of thee,
Whither shall I betake me, where subsist?
While yet we live, scarce one short hour perhaps,
Between us two let there be peace, both joining,
As joined in injuries, one enmity   925
Against a foe by doom express assigned us,
That cruel serpent: on me exercise not
Thy hatred for this misery befall'n,
On me already lost, me than thyself
More miserable; both have sinned, but thou   930
Against God only, I against God and thee,
And to the place of judgment will return,
There with my cries importune Heaven, that all
The sentence from thy head removed may light
On me, sole cause to thee of all this woe,   935
Me me only just object of his ire."
    She ended weeping, and her lowly plight,
Immovable till peace obtained from fault
Acknowledged and deplored, in Adam wrought
Commiseration; soon his heart relented   940
Towards her, his life so late and sole delight,
Now at his feet submissive in distress,
Creature so fair his reconcilement seeking,
His counsel whom she had displeased, his aid;
As one disarmed, his anger all he lost,   945
And thus with peaceful words upraised her soon.
    "Unwary, and too desirous, as before,
So now of what thou know'st not, who desir'st
The punishment all on thyself; alas,
Bear thine own first, ill able to sustain   950
His full wrath those thou feel'st as yet least part,
And my displeasure bear'st so ill. If prayers
Could alter high decrees, I to that place

---

926. *doom express:* explicit judgment. *assigned* modifies *enmity.*
931. Cf. Ps. 51.4: "Against thee, thee only, have I sinned, and done this evil in thy sight: that thou mightest be justi- fied when thou speakest, and be clear when thou judgest."
938. *Immovable:* (modifies *plight*) unalterable.

Would speed before thee, and be louder heard,
That on my head all might be visited, 955
Thy frailty and infirmer sex forgiv'n,
To me committed and by me exposed.
But rise, let us no more contend, nor blame
Each other, blamed enough elsewhere, but strive
In offices of love, how we may light'n 960
Each other's burden in our share of woe;
Since this day's death denounced, if aught I see,
Will prove no sudden, but a slow-paced evil,
A long day's dying to augment our pain,
And to our seed (O hapless seed!) derived." 965
    To whom thus Eve, recovering heart, replied.
"Adam, by sad experiment I know
How little weight my words with thee can find,
Found so erroneous, thence by just event
Found so unfortunate; nevertheless, 970
Restored by thee, vile as I am, to place
Of new acceptance, hopeful to regain
Thy love, the sole contentment of my heart
Living or dying, from thee I will not hide
What thoughts in my unquiet breast are ris'n, 975
Tending to some relief of our extremes,
Or end, though sharp and sad, yet tolerable,
As in our evils, and of easier choice.
If care of our descent perplex us most,
Which must be born to certain woe, devoured 980
By Death at last, and miserable it is
To be to others cause of misery,
Our own begotten, and of our loins to bring
Into this cursèd world a woeful race,
That after wretched life must be at last 985
Food for so foul a monster, in thy power
It lies, yet ere conception to prevent
The race unblest, to being yet unbegot.
Childless thou art, childless remain; so Death
Shall be deceived his glut, and with us two 990
Be forced to satisfy his rav'nous maw.
But if thou judge it hard and difficult,
Conversing, looking, loving, to abstain
From love's due rites, nuptial embraces sweet,
And with desire to languish without hope, 995
Before the present object languishing
With like desire, which would be misery
And torment less than none of what we dread,

---

959. *elsewhere:* i.e., in heaven, or "the place of judgment" (932).
960. *offices:* services, attentions.
961. Cf. Gal. 6.2: "Bear ye one another's burdens, and so fulfil the law of Christ."
965. *derived:* passed on. Cf. 77n.

969. *event:* consequence.
978. *As in our evils:* considering our afflictions.
979. I.e.: If concern for our descendants most disturbs us.
987. *prevent:* to keep from existing.

Then both ourselves and seed at once to free
From what we fear for both, let us make short,   1000
Let us seek Death, or he not found, supply
With our own hands his office on ourselves;
Why stand we longer shivering under fears,
That show no end but death, and have the power,
Of many ways to die the shortest choosing,   1005
Destruction with destruction to destroy."
    She ended here, or vehement despair
Broke off the rest; so much of death her thoughts
Had entertained, as dyed her cheeks with pale.
But Adam with such counsel nothing swayed,   1010
To better hopes his more attentive mind
Laboring had raised, and thus to Eve replied.
    "Eve, thy contempt of life and pleasure seems
To argue in thee something more sublime
And excellent than what thy mind contemns;   1015
But self-destruction therefore sought, refutes
That excellence thought in thee, and implies,
Not thy contempt, but anguish and regret
For loss of life and pleasure overloved.
Or if thou covet death, as utmost end   1020
Of misery, so thinking to evade
The penalty pronounced, doubt not but God
Hath wiselier armed his vengeful ire than so
To be forestalled; much more I fear lest death
So snatched will not exempt us from the pain   1025
We are by doom to pay: rather such acts
Of contumácy will provoke the Highest
To make death in us live: then let us seek
Some safer resolution, which methinks
I have in view, calling to mind with heed   1030
Part of our sentence, that thy seed shall bruise
The serpent's head; piteous amends, unless
Be meant, whom I conjecture, our grand foe
Satan, who in the serpent hath contrived
Against us this deceit: to crush his head   1035
Would be revenge indeed; which will be lost
By death brought on ourselves, or childless days
Resolved, as thou proposest; so our foe
Shall scape his punishment ordained, and we
Instead shall double ours upon our heads.   1040
No more be mentioned then of violence
Against ourselves, and wilful barrenness,
That cuts us off from hope, and savors only
Rancor and pride, impatience and despite,
Reluctance against God and his just yoke   1045
Laid on our necks. Remember with what mild

1007. *vehement:* intense, powerful.   1045. *Reluctance:* L *re* + *luctari* to
1031–32. Cf. 175–81n.   struggle.

And gracious temper he both heard and judged
Without wrath or reviling; we expected
Immediate dissolution, which we thought
Was meant by death that day, when lo, to thee   1050
Pains only in child-bearing were foretold,
And bringing forth, soon recompensed with joy,
Fruit of thy womb: on me the curse aslope
Glanced on the ground, with labor I must earn
My bread; what harm? Idleness had been worse;   1055
My labor will sustain me; and lest cold
Or heat should injure us, his timely care
Hath unbesought provided, and his hands
Clothed us unworthy, pitying while he judged;
How much more, if we pray him, will his ear   1060
Be open, and his heart to pity incline,
And teach us further by what means to shun
Th' inclement seasons, rain, ice, hail and snow,
Which now the sky with various face begins
To show us in this mountain, while the winds   1065
Blow moist and keen, shattering the graceful locks
Of these fair spreading trees; which bids us seek
Some better shroud, some better warmth to cherish
Our limbs benumbed, ere this diurnal star
Leave cold the night, how we his gathered beams   1070
Reflected, may with matter sere foment,
Or by collision of two bodies grind
The air attrite to fire, as late the clouds
Justling or pushed with winds rude in their shock
Tine the slant lightning, whose thwart flame driv'n down   1075
Kindles the gummy bark of fir or pine,
And sends a comfortable heat from far,
Which might supply the sun: such fire to use,
And what may else be remedy or cure
To evils which our own misdeeds have wrought,   1080
He will instruct us praying, and of grace
Beseeching him, so as we need not fear

1050–52. Cf. John 16.19–21: "Now Jesus [speaking to his disciples about his Second Coming] . . . said unto them, Do ye enquire among yourselves of what I said, A little while, and ye shall not see me: and again, a little while, and ye shall see me? Verily, verily, I say unto you, That ye shall . . . be sorrowful: but your sorrow shall be turned into joy. A woman when she is in travail hath sorrow, because her hour is come: but as soon as she is delivered of the child, she remembereth no more the anguish, for joy that a man is born into the world."
1053. *Fruit of thy womb*. Cf. Luke 1.41–42: "And it came to pass, that, when Elizabeth [the mother of John the Baptist] heard the salutation of Mary, the babe leaped in her womb; and Elizabeth was filled with the Holy Ghost: And she spake out with a loud voice, and said, Blessed art thou among women, and blessed is the fruit of thy womb."
1066. *shattering:* scattering.
1067–73. "Which bids us seek . . . how we may with kindling nurse to life (or activity) focused and reflected sunbeams [as with some natural equivalent of a burning glass], or how by striking together two bodies we may turn air to fire by the heat of friction." *shroud:* shelter. *foment:* nourish. *attrite:* L *ad* + *terere* to rub.
1075. *Tine:* kindle. *thwart:* slanting.
1078. *supply:* take the place of.

To pass commodiously this life, sustained
By him with many comforts, till we end
In dust, our final rest and native home.   1085
What better can we do, than to the place
Repairing where he judged us, prostrate fall
Before him reverent, and there confess
Humbly our faults, and pardon beg, with tears
Watering the ground, and with our sighs the air   1090
Frequenting, sent from hearts contrite, in sign
Of sorrow unfeigned, and humiliation meek.
Undoubtedly he will relent and turn
From his displeasure; in whose look serene,
When angry most he seemed and most severe,   1095
What else but favor, grace, and mercy shone?"
   So spake our father penitent, nor Eve
Felt less remorse: they forthwith to the place
Repairing where he judged them prostrate fell
Before him reverent, and both confessed   1100
Humbly their faults, and pardon begged, with tears
Watering the ground, and with their sighs the air
Frequenting, sent from hearts contrite, in sign
Of sorrow unfeigned, and humiliation meek.

1083. *commodiously:* conveniently.   ed), filling.
1091. *Frequenting:* (L *frequens* crowd-

Book XI

The Argument

The Son of God presents to his Father the prayers of our first parents now repenting, and intercedes for them: God accepts them, but declares that they must no longer abide in Paradise; sends Michael with a band of Cherubim to dispossess them; but first to reveal to Adam future things: Michael's coming down. Adam shows to Eve certain ominous signs; he discerns Michael's approach, goes out to meet him: the angel denounces their departure. Eve's lamentation. Adam pleads, but submits: the angel leads him up to a high hill, sets before him in vision what shall happen till the Flood.

Thus they in lowliest plight repentant stood
Praying, for from the mercy-seat above
Prevenient grace descending had removed
The stony from their hearts, and made new flesh
Regenerate grow instead, that sighs now breathed   5
Unutterable, which the spirit of prayer
Inspired, and winged for heav'n with speedier flight
Than loudest oratory: yet their port
Not of mean suitors, nor important less
Seemed their petition, than when th' ancient pair   10
In fables old, less ancient yet than these,
Deucalion and chaste Pyrrha to restore
The race of mankind drowned, before the shrine
Of Themis stood devout. To heav'n their prayers
Flew up, nor missed the way, by envious winds   15
Blown vagabond or frustrate: in they passed
Dimensionless through heav'nly doors; then clad
With incense, where the golden altar fumed,
By their great Intercessor, came in sight

XI.1. *stood:* remained.

2. *mercy-seat:* the golden cover of the Ark of the Covenant, which stood in the Holy of Holies of the Tabernacle of the Israelites. On it was sprinkled the blood of sacrificed animals on the day of atonement. See I.383–87n, and XII.249–56. Here, a metaphor for the place of expiation in heaven.

3. *Prevenient grace:* the grace of God acting before man wills to turn from sin or ask forgiveness.

4. *stony.* Cf. Ezek. 11.19: "I will take the stony heart out of their flesh, and will give them an heart of flesh."

5–7. Cf. Rom. 8.26: "Likewise the Spirit also helpeth our infirmities: for we know not what we should pray for as we ought: but the Spirit itself maketh intercession for us with groanings which cannot be uttered."

8–9. *port . . . important.* The root meaning of the L *portare*, "to bear or carry" informs the word play. The bearing, carriage, style of the prayers was dignified, and what they carried was of great import, significance, consequence.

10–14. In classical myth *Deucalion* (like Noah) and *Pyrrha*, his wife, the sole survivors of a universal flood, sought guidance from the oracle of *Themis*, goddess of justice.

16. *frustrate:* prevented from reaching its goal.

17–25. Cf. Rev. 8.3–4: "And another angel came and stood at the altar, having a golden censer; and there was given unto him much incense, that he should offer it with the prayers of all saints upon the golden altar which was before the throne. And the smoke of the incense, which came with the prayers of the saints, ascended up before God out of the angel's hand."

Before the Father's throne: them the glad Son   20
Presenting, thus to intercede began.
    "See Father, what first-fruits on earth are sprung
From thy implanted grace in man, these sighs
And prayers, which in this golden censer, mixed
With incense, I thy priest before thee bring,   25
Fruits of more pleasing savor from thy seed
Sown with contrition in his heart, than those
Which his own hand manuring all the trees
Of Paradise could have produced, ere fall'n
From innocence. Now therefore bend thine ear   30
To supplication, hear his sighs though mute;
Unskilful with what words to pray, let me
Interpret for him, me his advocate
And propitiation, all his works on me
Good or not good ingraft, my merit those   35
Shall perfet, and for these my death shall pay.
Accept me, and in me from these receive
The smell of peace toward mankind, let him live
Before thee reconciled, at least his days
Numbered, though sad, till death, his doom (which I   40
To mitigate thus plead, not to reverse)
To better life shall yield him, where with me
All my redeemed may dwell in joy and bliss,
Made one with me as I with thee am one."
    To whom the Father, without cloud, serene.   45
"All thy request for man, accepted Son,
Obtain, all thy request was my decree:
But longer in that Paradise to dwell,
The law I gave to nature him forbids:
Those pure immortal elements that know   50

20. *glad:* pleased; full of brightness or beauty (as in "the glad sun," IV.150).

22. *first-fruits:* an offering to God. Cf. Cain's offering, XI.435.

28. *manuring:* (OF *manouvrer*, from L *manu operari* to work by hand) cultivating.

32–36. Cf. 1 John 2.1–2: "And if any man sin, we have an advocate with the Father, Jesus Christ the righteous: And he is the propitiation for our sins."

44. Cf. John 17.11: "And now I am no more in the world, but these are in the world, and I come to thee. Holy Father, keep through thine own name those whom thou hast given me, that they may be one, as we are." John 17.21–23: "That they all may be one; as thou, Father, art in me, and I in thee, that they also may be one in us: that the world may believe that thou hast sent me. And the glory which thou gavest me I have given them; that they may be one, even as we are one: I in them, and thou in me, that they may be made perfect in one; and that the world may know that thou hast

sent me, and hast loved them, as thou hast loved me."

45. *without cloud.* See III.378–79.

50–57. Paradise is a perfect ecological system immune to entropy. When man introduces disorder (*distemper, unharmonious mixture foul* and *gross*), which is the same thing as impurity, the system (*Those pure immortal elements*, in perfect temper, i.e., mixture, balance), *ejects* the *gross, distempered* part, i.e., *man*, purging him off into the imperfect ecological system east of Eden, of postlapsarian history. There *corrupted* man would live in air less pure than that of Paradise, eat impure mortal food, and become a part of the processes of *dissolution* instigated by his original distempering, disordering, imbalancing sin. The central metaphor depends on the theory of humors; see "Physiology and Psychology," p. 391. The syntax of the passage would be clearer if in line 53 there were no comma after *distemper*, a comma after the first *gross*, and no comma after the second *gross*. Cf. 284–85.

No gross, no unharmonious mixture foul,
Eject him tainted now, and purge him off
As a distemper, gross to air as gross,
And mortal food, as may dispose him best
For dissolution wrought by sin, that first   55
Distempered all things, and of incorrupt
Corrupted. I at first with two fair gifts
Created him endowed, with happiness
And immortality: that fondly lost,
This other served but to eternize woe;   60
Till I provided death; so death becomes
His final remedy, and after life
Tried in sharp tribulation, and refined
By faith and faithful works, to second life,
Waked in the renovation of the just,   65
Resigns him up with heav'n and earth renewed.
But let us call to synod all the blest
Through heav'n's wide bounds; from them I will not hide
My judgments, how with mankind I proceed,
As how with peccant angels late they saw;   70
And in their state, though firm, stood more confirmed."
    He ended, and the Son gave signal high
To the bright minister that watched, he blew
His trumpet, heard in Oreb since perhaps
When God descended, and perhaps once more   75
To sound at general doom. Th' angelic blast
Filled all the regions: from their blissful bow'rs
Of amarantine shade, fountain or spring,
By the waters of life, where'er they sat
In fellowships of joy, the sons of light   80
Hasted, resorting to the summons high,
And took their seats; till from his throne supreme
Th' Almighty thus pronounced his sovran will.
    "O sons, like one of us man is become
To know both good and evil, since his taste   85
Of that defended fruit; but let him boast
His knowledge of good lost, and evil got,
Happier, had it sufficed him to have known
Good by itself, and evil not at all.
He sorrows now, repents, and prays contrite,   90
My motions in him; longer than they move,
His heart I know, how variable and vain

59. *fondlly:* foolishly.
64. *faithful works.* Cf. *CD*, I.xxii.B.
74. *Oreb.* See I.6n.
75. *general doom:* the Last Judgment. Cf. Matt. 24.31: "And he shall send his angels with a great sound of a trumpet, and they shall gather together his elect from the four winds, from one end of heaven to the other." 1 Cor. 15.52: "In a moment, in the twinkling of an eye, at the last trump: for the trumpet shall sound, and the dead shall be raised incorruptible, and we shall be changed."
77. *regions:* the lower, middle and upper air. See I.10–15n.
78. *amarantine.* See III.352n.
86. *defended:* forbidden.
91–93. I.e.: I know how variable and vain his heart will be when, after I cease sending my impulses, he is left to himself. *motions:* impulses. See *Prevenient grace*, line 3.

Self-left. Lest therefore his now bolder hand
Reach also of the Tree of Life, and eat,
And live forever, dream at least to live   95
Forever, to remove him I decree,
And send him from the garden forth to till
The ground whence he was taken, fitter soil.
  "Michael, this my behest have thou in charge,
Take to thee from among the Cherubim   100
Thy choice of flaming warriors, lest the Fiend
Or in behalf of man, or to invade
Vacant possession some new trouble raise:
Haste thee, and from the Paradise of God
Without remorse drive out the sinful pair,   105
From hallowed ground th' unholy, and denounce
To them and to their progeny from thence
Perpetual banishment. Yet lest they faint
At the sad sentence rigorously urged,
For I behold them softened and with tears   110
Bewailing their excess, all terror hide.
If patiently thy bidding they obey,
Dismiss them not disconsolate; reveal
To Adam what shall come in future days,
As I shall thee enlighten, intermix   115
My cov'nant in the woman's seed renewed;
So send them forth, though sorrowing, yet in peace:
And on the east side of the garden place,
Where entrance up from Eden easiest climbs,
Cherubic watch, and of a sword the flame   120
Wide-waving, all approach far off to fright,
And guard all passage to the Tree of life:
Lest Paradise a receptácle prove
To Spirits foul, and all my trees their prey,
With whose stol'n fruit man once more to delude."   125
  He ceased; and th' Archangelic Power prepared
For swift descent, with him the cohort bright
Of watchful Cherubim; four faces each
Had, like a double Janus, all their shape
Spangled with eyes more numerous than those   130
Of Argus, and more wakeful than to drowse,
Charmed with Arcadian pipe, the pastoral reed
Of Hermes, or his opiate rod. Meanwhile
To resalute the world with sacred light
Leucóthea waked, and with fresh dews embalmed   135

---

102. *in behalf of:* with regard to.
105. *remorse:* pity.
106. *denounce:* deliver a judgment of punishment.
108. *faint:* lose courage.
109. *urged:* carried out.
111. *excess:* transgression, enormity.
116. *Covenant.* See "Covenant," pp. 397–98, and *CD*, I.xxvii.A.

128–33. Cf. Ezek. 1.18, p. 379. *Janus:* a Roman god with two faces. Jealous Juno set *Argus,* with his hundred eyes, to watch Io, Jove's mistress, but *Hermes* with music and stories put Argus asleep. *opiate rod:* Hermes's sleep-producing caduceus.
135. *Leucothea:* goddess of the dawn.

The earth, when Adam and first matron Eve
Had ended now their orisons, and found
Strength added from above, new hope to spring
Out of despair, joy, but with fear yet linked;
Which thus to Eve his welcome words renewed.   140
    "Eve, easily may faith admit, that all
The good which we enjoy, from heav'n descends;
But that from us aught should ascend to heav'n
So prevalent as to concern the mind
Of God high-blest, or to incline his will,   145
Hard to belief may seem; yet this will prayer,
Or one short sigh of human breath, upborne
Ev'n to the seat of God. For since I sought
By prayer th' offended Deity to appease,
Kneeled and before him humbled all my heart,   150
Methought I saw him placable and mild,
Bending his ear; persuasion in me grew
That I was heard with favor; peace returned
Home to my breast, and to my memory
His promise, that thy seed shall bruise our foe;   155
Which then not minded in dismay, yet now
Assures me that the bitterness of death
Is past, and we shall live. Whence Hail to thee,
Eve rightly called, mother of all mankind,
Mother of all things living, since by thee   160
Man is to live, and all things live for man."
    To whom thus Eve with sad demeanor meek.
"Ill-worthy I such title should belong
To me transgressor, who for thee ordained
A help, became thy snare; to me reproach   165
Rather belongs, distrust and all dispraise:
But infinite in pardon was my Judge,
That I who first brought death on all, am graced
The source of life; next favorable thou,
Who highly thus to entitle me voutsaf'st,   170
Far other name deserving. But the field
To labor calls us now with sweat imposed,
Though after sleepless night; for see the morn,
All unconcerned with our unrest, begins
Her rosy progress smiling; let us forth,   175
I never from thy side henceforth to stray,
Where'er our day's work lies, though now enjoined
Laborious, till day droop; while here we dwell,
What can be toilsome in these pleasant walks?

144. *prevalent:* (L *prae* + *valere* to be strong or able) able to prevail.
157. Cf. 1 Sam. 15.32–33 [*NEB*]: "Then Samuel said, 'Bring Agag king of the Amalekites.' So Agag came to him with faltering steps and said, 'Surely the bitterness of death has passed.' Samuel said, 'Your sword has made women childless, and your mother of all women shall be childless too.' Then Samuel hewed Agag in pieces before the Lord at Gilgal."
159. *rightly called, mother.* Cf. Gen. 3.20, p. 354.

Here let us live, though in fall'n state, content."   180
So spake, so wished much-humbled Eve, but fate
Subscribed not; nature first gave signs, impressed
On bird, beast, air, air suddenly eclipsed
After short blush of morn; nigh in her sight
The bird of Jove, stooped from his airy tow'r,   185
Two birds of gayest plume before him drove:
Down from a hill the beast that reigns in woods,
First hunter then, pursued a gentle brace,
Goodliest of all the forest, hart and hind;
Direct to th' eastern gate was bent their flight.   190
Adam observed, and with his eye the chase
Pursuing, not unmoved to Eve thus spake.
    "O Eve, some further change awaits us nigh,
Which heav'n by these mute signs in nature shows
Forerunners of his purpose, or to warn   195
Us haply too secure of our discharge
From penalty, because from death released
Some days; how long, and what till then our life,
Who knows, or more than this, that we are dust,
And thither must return and be no more.   200
Why else this double object in our sight
Of flight pursued in th' air and o'er the ground
One way the selfsame hour? Why in the east
Darkness ere day's mid-course, and morning light
More orient in yon western cloud that draws   205
O'er the blue firmament a radiant white,
And slow descends, with something heav'nly fraught."
    He erred not, for by this the heav'nly bands
Down from a sky of jasper lighted now
In Paradise, and on a hill made alt,   210
A glorious apparition, had not doubt
And carnal fear that day dimmed Adam's eye.
Not that more glorious, when the angels met
Jacob in Mahanaim, where he saw
The field pavilioned with his guardians bright;   215
Nor that which on the flaming mount appeared
In Dothan, covered with a camp of fire,
Against the Syrian king, who to surprise
One man, assassin-like had levied war,

---

180. Cf. Phil. 4.11: "Not that I speak in respect of want: for I have learned, in whatsoever state I am, therewith to be content."

182. *signs:* omens.

183. *eclipsed:* darkened.

185. *bird of Jove:* eagle. *stooped:* (a term from falconry) swooped.

187. *beast that reigns:* lion.

196. *secure:* sure.

205. *orient:* bright, shining.

209. *jasper.* Cf. Rev. 4.3, p. 384.

210. *made alt:* (military term) came to a halt.

213–15. Cf. Gen. 32.1–2: "And Jacob went on his way, and the angels of God met him. And when Jacob saw them, he said, "This is God's host: and he called the name of that place Mahanaim."

216–20. The king of Syria, warring on Israel, sent a detachment to Dothan (where Elisha, the prophet, was miraculously publishing the war plans of the king) with orders to kill Elisha. But the Lord saved his prophet by surrounding him with "horses and chariots of fire." 2 Kings 6.8ff.

War unproclaimed. The princely Hierarch   220
In their bright stand, there left his powers to seize
Possession of the garden; he alone,
To find where Adam sheltered, took his way,
Not unperceived of Adam, who to Eve,
While the great visitant approached, thus spake.   225
　　"Eve, now expect great tidings, which perhaps
Of us will soon determine, or impose
New laws to be observed; for I descry
From yonder blazing cloud that veils the hill
One of the heav'nly host, and by his gait   230
None of the meanest, some great Potentate
Or of the Thrones above, such majesty
Invests him coming; yet not terrible,
That I should fear, nor sociably mild,
As Raphael, that I should much confide,   235
But solemn and sublime, whom not to offend,
With reverence I must meet, and thou retire."
He ended; and th' Archangel soon drew nigh,
Not in his shape celestial, but as man
Clad to meet man; over his lucid arms   240
A military vest of purple flowed
Livelier than Meliboean, or the grain
Of Sarra, worn by kings and heroes old
In time of truce; Iris had dipped the woof;
His starry helm unbuckled showed him prime   245
In manhood where youth ended; by his side
As in a glistering zodiac hung the sword,
Satan's dire dread, and in his hand the spear.
Adam bowed low, he kingly from his state
Inclined not, but his coming thus declared.   250
　　"Adam, Heav'n's high behest no preface needs:
Sufficient that thy prayers are heard, and Death,
Then due by sentence when thou didst transgress,
Defeated of his seizure many days
Giv'n thee of grace, wherein thou may'st repent,   255
And one bad act with many deeds well done
May'st cover: well may then thy Lord appeased
Redeem thee quite from Death's rapacious claim;
But longer in this Paradise to dwell
Permits not; to remove thee I am come,   260
And send thee from the garden forth to till
The ground whence thou wast taken, fitter soil."
　　He added not, for Adam at the news
Heart-strook with chilling gripe of sorrow stood,

220. *Hierarch.* See V.468n.
221. *bright stand:* shining formation, or station. *powers:* army, host.
227. *determine:* make an end.
240. *lucid:* shining.
242–43. Meliboea and Tyre (*Sarra*) were famous for their purple dye (*grain*).
244. *Iris:* goddess of the rainbow.
247. *zodiac:* girdle.
249. *state:* dignified standing.
254. *Defeated of his seizure:* (legal language) deprived of his possession.

That all his senses bound; Eve, who unseen   265
Yet all had heard, with audible lament
Discovered soon the place of her retire.
    "O unexpected stroke, worse than of Death!
Must I thus leave thee Paradise? thus leave
Thee native soil, these happy walks and shades,   270
Fit haunt of gods? where I had hope to spend,
Quiet though sad, the respite of that day
That must be mortal to us both. O flow'rs,
That never will in other climate grow,
My early visitation, and my last   275
At ev'n, which I bred up with tender hand
From the first op'ning bud, and gave ye names,
Who now shall rear ye to the sun, or rank
Your tribes, and water from th' ambrosial fount?
Thee lastly nuptial bower, by me adorned   280
With what to sight or smell was sweet; from thee
How shall I part, and whither wander down
Into a lower world, to this obscure
And wild, how shall we breathe in other air
Less pure, accustomed to immortal fruits?"   285
    Whom thus the Angel interrupted mild.
"Lament not Eve, but patiently resign
What justly thou hast lost; nor set thy heart,
Thus over-fond, on that which is not thine;
Thy going is not lonely, with thee goes   290
Thy husband, him to follow thou art bound;
Where he abides, think there thy native soil."
    Adam by this from the cold sudden damp
Recovering, and his scattered spirits returned,
To Michael thus his humble words addressed.   295
    "Celestial, whether among the Thrones, or named
Of them the highest, for such of shape may seem
Prince above princes, gently hast thou told
Thy message, which might else in telling wound,
And in performing end us; what besides   300
Of sorrow and dejection and despair
Our frailty can sustain, thy tidings bring,
Departure from this happy place, our sweet
Recess, and only consolation left
Familiar to our eyes, all places else   305
Inhospitable appear and desolate,
Nor knowing us nor known: and if by prayer
Incessant I could hope to change the will
Of him who all things can, I would not cease
To weary him with my assiduous cries: 310
But prayer against his absolute decree

267. *Discovered:* revealed.   293. *damp:* dejection.
272. *respite:* period of postponement.   309. *can:* is able to do, has knowledge
283. *to this:* compared with this.   of.

No more avails than breath against the wind,
Blown stifling back on him that breathes it forth:
Therefore to his great bidding I submit.
This most afflicts me, that departing hence,   315
As from his face I shall be hid, deprived
His blessed count'nance; here I could frequent,
With worship, place by place where he voutsafed
Presence Divine, and to my sons relate:
'On this mount he appeared, under this tree   320
Stood visible, among these pines his voice
I heard, here with him at this fountain talked:'
So many grateful altars I would rear
Of grassy turf, and pile up every stone
Of luster from the brook, in memory,   325
Or monument to ages, and thereon
Offer sweet-smelling gums and fruits and flow'rs:
In yonder nether world where shall I seek
His bright appearances, or footstep trace?
For though I fled him angry, yet recalled   330
To life prolonged and promised race, I now
Gladly behold though but his utmost skirts
Of glory, and far off his steps adore."
    To whom thus Michael with regard benign.
"Adam, thou know'st heav'n his, and all the earth,   335
Not this rock only; his omnipresence fills
Land, sea, and air, and every kind that lives,
Fomented by his virtual power and warmed:
All th' earth he gave thee to possess and rule,
No despicable gift; surmise not then   340
His presence to these narrow bounds confined
Of Paradise or Eden: this had been
Perhaps thy capital seat, from whence had spread
All generations, and had hither come
From all the ends of th' earth, to celebrate   345
And reverence thee their great progenitor.
But this preeminence thou hast lost, brought down

316. Cf. Gen. 4.14 "Behold, thou hast driven me out this day from the face of the earth; and from thy face shall I be hid; and I shall be a fugitive and a vagabond in the earth; and it shall come to pass, that every one that findeth me shall slay me." Ps. 27.9: "Hide not thy face far from me; put not thy servant away in anger: thou hast been my help; leave me not, neither forsake me, O God of my salvation."
332. *skirts:* outermost edges; but cf. III.380, where Milton's use may derive from a Hebrew word (in Isa. 6.1) meaning "the skirt of his robe" and implying God's glory. Cf. Exod. 33.23 and [*NEB*] Job 26.14.
335–38. Cf. Ps. 139.7–12: "Whither shall I go from thy spirit? or whither shall I flee from thy presence? If I ascend up into heaven, thou art there: if I make my bed in hell, behold, thou art there. If I take the wings of the morning, and dwell in the uttermost parts of the seas; Even there shall thy hand lead me, and thy right hand shall hold me. If I say, Surely the darkness shall cover me; even the night shall be light about me. Yea, the darkness hideth not from thee; but the night shineth as the day: the darkness and the light are both alike to thee." Jer. 23.24: "Can any hide himself in secret places that I shall not see him? saith the Lord. Do not I fill heaven and earth? saith the Lord." *Fomented:* nursed to life, nurtured. *virtual:* (L *virtus* strength) efficacious.

To dwell on even ground now with thy sons:
Yet doubt not but in valley and in plain
God is as here, and will be found alike   350
Present, and of his presence many a sign
Still following thee, still compassing thee round
With goodness and paternal love, his face
Express, and of his steps the track divine.
Which that thou may'st believe, and be confirmed,   355
Ere thou from hence depart, know I am sent
To show thee what shall come in future days
To thee and to thy offspring; good with bad
Expect to hear, supernal grace contending
With sinfulness of men; thereby to learn   360
True patience, and to temper joy with fear
And pious sorrow, equally inured
By moderation either state to bear,
Prosperous or adverse: so shalt thou lead
Safest thy life, and best prepared endure   365
Thy mortal passage when it comes. Ascend
This hill; let Eve (for I have drenched her eyes)
Here sleep below while thou to foresight wak'st,
As once thou slept'st while she to life was formed."
    To whom thus Adam gratefully replied.   370
"Ascend, I follow thee, safe guide, the path
Thou lead'st me, and to the hand of Heav'n submit,
However chast'ning, to the evil turn
My obvious breast, arming to overcome
By suffering, and earn rest from labor won,   375
If so I may attain." So both ascend
In the visions of God: it was a hill
Of Paradise the highest, from whose top
The hemisphere of earth in clearest ken
Stretched out to amplest reach of prospect lay.   380
Not higher that hill nor wider looking round,
Whereon for different cause the Tempter set
Our second Adam in the wilderness,
To show him all earth's kingdoms and their glory.
His eye might there command wherever stood   385
City of old or modern fame, the seat
Of mightiest empire, from the destined walls

362. *pious sorrow:* pity consistent with proper religious attitudes.
367. *drenched.* Cf. II.73 *the sleepy drench/Of that forgetful lake.*
374. *obvious:* exposed.
377. Cf. Ezek. 40.2: "In the visions of God brought he me into the land of Israel, and set me upon a very high mountain . . ."
379. *ken:* view.
381–84. In the temptations of Christ, which Milton recounted in *PR*, the devil took Christ "up into an exceeding high mountain and [showed] him all the king-

doms of the world, and the glory of them" (Matt. 4.8), and offered Christ "all these things" if Christ would "fall down and worship" him.
387–96. These *destined* (yet to come) cities were great capitals: *Cambalu* (Peking) of Cathay, a vaguely defined region in N China ruled by such khans as Genghis and Kubla; *Samarkand*, on the Oxus River, of the SW part of Tatary (now SW Russia), ruled by another khan, Tamburlaine (*Temir*); *Paquin* (Peking) of China (Milton's contemporaries were not sure whether Cambalu

Of Cambalu, seat of Cathaian Can,
And Samarkand by Oxus, Temir's throne,
To Paquin of Sinaean kings, and thence   390
To Agra and Lahore of Great Mogul
Down to the golden Chersonese, or where
The Persian in Ecbatan sat, or since
In Hispahan, or where the Russian Ksar
In Moscow, or the Sultan in Bizance,   395
Turkéstan-born; nor could his eye not ken
Th' empire of Negus to his utmost port
Ercoco and the less marítime kings
Mombaza, and Quiloa, and Melind,
And Sofala thought Ophir, to the realm   400
Of Congo, and Angola farthest south;
Or thence from Niger flood to Atlas mount
The kingdoms of Almansor, Fez and Sus,
Marocco and Algiers, and Tremisen;
On Europe thence, and where Rome was to sway   405
The world: in spirit perhaps he also saw
Rich Mexico the seat of Motezume,
And Cusco in Peru, the richer seat
Of Atabalipa, and yet unspoiled
Guiana, whose great city Geryon's sons   410
Call El Dorado: but to nobler sights
Michael from Adam's eyes the film removed
Which that false fruit that promised clearer sight
Had bred; then purged with euphrasy and rue
The visual nerve, for he had much to see;   415

---

and Paquin were the same city); *Agra* and *Lahore* of the *mogul* empire in India; *Ecbatan* (modern Hamadan) and *Hispahan* (modern Isfahan), of Persia (Iran); *Bizance* (Byzantium—modern Istanbul) of the Turkish empire, ruled by *sultans*, who came from *Turkestan* (a region now divided among Russia, China, and Afghanistan). *the golden Chersonese:* the Malay Peninsula, thought by some to be *Ophir*, the country from which Solomon got the gold for his temple. Other places had been suggested, among them *Sofala* (400).

397–404. On the African continent: the *empire* of the king (*Negus*) is Abyssinia; *Ercoco* (modern Arkiko) is on the Red Sea; *Mombaza* (modern Mombasa), *Melind* (modern Malindi), *Quiloa* (modern Kilwa) and *Sofala* are on the east coast; the S part of the W coast in Milton's time was called *Angola*; the territory between the *Niger* River and the *Atlas* Mountains (in N Morocco and Algeria), are the *kingdoms of Almansor* (a tenth century Mohammedan prince), i.e., the province of *Sus* and the cities of *Fez* and *Tremisen* (modern Tlemecen), which Milton thought of as capitals of small nations.

400. *Ophir.* Cf. 1 Kings 9.28: "And they came to Ophir, and fetched from thence gold, four hundred and twenty talents, and brought it to king Solomon." 1 Kings 10.11: "And the navy also of Hiram, that brought gold from Ophir, brought in from Ophir great plenty of almug trees, and precious stones."

406–11. *in spirit.* No matter how high the mount in Paradise, Adam could not see the other side of the sphere. Atahualpa (*Atabalipa*) was the Inca emperor defeated by Pizarro. *Guiana* was a region containing modern Surinam, Guyana, and French Guiana, part of Venezuela and part of Brazil; its capital, Manoa, was supposed by the Spanish (*Geryon's sons*) to be the residence of *El Dorado*, the Gilded King. *yet unspoiled:* in Milton's time, not yet plundered by the Spanish (unlike Mexico and Persia).

414. *euphrasy:* the herb "eyebright," like *rue* (another herb) believed to improve vision. Fowler notes that *euphrasy* comes from Gk *euphrasia* cheerfulness and that the word, like *rue*, may be a pun—that euphrasy and rue as joy and sorrow are "correlates of the 'joy' and 'pious sorrow' that Michael told Adam to temper, at 361ff."

And from the well of life three drops instilled.
So deep the power of these ingredients pierced,
Ev'n to the inmost seat of mental sight,
That Adam now enforced to close his eyes,
Sunk down and all his spirits became entranced: 420
But him the gentle angel by the hand
Soon raised, and his attention thus recalled.
      "Adam, now ope thine eyes, and first behold
Th' effects which thy original crime hath wrought
In some to spring from thee, who never touched   425
Th' excepted tree, nor with the snake conspired,
Nor sinned thy sin, yet from that sin derive
Corruption to bring forth more violent deeds."
      His eyes he opened, and beheld a field,
Part arable and tilth, whereon were sheaves   430
New-reaped, the other part sheep-walks and folds;
I' th' midst an altar as the landmark stood
Rustic, of grassy sord; thither anon
A sweaty reaper from his tillage brought
First-fruits, the green ear, and the yellow sheaf,   435
Unculled, as came to hand; a shepherd next
More meek came with the firstlings of his flock
Choicest and best; then sacrificing, laid
The inwards and their fat, with incense strewed,
On the cleft wood, and all due rites performed.   440
His off'ring soon propitious fire from heav'n
Consumed with nimble glance, and grateful steam;
The other's not, for his was not sincere;
Whereat he inly raged, and as they talked,
Smote him into the midriff with a stone   445
That beat out life; he fell, and deadly pale
Groaned out his soul with gushing blood effused.
Much at that sight was Adam in his heart
Dismayed, and thus in haste to th' angel cried.
      "O teacher, some great mischief hath befall'n   450
To that meek man, who well had sacrificed;
Is piety thus and pure devotion paid?"
      T' whom Michael thus, he also moved, replied.
"These two are brethren, Adam, and to come
Out of thy loins; th' unjust the just hath slain,   455
For envy that his brother's offering found
From Heav'n acceptance; but the bloody fact

---

416. Cf. Ps. 36.9: "For with thee is the fountain of life: in thy light shall we see light."
429–60. Cf. Gen. 4.1–16, pp. 356–57.
430. *tilth:* cultivated land.
432. *landmark:* boundary-marker.
433. *sord:* sward, turf.
435. *First-fruits.* Cf. 22.

436. *Unculled:* unselected; not, like Abel's the *choicest and best* (438).
439. *inwards:* innards.
441. *propitious:* indicative of God's favor.
442. *nimble glance:* quick flash.
457. *fact:* crime. Cf. IX.928.

Will be avenged, and th' other's faith approved
Lose no reward, thou here thou see him die,
Rolling in dust and gore." To which our sire.   460
    "Alas, both for the deed and for the cause!
But have I now seen death? Is this the way
I must return to native dust? O sight
Of terror, foul and ugly to behold,
Horrid to think, how horrible to feel!"   465
    To whom thus Michaël. "Death thou hast seen
In his first shape on man; but many shapes
Of Death, and many are the ways that lead
To his grim cave, all dismal; yet to sense
More terrible at th' entrance than within.   470
Some, as thou saw'st, by violent stroke shall die,
By fire, flood, famine; by intemperance more
In meats and drinks, which on the earth shall bring
Diseases dire, of which a monstrous crew
Before thee shall appear; that thou may'st know   475
What misery th' inabstinence of Eve
Shall bring on men." Immediately a place
Before his eyes appeared, sad, noisome, dark,
A lazar-house it seemed, wherein were laid
Numbers of all diseased, all maladies   480
Of ghastly spasm, or racking torture, qualms
Of heart-sick agony, all feverous kinds,
Convulsions, epilepsies, fierce catarrhs,
Intestine stone and ulcer, colic pangs,
Demoniac frenzy, moping melancholy   485
And moon-struck madness, pining atrophy,
Marasmus, and wide-wasting pestilence,
Dropsies, and asthmas, and joint-racking rheums.
Dire was the tossing, deep the groans, Despair
Tended the sick busiest from couch to couch;   490
And over them triumphant Death his dart
Shook, but delayed to strike, though oft invoked
With vows, as their chief good, and final hope.
Sight so deform what heart of rock could long
Dry-eyed behold? Adam could not, but wept,   495
Though not of woman born; compassion quelled
His best of man, and gave him up to tears
A space, till firmer thoughts restrained excess,
And scarce recovering words his plaint renewed.
    "O miserable mankind, to what fall   500
Degraded, to what wretched state reserved!

458–59. Cf. Heb. 11.4: "By faith Abel
offered unto God a more excellent sac-
rifice than Cain, by which he obtained
witness that he was righteous, God testi-
fying of his gifts: and by it he being
dead yet speaketh."

478. *sad:* lamentable.
479. *lazar-house:* house for lepers.
485–87. These lines were not in the
first edn. *pining atrophy, Marasmus:* all
three words mean "wasting away."
497. *best of man:* manliness, courage.

Better end here unborn. Why is life giv'n
To be thus wrested from us? Rather why
Obtruded on us thus? who if we knew
What we receive, would either not accept 505
Life offered, or soon beg to lay it down,
Glad to be so dismissed in peace. Can thus
Th' image of God in man created once
So goodly and erect, though faulty since,
To such unsightly sufferings be debased 510
Under inhuman pains? Why should not man,
Retaining still divine similitude
In part, from such deformities be free,
And for his Maker's image sake exempt?"
        "Their Maker's image," answered Michael, "then 515
Forsook them, when themselves they vilified
To serve ungoverned appetite, and took
His image whom they served, a brutish vice,
Inductive mainly to the sin of Eve.
Therefore so abject is their punishment, 520
Disfiguring not God's likeness, but their own,
Or if his likeness, by themselves defaced
While they pervert pure nature's healthful rules
To loathsome sickness, worthily, since they
God's image did not reverence in themselves." 525
        "I yield it just," said Adam, "and submit.
But is there yet no other way, besides
These painful passages, how we may come
To death, and mix with our connatural dust?"
        "There is," said Michael, "if thou well observe 530
The rule of not too much, by temperance taught
In what thou eat'st and drink'st, seeking from thence
Due nourishment, not gluttonous delight,
Till many years over thy head return:
So may'st thou live, till like ripe fruit thou drop 535
Into thy mother's lap, or be with ease
Gathered, not harshly plucked, for death mature:
This is old age; but then thou must outlive
Thy youth, thy strength, thy beauty, which will change
To withered weak and gray; thy senses then 540
Obtuse, all taste of pleasure must forgo,
To what thou hast, and for the air of youth
Hopeful and cheerful, in thy blood will reign
A melancholy damp of cold and dry
To weigh thy spirits down, and last consume 545
The balm of life." To whom our ancestor.

---

516. *vilified:* lowered.
519. *Inductive:* conducive.
524. *worthily:* deservedly.
544. *damp:* vapor; depression or dejection; but Milton suggests "humor," since in the theory of the humors melancholy was supposed to be *cold* (of the earth) and *dry* (of the air).
546. *balm:* balsam, "preservative essence, conceived by Paracelsus to exist in all organic bodies" *OED*.

"Henceforth I fly not death, nor would prolong
Life much, bent rather how I may be quit
Fairest and easiest of this cumbrous charge,
Which I must keep till my appointed day   550
Of rend'ring up, and patiently attend
My dissolution.' Michaël replied.
    "Nor love thy life, nor hate; but what thou liv'st
Live well, how long or short permit to Heav'n:
And now prepare thee for another sight."   555
    He looked and saw a spacious plain, whereon
Were tents of various hue; by some were herds
Of cattle grazing: others, whence the sound
Of instruments that made melodious chime
Was heard, of harp and organ; and who moved   560
Their stops and chords was seen: his volant touch
Instinct through all proportions low and high
Fled and pursued transverse the resonant fugue.
In other part stood one who at the forge
Laboring, two massy clods of iron and brass   565
Had melted (whether found where casual fire
Had wasted woods on mountain or in vale,
Down to the veins of earth, thence gliding hot
To some cave's mouth, or whether washed by stream
From underground) the liquid ore he drained   570
Into fit molds prepared; from which he formed
First his own tools; then, what might else be wrought
Fusile or grav'n in metal. After these,
But on the hither side a different sort
From the high neighboring hills, which was their seat,   575
Down to the plain descended: by their guise
Just men they seemed, and all their study bent
To worship God aright, and know his works
Not hid, nor those things last which might preserve
Freedom and peace to men: they on the plain   580
Long had not walked, when from the tents behold
A bevy of fair women, richly gay
In gems and wanton dress; to the harp they sung

---

551. *attend:* await.
    556–73. Cf. Gen. 4.20–22, p. 357.
    561–63. Milton describes the fugue and the playing of a fugue. *volant:* (L *volare* to fly) nimble. *touch:* skill in or style of playing an instrument. *Instinct:* instinctive, innate, untutored. *proportions:* (technical musical term) here, ratios of pitches; perhaps, scales. *Fled and pursued:* descriptive of both the player's hands and of the music. In a fugue (L *fugere* to flee) one variation of the theme seems to chase another. *transverse:* across either scales, or keyboard or strings. *resonant:* literally re-sounding, since in a fugue the same notes or theme(s) are, in a way, repeated.

566. *casual:* L *casus* fall, chance. *fire:* lightning.
    573. *Fusile or grav'n:* cast or sculptured.
    573–74. Turning from the descendants of Cain, Milton speaks of those of Seth, Adam's third son, who lived in the hills bordering Cain's plain, east of Eden, opposite the hill of Paradise.
    580. Here Milton begins the story of the *Giants of mighty bone* (642) based on Gen. 6.1–4 (pp. 357–58). Milton implies that the heroic race was the offspring of the descendants of Seth ("sons of God") and the descendants of Cain ("daughters of men").

Soft amorous ditties, and in dance came on:
The men though grave, eyed them, and let their eyes   585
Rove without rein, till in the amorous net
Fast caught, they liked, and each his liking chose;
And now of love they treat till th' evening star
Love's harbinger appeared; then all in heat
They light the nuptial torch, and bid invoke   590
Hymen, then first to marriage rites invoked;
With feast and music all the tents resound.
Such happy interview and fair event
Of love and youth not lost, songs, garlands, flow'rs,
And charming symphonies attached the heart   595
Of Adam, soon inclined to admit delight,
The bent of nature; which he thus expressed.
    "True opener of mine eyes, prime angel blest,
Much better seems this vision, and more hope
Of peaceful days portends, than those two past;   600
Those were of hate and death, or pain much worse,
Here nature seems fulfilled in all her ends."
    To whom thus Michael. "Judge not what is best
By pleasure, though to nature seeming meet,
Created, as thou art, to nobler end   605
Holy and pure, conformity divine.
Those tents thou saw'st so pleasant, were the tents
Of wickedness, wherein shall dwell his race
Who slew his brother; studious they appear
Of arts that polish life, inventors rare,   610
Unmindful of their Maker, though his spirit
Taught them, but they his gifts acknowledged none.
Yet they a beauteous offspring shall beget;
For that fair female troop thou saw'st, that seemed
Of goddesses, so blithe, so smooth, so gay,   615
Yet empty of all good wherein consists
Woman's domestic honor and chief praise;
Bred only and completed to the taste
Of lustful appetence, to sing, to dance,
To dress, and troll the tongue, and roll the eye.   620
To these that sober race of men, whose lives
Religious titled them the Sons of God,
Shall yield up all their virtue, all their fame
Ignobly, to the trains and to the smiles
Of these fair atheists, and now swim in joy,   625
(Erelong to swim at large) and laugh; for which
The world erelong a world of tears must weep."

588. *evening star:* Venus.
591. *Hymen:* god of marriage.
595. *symphonies:* concerted or har-
monious music. *attached:* seized.
596. *soon:* easily.
607–8. Cf. Ps. 84.10: "For a day in
thy courts is better than a thousand. I

had rather be a doorkeeper in the house
of my God, than to dwell in the tents of
wickedness."
618. *completed:* equipped.
619. *appetence:* appetite, desire.
620. *troll:* roll, wag.
624. *trains:* guile, wiles, trickery.

To whom thus Adam of short joy bereft.
"O pity and shame, that they who to live well
Entered so fair, should turn aside to tread   630
Paths indirect, or in the mid way faint!
But still I see the tenor of man's woe
Holds on the same, from woman to begin."
   "From man's effeminate slackness it begins,"
Said th' angel, "who should better hold his place   635
By wisdom, and superior gifts received.
But now prepare thee for another scene."
   He looked and saw wide territory spread
Before him, towns, and rural works between,
Cities of men with lofty gates and tow'rs,   640
Concourse in arms, fierce faces threat'ning war,
Giants of mighty bone, and bold emprise;
Part wield their arms, part curb the foaming steed,
Single or in array of battle ranged
Both horse and foot, nor idly must'ring stood;   645
One way a band select from forage drives
A herd of beeves, fair oxen and fair kine
From a fat meadow ground; or fleecy flock,
Ewes and their bleating lambs over the plain,
Their booty; scarce with life the shepherds fly,   650
But call in aid, which makes a bloody fray;
With cruel tournament the squadrons join;
Where cattle pastured late, now scattered lies
With carcasses and arms th' ensanguined field
Deserted: others to a city strong   655
Lay siege, encamped; by battery, scale, and mine,
Assaulting; others from the wall defend
With dart and jav'lin, stones and sulphurous fire;
On each hand slaughter and gigantic deeds.
In other part the sceptered heralds call   660
To council in the city gates: anon
Gray-headed men and grave, with warriors mixed,
Assemble, and harangues are heard, but soon
In factious opposition, till at last
Of middle age one rising, eminent   665
In wise deport, spake much of right and wrong,
Of justice, of religion, truth and peace,
And judgment from above: him old and young
Exploded, and had seized with violent hands,
Had not a cloud descending snatched him thence   670
Unseen amid the throng: so violence
Proceeded, and oppression, and sword-law
Through all the plain, and refuge none was found.

---

641. *Concourse:* (L *concurrere* to run together) encounter.
642. *emprise:* chivalric adventure.
656. I.e.: By battering, scaling, and tunneling under (the walls).

665. *one:* Enoch, who "walked with God: and he was not; for God took him" (Gen, 5.24). See 700–9n.
669. *Exploded.* See X.546n.

Adam was all in tears, and to his guide
Lamenting turned full sad; "O what are these,   675
Death's ministers, not men, who thus deal death
Inhumanly to men, and multiply
Ten-thousandfold the sin of him who slew
His brother; for of whom such massacre
Make they but of their brethren, men of men?   680
But who was that just man, whom had not Heav'n
Rescued, had in his righteousness been lost?"
    To whom thus Michael. "These are the product
Of those ill-mated marriages thou saw'st:
Where good with bad were matched, who of themselves   685
Abhor to join; and by imprudence mixed,
Produce prodigious births of body or mind.
Such were these giants, men of high renown;
For in those days might only shall be admired,
And valor and heroic virtue called;   690
To overcome in battle, and subdue
Nations, and bring home spoils with infinite
Manslaughter, shall be held the highest pitch
Of human glory, and for glory done
Of triumph, to be styled great conquerors,   695
Patrons of mankind, gods, and sons of gods,
Destroyers rightlier called and plagues of men.
Thus fame shall be achieved, renown on earth,
And what most merits fame in silence hid.
But he the sev'nth from thee, whom thou beheld'st   700
The only righteous in a world perverse,
And therefore hated, therefore so beset
With foes for daring single to be just,
And utter odious truth, that God would come
To judge them with his saints: him the Most High   705
Rapt in a balmy cloud with wingèd steeds
Did, as thou saw'st, receive, to walk with God
High in salvation and the climes of bliss,
Exempt from death; to show thee what reward
Awaits the good, the rest what punishment;   710
Which now direct thine eyes and soon behold."
    He looked, and saw the face of things quite changed;
The brazen throat of war had ceased to roar,
All now was turned to jollity and game,
To luxury and riot, feast and dance,   715
Marrying or prostituting, as befell,

700–9. Cf. Jude 14–15 "And Enoch also, the seventh from Adam, prophesied of these, saying, Behold, the Lord cometh with ten thousands of his saints, to execute judgment upon all, and to convince all that are ungodly among them of all their ungodly deeds which they have ungodly committed, and of all their hard speeches which ungodly sinners have spoken against him." Heb. 11.5: "By faith Enoch was translated that he should not see death; and was not found, because God had translated him: for before his translation he had this testimony, that he pleased God."

715. *luxury:* (L *luxus* excess) lust.

Rape or adultery, where passing fair
Allured them; thence from cups to civil broils.
At length a reverend sire among them came,
And of their doings great dislike declared,   720
And testified against their ways; he oft
Frequented their assemblies, whereso met,
Triumphs or festivals, and to them preached
Conversion and repentance, as to souls
In prison under judgments imminent: 725
But all in vain: which when he saw, he ceased
Contending, and removed his tents far off;
Then from the mountain hewing timber tall,
Began to build a vessel of huge bulk,
Measured by cubit, length, and breadth, and highth,   730
Smeared round with pitch, and in the side a door
Contrived, and of provisions laid in large
For man and beast: when lo a wonder strange!
Of every beast, and bird, and insect small
Came sevens and pairs, and entered in, as taught   735
Their order: last the sire and his three sons
With their four wives; and God made fast the door.
Meanwhile the southwind rose, and with black wings
Wide hovering, all the clouds together drove
From under heav'n; the hills to their supply   740
Vapor, and exhalation dusk and moist,
Sent up amain; and now the thickened sky
Like a dark ceiling stood; down rushed the rain
Impetuous, and continued till the earth
No more was seen; the floating vessel swum   745
Uplifted; and secure with beakèd prow
Rode tilting o'er the waves, all dwellings else
Flood overwhelmed, and them with all their pomp
Deep under water rolled; sea covered sea,
Sea without shore; and in their palaces   750
Where luxury late reigned, sea-monsters whelped
And stabled; of mankind, so numerous late,
All left, in one small bottom swum embarked.
How didst thou grieve then, Adam, to behold
The end of all thy offspring, end so sad,   755
Depopulation; thee another flood,

717. *passing fair.* Fowler notes a possible pun: "surpassing beauties" and "women passing by."
719. *a reverend sire:* Noah. Cf. Gen. 6–9, pp. 357–62. Christian interpretations appear in the NT; cf. 1 Pet. 3.19–21 [*NEB*]: "In the body [Christ] was put to death; in the spirit he was brought to life. And in the spirit he went and made his proclamation to the imprisoned spirits. They had refused obedience long ago, while God waited patiently in the days of Noah and the building of the ark, and in the ark a few persons, eight in all, were brought to safety through the water. This water prefigured the water of baptism through which you are now brought to safety." Cf. Heb. 11.7: "By faith Noah, being warned of God of things not seen as yet, moved with fear, prepared an ark to the saving of his house; by which he condemned the world, and became heir of the righteousness which is by faith."
723. *Triumphs:* pageants.
753. *swum:* floated.

Of tears and sorrow a flood thee also drowned,
And sunk thee as thy sons; till gently reared
By th' angel, on thy feet thou stood'st at last,
Though comfortless, as when a father mourns   760
His children, all in view destroyed at once;
And scarce to th' angel utter'dst thus thy plaint.
    "O visions ill foreseen! Better had I
Lived ignorant of future, so had borne
My part of evil only, each day's lot   765
Enough to bear; those now, that were dispensed
The burd'n of many ages, on me light
At once, by my foreknowledge gaining birth
Abortive, to torment me ere their being,
With thought that they must be. Let no man seek   770
Henceforth to be foretold what shall befall
Him or his children, evil he may be sure,
Which neither his foreknowing can prevent,
And he the future evil shall no less
In apprehension than in substance feel   775
Grievous to bear: but that care now is past,
Man is not whom to warn: those few escaped
Famine and anguish will at last consume
Wand'ring that wat'ry desert: I had hope
When violence was ceased, and war on earth,   780
All would have then gone well, peace would have crowned
With length of happy days the race of man;
But I was far deceived; for now I see
Peace to corrupt no less than war to waste.
How comes it thus? unfold, celestial guide,   785
And whether here the race of man will end."
    To whom thus Michael. "Those whom last thou saw'st
In triumph and luxurious wealth, are they
First seen in acts of prowess eminent
And great exploits, but of true virtue void;   790
Who having spilt much blood, and done much waste
Subduing nations, and achieved thereby
Fame in the world, high titles, and rich prey,
Shall change their course to pleasure, ease, and sloth,
Surfeit, and lust, till wantonness and pride   795
Raise out of friendship hostile deeds in peace.
The conquered also, and enslaved by war
Shall with their freedom lost all virtue lose
And fear of God, from whom their piety feigned
In sharp contést of battle found no aid   800
Against invaders; therefore cooled in zeal
Thenceforth shall practice how to live secure,

765–66. Cf. Matt. 6.34: "Take therefore no thought for the morrow: for the morrow shall take thought for the things of itself. Sufficient unto the day is the evil thereof."

Worldly or dissolute, on what their lords
Shall leave them to enjoy; for th' earth shall bear
More than enough, that temperance may be tried: 805
So all shall turn degenerate, all depraved,
Justice and temperance, truth and faith forgot;
One man except, the only son of light
In a dark age, against example good,
Against allurement, custom, and a world   810
Offended; fearless of reproach and scorn,
Or violence, he of their wicked ways
Shall them admonish, and before them set
The paths of righteousness, how much more safe,
And full of peace, denouncing wrath to come   815
On their impenitence; and shall return
Of them derided, but of God observed
The one just man alive; by his command
Shall build a wondrous ark, as thou beheld'st,
To save himself and household from amidst   820
A world devote to universal wrack.
No sooner he with them of man and beast
Select for life shall in the ark be lodged,
And sheltered round, but all the cataracts
Of heav'n set open on the earth shall pour   825
Rain day and night, all fountains of the deep
Broke up, shall heave the ocean to usurp
Beyond all bounds, till inundation rise
Above the highest hills: then shall this mount
Of Paradise by might of waves be moved   830
Out of his place, pushed by the hornèd flood,
With all his verdure spoiled, and trees adrift
Down the great river to the op'ning gulf,
And there take root an island salt and bare,
The haunt of seals and orcs, and sea-mews' clang.   835
To teach thee that God áttributes to place
No sanctity, if none be thither brought
By men who there frequent, or therein dwell.
And now what further shall ensue, behold."
    He looked, and saw the ark hull on the flood,   840
Which now abated, for the clouds were fled,
Driv'n by a keen north wind, that blowing dry
Wrinkled the face of deluge, as decayed;
And the clear sun on his wide wat'ry glass
Gazed hot, and of the fresh wave largely drew,   845
As after thirst, which made their flowing shrink
From standing lake to tripping ebb, that stole

810–11. *a world/Offended:* a displeased, unfriendly world.
815. *denouncing:* proclaiming.
821. *devote:* doomed.
833. I.e.: Down the Euphrates River

to the Persian Gulf.
835. *orcs:* whales, or sea monsters.
sea-mews: gulls. *clang:* shrill scream.
840. *hull:* drift.

With soft foot towards the deep, who now had stopped
His sluices, as the heav'n his windows shut.
The ark no more now floats, but seems on ground   850
Fast on the top of some high mountain fixed.
And now the tops of hills as rocks appear;
With clamor thence the rapid currents drive
Towards the retreating sea their furious tide.
Forthwith from out the ark a raven flies,   855
And after him, the surer messenger,
A dove sent forth once and again to spy
Green tree or ground whereon his foot may light;
The second time returning, in his bill
An olive leaf he brings, pacific sign: 860
Anon dry ground appears, and from his ark
The ancient sire descends with all his train;
Then with uplifted hands, and eyes devout,
Grateful to Heav'n, over his head beholds
A dewy cloud, and in the cloud a bow   865
Conspicuous with three listed colors gay,
Betok'ning peace from God, and cov'nant new.
Whereat the heart of Adam erst so sad
Greatly rejoiced, and thus his joy broke forth.
      "O thou who future things canst represent   870
As present, heav'nly instructor, I revive
At this last sight, assured that man shall live
With all the creatures, and their seed preserve.
Far less I now lament for one whole world
Of wicked sons destroyed, than I rejoice   875
For one man found so perfet and so just,
That God voutsafes to raise another world
From him, and all his anger to forget.
But say, what mean those colored streaks in heav'n,
Distended as the brow of God appeased,   880
Or serve they as a flow'ry verge to bind
The fluid skirts of that same wat'ry cloud,
Lest it again dissolve and show'r the earth?"
      To whom th' Archangel. "Dextrously thou aim'st;
So willingly doth God remit his ire,   885
Though late repenting him of man depraved,
Grieved at his heart, when looking down he saw
The whole earth filled with violence, and all flesh
Corrupting each their way; yet those removed,
Such grace shall one just man find in his sight,   890
That he relents, not to blot out mankind,
And makes a cov'nant never to destroy
The earth again by flood, nor let the sea
Surpass his bounds, nor rain to drown the world
With man therein or beast; but when he brings   895

866. *listed*: striped.

Over the earth a cloud, will therein set
His triple-colored bow, whereon to look
And call to mind his cov'nant: day and night,
Seed-time and harvest, heat and hoary frost
Shall hold their course, till fire purge all things new,   900
Both heav'n and earth, wherein the just shall dwell."

900. I.e., till the Millennium.

Book XII

The Argument

The angel Michael continues from the Flood to relate what shall succeed; then, in the mention of Abraham, comes by degrees to explain, who that Seed of the Woman shall be, which was promised Adam and Eve in the Fall; his incarnation, death, resurrection, and ascension; the state of the church till his second coming. Adam greatly satisfied and recomforted by these relations and promises descends the hill with Michael; wakens Eve, who all this while had slept, but with gentle dreams composed to quietness of mind and submission. Michael in either hand leads them out of Paradise, the fiery sword waving behind them, and the Cherubim taking their stations to guard the place.

> As one who in his journey bates at noon,
> Though bent on speed, so here the Archangel paused
> Betwixt the world destroyed and world restored,
> If Adam aught perhaps might interpose;
> Then with transition sweet new speech resumes.　　　　5
> 　　"Thus thou hast seen one world begin and end;
> And man as from a second stock proceed.
> Much thou hast yet to see, but I perceive
> Thy mortal sight to fail; objects divine
> Must needs impair and weary human sense:　　　　10
> Henceforth what is to come I will relate,
> Thou therefore give due audience, and attend.
> This second source of men, while yet but few,
> And while the dread of judgment past remains
> Fresh in their minds, fearing the Deity,　　　　15
> With some regard to what is just and right
> Shall lead their lives, and multiply apace,
> Laboring the soil, and reaping plenteous crop,
> Corn wine and oil; and from the herd or flock,
> Oft sacrificing bullock, lamb, or kid,　　　　20
> With large wine-offerings poured, and sacred feast,
> Shall spend their days in joy unblamed, and dwell
> Long time in peace by families and tribes
> Under paternal rule; till one shall rise
> Of proud ambitious heart, who not content　　　　25
> With fair equality, fraternal state,
> Will arrogate dominion undeserved

XII.1–5. Milton added these lines when Book X of the 1st edn. was divided to make Books XI and XII of the 2nd edn. *bates:* pauses for rest and refreshment. *transition:* (musical term) passing from one note or key to another.

7. *second stock:* i.e., from the old root and stump a new branch, which will become a *second* tree.

24. *one:* Nimrod. Cf. Gen. 10.8: "And Cush begat Nimrod: he began to be a mighty one in the earth. He was a mighty hunter before the Lord: wherefore it is said, Even as Nimrod the mighty hunter before the Lord. And the beginning of his kingdom was Babel . . .''

Over his brethren, and quite dispossess
Concord and law of nature from the earth;
Hunting (and men not beasts shall be his game)   30
With war and hostile snare such as refuse
Subjection to his empire tyrannous:
A mighty hunter thence he shall be styled
Before the Lord, as in despite of Heav'n,
Or from Heav'n claiming second sovranty;   35
And from rebellion shall derive his name,
Though of rebellion others he accuse.
He with a crew, whom like ambition joins
With him or under him to tyrannize,
Marching from Eden towards the west, shall find   40
The plain, wherein a black bituminous gurge
Boils out from under ground, the mouth of hell;
Of brick, and of that stuff they cast to build
A city and tow'r, whose top may reach to heav'n;
And get themselves a name, lest far dispersed   45
In foreign lands their memory be lost,
Regardless whether good or evil fame.
But God who oft descends to visit men
Unseen, and through their habitations walks
To mark their doings, them beholding soon,   50
Comes down to see their city, ere the tower
Obstruct heav'n tow'rs, and in derision sets
Upon their tongues a various spirit to raze
Quite out their native language, and instead
To sow a jangling noise of words unknown: 55
Forthwith a hideous gabble rises loud
Among the builders; each to other calls
Not understood, till hoarse, and all in rage,
As mocked they storm; great laughter was in heav'n
And looking down, to see the hubbub strange   60
And hear the din; thus was the building left
Ridiculous, and the work Confusion named."
    Whereto thus Adam fatherly displeased.
"O execrable son so to aspire
Above his brethren, to himself assuming   65
Authority usurped, from God not giv'n:
He gave us only over beast, fish, fowl
Dominion absolute; that right we hold
By his donation; but man over men

33–35. Milton's explanation of the Bib-
lical phrase *Before the Lord* is that Nim-
rod claimed either superiority to God or
power next only to God's.
    36. Bush notes that "the name *Nimrod*
was mistakenly linked with the Hebrew
verb meaning 'to rebel.'"
    38–62. Cf. Gen. 11.1–9, p. 362 and
III.466ff.
    41. *gurge:* whirlpool.

43. *cast:* plan.
    44. *A city:* Babylon.
    52. *in derision.* Cf. Ps. 2.4: "He that
sitteth in the heavens shall laugh: the
Lord shall have them in derision."
    53. *various:* divisive.
    62. *Confusion:* erroneously thought to
be the meaning of *Babel.*
    67–69. Cf. Gen. 9.2, p. 361.

He made not lord; such title to himself   70
Reserving, human left from human free.
But this usurper his encroachment proud
Stays not on man; to God his tower intends
Siege and defiance: wretched man! What food
Will he convey up thither to sustain   75
Himself and his rash army, where thin air
Above the clouds will pine his entrails gross,
And famish him of breath, if not of bread?"
        To whom thus Michael. "Justly thou abhorr'st
That son, who on the quiet state of men   80
Such trouble brought, affecting to subdue
Rational liberty; yet know withal,
Since thy original lapse, true liberty
Is lost, which always with right reason dwells
Twinned, and from her hath no dividual being: 85
Reason in man obscured, or not obeyed,
Immediately inordinate desires
And upstart passions catch the government
From reason, and to servitude reduce
Man till then free. Therefore since he permits   90
Within himself unworthy powers to reign
Over free reason, God in judgment just
Subjects him from without to violent lords;
Who oft as undeservedly enthrall
His outward freedom: tyranny must be,   95
Though to the tyrant thereby no excuse.
Yet sometimes nations will decline so low
From virtue, which is reason, that no wrong,
But justice, and some fatal curse annexed
Deprives them of their outward liberty,   100
Their inward lost: witness th' irreverent son
Of him who built the ark, who for the shame
Done to his father, heard this heavy curse,
'Servant of servants,' on his vicious race.
Thus will this latter, as the former world,   105
Still tend from bad to worse, till God at last
Wearied with their iniquities, withdraw
His presence from among them, and avert
His holy eyes; resolving from thenceforth
To leave them to their own polluted ways;   110
And one peculiar nation to select

77. *pine:* waste away.
82–101. *Rational liberty.* Milton begins a discussion of the relationship of right reason and Christian doctrine to civil and religious freedom—the idea of protestant Christian liberalism that is an important part of the poem's conclusion. Up to this point the words *free, freedom,* and *liberty,* in their political senses, have (with one exception) all occurred in speeches of Satan or in ironic references to him. Only here at the end does Milton use them unironically. Cf. X.307; XI.798; XII.82, 95, 100, 526. But see especially *CD*, paragraph 8 of its Preface p. 307, and I.xxvii.B; and "Reason," p. 392, and "Freedom," p. 397.
101–4. Cf. Gen. 9.21–25, p. 362.
111. *peculiar:* particular.

From all the rest, of whom to be invoked,
A nation from one faithful man to spring:
Him on this side Euphrates yet residing,
Bred up in idol-worship; O that men   115
(Canst thou believe?) should be so stupid grown,
While yet the patriarch lived, who scaped the Flood,
As to forsake the living God, and fall
To worship their own work in wood and stone
For gods! Yet him God the Most High voutsafes   120
To call by vision from his father's house,
His kindred and false gods, into a land
Which he will show him, and from him will raise
A mighty nation, and upon him show'r
His benediction so, that in his seed   125
All nations shall be blest; he straight obeys,
Not knowing to what land, yet firm believes:
I see him, but thou canst not, with what faith
He leaves his gods, his friends, and native soil
Ur of Chaldaea, passing now the ford   130
To Haran, after him a cumbrous train
Of herds and flocks, and numerous servitude;
Not wand'ring poor, but trusting all his wealth
With God, who called him, in a land unknown.
Canaan he now attains, I see his tents   135
Pitched about Sechem, and the neighboring plain
Of Moreh; there by promise he receives
Gift to his progeny of all that land;
From Hamath northward to the desert south
(Things by their names I call, though yet unnamed)   140
From Hermon east to the great western sea,
Mount Hermon, yonder sea, each place behold
In prospect, as I point them; on the shore
Mount Carmel; here the double-founted stream
Jordan, true limit eastward; but his sons   145
Shall dwell to Senir, that long ridge of hills.
This ponder, that all nations of the earth
Shall in his seed be blessed; by that seed
Is meant thy great Deliverer, who shall bruise
The Serpent's head; whereof to thee anon   150
Plainlier shall be revealed. This patriarch blest,
Whom 'faithful Abraham' due time shall call,

113. *one faithful man:* Abraham, meaning "Father of many nations." Cf. Gen. 11.31–32, p. 362, and 12.1–7, p. 363.
115. Cf. Joshua 24.2: "And Joshua said unto all the people, Thus saith the Lord God of Israel, Your fathers dwelt on the other side of the flood in old time, even Terah, the father of Abraham, and the father of Nachor: and they served other gods."
132. *servitude:* servants.
144. *Mount Carmel:* a mountain range near Haifa, on the Mediterranean shore of Israel. *double-founted:* having two sources, believed to be fountains called Jor and Dan.
152. *'faithful Abraham.'* Cf. Gen. 17.5: "Neither shall thy name any more be called Abram, but thy name shall be Abraham; for a father of many nations have I made thee." Gal. 3.9: "So then they which be of faith are blessed with faithful Abraham."

A son, and of his son a grandchild leaves,
Like him in faith, in wisdom, and renown;
The grandchild with twelve sons increased, departs   155
From Canaan, to a land hereafter called
Egypt, divided by the river Nile;
See where it flows, disgorging at seven mouths
Into the sea: to sojourn in that land
He comes invited by a younger son   160
In time of dearth, a son whose worthy deeds
Raise him to be the second in that realm
Of Pharaoh: there he dies, and leaves his race
Growing into a nation, and now grown
Suspected to a sequent king, who seeks   165
To stop their overgrowth, as inmate guests
Too numerous; whence of guests he makes them slaves
Inhospitably, and kills their infant males:
Till by two brethren (those two brethren call
Moses and Aaron) sent from God to claim   170
His people from enthralment, they return
With glory and spoil back to their promised land.
But first the lawless tyrant, who denies
To know their God, or message to regard,
Must be compelled by signs and judgments dire;   175
To blood unshed the rivers must be turned,
Frogs, lice and flies must all his palace fill
With loathed intrusion, and fill all the land;
His cattle must of rot and murrain die,
Botches and blains must all his flesh emboss,   180
And all his people; thunder mixed with hail,
Hail mixed with fire must rend th' Egyptian sky
And wheel on th' earth, devouring where it rolls;
What it devours not, herb, or fruit, or grain,
A darksome cloud of locusts swarming down   185
Must eat, and on the ground leave nothing green:
Darkness must overshadow all his bounds,
Palpable darkness, and blot out three days;
Last with one midnight stroke all the first-born
Of Egypt must lie dead. Thus with ten wounds   190
The river-dragon tamed at length submits
To let his sojourners depart, and oft
Humbles his stubborn heart, but still as ice
More hardened after thaw, till in his rage

153–64. The *son* was Isaac; the *grand-child*, Jacob, one of whose *twelve sons*, Joseph, *invited* (160) the Israelites to Egypt. The story is told in Gen. 21–50.

163–311. The story of Moses begins after the death of Joseph. The journey of the Israelites, led by Moses, from captivity to freedom in the *promised land* (172) begins in Exodus and ends in the last chapter of Deuteronomy with the death of Moses.

173–93. Cf. Exod. 7–13. *denies*: refuses.

180. *Botches*: boils. *blains*: blisters. *emboss*: cover with bosses or studs.

190–91. Cf. Ezek. 29.3: ". . . Pharaoh king of Egypt, the great dragon that lieth in the midst of his rivers . . ."

194–222. Cf. Exod. 13.17–22, p. 363; 14.5–31, pp. 364–65.

Pursuing whom he late dismissed, the sea   195
Swallows him with his host, but them lets pass
As on dry land between two crystal walls,
Awed by the rod of Moses so to stand
Divided, till his rescued gain their shore:
Such wondrous power God to his saint will lend,   200
Though present in his angel, who shall go
Before them in a cloud, and pillar of fire,
By day a cloud, by night a pillar of fire,
To guide them in their journey, and remove
Behind them, while th' obdúrate king pursues: 205
All night he will pursue, but his approach
Darkness defends between till morning watch;
Then through the fiery pillar and the cloud
God looking forth will trouble all his host
And craze their chariot wheels: when by command   210
Moses once more his potent rod extends
Over the sea; the sea his rod obeys;
On their embattled ranks the waves return,
And overwhelm their war: the race elect
Safe towards Canaan from the shore advance   215
Through the wild desert, not the readiest way,
Lest ent'ring on the Canaanite alarmed
War terrify them inexpert, and fear
Return them back to Egypt, choosing rather
Inglorious life with servitude; for life   220
To noble and ignoble is more sweet
Untrained in arms, where rashness leads not on.
This also shall they gain by their delay
In the wide wilderness, there they shall found
Their government, and their great senate choose   225
Through the twelve tribes, to rule by laws ordained:
God from the mount of Sinai, whose gray top
Shall tremble, he descending, will himself
In thunder lightning and loud trumpet's sound
Ordain them laws; part such as appertain   230
To civil justice, part religious rites
Of sacrifice, informing them, by types
And shadows, of that destined Seed to bruise
The Serpent, by what means he shall achieve
Mankind's deliverance. But the voice of God   235
To mortal ear is dreadful; they beseech

207. *defends:* holds off.
210. *craze:* crush, smash.
214. *war:* army.
217. *alarmed:* prepared to fight (modifies *Canaanite*).
223–69. Cf. Exod. 19.16–25, p. 366; 20.18–20, p. 367; 24.1–9, p. 367; 40.34–38, p. 368.
225. *senate:* the Seventy Elders. Cf. Num. 11.16–25.

232–33. *types:* (in theology) persons, objects, or events of OT history, prefiguring some persons or things revealed in the new dispensation. *shadows:* types, foreshadowings. In *CD* Milton refers to Moses as a type of Christ, Noah's ark as a type of baptism before the law, manna as a type of the Lord's Supper, the destruction of Jerusalem as a type of Christ's Second Coming. See *CD*, I.xxx.

That Moses might report to them his will,
And terror cease; he grants what they besought
Instructed that to God is no access
Without mediator, whose high office now   240
Moses in figure bears, to introduce
One greater, of whose day he shall foretell,
And all the Prophets in their age the times
Of great Messiah shall sing. Thus laws and rites
Established, such delight hath God in men   245
Obedient to his will, that he voutsafes
Among them to set up his tabernacle,
The Holy One with mortal men to dwell:
By his prescript a sanctuary is framed
Of cedar, overlaid with gold, therein   250
An ark, and in the ark his testimony,
The records of his cov'nant, over these
A mercy-seat of gold between the wings
Of two bright Cherubim, before him burn
Seven lamps as in a zodiac representing   255
The heav'nly fires; over the tent a cloud
Shall rest by day, a fiery gleam by night,
Save when they journey, and at length they come,
Conducted by his angel to the land
Promised to Abraham and his seed: the rest   260
Were long to tell, how many battles fought,
How many kings destroyed, and kingdoms won,
Or how the sun shall in mid-heav'n stand still
A day entire, and night's due course adjourn,
Man's voice commanding, 'Sun in Gibeon stand,   265
And thou moon in the vale of Aialon,
Till Israel overcome'; so call the third

240. *mediator:* Moses as mediator is a type of Christ. See 232–33n.

241. *in figure:* as a type. See 232–33n.

241–42. Cf. Deut. 18.15–19: "The Lord thy God will raise up unto thee a Prophet from the midst of thee, of thy brethren, like unto me; unto him ye shall hearken; According to all that thou desiredst of the Lord thy God in Horeb in the day of the assembly, saying, Let me not hear again the voice of the Lord my God, neither let me see this great fire any more, that I die not. And the Lord said unto me, They have well spoken that which they have spoken. I will raise them up a Prophet from among their brethren, like unto thee, and will put my words in his mouth; and he shall speak unto them all that I shall command him."

260. Cf. Gen. 22.17–18: "That in blessing, I will bless thee, and in multiplying I will multiply thy seed as the stars of the heaven, and as the sand which is upon the sea shore; and thy seed shall possess the gate of his enemies; And in thy seed shall all the nations of the earth be blessed; because thou hast obeyed my voice." Gen. 26.3: "Sojourn in this land, and I will be with thee, and will bless thee; for unto thee, and unto thy seed, I will give all these countries, and I will perform the oath which I sware unto Abraham thy father."

263–67. Cf. Joshua 10.12–13: "Then spake Joshua to the Lord in the day when the Lord delivered up the Amorites before the children of Israel, and he said in the sight of Israel, Sun, stand thou still upon Gibeon; and thou, Moon, in the valley of Ajalon. And the sun stood still, and the moon stayed, until the people had avenged themselves upon their enemies. Is not this written in the book of Jasher? So the sun stood still in the midst of heaven, and hasted not to go down about a whole day."

267. Cf. Gen. 32.28: "And he said, Thy name shall be called no more Jacob, but Israel: for as a prince hast thou power with God and with men, and hast prevailed."

From Abraham, son of Isaac, and from him
His whole descent, who thus shall Canaan win."
    Here Adam interposed. "O sent from heav'n,   270
Enlight'ner of my darkness, gracious things
Thou hast revealed, those chiefly which concern
Just Abraham and his seed: now first I find
Mine eyes true op'ning, and my heart much eased,
Erewhile perplexed with thoughts what would become   275
Of me and all mankind; but now I see
His day, in whom all nations shall be blest,
Favor unmerited by me, who sought
Forbidden knowledge by forbidden means.
This yet I apprehend not, why to those   280
Among whom God will deign to dwell on earth
So many and so various laws are giv'n;
So many laws argue so many sins
Among them; how can God with such reside?"
    To whom thus Michael. "Doubt not but that sin   285
Will reign among them, as of thee begot;
And therefore was law given them to evince
Their natural pravity, by stirring up
Sin against law to fight; that when they see
Law can discover sin, but not remove,   290
Save by those shadowy expiations weak,
The blood of bulls and goats, they may conclude
Some blood more precious must be paid for man,
Just for unjust, that in such righteousness
To them by faith imputed, they may find   295
Justification towards God, and peace
Of conscience, which the law by ceremonies
Cannot appease, nor man the moral part
Perform, and not performing cannot live.
So law appears imperfect, and but giv'n   300
With purpose to resign them in full time
Up to a better cov'nant, disciplined
From shadowy types to truth, from flesh to spirit,

---

277. *His day:* the age of Abraham. Adam mistakenly thinks God's covenant with Abraham constitutes a promise of paradise regained. It was to be only a type of Christ's *day*. Cf. John 8.56: "Your father Abraham rejoiced to see my day."

285–306. *law:* the Mosaic Law, referred to in 226, 230, and 244, i.e., the will of God revealed in Exodus, Leviticus, Numbers, and Deuteronomy, and designed to govern the behavior of man in all aspects of his life, private, civil, and religious. For the Christian view of this law see Rom. 3.19–28 and *CD*, I.xxvii.A. *pravity:* (L *pravus* crooked, bad) moral perversion. *shadowy expiations:* sacrifices that were types of Christ's sacrifice. Cf. Heb. 10.1: "For the law having a shadow of good things to come and not the very image of the things, can never with those sacrifices which they offered year by year continually make the comers thereunto perfect." *shadowy types.* See 232–33n. *works of law.* Cf. Gal. 2.16: "Knowing that man is not justified by the works of the law, but by the faith of Jesus Christ, even we have believed in Jesus Christ, that we might be justified by the faith of Christ, and not by the works of the law: for by the works of the law shall no flesh be justified." *faith:* faith in Christ by which the sinner is justified in the sight of God. Cf. *CD*, I.xx, and other uses of the word in this special sense: 409, 427, 488.

From imposition of strict laws, to free
Acceptance of large grace, from servile fear 305
To filial, works of law to works of faith.
And therefore shall not Moses, though of God
Highly beloved, being but the minister
Of law, his people into Canaan lead;
But Joshua whom the Gentiles Jesus call, 310
His name and office bearing, who shall quell
The adversary Serpent, and bring back
Through the world's wilderness long-wandered man
Safe to eternal paradise of rest.
Meanwhile they in their earthly Canaan placed 315
Long time shall dwell and prosper, but when sins
National interrupt their public peace,
Provoking God to raise them enemies:
From whom as oft he saves them penitent
By judges first, then under kings; of whom 320
The second, both for piety renowned
And puissant deeds, a promise shall receive
Irrevocable, that his regal throne
Forever shall endure; the like shall sing
All prophecy, that of the royal stock 325
Of David (so I name this king) shall rise
A Son, the Woman's Seed to thee foretold,
Foretold to Abraham, as in whom shall trust
All nations, and to kings foretold, of kings
The last, for of his reign shall be no end. 330
But first a long succession must ensue,
And his next son for wealth and wisdom famed,
The clouded Ark of God till then in tents
Wand'ring, shall in a glorious temple enshrine.

307–14. Cf. Deut. 34.1–6: "And Moses went up from the plains of Moab unto the mountain of Nebo, to the top of Pisgah, that is over against Jericho. And the Lord shewed him all the land of Gilead, unto Dan . . . and all the land of Judah, unto the utmost sea . . . And the Lord said unto him, This is the land which I sware unto Abraham, unto Isaac, and unto Jacob, saying, I will give it unto thy seed: I have caused thee to see it with thine eyes, but thou shalt not go over thither. So Moses the servant of the Lord died there in the land of Moab, according to the word of the Lord. And he buried him in a valley in the land of Moab, over against Beth-peor: but no man knoweth of his sepulchre unto this day." Cf. *CD*, I.xxvi. *therefore:* i.e., because Moses represents the Old Law, not the New, of which Joshua is the representative. *Joshua.* The Hebrew word *Yĕshūa*, meaning "savior," became *Iesous* in Greek, the language of the NT. As Moses's successor, Joshua led the Israelites over Jordan into the Promised Land.

His story is told in the book of Joshua. *who:* Christ.

315–30. This history is told in Judges, Samuel, and Kings. *The second:* David, with whom God made a covenant (*promise*) through the prophet Nathan, in 2 Sam. 7.16: "Thine house and thy kingdom shall be established for ever before thee: thy throne shall be established for ever." *All prophecy:* the books of the Prophets in the OT, esp. Isaiah, esp. 9.6–7, p. 374. Cf. Dan. 7.13–14: "I saw in the night visions, and, behold, one like the Son of man came with the clouds of heaven, and came to the Ancient of days, and they brought him near before him. And there was given him dominion, and glory, and a kingdom, that all people, nations, and languages, should serve him: his dominion is an everlasting dominion, which shall not pass away, and his kingdom that which shall not be destroyed."

332. *son:* Solomon, son of David.

334. *temple.* See 1 Kings 6 and 2 Chron. 3–4.

Such follow him, as shall be registered   335
Part good, part bad, of bad the longer scroll,
Whose foul idolatries and other faults
Heaped to the popular sum, will so incense
God, as to leave them, and expose their land,
Their city, his temple, and his holy ark   340
With all his sacred things, a scorn and prey
To that proud city, whose high walls thou saw'st
Left in confusion, Babylon thence called.
There in captivity he lets them dwell
The space of seventy years, then brings them back,   345
Rememb'ring mercy, and his cov'nant sworn
To David, stablished as the days of Heav'n.
Returned from Babylon by leave of kings
Their lords, whom God disposed, the house of God
They first re-edify, and for a while   350
In mean estate live moderate, till grown
In wealth and multitude, factious they grow;
But first among the priests dissension springs,
Men who attend the altar, and should most
Endeavor peace: their strife pollution brings   355
Upon the temple itself: at last they seize
The scepter, and regard not David's sons,
Then lose it to a stranger, that the true
Anointed King Messiah might be born
Barred of his right; yet at his birth a star   360
Unseen before in heav'n proclaims him come,
And guides the eastern sages, who inquire
His place, to offer incense, myrrh, and gold;
His place of birth a solemn angel tells
To simple shepherds, keeping watch by night;   365
They gladly thither haste, and by a choir
Of squadroned angels hear his carol sung.
A virgin is his mother, but his sire
The Power of the Most High; he shall ascend
The throne hereditary, and bound his reign   370
With earth's wide bounds, his glory with the heav'ns."
　　He ceased, discerning Adam with such joy
Surcharged, as had like grief been dewed in tears,
Without the vent of words, which these he breathed.

335–47. The Babylonian Captivity (sixth century B.C.) is described in 2 Kings 25, 2 Chron. 36, and Jer. 39 and 52.
338. I.e.: Added to the human faults of common people.
348. *kings:* Cyrus the Great, Darius, and Artaxerxes, the Persians under whom Jerusalem was rebuilt, as described in Ezra.
349. *disposed:* made well-disposed.
353–58. As told in the Apocryphal book of 2 Macabees. *sons:* descendants, *a*

stranger: Antipater, whom Julius Caesar appointed Procurator of Judea, and whose son Herod the Great ruled at the time of the birth of Christ.
360–71. Cf. Matt. 2 and Luke 2.
364. *solemn:* awe-inspiring.
369. *Power:* the Holy Ghost. Cf. *CD*, I.xiv.
370–71. Cf. Ps. 2.8: "Ask of me, and I shall give thee the heathen for thine inheritance, and the uttermost parts of the earth for thy possession." Cf. *CD*, I.xxxiii.C.

"O prophet of glad tidings, finisher   375
Of utmost hope! now clear I understand
What oft my steadiest thoughts have searched in vain,
Why our great expectation should be called
The Seed of Woman: Virgin Mother, hail,
High in the love of Heav'n, yet from my loins   380
Thou shalt proceed, and from thy womb the Son
Of God Most High; so God with man unites.
Needs must the Serpent now his capital bruise
Expect with mortal pain: say where and when
Their fight, what stroke shall bruise the Victor's heel."   385
To whom thus Michael. "Dream not of their fight,
As of a duel, or the local wounds
Of head or heel: not therefore joins the Son
Manhood to Godhead, with more strength to foil
Thy enemy; nor so is overcome   390
Satan, whose fall from heavn'n, a deadlier bruise,
Disabled not to give thee thy death's wound:
Which he who comes thy Saviour, shall recure,
Not by destroying Satan, but his works
In thee and in thy seed: nor can this be,   395
But by fulfilling that which thou didst want,
Obedience to the law of God, imposed
On penalty of death, and suffering death,
The penalty to thy transgression due,
And due to theirs which out of thine will grow: 400
So only can high justice rest apaid.
The law of God exact he shall fulfill
Both by obedience and by love, though love
Alone fulfill the law; thy punishment
He shall endure by coming in the flesh   405
To a reproachful life and cursèd death,
Proclaiming life to all who shall believe
In his redemption, and that his obedience
Imputed becomes theirs by faith, his merits
To save them, not their own, though legal works.   410
For this he shall live hated, be blasphemed,
Seized on by force, judged, and to death condemned
A shameful and accursed, nailed to the Cross
By his own nation, slain for bringing life;
But to the Cross he nails thy enemies,   415
The law that is against thee, and the sins

375. *finisher:* completer.
379–80. Cf. Luke 1.31–35, p. 381.
383. *capital:* (L *caput* head) involving loss of the head or life. *bruise:* crushing blow.
393. *recure:* heal.
396. *want:* lack.
401. *apaid:* satisfied.
403–4. Cf. Rom. 13.10: "Love worketh no ill to his neighbor: therefore love is

the fulfilling of the law."
409–10. I.e.: And that his merits save them, not their own obedience to the Old Law.
409. *Imputed:* See III.291n.
415–17. Cf. Col. 2.14: "Blotting out the handwriting of ordinances that was against us, which was contrary to us, and took it out of the way, nailing it to his cross."

Of all mankind, with him there crucified,
Never to hurt them more who rightly trust
In this his satisfaction; so he dies,
But soon revives, Death over him no power   420
Shall long usurp; ere the third dawning light
Return, the stars of morn shall see him rise
Out of his grave, fresh as the dawning light,
Thy ransom paid, which man from Death redeems,
His death for man, as many as offered life   425
Neglect not, and the benefit embrace
By faith not void of works: this God-like act
Annuls thy doom, the death thou shouldst have died,
In sin for ever lost from life; this act
Shall bruise the head of Satan, crush his strength   430
Defeating Sin and Death, his two main arms,
And fix far deeper in his head their stings
Than temporal death shall bruise the Victor's heel,
Or theirs whom he redeems, a death like sleep,
A gentle wafting to immortal life.   435
Nor after resurrection shall he stay
Longer on earth than certain times to appear
To his disciples, men who in his life
Still followed him; to them shall leave in charge
To teach all nations what of him they learned   440
And his salvation, them who shall believe
Baptizing in the profluent stream, the sign
Of washing them from guilt of sin to life
Pure, and in mind prepared, if so befall,
For death, like that which the Redeemer died.   445
All nations they shall teach; for from that day
Not only to the sons of Abraham's loins
Salvation shall be preached, but to the sons
Of Abraham's faith wherever through the world;
So in his seed all nations shall be blest.   450
Then to the heav'n of heav'ns he shall ascend
With victory, triumphing through the air
Over his foes and thine; there shall surprise
The Serpent, prince of air, and drag in chains
Through all his realm, and there confounded leave;   455
Then enter into glory, and resume
His seat at God's right hand, exalted high
Above all names in heav'n; and thence shall come,
When this world's dissolution shall be ripe,

---

419. *satisfaction:* payment of a penalty. See "The Fourtunate Fall," pp. 398–99.
425–26. I.e.: For as many as accept his offer of life. *Neglect:* (from L *nec* not + *legere* to pick up) slight, disregard.
427. *faith . . . works.* Cf. *CD*, I.xxii.B.
442. *profluent:* flowing.

445–50. Cf. Rom. 4.16; Gal. 3.7–9, 16; Eph. 4.11–12.
454–65. Cf. Rev. 20, pp. 386–87.
458–65. For Milton's orthodox belief in the Second Coming, the Millennium and Last Judgment, see *CD*, I.xxxiii. A,B,C. *quick:* living. The phrase comes from the Apostles' Creed.

With glory and power to judge both quick and dead,   460
To judge th' unfaithful dead, but to reward
His faithful, and receive them into bliss,
Whether in heav'n or earth, for then the earth
Shall all be Paradise, far happier place
Than this of Eden, and far happier days."   465
    So spake th' Archangel Michaël, then paused,
As at the world's great period; and our sire
Replete with joy and wonder thus replied.
    "O goodness infinite, goodness immense!
That all this good of evil shall produce,   470
And evil turn to good; more wonderful
Than that which by creation first brought forth
Light out of darkness! Full of doubt I stand,
Whether I should repent me now of sin
By me done and occasioned, or rejoice   475
Much more, that much more good thereof shall spring,
To God more glory, more good will to men
From God, and over wrath grace shall abound.
But say, if our Deliverer up to heav'n
Must reascend, what will betide the few   480
His faithful, left among th' unfaithful herd,
The enemies of truth; who then shall guide
His people, who defend? Will they not deal
Worse with his followers than with him they dealt?"
    "Be sure they will," said th' angel; "but from heav'n   485
He to his own a Comforter will send,
The promise of the Father, who shall dwell
His Spirit within them, and the law of faith
Working through love, upon their hearts shall write,
To guide them in all truth, and also arm   490
With spiritual armor, able to resist
Satan's assaults, and quench his fiery darts,
What man can do against them, not afraid,
Though to the death, against such cruelties

---

467. *great period:* at the end of the thousand years of the Millennium—end of the world.

469–78. See "The Fortunate Fall," pp. 398–99.

478. Cf. Rom. 5.20: "Moreover the law entered, that the offence might abound. But where sin abounded, grace did much more abound."

485–551. Milton's brief history of the Christian church, from the time of the Apostles to the Second Coming, contains many echoes from the NT, particularly from the letters of St. Paul to members of the earliest "churches," and reflects Milton's protestantism.

486. Cf. John 15.26: [Christ says] "But when the Comforter is come, whom I will send unto you from the Father, even the spirit of truth, which proceedeth from the Father, he shall testify of me."

489. Cf. Gal. 5.6: "For in Jesus Christ neither circumcision availeth any thing, nor uncircumcision; but faith which worketh by love." Heb. 8.10: "For this is the covenant that I will make with the house of Israel after those days, saith the Lord; I will put my laws into their mind, and write them in their hearts."

491–92. Cf. Eph. 6.11–16: "Put on the whole armour of God, that ye may be able to stand against the wiles of the devil. . . . Above all, taking the shield of faith, wherewith ye shall be able to quench all the fiery darts of the wicked."

493. Cf. Ps. 56.11: "In God have I put my trust: I will not be afraid what man can do unto me."

With inward consolations recompensed,   495
And oft supported so as shall amaze
Their proudest persecutors: for the Spirit
Poured first on his apostles, whom he sends
To evangelize the nations, then on all
Baptized, shall them with wondrous gifts endue   500
To speak all tongues, and do all miracles,
As did their Lord before them. Thus they win
Great numbers of each nation to receive
With joy the tidings brought from heav'n: at length
Their ministry performed, and race well run,   505
Their doctrine and their story written left,
They die; but in their room, as they forewarn,
Wolves shall succeed for teachers, grievous wolves,
Who all the sacred mysteries of heav'n
To their own vile advantages shall turn   510
Of lucre and ambition, and the truth
With superstitions and traditions taint,
Left only in those written records pure,
Though not but by the Spirit understood.
Then shall they seek to avail themselves of names,   515
Places and titles, and with these to join
Secular power, though feigning still to act
By spiritual, to themselves appropriating
The Spirit of God, promised alike and giv'n
To all believers; and from that pretense,   520
Spiritual laws by carnal power shall force
On every conscience; laws which none shall find
Left them enrolled, or what the Spirit within
Shall on the heart engrave. What will they then
But force the Spirit of Grace itself, and bind   525
His consort Liberty; what, but unbuild
His living temples, built by faith to stand,
Their own faith not another's: for on earth
Who against faith and conscience can be heard
Infallible? Yet many will presume: 530

497–502. Cf. Acts 2.4, 43: "And they [the apostles] were all filled with the Holy Ghost, and began to speak with other tongues [languages]. . . . and many wonders and signs were done by the apostles."

505. Cf. Heb. 12.1: "Wherefore seeing we also are compassed about with so great a cloud of witnesses, let us lay aside every weight, and the sin which doth so easily beset us, and let us run with patience the race that is set before us." 1 Cor. 9.24: "Know ye not that they which run in a race run all, but one receiveth the prize? So run, that ye may obtain."

508. *Wolves:* a common metaphor among Puritans for the corrupt clergy of the established church. Cf. Acts 20.29: "For I know this, that after my departing shall grievous wolves enter in among you, not sparing the flock."

515. *names:* honors.

516. *Places:* ranks, offices.

521. *carnal:* secular.

522–24. I.e.: Written in the Bible or, by the Holy Spirit, in the hearts of men.

525–26. Cf. 2 Cor. 3.17: "Now the Lord is that Spirit: and where the Spirit of the Lord is, there is liberty."

526–28. Cf. I.17–18, and 1 Cor. 3.17: "If any man defile the temple of God, him shall God destroy; for the temple of God is holy, which temple ye are."

Whence heavy persecution shall arise
On all who in the worship persevere
Of Spirit and Truth; the rest, far greater part,
Will deem in outward rites and specious forms
Religion satisfied; Truth shall retire   535
Bestuck with sland'rous darts, and works of faith
Rarely be found: so shall the world go on,
To good malignant, to bad men benign,
Under her own weight groaning, till the day
Appear of respiration to the just,   540
And vengeance to the wicked, at return
Of him so lately promised to thy aid,
The Woman's Seed, obscurely then foretold,
Now amplier known thy Saviour and thy Lord,
Last in the clouds from heav'n to be revealed   545
In glory of the Father, to dissolve
Satan with his perverted world, then raise
From the conflagrant mass, purged and refined,
New heav'ns, new earth, ages of endless date
Founded in righteousness and peace and love,   550
To bring forth fruits joy and eternal bliss."
    He ended; and thus Adam last replied.
"How soon hath thy prediction, seer blest,
Measured this transient world, the race of time,
Till time stand fixed: beyond is all abyss,   555
Eternity, whose end no eye can reach.
Greatly instructed I shall hence depart,
Greatly in peace of thought, and have my fill
Of knowledge, what this vessel can contain;
Beyond which was my folly to aspire.   560
Henceforth I learn, that to obey is best,
And love with fear the only God, to walk
As in his presence, ever to observe
His providence, and on him sole depend,
Merciful over all his works, with good   565

533. Cf. John 4.23–24: "But the hour cometh, and now is, when the true worshippers shall worship the Father in spirit and in truth."
539. Cf. Rom. 8.22: "For we know that the whole creation groaneth and travaileth in pain together until now."
540. *respiration:* rest, respite.
545–47. Cf. Matt. 24.30: "And then shall appear the sign of the Son of man in heaven: and then shall all the tribes of the earth mourn, and they shall see the Son of man coming in the clouds of heaven with power and great glory." 2 Thess. 1.7–8: "And to you who are troubled rest with us, when the Lord Jesus shall be revealed from heaven with his mighty angels, In flaming fire taking vengeance on them that know not God, and that obey not the gospel of our Lord Jesus Christ."
546. *dissolve:* cause to disappear from existence, consume.
549–51. Cf. Rev. 21, pp. 387–88.
555. Cf. Rev. 10.5–6: "And the angel which I saw stand upon the sea . . . sware . . . that there should be time no longer."
565–68. Cf. Ps. 145.9: "The Lord is good to all: and his tender mercies are over all his works." Rom. 12.21: "Be not overcome of evil, but overcome evil with good." 1 Cor. 1.27: "But God hath chosen the foolish things of the world to confound the wise; and God hath chosen the weak things of the world to confound the things which are mighty." Rev. 2.10: "Fear none of those things which thou

Still overcoming evil, and by small
Accomplishing great things, by things deemed weak
Subverting worldly strong, and worldly wise
By simply meek; that suffering for truth's sake
Is fortitude to highest victory,   570
And to the faithful death the gate of life;
Taught this by his example whom I now
Acknowledge my Redeemer ever blest."
   To whom thus also th' angel last replied:
"This having learnt, thou hast attained the sum   575
Of wisdom; hope no higher, though all the stars
Thou knew'st by name, and all th' ethereal powers,
All secrets of the deep, all nature's works,
Or works of God in heav'n, air, earth, or sea,
And all the riches of this world enjoy'dst,   580
And all the rule, one empire; only add
Deeds to thy knowledge answerable, add faith,
Add virtue, patience, temperance, add love,
By name to come called charity, the soul
Of all the rest: then wilt thou not be loath   585
To leave this Paradise, but shalt possess
A paradise within thee, happier far.
Let us descend now therefore from this top
Of speculation; for the hour precise
Exacts our parting hence; and see the guards,   590
By me encamped on yonder hill, expect
Their motion, at whose front a flaming sword,
In signal of remove, waves fiercely round;
We may no longer stay: go, waken Eve;
Her also I with gentle dreams have calmed   595
Portending good, and all her spirits composed
To meek submission: thou at season fit
Let her with thee partake what thou hast heard,
Chiefly what may concern her faith to know,
The great deliverance by her seed to come   600
(For by the Woman's Seed) on all mankind.
That ye may live, which will be many days,
Both in one faith unanimous though sad,
With cause for evils past, yet much more cheered
With meditation on the happy end."   605
   He ended, and they both descend the hill;
Descended, Adam to the bow'r where Eve

---

shalt suffer: behold, the devil shall cast some of you into prison, that ye may be tried; and ye shall have tribulation ten days: be thou faithful unto death, and I will give thee a crown of life."
  581–84. Cf. 2 Pet. 1.5–7: "And besides this, giving all diligence, add to your faith virtue; and to virtue knowledge;

And to knowledge temperance; and to temperance patience; and to patience godliness; And to godliness brotherly kindness; and to brotherly kindness charity."
  591–92. *expect/Their motion:* (military) await their marching orders.
  593. *remove.* (military) departure.

Lay sleeping ran before, but found her waked;
And thus with words not sad she him received.
    "Whence thou return'st, and whither went'st, I know;   610
For God is also in sleep, and dreams advise,
Which he hath sent propitious, some great good
Presaging, since with sorrow and heart's distress
Wearied I fell asleep: but now lead on;
In me is no delay; with thee to go,   615
Is to stay here; without thee here to stay,
Is to go hence unwilling; thou to me
Art all things under heav'n, all places thou,
Who for my wilful crime art banished hence.
This further consolation yet secure   620
I carry hence; though all by me is lost,
Such favor I unworthy am voutsafed,
By me the Promised Seed shall all restore."
    So spake our mother Eve, and Adam heard
Well pleased, but answered not; for now too nigh   625
Th' Archangel stood, and from the other hill
To their fixed station, all in bright array
The Cherubim descended; on the ground
Gliding metéorous, as evening mist
Ris'n from a river o'er the marish glides,   630
And gathers ground fast at the laborer's heel
Homeward returning. High in front advanced,
The brandished sword of God before them blazed
Fierce as a comet; which with torrid heat,
And vapor as the Libyan air adust,   635
Began to parch that temperate clime; whereat
In either hand the hast'ning angel caught
Our ling'ring parents, and to th' eastern gate
Led them direct, and down the cliff as fast
To the subjected plain; then disappeared.   640
They looking back, all th' eastern side beheld
Of Paradise, so late their happy seat,
Waved over by that flaming brand, the gate

615–19. Cf. Ruth 1.16: "And Ruth said, Intreat me not to leave thee, or to return from following after thee: for whither thou goest, I will go; and where thou lodgest, I will lodge: thy people shall be my people, and thy God my God." And cf. Eve's song of love to Adam before the Fall, IV.641ff.

629. *meteorous:* transiently or irregularly luminescent like a meteor—or like an ignis fatuus.

630. *marish:* marsh.

631–32. Cf. Gen. 3.19: "In the sweat of thy face shalt thou eat bread, till thou return unto the ground; for out of it wast thou taken: for dust thou art, and unto dust shalt thou return." Gen. 3.23: "Therefore the Lord God sent him forth from the garden of Eden, to till the ground from whence he was taken."

633. Cf. Gen. 3.24: "So he drove out the man; and he placed at the east of the garden of Eden Cherubims, and a flaming sword which turned every way, to keep the way of the tree of life."

635. *vapor:* smoke. *adust:* parched.

637–38. Cf. Gen. 19.15–16: "And when the morning arose, then the angels hastened Lot, saying, Arise, take thy wife, and thy two daughters, which are here; lest thou be consumed in the iniquity of the city. And while he lingered, the men laid hold upon his hand, and upon the hand of his wife, and upon the hand of his two daughters; the Lord being merciful unto him; and they brought him forth, and set him without the city."

640. *subjected:* lying below.

With dreadful faces thronged and fiery arms:
Some natural tears they dropped, but wiped them soon;   645
The world was all before them, where to choose
Their place of rest, and Providence their guide:
They hand in hand with wand'ring steps and slow,
Through Eden took their solitary way.

648. *hand in hand.* Cf. IV.321, 488–89, 689, 739; VIII. 510–11; IX.385, 1037.

A Note on the Text

The three authoritative texts of *Paradise Lost* are the manuscript of Book I, in the Morgan Library, in New York; the first edition, published in ten books, in 1667; and the second edition, in twelve books, in 1674. Though blind and dependent on the eyes of several copyists, Milton was remarkably successful in supervising the work of his printers, and as a result the text of the poem presents relatively few problems. Spelling and punctuation were not then as standardized as they are now. Manuscripts in Milton's own hand show that he was not consistent in his spelling; and authors in his time were generally in these matters at the mercy of the whims of copyists and printers. But Milton was fairly successful in seeing to it that in *Paradise Lost* his words and sentences were spelled and punctuated as he wished. In spelling he seems to have preferred forms that most clearly indicated his pronunciation of the word: he preferred *hunderd* to *hundred*. In punctuation, his aim was not to supply visual aids to his syntax, but to indicate the length of pauses between words or groups of words. A colon marked a pause shorter than that of a period and longer than that of a semicolon. Milton put commas where we would omit them, and omitted them where modern usage requires them. Readers should pause slightly where he puts them, and pause more briefly where the syntax, or modern usage, would seem to call for a comma. The capitalization and italicizing in the original texts reflect the tendency of the time to capitalize many nouns and some adjectives, and to set proper nouns in italic type.

In the second edition, on which my text is based, the opening lines look something like this:

> Of Mans First Disobedience, and the Fruit
> Of that Forbidden Tree, whose mortal tast
> Brought Death into the World, and all our woe,
> With loss of *Eden*, till one greater Man
> Restore us, and regain the blissful Seat,
> Sing Heav'nly Muse, that on the secret top
> Of *Oreb*, or of *Sinai*, didst inspire
> That Shepherd, who first taught the chosen Seed,
> In the Beginning how the Heav'ns and Earth
> Rose out of *Chaos:* Or if *Sion* Hill
> Delight thee more, and *Siloa*'s Brook that flow'd
> Fast by the Oracle of God; I thence
> Invoke thy aid to my adventrous Song,
> . . . .

In order to present a text as free as possible from meaningless distractions, I have normalized the spelling and capitalization and changed all italics to Roman. I have retained the apostrophe only where necessary, as in *heav'nly*; since one normally pronounces *evening*, *opening*, and *blustering* as dissyllabics, I have not retained the marked elisions Milton gave them. I have used apostrophes to mark elisions that Milton indicated simply by dropping the vowel, as in *adventrous*. I have spelled Milton's *rowl'd rolled*, because one pronounces both forms alike. I have retained some of Milton's peculiar spellings, such as *perfet*, *highth*, *maistry*, *voutsafe*, *lantskip*, *Ksar*, and *hunderd*. In normalizing the use of capitals, I have had to be somewhat arbitrary. Wherever Milton seems clearly to have intended a personification I have capitalized the word: *chaos, night,* and *nature,* for example, are therefore sometimes capitalized, sometimes not. I have distinguished the word *Spirit* when used to refer to an angel. In synonyms and epithets for God and Satan I have retained the capitals except where the speaker might not have been so proper. I have used quotation marks to set off all direct address.

With a few exceptions, noted below, I have followed the lead of several recent editors in retaining the punctuation of the original editions. The initial difficulties presented by Milton's punctuation disappear after a little practice in reading; and the advantages of being guided by Milton's notations are considerable. *Paradise Lost must* be read aloud, or at least clearly heard in the mind, and in general the punctuation helps one discover the complicated rhythms that distinguish the sound of the poem and emphasize its meanings. Though some of the marks must be assumed to be errors of the copyist or printer, my principle has been to change a mark only when the original pointing seemed both to be clearly erroneous and to make the meaning of the line unnecessarily obscure.

In the following list of emendations, the second of the two versions is that of the 1674 edition:

I.716	grav'n;] grav'n,	VI.847	eyes;] eyes,
II.282	where] were	VII.17	unreined] unrein'd,
II.444	escape?] escape.	VII.21	unsung,] unsung
II.688	replied:] reply'd,	VII.321	swelling] smelling
II.798	list,] list	VII.418	th' egg] the Egg
II.980	profound;] profound,	VII.451	soul] Foul
III.276	dear] dear,	VII.561	Resounded] Resounded,
III.475	black,] black		heard'st),] heardst)
III.507	Embellished;]	VII.588	Father,] Father(
	Imbellisht,	VII.601	sung:] sung,
III.645	unheard;] unheard,	VIII.16	compute] compute,
IV.131	comes] comes,	VIII.25	besides;] besides,
IV.345	them;] them,	VIII.71	right;] right,
IV.751	propriety] propriety,	VIII.194	wisdom;] Wisdom,
IV.773	on,] on	VIII.369	solitude?] solitude,
IV.824	prison;] prison,	VIII.372	thee?] thee,
IV.934	untried.] untri'd,	VIIII.373	ways?] wayes,
V.182	multiform,] multiform;	IX.133	woe:] woe,
V.197	souls:] Souls,	IX.199	voice;] voice,
V.587	bright.] bright,	IX.211	derides,] derides
V.811	ingrate,] ingrate	IX.687	knowledge:] knowledge?
VI.14	Empyreal;] Empyreal,		Threat'ner?]
VI.185	obeyed;] obey'd,		Threatner,
VI.200	mightiest:] mightiest,	IX.849	pass;] pass,
VI.203	heav'n] Heaven	IX.944	lose] loose
VI.251	once;] once,	IX.953	doom;] doom,
VI.269	rebellion!] Rebellion?	IX.1001	groan;] groan,
VI.271	false!] false.	IX.1002	loured,] lowr'd
VI.338	chariot,] Chariot;	IX.1058	Shame:] shame
VI.565	part:] part;	IX.1059	more.] more,
VI.594	rolled,] Rowl'd;	X. The	Death,] death
VI.595	arms;] Arms,	Argu-	
VI.624	many:] many,	ment,	
VI.772	throned,] Thron'd.	1.6	
VI.774	seen:] seen,		

X. The Argument, 1.24	condition,] condition	X.755	late] late,
		X.778	lap!] lap?
		X.801	he] he,
		X.841	like,] like
X.83	law:] Law	XI.80	joy,] joy:
X.95	cool,] coole	XI.91	him;] him,
X.99	declined;] declin'd,	XI.319	relate:] relate;
X.207	taken:] taken,	XI.472	famine;] famine,
X.285	waters,] Waters;	XI.736	sire] sire,
X.436	Casbeen:] *Casbeen*.	XI.787	¶] no ¶

Backgrounds and Sources

Selections from Milton's Prose

From Milton's Commonplace Book

Just a century ago someone discovered a 250-page notebook in which Milton (and after he was blind, his copyists) entered (in English and Latin) notes and quotations from his reading under such headings as moral evil, chastity, suicide, knowledge of literature, poetry, highway robbery, food, concubinage, usury, kings, liberty, games, war, and plagues. Here are six of these entries, in the English translation of Glenn McCrea, in Vol. XVIII of the Columbia Edition of the *Works of John Milton*.

In moral evil there can be mixed much of good and that with cunning skill; no one mixes poison with gall and hellibore, but with spice and savory dainties; so the Devil flavors his fatal concoction with the most pleasing gifts of God.

Why does God permit evil? So that reason can support virtue. For virtue is attested by evil, is illuminated and trained. As Lactantius says: that Reason and Judgement may have a field in which they may exercise themselves by choosing the things that are good and shunning the things that are evil; although even these reasons are not satisfactory.[1]

Why good men who are otherwise outstanding present the appearance in a striking degree of minds that are sluggish, small, and at first glance seem to be worth nothing. Lactantius replies: that they may have the means of exercising every day the greatest of the virtues, namely, patience.

A good man in some measure seems to excel even the angels, for the reason that housed in a weak and perishable body and struggling forever with desires, he nevertheless aspires to lead a life that resembles that of the heavenly host.

A man's courage depends not upon his body but upon his reason, which is for a human being the strongest safeguard and defense. This is clear from the fact that a man by this single help of reason masters even the strongest animals and is able if he so desires to do them harm.

A marvelous and very pleasing anecdote is told in Bede's History about an Englishman who suddenly by act of God became a poet.

1. The editor has revised McCrea's trans-
lation of this entry. The last clause seems
to be Milton's comment on Lactantius'
explanation.

Four Outlines for Tragedies on the Theme of *Paradise Lost*

From the Milton manuscripts in the Library of Trinity College, Cambridge. On pp. 35–41 of this fifty-page manuscript, containing, among other treasures, thirteen of Milton's minor poems in his own hand, are (also in Milton's hand) lists of subjects for plays or poems from English history and the Bible, and the following plans for tragedies on the subject of *Paradise Lost*.

[First Draft.]
the Persons

Michael
Heavenly Love
Chorus of Angels
Lucifer
Adam ⎫
Eve   ⎬ with the serpent
Conscience
Death
Labour ⎫
Sicknesse ⎪
Discontent ⎬ mutes.
Ignorance ⎪
   with others ⎭
Faith
Hope
Charity.

[Second Draft.]
the Persons

Moses
Justice
Mercie
Wisdome
Heavenly Love
Hesperus the Evening Starre
Chorus of Angels
Lucifer
Adam
Eve
Conscience
Labour ⎫
Sicknesse ⎪
Discontent ⎬ mutes
Ignorance ⎪
Feare ⎪
Death ⎭
Faith
Hope
Charity.

[Third Draft.]
Paradise Lost
The Persons

Moses προλογίζει recounting how he assum'd his true bodie, that it corrupts not because of his [*being*] with god in the mount declares the like of Enoch and Eliah, besides the purity of the place that certaine pure winds, dues, and clouds præserve it from corruption whence he hasts to the sight of god, tells they cannot se Adam in this state of innocence by reason of thire sin

[Act 1.]

Justice ⎫
Mercie ⎬ debating what should become of man if he fall
Wisdomme ⎭

Chorus of Angels sing a hymne of the creation

Act 2.

Heavenly love
Evening starre
Chorus sing the mariage song and describe Paradice

Act 3.

Lucifer contriving Adams ruine
Chorus feares for Adam and relates Lucifers rebellion and fall.

Act 4.

Adam ⎱
Eve ⎰ fallen

Conscience cites them to Gods Examination
Chorus bewails and tells the good Adam hath lost

Act 5.

Adam and Eve, driven out of Paradice præsented by an angel
  with

Labour ⎱
greife
hatred
Envie
warre
famine   mutes to whome he gives thire names
Pestilence   likewise winter, heat Tempest &c.
sicknesse
discontent
Ignorance
Feare
Death——— enterd into the world

Faith ⎱
Hope ⎰ comfort him and instruct him
Charity

Chorus breifly concludes.

[Fourth Draft.]
Adam unparadiz'd

  The angel Gabriel, either descending or entring, shewing since
this globe was created, his frequency as much on earth, as in
heavn, describes Paradise. next the Chorus shewing the reason of
his comming to keep his watch in Paradise after Lucifers rebellion
by command from god, & withall expressing his desire to see, &
know more concerning this excellent new creature man. the angel
Gabriel as by his name signifying a prince of power tracing para-

dise with a more free office passes by the station of the chorus & desired by them relates what he knew of man as the creation of Eve with thire love, & mariage. after this Lucifer appears after his overthrow, bemoans himself, seeks revenge on man the Chorus prepare resistance at his first approach at last after discourse of enmity on either side he departs wherat the chorus sings of the battell, & victorie in heavn against him, & his accomplices, as before after the first act was sung a hymn of the creation. heer again may appear Lucifer relating, & insulting in what he had don to the destruction of man. man next & Eve having by this time bin seduc't by the serpent appears confusedly cover'd with leaves conscience in a shape accuses him, Justice cites him to the place whither Jehova call'd for him in the mean while the chorus entertains the stage, & is inform'd by some angel the manner of his fall heer the chorus bewailes Adams fall. Adam then & Eve returne accuse one another but especially Adam layes the blame to his wife, is stubborn in his offence Justice appears reason with him convinces him the chorus admonisheth Adam, & bids him beware by Lucifers example of impenitence the Angel is sent to banish them out of paradise but before causes to passe before his eyes in Shapes a mask of all the evills of this life & world he is humbl'd relents, dispaires. at last appeares Mercy comforts him promises the Messiah, then calls in faith, hope, & charity, instructs him he repents gives god the glory, submitts to his penalty the chorus breifly concludes. compare this with the former draught.

From *Areopagitica*

In 1644 Milton addressed this argument "for the liberty of unlicensed printing, to the Parliament of England." The following passage is only one of several that touch on various topics of *Paradise Lost*.

Good and evil we know in the field of this world grow up together almost inseparably; and the knowledge of good is so involved and interwoven with the knowledge of evil, and in so many cunning resemblances hardly to be discerned, that those confused seeds which were imposed upon Pysche as an incessant labor to cull out, and sort asunder, were not more intermixed. It was from out the rind of one apple tasted, that the knowledge of good and evil, as two twins cleaving together, leaped forth into the world. And perhaps this is that doom which Adam fell into of knowing good and evil—that is to say, of knowing good by evil.

As therefore the state of man now is; what wisdom can there be to choose, what continence to forbear, without the knowledge of evil? He that can apprehend and consider vice with all her baits and seeming pleasures, and yet abstain, and yet distinguish, and yet prefer that which is truly better, he is the true warfaring Christian. I cannot praise a fugitive and cloistered virtue unexercised and unbreathed, that never sallies out and seeks her adversary, but slinks out of the race, where that immortal garland is to be run for, not without dust and heat. Assuredly we bring not innocence into the world, we bring impurity much rather; that which purifies us is trial, and trial is by what is contrary. That virtue therefore which is but a youngling in the contemplation of evil, and knows not the utmost that vice promises to her followers, and rejects it, is but a blank virtue, not a pure; her whiteness is but an excremental whiteness; which was the reason why our sage and serious poet Spenser, (whom I dare be known to think a better teacher than Scotus or Aquinas,) describing true temperance under the person of Guion, brings him in with his palmer through the cave of Mammon, and the bower of earthly bliss, that he might see and know, and yet abstain.

Autobiographical Passages

The first of these passages, from *The Reason of Church Government Urged Against Prelaty* (1642), is the conclusion of an introduction in which Milton explains why he has decided temporarily to abandon his career as a poet in order to engage in public debate. The second is from *An Apology Against a Pamphlet Called 'A Modest Confutation of the Animadversions upon the Remonstrant Against Smectymnuus'* (1642). Milton's tutor and friend Thomas Young was the *t y* of the five men whose initials spelled Smectymnuus (the double *u* was *w*). Their pamphlet had been answered by the *Remonstrant*, who in turn was answered by the *Animadversions*, which in turn had been answered by the *Confutation*, whose author had accused Milton of immoral conduct, including visits to bordellos. The tone and substance of this scurrilous attack account in part for the intensity of Milton's reply. Though Milton's tone is defensive, there is no reason to doubt the essential truth of the biographical facts. The third passage is from the translation by Robert Fellowes of *Joannis Miltoni Angli Pro Populo Anglicano Defensio Secunda* (The Second Defense of the English People), published in 1654, only three or four years before Milton began to write *Paradise Lost*. Here again Milton is responding to a vicious personal attack that accused him of moral depravity. Milton strikes back with passion, and his self-defense may be guilty of certain rationalizations, but again the facts are true and the autobiography invaluable.

From *The Reason of Church Government
Urged Against Prelaty* (1642)

Lastly, I should not choose this manner of writing, wherein knowing myself inferior to myself, led by the genial power of nature to another task, I have the use, as I may account, but of my left hand. And though I shall be foolish in saying more to this purpose, yet, since it will be such a folly, as wisest men go about to commit, having only confessed and so committed, I may trust with more reason, because with more folly, to have courteous pardon. For although a poet, soaring in the high reason of his fancies, with his garland and singing robes about him, might, without apology, speak more of himself than I mean to do; yet for me sitting here below in the cool element of prose, a mortal thing among many readers of no empyreal conceit, to venture and divulge unusual things of myself, I shall petition to the gentler sort, it may not be envy to me. I must say, therefore, that after I had for my first years, by the ceaseless diligence and care of my father, (whom God recompense!) been exercised to the tongues, and some sciences, as my age would suffer, by sundry masters and teachers, both at home and at the schools, it was found that whether aught was imposed me by them that had the overlooking, or betaken to of mine own choice in English, or other tongue, prosing or versing, but chiefly by this latter, the style, by certain vital signs it had, was likely to live. But much latelier in the private academies of Italy, whither I was favored to resort, perceiving that some trifles which I had in memory, composed at under twenty or thereabout, (for the manner is, that every one must give some proof of his wit and reading there,) met with acceptance above what was looked for; and other things, which I had shifted in scarcity of books and conveniences to patch up amongst them, were received with written encomiums, which the Italian is not forward to bestow on men of this side the Alps; I began thus far to assent both to them and divers of my friends here at home, and not less to an inward prompting which now grew daily upon me, that by labor and intense study, (which I take to be my portion in this life,) joined with the strong propensity of nature, I might perhaps leave something so written to aftertimes, as they should not willingly let it die. These thoughts at once possessed me, and these other; that if I were certain to write as men buy leases, for three lives and downward, there ought no regard be sooner had than to God's glory, by the honor and instruction of my country. For which cause, and not only for that I knew it would be hard to arrive at the second rank among the Latins, I applied myself to that resolution, which Ariosto followed against the persuasions of Bembo, to fix all the industry and art I could unite to the adorning of my native tongue; not to make verbal curiosities the end, (that were a toilsome vanity,) but to be an interpreter and relater of the best and sagest things among mine own citizens throughout this island in the mother dialect. That what the greatest and choicest wits of Athens, Rome, or modern Italy, and those Hebrews of old did for their country, I, in my proportion, with this over and above, of being a Christian, might do for mine; not caring to be once named abroad, though perhaps I could attain to that, but content with these British islands as my world; whose fortune hath hitherto been, that if the Athenians, as some say, made their small deeds great and renowned by their eloquent writers, England hath had her noble achievements made small by the unskilful handling of monks and mechanics.

Time serves not now, and perhaps I might seem too profuse to give any certain account of what the mind at home, in the spacious circuits of her musing, hath liberty to propose to herself, though of highest hope and hardest attempting; whether that epic form whereof the two poems of Homer, and those other two of Virgil and Tasso, are a diffuse, and the book of Job a brief model: or whether the rules of Aristotle herein are strictly to be kept, or nature to be followed, which in them that know art, and use judgment, is no transgression, but an enriching of art: and lastly, what king or knight, before the conquest, might be chosen in whom to lay the pattern of a Christian hero. And as Tasso gave to a prince of Italy his choice whether he would command him to write of Godfrey's expedition against the Infidels, or Belisarius against the Goths, or Charlemain against the Lombards; if to the instinct of nature and the emboldening of art aught may be trusted, and that there be nothing adverse in our climate, or the fate of this age, it haply would be no rashness, from an equal diligence and inclination, to present the like offer in our own ancient stories; or whether those dramatic constitutions, wherein Sophocles and Euripides reign, shall be found more doctrinal and exemplary to a nation. The scripture also affords us a divine pastoral drama in the Song of Solomon, consisting of two persons, and a double chorus, as Origen rightly judges. And the Apocalypse of St. John[1] is the majestic image of a high and stately tragedy, shutting up and intermingling her solemn scenes and acts with a sevenfold chorus of hallelujahs and harping symphonies: and this my opinion the grave authority of Pareus, commenting that book, is sufficient to confirm. Or if occasion shall lead, to imitate those magnific odes and hymns, wherein Pindarus and Callimachus are in most things worthy, some others in their frame judicious, in their matter most an end faulty. But those frequent songs throughout the law and prophets beyond all these, not in their divine argument alone, but in the very critical art of composition, may be easily made appear over all the kinds of lyric poesy to be incomparable. These abilities, wheresoever they be found, are the inspired gift of God, rarely bestowed, but yet to some (though most abuse) in every nation; and are of power, beside the office of a pulpit, to imbreed and cherish in a great people the seeds of virtue and public civility, to allay the

---

1. I.e., the Book of Revelation, in the Bible.

perturbations of the mind, and set the affections in right tune; to celebrate in glorious and lofty hymns the throne and equipage of God's almightiness, and what he works, and what he suffers to be wrought with high providence in his church; to sing victorious agonies of martyrs and saints, and deeds and triumphs of just and pious nations, doing valiantly through faith against the enemies of Christ; to deplore the general relapses of kingdoms and states from justice and God's true worship. Lastly, whatsoever in religion is holy and sublime, in virtue amiable or grave, whatsoever hath passon or admiration in all the changes of that which is called fortune from without, or the wily subtleties and refluxes of man's thoughts from within; all these things with a solid and treatable smoothness to paint out and describe. Teaching over the whole book of sanctity and virtue, through all the instances of example, with such delight to those especially of soft and delicious temper, who will not so much as look upon truth herself, unless they see her elegantly dressed; that whereas the paths of honesty and good life appear now rugged and difficult, though they be indeed easy and pleasant, they will then appear to all men both easy and pleasant, though they were rugged and difficult indeed. And what a benefit this would be to our youth and gentry, may be soon guessed by what we know of the corruption and bane which they suck in daily from the writings and interludes of libidinous and ignorant poetasters, who having scarce ever heard of that which is the main consistence of a true poem, the choice of such persons as they ought to introduce, and what is moral and decent to each one; do for the most part lay up vicious principles in sweet pills to be swallowed down, and make the taste of virtuous documents harsh and sour. But because the spirit of man cannot demean itself lively in this body, without some recreating intermission of labor and serious things, it were happy for the commonwealth, if our magistrates, as in those famous governments of old, would take into their care, not only the deciding of our contentious lawcases and brawls, but the managing of our public sports and festival pastimes; that they might be, not such as were authorized a while since, the provocations of drunkenness and lust, but such as may inure and harden our bodies by martial exercises to all warlike skill and performance; and may civilize, adorn, and make discreet our minds by the learned and affable meeting of frequent academies, and the procurement of wise and artful recitations, sweetened with eloquent and graceful enticements to the love and practice of justice, temperance, and fortitude, instructing and bettering the nation at all opportunities, that the call of wisdom and virtue may be heard everywhere, as Solomon saith: "She crieth without, she uttereth her voice in the streets, in the top of high places, in the chief concourse, and in the openings of the gates." Whether this may not be, not only in pulpits, but after another persuasive method, at set and solemn paneguries, in theatres, porches, or what other place or way may win most upon the people to receive at once both recreation and instruction, let them in authority consult. The thing which I had to say, and those intentions which have lived within me ever since I could conceive myself anything worth to my country, I return to crave excuse that urgent reason hath plucked from me, by an abortive and foredated discovery. And the accomplishment of them lies not but in a power above man's to promise; but that none hath by more studious ways endeavored, and with more unwearied spirit that none shall, that I dare almost aver of myself, as far as life and free leisure will extend; and that the land had once enfranchised herself from this impertinent yoke of prelaty, under whose inquisitorious and tyrannical duncery, no free and splendid wit can flourish. Neither do I think it shame to covenant with any knowing reader, that for some few years yet I may go on trust with him toward the payment of what I am now indebted, as being a work not to be raised from the heat of youth, or the vapors of wine; like that which flows at waste from the pen of some vulgar amorist, or the trencher fury of a rhyming parasite; nor to be obtained by the invocation of dame memory and her siren daughters, but by devout prayer to that eternal Spirit, who can enrich with all utterance and knowledge, and sends out his seraphim, with the hallowed fire of his altar, to touch and purify the lips of whom he pleases: to this must be added industrious and select reading, steady observation, insight into all seemly and generous arts and affairs; till which in some measure be compassed, at mine own peril and cost, I refuse not to sustain this expectation from as many as are not loth to hazard so much credulity upon the best pledges that I can give them. Although it nothing content me to have disclosed thus much beforehand, but that I trust hereby to make it manifest with what small willingness I endure to interrupt the pursuit of no less hopes than these, and leave a calm and pleasing solitariness, fed with cheerful and confident thoughts, to embark in a troubled sea of noises and hoarse disputes, put from beholding the bright countenance of truth in the quiet and still air of delightful studies, to come into the dim reflection of hollow antiquities sold by the seeming bulk, and there be fain to club quotations with men whose learning and belief lies in marginal stuffings, who, when they have, like good sumpters, laid ye down their horse-loads of citations and fathers at your door, with a rhapsody of who and who were bishops here or there, ye may take off their packsaddles, their day's work is done, and episcopacy, as they think, stoutly vindicated. Let any gentle apprehension, that can distinguish learned pains from unlearned drudgery imagine what pleasure or profoundness can be in this, or what honor to deal against such adversaries. But were it the meanest under-service, if God by his secretary conscience enjoin it, it were sad for me if I should draw back; for me especially, now when all men offer their aid to help, ease, and lighten the difficult labors of the church, to whose service, by the intentions of my parents and friends, I was destined of a child, and in mine own resolutions: till coming to some maturity of years, and perceiving what tyranny had invaded the church, that he who would take orders must subscribe slave, and take an oath withal, which, unless he took with a conscience that would retch, he must either straight perjure, or split his faith; I thought it better to prefer a blameless silence before the sacred office of speaking, bought and begun with servitude and forswearing. Howsoever, thus church-outed by the prelates, hence may appear the right I have to meddle in these matters, as before the necessity and constraint appeared.

From *An Apology Against a Pamphlet Called 'A Modest Confutation of the Animadversions upon the Remonstrant Against Smectymnuus'* (1642)

I had my time, readers, as others have, who have good learning bestowed upon them, to be sent to those places where, the opinion was, it might be soonest attained; and as the manner is, was not unstudied in those authors which are most commended. Whereof some were grave orators and historians, whose matter methought I loved indeed, but as my age then was, so I understood them; others were the smooth elegiac poets, whereof the schools are not scarce, whom both for the pleasing sound of their numerous[1] writing, which in imitation I found most easy, and most agreeable to nature's part in me, and for their matter, which what it is, there be few who know not, I was so allured to read, that no recreation came to me better welcome. For that it was then those years with me which are excused, though they be least severe, I may be saved the labor to remember ye. Whence having observed them to account it the chief glory of their wit, in that they were ablest to judge, to praise, and by that could esteem themselves worthiest to love those high perfections, which under one or other name they took to celebrate; I thought with myself by every instinct and presage of nature, which is not wont to be false, that what emboldened them to this task, might with such diligence as they used embolden me; and that what judgment, wit, or elegance was my share, would herein best appear, and best value itself, by how much more wisely, and with more love of virtue I should choose (let rude ears be absent) the object of not unlike praises. For albeit these thoughts to some will seem virtuous and commendable, to others

---

1. In poetic meters.

only pardonable, to a third sort perhaps idle; yet the mentioning of them now will end in serious.

Nor blame it, readers, in those years to propose to themselves such a reward, as the noblest dispositions above other things in this life have sometimes preferred: whereof not to be sensible when good and fair in one person meet, argues both a gross and shallow judgment, and withal an ungentle and swainish breast. For by the firm settling of these persuasions, I became, to my best memory, so much a proficient, that if I found those authors anywhere speaking unworthy things of themselves, or unchaste of those names which before they had extolled; this effect it wrought with me, from that time forward their art I still applauded, but the men I deplored; and above them all, preferred the two famous renowners of Beatrice and Laura,[2] who never write but honor of them to whom they devote their verse, displaying sublime and pure thoughts, without transgression. And long it was not after, when I was confirmed in this opinion, that he who would not be frustrate of his hope to write well hereafter in laudable things, ought himself to be a true poem; that is, a composition and pattern of the best and honorablest things; not presuming to sing high praises of heroic men, or famous cities, unless he have in himself the experience and the practice of all that which is praiseworthy. These reasonings, together with a certain niceness of nature, an honest haughtiness, and self-esteem either of what I was, or what I might be, (which let envy call pride,) and lastly that modesty, whereof, though not in the title-page, yet here I may be excused to make some beseeming profession; all these uniting the supply of their natural aid together, kept me still above those low descents of mind, beneath which he must deject and plunge himself, that can agree to saleable and unlawful prostitutions.

Next, (for hear me out now, readers), that I may tell ye whither my younger feet wandered; I betook me among those lofty fables and romances, which recount in solemn cantos the deeds of knighthood founded by our victorious kings, and from hence had in renown over all Christendom. There I read it in the oath of every knight, that he should defend to the expense of his best blood, or of his life, if it so befell him, the honor and chastity of virgin or matron; from whence even then I learned what a noble virtue chastity sure must be, to the defence of which so many worthies, by such a dear adventure of themselves, had sworn. And if I found in the story afterward, any of them, by word or deed, breaking that oath, I judged it the same fault of the poet, as that which is attributed to Homer, to have written indecent things of the gods. Only this my mind gave me, that every free and gentle spirit,

2. Dante and Petrarch.

without that oath, ought to be born a knight, nor needed to expect the gilt spur, or the laying of a sword upon his shoulder to stir him up both by his counsel and his arms, to secure and protect the weakness of any attempted chastity. So that even these books, which to many others have been the fuel of wantonness and loose living, I cannot think how, unless by divine indulgence, proved to me so many incitements, as you have heard, to the love and steadfast observation of that virtue which abhors the society of bordelloes.

Thus, from the laureat fraternity of poets, riper years and the ceaseless round of study and reading led me to the shady spaces of philosophy; but chiefly to the divine volumes of Plato, and his equal[3] Xenophon: where, if I should tell ye what I learnt of chastity and love. I mean that which is truly so, whose charming cup is only virtue, which she bears in her hand to those who are worthy; (the rest are cheated with a thick intoxicating potion, which a certain sorceress, the abuser of love's name, carries about;) and how the first and chiefest office of love begins and ends in the soul, producing those happy twins of her divine generation, knowledge and virtue. With such abstracted sublimities as these, it might be worth your listening, readers, as I may one day hope to have ye in a still time, when there shall be no chiding; not in these noises, the adversary, as ye know, barking at the door, or searching for me at the bordelloes, where it may be has lost himself, and raps up without pity the sage and rheumatic old prelates, with all her young Corinthian[4] laity, to inquire for such a one.

Last of all, not in time, but as perfection is last, that care was ever had of me, with my earliest capacity, not to be negligently trained in the precepts of the Christian religion: this that I have hitherto related, hath been to show, that though Christianity had been but slightly taught me, yet a certain reservedness of natural disposition, and moral discipline, learnt out of the noblest philosophy, was enough to keep me in disdain of far less incontinences than this of the bordello. But having had the doctrine of holy scripture unfolding those chaste and high mysteries, with timeliest care infused, that "the body is for the Lord, and the Lord for the body;"[5] thus also I argued to myself, that if unchastity in a woman, whom St. Paul terms the glory of man,[6] be such a scandal and dishonor, then certainly in a man, who is both the image and glory of God, it must, though commonly not so thought, be much more deflowering and dishonourable; in that he sins both against his own body, which is the perfecter sex, and his own glory, which is in the woman; and, that which is worst, against the image and glory of God, which is in himself. Nor did I slumber over that place express-

3. Contemporary.
4. Prostitutes were called Corinthians.

5. I Cor. 6.13.
6. I Cor. 11.7.

ing such high rewards of ever accompanying the Lamb with those
celestial songs to others inapprehensible, but not to those who were
not defiled with women,[7] which doubtless means fornication; for
marriage must not be called a defilement.

From *Joannis Miltoni Angli Pro Populo Anglicano Defensio Secunda*
(The Second Defense of the English People) (1654)

I will now mention who and whence I am. I was born at Lon-
don, of an honest family; my father was distinguished by the un-
deviating integrity of his life; my mother, by the esteem in which
she was held, and the alms which she bestowed. My father destined
me from a child to the pursuits of literature; and my appetite for
knowledge was so voracious, that, from twelve years of age, I
hardly ever left my studies, or went to bed before midnight. This
primarily led to my loss of sight. My eyes were naturally weak, and
I was subject to frequent head-aches; which, however, could not
chill the ardor of my curiosity, or retard the progress of my im-
provement. My father had me daily instructed in the grammar-
school, and by other masters at home. He then, after I had acquired
a proficiency in various languages, and had made a consid-
erable progress in philosophy, sent me to the University of
Cambridge. Here I passed seven years in the usual course of in-
struction and study, with the approbation of the good, and without
any stain upon my character, till I took the degree of Master of
Arts. After this I did not, as this miscreant feigns, run away into
Italy, but of my own accord retired to my father's house, whither I
was accompanied by the regrets of most of the fellows of the
college, who showed me no common marks of friendship and es-
teem. On my father's estate, where he had determined to pass the
remainder of his days, I enjoyed an interval of uninterrupted lei-
sure, which I entirely devoted to the perusal of the Greek and Latin
classics; though I occasionally visited the metropolis, either for the
sake of purchasing books, or of learning something new in mathe-
matics or in music, in which I, at that time, found a source of
pleasure and amusement. In this manner I spent five years till my
mother's death. I then became anxious to visit foreign parts, and
particularly Italy. My father gave me his permission, and I left
home with one servant. On my departure, the celebrated Henry
Wootton, who had long been king James's ambassador at Venice,
gave me a signal proof of his regard, in an elegant letter which he
wrote, breathing not only the warmest friendship, but containing
some maxims of conduct which I found very useful in my travels.
The noble Thomas Scudamore, king Charles's ambassador, to

7. Cf. Rev. 19.

whom I carried letters of recommendation, received me most cour-
teously at Paris. His lordship gave me a card of introduction to the
learned Hugo Grotius, at that time ambassador from the queen of
Sweden to the French court; whose acquaintance I anxiously de-
sired, and to whose house I was accompanied by some of his
lordship's friends. A few days after, when I set out for Italy, he
gave me letters to the English merchants on my route, that they
might show me any civilities in their power. Taking ship at Nice, I
arrived at Genoa, and afterwards visited Leghorn, Pisa, and Flor-
ence. In the latter city, which I have always more particularly
esteemed for the elegance of its dialect, its genius, and its taste, I
stopped about two months; when I contracted an intimacy with
many persons of rank and learning; and was a constant attendant
at their literary parties; a practice which prevails there, and tends so
much to the diffusion of knowledge, and the preservation of friend-
ship. No time will ever abolish the agreeable recollections which I
cherish of Jacob Gaddi, Carolo Dati, Frescobaldo, Cultellero,
Bonomatthai, Clementillo, Francisco, and many others. From
Florence I went to Siena, thence to Rome, where, after I had spent
about two months in viewing the antiquities of that renowned city,
where I experienced the most friendly attentions from Lucas Hol-
stein, and other learned and ingenious men, I continued my route
to Naples. There I was introduced by a certain recluse, with whom
I had travelled from Rome, to John Baptista Manso, marquis of
Villa, a nobleman of distinguished rank and authority, to whom
Torquato Tasso, the illustrious poet, inscribed his book on friend-
ship. During my stay, he gave me singular proofs of his regard: he
himself conducted me round the city, and to the palace of the
viceroy; and more than once paid me a visit at my lodgings. On my
departure he gravely apologized for not having shown me more
civility, which he said he had been restrained from doing, because I
had spoken with so little reserve on matters of religion. When I was
preparing to pass over into Sicily and Greece, the melancholy intel-
ligence which I received of the civil commotions in England made
me alter my purpose; for I thought it base to be travelling for
amusement abroad, while my fellow-citizens were fighting for lib-
erty at home. While I was on my way back to Rome, some mer-
chants informed me that the English Jesuits had formed a plot
against me if I returned to Rome, because I had spoken too freely
on religion; for it was a rule which I laid down to myself in those
places, never to be the first to begin any conversation on religion;
but if any questions were put to me concerning my faith, to declare
it without any reserve or fear. I, nevertheless, returned to Rome. I
took no steps to conceal either my person or my character; and for
about the space of two months I again openly defended, as I had
done before, the reformed religion in the very metropolis of popery.

By the favor of God, I got safe back to Florence, where I was received with as much affection as if I had returned to my native country. There I stopped as many months as I had done before, except that I made an excursion for a few days to Lucca; and, crossing the Apennines, passed through Bologna and Ferrara to Venice. After I had spent a month in surveying the curiosities of this city, and had put on board a ship the books which I had collected in Italy, I proceeded through Verona and Milan, and along the Leman lake to Geneva. The mention of this city brings to my recollection the slandering More, and makes me again call the Deity to witness, that in all those places in which vice meets with so little discouragement, and is practiced with so little shame, I never once deviated from the paths of integrity and virtue, and perpetually reflected that, though my conduct might escape the notice of men, it could not elude the inspection of God. At Geneva I held daily conferences with John Deodati, the learned professor of Theology. Then pursuing my former route through France, I returned to my native country, after an absence of one year and about three months; at the time when Charles, having broken the peace, was renewing what is called the episcopal war with the Scots, in which the royalists being routed in the first encounter, and the English being universally and justly disaffected, the necessity of his affairs at last obliged him to convene a parliament. As soon as I was able, I hired a spacious house in the city for myself and my books; where I again with rapture renewed my literary pursuits, and where I calmly awaited the issue of the contest, which I trusted to the wise conduct of Providence, and to the courage of the people. The vigor of the parliament had begun to humble the pride of the bishops. As long as the liberty of speech was no longer subject to control, all mouths began to be opened against the bishops; some complained of the vices of the individuals, others of those of the order. They said that it was unjust that they alone should differ from the model of other reformed churches; that the government of the church should be according to the pattern of other churches, and particularly the word of God. This awakened all my attention and my zeal. I saw that a way was opening for the establishment of real liberty; that the foundation was laying for the deliverance of man from the yoke of slavery and superstition; that the principles of religion, which were the first objects of our care, would exert a salutary influence on the manners and constitution of the republic; and as I had from my youth studied the distinctions between religious and civil rights, I perceived that if I ever wished to be of use, I ought at least not to be wanting to my country, to the church, and to so many of my fellow-Christians, in a crisis of so much danger; I therefore determined to relinquish the other pursuits in which I was engaged, and to transfer the whole force of my talents and my industry to this one important object. I accordingly wrote two books to a friend concerning the reformation of the church of England. Afterwards, when two bishops of superior distinction vindicated their privileges against some principal ministers, I thought that on those topics, to the consideration of which I was led solely by my love of truth, and my reverence for Christianity, I should not probably write worse than those who were contending only for their own emoluments and usurpations. I therefore answered the one in two books, of which the first is inscribed, Concerning Prelatical Episcopacy, and the other Concerning the Mode of Ecclesiastical Government; and I replied to the other in some Animadversions, and soon after in an Apology. On this occasion it was supposed that I brought a timely succor to the ministers, who were hardly a match for the eloquence of their opponents; and from that time I was actively employed in refuting any answers that appeared. When the bishops could no longer resist the multitude of their assailants, I had leisure to turn my thoughts to other subjects; to the promotion of real and substantial liberty; which is rather to be sought from within than from without; and whose existence depends, not so much on the terror of the sword, as on sobriety of conduct and integrity of life. When, therefore, I perceived that there were three species of liberty which are essential to the happiness of social life—religious, domestic, and civil; and as I had already written concerning the first, and the magistrates were strenuously active in obtaining the third, I determined to turn my attention to the second, or the domestic species. As this seemed to involve three material questions, the conditions of the conjugal tie, the education of the children, and the free publication of the thoughts, I made them objects of distinct consideration. I explained my sentiments, not only concerning the solemnization of the marriage, but the dissolution, if circumstances rendered it necessary; and I drew my arguments from the divine law, which Christ did not abolish, or publish another more grievous than that of Moses. I stated my own opinions, and those of others, concerning the exclusive exception of fornication, which our illustrious Selden has since, in his Hebrew Wife, more copiously discussed;[1] for he in vain makes a vaunt of liberty in the senate or in the forum, who languishes under the vilest servitude, to an inferior at home. On this subject, therefore, I published some books which were more particularly necessary at that time, when man and wife were often the most inveterate foes, when the man often staid to take care of his children at home, while the mother of the family was seen in the camp of the enemy, threatening death and destruction to her husband. I then discussed the principles of education in a summary

---

1. John Selden, whose *Uxor Ebraica* appeared in 1646.

manner, but sufficiently copious for those who attend seriously to the subject; than which nothing can be more necessary to principle the minds of men in virtue, the only genuine source of political and individual liberty, the only true safeguard of states, the bulwark of their prosperity and renown. Lastly, I wrote my Areopagitica, in order to deliver the press from the restraints with which it was encumbered; that the power of determining what was true and what was false, what ought to be published and what to be suppressed, might no longer be entrusted to a few illiterate and illiberal individuals, who refused their sanction to any work which contained views or sentiments at all above the level of the vulgar superstition. On the last species of civil liberty, I said nothing, because I saw that sufficient attention was paid to it by the magistrates; nor did I write anything on the prerogative of the crown, till the king, voted an enemy by the parliament, and vanquished in the field, was summoned before the tribunal which condemned him to lose his head. But when, at length, some presbyterian ministers, who had formerly been the most bitter enemies to Charles, became jealous of the growth of the independents, and of their ascendancy in the parliament, most tumultuously clamored against the sentence, and did all in their power to prevent the execution, though they were not angry, so much on account of the act itself, as because it was not the act of their party; and when they dared to affirm, that the doctrine of the protestants, and of all the reformed churches, was abhorrent to such an atrocious proceeding against kings; I thought that it became me to oppose such a glaring falsehood; and accordingly, without any immediate or personal application to Charles, I showed, in an abstract consideration of the question, what might lawfully be done against tyrants; and in support of what I advanced, produced the opinions of the most celebrated divines; while I vehemently inveighed against the egregious ignorance or effrontery of men, who professed better things, and from whom better things might have been expected. That book did not make its appearance till after the death of Charles; and was written rather to reconcile the minds of the people to the event, than to discuss the legitimacy of that particular sentence which concerned the magistrates, and which was already executed. Such were the fruits of my private studies, which I gratuitously presented to the church and to the state; and for which I was recompensed by nothing but impunity; though the actions themselves procured me peace of conscience, and the approbation of the good; while I exercised that freedom of discussion which I loved. Others, without labor or desert, got possession of honors and emoluments; but no one ever knew me either soliciting anything myself or through the medium of my friends, ever beheld me in a supplicating posture at the doors of the senate, or the levees of the great. I usually kept myself secluded at home, where my own property, part of which had been withheld during the civil commotions, and part of which had been absorbed in the oppressive contributions which I had to sustain, afforded me a scanty subsistence. When I was released from these engagements, and thought that I was about to enjoy an interval of uninterrupted ease, I turned my thoughts to a continued history of my country, from the earliest times to the present period.[2] I had already finished four books, when, after the subversion of the monarchy, and the establishment of a republic, I was surprised by an invitation from the council of state, who desired my services in the office for foreign affairs.

From *The Christian Doctrine*

Some time in the 1640s Milton began to collect notes in preparation for this work, *De Doctrina Christiana*. He began to write it shortly after he became blind, and he was probably working on it when he began *Paradise Lost*. Though he was still revising it at the time of the Restoration, it was practically complete by then and might soon have been published if the King had not returned and made publication imprudent if not impossible. The 735-page manuscript was discovered 150 years ago among the records in the Old State Paper Office in London. It was first published in 1825, by Charles R. Summer, who also translated it into English. The following selections (in Summer's translation) are taken from vols. 14–17 of the Columbia Edition of the **Works** of John Milton.

John Milton

ENGLISHMAN

To all the churches of Christ, and to all who profess the Christian Faith throughout the world, Peace, and the Recognition of the Truth, and Eternal Salvation in God the Father, and in our Lord Jesus Christ.

Since the commencement of the last century, when religion began to be restored from the corruptions of more than thirteen hundred years to something of its original purity, many treatises of theology have been published, conducted according to sounder principles, wherein the chief heads of Christian doctrine are set forth sometimes briefly, sometimes in a more enlarged and methodical order. I think myself obliged, therefore, to declare in the first instance why, if any works have already appeared as perfect as the nature of the subject will admit, I have not remained contented with them; or, if all my predecessors have treated it unsuccessfully,

2. Milton's *History of Britain, That part especially now called England. From the first Traditional Beginning, continued to* the *Norman Conquest* was published in 1670.

why their failure has not deterred me from attempting an undertaking of a similar kind.

If I were to say that I had devoted myself to the study of the Christian religion because nothing else can so effectually rescue the lives and minds of men from those two detestable curses, slavery and superstition, I should seem to have acted rather from a regard to my highest earthly comforts, than from a religious motive.

But since it is only to the individual faith of each that the Deity has opened the way of eternal salvation, and as he requires that he who would be saved should have a personal belief of his own, I resolved not to repose on the faith or judgment of others in matters relating to God; but on the one hand, having taken the grounds of my faith from divine revelation alone, and on the other, having neglected nothing which depended on my own industry, I thought fit to scrutinize and ascertain for myself the several points of my religious belief, by the most careful perusal and meditation of the Holy Scriptures themselves.

If therefore I mention what has proved beneficial in my own practice, it is in the hope that others, who have a similar wish of improving themselves, may be thereby invited to pursue the same method. I entered upon an assiduous course of study in my youth, beginning with the books of the Old and New Testament in their original languages, and going diligently through a few of the shorter systems of divines, in imitation of whom I was in the habit of classing under certain heads whatever passages of Scripture occurred for extraction, to be made use of hereafter as occasion might require. At length I resorted with increased confidence to some of the more copious theological treatises, and to the examination of the arguments advanced by the conflicting parties respecting certain disputed points of faith. But, to speak the truth with freedom as well as candor, I was concerned to discover in many instances adverse reasonings either evaded by wretched shifts, or attempted to be refuted, rather speciously than with solidity, by an affected display of formal sophisms, or by a constant recourse to the quibbles of the grammarians; while what was most pertinaciously espoused as the true doctrine, seemed often defended, with more vehemence than strength of argument, by misconstructions of Scripture, or by the hasty deduction of erroneous inferences. Owing to these causes, the truth was sometimes as strenuously opposed as if it had been an error or a heresy, while errors and heresies were substituted for the truth, and valued rather from deference to custom and the spirit of party than from the authority of Scripture.

According to my judgment, therefore, neither my creed nor my hope of salvation could be safely trusted to such guides; and yet it appeared highly requisite to possess some methodical tractate of Christian doctrine, or at least to attempt such a disquisition as might be useful in establishing my faith or assisting my memory. I deemed it therefore safest and most advisable to compile for myself, by my own labor and study, some original treatise which shuld be always at hand, derived solely from the word of God itself, and executed with all possible fidelity, seeing that I could have no wish to practice any imposition on myself in such a matter.

After a diligent perseverance in this plan for several years, I perceived that the strongholds of the reformed religion were sufficiently fortified, as far as it was in danger from the Papists, but neglected in many other quarters; neither competently strengthened with works of defence, nor adequately provided with champions. It was also evident to me, that, in religion as in other things, the offers of God were all directed, not to an indolent credulity, but to constant diligence, and to an unwearied search after truth; and that more than I was aware of still remained, which required to be more rigidly examined by the rule of Scripture, and reformed after a more accurate model. I so far satisfied myself in the prosecution of this plan as at length to trust that I had discovered, with regard to religion, what was matter of belief, and what only matter of opinion. It was also a great solace to me to have compiled, by God's assistance, a precious aid for my faith; or rather to have laid up for myself a treasure which would be a provision for my future life, and would remove from my mind all grounds for hesitation, as often as it behoved me to render an account of the principles of my belief.

If I communicate the result of my inquiries to the world at large; if, as God is my witness, it be with a friendly and benignant feeling towards mankind, that I readily give as wide a circulation as possible to what I esteem my best and richest possession, I hope to meet with a candid reception from all parties, and that none at least will take unjust offense, even though many things should be brought to light which will at once be seen to differ from certain received opinions. I earnestly beseech all lovers of truth, not to cry out that the Church is thrown into confusion by that freedom of discussion and inquiry which is granted to the schools, and ought certainly to be refused to no believer, since we are ordered "to prove all things," and since the daily progress of the light of truth is productive far less of disturbance to the Church, than of illumination and edification. Nor do I see how the Church can be more disturbed by the investigation of truth, than were the Gentiles by the first promulgation of the gospel; since so far from recommending or imposing anything on my own authority, it is my particular advice that every one should suspend his opinion on whatever points he may not feel himself fully satisfied, till the evidence of Scripture prevail, and persuade his reason into assent and faith. Concealment is not my object; it is to the learned that I address myself, or if it be thought that the learned are not the best umpires and judges of such things, I should at least wish to submit my opinions to men of a mature and manly understanding, possessing a thorough knowledge of the doctrines of the gospel; on whose judgments I should rely with far more confidence, than on those of novices in these matters. And whereas the greater part of those who have written most largely on these subjects have been wont to fill whole pages with explanations of their own opinions, thrusting into the margin the texts in support of their doctrine with a summary reference to the chapter and verse, I have chosen, on the contrary, to fill my pages even to redundance with quotations from Scripture, that so as little space as possible might be left for my own words, even when they arise from the context of revelation itself.

It has also been my object to make it appear from the opinions I shall be found to have advanced, whether new or old, of how much consequence to the Christian religion is the liberty not only of winnowing and sifting every doctrine, but also of thinking and even writing respecting it, according to our individual faith and persuasion; an inference which will be stronger in proportion to the weight and importance of those opinions, or rather in proportion to the authority of Scripture, on the abundant testimony of which they rest. Without this liberty there is neither religion nor gospel—force alone prevails—by which it is disgraceful for the Christian religion to be supported. Without this liberty we are still enslaved, not indeed, as formerly, under the divine law, but, what is worst of all, under the law of man, or to speak more truly, under a barbarous tyranny. But I do not expect from candid and judicious readers a conduct so unworthy of them, that like certain unjust and foolish men, they should stamp with the invidious name of heretic or heresy whatever appears to them to differ from the received opinions, without trying the doctrine by a comparison with Scripture testimonies. According to their notions, to have branded any one at random with this opprobrious mark, is to have refuted him without any trouble, by a single word. By the simple imputation of the name of heretic, they think that they have despatched their man at one blow. To men of this kind I answer, that in the time of the apostles, ere the New Testament was written, whenever the charge of heresy was applied as a term of reproach, that alone was considered as heresy which was at variance with their doctrine orally delivered, and that those only were looked upon as heretics, who according to Rom. xvi. 17, 18. "caused divisions and offenses contrary to the doctrine" of the apostles, "serving not our Lord Jesus Christ, but their own belly." By parity of reasoning therefore, since the compilation of the New Testament, I maintain that nothing but what is in contradiction to it can properly be called heresy.

For my own part, I adhere to the Holy Scriptures alone; I follow no other heresy or sect. I had not even read any of the works of heretics, so called, when the mistakes of those who are reckoned for orthodox, and their incautious handling of Scripture, first taught me to agree with their opponents whenever those opponents agreed with Scripture. If this be heresy, I confess with St. Paul, Acts xxiv. 14. "that after the way which they call heresy, so worship I the God of my fathers, believing all things which are written in the law and the prophets"; to which I add, whatever is written in the New Testament. Any other judges or paramount interpreters of the Christian belief, together with all implicit faith, as it is called, I, in common with the whole Protestant Church, refuse to recognize.

For the rest, brethren, cultivate truth with brotherly love. Judge of my present undertaking according to the admonishing of the Spirit of God, and neither adopt my sentiments, nor reject them, unless every doubt has been removed from your belief by the clear testimony of revelation. Finally, live in the faith of our Lord and Savior Jesus Christ. Farewell.

J.M.

Book I, Chapter II

OF GOD

[I. ii. A]

Though there be not a few who deny the existence of God, "for the fool hath said in his heart, There is no God," Psal. xiv. 1. yet the Deity has imprinted upon the human mind so many unquestionable tokens of himself, and so many traces of him are apparent throughout the whole of nature, that no one in his senses can remain ignorant of the truth. Job xii. 9. "who knoweth not in all these that the hand of Jehovah hath wrought this?" Psal. xix. 1. "the heavens declare the glory of God." Acts xiv. 17. "he left not himself without witness." xvii. 27, 28. "he is not far from every one of us." Rom. i. 19, 20. "that which may be known of God is manifest in them." and ii. 14, 15. "the Gentiles . . . show the work of the law written in their hearts, their conscience also bearing witness." 1 Cor. i. 21. "after that in the wisdom of God, the world by wisdom knew not God, it pleased God by the foolishness of preaching to save them that believe." There can be no doubt that every thing in the world, by the beauty of its order, and the evidence of a determinate and beneficial purpose which pervades it, testifies that some supreme efficient Power must have preexisted, by which the whole was ordained for a specific end.

There are some who pretend that nature or fate is this supreme Power: but the very name of nature implies that it must owe its birth to some prior agent, or, to speak properly, signifies in itself nothing; but means either the essence of a thing, or that general law which is the origin of every thing, and under which every thing acts; on the other hand, fate can be nothing but a divine decree emanating from some almighty power.

Further, those who attribute the creation of every thing to nature, must necessarily associate chance with nature as a joint divinity; so that they gain nothing by this theory, except that in the place of that one God, whom they cannot tolerate, they are obliged, however reluctantly, to substitute two sovereign rulers of affairs, who must almost always be in opposition to each other. In short, many visible proofs, the verification of numberless predictions, a multitude of wonderful works have compelled all nations to believe, either that God, or that some evil power whose name was unknown, presided over the affairs of the world. Now that evil should prevail over good, and be the true supreme power, is as unmeet as it is incredible. Hence it follows as a necessary consequence, that God exists.

Again: the existence of God is further proved by that feeling, whether we term it conscience, or right reason, which even in the worst of characters is not altogether extinguished. If there were no God, there would be no distinction between right and wrong; the estimate of virtue and vice would entirely depend on the blind opinion of men; none would follow virtue, none would be restrained from vice by any sense of shame, or fear of the laws, unless conscience or right reason did from time to time convince every one, however unwilling, of the existence of God, the Lord and ruler of all things, to whom, sooner or later, each must give an account of his own actions, whether good or bad.

* * *

[I. ii. B]

Our safest way is to form in our minds such a conception of God, as shall correspond with his own delineation and representation of himself in the sacred writings. For granting that both in the literal and figurative descriptions of God, he is exhibted not as he really is, but in such a manner as may be within the scope of our comprehensions, yet we ought to entertain such a conception of him, as he, in condescending to accommodate himself to our capacities, has shown that he desires we should conceive. For it is on this very account that he has lowered himself to our level, lest in our flights above the reach of human understanding, and beyond the written word of Scripture, we should be tempted to indulge in vague cogitations and subtleties.

There is no need then that theologians should have recourse here to what they call anthropopathy, a figure invented by the grammarians to excuse the absurdities of the poets on the subject of the heathen divinities. We may be sure that sufficient care has been taken that the Holy Scriptures should contain nothing unsuitable to the character or dignity of God, and that God should say nothing of himself which could derogate from his own majesty. It is better therefore to contemplate the Deity, and to conceive of him, not with reference to human passions, that is, after the manner of men, who are never weary of forming subtle imaginations respecting him, but after the manner of Scripture, that is, in the way wherein God has offered himself to our contemplation; nor should we think that he would say or direct anything to be written of himself, which is inconsistent with the opinion he wishes us to entertain of his character. Let us require no better authority than God himself for determining what is worthy or unworthy of him. If "it repented Jehovah that he had made man," Gen. vi. 6. and "because of their groanings," Judges ii. 18. let us believe that it did repent him, only taking care to remember that what is called repentance when applied to God, does not arise from inadvertency, as in men; for so he has himself cautioned us, Num. xxiii. 19. "God is not a man that he should lie, neither the son of man that he should repent." * * * If God be said "to have made man in his own image, after his likeness," Gen. i. 26. and that too not only as to his soul, but also as to his outward form (unless the same words have different significations here and in chap. v. 3. "Adam begat a son in his own likeness, after his image") and if God habitually assign to himself the members and form of man, why should we be afraid of attributing to him what he attributes to himself, so long as what is imperfection and weakness when viewed in reference to ourselves be considered as most complete and excellent when imputed to God? Questionless the glory and majesty of the Deity must have been so dear to him, that he would never say anything of himself which could be humiliating or degrading, and would ascribe to himself no personal attributes which he would not willingly have ascribed to him by his creatures. Let us be convinced that those have acquired the truest apprehension of the nature of God who submit their understandings to his word; considering that he has accommodated his word to their understandings, and has shown what he wishes their notion of the Deity should be.

Chapter III

DECREES OF THE DIVINE

* * *

[I. iii]

Hence it is absurd to separate the decrees or will of the Deity from his eternal counsel and foreknowledge, or to give them priority of order. For the foreknowledge of God is nothing but the wisdom of God, under another name, or that idea of every thing, which he had in his mind, to use the language of men, before he decreed anything.

We must conclude, therefore, that God decreed nothing absolutely, which he left in the power of free agents, a doctrine which is shown by the whole canon of Scripture.

*   *   *

It follows, therefore, that the liberty of man must be considered entirely independent of necessity, nor can any admission be made in favor of that modification of the principle which is founded on the doctrine of God's immutability and prescience. If there be any necessity at all, as has been stated before, it either determines free agents to a particular line of conduct, or it constrains them against their will, or it cooperates with them in conjunction with their will, or it is altogether inoperative. If it determine free agents to a particular line of conduct, man will be rendered the natural cause of all his actions, and consequently of his sins, and formed as it were with an inclination for sinning. If it constrain them against their will, man being subject to this compulsory decree becomes the cause of sins only *per accidens*, God being the cause of sins *per se*. If it co-operate with them in conjunction with their will, then God becomes either the principal or the joint cause of sins with man. If finally it be altogether inoperative, there is no such thing as necessity, it virtually destroys itself by being without operation. For it is wholly impossible, that God should have fixed by a necessary decree what we know at the same time to be in the power of man; or that that should be immutable which it remains for subsequent contingent circumstances either to fulfil or frustrate.

Whatever, therefore, was left to the free will of our first parents, could not have been decreed immutably or absolutely from all eternity; and questionless, the Deity must either have never left anything in the power of man, or he cannot be said to have determined finally respecting whatever was so left without reference to possible contingencies.

*   *   *

Seeing, therefore, that in assigning the gift of free will God suffered both men and angels to stand or fall at their own uncontrolled choice, there can be no doubt that the decree itself bore a strict analogy to the object which the divine counsel regarded, not necessitating the evil consequences which ensued, but leaving them contingent; hence the covenant was of this kind: If thou stand, thou shalt abide in Paradise; if thou fall, thou shalt be cast out; if thou eat not the forbidden fruit, thou shalt live; if thou eat, thou shalt die.

Hence, those who contend that the liberty of actions is subject to an absolute decree, erroneously conclude that the decree of God is the cause of his foreknowledge, and antecedent in order of time. If we must apply to God a phraseology borrowed from our own habits and understanding, to consider his decrees as consequent upon his foreknowledge seems more agreeable to reason, as well as to Scripture, and to the nature of the Deity himself, who, as has just been proved, decreed every thing according to his infinite wisdom by virtue of his foreknowledge.

* * *

To comprehend the whole matter in a few words, the sum of the argument may be thus stated in strict conformity with reason. God of his wisdom determined to create men and angels reasonable beings, and therefore free agents; foreseeing at the same time which way the bias of their will would incline, in the exercise of their own uncontrolled liberty. What then? shall we say that this foresight or foreknowledge on the part of God imposed on them the necessity of acting in any definite way? No more than if the future event had been foreseen by any human being. For what any human being has foreseen as certain to happen, will not less certainly happen than what God himself has predicted. Thus Elisha foresaw how much evil Hazael would bring upon the children of Israel in the course of a few years, 2 Kings viii. 12. Yet no one would affirm that the evil took place necessarily on account of the foreknowledge of Elisha; for had he never foreknown it, the event would have occurred with equal certainty, through the free will of the agent. In like manner nothing happens of necessity because God has foreseen it; but he foresees the event of every action, because he is acquainted with their natural causes, which, in pursuance of his own decree, are left at liberty to exert their legitimate influence. Consequently the issue does not depend on God who foresees it, but on him alone who is the object of his foresight. Since therefore, as has before been shown, there can be no absolute decree of God regarding free agents, undoubtedly the prescience of the Deity (which can no more bias free agents than the prescience of man, that is, not at all, since the action in both cases is intransitive, and has no external influence) can neither impose any necessity of itself, nor can it be considered at all as the cause of free actions. If it be so considered, the very name of liberty must be altogether abolished as an unmeaning sound; and that not only in matters of religion, but even in questions of morality and indifferent things. There can be nothing but what will happen necessarily, since there is nothing but what is foreknown by God.

* * *

From what has been said it is sufficiently evident, that free causes are not impeded by any law of necessity arising from the decree or prescience of God. There are some who in their zeal to oppose this doctrine, do not hesitate even to assert that God is himself the cause and origin of sin. Such men, if they are not to be looked upon as misguided rather than mischievous, should be ranked among the most abandoned of all blasphemers. An attempt to refute them, would be nothing more than an argument to prove that God was not the evil spirit.

Chapter IV

OF PREDESTINATION

[I. iv]

THE principal SPECIAL DECREE of God RELATING TO MAN is termed PREDESTINATION, whereby GOD IN PITY TO MANKIND, THOUGH FORESEEING THAT THEY WOULD FALL OF THEIR OWN AC-CORD, PREDESTINATED TO ETERNAL SALVATION BEFORE THE FOUNDA-TION OF THE WORLD THOSE WHO SHOULD BELIEVE AND CONTINUE IN THE FAITH; FOR A MANIFESTATION OF THE GLORY OF HIS MERCY, GRACE, AND WISDOM, ACCORDING TO HIS PURPOSE IN CHRIST.

It has been the practice of the schools to use the word predestination, not only in the sense of election, but also of reprobation. This is not consistent with the caution necessary on so momentous a subject, since wherever it is mentioned in Scripture, election alone is uniformly intended. * * * Hence it seems that the generality of commentators are wrong in interpreting the foreknowledge of God in these passages in the sense of prescience; since the prescience of God seems to have no connection with the principle or essence of predestination; for God has predestinated and elected whoever believes and continues in the faith. Of what consequence is it to us to know whether the prescience of God foresees who will, or will not, subsequently believe? for no one believes because God has foreseen his belief, but God foresees his belief because he was about to believe. Nor is it easy to understand how the prescience or foreknowledge of God with regard to particular persons can be brought to bear at all upon the doctrine of predestination, except for the purpose of raising a number of useless and utterly inapplicable questions. For why should God foreknow particular individuals, or what could he foreknow in them which should induce him to predestinate them in particular, rather than all in general, when the condition of faith, which was common to all mankind, had been once laid down. Without searching deeper into this subject, let us be contented to know nothing more than that God, out of his infinite mercy and grace in Christ, has predestinated to salvation all who should believe.

Chapter V

OF THE SON OF GOD

[I. v]

*   *   *

All these passages prove the existence of the Son before the world was made, but they conclude nothing respecting his generation from all eternity. The other texts which are produced relate only to his metaphorical generation, that is, to his resuscitation from the dead, or to his unction to the mediatorial office, according to St. Paul's own interpretation of the second Psalm: "I will declare the decree; Jehovah hath said unto me, Thou are my Son; this day have I begotten thee," which the apostle thus explains, Acts xiii. 32, 33. "God hath fulfilled the promise unto us their children, in that he hath raised up Jesus again; as it is also written in the second Psalm, Thou art my Son; this day have I begotten thee."

*   *   *

It is evident however upon a careful comparison and examination of all these passages, and particularly from the whole of the second Psalm, that however the generation of the Son may have taken place, it arose from no natural necessity, as is generally contended, but was no less owing to the decree and will of the Father than his priesthood or kingly power, or his resuscitation from the dead. Nor is it any objection to this that he bears the title of begotten, in whatever sense that expression is to be understood, or of God's *own Son*, Rom. viii. 32. For he is called the own Son of God merely because he had no other Father besides God, whence he himself said, that *God was his Father*, John v. 18. For to Adam God stood less in the relation of Father, than of Creator, having only formed him from the dust of the earth; whereas he was properly the Father of the Son made of his own substance. Yet it does not follow from hence that the Son is co-essential with the Father, for then the title of Son would be least of all applicable to him, since he who is properly the Son is not coeval with the Father, much less of the same numerical essence, otherwise the Father and the Son would be one person; nor did the Father beget him from any natural necessity, but of his own free will, a mode more perfect and more agreeable to the paternal dignity; particularly since the Father is God, all whose works, and consequently the works of generation, are executed freely according to his own good pleasure, as has been already proved from Scripture.

For questionless, it was in God's power consistently with the perfection of his own essence not to have begotten the Son, inasmuch as generation does not pertain to the nature of the Deity, who stands in no need of propagation; but whatever does not pertain to his own essence or nature, he does not effect like a natural agent from any physical necessity. If the generation of the Son proceeded from a physical necessity, the Father impaired himself by physically begetting a co-equal; which God could no more do than he could deny himself; therefore the generation of the Son cannot have proceeded otherwise than from a decree, and of the Father's own free will.

Chapter VII

OF THE CREATION

[I. vii. A]

The second species of external efficiency is commonly called CREATION. As to the actions of God before the foundation of the world, it would be the height of folly to inquire into them, and almost equally so to attempt a solution of the question. With regard to the account which is generally given from 1 Cor. ii. 7. "he ordained his wisdom in a mystery, even the hidden mystery which God ordained before the world"—or, as it is explained, that he was occupied with election and reprobation, and with decreeing other things relative to these subjects—it is not imaginable that God should have been wholly occupied from eternity in decreeing that which was to be created in a period of six days, and which, after having been governed in divers manners for a few thousand years, was finally to be received into an immutable state with himself, or to be rejected from his presence for all eternity.

That the world was created, is an article of faith: Heb. xi. 3. "through faith we understand that the worlds were framed by the word of God."

CREATION is that act whereby GOD THE FATHER PRODUCED EVERY THING THAT EXISTS BY HIS WORD AND SPIRIT, that is, BY HIS WILL, FOR THE MANIFESTATION OF THE GLORY OF HIS POWER AND GOODNESS.

* * *

[I. vii. B]

Thus far it has appeared that God the Father is the primary and efficient cause of things. With regard to the original matter of the universe, however, there has been much difference of opinion. Most of the moderns contend that it was formed from nothing, a basis as unsubstantial as that of their own theory. In the first place, it is certain that neither the Hebrew בָּרָא nor the Greek κτίζειν, nor the Latin *creare*, can signify to create out of nothing. On the contrary, these words uniformly signify to create out of matter. Gen. i. 21, 27. "God created . . . every living creature which the waters brought forth abundantly . . . male and female created he them." Isa. liv. 16. "behold, I have created the smith . . . I have created the waster to destroy." To allege, therefore, that creation signifies production out of nothing, is, as logicians say, to lay down premises without a proof; for the passages of Scripture commonly quoted for this purpose, are so far from confirming the received opinion, that they rather imply the contrary; namely, that all things were not made out of nothing. 2 Cor. iv. 6. "God, who commanded the light to shine out of darkness." That this darkness was far from being a mere negation, is clear from Isa. xlv. 7. "I am Jehovah; I form the light, and create darkness." If the darkness be nothing, God in creating darkness created nothing, or in other words, he created and did not create, which is a contradiction. Again, what we are required "to understand through faith" respecting "the worlds," is merely this, that "the things which were seen were not made of things which do appear." Heb. xi. 3. Now "the things which do not appear" are not to be considered as synonymous with nothing, for nothing does not admit of a plural, nor can a thing be made and compacted together out of nothing, as out of a number of things, but the meaning is, that they do not appear as they now are. The apocryphal writers, whose authority may be considered as next to that of the Scriptures, speak to the same effect. Wisd. xi. 17. "thy almighty hand that made the world of matter without form." 2 Macc. vii. 28. "God made the earth and all that is therein of things that were not." The expression in Matt. ii. 18. may be quoted, "the children of Rachel are not." This, however, does not mean properly that they are nothing, but that, according to a common Hebraism, they are no longer among the living.

It is clear then that the world was framed out of matter of some kind or other. For since action and passion are relative terms, and since, consequently, no agent can act externally, unless there be some patient, such as matter, it appears impossible that God could have created this world out of nothing; not from any defect of power on his part, but because it was necessary that something should have previously existed capable of receiving passively the exertion of the divine efficacy. Since, therefore, both Scripture and reason concur in pronouncing that all these things were made, not out of nothing, but out of matter, it necessarily follows, that matter must either have always existed independently of God, or have originated from God at some particular point of time. That matter should have been always independent of God, seeing that it is only a passive principle, dependent on the Deity, and subservient to him; and seeing, moreover, that, as in number, considered abstractedly, so also in time or eternity there is no inherent force or efficacy; that matter, I say, should have existed of itself from all eternity, is inconceivable. If on the contrary it did not exist from all eternity, it is difficult to understand from whence it derives its origin. There remains, therefore, but one solution of the difficulty, for which moreover we have the authority of Scripture, namely, that all things are of God. Rom. xi. 36. "for of him, and through him, and to him are all things." 1 Cor. viii. 6. "there is but one God, the Father, of whom are all things": where the same Greek preposition is used in both cases. Heb. ii. 11. "for both he that sanctifieth, and they who are sanctified, are all of one."

* * *

[I. vii. C]

Those who are dissatisfied because, according to this view, substance was imperfect, must also be dissatisfied with God for having originally produced it out of nothing in an imperfect state, and without form. For what difference does it make, whether God produced it in this imperfect state out of nothing, or out of himself? By this reasoning, they only transfer that imperfection to the divine efficiency, which they are unwilling to admit can properly be attributed to substance considered as an efflux of the Deity. For why did not God create all things out of nothing in an absolutely perfect state at first? It is not true, however, that matter was in its own nature originally imperfect; it merely received embellishment from the accession of forms, which are themselves material. And if it be asked how what is corruptible can proceed from incorruption, it may be asked in return how the virtue and efficacy of God can proceed out of nothing. Matter, like the form and nature of the angels itself, proceeded incorruptible from God; and even since the fall it remains incorruptible as far as concerns its essence.

But the same, or even a greater difficulty still remains, how that which is in its nature peccable can have proceeded (if I may so speak) from God? I ask in reply, how anything peccable can have originated from the virtue and efficacy which proceeded from God? Strictly speaking indeed it is neither matter nor form that sins; and yet having proceeded from God, and become in the power of another party, what is there to prevent them, inasmuch as they have now become mutable, from contracting taint and contamination through the enticements of the devil, or those which originate in man himself? It is objected, however, that body cannot emanate from spirit. I reply, much less then can body emanate from nothing. For spirit being the more excellent substance, virtually and essentially contains within itself the inferior one; as the spiritual and rational faculty contains the corporeal, that is, the sentient and vegetative faculty. For not even divine virtue and efficiency could produce bodies out of nothing, according to the commonly received opinion, unless there had been some bodily power in the substance of God; since no one can give to another what he does not himself possess. Nor did St. Paul hesitate to attribute to God something corporeal; Col. ii. 9. "in him dwelleth all the fulness of the Godhead bodily." Neither is it more incredible that a bodily power should issue from a spiritual substance, than that what is spiritual should arise from body; which nevertheless we believe will be the case with our own bodies at the resurrection. Nor, lastly, can it be understood in what sense God can properly be called infinite, if he be capable of receiving any accession whatever; which would be the case if anything could exist in the nature of things, which had not first been of God and in God.

* * *

[I. vii. D]

Creation is either of things invisible or visible.

The things invisible, or which are at least such to us, are, the highest heaven, which is the throne and habitation of God, and the heavenly powers, or angels.

Such is the division of the apostle, Col. i. 16. The first place is due to things invisible, if not in respect of origin, at least of dignity. For the highest heaven is as it were the supreme citadel and habitation of God. See Deut. xxvi. 15. I Kings viii. 27, 30. "heaven of heavens." Neh. ix. 6. Isa. lxiii. 15. "far above all heavens," Eph. iv. 10. where God "dwelleth in the light which no man can approach unto." 1 Tim. vi. 16. Out of this light it appears that pleasures and glories, and a kind of perpetual heaven, have emanated and subsist. Psal. xvi. 11. "at thy right hand there are pleasures for evermore." Isa. lvii. 15. "the high and lofty one that inhabiteth eternity, whose name is Holy; I dwell in the high and holy place."

It is improbable that God should have formed to himself such an abode for his majesty only at so recent a period as at the beginning of the world. For if there be any one habitation of God, where he diffuses in an eminent manner the glory and brightness of his majesty, why should it be thought that its foundations are only coeval with the fabric of this world, and not of much more ancient origin? At the same time it does not follow that heaven should be eternal, nor, if eternal, that it should be God; for it was always in the power of God to produce any effect he pleased at whatever time and in whatever manner seemed good to him. We cannot form any conception of light independent of a luminary; but we do not therefore infer that a luminary is the same as light, or equal in dignity. In the same manner we do not think that what are called "the back parts" of God, Exod. xxxiii. are, properly speaking, God; though we nevertheless consider them to be eternal. It seems more reasonable to conceive in the same manner of the heaven of heavens, the throne and habitation of God, than to imagine that God should have been without a heaven till the first of the six days of creation. At the same time I give this opinion, not as venturing to determine anything certain on such a subject, but rather with a view of showing that others have been too bold in affirming that the invisible and highest heaven was made on the first day, contemporaneously with that heaven which is within our sight. For since it was of the latter heaven alone, and of the visible world, that Moses undertook to write, it would have been foreign to his purpose to have said anything of what was above the world.

*   *   *

[I. vii. E]

It is generally supposed that the angels were created at the same time with the visible universe, and that they are to be considered as comprehended under the general name of "heavens." That the angels were created at some particular period, we have the testimony of Num. xvi. 22. and xxvii. 16. "God of the spirits," Heb. i. 7. Col. i. 16. "by him were all things created . . . visible and invisible, whether they be thrones," &c. But that they were created on the first, or on any one of the six days, seems to be asserted (like most received opinions) with more confidence than reason, chiefly on the authority of the repetition in Gen. ii. 1. "thus the heavens and the earth were finished, and all the host of them," unless we are to suppose that more was meant to be implied in the concluding summary than in the previous narration itself, and that the angels are to be considered as the host who inhabit the visible heavens. For when it is said Job xxxviii. 7. that they shouted for joy before God at the creation, it proves rather that they were then already in existence, than that they were then first created. Many at least of the Greek, and some of the Latin Fathers, are of opinion that angels, as being spirits, must have existed long before the material world; and it seems even probable, that the apostasy which caused the expulsion of so many thousands from heaven, took place before the foundations of this world were laid. Certainly there is no sufficient foundation for the common opinion, that motion and time (which is the measure of motion) could not, according to the ratio of priority and subsequence, have existed before this world was made; since Aristotle, who teaches that no ideas of motion and time can be formed except in reference to this world, nevertheless pronounces the world itself to be eternal.

*   *   *

[I. vii. F]

We may understand from other passages of Scripture, that when God infused the breath of life into man, what man thereby received was not a portion of God's essence, or a participation of the divine nature, but that measure of the divine virtue or influence, which was commensurate to the capabilities of the recipient. For it appears from Psal. civ. 29, 30. that he infused the breath of life into other living beings also: "thou takest away their breath, they die . . . thou sendest forth thy spirit, they are created"; whence we learn that every living thing receives animation from one and the same source of life and breath; inasmuch as when God takes back to himself that spirit or breath of life, they cease to exist. Eccles. iii. 19. "they have all one breath." Nor has the word "spirit" any other meaning in the sacred writings, but that breath of life which we inspire, or the vital, or sensitive, or rational faculty, or some action or affection belonging to those faculties.

Man having been created after this manner, it is said, as a consequence, that "man became a living soul"; whence it may be inferred (unless we had rather take the heathen writers for our teachers respecting the nature of the soul) that man is a living being, intrinsically and properly one and individual, not compound or separable, not, according to the common opinion, made up and framed of two distinct and different natures, as of soul and body, but that the whole man is soul, and the soul man, that is to say, a body, or substance individual, animated, sensitive, and rational; and that the breath of life was neither a part of the divine essence, nor the soul itself, but as it were an inspiration of some divine virtue fitted for the exercise of life and reason, and infused into the organic body; for man himself, the whole man, when finally created, is called in express terms "a living soul." Hence the word used in Genesis to signify "soul," is interpreted by the apostle, 1 Cor. xv. 45. "animal." Again, all the attributes of the body are assigned in common to the soul: the touch, Lev. v. 2, &c. "if a soul touch any unclean thing,"—the act of eating, vii. 18. "the soul that eateth of it shall bear his iniquity"; v. 20. "the soul that eateth of the flesh," and in other places:—hunger, Prov. xiii. 25. xxvii. 7.—thirst, xxv. 25. "as cold waters to a thirsty soul." Isa. xxix. 8.—capture, 1 Sam. xxiv. 11. "thou huntest my soul to take it." Psal. vii. 5. "let the enemy persecute my soul, and take it."

Where however we speak of the body as of a mere senseless stock, there the soul must be understood as signifying either the spirit, or its secondary faculties, the vital or sensitive faculty for instance. Thus it is as often distinguished from the spirit, as from the body itself. Luke i. 46, 47. 1 Thess. v. 23. "your whole spirit and soul and body." Heb. iv. 12. "to the dividing asunder of soul and spirit." But that the spirit of man should be separate from the body, so as to have a perfect and intelligent existence independently of it, is nowhere said in Scripture, and the doctrine is evidently at variance both with nature and reason, as will be shown more fully hereafter.

For the word "soul" is also applied to every kind of living being; Gen. i. 30. "to every beast of the earth," &c. "wherein there is life." vii. 22. "all in whose nostrils was the breath of life, of all that was in the dry land, died"; yet it is never inferred from these expressions that the soul exists separate from the body in any of the brute creation.

*   *   *

Man being formed after the image of God, it followed as a necessary consequence that he should be endued with natural wisdom, holiness, and righteousness. Gen. i. 27, 31. ii. 25. Eccles. vii. 29. Eph. iv. 24. Col. iii. 10. 2 Cor. iii. 18. Certainly without extraordinary wisdom he could not have given names to the whole animal creation with such sudden intelligence, Gen. ii. 20.

Chapter VIII

OF THE PROVIDENCE OF GOD, OR OF HIS GENERAL
GOVERNMENT OF THE UNIVERSE

*   *   *

[I. viii. A]

If, inasmuch as I do not address myself to such as are wholly ignorant, but to those who are already competently acquainted with the outlines of Christian doctrine, I may be permitted, in discoursing on the general providence of God, so far to anticipate the natural order of arrangement, as to make an allusion to a subject which belongs properly to another part of my treatise, that of sin, I might remark, that even in the matter of sin God's providence finds its exercise, not only in permitting its existence, or in withdrawing his grace, but also in impelling sinners to the commission of sin, in hardening their hearts, and in blinding their understandings.

*   *   *

[I. viii. B]

But though in these, as well as in many other passages of the Old and New Testament, God distinctly declares that it is himself who impels the sinner to sin, who hardens his heart, who blinds his understanding, and leads him into error; yet on account of the infinite holiness of the Deity, it is not allowable to consider him as in the smallest instance the author of sin. * * * For it is not the human heart in a state of innocence and purity, and repugnance to evil, that is induced by him to act wickedly and deceitfully; but after it has conceived sin, and when it is about to bring forth, he, in his character of sovereign disposer of all things, inclines and biases

it in this or that direction, or towards this or that object. * * *
Nor does God make that will evil which was before good, but the
will being already in a state of perversion, he influences it in such a
manner, that out of its own wickedness it either operates good for
others, or punishment for itself, though unknowingly, and with the
intent of producing a very different result. Prov. xvi. 9. "a man's
heart deviseth his way, but Jehovah directeth his steps." Thus Ezek.
xxi. 21, 22. when the king of Babylon stood at the parting of the
way in doubt whether he should go to war against the Ammonites
or against the Jews, God so ordered the divination, as to determine
him on going against Jerusalem. Or, to use the common simile, as a
rider who urges on a stumbling horse in a particular direction is the
cause of its increasing its speed, but not of its stumbling, so God,
who is the supreme governor of the universe, may instigate an evil
agent, without being in the least degree the cause of the evil. I shall
recur again to this simile hereafter. For example, God saw that the
mind of David was so elated and puffed up by the increase of his
power, that even without any external impulse he was on the point
of giving some remarkable token of his pride; he therefore excited
in him the desire of numbering the people: he did not inspire him
with the passion of vain glory, but impelled him to display in this
manner, rather than in any other, that latent arrogance of his heart
which was ready to break forth. God therefore was the author of
the act itself, but David alone was responsible for its pride and
wickedness. Further, the end which a sinner has in view is generally
something evil and unjust, from which God uniformly educes a
good and just result, thus as it were creating light out of darkness.
By this means he proves the inmost intentions of men, that is, he
makes man to have a thorough insight into the latent wickedness of
his own heart, that he may either be induced thereby to forsake his
sins, or if not, that he may become notorious and inexcusable in
the sight of all; or lastly, to the end that both the author and the
sufferer of the evil may be punished for some former transgression.
At the same time, the common maxim, that God makes sin sub-
servient to the punishment of sin, must be received with caution;
for the Deity does not effect his purpose by compelling any one to
commit crime, or by abetting him in it, but by withdrawing the
ordinary grace of his enlightening spirit, and ceasing to strengthen
him against sin. There is indeed a proverb which says, that he who
is able to forbid an action, and forbids it not, virtually commands
it. This maxim is indeed binding on man, as a moral precept; but it
is otherwise with regard to God. When, in conformity with the
language of mankind, he is spoken of as instigating, where he only
does not prohibit evil, it does not follow that he therefore bids it,
inasmuch as there is no obligation by which he is bound to forbid
it. Psal. lxxxi. 11, 12. "my people would not hearken to my voice,

and Israel would none of me: so I gave them up unto their own hearts' lust, and they walked in their own counsels." Hence it is said, Rom. i. 24. "wherefore God also gave them up to uncleanness"; that is, he left them to be actuated by their own lusts, to walk in them; for properly speaking God does not instigate, or give up, him whom he leaves entirely to himself, that is, to his own desires and counsels, and to the suggestions of his ever active spiritual enemy.

* * *

[I. viii. C]

To this view of providence must be referred what is called temptation, whereby God either tempts men, or permits them to be tempted by the devil or his agents.

Temptation is either for evil or for good.

An evil temptation is when God, as above described, either withdraws his grace, or presents occasions of sin, or hardens the heart, or blinds the understanding. This is generally an evil temptation in respect of him who is tempted, but most equitable on the part of the Deity, for the reasons above mentioned. It also serves the purpose of unmasking hypocrisy; for God tempts no one in the sense of enticing or persuading to sin (see James i. 13. as above), though there be some towards whom he deservedly permits the devil to employ such temptations. We are taught in the Lord's prayer to deprecate temptations of this kind; Matt. vi. 13. "lead us not into temptation, but deliver us from evil."

A good temptation is that whereby God tempts even the righteous for the purpose of proving them, not as though he were ignorant of the disposition of their hearts, but for the purpose of exercising or manifesting their faith or patience, as in the case of Abraham and Job; or of lessening their self-confidence, and reproving their weakness, that both they themselves may become wiser by experience, and others may profit by their example: as in the case of Hezekiah. 2 Chron. xxxii. 31. whom "God left"—partially, or for a time—"to try him, that he might know all that was in his heart." He tempted the Israelites in the wilderness with the same view. Deut. viii. 2. "to humble thee, and to prove thee, to know what was in thine heart, whether thou wouldest keep his commandments or no." Psal. lxvi. 10. "thou, O God, hast proved us, thou hast tried us as silver is tried." 1 Pet. i. 7. "that the trial of your faith . . . might be found unto praise." iv. 12. "beloved, think it not strange concerning the fiery trial which is to try you, as though some strange thing happened unto you." Rev. ii. 10. "behold, the devil shall cast some of you into prison, that ye may be tried."

This kind of temptation is therefore rather to be desired. * * *
God also promises a happy issue. 1 Cor. x. 13. "there hath no

temptation taken you but such as is common to man: but God is faithful, who will not suffer you to be tempted above that ye are able, but will with the temptation also make a way to escape, that ye may be able to bear it." James i. 12. "blessed is the man that endureth temptation; for when he is tried, he shall receive the crown of life."

Yet even believers are not always sufficiently observant of these various operations of divine providence, until they are led to investigate the subject more deeply, and become more intimately conversant with the word of God. Psal. lxxiii. 2, 17. "my feet were almost gone . . . until I went into the sanctuary of God: then understood I their end." Dan. xii. 10. "many shall be purified, and made white, and tried; but the wicked shall do wickedly: and none of the wicked shall understand, but the wise shall understand."

Chapter IX

OF THE SPECIAL GOVERNMENT OF ANGELS

* * *

[I. ix. A]

Angels are either good or evil, Luke ix. 26. viii. 2. for it appears that many of them revolted from God of their own accord before the fall of man. John viii. 44. "he abode not in the truth, because there is no truth in him: when he speaketh a lie, he speaketh of his own, for he is a liar and the father of it." 2 Pet. ii. 4. "God spared not the angels that sinned." Jude 6. "the angels which kept not their first estate." 1 John iii. 8. "the devil sinneth from the beginning." Psal. cvi. 37. "they sacrificed unto devils."

Some are of opinion that the good angels are now upheld, not so much by their own strength, as by the grace of God. 1 Tim. v. 21. "the elect angels," that is, who have not revolted. Eph. i. 10. "that he might gather together in one all things in Christ, both which are in heaven and which are on earth." Job iv. 18. "his angels he charged with folly." See also xv. 15. Hence arises, in their opinion, the delighted interest which the angels take in the mystery of man's salvation; 1 Pet. i. 12. "which things the angels desire to look into." Eph. iii. 10. "that now unto the principalities and powers in heavenly places might be known by the church the manifold wisdom of God." Luke ii. 13, 14. "a multitude of the heavenly host praising God," namely, on account of the birth of Christ. xv. 10. "there is joy in the presence of the angels of God over one sinner that repenteth." They assign the same reason for their worshipping Christ. Heb. i. 6. "let all the angels of God worship him." Matt. iv.

11. "angels came and ministered unto him." Philipp. ii. 10. "at the name of Jesus every knee should bow, of things in heaven—." 2 Thess. i. 7. "the Lord Jesus shall be revealed from heaven with his mighty angels." 1 Pet. iii. 22. "angels being made subject unto him." Rev. v. 11, 12. "worthy is the Lamb that was slain." It seems, however, more agreeable to reason, to suppose that the good angels are upheld by their own strength no less than man himself was before his fall; that they are called "elect," in the sense of beloved, or excellent; that it is not from any interest of their own, but from their love to mankind, that they desire to look into the mystery of our salvation; that they are not comprehended in the covenant of reconciliation; that, finally, they are included under Christ as their head, not as their Redeemer.

For the rest, they are represented as standing dispersed around the throne of God in the capacity of ministering agents. * * * Praising God. * * *

They are obedient to God in all respects. * * *

Their ministry relates especially to believers. * * *

Seven of these, in particular, are described as traversing the earth in the execution of their ministry. Zech. iv. 10. "those seven are the eyes of Jehovah which run to and fro through the whole earth." Rev. v. 6. "which are the seven Spirits of God sent forth into all the earth." See also i. 4. and iv. 5.

It appears also probable that there are certain angels appointed to preside over nations, kingdoms, and particular districts. * * *

They are sometimes sent from heaven as messengers of the divine vengeance, to punish the sins of men. They destroy cities and nations. * * * Hence they are frequently represented as making their appearance in the shape of an armed host.

* * *

[I. ix. B]

There appears to be one who presides over the rest of the good angels, to whom the name of Michael is often given. Josh. vi. 14. "as captain of the host of Jehovah am I come." Dan. x. 13. "Michael, one of the chief princes, came to help me." xii. 1. "Michael shall stand up, the great prince." Rev. xii. 7, 8. "Michael and his angels fought against the dragon." It is generally thought that Michael is Christ. But Christ vanquished the devil, and trampled him under foot singly; Michael, the leader of the angels, is introduced in the capacity of a hostile commander waging war with the prince of the devils, the armies on both sides being drawn out in battle array, and separating after a doubtful conflict. * * *

The good angels do not look into all the secret things of God, as the Papists pretend; some things indeed they know by revelation, and others by means of the excellent intelligence with which they are gifted; there is much, however, of which they are ignorant. An angel is introduced inquiring Dan. viii. 13. "how long shall be the vision?" xii. 6. "how long shall it be to the end of these wonders?" Matt. xxiv. 36. "of that day knoweth no man, no not even the angels in heaven." Eph. iii. 10. "to the intent that now unto the principalities and powers in heavenly places might be known by the church the manifold wisdom of God." Rev. v. 3. "no man in heaven was able to open the book."

The evil angels are reserved for punishment. Matt. viii. 29. "art thou come hither to torment us before the time?" 2 Pet. ii. 4. "God cast them down to hell, and delivered them into chains of darkness, to be reserved unto judgment." Jude 6. "he hath reserved them in everlasting chains under darkness unto the judgment of the great day." 1 Cor. vi. 3. "know ye not that we shall judge angels?" Matt. xxv. 41. "everlasting fire, prepared for the devil and his angels." Rev. xx. 10. "they shall be tormented for ever and ever."

They are sometimes, however, permitted to wander throughout the whole earth, the air, and heaven itself, to execute the judgments of God. * * * They are even admitted into the presence of God. Job i. 6. ii. 1. 1 Kings xxii. 21. "there came forth a spirit, and stood before Jehovah." Zech. iii. 1. "he showed me Joshua the high priest standing before the angel of Jehovah, and Satan standing at his right hand to resist him." Luke x. 18. "I beheld Satan as lightning fall from heaven." Rev. xii. 12. "woe to the inhabitants of the earth, for the devil is come down unto you." Their proper place, however, is the bottomless pit, from which they cannot escape without permission. Luke viii. 31. "they besought him that he would not command them to go out into the deep." Matt. xii. 43. "he walketh through dry places, seeking rest, and findeth none." Mark v. 10. "he besought him much that he would not send them away out of the country." Rev. xx. 3. "and cast him into the bottomless pit, and shut him up." Nor can they do anything without the command of God. Job i. 12. "Jehovah said unto Satan, Behold, all that he hath is in thy power." * * *

Their knowledge is great, but such as tends rather to aggravate than diminish their misery; so that they utterly despair of their salvation. Matt. viii. 29. "what have we to do with thee, Jesus, thou Son of God? art thou come hither to torment us before the time?" See also Luke iv. 24. James ii. 19. "the devils believe and tremble," knowing that they are reserved for punishment, as has been shown.

The devils also have their prince. Matt. xii. 24. "Beelzebub, the prince of the devils." See also Luke xi. 15. Matt. xxv. 41. "the devil and his angels." Rev. xii. 9. "the great dragon was cast out . . . and his angels." They retain likewise their respective ranks. Col. ii. 15. "having spoiled principalities and powers." Eph. vi. 12. "against principalities, against powers." Their leader is the author of all

wickedness, and the opponent of all good. Job i. and ii. Zech. iii. 1.
"Satan." John viii. 44. "the father of lies." 1 Thess. ii. 18. "Satan
hindered us." Acts v. 3. "Satan hath filled thine heart." Rev. xx. 3,
8. "that he should deceive the nations no more." Eph. ii. 2. "the
spirit that now worketh in the children of disobedience." Hence he
has obtained many names corresponding to his actions. He is fre-
quently called "Satan," that is, an enemy or adversary. Job i. 6. 1
Chron. xxi. 1. "the great dragon, that old serpent, the devil," that
is, the false accuser, Rev. xii. 9. "the accuser of the brethren," v.
10. "the unclean spirit," Mat. xii. 43. "the tempter," iv. 3. "Abad-
don, Apollyon," that is, the destroyer, Rev. ix. 11. "a great red
dragon," xii. 3.

Chapter X

OF THE SPECIAL GOVERNMENT OF MAN BEFORE THE FALL, INCLUDING
THE INSTITUTIONS OF THE SABBATH AND OF MARRIAGE

[I. x. A]

The Providence of God as regards mankind, relates to man either
in his state of rectitude, or since his fall.

With regard to that which relates to man in his state of rectitude,
God, having placed him in the garden of Eden, and furnished him
with whatever was calculated to make life happy, commanded him,
as a test of his obedience, to refrain from eating of the single tree
of knowledge of good and evil, under penalty of death if he should
disregard the injunction. Gen. i. 28. "subdue the earth, and have
dominion—." ii. 15–17. "he put him into the garden of Eden . . .
of every tree in the garden thou mayest freely eat; but in the day
that thou eatest of the tree of the knowledge of good and evil, thou
shalt surely die."

This is sometimes called "the covenant of works," though it does
not appear from any passage of Scripture to have been either a
covenant, or of works. No works whatever were required of Adam;
a particular act only was forbidden. It was necessary that some-
thing should be forbidden or commanded as a test of fidelity, and
that an act in its own nature indifferent, in order that man's obedi-
ence might be thereby manifested. For since it was the disposition
of man to do what was right, as a being naturally good and holy, it
was not necessary that he should be bound by the obligation of a
covenant to perform that to which he was of himself inclined; nor
would he have given any proof of obedience by the performance of
works to which he was led by a natural impulse, independently of
the divine command. Not to mention, that no command, whether
proceeding from God or from a magistrate, can properly be called

a covenant, even where rewards and punishments are attached to it; but rather an exercise of jurisdiction.

The tree of knowledge of good and evil was not a sacrament, as it is generally called; for a sacrament is a thing to be used, not abstained from: but a pledge, as it were, and memorial of obedience.

It was called the tree of knowledge of good and evil from the event; for since Adam tasted it, we not only know evil, but we know good only by means of evil. For it is by evil that virtue is chiefly exercised, and shines with greater brightness.

* * *

[I. x. B]

Seeing, however, that man was made in the image of God, and had the whole law of nature so implanted and innate in him, that he needed no precept to enforce its observance, it follows, that if he received any additional commands, whether respecting the tree of knowledge, or the institution of marriage, these commands formed no part of the law of nature, which is sufficient of itself to teach whatever is agreeable to right reason, that is to say, whatever is intrinsically good. Such commands therefore must have been founded on what is called positive right, whereby God, or any one invested with lawful power, commands or forbids what is in itself neither good nor bad, and what therefore would not have been obligatory on any one, had there been no law to enjoin or prohibit it.

Chapter XI

OF THE FALL OF OUR FIRST PARENTS, AND OF SIN

[I. xi. A]

The Providence of God as regards the fall of man, is observable in the sin of man, and the misery consequent upon it, as well as in his restoration.

SIN, as defined by the apostle, is ἀνομία, or "the transgression of the law," 1 John iii. 4.

By the law is here meant, in the first place, that rule of conscience which is innate, and engraven upon the mind of man; secondly, the special command which proceeded out of the mouth of God (for the law written by Moses was long subsequent), Gen. ii. 17. "thou shalt not eat of it." Hence it is said, Rom. ii. 12. "as many as have sinned without law, shall also perish without law."

Sin is distinguished into THAT WHICH IS COMMON TO ALL MEN, and THE PERSONAL SIN OF EACH INDIVIDUAL.

THE SIN WHICH IS COMMON TO ALL MEN IS THAT WHICH OUR FIRST

PARENTS, AND IN THEM ALL THEIR POSTERITY COMMITTED, WHEN, CASTING OFF THEIR OBEDIENCE TO GOD, THEY TASTED THE FRUIT OF THE FORBIDDEN TREE.

OUR FIRST PARENTS. Gen. iii. 6. "the woman took of the fruit thereof, and did eat, and gave also unto her husband with her, and he did eat." Hence 1 Tim. ii. 14. "Adam was not deceived, but the woman being deceived, was in the transgression." This sin originated, first, in the instigation of the devil, as is clear from the narrative in Gen. iii. and from 1 John iii. 8. "he that committeth sin is of the devil, for the devil sinneth from the beginning." Secondly, in the liability to fall with which man was created, whereby he, as the devil had done before him, "abode not in the truth," John viii. 44. nor "kept his first estate, but left his own habitation," Jude 6. If the circumstances of this crime are duly considered, it will be acknowledged to have been a most heinous offense, and a transgression of the whole law. For what sin can be named, which was not included in this one act? It comprehended at once distrust in the divine veracity, and a proportionate credulity in the assurances of Satan; unbelief; ingratitude; disobedience; gluttony; in the man excessive uxoriousness, in the woman a want of proper regard for her husband, in both an insensibility to the welfare of their offspring, and that offspring the whole human race; parricide, theft, invasion of the rights of others, sacrilege, deceit, presumption in aspiring to divine attributes, fraud in the means employed to attain the object, pride, and arrogance.

* * *

[I. xi. B]

It is, however, a principle uniformly acted upon in the divine proceedings, and recognized by all nations and under all religions from the earliest period, that the penalty incurred by the violation of things sacred (and such was the tree of knowledge of good and evil) attaches not only to the criminal himself, but to the whole of his posterity, who thus become accursed and obnoxious to punishment. It was thus in the deluge, and in the destruction of Sodom; in the swallowing up of Korah, Num. xvi. 27–32. and in the punishment of Achan, Josh. vii. 24, 25. In the burning of Jericho the children suffered for the sins of their fathers, and even the cattle were devoted to the same slaughter with their masters, Josh. vi. 21. A like fate befell the posterity of Eli the priest, 1 Sam. ii. 31, 33, 36. and the house of Saul, 2 Sam. xxi. 1, &c. because their father had slain the Gibeonites.

God declares this to be the method of his justice, Exod. xx. 5. "visiting the iniquity of the fathers upon the children, unto the third and fourth generation of them that hate me." Num. xiv. 33. "your children shall wander in the wilderness forty years, and bear your whoredoms"; they themselves, however, not being guiltless. He himself explains the principle by which this justice is regulated, Lev. xxvi. 39. "they that are left of you shall pine away in their iniquity . . . and also in the iniquities of their fathers shall they pine away with them." 2 Kings xvii. 14. "they hardened their necks, like to the necks of their fathers." Ezek. xviii. 4. "behold, all souls are mine; as the soul of the father, so also the soul of the son is mine; the soul that sinneth it shall die." The difficulty is solved with respect to infants, by the consideration that all souls belong to God; that these, though guiltless of actual sin, were the offspring of sinful parents, and that God foresaw that, if suffered to live, they would grow up similar to their parents. With respect to others, it is obviated by the consideration, that no one perishes, except he himself sin. Thus Agag and his people were smitten for the crime of their fathers, four hundred years after their ancestors had lain wait for Israel in the way, when he came up out of Egypt, 1 Sam. xv. 2, 3. but at the same time they were themselves justly obnoxious to punishment for sins of their own, v. 33. So too Hoshea king of Israel was better than the kings that were before him, but having fallen into the idolatry of the Gentiles, he was punished at once for his own sins and for those of his fathers, by the loss of his kingdom.

*   *   *

[I. xi. C]

Subjects also are afflicted for the sins of their rulers; thus the whole of Egypt was smitten for the offence of Pharaoh.

*   *   *

We may add, that even just men have not thought it inconsistent with equity to visit offenses against themselves, not only on the offender, but on his posterity. Thus Noah scrupled not to pronounce the condemnation of Canaan for the wickedness of his father Ham, Gen. ix. 25.

This principle of divine justice in the infliction of piacular punishments was not unknown to other nations, nor was it ever by them accounted unjust. So Thucydides, Book I. "The murderers and their descendants are held to be accursed, and offenders against the Goddess." And Virgil, *Æneid* I.

> "Could not Pallas burn
> The Argives' fleet, and drown them in the deep,
> For one man's guilt?"

The same might be easily shown by a multitude of other Pagan testimonies and examples.

Again, the possessions and right of citizenship of one convicted of high treason, a crime between man and man, are forfeited, not only as respects himself, but all his posterity; and legal authorities decide similarly in other analogous cases. We all know what are the recognized rights of war, not only with regard to the immediate parties themselves, but all who fall into the power of the enemy, such as women and children, and those who have contributed nothing to the progress of the war either in will or deed.

*   *   *

Both kinds of sin, as well that which is common to all, as that which is personal to each individual, consist of the two following parts, whether we term them gradations, or divisions, or modes of sin, or whether we consider them in the light of cause and effect; namely, evil concupiscence, or the desire of sinning, and the act of sin itself. James i. 14, 15. "every man is tempted, when he is drawn away of his own lust, and enticed: then when lust hath conceived, it bringeth forth sin." This is not ill expressed by the poet:
"Mars sees her, seeing he desires, desiring he enjoys her."
Evil concupiscence is that of which our original parents were first guilty, and which they transmitted to their posterity, as sharers in the primary transgression, in the shape of an innate propensity to sin.

*   *   *

The first who employed the phrase ORIGINAL SIN is said to have been Augustine in his writings against Pelagius; probably because in the *origin*, that is, in the generation of man, it was handed down from our first parents to their posterity. If, however, this were his meaning, the term is too limited; for that evil concupiscence, that law of sin, was not only naturally bred in us, but dwelt also in Adam after the fall, in whom it could not properly be called original.

This general depravity of the human mind and its propensity to sin is described Gen. vi. 5. "God saw that every imagination of the thoughts of his heart was only evil continually." viii. 21. "the imagination of man's heart is evil from his youth." Jer. xvii. 9. "the heart is deceitful above all things." Matt. xv. 19. "out of the heart proceed evil thoughts, murders," &c. Rom. vii. 14. "the law is spiritual, but I am carnal." Rom, viii. 7. "the carnal mind is enmity against God." Gal. v. 17. "the flesh lusteth against the Spirit." Eph. iv. 22. "the old man which is corrupt according to the deceitful lusts."

Chapter XII

OF THE PUNISHMENT OF SIN

[I. xii. A]

Thus far of Sin. After sin came death, as the calamity or punishment consequent upon it. Gen. ii. 17. "in the day that thou eatest thereof thou shalt surely die." Rom. v. 12. "death entered by sin." vi. 23. "the wages of sin is death." vii. 5. "the motions of sins did work in our members to bring forth fruit unto death."

Under the head of death, in Scripture, all evils whatever, together with every thing which in its consequences tends to death, must be understood as comprehended; for mere bodily death, as it is called, did not follow the sin of Adam on the self-same day, as God had threatened.

Hence divines, not inappropriately, reckon up four several degrees of death. The first, as before said, comprehends ALL THOSE EVILS WHICH LEAD TO DEATH, AND WHICH IT IS AGREED CAME INTO THE WORLD IMMEDIATELY UPON THE FALL OF MAN, the most important of which I proceed to enumerate. In the first place, guiltiness; which, though in its primary sense it is an imputation made by God to us, yet is it also, as it were, a commencement or prelude of death dwelling in us, by which we are held as by a bond, and rendered subject to condemnation and punishment. * * * It is attended likewise with the sensible forfeiture of the divine protection and favor; whence results a diminution of the majesty of the human countenance, and a conscious degradation of mind. Gen. iii. 7. "they knew that they were naked." Hence the whole man becomes polluted: Tit. i. 15. "even their mind and conscience is defiled": whence arises shame: Gen. iii. 7. "they sewed fig-leaves together, and made themselves aprons." Rom. vi. 21. "what fruit had ye then in those things whereof ye are now ashamed? for the end of those things is death."

The second degree of death is called SPIRITUAL DEATH; by which is meant the loss of divine grace, and that of innate righteousness, wherein man in the beginning lived unto God. * * *

And this death took place not only on the very day, but at the very moment of the fall. They who are delivered from it are said to be "regenerated," to be "born again," and to be "created afresh"; which is the work of God alone, as will be shown in the chapter on Regeneration.

This death consists, first, in the loss, or at least in the obscuration to a great extent of that right reason which enabled man to discern the chief good, and in which consisted as it were the life of the understanding. * * * It consists, secondly, in that deprivation of righteousness and liberty to do good, and in that slavish subjection to sin and the devil, which constitutes, as it were, the death of the will. John viii. 34. "whosoever committeth sin, is the servant of sin." All have committed sin in Adam; therefore all are born servants of sin. Rom. vii. 14. "sold under sin." * * * Lastly, sin is its own punishment, and produces, in its natural consequences, the death of the spiritual life; more especially gross and habitual sin. Rom. i. 26. "for this cause God gave them up unto vile affections."

The reason of this is evident; for in proportion to the increasing amount of his sins, the sinner becomes more liable to death, more miserable, more vile, more destitute of the divine assistance and grace, and farther removed from his primitive glory. It ought not to be doubted that sin in itself alone is the heaviest of all evils, as being contrary to the chief good, that is, to God; whereas punishment seems to be at variance only with the good of the creature, and not always with that.

It cannot be denied, however, that some remnants of the divine image still exist in us, not wholly extinguished by this spiritual death. This is evident, not only from the wisdom and holiness of many of the heathen, manifested both in words and deeds, but also from what is said Gen. ix. 2. "the dread of you shall be upon every beast of the earth." v. 6. "whoso sheddeth man's blood, by man shall his blood be shed; for in the image of God made he man." These vestiges of original excellence are visible, first, in the understanding. Psal. xix. 1. "the heavens declare the glory of God"; which could not be, if man were incapable of hearing their voice. Rom. i. 19, 20. "that which may be known of God is manifest in them . . . for the invisible things of him from the creation of the world are clearly seen." v. 32. "who knowing the judgment of God." ii. 15. "which show the work of the law written in their hearts."

*   *   *

[I. xii. B]

There can be no doubt that for the purpose of vindicating the justice of God, especially in his calling of mankind, it is much better to allow to man (whether as a remnant of his primitive state, or as restored through the operation of the grace whereby he is called) some portion of free will in respect of good works, or at least of good endeavors, rather than in respect of things which are indifferent. For if God be conceived to rule with absolute disposal all the actions of men, natural as well as civil, he appears to do nothing which is not his right, neither will any one murmur against such a procedure. But if he inclines the will of man to moral good or evil, according to his own pleasure, and then rewards the good, and punishes the wicked, the course of equity seems to be disturbed; and it is entirely on this supposition that the outcry against divine justice is founded. It would appear, therefore, that God's general government of the universe, to which such frequent allusion is made, should be understood as relating to natural and civil concerns, to things indifferent and fortuitous, in a word, to anything rather than to matters of morality and religion. And this is confirmed by many passages of Scripture. 2 Chron. xv. 12, 14. "they entered into a covenant to seek Jehovah the God of their fathers with all their heart, and with all their soul: and they sware unto Jehovah." Psal. cxix. 106. "I have sworn, and I will perform it, that I will keep thy righteous judgments." For if our personal religion were not in some degree dependent on ourselves, and in our own power, God could not properly enter into a covenant with us; neither could we perform, much less swear to perform, the conditions of that covenant.

Chapter XIV

OF MAN'S RESTORATION AND OF CHRIST AS REDEEMER

[I. xiv]

* * *

This incarnation of Christ, whereby he, being God, took upon him the human nature, and was made flesh, without thereby ceasing to be numerically the same as before, is generally considered by theologians as, next to the Trinity in Unity, the greatest mystery of our religion. Of the mystery of the Trinity, however, no mention is made in Scripture; whereas the incarnation is frequently spoken of as a mystery. * * *

Since then this mystery is so great, we are admonished by that very consideration not to assert anything respecting it rashly or presumptuously, on mere grounds of philosophical reasoning; not to add to it anything of our own; not even to adduce in its behalf any passage of Scripture of which the purport may be doubtful, but to be contented with the clearest texts, however few in number. If we listen to such passages, and are willing to acquiesce in the simple truth of Scripture, unincumbered by metaphysical comments, to how many prolix and preposterous arguments shall we put an end! how much occasion of heresy shall we remove! how many ponderous volumes of dabblers in theology shall we cast out, purging the temple of God from the contamination of their rubbish! Nothing would be more plain, and agreeable to reason, nothing more suitable to the understanding even of the meanest individual, than such parts of the Christian faith as are declared in Scripture to be necessary for salvation, if teachers, even of the reformed church, were as yet sufficiently impressed with the propriety of insisting on nothing but divine authority in matters relating to God, and of limiting themselves to the contents of the sacred volume. What is essential would easily appear, when freed from the perplexities of controversy; what is mysterious would be suffered to remain inviolate, and we should be fearful of overstepping the bounds of propriety in its investigation.

The incarnation of Christ consists of two parts; his conception and his nativity. Of his conception the efficient cause was the Holy Spirit. Matt. i. 20. "that which is conceived in her, is of the Holy Ghost." Luke i. 35. "the Holy Ghost shall come upon thee, and the power of the Highest shall overshadow thee"; by which words I am inclined to understand the power and spirit of the Father himself, as has been shown before; according to Psal. xl. 6, 7. compared with Heb. x. 5, 6. "a body hast thou prepared me."

The object of this miraculous conception was to obviate the contamination consequent upon the sin of Adam. Heb. vii. 26. "such an high priest became us, who is holy, harmless, undefiled, separate from sinners."

Chapter XVI

OF THE MINISTRY OF REDEMPTION

[I. xvi]

*   *   *

THE SATISFACTION OF CHRIST IS THE COMPLETE REPARATION MADE BY HIM IN HIS TWOFOLD CAPACITY OF GOD AND MAN, BY THE FULFILMENT OF THE LAW, AND PAYMENT OF THE REQUIRED PRICE FOR ALL MANKIND.

*   *   *

BY PAYMENT OF THE REQUIRED PRICE FOR, that is to say, INSTEAD OF ALL MANKIND. Matt. xx. 28. "a ransom for many." 1 Cor. vi. 20. "ye are bought with a price." 1 Tim. ii. 6. "a ransom for all." The expressions in the Greek clearly denote the substitution of one person in the place of another. 1 Pet. i. 18. "ye were redeemed . . . with the precious blood of Christ, as of a lamb." Rom. v. 10. "we were reconciled to God by the death of his Son." iv. 25. "for our offences." 1 Cor. xv. 3. "for our sins." 2 Cor. v. 21. "for us." Tit. ii. 14. "for us, that he might redeem us." See also Gal. i. 4. Heb. vii. 22. "a surety." x. 12. "one sacrifice for sins." v. 29. "who hath trodden under foot the Son of God, and hath counted the blood of the covenant, wherewith he was sanctified, an unholy thing." It is in vain that the evidence of these texts is endeavored to be evaded by those who maintain that Christ died, not in our stead, and for our redemption, but merely for our advantage in the abstract, and as an example to mankind. At the same time I confess myself unable to perceive how those who consider the Son as of the same essence with the Father, can explain either his incarnation, or his satisfaction.

*   *   *

Chapter XVIII

OF REGENERATION

[I. xviii]

The intent of SUPERNATURAL RENOVATION is not only to restore man more completely than before to the use of his natural faculties, as regards his power to form right judgment, and to exercise free will; but to create afresh, as it were, the inward man, and infuse from above new and supernatural faculties into the minds of the renovated. This is called REGENERATION, and the regenerate are said to be PLANTED IN CHRIST.

REGENERATION IS THAT CHANGE OPERATED BY THE WORD AND THE SPIRIT, WHEREBY THE OLD MAN BEING DESTROYED, THE INWARD MAN IS REGENERATED BY GOD AFTER HIS OWN IMAGE, IN ALL THE FACULTIES OF HIS MIND, INSOMUCH THAT HE BECOMES AS IT WERE A NEW CREATURE, AND THE WHOLE MAN IS SANCTIFIED BOTH IN BODY AND SOUL, FOR THE SERVICE OF GOD, AND THE PERFORMANCE OF GOOD WORKS.

* * *

The external cause of regeneration or sanctification is the death and resurrection of Christ. Eph. ii. 4, 5. "when we were dead in sins, God hath quickened us together with Christ." * * *

Sanctification is attributed also to faith. Acts xv. 9. "purifying their hearts by faith"; not that faith is anterior to sanctification, but because faith is an instrumental and assisting cause in its gradual progress.

Chapter XIX

OF REPENTANCE

[I. xix]

THE effects of regeneration are REPENTANCE and FAITH. REPENTANCE, or rather that higher species of it called in Greek μετάνοια, is THE GIFT OF GOD, WHEREBY THE REGENERATE MAN PERCEIVING WITH SORROW THAT HE HAS OFFENDED GOD BY SIN, DETESTS AND AVOIDS IT, HUMBLY TURNING TO GOD THROUGH A SENSE OF THE DIVINE MERCY, AND HEARTILY STRIVING TO FOLLOW RIGHTEOUSNESS.

* * *

By a comparison of these and similar texts, we may distinguish certain progressive steps in repentance; namely, conviction of sin, contrition, confession, departure from evil, conversion to good: all which, however, belong likewise in their respective degrees to the repentance of the unregenerate.

* * *

Repentance is either general, which is also called conversion, when a man is converted from a state of sin to a state of grace; or particular, when one who is already converted repents of some individual sin. General repentance is either primary or continued; from which latter even the regenerate are not exempt, through their sense of in-dwelling sin.

Chapter XX

OF SAVING FAITH

[I. xx]

The other effect of regeneration is SAVING FAITH. SAVING FAITH IS A FULL PERSUASION OPERATED IN US THROUGH THE GIFT OF GOD, WHEREBY WE BELIEVE, ON THE SOLE AUTHORITY OF THE PROMISE ITSELF, THAT WHATSOEVER THINGS HE HAS PROMISED IN CHRIST ARE OURS, AND ESPECIALLY THE GRACE OF ETERNAL LIFE.

* * *

Hence, as was shown in the fifth chapter, the ultimate object of faith is not Christ the Mediator, but God the Father; a truth, which the weight of scripture evidence has compelled divines to acknowledge. For the same reason it ought not to appear wonderful if many, both Jews and others, who lived before Christ, and many also who have lived since his time, but to whom he has never been revealed, should be saved by faith in God alone; still however through the sole merits of Christ, inasmuch as he was given and slain from the beginning of the world, even for those to whom he was not known, provided they believed in God the Father. Hence honorable testimony is borne to the faith of the illustrious patriarchs who lived under the law, Abel, Enoch, Noah, &c. though it is expressly stated that they believed only in God, Heb. xi.

Chapter XXII

OF JUSTIFICATION

[I. xxii. A]

JUSTIFICATION IS THE GRATUITOUS PURPOSE OF GOD, WHEREBY THOSE WHO ARE REGENERATE AND INGRAFTED IN CHRIST ARE ABSOLVED FROM SIN AND DEATH THROUGH HIS MOST PERFECT SATISFACTION, AND ACCOUNTED JUST IN THE SIGHT OF GOD, NOT BY THE WORKS OF THE LAW, BUT THROUGH FAITH.

* * *

As therefore our sins are imputed to Christ, so the merits or righteousness of Christ are imputed to us through faith. 1 Cor. i. 30. "of him are ye in Christ Jesus, who of God is made unto us wisdom, and righteousness, and sanctification, and redemption." 2 Cor. v. 21. "he hath made him to be sin for us who knew no sin, that we might be made the righteousness of God in him." Rom. iv. 6. "even as David also describeth the blessedness of the man unto whom God imputeth righteousness without works." v. 19. "for as by one man's disobedience many were made sinners, so by the obedience of one shall many be made righteous." It is evident therefore that justification, in so far as we are concerned, is gratuitous; in so far as Christ is concerned, not gratuitous; inasmuch as Christ paid the ransom of our sins, which he took upon himself by imputation, and thus of his own accord, and at his own cost, effected their expiation; whereas man, paying nothing on his part, but merely believing, receives as a gift the imputed righteousness of Christ. Finally, the Father, appeased by this propitiation, pronounces the justification of all believers. A simpler mode of satisfaction could not have been devised, nor one more agreeable to equity.

Hence we are said to be "clothed" with the righteousness of Christ. Rev. xix. 8. "to her was granted that she should be arrayed in fine linen, clean and white; for the fine linen is the justification of the saints."

* * *

[I. xxii. B]

An important question here arises, which is discussed with much vehemence by the advocates on both sides; namely, whether faith alone justifies? Our divines answer in the affirmative; adding, that works are the effects of faith, not the cause of justification, Rom. iii. 24, 27, 28. Gal. ii. 16, as above. Others contend that justification is not by faith alone, on the authority of James ii. 24. "by works a man is justified, and not by faith only." As however the two opinions appear at first sight inconsistent with each other, and incapable of being maintained together, the advocates of the former, to obviate the difficulty arising from the passage of St. James, allege that the apostle is speaking of justification in the sight of men, not in the sight of God. But whoever reads attentively from the fourteenth verse to the end of the chapter, will see that the apostle is expressly treating of justification in the sight of God. For the question there at issue relates to the faith which profits, and which is a living and a saving faith; consequently it cannot relate to that which justifies only in the sight of men, inasmuch as this latter may be hypocritical. When therefore the apostle says that we are justified by works, and not by faith only, he is speaking of the faith which profits, and which is a true, living, and saving faith. * * *

We are justified therefore by faith, but by a living, not a dead faith; and that faith alone which acts is counted living; James ii. 17, 20, 26. Hence we are justified by faith without the works of the law, but not without the works of faith; inasmuch as a living and true faith cannot consist without works, though these latter may differ from the works of the written law. Such were those of Abraham and Rahab, the two examples cited by St. James in illustration of the works of faith, when the former was prepared to offer up his son, and the latter sheltered the spies of the Israelites. * * *

This interpretation, however, affords no countenance to the doctrine of human merit, inasmuch as both faith itself and its works are the works of the Spirit, not our own. Eph. ii. 8–10. "by grace are ye saved through faith; and that not of yourselves, it is the gift of God; not of works, lest any man should boast: for we are his workmanship, created in Christ Jesus unto good works, which God hath before ordained that we should walk in them." In this passage the works of which a man may boast are distinguished from those which do not admit of boasting, namely, the works of faith. So Rom. iii. 27, 28. "where is boasting then? it is excluded: by what law? of works? nay, but by the law of faith." Now what is the law of faith, but the works of faith? * * *

Nor does this doctrine derogate in any degree from Christ's satisfaction; inasmuch as, our faith being imperfect, the works which proceed from it cannot be pleasing to God, except in so far as they rest upon his mercy and the righteousness of Christ, and are sustained by that foundation alone. Philipp. iii. 9. "that I may be found of him, not having mine own righteousness, which is of the law, but that which is through the faith of Christ, the righteousness which is of God by faith." Tit. iii. 5–7. "not by works of righteousness which we have done, but according to his mercy he saved us, by the washing of regeneration and renewing of the Holy Ghost, which he shed on us abundantly through Jesus Christ our Savior; that being justified by his grace, we should be made heirs—."

* * *

Chapter XXVI

OF THE MANIFESTATION OF THE COVENANT OF GRACE;
INCLUDING THE LAW OF GOD

[I. xxvi]

* * *

THE LAW OF GOD is either written or unwritten.

The unwritten law is no other than that law of nature given

340 · *Selections from Milton's Prose*

originally to Adam, and of which a certain remnant, or imperfect illumination, still dwells in the hearts of all mankind; which, in the regenerate, under the influence of the Holy Spirit, is daily tending towards a renewal of its primitive brightness. Rom. i. 19. "God hath showed it unto them." v. 32. "who knowing the judgment of God, that they which commit such things are worthy of death, not only do the same, but have pleasure in them that do them." ii. 14, 15. "the Gentiles, which have not the law, do by nature the things contained in the law, these having not the law, are a law unto themselves; which show the work of the law written in their hearts."

Hence "the law" is often used for heavenly doctrine in the abstract, or the will of God, as declared under both covenants. Jer. xxxi. 33. "I will put my law in their inward parts." John x. 34. "is it not written in your law, I said, Ye are gods?" though the passage alluded to is found in the Psalms, not in the law properly so called.

* * *

THE MOSAIC LAW WAS A WRITTEN CODE CONSISTING OF MANY PRECEPTS, INTENDED FOR THE ISRAELITES ALONE, WITH A PROMISE OF LIFE TO SUCH AS SHOULD KEEP THEM, AND A CURSE ON SUCH AS SHOULD BE DISOBEDIENT; TO THE END THAT THEY, BEING LED THEREBY TO AN ACKNOWLEDGMENT OF THE DEPRAVITY OF MANKIND, AND CONSEQUENTLY OF THEIR OWN, MIGHT HAVE RECOURSE TO THE RIGHTEOUSNESS OF THE PROMISED SAVIOR; AND THAT THEY, AND IN PROCESS OF TIME ALL OTHER NATIONS, MIGHT BE LED UNDER THE GOSPEL FROM THE WEAK AND SERVILE RUDIMENTS OF THIS ELEMENTARY INSTITUTION TO THE FULL STRENGTH OF THE NEW CREATURE, AND A MANLY LIBERTY WORTHY THE SONS OF GOD. Heb. ix. 8, &c. as above.

* * *

Thus the imperfection of the law was manifested in the person of Moses himself; for Moses, who was a type of the law, could not bring the children of Israel into the land of Canaan, that is, into eternal rest; but an entrance was given to them under Joshua, or Jesus.

Chapter XXVII

OF THE GOSPEL AND CHRISTIAN LIBERTY

[I. xxvii. A]

THE GOSPEL is THE NEW DISPENSATION OF THE COVENANT OF GRACE, FAR MORE EXCELLENT AND PERFECT THAN THE LAW, ANNOUNCED FIRST OBSCURELY BY MOSES AND THE PROPHETS, AFTERWARDS IN THE CLEAREST TERMS BY CHRIST HIMSELF, AND HIS

APOSTLES AND EVANGELISTS, WRITTEN SINCE BY THE HOLY SPIRIT
IN THE HEARTS OF BELIEVERS, AND ORDAINED TO CONTINUE EVEN TO
THE END OF THE WORLD, CONTAINING A PROMISE OF ETERNAL LIFE
TO ALL IN EVERY NATION WHO SHALL BELIEVE IN CHRIST WHEN
REVEALED TO THEM, AND A THREAT OF ETERNAL DEATH TO SUCH AS
SHALL NOT BELIEVE.

* * *

On the introduction of the gospel, or new covenant through faith
in Christ, the whole of the preceding covenant, in other words the
entire Mosaic law, was abolished. Jer. xxxi. 31–33. as above. Luke
xvi. 16. "the law and the prophets were until John." Rom. vii.
7. * * * "I had not known sin but by the law," that is, the whole
law, for the expression is unlimited, "for I had not known lust,
except the law had said, Thou shalt not covet." It is in the deca-
logue that the injunction here specified is contained; we are there-
fore absolved from subjection to the decalogue as fully as to the
rest of the law. * * * Tit. i. 15. "unto the pure all things are pure;
but unto them that are defiled and unbelieving is nothing pure, but
even their mind and conscience is defiled." * * * 2 Cor. iii. 3.
"not in tables of stone, but in fleshy tables of the heart." v. 6–8.
"ministers of the new testament, not of the letter, but of the spirit;
for the letter killeth, but the spirit giveth life.

* * *

It is generally replied, that all these passages are to be understood
only of the abolition of the ceremonial law. This is refuted, first, by
the definition of the law itself, as given in the preceding chapter, in
which are specified all the various reasons for its enactment: if
therefore, of the causes which led to the enactment of the law
considered as a whole, every one is revoked or obsolete, it follows
that the whole law itself must be annulled also. The principal
reasons then which are given for the enactment of the law are as
follows: that it might call forth and develop our natural depravity;
that by this means it might work wrath; that it might impress us
with a slavish fear through consciousness of divine enmity, and of
the handwriting of accusation that was against us; that it might be
a schoolmaster to bring us to the righteousness of Christ; and
others of a similar description. Now the texts quoted above prove
clearly, both that all these causes are now abrogated, and that they
have not the least connection with the ceremonial law.

First then, the law is abolished principally on the ground of its
being a law of works; that it might give place to the law of grace.
Rom. iii. 27. "by what law? of works? nay, but by the law of faith."
xi. 6. "if by grace, then is it no more of works; otherwise grace is
no more grace." Now the law of works was not solely the ceremo-
nial law, but the whole law.

* * *

To these considerations we may add, that that law which not only cannot justify, but is the source of trouble and subversion to believers; which even tempts God if we endeavor to perform its requisitions; which has no promise attached to it, or, to speak more properly, which takes away and frustrates all promises, whether of inheritance, or adoption, or grace, or of the Spirit itself; nay, which even subjects us to a curse; must necessarily have been abolished. If then it can be shown that the above effects result, not from the ceremonial law alone, but from the whole law, that is to say, the law of works in a comprehensive sense, it will follow that the whole law is abolished; and that they do so result, I shall proceed to show from the clearest passages of Scripture.

*   *   *

It is to be observed, however, that the sum and essence of the law is not hereby abrogated; its purpose being attained in that love of God and our neighbor, which is born of the Spirit through faith. It was with justice therefore that Christ asserted the permanence of the law, Matt. v. 17. "think not that I am come to destroy the law, or the prophets; I am not come to destroy, but to fulfil." Rom. iii. 31. "do we then make void the law through faith? God forbid: yea, we establish the law." viii. 4. "that the righteousness of the law might be fulfilled in us, who walk not after the flesh, but after the Spirit."

The common objection to this doctrine is anticipated by St. Paul himself, who expressly teaches that by this abrogation of the law, sin, if not taken away, is at least weakened rather than increased in power: Rom. vi. 14, 15. "sin shall not have dominion over you; for ye are not under the law, but under grace: what then? shall we sin, because we are not under the law, but under grace? God forbid." Therefore, as was said above, the end for which the law was instituted, namely, the love of God and our neighbor, is by no means to be considered as abolished; it is the tablet of the law, so to speak, that is alone changed, its injunctions being now written by the Spirit in the hearts of believers with this difference, that in certain precepts the Spirit appears to be at variance with the letter, namely, wherever by departing from the letter we can more effectually consult the love of God and our neighbor.

*   *   *

[I. xxvii. B]

From the abrogation, through the gospel, of the law of servitude, results Christian liberty; though liberty, strictly speaking, is the peculiar fruit of adoption, and consequently was not unknown during the time of the law, as observed in the twenty-third chapter. Inasmuch, however, as it was not possible for our liberty either to be perfected or made fully manifest till the coming of Christ our deliverer, liberty must be considered as belonging in an especial manner to the gospel, and as consorting therewith: first, because truth is principally known by the gospel, John i. 17. "grace and truth came by Jesus Christ," and truth has an essential connection with liberty; viii. 31, 32. "if ye continue in my word, then are ye my disciples indeed; and ye shall know the truth, and the truth shall make you free." v. 36. "if the Son therefore shall make you free, ye shall be free indeed." Secondly, because the peculiar gift of the gospel is the Spirit; but "where the Spirit of the Lord is, there is liberty," 2 Cor. iii. 17.

CHRISTIAN LIBERTY is that whereby WE ARE LOOSED AS IT WERE BY ENFRANCHISEMENT, THROUGH CHRIST OUR DELIVERER, FROM THE BONDAGE OF SIN, AND CONSEQUENTLY FROM THE RULE OF THE LAW AND OF MAN; TO THE INTENT THAT BEING MADE SONS INSTEAD OF SERVANTS, AND PERFECT MEN INSTEAD OF CHILDREN, WE MAY SERVE GOD IN LOVE THROUGH THE GUIDANCE OF THE SPIRIT OF TRUTH.

*   *   *

Neither this reason, therefore, nor a pretended consideration for the weaker brethren, afford a sufficient warrant for those edicts of the magistrate which constrain believers, or deprive them in any respect of their religious liberty. For so the apostle argues 1 Cor. ix. 19. "though I be free from all men, yet have I made myself servant unto all"; I was not made so by others, but became so of my own accord; "free from all men," and consequently from the magistrate, in these matters at least. When the magistrate takes away this liberty, he takes away the gospel itself; he deprives the good and the bad indiscriminately of their privilege of free judgment, contrary to the spirit of the well known precept, Matt. xiii. 29, 30. "lest while ye gather up the tares ye root up also the wheat with them: let both grow together until the harvest."

Chapter XXX

OF THE HOLY SCRIPTURES

[I. xxx]

*   *   *

The Scriptures, therefore, partly by reason of their own simplicity, and partly through the divine illumination, are plain and perspicuous in all things necessary to salvation, and adapted to the instruction even of the most unlearned, through the medium of diligent and constant reading. Psal. xix. 7. "the law of Jehovah is perfect, converting the soul; the testimony of Jehovah is sure, making wise the simple." cxix. 105. "thy word is a lamp unto my feet, and a light unto my path." v. 130. "the entrance of thy words giveth light, it giveth understanding unto the simple"; whence it follows that the liberty of investigating Scripture thoroughly is granted to all. v. 18. "open thou mine eyes, that I may behold wondrous things out of thy law." Luke xxiv. 45. "then opened he their understanding, that they might understand the scriptures." * * *

If then the Scriptures be in themselves so perspicuous, and sufficient of themselves "to make men wise unto salvation through faith," that "the man of God may be perfect, thoroughly furnished unto all good works," through what infatuation is it, that even Protestant divines persist in darkening the most momentous truths of religion by intricate metaphysical comments, on the plea that such explanation is necessary; stringing together all the useless technicalities and empty distinctions of scholastic barbarism, for the purpose of elucidating those Scriptures, which they are continually extolling as models of plainness? As if Scripture, which possesses in itself the clearest light, and is sufficient for its own explanation, especially in matters of faith and holiness, required to have the simplicity of its divine truths more fully developed, and placed in a more distinct view, by illustrations drawn from the abstrusest of human sciences, falsely so called.

* * *

No passage of Scripture is to be interpreted in more than one sense; in the Old Testament, however, this sense is sometimes a compound of the historical and typical, as in Hosea xi. 1. compared with Matt. ii. 15. "out of Egypt have I called my son," which may be explained in a double sense, as referring partly to the people of Israel, and partly to Christ in his infancy.

* * *

The requisites for the public interpretation of Scripture have been laid down by divines with much attention to usefulness, although they have not been observed with equal fidelity. They consist in knowledge of languages; inspection of the originals; examination of the context; care in distinguishing between literal and figurative expressions; consideration of cause and circumstance, of antecedents and consequents; mutual comparison of texts; and regard to the analogy of faith. Attention must also be paid to the frequent anomalies of syntax; as for example, where the relative does not refer to the immediate antecedent, but to the principal word in the sentence, though more remote. * * * Lastly, no inferences from the text are to be admitted, but such as follow necessarily and plainly from the words themselves; lest we should be constrained to receive what is not written for what is written, the shadow for the substance, the fallacies of human reasoning for the doctrines of God: for it is by the declarations of Scripture, and not by the conclusions of the schools, that our consciences are bound.

Every believer has a right to interpret the Scriptures for himself, inasmuch as he has the Spirit for his guide, and the mind of Christ is in him; nay, the expositions of the public interpreter can be of no use to him, except so far as they are confirmed by his own conscience.

*   *   *

Hence, although the external ground which we possess for our belief at the present day in the written word is highly important, and, in most instances at least, prior in point of reception, that which is internal, and the peculiar possession of each believer, is far superior to all, namely, the Spirit itself. * * *

Previously to the Babylonish captivity, the law of Moses was preserved in the sacred repository of the ark of the covenant; after that event, it was committed to the trust and guardianship of the priests and prophets, as Ezra, Zechariah, Malachi, and other men taught of God. There can be no doubt that these handed down the sacred volumes in an uncorrupted state to be preserved in the temple by the priests their successors, who were in all ages most scrupulous in preventing alterations, and who had themselves no grounds of suspicion to induce them to make any change. With regard to the remaining books, particularly the historical, although it be uncertain by whom and at what time they were written, and although they appear sometimes to contradict themselves on points of chronology, few or none have ever questioned the integrity of their doctrinal parts. The New Testament, on the contrary, has come down to us as before observed through the hands of a multitude of persons, subject to various temptations; nor have we in any instance the original copy in the author's hand-writing, by which to correct the errors of the others. Hence Erasmus, Beza, and other learned men, have edited from the different manuscripts what in their judgment appeared most likely to be the authentic readings. It is difficult to conjecture the purpose of Providence in committing the writings of the New Testament to such uncertain and variable guardianship, unless it were to teach us by this very circumstance that the Spirit which is given to us is a more certain guide than Scripture, whom therefore it is our duty to follow.

*   *   *

Chapter XXXIII

OF PERFECT GLORIFICATION, INCLUDING THE SECOND ADVENT OF
CHRIST, THE RESURRECTION OF THE DEAD, AND THE
GENERAL CONFLAGRATION

[I. xxxiii. A]

Its fulfilment and consummation will commence from the period of Christ's second coming to judgment, and the resurrection of the dead. * * *

THE COMING OF THE LORD TO JUDGMENT, when he shall judge the world with his holy angels, was predicted, first, by Enoch and the prophets; afterwards by Christ himself and his apostles. Jude 14, 15. "Enoch also, the seventh from Adam, prophesied of these, saying, Behold, the Lord cometh with ten thousand of his saints, to execute judgment upon all, and to convince all that are ungodly among them of all their ungodly deeds which they have ungodly committed, and of all their hard speeches which ungodly sinners have spoken against him." Dan. vii. 22. "until the Ancient of days came, and judgment was given to the saints of the most High." Matt. xxv. 31. "the Son of man shall come in his glory, and all the holy angels with him." Acts i. 11. "this same Jesus . . . shall so come in like manner as ye have seen him go into heaven." x. 42. "it is he which was ordained of God to be the judge of quick and dead." xvii. 31. "he hath appointed a day in the which he will judge the world in righteousness by that man whom he hath ordained . . . in that he hath raised him from the dead." 2 Thess. i. 7, 8. "the Lord Jesus shall be revealed from heaven with his mighty angels."

The day and hour of Christ's coming are known to the Father only. Matt. xxiv. 36. Mark xiii. 32. "of that day and that hour knoweth no man." * * *

Hence it will be sudden. Matt. xxv. 6. "at midnight there was a cry made, Behold, the bridegroom cometh; go ye out to meet him." * * *

Certain signs however are pointed out by Christ and his apostles as indicative of its approach; Matt. xxiv. 3–27. Mark xiii. Luke xxi. These signs are either general or peculiar.

The general signs are those which relate equally to the destruction of Jerusalem, the type of Christ's advent, and to the advent itself; such as false prophets, false Christs, wars, earthquakes, persecutions, pestilence, famine, and the gradual decay of faith and charity, down to the very day itself. Matt. xxiv. 3–27. 2 Tim. iii. 1, &c.

The peculiar signs are, first, an extreme recklessness and impiety, and an almost universal apostasy. Luke xviii. 8. "when the Son of man cometh, shall he find faith on the earth?" 2 Thess. ii. 3. "that day shall not come, except there come a falling away first." Compare also 1 Tim. iv. 1.

Secondly, the revealing of antichrist, and his destruction by the spirit of the mouth of Christ. 2 Thess. ii. 3. "that man of sin shall be revealed, the son of perdition—." v. 8. "and then shall that Wicked be revealed, whom the Lord shall consume with the spirit of his mouth, and shall destroy with the brightness of his coming."

* * *

[I. xxxiii. B]

The second advent of Christ will be followed by the resurrection of the dead and the last judgment.

A belief in the RESURRECTION OF THE DEAD existed even before the time of the gospel. Job xix. 25, 26, &c. "I know that my Redeemer liveth, and that he shall stand at the latter day upon the earth; and though after my skin worms destroy this body, yet in my flesh I shall see God." Psal. xvi. 10, &c. "thou wilt not leave my soul in hell."

* * *

To these testimonies from Scripture, may be added several arguments from reason in support of the doctrine. First, the covenant with God is not dissolved by death. Matt. xxii. 32. "God is not the God of the dead, but of the living." Secondly, "if there be no resurrection of the dead, then is Christ not risen," 1 Cor. xv. 13–20. v. 23. "every man in his own order; Christ the first-fruits, afterward they that are Christ's at his coming." John xi. 25. "Jesus said unto her, I am the resurrection and the life." Thirdly, were there no resurrection, the righteous would be of all men most miserable, and the wicked, who have a better portion in this life, most happy; which would be altogether inconsistent with the providence and justice of God.

* * *

[I. xxxiii. C]

THE LAST JUDGMENT is that wherein CHRIST WITH THE SAINTS, ARRAYED IN THE GLORY AND POWER OF THE FATHER, SHALL JUDGE THE EVIL ANGELS, AND THE WHOLE RACE OF MANKIND.

* * *

Coincident, as appears, with the time of this last judgment—I use the indefinite expression time, as the word day is often employed to denote any given period, and as it is not easily imaginable that so many myriads of men and angels should be assembled and sentenced within a single day—beginning with its commencement, and extending a little beyond its conclusion, will take place that glorious reign of Christ on earth with his saints, so often promised in Scripture, even until all his enemies shall be subdued. His kingdom of grace, indeed, which is also called "the kingdom of heaven," began with his first advent, when its beginning was proclaimed by John the Baptist, as appears from testimony of Scripture; but his kingdom of glory will not commence till his second advent. Dan. vii. 13, 14. "behold, one like the Son of man came with the clouds of heaven . . . and there was given him dominion and glory, and a kingdom"; "given him," that is, from the time when he came with the clouds of heaven (in which manner his final advent is uniformly described) not to assume our nature, as Junius interprets it, (for then he would have been like the Son of man before he became man, which would be an incongruity) but to execute judgment; from the period so indicated, to the time when he should lay down the kingdom, 1 Cor. xv. 24. "then cometh the end," of which more shortly. That this reign will be on earth, is evident from many passages. * * * It appears that the "judgment" here spoken of will not be confined to a single day, but will extend through a great space of time; and that the word is used to denote, not so much a judicial inquiry properly so called, as an exercise of dominion; in which sense Gideon, Jephthah, and the other judges are said to have judged Israel during many years. * * *

After the expiration of the thousand years Satan will rage again, and assail the church at the head of an immense confederacy of its enemies; but will be overthrown by fire from heaven, and condemned to everlasting punishment. Rev. xx. 7–9. "when the thousand years are expired, Satan shall be loosed out of his prison, and shall go out to deceive the nations which are in the four quarters of the earth, Gog and Magog, to gather them together to battle . . . and they compassed the camp of the saints about, and the beloved city; and fire came down from God out of heaven, and devoured them." * * *

After the evil angels and chief enemies of God have been sentenced, judgment will be passed upon the whole race of mankind. * * *

Then, as appears, will be pronounced that sentence, Matt. xxv. 34. "COME, YE BLESSED OF MY FATHER, INHERIT THE KINGDOM PREPARED FOR YOU FROM THE FOUNDATION OF THE WORLD." v. 41. "DEPART FROM ME, YE CURSED, INTO EVERLASTING FIRE, PREPARED FOR THE DEVIL AND HIS ANGELS."

The passing of the sentence will be followed by its execution; that is to say, by the punishment of the wicked, and the perfect glorification of the righteous. * * *

The second death is so termed with reference to the first, or death of the body. For the three other, or preparatory degrees of death, see chap. xiii. On the punishment of sin. The fourth and last gradation is that of which we are now speaking, namely, eternal death, or the punishment of the damned.

Under this death may be included the destruction of the present unclean and polluted world itself, namely, its FINAL CONFLAGRATION. Whether by this is meant the destruction of the substance of the world itself, or only a change in the nature of its constituent parts, is uncertain, and of no importance to determine; respecting the event itself, we are informed, so far as it concerns us to know, Job xiv. 12. "till the heavens be no more." Psal. cii. 26. "they shall perish." Isa. xxxiv. 4. "the heavens shall be rolled together as a scroll, and all their host shall fall down." * * *

The second death, or the punishment of the damned, seems to consist partly in the loss of the chief good, namely, the favor and protection of God, and the beatific vision of his presence, which is commonly called the punishment of loss; and partly in eternal torment, which is called the punishment of sense. Matt. xxv. 41. "depart from me, ye cursed, into everlasting fire, prepared for the devil and his angels."

* * *

[I. xxxiii. D]

The place of punishment is called HELL; "Tophet," Isa. xxx. 33. "hell fire," Matt. v. 22. and still more distinctly x. 28. "outer darkness," viii. 12. xxii. 13. xxv. 30. "a furnace of fire," xiii. 42. "Hades," Luke xvi. 23; and elsewhere: "a place of torment," v. 28. "the bottomless pit," Rev. ix. 1. "the lake of fire," xx. 15. "the lake which burneth with fire and brimstone," xxi. 8. Hell appears to be situated beyond the limits of this universe. Luke xvi. 26. "between us and you there is a great gulf fixed, so that they which would pass from hence to you cannot." Matt. viii. 12. "outer darkness." Rev. xxii. 14, 15. "they may enter in through the gates into the city; for without are dogs." Nor are reasons wanting for this locality; for as the place of the damned is the same as that prepared for the devil and his angels, Matt. xxv. 41. in punishment of their apostasy, which occurred before the fall of man, it does not seem probable that hell should have been prepared within the limits of this world, in the bowels of the earth, on which the curse had not as yet passed. This is said to have been the opinion of Chrysostom, as likewise of Luther and some later divines. Besides, if, as has been shown from various passages of the New Testament, the whole world is to be finally consumed by fire, it follows that hell, being situated in the center of the earth, must share the fate of the surrounding universe, and perish likewise; a consummation more to be desired than expected by the souls in perdition.

Thus far of the punishment of the wicked; it remains to speak of the perfect glorification of the righteous.

Perfect glorification consists in eternal life and perfect happiness, arising chiefly from the divine vision. It is described Psal. xvi. 11. "thou wilt show me the path of life; in thy presence is fulness of joy; at thy right hand there are pleasures for evermore." xvii. 15. "I will behold thy face in righteousness; I shall be satisfied, when I awake, with thy likeness." Dan. xii. 3. "they that be wise shall shine as the brightness of the firmament, and they that turn many to righteousness as the stars for ever and ever." Matt. xiii. 43. "then shall the righteous shine forth as the sun in the kingdom of their

Father." xxii. 30. "they are as the angels of God in heaven." v. 8. "blessed are the pure in heart, for they shall see God." 1 Cor. ii. 9. "as it is written, Eye hath not seen, nor ear heard, neither have entered into the heart of man, the things which God hath prepared for them that love him."

* * *

[I. xxxiii. E]

It appears that all the saints will not attain to an equal state of glory. Dan. xii. 3. "they that be wise shall shine as the brightness of the firmament, and they that turn many to righteousness as the stars for ever and ever." Matt. xx. 23. "to sit on my right hand and on my left is not mine to give, but it shall be given to them for whom it is prepared of my Father." 1 Cor. xv. 41, 42. "there is one glory of the sun, and another glory of the moon, and another glory of the stars; for one star differeth from another star in glory: so also is the resurrection of the dead."

* * *

Our glorification will be accompanied by the renovation of heaven and earth, and of all things therein adapted to our service or delight, to be possessed by us in perpetuity.

Book II, Chapter XV

OF THE RECIPROCAL DUTIES OF MAN TOWARDS HIS NEIGHBOR; AND SPECIALLY OF PRIVATE DUTIES

[II. xv]

* * *

Under domestic duties are comprehended the reciprocal obligations of husband and wife, parent and child, brethren and kinsmen, master and servant.

THE DUTIES OF HUSBAND AND WIFE are mutual or personal.

Mutual duties. 1 Cor. vii. 3. "let the husband render unto the wife due benevolence, and likewise also the wife unto the husband."

The personal duties appertaining to either party respectively are, first, those of the husband. Exod. xxi. 10, 11. "her food, her raiment, and her duty of marriage shall he not diminish; and if he do not these three unto her," &c. Prov. v. 18, 19. "rejoice with the wife of thy youth." Esther i. 22. "every man should bear rule in his own house." 1 Cor. xi. 3. "I would have you know that the head of every man is Christ, and the head of the woman is the man." Eph. v. 25. "husbands, love your wives, even as Christ also loved the church." Col. iii. 19. "husbands, love your wives, and be not bitter against them." 1 Pet. iii. 7. "likewise, ye husbands, dwell with them according to knowledge, giving honor unto the wife, as unto the weaker vessel." The contrary is reproved Mal. ii. 13, 14, &c. "Jehovah hath been witness between thee and the wife of thy youth, against whom thou hast dealt treacherously—." Prov. v. 20, 21. "why wilt thou, my son, be ravished with a strange woman?"

Personal duties of the wife. Prov. xiv. 1. "every wise woman buildeth her house." xix. 14. "a prudent wife is from Jehovah." xxxi. 11, &c. "the heart of her husband doth safely trust in her." 1 Cor. xi. 3, &c. "the woman is the glory of the man; for the man is not of the woman, but the woman of the man." Eph. v. 22–24. "wives, submit yourselves unto your own husbands, as unto the Lord; for the husband is the head of the wife, even as Christ is the head of the church, and he is the Savior of the body; therefore as the church is subject unto Christ, so let the wives be to their own husbands in every thing." Col. iii. 18. "wives, submit yourselves unto your own husbands, as it is fit in the Lord." Tit. ii. 4, 5. "that they may teach the young women to be sober, to love their husbands, to love their children, to be discreet, chaste, keepers at home, good, obedient to their own husbands, that the word of God be not blasphemed." 1 Pet. iii. 1, &c. "likewise, ye wives, be in subjection to your own husbands," &c. The same is implied in the original formation of the woman: Gen. ii. 22. "the rib which Jehovah had taken from man, made he a woman"; it cannot therefore be fitting that a single member, and that not one of the most important, should be independent of the whole body, and even of the head. Finally, such is the express declaration of God: Gen. iii. 16. "he shall rule over thee."

Offences against these duties. Exod. iv. 25. "a bloody husband art thou to me." Job ii. 9. "then said his wife unto him, Dost thou still retain thine integrity?" &c. 2 Sam. vi. 20. "Michal the daughter of Saul came out to meet David, and said," &c. Prov. ix. 13. "a foolish woman is clamorous." vii. 11. "her feet abide not in her house." xiv. 1. "the foolish plucketh it down with her hands." xix. 13. "the contentions of a wife are a continual dropping." See also xxvii. 15. xxi. 9. "it is better to dwell in a corner of the house top, than with a brawling woman in a wide house." v. 19. "it is better to dwell in the wilderness, than with a contentious and an angry woman." See also xxv. 24. Eccles. vii. 26. "I find more bitter than death the woman whose heart is snares and nets, and her hands as bands: whoso pleaseth God shall escape from her, but the sinner shall be taken by her." Above all, adultery: Deut. xxii. 14, 20. "I took this woman, and when I came unto her, I found her not a maid . . . if this thing be true," &c.

Selections from Books
of the Bible

Milton was three years old when the Authorized Version of the Bible was first published in 1611, and throughout his life he used a copy printed in 1612. Of course he read and consulted many versions. The thousands of quotations in the *Christian Doctrine*, for example, are from the Junius-Tremelius Latin Bible in a Geneva edition of 1630, though Milton must have owned a copy of the Vulgate as well. And he read the Old Testament in Hebrew and the New Testament in Greek. But most of the verbal echoes of the Bible in *Paradise Lost* are in the language of the King James Version. (See Harris Fletcher, *The Use of the Bible in Milton's Prose*, and James Sims, *The Bible in Milton's Epics*.) The selections from Job, Romans, and Corinthians are from *The New English Bible* (New York: Oxford University Press, 1971), which is sometimes clearer than the Authorized Version. But all the others are in the language of the version that Milton probably knew largely by heart.

The Book of Genesis

CHAPTER 1

In the beginning God created the heaven and the earth. And the earth was without form, and void; and darkness was upon the face of the deep. And the spirit of God moved upon the face of the waters. And God said, "Let there be light": and there was light. And God saw the light, that it was good: and God divided the light from the darkness. And God called the light Day, and the darkness he called Night. And the evening and the morning were the first day.

6 And God said, "let there be a firmament in the midst of the waters, and let it divide the waters from the waters". And God made the firmament, and divided the waters which were under the firmament from the waters which were above the firmament: and it was so. And God called the firmament Heaven. And the evening and the morning were the second day.

9 And God said, "let the waters under the heaven be gathered together unto one place, and let the dry land appear": and it was so. And God called the dry land Earth; and the gathering together of the waters called he Seas: and God saw that it was good. And God said, "Let the earth bring forth grass, the herb yielding seed, and the fruit tree yielding fruit after his kind, whose seed is in itself, upon the earth": and it was so. And the earth brought forth grass, and herb yielding seed after his kind, and the tree yielding fruit, whose seed was in itself, after his kind: and God saw that it was good. And the evening and the morning were the third day.

14 And God said, "Let there be lights in the firmament of the heaven to divide the day from the night; and let them be for signs, and for seasons, and for days, and years: and let them be for lights in the firmament of the heaven to give light upon the earth": and it was so. And God made two great lights; the greater light to rule the day, and the lesser light to rule the night: he made the stars also. And God set them in the firmament of the heaven to give light upon the earth, and to rule over the day and over the night, and to divide the light from the darkness: and God saw that it was good. And the evening and the morning were the fourth day.

20 And God said, "Let the waters bring forth abundantly the moving creature that hath life, and fowl that may fly above the earth in the open firmament of heaven". And God created great whales, and every living creature that moveth, which the waters brought forth abundantly, after their kind, and every winged fowl after his kind: and God saw that it was good. And God blessed them, saying, "Be fruitful, and multiply, and fill the waters in the seas, and let fowl multiply in the earth". And the evening and the morning were the fifth day.

24 And God said, "Let the earth bring forth the living creature after his kind, cattle, and creeping thing, and beast of the earth after his kind": and it was so. And God made the beast of the earth after his kind, and cattle after their kind, and every thing that creepeth upon the earth after his kind: and God saw that it was good. And God said, "Let us make man in our image, after our likeness: and let them have dominion over the fish of the sea, and over the fowl of the air, and over the cattle, and over all the earth, and over every creeping thing that creepeth upon the earth". So God created man in his own image, in the image of God created he him; male and female created he them. And God blessed them, and God said unto them, "Be fruitful, and multiply, and replenish the earth, and subdue it: and have dominion over the fish of the sea, and over the fowl of the air, and over every living thing that moveth upon the earth". And God said, "Behold, I have given you every herb bearing seed, which is upon the face of all the earth, and every tree, in the which is the fruit of a tree yielding seed; to you it shall be for meat. And to every beast of the earth, and to every fowl of the air, and to every thing that creepeth upon the earth, wherein there is life, I have given every green herb for meat:" and it was so. And God saw every thing that he had made, and, behold, it was very good. And the evening and the morning were the sixth day.

CHAPTER 2

Thus the heavens and the earth were finished, and all the host of them. And on the seventh day God ended his work which he had made; and he rested on the seventh day from all his work which he had made. And God blessed the seventh day, and sanctified it: because that in it he had rested from all his work which God created and made.

4 These are the generations of the heavens and of the earth when they were created, in the day that the LORD God made the earth and the heavens, and every plant of the field before it was in the earth, and every herb of the field before it grew: for the LORD God had not caused it to rain upon the earth, and there was not a man to till the ground. But there went up a mist from the earth, and watered the whole face of the ground. And the LORD God formed man of the dust of the ground, and breathed into his nostrils the breath of life; and man became a living soul. And the LORD God planted a garden eastward in Eden; and there he put the man whom he had formed. And out of the ground made the LORD God to grow every tree that is pleasant to the sight, and good for food; the tree of life also in the midst of the garden, and the tree of knowledge of good and evil. 10 And a river went out of Eden to water the garden; and from thence it was parted, and became into four heads. The name of the first is Pison: that is it which compasseth the whole land of Havilah, where there is gold; and the gold of that land is good: there is bdellium and the onyx stone. And the name of the second river is Gihon: the same is it that compasseth the whole land of Ethiopia. And the name of the third river is Hiddekel: that is it which goeth toward the east of Assyria. And the fourth river is Euphrates. And the LORD God took the man, and put him into the garden of Eden to dress it and to keep it. And the LORD God commanded the man, saying, "Of every tree of the garden thou mayest freely eat: but of the tree of the knowledge of good and evil, thou shalt not eat of it: for in the day that thou eatest thereof thou shall surely die".

18 And the LORD God said, "It is not good that the man should be alone; I will make him an help meet for him". And out of the ground the LORD God formed every beast of the field, and every fowl of the air; and brought them unto Adam to see what he would call them: and whatsoever Adam called every living creature, that was the name thereof. And Adam gave names to all cattle, and to the fowl of the air, and to every beast of the field; but for Adam there was not found an help meet for him. And the LORD God caused a deep sleep to fall upon Adam, and he slept: and he took one of his ribs, and closed up the flesh instead thereof; and the rib, which the LORD God had taken from man, made he a woman, and brought her unto the man. And Adam said, "This is now bone of my bones, and flesh of my flesh: she shall be called Woman, because she was taken out of Man". Therefore shall a man leave his father and his mother, and shall cleave unto his wife: and they

shall be one flesh. And they were both naked, the man and his wife, and were not ashamed.

CHAPTER 3

Now the serpent was more subtil than any beast of the field which the LORD God had made. And he said unto the woman, "Yea, hath God said, 'Ye shall not eat of every tree of the garden'?" And the woman said unto the serpent, "We may eat of the fruit of the trees of the garden: but of the fruit of the tree which is in the midst of the garden, God hath said, 'Ye shall not eat of it, neither shall ye touch it, lest ye die' ". And the serpent said unto the woman, "Ye shall not surely die: for God doth know that in the day ye eat thereof, then your eyes shall be opened, and ye shall be as gods, knowing good and evil". And when the woman saw that the tree was good for food, and that it was pleasant to the eyes, and a tree to be desired to make one wise, she took of the fruit thereof, and did eat, and gave also unto her husband with her; and he did eat. And the eyes of them both were opened, and they knew that they were naked; and they sewed fig leaves together, and made themselves aprons. And they heard the voice of the LORD God walking in the garden in the cool of the day: and Adam and his wife hid themselves from the presence of the LORD God amongst the trees of the garden. 10 And the LORD God called unto Adam, and said unto him, "Where art thou?" And he said, "I heard thy voice in the garden, and I was afraid, because I was naked; and I hid myself". And he said, "Who told thee that thou wast naked? Hast thou eaten of the tree, whereof I commanded thee that thou shouldest not eat?" And the man said, "The woman whom thou gavest to be with me, she gave me of the tree, and I did eat". And the LORD God said unto the woman, "What is this that thou hast done?" And the woman said, "The serpent beguiled me, and I did eat". And the LORD God said unto the serpent, "Because thou hast done this, thou art cursed above all cattle, and above every beast of the field; upon thy belly shalt thou go, and dust shalt thou eat all the days of thy life: and I will put enmity between thee and the woman, and between thy seed and her seed; it shall bruise thy head, and thou shalt bruise his heel". Unto the woman he said, "I will greatly multiply thy sorrow and thy conception; in sorrow thou shalt bring forth children; and thy desire shalt be to thy husband, and he shall rule over thee". And unto Adam he said, "Because thou hast hearkened unto the voice of thy wife, and hast eaten of the tree, of which I commanded thee, saying, Thou shalt not eat of it: cursed is the ground for thy sake; in sorrow shalt thou eat of it all the days of thy life; thorns also and thistles shall it bring forth to thee; and thou shalt eat the herb of the field; in the sweat of thy face shalt thou eat bread, till thou return unto the ground; for out of it wast thou taken: for dust thou art, and unto dust shalt thou return". And Adam called his wife's name Eve; because she was the mother of all living. Unto Adam also and to his wife did the LORD God make coats of skins, and clothed them.

22 And the LORD God said, "Behold, the man is become as one of us, to know good and evil: and now, lest he put forth his hand, and take also of the tree of life, and eat, and live for ever": therefore the LORD God sent him forth from the garden of Eden, to till the ground from whence he was taken. So he drove out the man; and he placed at the east of the garden of Eden Cherubims, and a flaming sword which turned every way, to keep the way of the tree of life.

CHAPTER 4

And Adam knew Eve his wife; and she conceived, and bare Cain, and said, "I have gotten a man from the LORD". And she again bare his brother Abel. And Abel was a keeper of sheep, but Cain was a tiller of the ground. And in process of time it came to pass, that Cain brought of the fruit of the ground an offering unto the LORD. And Abel, he also brought of the firstlings of his flock and of the fat thereof. And the LORD had respect unto Abel and to his offering: but unto Cain and to his offering he had not respect. And Cain was very wroth, and his countenance fell. And the LORD said unto Cain, "Why art thou wroth? and why is thy countenance fallen? If thou doest well, shalt thou not be accepted? and if thou doest not well, sin lieth at the door. And unto thee shall be his desire, and thou shalt rule over him." And Cain talked with Abel his brother: and it came to pass, when they were in the field, that Cain rose up against Abel his brother, and slew him. And the LORD said unto Cain, Where is Abel thy brother?" And he said, "I know not: Am I my brother's keeper?" 10 And he said, "What hast thou done? the voice of thy brother's blood crieth unto me from the ground. And now art thou cursed from the earth, which hath opened her mouth to receive thy brother's blood from thy hand; when thou tillest the ground, it shall not henceforth yield unto thee her strength; a fugitive and a vagabond shalt thou be in the earth." And Cain said unto the LORD, "My punishment is greater than I can bear. Behold, thou hast driven me out this day from the face of the earth; and from thy face shall I be hid; and I shall be a fugitive and a vagabond in the earth; and it shall come to pass, that every one that findeth me shall slay me." And the LORD said unto him, "Therefore whosoever slayeth Cain, vengeance shall be taken on him sevenfold". And the LORD set a mark upon Cain, lest any finding him should kill him.

16 And Cain went out from the presence of the Lord, and dwelt in the land of Nod, on the east of Eden. And Cain knew his wife; and she conceived, and bare Enoch: and he builded a city, and called the name of the city, after the name of his son, Enoch. And unto Enoch was born Irad: and Irad begat Mehujael: and Mehujael begat Methusael: and Methusael begat Lamech. And Lamech took unto him two wives: the name of the one was Adah, and the name of the other Zillah. And Adah bare Jabal: he was the father of such as dwell in tents, and of such as have cattle. And his brother's name was Jubal: he was the father of all such as handle the harp and organ. And Zillah, she also bare Tubal-cain, an instructer of every artificer in brass and iron: and the sister of Tubal-cain was Naamah. And Lamech said unto his wives,

> "Adah and Zillah, Hear my voice;
> Ye wives of Lamech, hearken unto my speech:
> For I have slain a man to my wounding,
> And a young man to my hurt.
> If Cain shall be avenged sevenfold,
> Truly Lamech seventy and sevenfold."

And Adam knew his wife again; and she bare a son, and called his name Seth: "For God", said she, "hath appointed me another seed instead of Abel, whom Cain slew." And to Seth, to him also there was born a son; and he called his name Enos: then began men to call upon the name of the Lord.

CHAPTER 5.1–5

This is the book of the generations of Adam. In the day that God created man, in the likeness of God made he him; male and female created he them; and blessed them, and called their name Adam, in the day when they were created. And Adam lived an hundred and thirty years, and begat a son in his own likeness, after his image; and called his name Seth: and the days of Adam after he had begotten Seth were eight hundred years: and he begat sons and daughters: and all the days that Adam lived were nine hundred and thirty years: and he died.

CHAPTER 6

And it came to pass, when men began to multiply on the face of the earth, and daughters were born unto them, that the sons of God saw the daughters of men that they were fair; and they took them wives of all which they chose. And the Lord said, "My spirit shall not always strive with man, for that he also is flesh: yet his days shall be an hundred and twenty years". There were giants in the earth in those days; and also after that, when the sons of God came in unto the daughters of men, and they bare children to them, the same became mighty men which were of old, men of renown. And GOD saw that the wickedness of man was great in the earth, and that every imagination of the thoughts of his heart was only evil continually. And it repented the LORD that he had made man on the earth, and it grieved him at his heart. And the LORD said, "I will destroy man whom I have created from the face of the earth; both man, and beast, and the creeping thing, and the fowls of the air; for it repenteth me that I have made them". But Noah found grace in the eyes of the LORD.

9 These are the generations of Noah: Noah was a just man and perfect in his generations, and Noah walked with God. And Noah begat three sons, Shem, Ham, and Japheth. The earth also was corrupt before God, and the earth was filled with violence. And God looked upon the earth, and, behold, it was corrupt; for all flesh had corrupted his way upon the earth.

13 And God said unto Noah, "The end of all flesh is come before me; for the earth is filled with violence through them; and, behold, I will destroy them with the earth. Make thee an ark of gopher wood; rooms shalt thou make in the ark, and shalt pitch it within and without with pitch. And this is the fashion which thou shalt make it of: The length of the ark shall be tree hundred cubits, the breadth of it fifty cubits, and the height of it thirty cubits. A window shalt thou make to the ark, and in a cubit shalt thou finish it above; and the door of the ark shalt thou set in the side thereof; with lower, second, and third stories shalt thou make it. And, behold, I, even I, do bring a flood of waters upon the earth, to destroy all flesh, wherein is the breath of life, from under heaven; and every thing that is in the earth shall die. But with thee will I establish my covenant; and thou shalt come into the ark, thou, and thy sons, and thy wife, and thy sons' wives with thee. And of every living thing of all flesh, two of every sort shalt thou bring into the ark, to keep them alive with thee; they shall be male and female. Of fowls after their kind, and of cattle after their kind, of every creeping thing of the earth after his kind, two of every sort shall come unto thee, to keep them alive. And take thou unto thee of all food that is eaten, and thou shalt gather it to thee; and it shall be for food for thee, and for them." Thus did Noah; according to all that God commanded him, so did he.

CHAPTER 7

And the LORD said unto Noah, "Come thou and all thy house into the ark; for thee have I seen righteous before me in this generation. Of every clean beast thou shalt take to thee by sevens, the male and his female: and of beasts that are not clean by two, the male and his female. Of fowls also of the air by sevens, the male and the female; to keep seed alive upon the face of all the earth. For yet seven days, and I will cause it to rain upon the earth forty days and forty nights; and every living substance that I have made will I destroy from off the face of the earth." And Noah did according unto all that the LORD commanded him.

6 And Noah was six hundred years old when the flood of waters was upon the earth. And Noah went in, and his sons, and his wife, and his sons' wives with him, into the ark, because of the waters of the flood. Of clean beasts, and of beasts that are not clean, and of fowls, and of every thing that creepeth upon the earth, there went in two and two unto Noah into the ark, the male and the female, as God had commanded Noah. And it came to pass after seven days, that the waters of the flood were upon the earth. In the six hundredth year of Noah's life, in the second month, the seventeenth day of the month, the same day were all the fountains of the great deep broken up and the windows of heaven were opened. And the rain was upon the earth forty days and forty nights. In the selfsame day entered Noah, and Shem, and Ham, and Japheth, the sons of Noah, and Noah's wife, and the three wives of his sons with them, into the ark; they, and every beast after his kind, and all the cattle after their kind, and every creeping thing that creepeth upon the earth after his kind, and every fowl after his kind, every bird of every sort. And they went in unto Noah into the ark, two and two of all flesh, wherein is the breath of life. 16 And they that went in, went in male and female of all flesh, as God had commanded him: and the LORD shut him in. And the flood was forty days upon the earth; and the waters increased, and bare up the ark, and it was lift up above the earth. And the waters prevailed, and were increased greatly upon the earth; and the ark went upon the face of the waters. And the waters prevailed exceedingly upon the earth; and all the high hills, that were under the whole heaven, were covered. Fifteen cubits upward did the waters prevail; and the mountains were covered. And all flesh died that moved upon the earth, both of fowl, and of cattle, and of beast, and of every creeping thing that creepth upon the earth, and every man: all in whose nostrils was the breath of life, of all that was in the dry land, died. And every living substance was destroyed which was upon the face of the ground, both man, and cattle, and the creeping things, and the fowl of the heaven; and they were destroyed from the earth: and Noah only remained alive, and they that were with him in the ark. And the waters prevailed upon the earth an hundred and fifty days.

CHAPTER 8

And God remembered Noah, and every living thing, and all the cattle that was with him in the ark: and God made a wind to pass over the earth, and the waters assuaged; the fountains also of the deep and the windows of heaven were stopped, and the rain from heaven was restrained; and the waters returned from off the earth continually: and after the end of the hundred and fifty days the waters were abated. And the ark rested in the seventh month, on the seventeenth day of the month, upon the mountains of Ararat. And the waters decreased continually until the tenth month: in the tenth month, on the first day of the month, were the tops of the mountains seen. And it came to pass at the end of forty days, that Noah opened the window of the ark which he had made: and he sent forth a raven, which went forth to and fro, until the waters were dried up from off the earth. 8 Also he sent forth a dove from him, to see if the waters were abated from off the face of the ground; but the dove found no rest for the sole of her foot, and she returned unto him into the ark, for the waters were on the face of the whole earth: then he put forth his hand, and took her, and pulled her in unto him into the ark. And he stayed yet other seven days; and again he sent forth the dove out of the ark; and the dove came in to him in the evening; and, lo, in her mouth was an olive leaf pluckt off: so Noah knew that the waters were abated from off the earth. And he stayed yet other seven days; and sent forth the dove; which returned not again unto him any more. And it came to pass in the six hundredth and first year, in the first month, the first day of the month, the waters were dried up from off the earth: and Noah removed the covering of the ark, and looked, and, behold, the face of the ground was dry. And in the second month, on the seven and twentieth day of the month, was the earth dried.

15 And God spake unto Noah, saying, "Go forth of the ark, thou, and thy wife, and thy sons, and thy sons' wives with thee. Bring forth with thee every living thing that is with thee, of all flesh, both of fowl, and of cattle, and of every creeping thing that creepeth upon the earth; that they may breed abundantly in the earth, and be fruitful, and multiply upon the earth." And Noah went forth, and his sons, and his wife, and his sons' wives with him: every beast, every creeping thing, and every fowl, and whatsoever creepeth upon the earth, after their kinds, went forth out of the ark. And Noah builded an altar unto the LORD; and took of every clean beast, and of every clean fowl, and offered burnt offerings on the altar. And the LORD smelled a sweet savour; and the LORD said in his heart, "I will not again curse the ground any more for man's sake; for the imagination of man's heart is evil from his

youth; neither will I again smite any more every thing living, as I have done. While the earth remaineth, seedtime and harvest, and cold and heat, and summer and winter, and day and night shall not cease."

And God blessed Noah and his sons, and said unto them, "Be fruitful, and multiply, and replenish the earth. And the fear of you and the dread of you shall be upon every beast of the earth, and upon every fowl of the air, upon all that moveth upon the earth, and upon all the fishes of the sea; into your hand are they delivered. Every moving thing that liveth shall be meat for you; even as the green herb have I given you all things. But flesh with the life thereof, which is the blood thereof, shall ye not eat. And surely your blood of your lives will I require; at the hand of every beast will I require it, and at the hand of man; at the hand of every man's brother will I require the life of man. Whoso sheddeth man's blood, by man shall his blood be shed: for in the image of God made he man. And you, be ye fruitful, and multiply; bring forth abundantly in the earth, and multiply therein."

8 And God spake unto Noah, and to his sons with him, saying "And I, behold, I establish my covenant with you, and with your seed after you; and with every living creature that is with you, of the fowl, of the cattle, and of every beast of the earth with you; from all that go out of the ark, to every beast of the earth. And I will establish my covenant with you; neither shall all flesh be cut off any more by the waters of a flood; neither shall there any more be a flood to destroy the earth." And God said, "This is the token of the covenant which I make between me and you and every living creature that is with you, for perpetual generations: I do set my bow in the cloud, and it shall be for a token of a covenant between me and the earth. And it shall come to pass, when I bring a cloud over the earth, that the bow shall be seen in the cloud: and I will remember my covenant, which is between me and you and every living creature of all flesh; and the waters shall no more become a flood to destroy all flesh. And the bow shall be in the cloud; and I will look upon it, that I may remember the everlasting covenant between God and every living creature of all flesh that is upon the earth." And God said unto Noah, "This is the token of the covenant, which I have established between me and all flesh that is upon the earth".

18 And the sons of Noah, that went forth of the ark, were Shem, and Ham, and Japheth: and Ham is the father of Canaan. These are the three sons of Noah: and of them was the whole earth overspread.

And Noah began to be an husbandman, and he planted a vineyard: and he drank of the wine, and was drunken; and he was uncovered within his tent. And Ham, the father of Canaan, saw the nakedness of his father, and told his two brethren without. And Shem and Japheth took a garment, and laid it upon both their shoulders, and went backward, and covered the nakedness of their father; and their faces were backward, and they saw not their father's nakedness. And Noah awoke from his wine, and knew what his younger son had done unto him. And he said,

> "Cursed be Canaan;
> A servant of servants shall he be unto his breathren".

And he said,

> "Blessed be the LORD God of Shem;
> And Canaan shall be his servant.
> God shall enlarge Japheth,
> And he shall dwell in the tents of Shem;
> And Canaan shall be his servant."

And Noah lived after the flood three hundred and fifty years. And all the days of Noah were nine hundred and fifty years: and he died.

CHAPTER 11.1–9, 31–32

And the whole earth was of one language, and of one speech. And it came to pass, as they journeyed from the east, that they found a plain in the land of Shinar; and they dwelt there. And they said one to another, "Go to, let us make brick, and burn them throughly." And they had brick for stone, and slime had they for morter. And they said, "Go to, let us build us a city and a tower, whose top may reach unto heaven; and let us make us a name, lest we be scattered abroad upon the face of the whole earth". And the LORD came down to see the city and the tower, which the children of men builded. And the LORD said, "Behold, the people is one, and they have all one language; and this they begin to do: and now nothing will be restrained from them, which they have imagined to do. Go to, let us go down, and there confound their language, that they may not understand one another's speech." So the LORD scattered them abroad from thence upon the face of all the earth: and they left off to build the city. Therefore is the name of it called Babel; because the LORD did there confound the language of all the earth: and from thence did the LORD scatter them abroad upon the face of all the earth.

* * *

And Terah took Abram his son, and Lot the son of Haran his son's son, and Sarai his daughter in law, his son Abram's wife; and they went forth with them from Ur of the Chaldees, to go into the land of Canaan; and they came unto Haran, and dwelt there. And the days of Terah were two hundred and five years: and Terah died in Haran.

Now the Lord had said unto Abram, "Get thee out of thy country, and from thy kindred, and from thy father's house, unto a land that I will shew thee: and I will make of thee a great nation, and I will bless thee, and make thy name great; and thou shalt be a blessing: and I will bless them that bless thee, and curse him that curseth thee: and in thee shall all families of the earth be blessed." So Abram departed, as the Lord had spoken unto him; and Lot went with him: and Abram was seventy and five years old when he departed out of Haran. And Abram took Sarai his wife, and Lot his brother's son, and all their substance that they had gathered, and the souls that they had gotten in Haran; and they went forth to go into the land of Canaan; and into the land of Canaan they came. And Abram passed through the land unto the place of Sichem, unto the plain of Moreh. And the Canaanite was then in the land. And the Lord appeared unto Abram, and said, "Unto thy seed will I give this land": and there builded he an altar unto the Lord, who appeared unto him.

The Book of Exodus

And it came to pass, when Pharaoh had let the people go, that God led them not through the way of the land of the Philistines, although that was near; for God said, "Lest peradventure the people repent when they see war, and they return to Egypt": but God led the people about, through the way of the wilderness of the Red sea: and the children of Israel went up harnessed out of the land of Egypt. And Moses took the bones of Joseph with him: for he had straitly sworn the children of Israel, saying, "God will surely visit you; and ye shall carry up my bones away hence with you". And they took their journey from Succoth, and encamped in Etham, in the edge of the wilderness. And the Lord went before them by day in a pillar of a cloud, to lead them the way; and by night in a pillar of fire, to give them light; to go by day and night: he took not away the pillar of the cloud by day, nor the pillar of fire by night, from before the people.

And it was told the king of Egypt that the people fled: and the heart of Pharaoh and of his servants was turned against the people, and they said, "Why have we done this, that we have let Israel go from serving us?" And he made ready his chariot, and took his people with him: and he took six hundred chosen chariots, and all the chariots of Egypt, and captains over every one of them. And the LORD hardened the heart of Pharaoh king of Egypt, and he pursued after the children of Israel: and the children of Israel went out with an high hand. But the Egyptians pursued after them, all the horses and chariots of Pharaoh, and his horsemen, and his army, and overtook them encamping by the sea, beside Pi-hahiroth, before Baal-zephon. And when Pharaoh drew nigh, the children of Israel lifted up their eyes, and, behold, the Egyptians marched after them; and they were sore afraid: and the children of Israel cried out unto the LORD. And they said unto Moses, "Because there were no graves in Egypt, hast thou taken us away to die in the wilderness? wherefore hast thou dealt thus with us, to carry us forth out of Egypt? Is not this the word that we did tell thee in Egypt, saying, Let us alone, that we may serve the Egyptians? For it had been better for us to serve the Egyptians, than that we should die in the wilderness." And Moses said unto the people, "Fear ye not, stand still, and see the salvation of the LORD, which he will shew to you to day: for the Egyptians whom ye have seen to day, ye shall see them again no more for ever. The LORD shall fight for you, and ye shall hold your peace."

15 And the LORD said unto Moses, "Wherefore criest thou unto me? speak unto the children of Israel, that they go forward: but lift thou up thy rod, and stretch out thine hand over the sea, and divide it: and the children of Israel shall go on dry ground through the midst of the sea. And I, behold, I will harden the hearts of the Egyptians, and they shall follow them: and I will get me honour upon Pharaoh, and upon all his host, upon his chariots, and upon his horsemen. And the Egyptians shall know that I am the LORD, when I have gotten me honour upon Pharaoh, upon his chariots, and upon his horsemen." And the angel of God, which went before the camp of Israel, removed and went behind them; and the pillar of the cloud went from before their face, and stood behind them: and it came between the camp of the Egyptians and the camp of Israel; and it was a cloud and darkness to them, but it gave light by night to these: so that the one came not near the other all the night. And Moses stretched out his hand over the sea; and the LORD caused the sea to go back by a strong east wind all that night, and made the sea dry land, and the waters were divided. And the

children of Israel went into the midst of the sea upon the dry ground: and the waters were a wall unto them on their right hand, and on their left. And the Egyptians pursued, and went in after them to the midst of the sea, even all Pharaoh's horses, his chariots, and his horsemen. And it came to pass, that in the morning watch the LORD looked unto the host of the Egyptians through the pillar of fire and of the cloud, and troubled the host of the Egyptians, and took off their chariot wheels, that they drave them heavily: so that the Egyptians said, "Let us flee from the face of Israel; for the LORD fighteth for them against the Egyptians".

26 And the LORD said unto Moses, "Stretch out thine hand over the sea, that the waters may come again upon the Egyptians, upon their chariots, and upon their horsemen". And Moses stretched forth his hand over the sea, and the sea returned to his strength when the morning appeared; and the Egyptians fled against it; and the LORD overthrew the Egyptians in the midst of the sea. And the waters returned, and covered the chariots, and the horsemen, and all the host of Pharaoh that came into the sea after them; there remained not so much as one of them. But the children of Israel walked upon dry land in the midst of the sea; and the waters were a wall unto them on their right hand, and on their left. Thus the LORD saved Israel that day out of the hand of the Egyptians; and Israel saw the Egyptians dead upon the sea shore. And Israel saw that great work which the LORD did upon the Egyptians: and the people feared the LORD, and believed the LORD, and his servant Moses.

CHAPTER 19.1–9, 16–25

In the third month, when the children of Israel were gone forth out of the land of Egypt, the same day came they into the wilderness of Sinai. For they were departed from Rephidim, and were come to the desert of Sinai, and had pitched in the wilderness; and there Israel camped before the mount. And Moses went up unto God, and the LORD called unto him out of the mountain, saying, "Thus shalt thou say to the house of Jacob, and tell the children of Israel; 'Ye have seen what I did unto the Egyptians, and how I bare you on eagles' wings, and brought you unto myself. Now therefore, if ye will obey my voice indeed, and keep my covenant, then ye shall be a peculiar treasure unto me above all people: for all the earth is mine: and ye shall be unto me a kingdom of priests, and an holy nation.' These are the words which thou shalt speak unto the children of Israel." And Moses came and called for the elders of the people, and laid before their faces all these words which the LORD commanded him. And all the people answered together, and said, "All that the LORD hath spoken we will do". And Moses returned the words of the people unto the Lord. And the Lord said unto Moses, "Lo, I come unto thee in a thick cloud, that the people may hear when I speak with thee, and believe thee for ever". And Moses told the words of the people unto the Lord.

*   *   *

And it came to pass on the third day in the morning, that there were thunders and lightnings, and a thick cloud upon the mount, and the voice of the trumpet exceeding loud; so that all the people that was in the camp trembled. And Moses brought forth the people out of the camp to meet with God; and they stood at the nether part of the mount. And mount Sinai was altogether on a smoke, because the Lord descended upon it in fire: and the smoke thereof ascended as the smoke of a furnace, and the whole mount quaked greatly. And when the voice of the trumpet sounded long, and waxed louder and louder, Moses spake, and God answered him by a voice. And the Lord came down upon mount Sinai, on the top of the mount: and the Lord called Moses up to the top of the mount; and Moses went up. And the Lord said unto Moses, "Go down, charge the people, lest they break through unto the Lord to gaze, and many of them perish. And let the priests also, which come near to the Lord, sanctify themselves, lest the Lord break forth upon them." And Moses said unto the Lord, "The people cannot come up to mount Sinai: for thou chargedst us, saying, 'Set bounds about the mount, and sanctify it' ". And the Lord said unto him, "Away, get thee down, and thou shalt come up, thou, and Aaron with thee: but let not the priests and the people break through to come up unto the Lord, lest he break forth upon them". So Moses went down unto the people, and spake unto them.

CHAPTER 20.1—21

And God spake all these words, saying,

"I am the Lord thy God, which have brought thee out of the land of Egypt, out of the house of bondage.

"Thou shalt have no other gods before me.

"Thou shalt not make unto thee any graven image, or any likeness of any thing that is in heaven above, or that is in the earth beneath, or that is in the water under the earth: thou shalt not bow down thyself to them, nor serve them: for I the Lord thy God am a jealous God, visiting the iniquity of the fathers upon the children unto the third and fourth generation of them that hate me; and shewing mercy unto thousands of them that love me, and keep my commandments.

"Thou shalt not take the name of the Lord thy God in vain; for the Lord will not hold him guiltless that taketh his name in vain.

9 "Remember the sabbath day, to keep it holy. Six days shalt thou labour, and do all thy work: but the seventh day is the sabbath of the LORD thy God: in it thou shalt not do any work, thou, nor thy son, nor thy daughter, thy manservant, nor thy maidservant, nor thy cattle, nor thy stranger that is within thy gates: for in six days the LORD made heaven and earth, the sea, and all that in them is, and rested the seventh day: wherefore the LORD blessed the sabbath day, and hallowed it.

"Honour thy father and thy mother: that thy days may be long upon the land which the LORD thy God giveth thee.

"Thou shalt not kill.

"Thou shalt not commit adultery.

"Thou shalt not steal.

"Thou shalt not bear false witness against thy neighbour.

"Thou shalt not covet thy neighbour's house, thou shalt not covet thy neighbour's wife, nor his manservant, nor his maidservant, nor his ox, nor his ass, nor any thing that is thy neighbour's."

18 And all the people saw the thunderings, and the lightnings, and the noise of the trumpet, and the mountain smoking: and when the people saw it, they removed, and stood afar off. And they said unto Moses, "Speak thou with us, and we will hear: but let not God speak with us, lest we die". And Moses said unto the people, "Fear not: for God is come to prove you, and that his fear may be before your faces, that ye sin not". And the people stood afar off, and Moses drew near unto the thick darkness where God was.

CHAPTER 24

And he said unto Moses, "Come up unto the LORD, thou, and Aaron, Nadab, and Abihu, and seventy of the elders of Israel; and worship ye afar off. And Moses alone shall come near the LORD: but they shall not come nigh; neither shall the people go up with him." And Moses came and told the people all the words of the LORD, and all the judgments: and all the people answered with one voice, and said, "All the words which the LORD hath said will we do". And Moses wrote all the words of the LORD, and rose up early in the morning, and builded an altar under the hill, and twelve pillars, according to the twelve tribes of Israel. 5 And he sent young men of the children of Israel, which offered burnt offerings, and sacrificed peace offerings of oxen unto the LORD. And Moses took half of the blood, and put it in basons; and half of the blood he sprinkled on the altar. And he took the book of the covenant, and read in the audience of the people: and they said, "All that the LORD hath said will we do, and be obedient". And Moses took the blood, and sprinkled it on the people, and said, "Behold the blood of the covenant, which the LORD hath made with you concerning all these words". Then went up Moses, and Aaron, Nadab, and Abihu, and seventy of the elders of Israel: and they saw the God of Israel: and there was under his feet as it were a paved work of a sapphire stone, and as it were the body of heaven in his clearness. And upon the nobles of the children of Israel he laid not his hand: also they saw God, and did eat and drink.

12 And the LORD said unto Moses, "Come up to me into the mount, and be there: and I will give thee tables of stone, and a law, and commandments which I have written; that thou mayest teach them". And Moses rose up, and his minister Joshua: and Moses went up into the mount of God. And he said unto the elders, "Tarry ye here for us, until we come again unto you: and, behold, Aaron and Hur are with you: if any man have any matters to do, let him come unto them". And Moses went up into the mount, and a cloud covered the mount. And the glory of the LORD abode upon mount Sinai, and the cloud covered it six days: and the seventh day he called unto Moses out of the midst of the cloud. And the sight of the glory of the LORD was like devouring fire on the top of the mount in the eyes of the children of Israel. And Moses went into the midst of the cloud, and gat him up into the mount: and Moses was in the mount forty days and forty nights.

CHAPTER 40.34–38

Then a cloud covered the tent of the congregation, and the glory of the LORD filled the tabernacle. And Moses was not able to enter into the tent of the congregation, because the cloud abode thereon, and the glory of the LORD filled the tabernacle. And when the cloud was taken up from over the tabernacle, the children of Israel went onward in all their journeys: but if the cloud were not taken up, then they journeyed not till the day that it was taken up. For the cloud of the LORD was upon the tabernacle by day, and fire was on it by night, in the sight of all the house of Israel, throughout all their journeys.

The Book of Job†

CHAPTER 26.5–13

In the underworld the shades writhe in fear,
the waters and all that live in them are struck with terror.
Sheol is laid bare,
and Abaddon uncovered before him.
God spreads the canopy of the sky over chaos

† From *The New English Bible*. © The Delegates of the Oxford University Press and the Syndics of the Cambridge University Press, 1961, 1970. Reprinted by permission.

and suspends earth in the void.
He keeps the waters penned in dense cloud-masses,
and the clouds do not burst open under their weight.
He covers the face of the full moon,
unrolling his clouds across it.
He has fixed the horizon on the surface of the waters
at the farthest limit of light and darkness.
The pillars of heaven quake
and are aghast at his rebuke.
With his strong arm he cleft the sea-monster,
and struck down the Rahab by his skill.
At his breath the skies are clear,
and his hand breaks the twisting sea-serpent.

CHAPTER 38.1–34

Then the LORD answered Job out of the tempest:

Who is this whose ignorant words
cloud my design in darkness?
Brace yourself and stand up like a man;
I will ask questions, and you shall answer.
Where were you when I laid the earth's foundations?
Tell me, if you know and understand.
5   Who settled its dimensions? Surely you should know.
Who stretched his measuring-line over it?
On what do its supporting pillars rest?
Who set its corner-stone in place,
when the morning stars sang together
and all the sons of God shouted aloud?
Who watched over the birth of the sea,
when it burst in flood from the womb?—
when I wrapped it in a blanket of cloud
and cradled it in fog,
when I established its bounds,
fixing its doors and bars in place,
and said, 'Thus far shall you come and no farther,
and here your surging waves shall halt.'
12   In all your life have you ever called up the dawn
or shown the morning its place?
Have you taught it to grasp the fringes of the earth
and shake the Dog-star from its place;
to bring up the horizon in relief as clay under a seal,
until all things stand out like the folds of a cloak,
when the light of the Dog-star is dimmed
and the stars of the Navigator's Line go out one by one?
Have you descended to the springs of the sea
or walked in the unfathomable deep?
Have the gates of death been revealed to you?
Have you ever seen the door-keepers of the
        place of darkness?

Have you comprehended the vast expanse of the world?
Come, tell me all this, if you know.
Which is the way to the home of light
and where does darkness dwell?
20 And can you then take each to its appointed bound
and escort it on its homeward path?
Doubtless you know all this; for you were born already,
so long is the span of your life!

Have you visited the storehouse of the snow
or seen the arsenal where hail is stored,
which I have kept ready for the day of calamity,
for war and for the hour of battle?
By what paths is the heat spread abroad
or the east wind carried far and wide over the earth?
Who has cut channels for the downpour
and cleared a passage for the thunderstorm,
for rain to fall on land where no man lives
and on the deserted wilderness,
clothing lands waste and derelict with green
and making grass grow on thirsty ground?
Has the rain a father?
Who sired the drops of dew?
29 Whose womb gave birth to the ice,
and who was the mother of the frost from heaven,
which lays a stony cover over the waters
and freezes the expanse of ocean?
Can you bind the cluster of the Pleiades
or loose Orion's belt?
Can you bring out the signs of the zodiac in their season
or guide Aldebaran and its train?
Did you proclaim the rules that govern the heavens,
or determine the laws of nature on earth?

Psalm 104

Bless the Lord, O my soul.
O Lord my God, thou art very great;
Thou art clothed with honour and majesty.
Who coverest thyself with light as with a garment:
Who stretchest out the heavens like a curtain:
Who layeth the beams of his chambers in the waters:
Who maketh the clouds his chariot:
Who walketh upon the wings of the wind:
Who maketh his angels spirits;
His ministers a flaming fire:
5 Who laid the foundations of the earth,
That it should not be removed for ever.
Thou coveredst it with the deep as with a garment:
The waters stood above the mountains.

At thy rebuke they fled:
At the voice of thy thunder they hasted away.
They go up by the mountains; they go down
    by the valleys
Unto the place which thou hast founded for them.
Thou hast set a bound that they may not pass over;
That they turn not again to cover the earth.

10 He sendeth the springs into the valleys,
Which run among the hills.
They give drink to every beast of the field:
The wild asses quench their thirst.
By them shall the fowls of the heaven have
    their habitation,
Which sing among the branches.
He watereth the hills from his chambers:
The earth is satisfied with the fruit of thy works.
He causeth the grass to grow for the cattle,
And herb for the service of man:
That he may bring forth food out of the earth;

15 And wine that maketh glad the heart of man,
And oil to make his face to shine,
And bread which strengtheneth man's heart.
The trees of the Lord are full of sap;
The cedars of Lebanon, which he hath planted;
Where the birds make their nests:
As for the stork, the fir trees are her house.
The high hills are a refuge for the wild goats;
And the rocks for the conies.
He appointed the moon for seasons:
The sun knoweth his going down.

20 Thou makest darkness, and it is night:
Wherein all the beasts of the forest do creep forth.
The young lions roar after their prey,
And seek their meat from God.
The sun ariseth, they father themselves together,
And lay them down in their dens.
Man goeth forth unto his work
And to his labour until the evening.
O Lord, how manifold are thy works!
In wisdom hast thou made them all:
The earth is full of thy riches.

25 So is this great and wide sea,
Wherein are things creeping innumerable,
Both small and great beasts.
There go the ships:
There is that leviathan, whom thou hast made
    to play therein.
These wait all upon thee:
That thou mayest give them their meat in
    due season.
That thou givest them they gather:

Thou openest thine hand, they are filled with good.
Thou hidest thy face, they are troubled:
Thou takest away their breath, they die,
And return to their dust.

30 Thou sendest forth thy spirit, they are created:
And thou renewest the face of the earth.
The glory of the Lord shall endure for ever:
The Lord shall rejoice in his works.
He looketh on the earth, and it trembleth:
He toucheth the hills, and they smoke.
I will sing unto the Lord as long as I live:
I will sing praise to my God while I have my being.
My meditation of him shall be sweet:
I will be glad in the Lord.
Let the sinners be consumed out of the earth,
And let the wicked be no more.
Bless thou the Lord, O my soul.
Praise ye the Lord.

Psalm 148

Praise ye the Lord.
Praise ye the Lord from the heavens:
Praise him in the heights.
Praise ye him, all his angels:
Praise ye him, all his hosts.
Praise ye him, sun and moon:
Praise him, all ye stars of light.
Praise him, ye heavens of heavens,
And ye waters that be above the heavens.
Let them praise the name of the Lord:
For he commanded, and they were created.
He hath also stablished them for ever and ever:
He hath made a decree which shall not pass.
Praise the Lord from the earth,
Ye dragons, and all deeps:
Fire, and hail; snow, and vapour;
Stormy wind fulfilling his word:
Mountains, and all hills;
Fruitful trees, and all cedars:
Beasts, and all cattle;
Creeping things, and flying fowl:
Kings of the earth, and all people;
Princes, and all judges of the earth:
Both young men, and maidens;
Old men, and children:
Let them praise the name of the Lord:
For his name alone is excellent;
His glory is above the earth and heaven.

He also exalteth the horn of his people,
The praise of all his saints;
Even of the children of Israel, a people near unto him.
Praise ye the LORD.

The Book of Isaiah

CHAPTER 6.1–9

In the year that king Uzziah died I saw also the Lord sitting upon a throne, high and lifted up, and his train filled the temple. Above it stood the seraphims: each one had six wings; with twain he covered his face, and with twain he covered his feet, and with twain he did fly. And one cried unto another, and said,

> "Holy, holy, holy, is the LORD of hosts:
> The whole earth is full of his glory".

And the posts of the door moved at the voice of him that cried, and the house was filled with smoke. Then said I, "Woe is me! for I am undone; because I am a man of unclean lips, and I dwell in the midst of a people of unclean lips: for mine eyes have seen the King, the LORD of hosts". Then flew one of the seraphims unto me, having a live coal in his hand, which he had taken with the tongs from off the altar: and he laid it upon my mouth, and said, "Lo, this hath touched thy lips; and thine iniquity is taken away, and thy sin purged". Also I heard the voice of the Lord, saying, "Whom shall I send, and who will go for us?" Then said I, "Here am I; send me". And he said, "Go, and tell this people,

> 'Hear ye indeed, but understand not;
> And see ye indeed, but perceive not'.

CHAPTER 7.10–14

Moreover the LORD spake again unto Ahaz, saying,

> "Ask thee a sign of the LORD thy God;
> Ask it either in the depth, or in the height above".

But Ahaz said, "I will not ask, neither will I tempt the LORD". And he said,

> "Hear ye now, O house of David;
> Is it a small thing for you to weary men,
>   but will ye weary my God also?
> Therefore the Lord himself shall give you a sign;
> Behold, a virgin shall conceive, and bear a son,
> And shall call his name Immanuel.

The people that walked in darkness
    have seen a great light:
They that dwell in the land of the shadow of death,
    upon them hath the light shined.
Thou hast multiplied the nation,
    and not increased the joy;
They joy before thee according to the joy in harvest,
And as men rejoice when they divide the spoil.
For thou hast broken the yoke of his burden,
    and the staff of his shoulder,
The rod of his oppressor, as in the day of Midian.
For every battle of the warrior is with confused noise,
And garments rolled in blood;
But this shall be with burning and fuel of fire.
For unto us a child is born, unto us a son is given:
And the government shall be upon his shoulder:
And his name shall be called Wonderful, Counsellor,
    The Mighty God,
The Everlasting Father, The Prince of Peace.
Of the increase of his government and peace
    there shall be no end,
Upon the throne of David, and upon his kingdom,
To order it, and to establish it with judgment
    and with justice
From henceforth even for ever.
The zeal of the Lord of hosts will perform this.

For the Lord will have mercy on Jacob,
And will yet choose Israel,
And set them in their own land:
And the strangers shall be joined with them,
And they shall cleave to the house of Jacob.
And the people shall take them, and bring them
    to their place:
And the house of Israel shall possess them in the land
    of the Lord
For the servants and handmaids:
And they shall take them captives,
    whose captives they were;
And they shall rule over their oppressors.

And it shall come to pass in the day that the Lord shall give thee rest from thy sorrow, and from thy fear, and from the hard bondage wherein thou wast made to serve, that thou shalt take up this proverb against the king of Babylon, and say,

"How hath the oppressor ceased! the golden city ceased!
5   The LORD hath broken the staff of the wicked, and
      the sceptre of the rulers.
He who smote the people in wrath with a continual stroke,
He that ruled the nations in anger, is persecuted, and
      none hindereth.
The whole earth is at rest, and is quiet: they break
      forth into singing.
Yea, the fir trees rejoice at thee, and the cedars
      of Lebanon, saying,
'Since thou art laid down, no feller is come up against us'.
Hell from beneath is moved for thee to meet thee at
      thy coming:
It stirreth up the dead for thee, even all the chief ones
      of the earth;
It hath raised up from their thrones all the kings of
      of the nations.
10   All they shall speak and say unto thee,
    'Art thou also become weak as we?
      art thou become like unto us?'
The pomp is brought down to the grave, and the noise
      of thy viols:
The worm is spread under thee, and the worms cover thee.
How art thou fallen from heaven. O Lucifer,
      son of the morning!
How art thou cut down to the ground, which didst
      weaken the nations!
For thou hast said in thine heart, 'I will ascend into heaven,
I will exalt my throne above the stars of God:
I will sit also upon the mount of the congregation,
      in the sides of the north:
I will ascend above the heights of the clouds; I will be
      like the Most High'.
15   Yet thou shalt be brought down to hell, to the
      sides of the pit.
They that see thee shall narrowly look upon thee,
      and consider thee, saying,
'Is this the man that made the earth to tremble,
      that did shake kingdoms;
That made the world as a wilderness, and destroyed
      the cities thereof;
That opened not the house of his prisoners?'
All the kings of the nations, even all of them,
Lie in glory, every one in his own house.
But thou art cast out of thy grave like an abominable
      branch,
And as the rainment of those that are slain, thrust through
      with a sword,
That go down to the stones of the pit;
      as a carcase trodden under feet.
Thou shalt not be joined with them in burial,

Because thou hast destroyed thy land, and slain thy people:
The seed of evil doers shall never be renowned.
Prepare slaughter for his children for the
      iniquity of their fathers;
That they do not rise, nor possess the land,
Nor fill the face of the world with cities."

CHAPTER 40

"Comfort ye, comfort ye my people," saith your God.
"Speak ye comfortably to Jerusalem, and cry unto her,
That her warfare is accomplished,
That her iniquity is pardoned:
For she hath received of the LORD's hand double
      for all her sins."

3   The voice of him that crieth in the wilderness, "Prepare
          ye the way of the LORD,
Make straight in the desert a highway for our God.
Every valley shall be exalted,
And every mountain and hill shall be made low:
And the crooked shall be made straight,
And the rough places plain:
And the glory of the LORD shall be revealed,
And all flesh shall see it together:
For the mouth of the LORD hath spoken it."
The voice said, "Cry".
And he said, "What shall I cry?"
"All flesh is grass.
And all the goodliness thereof is as the flower of the field:
The grass withereth, the flower fadeth:
Because the spirit of the LORD bloweth upon it:
Surely the people is grass.
The grass withereth, the flower fadeth:
But the word of our God shall stand for ever."

9   O Zion, that bringest good tidings, get thee up into
          the high mountain;
O Jerusalem, that bringest good tidings, lift up thy voice
          with strength;
Lift it up, be not afraid;
Say unto the cities of Judah, "Behold your God!"
Behold, the Lord GOD will come with strong hand,
And his arm shall rule for him:
Behold, his reward is with him,
And his work before him.
He shall feed his flock like a shepherd:
He shall gather the lambs with his arm,
And carry them in his bosom,

And shall gently lead those that are with young.

12 Who hath measured the waters in the hollow of his hand,
And meted out heaven with the span,
And comprehended the dust of the earth in a measure,
And weighed the mountains in scales,
And the hills in a balance?
Who hath directed the spirit of the LORD,
Or being his counsellor hath taught him?
With whom took he counsel, and who instructed him,
And taught him in the path of judgment,
And taught him knowledge,
And shewed to him the way of understanding?
Behold, the nations are as a drop of a bucket,
And are counted as the small dust of the balance:
Behold, he taketh up the isles as a very little thing.
And Lebanon is not sufficient to burn,
Nor the beasts thereof sufficient for a burnt offering.
All nations before him are as nothing;
And they are counted to him less than nothing, and vanity.
18 To whom then will ye liken God?
Or what likeness will ye compare unto him?
The workman melteth a graven image,
And the goldsmith spreadeth it over with gold,
And casteth silver chains.
He that is so impoverished that he hath no oblation
        chooseth a tree that will not rot;
He seeketh unto him a cunning workman
To prepare a graven image, that shall not be moved.
Have ye not known? have ye not heard?
Hath it not been told you from the beginning?
Have ye not understood from the foundations of the earth?
22 It is he that sitteth upon the circle of the earth,
And the inhabitants thereof are as grasshoppers;
That stretcheth out the heavens as a curtain,
And spreadeth them out as a tent to dwell in:
That bringeth the princes to nothing;
He maketh the judges of the earth as vanity.
Yea, they shall not be planted;
Yea, they shall not be sown:
Yea, their stock shall not take root in the earth:
And he shall also blow upon them, and they shall wither,
And the whirlwind shall take them away as stubble.
"To whom then will ye liken me, or shall I be equal?"
        saith the Holy One.
Lift up your eyes on high.
And behold who hath created these things,
That bringeth out their host by number:
He calleth them all by names
By the greatness of his might, for that he is
        strong in power;

Not one faileth.

27 Why sayest thou, O Jacob, and speakest, O Israel,
"My way is hid from the Lord,
And my judgment is passed over from my God"?
Hast thou not known? hast thou not heard,
That the everlasting God, the Lord,
The Creator of the ends of the earth,
Fainteth not, neither is weary?
There is no searching of his understanding.
He giveth power to the faint;
And to them that have no might he increaseth strength.
Even the youths shall faint and be weary,
And the young men shall utterly fall:
But they that wait upon the Lord shall
    renew their strength;
They shall mount up with wings as eagles;
They shall run, and not be weary;
And they shall walk, and not faint.

The Book of Ezekiel

CHAPTER 1

Now it came to pass in the thirtieth year, in the fourth month, in the fifth day of the month, as I was among the captives by the river of Chebar, that the heavens were opened, and I saw visions of God. In the fifth day of the month, which was the fifth year of king Jehoiachin's captivity, the word of the Lord came expressly unto Ezekiel the priest, the son of Buzi, in the land of the Chaldeans by the river Chebar; and the hand of the Lord was there upon him. 4 And I looked, and, behold, a whirlwind came out of the north, a great cloud, and a fire unfolding itself, and a brightness was about it, and out of the midst thereof as the colour of amber, out of the midst of the fire. Also out of the midst thereof came the likeness of four living creatures. And this was their appearance; they had the likeness of a man. And every one had four faces, and every one had four wings. And their feet were straight feet; and the sole of their feet was like the sole of a calf's foot: and they sparkled like the colour of burnished brass. And they had the hands of a man under their wings on their four sides; and they four had their faces and their wings. Their wings were joined one to another; they turned not when they went; they went every one straight forward. 10 As for the likeness of their faces, they four had the face of a man, and the face of a lion, on the right side: and they four had the face of an ox on the left side; they four also had the face of an eagle. Thus were their faces: and their wings were stretched upward; two wings of every one were joined one to another, and two covered their bodies. And they went every one straight forward: whither the spirit was to go, they went; and they turned not when they went. As for the likeness of the living creatures, their appearance was like burning coals of fire, and like the appearance of lamps: it went up and down among the living creatures; and the fire was bright, and out of the fire went forth lightning. And the living creatures ran and returned as the appearance of a flash of lightning. 16 Now as I beheld the living creatures, behold one wheel upon the earth by the living creatures, with his four faces. The appearance of the wheels and their work was like unto the colour of a beryl: and they four had one likeness: and their appearance and their work was as it were a wheel in the middle of a wheel. When they went, they went upon their four sides: and they turned not when they went. As for their rings, they were so high that they were dreadful; and their rings were full of eyes round about them four. And when the living creatures went, the wheels went by them: and when the living creatures were lifted up from the earth, the wheels were lifted up. 20 Whithersoever the spirit was to go, they went, thither was their spirit to go; and the wheels were lifted up over against them: for the spirit of the living creature was in the wheels. When those went, these went; and when those stood, these stood; and when those were lifted up from the earth, the wheels were lifted up over against them: for the spirit of the living creature was in the wheels. And the likeness of the firmament upon the heads of the living creature was as the colour of the terrible crystal, stretched forth over their heads above. And under the firmament were their wings straight, the one toward the other: every one had two, which covered on this side, and every one had two, which covered on that side, their bodies. And when they went, I heard the noise of their wings, like the noise of great waters, as the voice of the Almighty, the voice of speech, as the noise of an host: when they stood, they let down their wings. And there was a voice from the firmament that was over their heads, when they stood, and had let down their wings. 26 And above the firmament that was over their heads was the likeness of a throne, as the appearance of a sapphire stone: and upon the likeness of the throne was the likeness as the appearance of a man above upon it. And I saw as the colour of amber, as the appearance of fire round about within it, from the appearance of his loins even upward, and from the appearance of his loins even downward, I saw as it were the appearance of fire, and it had brightness round about. As the appearance of the bow that is in the cloud in the day of rain, so was the appearance of the brightness round about. This was the appearance of the likeness of the glory of the LORD. And when I saw it, I fell upon my face, and I heard a voice of one that spake.

The Gospel According to St. Matthew

CHAPTER 1.18–25

Now the birth of Jesus Christ was on this wise: When as his mother Mary was espoused to Joseph, before they came together, she was found with child of the Holy Ghost. Then Joseph her husband, being a just man, and not willing to make her a publick example, was minded to put her away privily. But while he thought on these things, behold, the angel of the Lord appeared unto him in a dream, saying, "Joseph, thou son of David, fear not to take unto thee Mary thy wife: for that which is conceived in her is of the Holy Ghost. And she shall bring forth a son, and thou shalt call his name JESUS: for he shall save his people from their sins." Now all this was done, that it might be fulfilled which was spoken of the Lord by the prophet, saying,

"Behold, a virgin shall be with child, and shall bring forth a son,
And they shall call his name Emmanuel,"

which being interpreted is, God with us. Then Joseph being raised from sleep did as the angel of the Lord had bidden him, and took unto him his wife: and knew her not till she had brought forth her firstborn son: and he called his name JESUS.

The Gospel According to St. Mark

CHAPTER 12.28–31

And one of the scribes came, and having heard them reasoning together, and perceiving that he had answered them well, asked him, "Which is the first commandment of all?" And Jesus answered him, "The first of all the commandments is, 'Hear, O Israel; The Lord our God is one Lord: and thou shalt love the Lord thy God with all thy heart, and with all thy soul, and with all thy mind, and with all thy strength:' this is the first commandment. And the second is like, namely this, "Thou shalt love thy neighbour as thyself'. There is none other commandment greater than these."

CHAPTER 13.24–27

"But in those days, after that tribulation, the sun shall be darkened, and the moon shall not give her light, and the stars of heaven shall fall, and the powers that are in heaven shall be shaken. And then shall they see the Son of man coming in the clouds with great power and glory. And then shall he send his angels, and shall gather together his elect from the four winds, from the uttermost part of the earth to the uttermost part of heaven.

The Gospel According to St. Luke

CHAPTER 1.26–35

And in the sixth month the angel Gabriel was sent from God unto a city of Galilee, named Nazareth, to a virgin espoused to a man whose name was Joseph, of the house of David; and the virgin's name was Mary. And the angel came in unto her, and said, "Hail, thou that art highly favoured, the Lord is with thee: blessed art thou among women". And when she saw him, she was troubled at his saying, and cast in her mind what manner of salutation this should be. And the angel said unto her, "Fear not, Mary: for thou hast found favour with God. And, behold, thou shalt conceive in thy womb, and bring forth a son, and shalt call his name JESUS. He shall be great and shall be called the Son of the Highest: and the Lord God shall give unto him the throne of his father David: and he shall reign over the house of Jacob for ever; and of his kingdom there shall be no end." Then said Mary unto the angel, "How shall this be, seeing I know not a man?" And the angel answered and said unto her, "The Holy Ghost shall come upon thee, and the power of the Highest shall overshadow thee: therefore also that holy thing which shall be born of thee shall be called the Son of God.

The Gospel According to St. John

CHAPTER 1.1–4

In the beginning was the Word, and the Word was with God, and the Word was God. The same was in the beginning with God. All things were made by him; and without him was not any thing made that was made. In him was life; and the life was the light of men.

CHAPTER 3.16–21

For God so loved the world, that he gave his only begotten Son, that whosoever believeth in him should not perish, but have everlasting life. For God sent not his Son into the world to condemn the world; but that the world through him might be saved. He that believeth on him is not condemned: but he that believeth not is condemned already, because he hath not believed in the name of the only begotten Son of God. And this is the condemnation, that light is come into the world, and men loved darkness rather than light, because their deeds were evil. For every one that doeth evil hateth the light, neither cometh to the light, lest his deeds should be reproved. But he that doeth truth cometh to the light, that his deeds may be made manifest, that they are wrought in God.

The Letter of Paul to the Romans†

CHAPTER 3.19–28

Now all the words of the law are addressed, as we know, to those who are within the pale of the law, so that no one may have anything to say in self-defence, but the whole world may be exposed to the judgement of God. For (again from Scripture) 'no human being can be justified in the sight of God' for having kept the law: law brings only the consciousness of sin.

But now, quite independently of law, God's justice has been brought to light. The Law and the prophets both bear witness to it: it is God's way of righting wrong, effective through faith in Christ for all who have such faith—all, without distinction. For all alike have sinned, and are deprived of the divine splendour, and all are justified by God's free grace alone, through his act of liberation in the person of Christ Jesus. For God designed him to be the means of expiating sin by his sacrificial death, effective through faith. God meant by this to demonstrate his justice, because in his forbearance he had overlooked the sins of the past—to demonstrate his justice now in the present, showing that he is himself just and also justifies any man who puts his faith in Jesus.

What room then is left for human pride? It is excluded. And on what principle? The keeping of the law would not exclude it, but faith does. For our argument is that a man is justified by faith quite apart from success in keeping the law.

CHAPTER 6.1–11

What are we to say, then "Shall we persist in sin, so that there may be all the more grace? No, no! We died to sin: how can we live in it any longer? Have you forgotten that when we were baptized into union with Christ Jesus we were baptized into his death? By baptism we were buried with him, and lay dead, in order that, as Christ was raised from the dead in the splendour of the Father, so also we might set our feet upon the new path of life.

For if we have become incorporate with him in a death like his,

† From *The New English Bible.* © The Delegates of the Oxford University Press and the Syndics of the Cambridge University Press, 1961, 1970. Reprinted by permission.

we shall also be one with him in a resurrection like his. We know that the man we once were has been crucified with Christ, for the destruction of the sinful self, so that we may no longer be the slaves of sin, since a dead man is no longer answerable for his sin. But if we thus died with Christ, we believe that we shall also come to life with him. We know that Christ, once raised from the dead, is never to die again: he is no longer under the dominion of death. For in dying as he died, he died to sin, once for all, and in living as he lives, he lives to God. In the same way you must regard yourselves as dead to sin and alive to God, in union with Christ Jesus.

The First Letter of Paul to the Corinthians†

CHAPTER 11.3–12

But I wish you to understand that, while every man has Christ for his Head, woman's head is man, as Christ's Head is God. A man who keeps his head covered when he prays or prophesies brings shame on his head; a woman, on the contrary, brings shame on her head if she prays or prophesies bare-headed; it is as bad as if her head were shaved. If a woman is not to wear a veil she might as well have her hair cut off; but if it is a disgrace for her to be cropped and shaved, then she should wear a veil. A man has no need to cover his head, because man is the image of God, and the mirror of his glory, whereas woman reflects the glory of man. For man did not originally spring from woman, but woman was made out of man; and man was not created for woman's sake, but woman for the sake of man; and therefore it is woman's duty to have a sign of authority on her head, out of regard for the angels. And yet, in Christ's fellowship woman is as essential to man as man to woman. If woman was made out of man, it is through woman that man now comes to be; and God is the source of all.

CHAPTER 15.21–28, 51–58

For since it was a man who brought death into the world, a man also brought resurrection of the dead. As in Adam all men die, so in Christ all will be brought to life; but each in his own proper place: Christ the firstfruits, and afterwards, at his coming, those who belong to Christ. Then comes the end, when he delivers up the kingdom to God the Father, after abolishing every kind of domination, authority, and power. For he is destined to reign until God has put all enemies under his feet; and the last enemy to be abol-

† From *The New English Bible.* © The Delegates of the Oxford University Press and the Syndics of the Cambridge University Press, 1961, 1970. Reprinted by permission.

ished is death. Scripture says, 'He has put all things in subjection under his feet.' But in saying 'all things,' it clearly means to exclude God who subordinates them; and when all things are thus subject to him, then the Son himself will also be made subordinate to God who made all things subject to him, and thus God will be all in all.

* * *

Listen! I will unfold a mystery: we shall not all die, but we shall all be changed in a flash, in the twinkling of an eye, at the last trumpet-call. For the trumpet will sound, and the dead will rise immortal, and we shall be changed. This perishable being must be clothed with the imperishable, and what is mortal must be clothed with immortality. And when our mortality has been clothed with immortality, then the saying of Scripture will come true: 'Death is swallowed up; victory is won!' 'O Death, where is your victory? O Death, where is your sting?' The sting of death is sin, and sin gains its power from the law; but, God be praised, he gives us the victory through our Lord Jesus Christ.

Therefore, my beloved brothers, stand firm and immovable, and work for the Lord always, work without limit, since you know that in the Lord your labour cannot be lost.

The Revelation of St. John the Divine

CHAPTER 4

After this I looked, and, behold, a door was opened in heaven: and the first voice which I heard was as it were of a trumpet talking with me; which said, "Come up hither, and I will shew thee things which must be hereafter". And immediately I was in the spirit: and, behold, a throne was set in heaven, and one sat on the throne. And he that sat was to look upon like a jasper and a sardine stone: and there was a rainbow round about the throne, in sight like unto an emerald. And round about the throne were four and twenty seats: and upon the seats I saw four and twenty elders sitting, clothed in white raiment; and they had on their heads crowns of gold. And out of the throne proceeded lightnings and thunderings and voices: and there were seven lamps of fire burning before the throne, which are the seven Spirits of God. And before the throne there was a sea of glass like unto crystal: and in the midst of the throne, and round about the throne, were four beasts full of eyes before and behind. And the first beast was like a lion, and the second beast like a calf, and the third beast had a face as a man, and the fourth beast was like a flying eagle. And the four beasts had each of them six wings about him; and they were full of eyes within: and they rest not day and night, saying, "Holy, holy, holy, Lord God Almighty, which was, and is, and is to come". And when those beasts give glory and honour and thanks to him that sat on the throne, who liveth for ever and ever, the four and twenty elders fall down before him that sat on the throne, and worship him that liveth for ever and ever, and cast their crowns before the throne, saying, "Thou art worthy, O Lord, to receive glory and honour and power: for thou hast created all things, and for thy pleasure they are, and were created".

CHAPTER 5.11

And I beheld, and I heard the voice of many angels round about the throne and the beasts and the elders: and the number of them was ten thousand times ten thousand, and thousands of thousands;

CHAPTER 6.8, 15–17

And I looked, and behold a pale horse: and his name that sat on him was Death, and Hell followed with him. And power was given unto them over the fourth part of the earth, to kill with sword, and with hunger, and with death, and with the beasts of the earth.

* * *

And the kings of the earth, and the great men, and the rich men, and the chief captains, and the mighty men, and every bondman, and every free man, hid themselves in the dens and in the rocks of the mountains; and said to the mountains and rocks, "Fall on us, and hide us from the face of him that sitteth on the throne, and from the wrath of the Lamb: for the great day of his wrath is come; and who shall be able to stand?"

CHAPTER 12.3–12

And there appeared another wonder in heaven; and behold a great red dragon, having seven heads and ten horns, and seven crowns upon his heads. And his tail drew the third part of the stars of heaven, and did cast them to the earth: and the dragon stood before the woman which was ready to be delivered, for to devour her child as soon as it was born. And she brought forth a man child, who was to rule all nations with a rod of iron: and her child was caught up unto God, and to his throne. And the woman fled into the wilderness, where she hath a place prepared of God, that they should feed her there a thousand two hundred and threescore days.

And there was war in heaven: Michael and his angels fought against the dragon; and the dragon fought and his angels, and prevailed not; neither was their place found any more in heaven. And the great dragon was cast out, that old serpent, called the

Devil, and Satan, which deceiveth the whole world: he was cast out into the earth, and his angels were cast out with him. And I heard a loud voice saying in heaven, "Now is come salvation, and strength, and the kingdom of our God, and the power of his Christ: for the accuser of our brethren is cast down, which accused them before our God day and night. And they overcame him by the blood of the Lamb, and by the word of their testimony; and they loved not their lives unto the death. Therefore rejoice, ye heavens, and ye that dwell in them. Woe to the inhabiters of the earth and of the sea! for the devil is come down unto you, having great wrath, because he knoweth that he hath but a short time."

CHAPTER 20

And I saw an angel come down from heaven, having the key of the bottomless pit and a great chain in his hand. And he laid hold on the dragon, that old serpent, which is the Devil, and Satan, and bound him a thousand years, and cast him into the bottomless pit, and shut him up, and set a seal upon him, that he should deceive the nations no more, till the thousand years should be fulfilled: and after that he must be loosed a little season.

And I saw thrones, and they sat upon them, and judgment was given unto them: and I saw the souls of them that were beheaded for the witness of Jesus, and for the word of God, and which had not worshipped the beast, neither his image, neither had received his mark upon their foreheads, or in their hands; and they lived and reigned with Christ a thousand years. But the rest of the dead lived not again until the thousand years were finished. This is the first resurrection. Blessed and holy is he that hath part in the first resurrection: on such the second death hath no power, but they shall be priests of God and of Christ, and shall reign with him a thousand years.

7 And when the thousand years are expired, Satan shall be loosed out of his prison, and shall go out to deceive the nations which are in the four quarters of the earth, Gog and Magog, to gather them together to battle: the number of whom is as the sand of the sea. And they went up on the breadth of the earth, and compassed the camp of the saints about, and the beloved city: and fire came down from God out of heaven, and devoured them. And the devil that deceived them was cast into the lake of fire and brimstone, where the beast and the false prophet are, and shall be tormented day and night for ever and ever.

And I saw a great white throne, and him that sat on it, from whose face the earth and the heaven fled away; and there was found no place for them. And I saw the dead, small and great, stand before God; and the books were opened: and another book was opened, which is the book of life: and the dead were judged out of those things which were written in the books, according to their works. And the sea gave up the dead which were in it; and death and hell delivered up the dead which were in them: and they were judged every man according to their works. And death and hell were cast into the lake of fire. This is the second death. And whosoever was not found written in the book of life was cast into the lake of fire.

CHAPTER 21

And I saw a new heaven and a new earth: for the first heaven and the first earth were passed away; and there was no more sea. And I John saw the holy city, new Jerusalem, coming down from God out of heaven, prepared as a bride adorned for her husband. And I heard a great voice out of heaven saying, "Behold, the tabernacle of God is with men, and he will dwell with them, and they shall be his people, and God himself shall be with them, and be their God. And God shall wipe away all tears from their eyes; and there shall be no more death, neither sorrow, nor crying, neither shall there be any more pain: for the former things are passed away." And he that sat upon the throne said, "Behold, I make all things new". And he said unto me, "Write: for these words are true and faithful". And he said unto me, "It is done. I am Alpha and Omega, the beginning and the end. I will give unto him that is athirst of the fountain of the water of life freely. He that overcometh shall inherit all things; and I will be his God, and he shall be my son. But the fearful, and unbelieving, and the abominable, and murderers, and whoremongers, and sorcerers, and idolaters, and all liars, shall have their part in the lake which burneth with fire and brimstone: which is the second death."

9 And there came unto me one of the seven angels which had the seven vials full of the seven last plagues, and talked with me, saying, "Come hither, I will shew thee the bride, the Lamb's wife." And he carried me away in the spirit to a great and high mountain, and shewed me that great city, the holy Jerusalem, descending out of heaven from God, having the glory of God: and her light was like unto a stone most precious, even like a jasper stone, clear as crystal; and had a wall great and high, and had twelve gates, and at the gates twelve angels, and names written thereon, which are the names of the twelve tribes of the children of Israel: on the east three gates; on the north three gates; on the south three gates; and on the west three gates. And the wall of the city had twelve foundations, and in them the names of the twelve apostles of the Lamb. And he that talked with me had a golden reed to measure the city, and the gates thereof, and the wall thereof. And the city lieth four-

square, and the length is as large as the breadth: and he measured the city with the reed, twelve thousand furlongs. The length and the breadth and the height of it are equal. And he measured the wall thereof, an hundred and forty and four cubits, according to the measure of a man, that is, of the angel. And the building of the wall of it was of jasper: and the city was pure gold, like unto clear glass. And the foundations of the wall of the city were garnished with all manner of precious stones. The first foundation was jasper; the second, sapphire; the third, a chalcedony; the fourth, an emerald; the fifth, sardonyx; the sixth, sardius; the seventh, chrysolite; the eighth, beryl; the ninth, a topaz; the tenth, a chrysoprasus; the eleventh, a jacinth; the twelfth, an amethyst. *21* And the twelve gates were twelve pearls; every several gate was of one pearl: and the street of the city was pure gold, as it were transparent glass. And I saw no temple therein: for the Lord God Almighty and the Lamb are the temple of it. And the city had no need of the sun, neither of the moon, to shine in it: for the glory of God did lighten it, and the Lamb is the light thereof. And the nations of them which are saved shall walk in the light of it: and the kings of the earth do bring their glory and honour into it. And the gates of it shall not be shut at all by day: for there shall be no night there. And they shall bring the glory and honour of the nations into it. And there shall in no wise enter into it any thing that defileth, neither whatsoever worketh abomination, or maketh a lie: but they which are written in the Lamb's book of life.

CHAPTER 22.1–5

And he shewed me a pure river of water of life, clear as crystal, proceeding out of the throne of God and of the Lamb. In the midst of the street of it, and on either side of the river, was there the tree of life, which bare twelve manner of fruits, and yielded her fruit every month: and the leaves of the tree were for the healing of the nations. And there shall be no more curse: but the throne of God and of the Lamb shall be in it; and his servants shall serve him: and they shall see his face; and his name shall be in their foreheads. And there shall be no night there; and they need no candle, neither light of the sun; for the Lord God giveth them light: and they shall reign for ever and ever.

Background Notes on Certain Important Concepts and Topics in *Paradise Lost*

The Universe

The world of *Paradise Lost* was created out of that part of chaos which was ensphered by God's act of turning a great pair of golden compasses. The resulting spherical shell, made of an impenetrable and immobile substance, was suspended from heaven by a golden chain fastened to heaven's floor at a point near heaven's gate and at the head of a flight of retractable stairs that led down to the top of the sphere. There the chain was fastened at a point near an opening, through which God could look down into the universe from his heavenly throne and through which would pass all traffic between earth and heaven or hell. Hell was a separate enclosure within chaos situated below the universe at a distance equal to the diameter of the universe.

Milton did not believe that the universe was created from nothing. It was made from whatever was contained in what the Bible called "the deep," a synonym for *abyss* (a Greek word meaning "bottomless," therefore infinite). *Chaos* also meant a "yawning gulf," and carried the connotations of emptiness and formlessness. But Milton conceived of it as containing something out of which matter could be formed, and he thought of the process as *ordering*, a word whose root means "to begin." Forces or primordial matter were ordered. The first phenomenon within the universe was light. The next was the separation of the waters into two concentric spheres by means of the "firmament," a word which in Hebrew is related to the idea of expansion and to the idea of a vault. Milton followed convention in using *sky, vault, expanse, heaven* or *heavens,* and *firmament* synonymously. The inner sphere of waters contained what would become the earth; the outer sphere of waters became the "chrystalline waters" that formed a cover for the outer shell of the universe. Both the universe and the earth floated, so to speak, in a kind of uterine fluid, the outer waters protecting the universe from chaos, the inner furnishing nourishment for the earth.

Next, the continents emerged from the waters covering the earth, and vegetation was created. Then, within the firmament, the space between earth and the outer shell of the universe, God put ten concentric transparent and immaterial spheres. Milton did not pretend to know whether the center of this set of spheres was the earth or the sun, and none of his astronomical descriptions or allusions commits him to one or the other of the possibilities. As earthbound readers we tend to imagine the easier Ptolemaic arrangement, which puts our standpoint, the earth, at the center, surrounded by the spheres of the moon, Mercury, Venus, the sun, Mars, Jupiter, and Saturn. Beyond Saturn is the sphere of the "fixed stars," among them the twelve constellations that constitute the signs of the zodiac. Before the Fall this zone (meaning "belt"), about 18° wide, revolved around the earth parallel with the equator, and within its boundaries moved (as they still do) the sun and all the "other" planets—each at a different speed (and in some cases, apparently, not always in the same direction). The twelve constellations that stud this belt are set about 30° apart, and during the course of a year the sun, revolving at a different speed from that of the zodiac, passes through each of the twelve signs. At creation the sun was thought to have been "in" Aries, that is to have been travelling in a position between earth and the constellation of Aries. Aries is the sign in which (until recently) the sun travelled from March 21 to April 20—in the northern hemisphere, the first month of spring.

But Eden was perpetually in spring because before the Fall the plane of the earth's equator coincided with the plane of the sun's orbit (or, in a heliocentric system, the plane of the earth's equator would always intersect the sun)—hence there were no solstices, but perpetual equinox and, at the latitude of Eden, perpetual temperate or spring-like weather. After the Fall, the earth was tipped on its axis, and the cycle of seasons was introduced—with its painful extremes of temperature. The sun continued to travel in the zodiac, but now, for the earthly observer, that path across the heavens moved slowly during the year from south to north to south, so that at noon in January in our hemisphere the sun, and the constellation of Capricorn (the Goat), with which it is in conjunction, were "low" in the sky, and in June the sun and Cancer (the Crab) were "high." Before the Fall all astrological patterns of relationships between the planets and the stars were benign; after the Fall, God sent angels down to instruct the stars and planets how in certain astrological relationships to rain down on earth various malign "influences"—meteorological, natural, physiological, and psychological.

Beyond the sphere of the fixed stars were two more spheres: the "crystalline" (III.482)—invented by a thirteenth-century astronomer to account for a celestial phenomenon that later proved to be an error in observation—and the *primum mobile*, or "rhomb" (VIII.134), which somehow moved all the spheres within it.

The space between the surface of the earth and shell of the universe was conceived of by the ancients as consisting of two main divisions separated by the sphere of the moon. What was within that sphere (sublunar) was made of the four elements of earth, air, fire, and water. What was above or beyond the moon's sphere was made of a fifth element called "quintessence." The planets and stars were made of this "most pure" element, as was the atmosphere or ether of the upper world. The sublunar atmosphere of the earth was bounded by a sphere (or "region") of fire, and between this region and the surface of the earth there were three regions of air, the one nearest the region of fire being very hot and the one nearest the earth being warm from the heat of the sun reflected from the earth's surface. The middle, very cold region, barely penetrated by the tallest mountains, was the home of the imaginary Greek gods, and was the source of weather: clouds, rain and snow, winds, thunder, and lightning. Meteors were generated in the upper, or third, region of air.

When on the last two days of Creation God made animals and human life, he continued the basic process of ordering forces and sublunar elements of water, earth, air, and fire (See "Physiology and Psychology," below).

The universe (meaning "the whole turning") revolved on an axis running parallel to the floor of Heaven so that when God looked down through the opening at the "top" of the stationary shell he was directly above the Garden of Eden. And the revolving planets and constelllations, like clockwork, marked time in units of days, months, and years.

From man's point of view the most compelling of all the parts of his universe was the sun, in which on the fourth day of Creation God concentrated the light which he created on the first day, and *Paradise Lost* is full of evidence of man's ancient belief that the sun was the immediate source of all physical energy, the maker or sire of all phenomena: mineral, vegetable, and animal.

Physiology and Psychology

Just as the cosmology of *Paradise Lost* allowed for the possible truth of the discoveries of Galileo and Copernicus, none of the poem's assumptions about human physiology does violence to the implications of Harvey's discoveries of the circulation of the blood. One of the four humors (literally "fluids") of the body, blood was the means of distributing the other three humors (black bile, yellow bile, and phlegm), as well as the spirits ("vapors") that performed the functions of what we might now call the nervous system. A person's temper (or humor) depended on how the humors in him were tempered (literally "mixed"). Melancholy, for example, was the result of a disproportionally large amount of black bile. As in the creation of the universe, so in the the creation of life, heat and moisture were determining factors, and all organisms consisted of variously proportioned and arranged elements. The four humors were associated with the four elements in that each humor was either moist (water) or dry (air) and cold (earth) or hot (fire). Both tempermentally and physiologically phlegmatic people were cold and moist; sanguine, hot and moist; choleric, hot and dry; melancholy, cold and dry. The art (practice) of medicine and the science (knowledge) of biology developed elaborate theories of pathology based on the theory of the humors.

Spirits or vapors, the active principles of life, were of three kinds—natural, animal, and intellectual. Natural spirits (generated in animals in the liver) controlled the basic vital functions of the body (e.g., digestion); animal spirits (generated in the heart) carried sense perceptions to the brain, and directions from the brain to the muscles; intellectual spirits controlled and communicated to the body the commands of the faculties of reason and will. The souls of vegetable life had only natural, vital spirits to work with. In animal souls, both vital and sensitive spirits operated. Human souls had all three—vital, sensitive, and intellectual.

The psychology of Milton's time was similarly neat and simple. The brain, seat of mental *faculties* (literally the "powers to act") consisted of three cells. To the first cell, that of the fancy (literally *phantasia*, or "imagination") the spirits communicated the messages from the five senses. The fancy passed these impressions on to the second cell, that of reason, which acted upon the image (creating perhaps what we might call an idea) before passing it on to the third cell, that of the faculty of memory. Sleep was a condition in which the second faculty ceased to operate, and dreams were a product of the first and third faculties, uncensored or unrationalized by the reason, which in healthy wakefulness was what controlled the will. (Cf. V. 100–113) Milton did not believe in the existence of a human soul apart from the live body in which it operated. (Cf. X. 782–93n.)

One way to describe the Fall and its consequences is to call them a distempering and a disturbance of the perfect balance in the mixture of elements and forces in all aspects of the world, which God created perfect. When Nature sighed "through all her works" (IX.783 and 1001) at the time of the Fall, storms as well as stomach-aches, earthquakes as well as shivers, extremes of heat and cold as well as manic and depressive states of mind—all forms of disequilibrium—began to plague mankind.

Reason

The Cambridge Platonists, a group of thinkers contemporary with Milton, who opposed the mechanistic, deterministic, atheistic ideas of Thomas Hobbes, called reason "the candle of the Lord," and believed that this light was innate in every man. The light was not only what we call conscience in ethical matters but also that intuitive intelligence by means of which we discern the laws of nature—as distinct from what Raphael calls "discursive" reason, or what we loosely call logic, or the human faculty by which we figure things out, or arrive at conclusions from a set of data. Milton's Raphael agrees with the Cambridge Platonists that the difference between faith and reason is only a matter of degree. He tells Adam that man depends most on discursive reason, whereas angels depend most on intuition, "Differing but in degree." Even after the Fall man was left with enough unimpaired reason (of both kinds) to know God's will, to see the difference between right and wrong. Sir Philip Sidney was thinking of *ratio recta*, or right reason, when he said, "Our erected wit maketh us know what perfection is, and yet our infected will keepeth us from reaching unto it." See also, under "Freedom," below.

The Scale of Nature

Nature, meaning sometimes the forces and processes that produce everything according to the laws of nature (which include what we call physical laws), sometimes simply those laws, and sometimes all that Nature produces—Nature, after the Fall, did not wholly lose her original power to produce and control natural, perfect, ordered phenomena, any more than Satan lost all his original brightness or man all his power to reason or to intuit natural law and God's will. What was left to fallen man was all the glories of the natural world and of humanity as we know them—that is, the glories that help us understand the perfection of the paradise we lost.

Milton's concept of nature, animate and inanimate, is not so mechanical as our simplifications of seventeenth-century "science" make it sound. The force in Mother Nature is identical with the force of God the Father as Abdiel suggests (VI.174) when he argues that wise and happy angels "serve whom God ordains,/Or nature; God and nature bid the same." Both are benevolent, or in Milton's diction, provident (i.e. seeing or planning ahead—exercising loving care and guardianship). And in this best of all possible universes everything had been thought of—no thing, being, or force had been omitted. This idea of perfection as completeness goes back to Plato, and as elaborated by the Renaissance Platonists was well known to Milton. Sometimes called the concept of plenitude, it is a help to the understanding of the idea of good in *Paradise Lost*. God's goodness was in giving every conceivable thing. The gift was not a static complex, or inorganic mechanism. Its chief characteristic was not its matter, but its activity and, in one of Milton's favorite words, its variety. As Raphael tells Adam, God made of one primordial matter, "various forms, various degrees/ Of substance, and in things that live, of life."

The arrangement of all the things in the universe, their articulation with one another, had been conceived as a dynamic hierarchy, from lowest or simplest or least good (not of course to be confused with bad or not good) to the highest, the perfect (full or complete) or best, which was God Himself. In the scale of nature each form or creature (created thing) incorporated the virtues of all the forms beneath it. Satan knew that in man were "summed up" all the lower forms of "growth, sense, reason"— that is, of all vegetable, animal, and human life (IX.112). Everything, therefore, was served by what was below it and in turn served what was above it. The two most common metaphors for this arrangement were a chain and a ladder or stairway (the basic meaning of *scale*—as in a musical scale). The golden chain of II. 1005 and 1051, by which the universe hangs from heaven, symbolized "the universal concord and sweet union of all things which Pythagoras poetically figures as harmony." The history and meaning of ideas about the scale of nature are the subject of Arthur O. Lovejoy's famous book, *The Great Chain of Being*.

The scale, or ladder, or stairs as a symbol appears near the chain as a second connection between heaven and the universe. Milton associated it with the ladder on which Jacob dreamed he saw "Angels ascending and descending" (III.510). The stairway was an appropriate symbol for the ascending scale on which, before the Fall, natural forms might by a sort of evolution change to a higher form, as God intended human beings eventually to evolve into angels ("Each stair was mysteriously meant"). The completeness, variety, and upward motion of all the phenomena on nature's scale are clearly implied by Raphael in his lectures to Adam in Book V (404 ff., and 469 ff.).

From the point of view of man the two most interesting positions on the scale of nature were those directly below and above him. Though Milton tells us that what distinguishes men from other animals is that men stand up straight (and can thereby look up toward heaven) and that they can smile, one of the central themes of *Paradise Lost* is that man's reason is his most godlike and distinguishing characteristic ("smiles from reason flow" IX.239).

Angels

Adam is humanly curious about the nature of the creatures who are just a little above him on the divine scale, and the angelology of *Paradise Lost* is contained chiefly in Raphael's responses to Adam's questions. In these descriptive passages (cf. V.401 ff., 461 ff., VI.344 ff., VIII.614 ff.), Milton again drew eclectically upon the large body of theory that had been accumulating for centuries, and added a few speculations of his own. The scale of nature is extended beyond the boundary of the universe; angels are a link between human beings and God. They are "pure/Intelligential substances" as distinct from "rational" beings. In their preponderance of intuitive reason they include all the discursive reason of mankind. They have bodies, but these are made not of earth, air, fire, and water, but of the "fifth" element called, "ether"; like everything beyond the lunar sphere, including heaven itself, they are quintessential and ethereal. Compared with men they are pure spirit; compared with God they are natural (his creatures). But in their fiery or airy bodies, in their form as pure spirit ("liquid texture" meaning non-solid), they retain all the qualities and powers of human beings. They eat, make love (a notion original with Milton) and enjoy all the sensations of the five senses, but the seats, or the mechanisms, of their senses are not localized in organs: angels feel, see, hear, taste, and smell with their whole being. Like prelapsarian Adam they are immortal, but unlike men they are in their insubstantiality literally invulnerable. Tending as they do toward the unity of God, they are in their relative perfection simpler in organization than man. Unlike God, they cannot be in two places at the same time, but unlike man they can travel with unimaginable speed, and can assume either sex and any size or shape. They move freely from heaven to earth and, like Plato's daemons, or "attendant spirits," they can inhabit planets. They may in fact be stars. Their dance is like the movement of the heavenly bodies, and their song is like the Platonic harmony of the spheres. As they are ministered unto by God, so they minister unto men—as agents of divine providence. Or as fallen angels or evil spirits, they try to pervert man.

To Adam (and to Milton and his Muse) they appear as they are described in the Bible—shining, beautiful, winged. In asserting that God created them before he created the universe and that his purpose in creating man was to fill the ranks vacated by the fallen angels, Milton followed theological speculations well-known to his readers. Even his conviction that the good angels remained loyal by an act of their own free will, though a minority opinion, was not original.

In the chapter on angels in his *De Doctrina Christiana*, Milton collected all the facts the Bible supplies: angels are either good or evil; they stand "dispersed around the throne of God in the capacity of ministering agents"; Michael seems to be the chief of the good angels; all bad angels will be punished, but some are allowed to execute God's judgment on men; bad angels are ruled by Satan, and they retain in hell their respective ranks. Though *Paradise Lost* goes far beyond the Bible in describing the nature, history, and personalities of the angels, Milton rejected or modified most of the theories that were the product of centuries of speculation by Jewish and Christian writers of the occult. He did not accept the standard hierarchial ordering of the ranks of angels into three degrees, or "choirs," each consisting of three ranks: Seraphim, Cherubim, Thrones; Dominions, Virtues, Powers; Principalities, Archangels, Angels. This hierarchy descending from Seraphim to Angels was the invention of an early Christian writer and had been the subject of centuries of speculation made possible by the lack of scriptural authority. Angels, Seraphim, and Cherubim appear throughout the Bible; but Thrones, Dominions, Virtues, Powers and Principalities occur chiefly in the letters of St. Paul and are not there defined or distinguished; Archangels are mentioned only twice in the Bible.

Milton referred to certain leading or commanding angels as Archangels—Michael, first in command of God's Army, Gabriel, second in command, and Satan in the battle in heaven, as well as Uriel, the viceroy of the sun, and Raphael, God's chief minister. But there seems to be no reason for the titles assigned to the other angels, some of whom are called by several titles. The five New Testament titles, Thrones, Dominions (or Dominations), Virtues, Powers, and Principalities (or Princedoms), which Satan was so fond of rolling off his tongue when addressing his followers, are all words for power and authority, and all the angels in *Paradise Lost*, in Heaven and Hell, seem to live in feudal systems where everyone has a title, a province, and a responsibility to a superior lord and ultimately to a King, but nothing quite that explicit appears in *Paradise Lost*.

Most of the given names of the angels in *Paradise Lost* come from the Bible or the Apocrypha, but some appear only in early Jewish and Christian occult writings. The names of the twelve chief followers of Satan are annotated in this text of *Paradise Lost*; Beelzebub, Moloch, Belial, Mammon, Chemos, Astoreth, Thammuz, Dagon, Rimmon, Osiris, Isis, and Orus. The seven other fallen angels in *Paradise Lost* are: *Andramalec*, a sun-god; *Ariel*, a version of Mars; *Arioc*, identified by commentators as a "spirit of revenge;" *Asmadai*, or *Asmadeus*, a devil mentioned in the Book of Tobit; *Azazel*, whose name, mentioned in the Old Testament, means "scapegoat," and who was said by commentators to be one of Satan's four standard-bearers; *Nizroch*, an Assyrian idol named in the Old Testament; and *Ramiel*, one of the angels who had intercourse with "the daughters of men" (apocryphal Book of Enoch I, vi. 7).

Of the good angels only nine appear in *Paradise Lost*: *Michael*, a great prince whom Daniel, in the Old Testament, sees in a vision as the deliverer of the Children of Israel, becomes an archangel in Jude, in the New Testament, and in Rev. 12.7 he "and his angels fought against the dragon;" *Gabriel*, an interpreter of one of Daniel's visions and, in Luke 1.19 and 26, an angel and messenger of God, was made by commentators a military leader, and guardian of Paradise; *Raphael* appears in the apocryphal Book of Tobit as a helpful angel; *Uriel*, meaning "light of God," is named only in the Apocrypha, but commentators had identified him as one of the "eyes of the Lord." These four archangels were said by the commentators to rule the four corners of the earth—about all of them there was a certain amount of occult speculation. The five other loyal angels are: *Abdiel*, a seraph, whose name (meaning 'servant of God') appears as that of a human being in the Old Testament; *Ithuriel*, like the remaining three, a cherub, does not appear in the Bible or the Apocrypha—the word means "discovery of God;"

Uzziel ("strength of God") appears as a human being in the Old Testament, but commentators had made him, like Uriel, one of the seven "eyes of the Lord"; *Zephon* ("searcher of secrets") is a human being in the Old Testament; and *Zophiel* means "spy of God," but not much else is known about him. Angelology began with the Jewish commentators and was made more confusing by Christian commentators. Robert West's *Milton and the Angels* is the last word on the subject.

God

Milton's God personifies "eternal providence." He foresees—cf. Latin *pro* (before) + *videre* (to see)—and provides everything, including his son, Christ, by whose agency God's will was manifested in the creation of the world, and by whose love God's justice and mercy and grace are manifested and man's salvation is effected. The Christian concept of the Trinity (by which the Father, Son, and Holy Spirit are both three and one) was not important in Milton's theology, and the mystery of the incarnation, crucifixion, and resurrection of Christ, though alluded to in *Paradise Lost*, is not part of the narrative.

Milton had little patience with metaphysical speculation of the kind practiced by Scholastic philosophers, or with other "vague cogitations and subtleties." Nonetheless, in justifying God's ways, Milton could not avoid being theological, and hence could not help asserting or implying things about God that were just as debatable in Milton's time as they had been for centuries before and are still today, three centuries later. Some of these are not crucial to the understanding or enjoyment of the poem, but a few that are central to its argument deserve to be understood and in our time may need explanation. The first of these is the relationship of God's foreknowledge to man's freedom.

In foreknowing all events God did not cause them. He made man capable of falling, knew he would fall, but did not make him fall. Thus foreknowledge is not the same as predestination in its general sense. (Milton did not believe in predestination in its special Calvinistic sense—that God decided from the beginning which individuals would be damned and which saved.) Next to the gift of life itself, Milton thought God's greatest gift to man was reason and the freedom to exercise that reason in the act of choosing. A man incapable of making a mistake would have been a man incapable of significant decisions, incapable of enjoying a sense of achievement, and incapable of the God-like pleasure of freely making a gift—as in the joy of giving thanks. Such a man, incapable of true obedience to God, would have no human dignity, or worth, as Milton defined those terms.

It would have been illogical to make man free to choose and at the same time not free to make wrong choices. And Milton believed God incapable of acting illogically. This argument seems sophistical to those who feel that a good God would not have made man capable of doing anything that would have undesirable consequences—that a good God would not have spoiled Paradise by planting the Tree and requiring obedience—or have allowed Satan to revolt—or Christ to suffer. Milton was, of course, aware of such objections. In fact, *Paradise Lost* is an attempt to meet them. (Cf. *Christian Doctrine*, I. iii.).

Freedom

Man's liberty before and after the Fall depended upon his following the dictates of the two-fold, God-given power (i.e. virtue) of reason (XII.79 ff.), which must govern his will. In *Paradise Lost* when Abdiel, the faithful angel, returned to Heaven after his encounter with Satan, God characterized the fallen angels as those who "refuse/Right reason for their law." And though in the war in Heaven the good angels employ force against the rebel angels, the victory is achieved only by Christ, the personification of reason, the *Logos*. Reason, like love, is a form of obedience. As Abdiel tells Satan, servitude or slavery is simply a state in which men "serve the unwise"; and Gabriel in his preview of postlapsarian history, expresses Milton's own protestant liberal conviction that no man should forfeit his God-given freedom to any other man, but should preserve his liberty to serve God according to the dictates of his reason and in the light of the candle of the Lord. When, after Raphael's instruction, Adam tries to make Eve understand the nature of their freedom in Paradise, he applies the same freedom-through-obedience formula to the relationship between the will and the reason (or judgment). Man's will is free as long as it obeys reason, but it may become enslaved to irrational forces if it disobeys reason. When reason errs, misjudges, mistakes, it will misinform and misdirect the will, but in following the false dictates of reason the will does not cease to be free.

Justifying his own ways, God says in Book III that both acts of reason and acts of will are forms of choice, implying that when human beings choose, both will and reason are involved, whereas choice in animals is simply an act of will. Therefore, presumably, if animals can be said to obey, their obedience is irrational—predetermined, so to speak—and their lives are not blessed with the freedom (or the responsibility) that is a corollary of the gift of reason.

Covenant

Covenant is the word used by translators of the Old Testament for the Hebrew word *berith*, meaning a relationship between two parties and the terms thereof. God's covenants with the Patriarchs Noah, Abraham, Isaac, and Jacob, and through Moses with Israel (Gen. 6.18, 9.9, 17.1 ff.; Exod. 24.7, 8) were collectively called by Christian writers the Old Covenant—with special reference to the institution of the Mosiac Law as well as to the Law itself and its observance. The Greek word *diatheke*, used to translate the Hebrew *berith*, carried the meaning of *testamant*, as in "last will and testament," and hence the New Covenant, prophesied by Jeremiah (31.31) and interpreted by Luke and Paul in the Greek New Testament as God's promise of salvation to all believers in Christ, was called the New Testament. Eventually the Christian books of the Bible were called the New Testament, and the pre-Christian books, the Old Testament. The New Covenant (that all believers in Christ would be saved by faith) was thought by Protestants to have superseded, or "renewed" (XI.116), though not entirely to have replaced, the Old Covenant, which applied only to the Jews and was fulfilled by obedience to the Law.

Knowledge

Though in the poem Milton follows the Bible in calling the forbidden tree the Tree of Knowledge, in *Christian Doctrine* he said he thought the tree was so named from the event. The consequence of eating was knowledge of a certain kind—knowledge of good that could be gained only by knowing evil. God did not forbid Adam and Eve from Knowledge of anything that was within their power to understand, and what that limitation meant Adam seemed generally to know even before Raphael tried to make it more explicit (see VII.126 and VIII.119, 188). Milton recognized in perfect Adam a thirst for knowledge which is best understood as a passion for contemplating God's works for the right purpose—that of knowing God and glorifying him. Part of the sin in the act of the Fall was a desire for a knowledge equal to God's, or a knowledge of things purposely placed beyond man's comprehension. It was not the desire to know, but the aggressive attempt to exceed their own humanity that was sinful. How much knowledge was open to men and angels, and under what conditions, was clear to Uriel (see III.694). In *Christian Doctrine* Milton said that "love and obedience are always the best guides to knowledge." When the thirst for knowledge was motivated and limited by love and obedience, it could not be excessive nor could God be said to have forbidden it. What was forbidden was simply eating the fruit of the Tree and, by implication, the disobedient motives that perverted Adam's and Eve's God-given desire to know as much as they could about God's works.

The Fortunate Fall

Instead of the kind of knowledge they sought when they fell, Adam and Eve gained two other kinds: the knowledge of evil and the knowledge of God's providence to which Adam responds when he wonders at the end of the poem whether he should be sorry or glad about his fall.

> Full of doubt I stand,
> Whether I should repent me now of sin
> By me done and occasioned, or rejoice
> Much more, that much more good thereof shall spring,
> To God more glory, more good will to men
> From God, and over wrath grace shall abound.

That is Milton's version of the idea expressed in the Mass for Holy Saturday: *O felix culpa quae talem ac tantum meruit habere redemptorum*—"O blessed sin (or crime) that was rewarded by so good and so great a redeemer!" In a famous essay Arthur O. Lovejoy calls it "The Paradox of the Fortunate Fall," but Milton makes it less a paradox by having Adam say only that he is uncertain how he should feel. The poem does not convince us that Adam should be glad he fell—only that Christians may be glad that the consequences were so good for mankind. The final justification of

God's ways is the manifestation of his grace in the redemption of man through the incarnation and crucifixion of Christ—"whereby man, being delivered from sin and death . . . is raised to a far more excellent state of grace and glory than that from which he had fallen" (*CD*, I.xiv). The words *pay, price, ransom,* and *redeem* are part of the Biblical metaphor in which Christ's death is seen as the price paid as ransom to free man from the bondage of Satan, sin, and death into which Adam sold himself and all his progeny by his disobedience. But according to a less primitive metaphor, also Biblical, the divine court of justice demanded that someone pay the penalty for breaking the law. The act of reparation must be equal to the crime—only the greatness of Christ's goodness could compensate for the greatness of Adam's crime. So by his death Christ was believed to have fulfilled the law (cf. "satisfaction," III.212) and to have paid "the required price for all mankind" (*CD*, I.xvi—cf. "deadly forfeiture and ransom set," *PL*, III.221). In this act of atonement, Christ restored to man the possibility of eternal life (as in Paradise), freed him from the inherited guilt of Adam's sin, and made him more aware of God's infinite love than he had been before.

The word *grace* has a complicated history, having in earlier forms meant praise, favor, charm, and thanks. In its Christian sense it is related to the idea in the title used for certain noblemen, as in "His Grace," for Christian grace is among other things a characteristic of an action done out of magnanimity and generosity by a person of power and position without regard to the merits of the person who benefits from the act. God's grace is a gift, which by definition is something that does not have to be given and something that makes the receiver grateful, or for which he may "say grace"—and in the possession of which he may be said to be in a "state of grace." So in the poem God's providence is made to seem just by the conclusion of the *great argument,* or story: Satan fell because he thought he merited more than he got, and Adam in his redemption got more than he merited. As Addison said long ago, in the end "Satan is represented as miserable in the heights of his triumph, and Adam triumphant in the heights of his misery."

Paradise

The visual image of Paradise is highly generalized, but its outlines are fairly clear, even from the shifting point of view of Satan, who either walks or flies low as he moves into Eden. It is an elevated, enclosed garden or park occupying the level top (*champaign head*) of a steep, rugged (*savage*) circular hill whose sides are covered by a *brake, wilderness,* or *thicket* consisting of *shrubs and tangling bushes,* over which grow trees of various kinds (cf. *woody mountain,* VIII.303) arranged in rows and tiers (*ranks*) like the seats in amphitheatres (except that they curve the wrong way). A natural earth wall covered by vegetation in such a way as to look like a hedge row (*rural mound*) surrounds the plateau at its edge. The *hairy* sides of the *shaggy hill* (which have reminded one unfortunate critic of the *mons veneris*) are a part of a metaphorical head wearing a colorful crown consisting of the green band of the wall and, within that, a circle of fruit trees whose blossoms and golden fruit are mixed with *gay enameled colors* (*enameled* meant both "variegated" and "glossy."), the whole work of natural art illuminated by the blazing light of the sun. The image suggests the wealth and power of Adam (who rules over his *nether empire* (145), as well as the beauty and security of his pastoral garden. Milton's description, as Fowler says, "assimilates and refines upon the whole European tradition of paradises, gardens, pleasances, fortunate isles, and lands of the blessed. . . ." Parts of the description are taken from the descriptions of gardens in Sidney's *Arcadia* and Spenser's *Faerie Queene*. European gardens in the seventeenth century were private parks on estates, carefully and ingeniously planted in geometrical patterns, and stocked for the pleasure of their privileged owners. They had become among other things, idealized setting for contemplation and philosophical diaglogue. But in the older, middle-Eastern tradition they carried associations of sensual pleasure, and in the Bible the physical pleasures of sex are described in "garden" imagery; see The Song of Solomon 4. 1–16 [NEB]:

> How beautiful are your breasts, my sister, my bride!
>   Your love is more fragrant than wine,
>   and your perfumes sweeter than any spices.
> Your lips drop sweetness like the honeycomb, my bride,
>   syrup and milk are under your tongue,
>   and your dress has the scent of Lebanon.
>   Your two cheeks are an orchard of pomegranates,
>   an orchard full of rare fruits:
> spikenard and saffron, sweet-cane and cinnamon
>   with every incense-bearing tree,
>   myrrh and aloes
>   with all the choicest spices.
> My sister, my bride, is a garden close-locked,
> a garden close-locked, a fountain sealed.

Bride

> The fountain in my garden is a spring of running water
>   pouring down from Lebanon.
> Awake, north wind, and come, south wind;
> blow upon my garden that its perfumes may pour forth,
>   that my beloved may come to his garden
>   and enjoy its rare fruits.

Milton echoes this metaphor in *enclosure*, and in the *native perfumes*, *balmy spoils*, and *Sabean odors from the spicy shore*.

Truth and Poetry

Milton did not believe that the Biblical commentators on whose works he drew for certain details in *Paradise Lost* were authoritative. In fact at one point he mentions his disagreement with "the common gloss/Of theologians." Their speculations and their elaborations and extensions of the Bible were, like pagan myths, secular history, and popular science, simply material which a poet could feel free to use when it did not conflict with anything in the Bible. Like practically everyone else in his time, Milton had no doubt of the literal, factual, historical truth of everything in the Bible. And nothing in *Paradise Lost* disagrees with anything in the Bible.

But of course there is much in the poem that is not in the Bible. He undertook to do what the Bible was not intended to do and what no one before him had done—to put the whole story of man in an epic poem. And in adding all the detail necessary for this imaginative elaboration of the Biblical history he knew he was not committing an impiety. It had been a commonplace among religious teachers that the truth had often to be accommodated to the understanding of men—even as Christ had told the truth by telling parables. And many of the Greek and Roman myths had long been interpreted as simply pagan corruptions of biblical truth: the revolt of the Greek gods was a pagan version of the revolt of the angels; Hercules, a pagan version of Samson; Deucalion, of Noah; Prometheus, of Adam; Apollo, of Christ, etc. Raphael's rationale for his narrative method in the "epic poem" he sings to Adam is essentially Milton's (see V.563). If we can know supernatural things by assuming that natural things are imperfect representations of them, we can know characters and events in history by assuming that they were much like those of the present. And if events narrated in the Old Testament are only shadows or types of the truth revealed in the New Testament (see "From shadowy types to truth, from flesh to spirit," XII.303), then the imagined detail of the poem may convey general truths of a higher order. Milton hoped that his prayers to the divine Muse were answered—that what he was inspired to write was as true as the story which Moses, the first historical poet, was inspired by God to write, in the first five books of the Bible. To entertain such hopes was not, of course, to believe that *Paradise Lost* had the authority of the Bible.

As for the truth of the implied religious doctrine of the poem, Milton believed that it could all be substantiated by the Scriptures, in the manner in which he substantiated all his conclusions in his own theological treatise, *De Doctrina Christiana*. In that prose work Milton arrived at some conclusions that would have been considered heresy by the Church of England as well as other churches. But the heresies that theological scholars may be able to discover in *Paradise Lost* are not obvious to the common reader.

Criticism

Modern Criticism

NORTHROP FRYE

The Story of All Things†

I suppose anyone proposing to deliver a series of lectures on *Paradise Lost* ought to begin with some explanation of why he is not deterred from doing so by the number of his predecessors. If my predecessors had all failed, I could at least claim the merit of courage, like the youngest adventurer of so many folk tales who is also the brashest and most bumptious of the whole series. But many of them have succeeded better than I expect to do, and I have no knowledge of Milton sufficiently detailed to add to the body of Milton scholarship or sufficiently profound to alter its general shape. I am talking about Milton because I enjoy talking about Milton, and while I may have begun the subject of these lectures late, it was not long in choosing. Huron College is a hundred years old, and though I find, on checking the dates, that I have not been teaching Milton for quite that long, I have been teaching him long enough to have incorporated him as a central part of my own literary experience. Consequently I feel that I can approach Milton with some sense of proportion based on the fact that his proportions are gigantic. Every student of Milton has been rewarded according to his efforts and his ability: the only ones who have abjectly failed with him are those who have tried to cut him down to size—their size—and that mistake at least I will not make.

The second edition of *Paradise Lost* opened with two complimentary poems addressed to Milton, one in English by Andrew Marvell and one in Latin by Samuel Barrow. The Barrow poem begins with a rhetorical question. When you read this wonderful poem, he says, what do you read but the story of all things? For the story of all things from their first beginnings to their ultimate ends are contained within this book:

> Qui legis Amissam Paradisum, grandia magni
>   Carmina Miltoni, quid nisi cuncta legis?
> Res cunctas, et cunctarum primordia rerum,
>   Et fata, et fines continet iste liber.

Implicit in what Barrow says is a standard Renaissance critical theory. It will be familiar to most readers, but I need it again

† From *The Return of Eden: Five Essays on Milton's Epics* (Toronto, University of Toronto Press, 1965), pp. 3–31. By permission of the University of Toronto Press.

because its elements reappear as structural principles in *Paradise Lost*. It was generally assumed that in literature there were inherently major genres and minor genres. Minor poets should stick to the minor genres, and should confine themselves to pastorals or to love lyrics. Minor genres were for poets of minor talents, or for professional poets learning their trade, or for poets too high in social rank to be much interested in publication or in any kind of poetic utterance beyond the kind of graceful conventional verse that is really a form of private correspondence. The major poets were those for whom the major genres were reserved; and of these, the most important in Renaissance theory were epic and tragedy.

The epic, as Renaissance critics understood it, is a narrative poem of heroic action, but a special kind of narrative. It also has an encyclopaedic quality in it, distilling the essence of all the religious, philosophical, political, even scientific learning of its time, and, if completely successful, the definitive poem for its age. The epic in this sense is not a poem by a poet, but that poet's poem: he can never complete a second epic unless he is the equal of Homer, and hence the moment at which the epic poet chooses his subject is the crisis of his life. To decide to write an epic of this kind is an act of considerable courage, because if one fails, one fails on a colossal scale, and the echo of ridicule may last for centuries. One thinks of what the name "Blackmore" still suggests to students of English literature, many of whom have not read a line of Blackmore's epics. Further, the epic can only be completed late in life, because of the amount of sheer scholarship it is compelled to carry. In Gabriel Harvey's phrase, major poets should be "curious universal scholars," but it takes time to mature a scholar and still more time to unite scholarship with poetic skill. Of course this theory implies that Homer was a poet of encyclopaedic learning, but it was almost a critical commonplace to assume that he was: William Webbe, for example, speaks of "Homer, who as it were in one sum comprehended all knowledge, wisdom, learning and policy that was incident to the capacity of man."

The epic, as a poem both narrative and encyclopaedic, is to be distinguished from the long poem which is simply one or the other. A narrative poet, as such, is a story-teller, and a story-teller is in the position of a modern novelist: the more stories he tells the more successful he is. One thinks of Ariosto's *Orlando Furioso* and of the question addressed to the author by the Cardinal who was supposed to be his patron: "Where did you find all these silly stories, Messer Lodovico?" This remark, however inadequate as criticism, does indicate something of the quality of the romance genre that Ariosto was using, for the romance tends to become an endless poem, going on from one story to another until the author runs out of stories to tell. The encyclopaedic poem, again, was a favourite genre of the Renaissance. The two poets of this group whom we should now rank highest, Lucretius and Dante, were somewhat disapproved of in Protestant England on ideological grounds, and a more tangible influence on Milton was *La Sepmaine* of du Bartas, which displayed so much knowledge of the creation that its author was compelled to expand the divine activity into two weeks. Some other encyclopaedic poems, such as Palingenius' *Zodiac of Life*, which, as translated by Barnabe Googe, may have been one of Shakespeare's school books, were based on rather facile organizing schemes—in other words their scholarship was a matter of content rather than of poetic structure. Romances, particularly *The Faerie Queene*, could also achieve an encyclopaedic quality by virtue of being allegorical, when they not only told stories but when their stories meant things in moral philosophy and political history— "Where more is meant than meets the ear," as Milton says.

But although there were many encyclopaedic poems and many romances and narratives, and although the authors of both genres were highly respected, still the central form with the greatest prestige was the epic. And the ideal, the huge, impossible ideal, would be a poem that derived its structure from the epic tradition of Homer and Virgil and still had the quality of universal knowledge which belonged to the encyclopaedic poem and included the extra dimension of reality that was afforded by Christianity. Now, says Samuel Barrow, who would ever have thought that anyone could actually bring off such a poem? But it's been done, and by an English poet too:

> Haec qui speraret quis crederet esse futurum?
> Et tamen haec hodie terra Britanna legit.

For in the seventeenth century, writing such a poem in English was still a patriotic act, with a certain amount of conscious virtue about it, as writing poetry on this side of the American border has now. The first critical statement ever made about *Paradise Lost*, therefore, tells us that *Paradise Lost* is among other things a technical *tour de force* of miraculous proportions.

That Milton was fully aware of the size and scope of what he was attempting, and that he shared the assumptions of his age about the importance of the epic, hardly need much demonstrating. For him, of course, the responsibilities entailed by the possession of major poetic talent were only incidentally literary: they were primarily religious. The word "talent" itself is a metaphor from a parable of Jesus that seems to associate the religious and the creative aspects of life, a parable that was never long out of Milton's mind. The analogy between the Christian and the creative life extends even further. A Christian has to work hard at living a Christian life, yet the essential act of that life is the surrender of the will; a poet must work hard at his craft, yet his greatest achievements are not his, but inspired.

Milton's first major poem, the one we know as the Nativity Ode, ends its prelude with the self-addressed exhortation:

> And join thy voice unto the angel choir
> From out his secret altar touched with hallowed fire.

In a sense this is the key signature, so to speak, of Milton's poetry: his ambition as a poet is to join the tradition of inspired prophetic speech that began with the great commission to Isaiah. When he speaks in *Paradise Lost* of wanting to justify the ways of God to men, he does not mean that he wishes to do God a favour by rationalizing one of God's favourite parables: he means that *Paradise Lost* is a sacrificial offering to God which, if it is accepted, will derive its merit from that acceptance. The Nativity Ode is closely related to the Sixth Elegy, addressed to Diodati, where Milton distinguishes the relaxed life permitted the minor poet who writes of love and pleasure from the austerity and rigorous discipline imposed by major powers. One is a secular and the other a priestly or dedicated life. The reason for the discipline is not so much moral as spiritually hygienic. To be a fit vessel of inspiration the poet must be as genuinely pure as the augur or pagan priest was ceremonially pure:

> Qualis veste nitens sacra, et lustralibus undis
> Surgis ad infensos augur iture Deos.
> [Elegy VI, ll. 65–66]

After the first period of Milton's poetry had reached its climax with the two great funeral elegies, *Lycidas* and *Epitaphium Damonis*, Milton started making plans for poetry in the major genres —perhaps part of the meaning of the "fresh woods and pastures new" at the end of *Lycidas*. His *Reason of Church Government*, in a famous passage, mentions in particular three genres, the tragedy, the "diffuse" or full-length epic, and the "brief" epic. This last is still a somewhat undeveloped conception in criticism, though examples of it in English literature stretch from *Beowulf* to *The Waste Land*. One cannot help noticing the similarity between this list of three major genres and the *Samson Agonistes, Paradise Lost* and *Paradise Regained* produced so many years later. At that time, Milton tells us, he was thinking of Arthur as the subject for his "diffuse" epic. But of course he had still many years to wait before he could give his full attention to writing it. The simultaneous pull in Milton's life between the impulse to get at his poem and finish it and the impulse to leave it until it ripened sufficiently to come by itself must have accounted for an emotional tension in Milton of a kind that we can hardly imagine. That the tension was there seems certain from the way in which the temptation to premature action remains so central a theme in his poetry. The tension reached a crisis with his blindness, yet his blindness, as he had perhaps begun to realize by the time he wrote *Defensio Secunda,* eventually gave him, as deafness did Beethoven, an almost preternatural concentration, and was what finally enabled him to write of heaven, hell and the unfallen world on his own terms.

In the same passage of *The Reason of Church Government* Milton speaks of doing something for his own nation of the same kind as Homer and Virgil, "with this over and above, of being a Christian." This additional advantage means for him partly a technical poetic advantage as well. For what gave the encyclopaedic poem such prestige in Christian civilization was the encyclopaedic shape of Christian philosophy and theology, a shape derived ultimately from the shape of the Bible. The Bible, considered in its literary aspect, is a definitive encyclopaedic poem starting with the beginning of time at the creation, ending with the end of time at the Last Judgment, and surveying the entire history of man, under the symbolic names of Adam and Israel, in between. Explicitly Christian poetry had moved within this framework from earliest times. Bede's *Ecclesiastical History,* one of the authorities used by Milton for his history of Britain, tells how English poetry began with the poet Caedmon, who was ordered by an angel to sing him something. Being inspired by a Christian muse, Caedmon began promptly with a paraphrase of the first verses of Genesis on the creation, worked his way down through the Exodus and the main episodes of the Old Testament to the Incarnation, and went on to the Last Judgment and the life eternal. The dramatic cycles of the Middle Ages are another example of the effect of the shape of the Bible on English literature.

The sermon, in Milton's day, constituted a kind of oral epic tradition dealing with the same encyclopaedic myth. The proverbially long Puritan sermons, divided into anything from eighteen to twenty-five divisions, usually owed their length to a survey of the divine plan of salvation as it unrolled itself from the earliest prelapsarian decrees to the eventual consummation of all things. This oral tradition has been embedded in *Paradise Lost* in the four hundred lines of the third book which constitute a sermon of this type preached by God himself. The speech of Michael, which takes up most of the last two books of *Paradise Lost,* is a summary of the Bible from the murder of Abel to the vision of John in Patmos in which the biblical myth takes the form of a miniature epic or epyllion, and as such pulls together and restates all the major themes of the poem, like a stretto in a fugue.

Renaissance critics believed that there were major and minor genres for prose as well as for poetry, as they made much less of the technical distinction between prose and verse than we do. In prose the major genres were mainly those established by Plato: the Socratic dialogue form, and the description of the ideal commonwealth. Such works as Sidney's *Arcadia* were highly praised because they were felt to belong to this tradition, as we can see in the discussion of the *Arcadia* in the opening chapter of Fulke Greville's biography of Sidney. But the Renaissance was above all a great age of educational theory, and its educational theory, to which Milton contributed, was based squarely on the two central facts of Renaissance society, the prince and the courtier or magistrate. Hence the educational treatise, which normally took the form of the ideal education of prince, courtier or magistrate, had even greater prestige in Renaissance eyes than the description of the ideal commonwealth.

The Classical pattern for the treatise on the ideal education of the prince had been established by Xenophon in the *Cyropaedia*, which Sidney describes as "an absolute heroical poem," thus implying that it represents the prose counterpart of the encyclopaedic epic. Spenser, in the letter to Raleigh which introduces *The Faerie Queene*, makes it clear that this encyclopaedic prose form is also a part of the conception of his poem, and speaks of his preference for Xenophon's form to Plato's, for a practicable as compared to an impossible ideal. Milton also shows a touch of impatience with Plato and with what he calls Plato's "airy burgomasters," and we should expect him to be of Spenser's mind in this matter. And just as the encyclopaedic shape of the Bible is condensed into the speech of Michael, so the speech of Raphael versifies a major prose genre, for the colloquy of Raphael and Adam is a Socratic dialogue without irony, a symposium with unfermented wine, a description of an ideal commonwealth ending with the expulsion of undesirables, and (for Adam is the king of men) a cyropaedia, or manual of royal discipline. It is essentially the education of Adam, and it covers a vast amount of knowledge, both natural and revealed.

The tradition of the epic was, of course, established by Homer in the *Iliad* and the *Odyssey*, but these two epics represent different structural principles. Many Classical scholars have noted that the *Iliad* is closer in form to Greek tragedy than it is to the *Odyssey*. The *Odyssey*, the more typically epic pattern, is the one followed more closely by Virgil in the *Aeneid* and by Milton in *Paradise Lost*. Of the characteristics which the *Odyssey*, the *Aeneid* and *Paradise Lost* have in common, three are of particular importance.

In the first place, there are, in the form in which we have them, twelve books, or a multiple of twelve. Milton published the first edition of *Paradise Lost* in ten books to demonstrate his contempt for tradition, and the second edition in twelve to illustrate the actual proportions of the poem. He had been preceded in his conversion to a duodecimal system by Tasso, who had expanded the twenty cantos of *Gerusalemme Liberata* into the twenty-four of *Gerusalemme Conquistata*. Spenser, too, is preoccupied with twelves: each book has twelve cantos and the total number of books planned was either twelve or twenty-four. We shall try to suggest in a moment that the association of Milton's epic with this sacred and zodiacal number may be less arbitrary than it looks.

Secondly, the action of both the *Odyssey* and the *Aeneid* splits neatly in two. The first twelve books of the *Odyssey* deal with the wanderings of the hero, with the journey through wonderlands of marvels and terrors, the immemorial quest theme. The next twelve books never leave Ithaca (except for the Katabasis at the end, in a part of the poem often considered a later addition), and their action is that of a typical comedy of recognition and intrigue, as the unknown and ridiculed beggar eventually turns out to be the returning hero. The first six books of the *Aeneid* have a similar quest pattern; the next six, the account of the struggle of Aeneas with the Italian warlords, also has the structure of romantic comedy, full of compacts, ordeals and other traditional features of comic action, and ending in success, marriage, and the birth of a new society. In both epics the main interest shifts half way from the hero's private perils to his social context. In the letter to Raleigh, Spenser, with a reference to Tasso, also distinguishes private or princely from public or kingly virtues in the epic theme. This division of narrative between a quest theme and a theme of the settling of a social order has a biblical parallel in the story of the Exodus, where forty years of Israel's wandering in the wilderness are followed by the conquest and settlement of the Promised Land. Milton preserves the traditional feature of a split in the middle of the action when, at the beginning of Book Seven, he says that the action for the second half of the poem will be confined to the earth. The order in *Paradise Lost* is the reverse of the biblical one, as it starts with the Promised Land and ends in the wilderness; but the biblical order is preserved when we add *Paradise Regained* to the sequence.

But of course of all the traditional epic features, the most important is that of beginning the action *in medias res*, in Horace's phrase, at a dramatically well-advanced point and then working back simultaneously to the beginning and forward to the end. If we ask beginning and end of what, the answer is, beginning and end of the total action, of which only a part may be presented in the actual poem. This total action is cyclical in shape: it almost has to be because of the nature of the quest theme. The hero goes out to do something, does it, and returns. In the *Odyssey*, the total action begins when Odysseus leaves Ithaca and goes off to the Trojan War, and it ends when he gets back to Ithaca as master of his house again. Matters are less simple in the *Iliad,* but even there the total movement of the Greeks out to Troy and back home again is clearly in the background. In the *Aeneid* there is what from Milton's point of view is a most important advance in this conception of a total cyclical action. Here the total action begins and ends, not at precisely the same point, but at the same point renewed and transformed by the heroic action itself. That is, the toal action of the *Aeneid* begins when Aeneas leaves Troy collapsing in flames, losing his wife; and it ends with the new Troy established at Rome, Aeneas remarried and the household gods of the defeated Troy set up once again in a new home. The end is the beginning as recreated by the heroism of Aeneas.

We notice that the trick of beginning the action at a dramatically well-advanced point is not done entirely at random. The *Odyssey* begins with Odysseus at the furthest point from home, on the island of Calypso, subjected to the temptations of Penelope's only formidable rival. The action of the *Aeneid* similarly begins with Aeneas' shipwreck on the shores of Carthage, the *Erbfeind* or hereditary enemy of Rome and the site of the citadel of Juno, Aeneas' implacable enemy. Similarly, the action of *Paradise Lost* begins at the furthest possible point from the presence of God, in hell. The cycle which forms the total background action of *Paradise Lost* is again the cycle of the Bible. It begins where God begins, in an eternal presence, and it ends where God ends, in an eternal presence. The foreground action begins *in medias res*, translated by Milton in his Argument as "in the midst of things," with Satan already fallen into hell, and it works from there back to the beginning and forward to the end of the total action. The foreground action deals with the conspiracy of Satan and the fall of Adam and Eve, and the two speeches of the two angels deal with the rest of the cycle. Raphael begins with what is chronologically the first event in the poem, the showing of Christ to the angels, and brings the action down to the point at which the poem begins. After Adam's fall, Michael picks up the story and summarizes the biblical narrative through to the Last Judgment, which brings us back again to the point at which God is all in all. The epic narrative thus consists of a foreground action with two great flanking speeches where the action is reported by messengers (*aggeloi*) putting it in its proper context.

We notice that in the Classical epics there are two kinds of revelation. There is the kind that comes from the gods above, when Athene or Venus appears to the hero at a crucial point with words of comfort or advice. There is nothing mysterious about these appearances: they happen in broad daylight and their function is to illuminate the present situation. Athene appears in the disguise of Mentor to give Telemachus the kind of advice that a wise and kindly human being would also give. There is another kind of revelation which is sought from gods below. Telemachus gains it by disguising himself as a seal and catching Proteus; Odysseus gains it by a complicated and sinister ritual of sacrifice, the spilling of blood, ghosts and darkness. There are strong hints that knowledge obtained in this way is normally forbidden knowledge, and it does not illuminate a present situation: it is specifically knowledge about the future. It is knowledge about his own future that Odysseus seeks when he calls up Teiresias from hell; it is knowledge of the future of Rome that Aeneas gets when he descends, though with less ritual elaboration, into the cave guarded by the Sibyl. The association of future and forbidden knowledge is carried even further in Dante's *Inferno*, because the people in Dante's hell have knowledge of the future but not of the present.

The kind of knowledge given to Adam in Michael's speech is essentially a knowledge of the future, of what is going to happen. It is intended to be consoling, although Adam collapses twice under the ordeal of being consoled, and the fact that knowledge of the future is possible means of course that the freedom of human will has been mortally injured. The suggestion is clearly that such knowledge of the future is a part of the forbidden knowledge which Adam should never have had in the first place, knowledge which God is willing to give him but which Satan would have cheated him out of. Human life now is in large part a dialectic between revelation and the knowledge of good and evil, and this dialectic is represented in *Paradise Lost* by the contrast between God the Father and Adam after his fall. God the Father sits in heaven and foreknows what will happen, but, as he carefully explains, not forcing it to happen. Below him is Adam in a parody of that situation, foreknowing what is going to happen to the human race in consequence of his fall, but unable in the smallest degree to interfere with or alter the course of events.

The foreground action, the conspiracy of Satan and its consequences, forms a kind of mock-Telemachia in counterpoint to the main epic action to be considered in a moment, a parable of a prodigal son who does not return. Technically, however, the foreground action presents a sharp focusing of attention which brings it close to dramatic forms. The fall itself is conceived in the form of tragedy, the great rival of epic in Renaissance theory, yet almost the antithesis of the epic, as it demanded a concentrated unity of action which seems the opposite of the epic's encyclopaedic range. The ninth book represents a crystallization of Milton's earlier plans for treating the fall of man in tragic form, with Satan as a returning spirit of vengeance persuading Eve into a foreshortened compliance much as Iago does Othello. Nature, sighing through all her works, occupies the place of the chorus.

At the opening of the poem we find ourselves plunged into the darkness of hell and eventually, after our pupils have expanded, look around and see one or two lights glaring. We then realize that these are eyes, and a number of huge clouded forms begin to come out of a kind of sea and gather on a kind of shore. Throughout the first two books we move through shadowy and indefinite gloom, and then, at the opening of the third, are plunged quite as suddenly into blinding light, where only after our pupils have contracted again can we observe such details as the pavement of heaven which "Impurpled with celestial roses smiled." We feel that such intensities are appropriate to a poet who is not only blind but baroque, and who, if he never saw the shadows of Rembrandt or the sunlight of Claude, still reflects his age's interest in chiaroscuro. But the principle *ut pictura poesis* can only be expressed in verbal spectacle, and we should also realize the extent to which the dramatic form of the Jonsonian masque has informed these first three books, a dark and sinister antimasque being followed by a splendid vision of ordered glory. The masque vision moves slowly from heaven down through the starry spheres to Eden; the antimasque modulates into the ludicrous disorder of the Limbo of Vanities, and disappears until it is recalled by Raphael's narrative of an earlier expulsion from heaven.

There is, then, with the dramatic foreground action and the speeches of Raphael and Michael filling in the beginning and end of the total background action, a kind of formal symmetry of a type that we might not expect in a poem that we have just called baroque. I think that this formal symmetry can be carried much further, and I should like to divide the total action in a way which I think best illustrates it. Some of the divisions take up several books and others only a few lines, but that is of no importance. Most of the shorter ones are from the Bible, and Milton expected his reader to be able to give them their due importance. Let us visualize the dial of a clock, with the presence of God where the figure 12 is. The first four figures of the dial represent the four main events of the speech of Raphael. First comes the first epiphany or manifestation of Christ, when God the Father shows his Son to the angels and demands that they worship him. This is the chronological beginning of the total action, as already remarked. Next, at 2 on the dial, comes the second epiphany of Christ at the end of the war in heaven, when on the third day he tramples on the rebel angels and manifests himself in triumph and wrath. The third stage is the creation of the natural order, as described by Milton in his extraordinarily skilful paraphrase of the Genesis account. The fourth phase is the creation of the human order, with the forming of the bodies of Adam and Eve, in the account of which Adam takes over from Raphael.

After this the foreground action moves across the lower part of the dial. At the figure 5 comes the conspiracy of Satan, ending in his pact with Sin and Death. The generation of Death from Satan is a parody of the generation of the Son from the Father which starts off the action, Death being, so to speak, the Word of Satan. At 6, the nadir of the action, comes the tragic catastrophe, the fall of Adam and Eve, the fall, that is, of the human order established by God. Next, at 7, comes the fall of the natural order, which is really a part of the fall of Adam and Eve, and is described in Book Ten as the triumph of Sin and Death, corresponding to Satan's pact with them at 5.

The next four stages are the ones covered by the speech of Michael: they correspond to the four that we found in the speech of Raphael, but are in roughly the reverse order. First, at 8, comes the re-establishing of the natural order at the time of the flood, when it is promised with the symbol of the rainbow that seedtime and harvest will not fail until the end of the world. Next, at 9, comes the re-establishing of the human order, when the law is given to Israel and the prototype of Jesus, Joshua, who has the same name as Jesus, takes possession of the Promised Land. Next, at 10, comes the third epiphany of Christ, the Incarnation properly speaking, which again is an epiphany ending with the triumph over death and hell in a three-day battle. Next, at 11, comes the fourth epiphany of Christ, the Last Judgment, again an epiphany of triumph and wrath, when the final separation is made between the orders of heaven and of hell. At 12, we come back again to the point prophesied by God himself in his speech in Book Three, when he says that there will come a time when he will lay by his sceptre and "God shall be all in all." The final point in the vast cycle is the same point as the beginning, yet not the same point, because, as in the *Aeneid*, the ending is the starting point renewed and transformed by the heroic quest of Christ. Thus there can be only one cycle, not an endless series of them. To summarize:

1. First epiphany of Christ: generation of Son from Father.
2. Second epiphany of Christ: triumph after three-day conflict.
3. Establishment of the natural order in the creation.
4. Establishment of the human order: creation of Adam and Eve.
5. Epiphany of Satan, generating Sin and Death.
6. Fall of the human order.
7. Fall of the natural order: triumph of Sin and Death.
8. Re-establishment of the natural order at the end of the flood.
9. Re-establishment of the human order with the giving of the law.
10. Third epiphany of Christ: the Word as gospel.
11. Fourth epiphany of Christ: the apocalypse or Last Judgment.

There are four orders of existence in *Paradise Lost*, the divine order, the angelic order, the human order and the demonic order. Being an epic, *Paradise Lost* has to deal with the traditional theme of the epic, which is the theme of heroic action. In order to under-stand what heroic action was to Milton we have to think what a Christian poet would mean by the conception of heroic action: that is, we have to ask ourselves what for Milton a hero was, and, even more important, what an act was. Milton says clearly in *The Chris-tian Doctrine* what he means by an act. An act is the expression of the energy of a free and conscious being. Consequently all acts are good. There is no such thing, strictly speaking, as an evil act; evil or sin implies deficiency, and implies also the loss or lack of the power to act. There is a somewhat unexpected corollary of this: if all acts are good, then God is the source of all real action. At the same time, as Milton says, or rather as his sentence structure says in spite of him, it is almost impossible to avoid speaking of evil acts:

> It is called actual sin, not that sin is properly an action, for in reality it implies defect; but because it commonly consists in some act. For every act is in itself good; it is only its irregularity, or deviation from the line of right, which properly speaking is evil.

What happens when Adam eats the forbidden fruit, then, is not an act, but the surrendering of the power to act. Man is free to lose his freedom, and there, obviously, his freedom stops. His position is like that of a man on the edge of a precipice—if he jumps it appears to be an act, but it is really the giving up of the possibility of action, the surrendering of himself to the law of gravitation which will take charge of him for the brief remainder of his life. In this surrendering of the power to act lies the key to Milton's con-ception of the behaviour of Adam. A typically fallen human act is something where the word "act" has to be in quotation marks. It is a pseudo-act, the pseudo-act of disobedience, and it is really a refusal to act at all.

Implied in this argument is a curious paradox between the dra-matic and the conceptual aspects of the temptation scenes in Mil-ton's poetry. In a temptation somebody is being persuaded to do something that looks like an act, but which is really the loss of the power to act. Consequently, the abstaining from this kind of pseudo-activity is often the sign that one possesses a genuine power of action. The Lady in *Comus*, for example, has a somewhat uninter-esting dramatic role: she is, in fact, paralyzed, and, dramatically, says little except an eloquent and closely reasoned paraphrase of "no." Comus attracts a good deal more of our sympathy because his arguments are specious, and therefore dramatically more inter-esting. Yet we have to realize that the real situation is the opposite of the dramatic one. It is Comus who represents passion, which is the opposite of action; it is the Lady who holds to the source of all freedom of action. The same situation is even more sharply mani-

fested in the role of Jesus in *Paradise Regained*, where Jesus be-
haves, for four books, like a householder dealing with an importu-
nate salesman. Yet again what is actually going on is the opposite
of what appears to be going on. Satan, who seems so lively and
resourceful, is the power that moves toward the cessation of all
activity, a kind of personal entropy that transforms all energy into
a heat-death.

The typical demonic "act" is not a real act either, but it is a much
more concentrated parody of divine action. It has the quality not of
disobedience but of rebellion, and it differs from the human act in
that it involves rivalry, or attempted rivalry, with God. The appear-
ance of Nimrod at the beginning of the last book of *Paradise Lost*
represents the coming into human life of the demonic, of the ability
to worship devils, of turning to Satan for one's conception of the
kingdom and the power and the glory, instead of to God. What
Satan himself manifests in *Paradise Lost* is this perverted quality of
parody-heroism, of which the essential quality is destructiveness.
Consequently it is to Satan and his followers that Milton assigns the
conventional and Classical type of heroism. Satan, like Achilles, re-
tires sulkily in heaven when a decision appears to be favouring
another Son of God, and emerges in a torrent of wrath to wreak
vengeance. Like Odysseus, he steers his way with great cunning
between the Scylla-like Sin and the Charybdis-like Death; like the
knights errant of romance, he goes out alone on a perilous quest to
an unknown world. The remark the devils make about the war in
heaven, that they have sustained the war for a day "And, if one
day, why not eternal days?" opens up a perverted vision of eternity
as a Valhalla of endless strife.

It is only the divine that can really act, by Milton's own defini-
tion of an act, and the quality of the divine act reveals itself in
Paradise Lost as an act of creation, which becomes an act of re-
creation or redemption after the fall of man. Christ, therefore, who
creates the world and then recreates or redeems man, is the hero of
Paradise Lost simply because, as the agent or acting principle of the
Father, he is ultimately the only actor in the poem.

The angelic order is there to provide models for human action.
They have superior intellectual and physical powers which man
may eventually attain, but in *Paradise Lost* they are moral models
only. They form a community of service and obedience, often
doing things meaningless to them except that as the will of God
they have meaning. They are ministers of responsibility (Gabriel),
instruction (Raphael), command (Michael) or vigilance (Uriel).
The figure of the tense, waiting angels, listening for the Word to
speak and motionless until it does, appears in the last line of the
Nativity Ode and again in the last line of the sonnet on the poet's
blindness. Such angels are, as the angel says to John at the end of

the Bible, fellow servants of mankind: there is nothing in Milton of Rilke's "schrecklich" angel.

More important than any of these, for the theme of heroism, is Abdiel, who remains faithful to God in the midst of the revolted angels. Abdiel, like many people of unimpeachable integrity, is not a very attractive character, but everything he says in the poem is of the highest importance. The speech which he makes to Satan at the time of the war in heaven indicates that he is establishing the pattern of genuine heroism that is later to be exhibited in the life of Christ, the "better part of fortitude" which consists primarily in obedience and endurance and in the kind of courage that is willing to suffer under ridicule and contempt and a chorus of opposition. As Abdiel says to Satan, after being restored to the faithful angels, "My sect thou seest." This pattern is followed in the biblical visions which Michael shows to Adam: in the story of Enoch, the one just man who stands out against all the vice of his time, and receives the angelic reward of direct transportation to heaven, and in Noah, who is similarly the one just man of his time and is saved from an otherwise total destruction. It could have been exemplified by Lot in Sodom, which is referred to briefly by Milton. This is the pattern which is followed by the prophets and apostles, and nobody else is entitled to be called heroic.

Doubtless the faithful angels could have defeated the rebels by themselves, but the symbolism of the three-day war in heaven is designed to show that the total angelic power of action is contained in the Son of God. The angels have no strength that does not come from God, and the devils have no strength against God at all. It is difficult not to feel that the entire war in heaven is a huge practical joke to the Father, all the more of one because of the seriousness with which the devils take it. The admiring description of the size of Satan's spear and shield in Book One has two perspectives: from man's point of view Satan is incalculably strong, but from God's point of view he is only a lubber fiend. God's own conception of strength is represented by the infant Christ of the Nativity Ode, the genuine form of Hercules strangling the serpent in his cradle, physically weak and yet strong enough to overcome the world.

In this world spiritual strength, being a direct gift of God, is not necessarily accompanied by physical strength, though it is normally accompanied by physical invulnerability. This condition is the condition of chastity, traditionally a magical strength in romance, and the theme of the magic of chastity runs all through Milton. The Lady cannot be hurt by Comus because of the "hidden strength" of her chastity. Samson owes his physical strength to his chastity, to his observance of his Nazarite vow: as he says bitterly, God hung his strength in his hair. He loses his chastity when he tells Delilah what his secret is. Such chastity does not in his case imply virginity or even continence: two marriages to Philistine women do not affect it, nor apparently does even a visit to a Philistine harlot, which Milton ignores, though he read about it in the Book of Judges. Adam and Eve have been given more than mortal strength by their chastity, which is also not affected by sexual intercourse: they lose their chastity only by eating of the forbidden tree. A reference to Samson in Book Nine establishes the link in the symbolism of chastity between the two.

Like most morally coherent writers, Milton is careful to distinguish the human from the demonic, even when what he is showing is the relation between them. As it may be difficult to feel this distinction without examples we may take an analogy from Shakespeare. Cleopatra in Shakespeare is all the things that the critics of Milton say Eve is. She is vain and frivolous and light-minded and capricious and extravagant and irresponsible and a very bad influence on Antony, who ought to be out chasing Parthians instead of wasting his time with her. She is morally a most deplorable character, yet there is something about her which is obstinately likable. Perhaps that makes her more dangerous, but it's no good: we cannot feel that Cleopatra is evil in the way that Goneril and Regan are evil. For one thing, Cleopatra can always be unpredictable, and as long as she can be that she is human. Goneril and Regan are much closer to what is meant in religion by lost souls, and what that means dramatically is that they can no longer be unpredictable. Everything they do or say is coarse and ugly and cruel, but still it also has about it something of the stylized grandeur of the demonic, something of the quality that Milton's devils have and that his human beings do not have. At the same time Cleopatra is a part of something far more sinister than herself: this comes out in the imagery attached to Egypt, if not in the characterization attached to her. Putting the two together, what we see is the human contained by the demonic, a fascinating creature of infinite variety who is still, from another point of view, sprung from the equivocal generation of the Nile.

It is the same with Adam and Eve. Theologically and conceptually, they have committed every sin in the calendar. In *The Christian Doctrine* Milton sets it all down: there was nothing bad that they omitted to do when they ate that wretched apple:

It comprehended at once distrust in the divine veracity, and a proportionate credulity in the assurances of Satan; unbelief; ingratitude; disobedience; gluttony; in the man excessive uxoriousness, in the woman a want of proper regard for her husband, in both an insensibility to the welfare of their offspring, and that offspring the whole human race; parricide, theft, invasion of the rights of others, sacrilege, deceit, presumption in aspiring to divine attributes, fraud in the means employed to attain the object, pride, and arrogance.

Yet this is something that it is wholly impossible for us to feel or realize dramatically, nor does Milton attempt to make us do so. Eve may have been a silly girl but she is still our general mother, still quite obviously the same kind of human being that we are. What has happened is that human life is now attached to the demonic, this being one of the points made by Michael, especially in the vision of Nimrod, the archetypal tyrant, the tyrant being one of the clearest examples of a human being who has given himself up to the demonic.

The fact that conventional heroism, as we have it in Classical epic and medieval and Renaissance romance, is associated with the demonic in Milton means, of course, that *Paradise Lost* is a profoundly anti-romantic and anti-heroic poem. Most of us live our lives on a roughly human level, but if we meet with some setback, snub, imposed authority or other humiliation we are thrown back on something that will support and console us, and unless we are saints that something is likely to be the ego. The sombre, brooding, humourless ego, with its "high disdain from sense of injured merit" drives us to look for compensation, perhaps by identifying ourselves with some irresistible hero. If in this state we read Milton, we shall find his Satan, so far from being the author of evil, a congenial and sympathetic figure. If we later regain a better sense of proportion, we may understand something of the profundity and accuracy of Milton's conception of evil.

Satan is a rebel, and into Satan Milton has put all the horror and distress with which he contemplated the egocentric revolutionaries of his time, who stumbled from one party to another and finally ended precisely where they had started, in a cyclical movement with no renewal. There is an almost uncanny anticipation of some of the moods of later Romanticism, also an age of egocentric revolutionaries. In particular, there is a quality in Milton's treatment of the demonic world that can only be called Wagnerian: in the unvarying nobility of the rhetoric, in the nihilistic heroic action that begins and ends in the lake of fire, in the *Götterdämmerung* motif in the music of hell:

> Others, more mild,
> Retreated in a silent valley, sing
> With notes angelical to many a harp
> Their own heroic deeds, and hapless fall
> By doom of battle, and complain that Fate
> Free virtue should enthrall to force or chance.

This is not to say that Wagner is a demonic artist, any more than that Milton is a Satanist, only that there are demonic elements portrayed in Wagner that some very evil people have found, as many have found Satan, irresistibly attractive.

The anti-heroic tendency in Milton is, however, less complicated than his attitude to myth, of which it forms part. When a literary critic says that the story of the fall of man is a myth, he is not making any statement about the truth of its content, merely that it is a certain kind of story; but still his feeling about its truth is coloured by this very shift of attention from its content to its form. But Milton is never tired of stressing the difference in ethical content between the truth of the Bible and the fables of the heathen, and obviously the story of the fall would never have interested him if he had not believed it to be as literally true as the events of his own life. The story of *Paradise Lost* is a myth in the sense that the action or narrative movement (*mythos*) is provided by a divine being: the essential content is human, and as credible and plausible as Milton's source would allow him to make it. The marvels and grotesqueries of the poem, such as the building of Pandemonium or the Limbo of Vanities, are mostly demonic, and form a contrast to the central action. In modern literature a writer may use a mythical subject because it affords him an interesting and traditional story pattern, as Cocteau does in *Orphée* or Giraudoux in *Antigone*. In Tolstoy's *Resurrection* we have a purely realistic narrative which assumes a shape with the religious significance indicated in the title. Milton's attitude to myth in *Paradise Lost* is much closer, temperamentally and technically, to Tolstoy than it is to Cocteau or Giraudoux.

Myths differ from folk tales or legends in having a superior kind of importance attached to them, and this in turn makes them stick together and form mythologies. A fully developed mythology thus tends, as the Bible does, to take an encyclopaedic shape. Ovid's *metamorphoses*, for example, starts with creation and flood stories and works its way down to Julius Caesar as the Bible does to Jesus. Milton's exhaustive use of Ovid is often sympathetic, but evidently he finds in the Ovidian theme of metamorphosis, the identifying of a human figure with an object in nature, the point at which polytheism becomes obvious idolatry. The demonic action of *Paradise Lost* ends with an Ovidian metamorphosis in which the devils are changed to serpents. Satan has taken the form of the serpent; he finds in hell that he cannot get rid of it, but is still a serpent; the devils in looking at him become serpents too:

> what they saw
> They felt themselves now changing.

There is a clear recall of the remark about idols in the 115th Psalm: "they that make them are like unto them."

For us, the mythological imagination is really part of the poetic imagination: the instinct to identify a human figure with a natural object, which gives mythology its sun gods and tree gods and ocean gods, is the same instinct that is described by Whitman:

> There was a child went forth every day,
> And the first object he look'd upon, that object he became,
> And that object became part of him for the day or a certain part
>   of the day,
> Or for many years or stretching cycles of years.

The author of *Lycidas* would have understood this very well; but a question not relevant to Whitman is relevant to Milton: is this identifying consciousness centered in the ego, as Satan's intelligence is, or not? To identify one's consciousness directly with the works of God in our present world, for Milton, is to enter the forest of Comus on Comus' own terms, to unite ourselves to a sub-moral, sub-conscious, sub-human existence which is life to the body but death to the soul. The free intelligence must detach itself from this world and unite itself to the totality of freedom and intelligence which is God in man, shift its centre of gravity from the self to the presence of God in the self. Then it will find the identity with nature it appeared to reject: it will participate in the Creator's view of a world he made and found good. This is the relation of Adam and Eve to Eden before their fall. From Milton's point of view, the polytheistic imagination can never free itself from the labyrinths of fantasy and irony, with their fitful glimpses of inseparable good and evil. What Milton means by revelation is a consolidated, coherent, encyclopaedic view of human life which defines, among other things, the function of poetry. Every act of the free intelligence, including the poetic intelligence, is an attempt to return to Eden, a world in the human form of a garden, where we may wander as we please but cannot lose our way.

STANLEY EUGENE FISH

Discovery as Form in *Paradise Lost*†

I

Recently I have argued that the true center of *Paradise Lost* is the reader's consciousness of the poem's *personal* relevance, and that the arc of the poem describes, in addition to the careers of the characters, the education of its readers.[1] This education proceeds

† From *New Essays on "Paradise Lost"* edited by Thomas Kranidas, (Berkeley, University of California Press, 1971), pp. 1–14. Reprinted by permission of the Regents of the University of California.

The author's footnotes have been renumbered and one has been deleted.
1. *Surprised by Sin: The Reader in Paradise Lost* (London and New York, 1967).

in two stages: in the first, the reader is brought face to face with the corruption within him, as he is made aware of the confusion reigning in his scale of values and of the inadequacy of his perceptions; in the second, he is invited to cooperate with the poem's effort to effect his regeneration, invited, in Milton's words, to purge his "intellectual ray" until it is once more "fit and proportionable to Truth the object, and end of it, as the eye of the thing visible."[2] These stages correspond to the stages of Plato's dialectic, the inducing in the respondent of a "healthy perplexity" followed by the refinement of his inner eye to the point where it recognizes and embraces the Supreme Good;[3] and the poem's operation is analogous to that of the Mosaic Law which, we are told in *The Christian Doctrine*, calls forth "our natural depravity, that by this means it might . . . bring us to the righteousness of Christ."[4] In its potential effect, then, *Paradise Lost* may claim the status of what Bunyan calls a "work of grace" in the soul; for it gives the sinner "conviction of sin, especially of the defilement of his nature, and the sin of unbelief."[5]

This description of *Paradise Lost*, as a poem concerned with the self-education of its readers, if it is accepted, throws a new light on some old questions. Specifically, it dictates a reorientation of the debate concerning the structure or form of the poem; for if the meaning of the poem is to be located in the reader's experience of it, the form of the poem is the form of that experience; and the outer or physical form, so obtrusive, and, in one sense, so undeniably there, is, in another sense, incidental and even irrelevant. This is a deliberately provocative thesis, the defense of which will be the concern of the following pages; and I would like to begin by explaining more fully what is meant by the phrase "the form of the reader's experience."

The stages of this experience mark advances in the reader's understanding, in the refining of his vision rather than in the organization of material. In *Paradise Lost, things* are not being clarified or ordered; rather, *eyes* are being made capable of seeing things as they truly are already in the clarity of God's order. The process, and its relationship to a truth that is evident to those who have eyes to see it, is adumbrated in this passage from *Of Reformation*:

> The very essence of Truth is plainnesse, and brightnes; the darknes and crookednesse is our own. . . . If our *understanding* have a film of *ignorance* over it, or be blear with gazing on other false glisterings, what is that to Truth? If we will but purge with

2. Milton, *Complete Prose Works*, Vol. I, ed. D. M. Wolfe, New Haven, 1953), p. 566.
3. See Robert Cushman, *Therapeia* (Chapel Hill, N.C., 1958), p. 89.
4. *The Works of John Milton*, ed. F. A. Patterson *et al.* (New York, 1933), XVI, 131.
5. *The Pilgrim's Progress*, ed. J. B. Wharey, rev. R. Sharrock (Oxford, 1960), pp. 82–83.

sovrain eyesalve that intellectual ray which *God* hath planted in us, then we would beleeve the Scriptures protesting their own plainnes.[6]

In Augustine's *On Christian Doctrine* the Scriptures themselves are the instrument by which the understanding can be made proportional to their plainness; and Augustine's description of what happens to the attentive reader of God's word is not unlike my description of the reader's experience in *Paradise Lost*:

> The student first will discover in the Scriptures that he has been enmeshed in the love of this world. . . . Then . . . that fear which arises from the thought of God's judgment . . . will force him to lament his own situation. . . . And by means of this affection of the spirit he will extract himself from all mortal joy in transitory things . . . and turn toward the love of eternal things . . . he purges his mind, which is rising up and protesting in the appetite for inferior things, of its contaminations.[7]

Augustine then describes five steps or stages leading to a sixth where the aspirant "cleanses that eye through which God may be seen, in so far as He can be seen by those who die to the world as much as they are able." "From fear to wisdom," he concludes, "the way extends through these steps."

To some extent Augustine's "steps" suggest a regular and predictable, that is, linear, progression to wisdom; but, of course, the movement from one step to the next cannot be predicted or charted since the operative factor is the "purging of the mind" or "the cleansing of the eye"; and the extent to which the mind is distracted by the appeal of transitory things, and, consequently, the period of time which must elapse before the eyes are made clear, will vary with the individual, who dies to the world as much as *he* is able. Nor will progress be regular (linear) within the discrete stages enumerated by Augustine. In how many differing contexts must the eye be challenged to distinguish true beauty from the "false glisterings" of "fair outsides" before it is able to see what is and is not truly beautiful *immediately*? No one answer will serve for all eyes. In Plato's dialectic, A. E. Taylor explains, the apprehension of Reality "comes as a sudden 'revelation' though it is not to be had without the long preliminary process of travail of thought."[8] Taylor's point is that the relationship between the "travail of thought" and the "revelation" is indeterminate, partly because the thing to be known cannot be known by "discursive knowledge about it," and partly because, as Robert Cushman observes, the effort that must be expended "to disengage the mind from preoccupation with sen-

6. Milton, *Complete Prose Works*, I, 566.
7. *On Christian Doctrine*, trans. D. W. Robertson (New York, 1958), pp. 39–40.
8. *Plato: The Man and his Work* (Meridian Books, New York, 1957), p. 231.

sibles" will be in proportion to the strength of the "fetters" binding the individual mind to earthly perception.[9]

Consider the case of Samson, whose experience in Milton's verse drama parallels that of the reader in *Paradise Lost*. When Manoa quarrels with God's dispensing of justice—"methinks whom God hath chosen once/. . . He should not so o'erwhelm" (11.368–370)—Samson answers firmly "Appoint not heavenly disposition" (1.373). But within a few lines he too begins to appoint heavenly disposition when he declares himself ineligible for service to God in his present condition—"To what can I be useful?"—for, in effect, he is putting limits on God's ability to use him. No straight line can describe Samson's spiritual journey. At times, as in this instance, he seems to make an advance toward understanding, only in the next minute to embrace in another guise the error he has just rejected. When clarity of vision does come to Samson, we can look back and see a series of starts (gestures) toward it—intimations, partial illuminations—but no chartable and visible progression. Let me here anticipate a later argument by pointing out that since the concern of the play is Samson's regeneration, Dalila, Harapha, the messenger, the Chorus, and Manoa are important, not for themselves, but for the opportunities they bring to Samson's laboring mind.

In *Paradise Lost*, the reader is repeatedly forced to acknowledge the unworthiness of values and ideals he had previously admired, yet, like Samson, he will often fall into the same admiration when the context changes slightly. To take as an example something I have treated at length elsewhere, in the early books: Satan's false heroism draws from the reader a response that is immediately challenged by the epic voice, who at the same time challenges the concept of heroism in which the response is rooted. Subsequently, Satan's apparent heroism is discredited by covert allusions to other heroes in other epics, by his ignoble accommodation to the "family" he meets at the gates of Hell, by his later discoveries squatting at the ear of Eve in the form of a toad, and, most tellingly, by his own self-revelations in the extended soliloquy that opens Book IV. At *some point* during this sequence of actions, the reader becomes immune to the Satanic appeal because he has learned what it is, or to be more precise, what it is not. "Some point," however, will be a different point for each reader, depending on the extent to which he is committed to the false ideal Satan exemplifies. Nor will the progress of any reader—of whatever capacity—be regular, since the learning of an individual lesson is not a guarantee against falling into a generic error. The reader who in Book I is led to resist the sophistries of the Satanic line when they are offered directly, may not recognize them in Book II when they are put forward in the Grand Council, especially if he has surrendered too much of his

9. Cushman, *op. cit.*, pp. 163, 166.

attention to the thrust and parry of the debate, that is, to the strategy rather than to the morality of the scene. And this same reader, when he is presented with a true hero in the person of Abdiel, is likely to admire him for the wrong reasons. That is to say, his response to Abdiel's action at the close of Book V will be a response to the melodramatic aspect of the situation—a lone figure rising to assert himself against innumerable foes—and therefore a response not enough differentiated from that originally given to the now discredited Satan. In Book VI, during the War in Heaven, the reader is given the opportunity to distinguish Abdiel's heroism from the *incidental* circumstances of its exercise. So that, at *some point* in the course of his struggles with the interpretative problems raised by the battle, the reader discovers the naked essence of heroism itself. It is important to realize that the poem does not move to this revelation; it has been there from the first, plainly visible to the eye capable of seeing it. It is the reader who moves, or advances, until his cleansed eye can see what has always been there. At least the reader is given the *opportunity* to advance. He may not take it, and so remain a captive of his clouded vision. It follows, then, that between Books I and VI Satan does not change at all. His degradation is a critical myth. The reader's capacity to see him clearly changes, although that change is gradual and fitful, uneven, unchartable, to some extent invisible, not easily separated from parallel changes in the reader's capacity to see other things clearly— virtue, heroism, love, beauty. (I am thinking, for example, of the contrast between the good and bad poetry of Satan's and God's speeches. I leave you to apply the labels.)

If Satan has not moved or altered, the only alteration being the reader's, it follows that the episodes in which Satan appears are not important for any light they throw on *him*, or for the challenges they present to *him*, but for the function they serve as a whetstone to the reader's laboring mind. Moreover the action of the poem is taking place in that mind, not in the narrative, whose world is static. For, strictly speaking, the plot of *Paradise Lost*, in the sense of a linear movement toward a dramatic and moral climax—the Fall—does not exist; simply because the concept of free will, as Milton defines it, precludes the usual process of decision—the interplay between circumstance, motivation, and choice—which in other works fills up a plot. The decision of an absolutely free will cannot be determined by forces outside it, and, in a causal sense, such a decision has no antecedents. I would suggest that the point of the scenes in Paradise from Book IV to Book IX is their irrelevance, as determining factors, to the moment of crisis experienced by the characters; and the action taking place in these scenes is the reader's discovery or comprehension of that irrelevance. In the middle books, and especially at those points where Milton has been accused of "necessary faking"—the phrase is Tillyard's[1]—the reader is presented with a series of "interpretative choices." On the surface, the account of Eve's infatuation with her reflected image, and the fact of her dream, and of Adam's admission to Raphael of his weakness, seem to deny the freedom of the unfallen will by circumscribing our first parents in what Watkins[2] has termed a "network of circumstance." Yet in each instance Milton provides evidence that makes it possible for the reader to disengage these incidents from the Fall—I am thinking for example of Adam's statement, "Evil into the mind of God or Man/May come and go . . . and leave/No spot . . . behind"—and finally to see them as moving away from, rather than toward, that crisis. This is the poet's solution to the problem of building a poem around an event that has no antecedents. He gives us a plot without a middle—Adam and Eve fall spontaneously—but he allows for a *psychological* middle, a middle to the reading experience, by leaving it to us to discover that the narrative middle does not, indeed could not, exist.

II

Now, for the obvious question: if the poem does not move, but the reader moves, if there is no plot except for the plot of the reader's education, and if the true form of the poem is the form of the individual reader's experience rather than the visible form represented by the division into twelve books; if, in sum, the action is interior, taking place inside the reader's mind, what is the function of the exterior form? Why is it there? What do we say, for instance, about the intricate patterning of words and phrases continually being uncovered by modern criticism? There are several answers to this question. The divisions in the narrative, in the physical artifact called *Paradise Lost*, mark out areas within which the process of regeneration can go forward, while the instances of parallelism provide "stations" at which the progress of the process can be checked. When the reader comes across a word or a phrase that recalls him to an earlier point in the poem, he is not being asked to compare the contents of two scenes now juxtaposed in his mind, but to apply whatever insights he has gained in the *psychological* interim to the single content these two scenes share. That is to say, the meaning of the parallel is determined not by its existence but by the success the reader has had in purging his intellectual ray. Anyone, even a computer, can point out echoes. Only a reader who has learned, only a reader with a cleansed eye, can create their meaning. *He* does it, not the poem. Echoes and cross-references are not

1. E. M. W. Tillyard, *Studies in Milton* (London, 1951), p. 10 [*Editor*].
2. W. B. C. Watkins, *An Anatomy of Milton's Verse* (Baton Rouge, 1955) [*Editor*].

saying, "Look at this." They are saying, "Do you know what to make of this *now*?"[3] The important time in the poem is psychological time. In the time consumed while reading, the poem is not developing, the reader is (or he isn't). And any significance one can attach to the sequence of events is to be found not in their relationship to the narrative situation—whose temporal structure, as many have observed, is confused—but to the reader's situation. Milton in effect tells us this when God sends Raphael down to warn Adam in Book V. In this way, the epic voice explains, "God fulfills all justice." But God here fulfills more than justice if Adam is meant, because Adam is sufficient to his test without Raphael's warning. Justice is being done to the reader, who is being given the opportunity Adam does not need, although what Adam will do in Book IX created the imperfection that makes it necessary for the reader to *now* have the opportunity. When at the end of Book VI the phrase "nine days they fell" returns us to the opening lines of Book I, our attention is not being called to what has happened to Satan since he was first expelled (of course nothing has happened to Satan), but to what has happened to ourselves. Satan is in the same place; we, one hopes, are not. Thus, this halfway point in *Paradise Lost* (in its outer form, that is) *is* there for a reason; it does mark the end of something, not, however, of something going on in the world of the characters (in that context we are right back where we started), but of something going on in the world of the reader. This, in fact, is the end of the poet's attempt to refine the reader's sense of what true heroism is. And later in Book IX the superficial nobility of Adam's gesture will pose once again the same question, "Do you understand now?" And in his response the reader will give his answer.

What I have said here with reference to the single problem of heroism applies to other problems and to other patternings. In Book III, God delivers a speech whose arguments, if they are understood, assure a correct reading of the crucial scene in Book IX. At irregular intervals, phrases from this "ur speech" are repeated (I am thinking especially of "sufficient to have stood, though free to fall"), and each repetition asks a silent question, "Do you understand *now*?" In the intervals between repetitions, the same question is posed indirectly by the events of the narrative. When Eve questions the perfection of her situation ("frail is our happiness if this be so"), she betrays a complete misunderstanding of the concepts God has been at pains to define, and thus her speech becomes a negative test of the reader. That is, the reader's

3. Again we find an analogue in the dialectic of Plato, where apparent progressions and/or digressions unexpectedly return to the point of origin, and the hapless respondent is asked to reassess his original position in the light of the truth he has ascended to, or, as is the case in most of the dialogues, in the light of the truth Socrates has drawn out of him.

ability to perceive the fallacies in her argument measures the extent to which he *now* understands God's logic. And once again we return to a point made earlier: since the misconceptions Eve entertains here cannot affect her performance at the moment of temptation ("the seat of temptation is in the will, not in the understanding"), her speech is more important for the reader's state of mind than for her own; in relationship to the Fall, her state of mind does not matter. It is the reader who has the most at stake in the scenes preceding the crisis; and the patterns, the repetitions, the time passing—they are all for him.

In addition to providing the reader with stations at which he may check his progress, and with cases or problems whose consideration is the vehicle of that progress, the poem's Aristotelian superstructure—beginning, middle, end—has a negative value as one form of a way of knowing Milton believes to be inferior or secondary. Plato makes a distinction between knowledge "by way of division," that is, knowledge whose end is the clarification of objects in the material world (*dianoia*), and knowledge by illumination, knowledge whose end is the recognition of a suprasensible reality (*episteme*); and this distinction corresponds to that made by Augustine and other theologians between *scientia* and *sapientia*. In one sphere, the mind, with the help of certain aids—deductive logic, enumeration, denotation—performs a refining operation on the data of experience; in the other, the mind itself is led to transcend the flux of experience and to reinterpret it in the light of the reality to which it has ascended. True knowledge, then, is not reached by following a chain of inferences or by accurately labeling *things* (although inference and labeling may have some part in the attainment of it), but is the possession of the mind that has been made congruent with it; true knowledge cannot be brought to the mind (it is not transmissable), the mind must be brought to it; to the point where there is no longer any need for the aid logical inference can offer. One must take care not to extend illegitimately the province of *scientia* and so fail to distinguish between that which can be seen and measured by the physical eye and that which reveals itself only to the inner eye of the aspiring soul. It is this danger to which Milton deliberately exposes his reader when he suggests in the opening lines that the purpose of his poem is to provide a verifiable answer to the question "What cause?"; in its position, this question holds out a promise that proves in the course of the poem to be false, the promise that if the reader follows Milton's argument, from its beginning to its middle to its end, he will find the answer and along with it a rational justification of God's ways, awaiting him, as it were, at the end of a syllogism. But this is not the case. The promise is given so that its falseness can be more forcefully exposed and so that the reader can learn not to rely on the way of knowing it assumes, but to rely instead on illumination and revelation. Just as the search for cause and for a rational justification is an attempt to confine God within the limits of formal reasoning, and is thus a temptation, so is the temporal-spatial structure of the poem, by means of which that search is supposedly to be conducted, a temptation, since the reader may fall into the error of looking to *it* as a revealer of meaning: that is, to the limited and distorting, though organized, picture of reality it presents, rather than to the inner light developing within him. (The more the inner light develops, of course, the less a temptation the outer formal structure will offer, since the reader's need of it, or of anything else, will progressively lessen.) The reader's situation parallels Adam's and Eve's, who are also tempted to look to the organization of experience, and to the meaning conferred on things by accidents of time and space, for guidance, rather than to revelation. So that, in summary, what we can call the outer form of the poem—twelve books, a regular plot line, the illusion of cause and effect—is (1) unnecessary (finally) to correct perception, and (2) a temptation, since dependence on it is enslavement to it and to the earthly (rational) perspective of which it is one manifestation. In other words, part of the poem's lesson is the superfluousness of the mold of experience—of space and time—to the perception of what is true; and thus the epic's outer form, inasmuch as it is the area within which the inner eye is purified, is the vehicle of its own abandonment. Like the hierarchical structure of the early Church as it is described in *The Reason of Church-government*, the outer form of the poem is a "scaffolding" which "so soon as the building is finished" is but a "troublesome disfigurement" that is to be cast aside.[4] And this casting aside is imitated in the *conceptual* movement of *Paradise Lost* by the rejection of the external trappings of a public heroism in favor of a better heroism whose successes are not visible to the physical eye.

III

And what does the reader who has reached this point discover at the end of his labors? The truth, of course, or Truth, as it awaits those who have climbed the Platonic ladder: the Supreme Good concerning which nothing can be predicated, since it is the basis of all predication; "a principle that requires justification and explanation by reference to nothing besides itself,"[5] because it is the basis of justification and that in the light of which all else is to be explained; a good whose value cannot be measured because it is the measure (or norm) of value. In Milton's poem, the position occu-

4. Milton, *Complete Prose Works*, I, 791.   *posium*, 211b.
5. Cushman, *op. cit.*, p. 177. See *Sym-*

pied by Plato's Supreme Good is occupied by Christ, whose action in Book XII—taking place not there but everywhere, not at one point in time, but at all points—is the measure of all other actions and the embodiment of everything that is truly valuable.

I began this paper by suggesting that the physical form of *Paradise Lost* has only an oblique relationship to its true form, which I identified with the form of the reader's experience. That experience, however, does not lend itself to the kind of description one usually associates with the word "formal"; here are no readily discernible beginning, middle, and end, no clearly marked transitions, no moments of crisis at which issues are preeminently resolved; instead, the form, if it can be called that, follows the convolutions of the reader's education, now describing an advance, now a backsliding, at one moment pointing upward, at another, downward, at a third, in both directions at once. Still, there is a pattern into which the experiences of all successful readers fall (although there are as many variations within it as there are readers) and we are now in a position to trace out that pattern:

(1) During the poem, the reader is being forced by the verse to sharpen his moral and spiritual perceptions to the point where they are answerable to those essences of which he has hitherto had only an imperfect and partial knowledge. This refining process is desultory and wandering, concerned randomly with the entire range of moral abstractions.

(2) At regular intervals, the reader is asked to assess his progress, asked if he is able to recognize the true form of one of these abstractions.

(3) There are in the poem two places where the answerability of the reader's vision to the *unity* of the conceptions he has been considering singly is tested: first in Book IX when Adam violates all of the values with whose identification the poem has been concerned—significantly he sins in their name and this "misnaming" becomes the legacy he leaves his sons—and again in Book XII when Christ restores to these much abused terms their true, that is spiritual, meaning.

The experience of the entire poem, then, moves toward this moment when the arc of the narrative action and the end of the reader's education coincide. (It is no accident that Adam's understanding is made perfect at the point where Christ is brought before his eyes at the end of a process very much like the education of the reader.) Knowledge of Christ is the end of all the smaller investigations and searches that go on in the body of the poem, investigations of the nature of heroism, love, beauty, innocence, happiness. He is the measure of them all and His essence *informs* them all. He gives form to the universe and to everything in it, including the things in this poem, including the poem itself. In an ultimate sense,

He is the poem's true form,[6] and His relationship to the temporal-spatial structure of the poem is a reflection of His relationship to the temporal-spatial structure of post-Edenic experience. He enters both structures at once to fulfill them and to supersede them as conveyors of meaning by making good on the promises they could not keep. The promise to justify God's ways to men, for instance, cannot, we discover, be fulfilled within the rational and linear framework of the physical *Paradise Lost*; but it *is* fulfilled when the reader, who has been led to an intuitive understanding of Christ's significance, understands, at that moment, how much the mercy of God exceeds the requirements of reason. (Mercy, the word taking flesh and sacrificing itself, is unreasonable.)

For the reader who has been so led, the poem no longer has any parts; rather, like the universe God sees from his prospect high, it constitutes a unity, infused at every point with a single stable meaning. This meaning is apprehended through what become its parts when one is limited to anything but an all-inclusive glance. As the reader moves (irregularly) toward this illuminative height, the divisions into books and episodes, and all other markers indicating subordination and emphasis, recede into the background and reveal themselves finally as artificial heighteners of what is self-evident to the purged eye.[7] The units of the poem are now interchangeable, one with another, receptacles all of the good and merciful news Christ proclaims in Book XII. The illusion of a multiplicity of parts, or even of a clash of values (i.e., love vs. obedience), is now seen to have been the creation of the distorting perspective of local contexts, a perspective that no longer delimits the horizons of the reader's vision. In short, the reader who finally knows Christ will experience none of the difficulties associated with Milton's poem; although, paradoxically, it is these difficulties (tests, trials, temptations) as they have been encountered in those (illusory) parts which have led him to that knowledge.[8]

---

6. William Madsen makes a similar point in a review of Frye's *The Return of Eden*: "If it is formal symmetry we are looking for in *Paradise Lost*, the nearest approach to it is provided by the image of Christ which radiates from the exact center of the poem" (*Criticism* [Fall, 1966], p. 393). See also C. A. Patrides, *Milton and the Christian Tradition* (Oxford, 1966), p. 260: "I am persuaded that the God-man in *Paradise Lost* . . . renders coherence to the entire epic."

7. In this overview the argument concerning the poem's crisis is resolved, or, to be more precise, dismissed. Since every moment at which there is the possibility of seeing or not seeing truly (that is, every moment) is a crisis—that statement applies also to Adam and Eve—the concept becomes meaningless. Some "crises" are

merely (and accidentally) made spectacular. See Jackson Cope's description of the poem as having no "center from which one might measure the distances relating beginning, middle, end, or 'crisis' " (*The Metaphoric Structure of Paradise Lost* [Baltimore, 1962], p. 77). See also G. A. Wilkes, *The Thesis of Paradise Lost* (Melbourne, 1961), p. 42: "The weight of Milton's conception is not poised on one episode . . . its weight is distributed through the whole structure."

8. Wilkes argues that these local difficulties are finally "submerged" in the wholeness of the "great argument." What he does not see is that they do exist for the reader while he is *inside* the poem, and that they *lead* him to comprehend the "great argument."

This leads me naturally to the question some of my readers will have been asking. If knowledge of Christ is sufficient to all our needs, including the needs *Paradise Lost* speaks to, what claim does the poem have on us beyond a successful first reading? The answer is bound up in the inability of the fallen mind to prolong the moment of vision to which dialectical self-examination can occasionally bring it. Augustine's spiritual history is a case in point:

> And now came I to have a sight of those invisible things of thee, which are understood by those things which are made. But I was not able to fix mine eye long upon them: but my infirmity being beaten back again, I was turned to my wonted fancies; carrying along with me no more but a liking of those new thoughts in my memory, and an appetite, as it were, to the meat I had smelt.[9]

The perishability of the insight that awaits us at the end of *Paradise Lost* assures the poem's continuing relevance. We may have succeeded to some degree in purging our intellectual ray, but the "film of ignorance" is not so easily removed, and a "sovrain eyesalve" may be needed again. And in that (certain) event, the first reading holds out the promise of another success. In the meantime, the abandoned outer form—which has been the vehicle for the apprehension of meaning, although meaning is not imbedded *in* it—remains as an area within which the interior journey can be renegotiated. With Adam, we exit from the poem into experience; but we can return to it, as he returns to the memory of Paradise, for strength and sustenance.

ALBERT COOK

Milton's Abstract Music†

The poets of the recent past have often wanted their personal rhythms to resemble the spoken language, or a prose not too far from cultivated speech. The bias if strong enough can lead to the rejection of blank verse itself as improper to American English. But one need not go so far as William Carlos Williams in pleading for the primacy of speech in a personal voice in order to feel cool towards Milton, whose verse is easily recognized as based on some personal rhythm quite remote from speech (or so he may seem to us; to Dr. Johnson, Milton's blank verse was too close to the spoken language, verse for the eye). Milton's imperious lulling of

---

9. Quoted by Louis Martz, *The Paradise Within* (New Haven, 1964), p. 50.
† The first part of an essay published in the *University of Toronto Quarterly*,

XXIX (1959–60), 370–78. Reprinted by permission of the author and the University of Toronto Press.

diction and syntax towards Latin has been pondered and assessed; since sound and sense wed indissolubly in a poem, we should expect to find, fusing Milton's invented sense, some general harmonics of sound beyond Bridges' discrimination of his syllabic laws or Arnold Stein's subtle analysis of tone colour in *Paradise Lost*.[1]

A speaking voice will give varying emphasis to the accents of verse, and an acomplished poet will orchestrate these variations:

> It is the *cause*, it is the *cause*, my *soul*; . . .

The second "cause," rising against Othello's attempt to stifle it by logically needless repetition, will be emphasized over the first "cause," as both over "soul," though these three accents stand out against (and gain firmness by contrast with) the indecision in the hovering accent on the first "it" and the second "is."

The dramatic setting of this line, and the mastery of Shakespeare, enlivens the play among these accents beyond the pattern of the metre, in which all the accents are theoretically equivalent (or at least patterned more regularly than speech rhythms allow). Yet normally, in fact almost always, one can distinguish one major accent, and often three "more important" accents, in a line of verse:

> Bare *ruin'd* choirs where late the sweet birds sang. . . .
> [Possibly "bare" or "choirs," depending on interpretation.]
>
> Thoughts that do often lie too *deep* for tears. . . .
>
> Or suck'd on *coun*try pleasures, childishly. . . .
>
> Like a patient *e*therized upon a table. . . .
>
> In the gloom the gold *ga*thers the light against it. . . .
> [Possibly "against," or even "gloom."]

It is a great mark of Milton's rhythm that, contrary to the practice of almost any other verse writers in English, including his own imitators in the eighteenth and nineteenth centuries, Milton carries his verse so far away from speech that one can seldom find in *Paradise Lost* a line where only three of the accents stand out over the other two, and never, I believe, a line in which one can distinguish a single major accent alone.

> *Who first seduc'd* them to that *fowl* re*volt*?
> The in*fer*nal Serpent; *he* it was, whose *guile*
> Stird up with *E*nvy and Re*venge*, dec*eiv'd*
> The *Mo*ther of Man*kinde*, what time his *Pride*
> Had *cast* him *out* from *Heav'n*, with *all* his *Host*
> Of *R*ebel Angels, by whose aid a*spir*ing

1. Robert Bridges, *Milton's Prosody* (Oxford, 1921); Arnold Stein, *Answerable Style* (Minneapolis, 1953) [*Editor*].

To *set* him*self* in *Glo*ry a*bove* his *Peers*,
He *trust*ed to have *equal'd* the *most High*,
If he op*pos'd*; and with am*bitious aim*
A*gainst* the *Throne* and *Mon*archy of *God*
*Rais'd im*pious *War* in *Heav'n* and *Battle proud*
With *vain* at*tempt*. *Him* the *Almighty Power*
*Hurld head*long *flam*ing from th' *Eth*ereal *Skie*
With *hide*ous *ruine* and com*bus*tion *down*
To *bottom*less per*dition*, *there* to *dwell*
In Ada*man*tine *Chains* and *pe*nal *Fire*
Who *durst* de*fie* th' Om*nip*otent to *Arms*.

If sense is necessarily the guide to the major accents, a single word cannot here be settled on as definitely more prominent in stress than the others. Even allowing latitude of interpretation for more usual poems, primacy is still assigned to a single accent at the expense of others: if one argues that the first "cause" receives most stress in the line from *Othello*, then the second receives less; if one argues that they both receive the same, a persuasive interpretation, the line is given a strikingly abnormal reading, and "soul" is still put into the background—unless one assigns it primacy; but all three cannot have equal value here—and this is precisely the way we must read the lines of *Paradise Lost*.

As we inspect the sense of the first line, "who" calls for stress because of the magnitude of the question; "first" because of the tremendous action initiated here, the subject of the poem, "Of Man's *first* disobedience"; "seduc'd" because of the fantastic treachery involved; "fowl" because of the enormity of the act; "revolt" because of the all-embracing nature of what the sin was directed against. The sense of the line seems simultaneously to concentrate in almost each accented word, and so on through this quotation as I have marked it, and on through the poem. This passage, in fact, illustrates rather more normal latitude of accent than is to be found in the prayers and invocations of the poem, which present nearly unbroken series of five major accents to the line. The voice to read this poetry must almost never flag in soaring, however it modulates: a strong-ribbed structure of accents constantly buoys up line by line the mighty periods.

The rhythmic effect which Milton gains by assigning all his accents nearly equal value is unusually special, as compared, for example, with French verse. In that convention the accents have an equality not of prominence, as in Milton, but of uninsistence. While Milton achieves a strenuous personal rhythm which heightens each of the individual accented syllables over the unaccented, the French convention tends to level the difference between accented and unaccented syllables, giving the whole poem line by line a rhythm that subdues the sense to wear its convention like a uniform. A similar effect is to be found in Italian poetry, even that which Milton imitated, as F. T. Prince points out (*The Italian Element in Milton's Verse*), in seeking a Virgilian grandiosity and *durezza*. Accents are levelled, not heightened, too, in the English verse of Chaucer, which echoes French conventions:

> Your ÿen two wol slee me sodenly;
> I may the beautee of hem not sustene,
> So woundeth hit thourghout my herte kene.

Spenser, also, in his equality of accent, resembles an Italian and French limpidity more than the Miltonic grandeur:

> A gentle knight was pricking on the plaine,
> Ycladd in mightie armes and silver shielde,
> Wherein old dints of deepe woundes did remaine,
> The cruell markes of many a bloody fielde;
> Yet armes till that time did he never wield
> His angry steede did chide his foming bitt,
> As much disdayning to the curbe to yielde:
> Full jolly knight he seemes, and faire did sitt,
> As one for knightly giusts and fierce encounters fitt.

No sooner have we stepped within the faerie forest, than all designations exist on the same allegorical level; and as the concrete stands throughout in a one-to-one relation to the abstract, so Spenser's syllabic convention operates to keep each word of the sentence, and here each line of the stanza too, patterned to an identical and formal emphasis. Even the rhythm has the two-dimensionality of the sort of mediaeval tapestry to which *The Faerie Queene* has often been compared.

Milton began with Spenser, and began by going beyond Spenser; we find an allegorical pattern in *L'Allegro* and *Il Penseroso* stated at the beginning of each poem and violated by the main contrasts between light and dark almost as soon as the broken, tuning-up rhythms of each poem's introduction have been toned off to the prevailing tetrameter line. *Paradise Lost* sets a poetic problem more simple in its generality than that of Spenser's epic and more directly spiritual—man instead of twelve virtues; angels and devils instead of maids, giants, and castles. And the poem enunciates more thoroughly a literal but unknowable truth; given Spenser's conception detail may be proliferated on a relatively simple principle, but Milton must at every point solve anew the problem of representing the unfallen Adam of Genesis through a fallen imagination.

The uniqueness of Milton's rhythm—what Eliot calls "the peculiar feeling, almost a physical sensation of a breathless leap, communicated by Milton's long periods, and by his alone"[2]—derives from what it expresses, an imaginative conception which

2. T. S. Eliot, "Milton," in *On Poetry and Poets* (London, 1957), p. 179 [*Editor*].

creates an equivalence among the verbal terms and their accents which the terms may not rest back on, as Spenser's are allowed to do by the syllabic norms and by his conception. In *Paradise Lost*, every accented word stands out when spoken as the major one in the line, pulling against the rise of the accents, equally strong, which precede and follow. This creates a kind of tension analogous to the conflict of physical forces found in the structure of a baroque dome, whose mathematics, Siegfried Giedion tells us, introduces a new complexity of interrelated forces into architecture. Or, as Milton says in another connection:

> As in an Organ from one blast of wind
> To many a row of Pipes the sound-board breathes.

(We remember that the baroque period is also the high point for that instrument in church music.)

Thus Adam may be general Man (which his name, Milton was aware, means in Hebrew) by virtue of inhabiting a world where everything concrete, in the Garden and elsewhere, can be at once abstract and irrevocably concrete; where every aspect of speech and idea gains importance without suppressing the importance of another, just as angels gain rather than lose (as Satan wrongly thought) by the preeminence of the Son in Heaven. A rhythmic provisionality—the accent is major only while spoken—governs this mortal representation of "things invisible to mortal sight." And just so a rhythmic assertion—the accent is major while it occurs— governs the poetic union which attempts "things unattempted yet in prose or rhyme." We may note, in fact, that the "things" are unattempted even by the inspired, and superior (Milton would surely say), prose of Genesis, because Scripture, in being inspired by the Holy Ghost, does not have to work within the limit of a fallen imagination. Milton expresses this limit, I believe, by his doubling of Urania, the classical muse, with the Holy Spirit, and by calling Moses a shepherd in the Theocritan as well as the New Testament sense. Moses is seen partly as such a shepherd, within the poem; and Milton, in not being a writer of Scripture but a poet following classical conventions, cannot help *as a poet* seeing the Holy Spirit partly through Urania.

The rhythms of *Paradise Lost* are simultaneously rapt with feeling and, as Arnold Stein says, "an integral part of the high, unwavering illusion of mystical motionlessness." We may inspect another passage to see how this rhythmic intussusception arrives at its "breathless leap" (Eliot) of "no middle flight" (Milton):

> Him th' Almighty Power
> Hurl'd headling flaming from th' Ethereal Skie
> With hideous ruine and combustion down
> To bottomless perdition, there to dwell

> In Adamantine Chains and penal Fire
> Who durst defie th' Omnipotent to Arms.
> Nine time the Space that measures Day and Night
> To mortal men, he with his horrid crew
> Lay vanquisht, rowling in the fiery Gulfe
> Confounded though immortal.

"Now the first thing to notice," Rajan[3] says of this passage, "is its preponderance of stock epithets. 'Hideous' does not limit the suggestions of 'ruine' and 'penal' does little to control our reaction to 'Fire.' Perdition has always been 'bottomless' and chains in poetry are usually 'Adamantine.' The associations of these words moreover are not developed but accumulated. 'Fire', 'Combustion', 'flaming' and in this context 'perdition' all suggest much the same thing and a similar grouping can be made of 'ethereal', 'down', 'bottomless', and 'headlong'." And Rajan goes on to notice that there is a repetition of *m* and *n* sounds, often in conjunction with *i* and *o*, which "convey irresistibly the terror of Satan's downfall." We might add that this "terror" which Rajan hears in the phonemes, the terror of the distance, the (plastic and infinite) measure of the fall, also gets into the tone of the poetry's sound through the strength of each primary accent, because these accents are not levelled off as in French, but are each successively primary. The headlong rush is the more precipitate for the dominance of the accent on "headlong" while the word is being spoken and the equally dominant accent on "ethereal," which, so to speak, keeps the sky aloft, tonally and geographically, and produces a kind of leaped gap of sound in which the word "flaming," equally accented, can blaze the more by being set, in wrenched sound as in visual image, against the "ethereal sky."

So Rajan's point about Milton's diction, that its terms tend to interfuse, "hideous" tending to complement "ruine" rather than limiting it (the way *modifiers* usually work), is reinforced by the similar action of the major accents in the sound, which give "hideous" and "ruine" the successive major emphasis. A particular poetic force, then, may be seen to reside in the famous Miltonic vagueness, noted perhaps first by Macaulay and berated by modern critics who value precision highly. Milton gives us not precision, but inter-echoing overtones, in sound and in sense. He does so because his poetic purposes are those not of precision—categorizing the attitudes of sin, repentance, and virtue like Dante, organizing the gestures of virtue and vice like Spenser—but of generality:

> Man's First Disobedience and the Fruit
> Of that Forbidden Tree whose mortal taste
> Brought Death into the World and all our woe.

3. B. Rajan, *"Paradise Lost" and the Seventeenth Century Reader* (London, 1947), p. 112 [*Editor*].

Here the terms "Man," "Fruit," "Tree," etc., are given more generality even than allegory (though Milton allows himself to capitalize them for quasi-allegorical emphasis): allegory implies system, and system a specification of function which Milton's whole poetic effort in *Paradise Lost* is to avoid.

If we introduce Valéry's idea, that a poet in some sense invents the meanings of the words he uses, then we may see that Milton's inventions are strengthened by the privacy of his diction. The word in a poem gets its particular newness, or at least its freshness, by appearing in vivid conjunction with other words. Milton's practice operates, we may say, only to free the words from a prose limitation, to allow them to assert their conjunction the more forcibly as a way of representing the plastic qualities of Man's theological experience.

In a world where God is known by analogies, "things invisible to mortal sight" must appear in a form mortal sight (physical and spiritual) can compass. God is Light, the invocation to Book III elaborates, and God (the Son) is a Word to such a degree that it is the Son, in the part of Book VII which puzzles some commentators, who goes forth as the agent of the Creation, presumably because the Creation is performed through Words ("Let there be light . . ."), and for God, Word is Act. There are for Milton the Word—Scripture—and words—those of his "private" language. To comment on Scripture in a poem is a perilous act, and a difficult one. One is following the Revealed with the fallen Imagination; therefore what one sees dazzles. The generality of light carries one over, but its generality is factitious; Adam imagined in a poem written by a post-lapsarian poet can be Man by the same sort of supposition that Moses can be spoken of as like Theocritus.

Milton's universe is as plastic as the sounds that describe it: a Dantesque diagram cannot be made of it. "First"—of disobedience or of parents—is used in the double sense of "original" and of "primal," and the elaborate voice is at once building the general (but lost) original situation, and regretting the lost (but always present) primal condition. The world itself is seen as a transmuted Eden; poetic analogies from the fallen world are used to portray the unfallen. It is in a description of the Garden that the famous simile is introduced about Proserpina, with its implied comparison to Eve:

> The Birds thir quire apply; aires, vernal aires,
> Breathing the smell of field and grove, attune
> The trembling leaves, while Universal *Pan*
> Knit with the *Graces* and the *Hours* in dance
> Led on th'Eternal Spring. Not that faire field
> Of *Enna*, where *Proserpin* gathring flowrs
> Her self a fairer Floure by gloomie Dis

> Was gatherd, which cost Ceres all that pain
> To seek her through the world; nor that sweet Grove
> Of *Daphne* by the *Orontes*, and th'inspir'd
> *Castalian* Spring might with this Paradise
> Of *Eden* strive; . . .

The simile is prepared for rhythmically by a pair of clauses just two lines long apiece, each introduced, as often in English and Latin verse, by a cadence somewhat shorter than those that follow. The effect of a cadenced rise between the short phrase and the longer ones is emphasized by the rhythmic connotation of the semicolon in the first line, which tends to hold the voice rather than stop it as a period would do; and also by the shorter rise from "aires" to "vernal aires" (itself a kind of delayed near-rhyme to "faire" in the first clause of the simile sentence) at the beginning of the first longer clause. In addition, there is an abrupt shift in tense from the present of the first clause, "attune," to the past of the second, "led," which trails the sense, with the voice, off in letting the garden not hold its immediate present tense. (This is prepared for, also, by the participial phrases, the present of "breathing" and the past of "knit.")[4] Pan, then, in Adam's time and in the present of the poem, is at once factitious like the poem (Milton does not "believe in" the classical gods), and "universal," this word being but an expansion of the Greek meaning of Pan.

The voice quickens powerfully to pick up the beginning of the simile in the middle of the line, the more that it must leap the distance of the denial in "Not" (in which we also have perhaps the trope of preterition: to say the field is not so beautiful would be a way of hinting that in some sense it is). In this plastic world that Milton depicts, a part of the simile, Proserpina, moves to the centre and assumes some of the purport's freedom (the original comparison was of quality between a field and a grove). Proserpina's connection with Enna is rhythmically insisted on, by the strong enjambent from the line before, and by the major accent on each. She herself enforces the meaning, being compared to a flower with the same word—"fair"—which had governed the initial comparison of one garden to another. The world of the simile is allowed to expand and include Ceres' search, because the rhythm and the sense of the poem add a feeling of constant flight, in their breathless sound. This search is a constant simile for the conception of the poem and will always suggest the poetic comparison at the end of this passage, here that of the Castalian spring where the poet drank to be "inspir'd." We should note that "inspir'd" is the first

---

4. Lowry Nelson finds this shift in tense characteristic of what he and others call Baraoque verse. "Góngora and Milton: Toward a Definition of the Baroque," *Comparative Literature* (1954), 53–63.

endword not a monosyllable since "Dis" (or, if "flowrs" may seem monosyllabic by being printed so, since "Pan"). Thus rhythmically we are made aware that it is by such a poem that we can imaginatively transcend "all that pain," our own being like Ceres'. It is but another line to the ending assonance of Paradise, expanding into its Hebrew equivalent (Eden, pleasant garden) in the next half-line, again through preterition ("nor . . . might . . . strive"). The loss implied, rhythmically, and also in sense, as Empson notes, by the word "all," is counterbalanced by this half line and is not as regretful as it would be if Milton had ended on "Paradise," with some such line as: "Castalian Spring might match this Paradise." The whole passage—and the poem—is such a trope as we find in the word "inspired," applied by metonymy to the spring, when actually referring to the poet who drinks the spring: so, Milton implies, Eden is actualized in the poem, a poem as lofty in its "no middle flight" as the Castalian spring is at "high" Delphi against the crags of Parnassus. Moses is "inspired" by the Holy Ghost and writes truth about Eden; Milton is "inspired" to a poetic fiction that offers what of Eden can be approached by a fallen imagination.

The whole poem, in its sound, fuses the imaginative perception of Paradise with sorrow for its loss. The central idea and the language—which it took Milton so much of his lifetime to arrive at—create the forceful succession of major accents, the idiosyncratic tendency to generality and repetition in the diction, and the rhetorically "incoherent" expansiveness of the similes. These derive from the central insight of sound which Empson has attributed to the word "all" as a tonal equivalent for both the poem's cosmological scope and its *lacrimae rerum* (*Structure of Complex Words*, chap. IV):

> In a stylist, the word presumes economy of means; it raises the thing in hand absolutely without needing to list all the others. The sound rolls the tongue from back low (the inner man) to front high (throwing him out and upward), and the vowel is the "organ" note for which Milton is praised or the Virgilian moan at the sorrow inherent in the whole story.

Paradise Lost is "emotive" in Empson's terms; it is like music. And since its poetic idea of fallen humanity is a central abstraction, its music tends to be abstract in a way to be found only in Milton's work, and then only in *Paradise Lost* and the later sonnets.

*   *   *

CHRISTOPHER RICKS

Milton's Grand Style†

[*The Successful Metaphor*]

The dignity of the epic is not compatible with such metaphors as are boldly and explosively new. But there is more than one kind of verbal life, and both his temperament and his respect for literary decorum impelled Milton to choose to bring ancient metaphors back to life rather than to forge new ones. The magnificent powers of Donne and Hopkins are sometimes in danger of making us silently assume that all our respect should go to the pioneer and none to the historian. Sometimes it even seems to be implied that it is only the pioneer who is 'sincere'. But each has value, and each has his apt style. Milton, like all epic poets, is concerned mainly to lead us back, not to blaze new trails. And the vigour of his words is a matter of his leading us back to the riches buried in them.

At its simplest, such a use of language does no more (and no less) than make words mean what they ought to mean. Dr. Davie has pointed out how often the verbal activity of the eighteenth-century poets is a matter of bringing dead metaphors to life. The poet takes a word or a phrase which has become slack or empty, and puts it into a context which suddenly brings back to life the original force. So any of us can now talk of 'goading' someone into a fury—but it is for Pope to say how his wit will 'goad the prelate slumbering in his stall', where the double aptness of *stall* (to prelate and to ox) tautens the whole line and puts the sting back into *goad*. Such a use of words might be thought to be particularly the method of those who seek to be original with the minimum of alteration— but it is very common in Milton, and ought to remind us of the balance between his notable idiosyncrasy of style and his observance of decorum. His admiration for the traditional is as much a matter of language as of epic machinery or convention.

Milton's Grand Style, in other words, has something in common with Goldsmith as well as with Hopkins. Dr. Davie points out how 'Goldsmith enlivens the metaphor gone dead in the locution "smiling land" ' (where smiling is 'beautiful', as in the Latin *ridere*):

> While scourg'd by famine from the smiling land,
> The mournful peasant leads his humble band

† From *Milton's Grand Style* (Oxford, The Clarendon Press, 1963), pp. 57–66, 132–38, 142–50. By permission of The Clarendon Press, Oxford. The author's footnotes have been renumbered and one has been deleted. All changes by the editor appear in brackets.

—where the land is 'seen to smile with heartless indifference on the ruined peasant'.[1] But Milton, too, had seen the ominous possibilities in the beautiful convention of the 'smiling' of nature. It is explicit in Eve's words after the Fall:

> for see the Morn,
> All unconcern'd with our unrest, begins
> Her rosie progress smiling.   (XI. 173–75)[2]

And it is implicit at that earlier tragic moment when Adam's faltering heart divines the ill which Eve is to conceal under a blithe countenance:

> by the Tree
> Of Knowledge he must pass, there he her met,
> Scarse from the Tree returning; in her hand
> A bough of fairest fruit that downie smil'd.   (IX. 848–51)

Once again the smile is 'all unconcern'd with our unrest', or (in Dr. Davie's words) one of 'heartless indifference'. And once again the metaphor is enlivened, without shock and with the dignity suited to the Grand Style.

The metaphor is usually faded, too, when *transport* is given the extended sense of 'to carry away with emotion'. In Milton's hands, indeed in any poet's, it often might seem to mean no more than 'with one's emotions out of control'. But Milton re-establishes the power of the original metaphor, by setting the word in a context which stresses the physical roots of the emotional meaning, so that we see a *transport* as something that does literally and powerfully *move* you. So it is when God sees Satan 'coasting the wall of Heav'n':

> Onely begotten Son, seest thou what rage
> Transports our adversarie, whom no bounds
> Prescrib'd, no barrs of Hell, nor all the chains
> Heapt on him there, nor yet the main Abyss
> Wide interrupt can hold; so bent he seems
> On desperat revenge, that shall redound
> Upon his own rebellious head. And now
> Through all restraint broke loose he wings his way
> Not farr off Heav'n . . .   (III. 80–88)

God at this moment is not concerned primarily with Satan's emotions, but with the desperate physical energy of his journey. And the whole passage is superbly expressive of such energy. In diction: 'broke loose he wings his way'. And in syntax: notice how the crucial verb *can hold* flies triumphantly free, at the very end of its clause, from the grip of the previous twenty-two words of

---

1. *The Deserted Village*, lines 299–300; [Donald Davie,] *Purity of Diction in*   *English Verse* (1952), pp. 50–51.
2. There is a similar effect at v. 122–24.

heaped chains. It is the superb syntax of 'can hold' which is prior to, and the condition of, the lines' magnificent sound which Mr. Empson praised.[3]

The result of these effects is that when God says

> seest thou what rage
> Transports our adversarie,

the words compress his knowledge of Satan's single motive with his observation of his escape from Hell. After all, it is literally true that rage *transports* Satan.

This may seem over-ingenious, but there is substantiation in another famous passage where once again the powerful physical meaning reinforces the emotional one—emotion itself being a form of motion. Satan is entranced by the beauty of Eve, and for a moment he stands abstracted from his own evil. Then,

> Thoughts, *whither have ye led me*, with what sweet
> Compulsion thus *transported* to forget
> What *hither brought us* . . .   (IX. 473–75)

Surely the italicized sequence insists on our taking 'transported' as very much more than a synonym for 'out of control'. And 'compulsion', too, renews its original *drive*.

That Milton was particularly fond of this complex of ideas is clear from Adam's tribute to Eve, when 'transported', 'commotion', and 'unmov'd' all renew their original movement:

> But here
> Farr otherwise, transported I behold,
> Transported touch; here passion first I felt,
> Commotion strange, in all enjoyments else
> Superiour and unmov'd.   (VIII. 528–32)

The words have a similar unobtrusive and dignified energy when, during the temptation of Eve, Satan is described as 'the spirited sly Snake' (IX. 613). Obviously the main meaning is 'possessed by a spirit', for which the *O.E.D.* quotes the phrase. And spirited is used elsewhere in the poem to mean exactly that (III. 717). But the other meaning ('brisk, blithe') is not left out. Plainly the meanings co-exist in a synonym like 'animated', and Milton is taking advantage of both of them. The very next mention of the snake describes it as 'the wilie Adder, blithe and glad', *spirited* in the modern sense. And the 'evil Spirit' returns explicitly in the simile which follows, that of the *ignis fatuus*.

The degeneration of the transcendent brightness of Satan to that of a will-of-the-wisp is summed up in the way that Milton uses the word 'glory'. By stressing the sense of 'brightness, halo', he makes it

---

3. [William Empson,] *Milton's God*, p. 119.

clear that there is no true glory except that of God's goodness, and that Satan has only what—in a superbly shrivelling phrase—he calls 'permissive glory' (x. 451),[4] that is, 'false glitter'. We need to see the halo in the *glory* of the famous lines on Satan:

> his form had yet not lost
> All her Original brightness, nor appear'd
> Less then Arch Angel ruind, and th' excess
> Of Glory obscur'd: As when the Sun new ris'n
> Looks through the Horizontal misty Air
> Shorn of his Beams ... (1. 591–96)[5]

There the context all bears on *glory*, insisting that it is literal as well as moral. So it is too when Beelzebub despairs of 'all our Glory extinct' (1.141). It was Patrick Hume, in 1695, who made the apt comment: 'put out, as a Flame, or any thing that burns and shines, a word well expressing the loss of that Angelick Beauty, which like a Glory attended on their Innocency, which by their foul Rebellion they had forfeited. . . . *Extinctus* is used in the same Metaphorical manner by *Virgil*.'[6]

It was the eighteenth-century editors who grasped the nature of the style, perhaps because the eighteenh-century poets owed so much to it. (The poets who merely imitated it are anoher and sadder matter.) Jonathan Richardson insisted that Milton's 'Sense is Crouded So Close, that Those who have been us'd to be indulg'd with Words and Sentences to Play withall, will find no Such Here; they must Attend Diligently, or Somthing Material will pass away'.[7]

So when we hear that the heathen gods 'with their darkness durst *affront* his light' (1. 391), Richardson brings out the force: 'This Word Carries a Stronger Sense than what is Commonly intended by it, though it also has That; it is from the *Italian Affrontare*, to Meet Face to Face; an Impudent Braving.'[8]

'Front' is still used by Milton in the sense of forehead, face to face; and the 'Stronger Sense' returns when Eve—as often—makes explicit what the poet had elsewhere muted. Her confidence rings with too emphatic a set of repetitions when she says that it will not matter even if the devil does tempt her:

> onely our Foe
> Tempting affronts us with his foul esteem
> Of our integritie: his foul esteeme
> Sticks no dishonor on our Front, but turns
> Foul on himself. (ix. 327–31)

---

4. For a similar effect compare 'Forc't Halleluiahs' (ii. 243).
5. Cleanth Brooks analyses this passage, 'Milton and the New Criticism', *Sewanee Review* (1951).
6. *Poetical Works of Milton, Annotations*
by *P.H.* (1695), p. 11.
7. *Explanatory Notes and Remarks on Milton's "Paradise Lost"* (1734), p. clxxvii [*Editor*].
8. p. 29.

There one can notice the precision which the word 'integrity' still had. For Milton it really does mean completeness, unity, wholeness —just as the world *whole* has the same root as the word holy. 'Our integritie': it is that innocent unity which Eve breaks when she wilfully withdraws her hand from her husband's. In the same way, when Satan corrupts the angels in Heaven, Milton brings out the full force of integrity by setting it against 'ambiguous': Satan

> casts between
> Ambiguous words and jealousies, to sound
> Or taint integritie . . .   (v. 699–701)

Such mastery of the context does more than anyting else can to invigorate language while still preserving decorum.

The inspiration of words that would otherwise be half-dead is inseparable from Milton's famous liking for using words with their original Latin meaning. Of course one must first put aside those 'Latinisms' which are no more than completely normal seventeenth-century English (say, *admire* as 'wonder at'); and then concentrate on what seem acts of choice by Milton. Sometimes a Miltonic usage may be of extreme rarity; and the question is simple. At other times, his deviation may be slight; but one should not put aside as critically irrelevant those moments when he seems to prefer what was apparently by then an unusual or a less usual application. Any critic is in danger of finding unique beauty in what was a casual or common usage; but any linguist is in danger of implying that in the past everybody wrote equally well.

Milton's Latinate usages are curiously open both to Mark Pattison's irrelevant praise (reading Milton as 'the last reward of consummated scholarship'), and to Dr. Leavis's equally irrelevant blame ('a callousness to the intrinsic nature of English'). Everything depends, as usual, on the particular case; on whether there is anything gained, in terms of meaning as well as sound, by his choosing to be Latinate. Is he simply being pedantic? Landor commented darkly, 'He soon begins to give the learned and less obvious signification to English words'.[9]

The extra meaning which Milton finds comes clearly from the fact that he does not discard the English meaning. As Raleigh said, 'He was not content to revive the exact classical meaning in place of the vague or weak English acceptation; he often kept both senses, and loaded the word with two meanings at once.'[1] What we have is not a pompous substitution, or an antiquarian delight in a remoter meaning, but an addition to the meaning, sometimes one of emphasis, sometimes one of refinement. Such Anglo-Latinisms are not the property of Milton alone, and often they are simple enough. So every schoolboy knows that when Satan falls 'With hideous

---

9. *Works*, ed. Welby, v. 238.   1. [Walter Raleigh,] *Milton*, p. 209.

ruine and combustion down' (i. 46), *ruine* includes the literal falling of the Latin. Or that when the reed for the gunpowder is described as 'pernicious with one touch to fire' vi. 520), *pernicious* is both 'destructive' and 'swift'.

But the effect can be much subtler. Dr. Davie's point about metaphor was anticipated by Thomas Newton in 1749, in commenting on the moment when Satan and the other devils turn into serpents:

> His Armes clung to his Ribs, his Leggs entwining
> Each other, till *supplanted* down he fell.   (x. 512–13)

'We may observe here', said Newton, 'a singular beauty and elegance in Milton's language, and that is his using words in their strict and litteral sense, which are commonly apply'd to a metaphorical meaning, whereby he gives peculiar force to his expressions, and the litteral meaning appears more new and striking than the metaphor itself. We have an instance of this in the word *supplanted*, which is deriv'd from the Latin *supplanto*, to trip up one's heels or overthrow . . . and there are abundance of other examples in several parts of this work, but let it suffice to have taken notice of it here once for all.'[2]

This is a very fine critical comment, but it is perhaps not explicit enough as to why Milton here uses *supplanted* with its physical meaning. The applied moral meaning is in the background, and provides the grim irony with which Satan is always seen—Satan, on whom always evil 'recoils', on whose head revenge 'redounds'. Satan is the great supplanter: 'He set upon our fyrst parentes in paradyse, and by pride supplanted them' (More, 1522).[3] In *Paradise Regained* (iv. 607), too, the word itself reminds us of this. So 'supplanted' here is a succinct and telling comment on the reason for Satan's being overthrown (hoist with his own petard), at the very some moment as it tells us that he *was* overthrown:

> Immediate are the Acts of God, more swift
> Then time or motion, but to human ears
> Cannot without process of speech be told.   (vii. 17–68)

Milton's process of speech is so compact that it can even reflect divine immediacy, the divine moment that instantaneously judges crime *and* punishment. Milton's phrase has what Raphael, in an excellent phrase, called 'Speed almost Spiritual'.

An equally acute comment by Newton (expanding a note by

---

2. ii. 252. Compare Arnold Stein on the release of the original metaphor in 'By Haralds voice *explain'd*'. 'compared with the more primitive meaning, the derived meaning tends to be abstract, the accepted equivalent of the familiar result or even process of an action, but with no physical or imaginative sense of the very happening of that process' (*Answerable Style*, p. 147).

3. *O.E.D.* 2: 'To cause to fall', from 1340. It also cites *c.* 1610, *Women Saints:* 'The divell envying these her vertuous studies, thought to supplant her.'

448 · *Christopher Ricks*

Hume) brings home that Milton's reaching down to the roots is certainly not limited to Latinisms. During the council in Hell, Beelzebub yearns to destroy God's

> whole Creation, or possess
> All as our own, and drive as we were driven,
> The punie habitants.   (II. 365–67)

Hume's gloss ran: 'The weak infirm Possessors, the late made Inmates of this new World: *Puisné*, born since, created long since us, Angelick Beings boasting Eternity.'[4] And Newton developed the point: 'It is possible that the author by *puny* might mean no more than weak or little; but yet if we reflect how frequently he uses words in their proper and primary signification, it seems probable that he might include likewise the sense of the French (from whence it is deriv'd) *puis né*, born since, created long after us.'[5] Again it is only a matter of making more explicit the double meaning which Hume and Newton so admirably fasten on. That Man was 'born since' the fallen angels is precisely the great reason why they hate him. The hatred and its cause were clear enough from the way in which Beelzebub introduced the subject of Man in this same speech:

> some new Race call'd Man, about this time
> To be created like to us, though less
> In power and excellence, but favour'd more
> Of him who rules above.   (II. 348–51)

The mixture of envy and contempt comes out in the bitter placing of 'less' and 'more'. And the same feelings stir Satan to cry out against

> this new Favorite
> Of Heav'n, this Man of Clay, Son of despite,
> Whom us the more to spite his Maker rais'd
> From dust: spite then with spite is best repaid.   (IX. 175–78)

That men are 'the punie habitants', then, superbly compresses Beelzebub's contemptuous reasons for hating them (new favourites) *and* his reasons for revenge: they are weak. To the fallen angels, men are weak just because they are a sort of divine afterthought, a poor attempt, to make up the numbers in Heaven. The comment of Hume and Newton on this one word radiates into the whole of the poem—a mark of good criticism and of a great poem.

* * *

4. p. 65.
5. [Thomas Newton, ed. *Paradise Lost* (1749),] i. 105. The survival of the form 'puisne' make a ready awareness of the derivation of *puny* likely. Moreover, the seventeenth-century sense of 'junior' will have pointed towards Milton's usage.

[*Simile and Cross-Reference*]

* * *

Macaulay has an excellent commentary on the Miltonic style:
'The most striking characteristic of the poetry of Milton is the
extreme remoteness of the associations by means of which it acts
on the reader. Its effect is produced, not so much by what it
expresses, as by what it suggests; not so much by the ideas which it
directly conveys, as by other ideas which are connected with them.
He electrifies the mind through conductors.'
   This is certainly to the point. But unfortunately the examples of
the principle at work which Macaulay offered reduce the process to
a kind of divine wool-gathering. Of the allusions, for instance, he
says: 'A third [name] evokes all the dear classical recollections of
childhood, the schoolroom, the dog-eared Virgil, the holiday, and
the prize.'[1] This may pass as autobiography, but not as criticism of
Milton. To understand the particular moments when Milton 'elec-
trifies the mind through conductors', we do better to turn to the
eighteenth century.
   It was clear to Richardson that Milton's allusions often merited
close and imaginative examination. For one thing, it was Richard-
son's general belief that 'he Expresses himself So Concisely, Em-
ploys Words So Sparingly, that whoever will Possess His Ideas must
Dig for them, and Oftentimes pretty far below the Surface'.[2] And
Richardson was able to put the principle to work in the service of
subtle examples. As when the corner of Eden cultivated by Eve is
compared to three famous gardens:

> Spot more delicious then those Gardens feign'd
> Or of reviv'd Adonis, or renownd
> Alcinous, host of old Laertes Son,
> Or that, not Mystic, where the Sapient King
> Held dalliance with his faire Egyptian Spouse.   (IX. 439–43)

Richardson fastened on *Adonis*: 'The Circumstance of these Gar-
dens of *Adonis* being to Last but a very little while, which even
became a Proverb among the Ancients, adds a very Pathetick pro-
priety to the Simile: Still More, as that 'tis not the Whole Garden
of *Eden* which is Now spoken of, but that One *Delicious Spot*
where *Eve* was, This *Flowrie Plat* and This was of her Own Hand,
as those Gardens of *Adonis* were always of the Hands of those
Lovely Damsels, Less Lovely yet than She.'[3]
   This is finely said. Yet the most important of the gardens is the
last: that which, not mythical, refers to Solomon and Pharaoh's

1. *Literary and Historical Essays* (1934),   2. p. cxliv.
pp. 9–11.   3. p. 416.

450 · Christopher Ricks

daughter. Its main purpose is to invoke the beauties of that garden —yet this seems to be very perfunctorily performed, since there is not a word of description. If the beauty of the garden were the sole reason for the allusion, we might be tempted to think that here is epic allusion of the rather empty kind—Milton finding it easier to refer than to create.

But it is significant that the passage which moved Bentley to just such a protest should be the comparison of Paradise and the field of Enna: 'And then, in stead of painting out their several Beauties, as a Pretense for their rivaling Paradise; you give us their bare Names, with some fabulous Story to them, not denoting at all any Beauty.'[4] The answer to this is Mr. Lewis's observation that the real point of the comparison is that Eve is like Proserpin. And there is the same 'subterranean virtue' in the mention of Solomon's garden. The allusion includes more than beauty: it recalls how a man of great wisdom showed his famous inability to resist a woman. Solomon is a type of Adam, and the allusion has the oblique but powerful purpose of predicting the Fall.

Solomon was traditionally linked with Adam—as at the end of *Sir Gawain and the Green Knight*. Indeed, in Milton's Trinity College manuscripts, one of the entries in the list of subjects for tragedy refers to 'Salomon Gynæcocratomenus', Solomon Woman-governed. Moreover, the account of the heathen gods includes an emphatic mention of

> that uxorious King, whose heart though large,
> Beguil'd by fair Idolatresses, fell
> To Idols foul.   (i. 444–46)

Here the aptness to the Fall hardly needs underlining. 'Solomon is "Beguil'd by fair Idolatresses" just as Adam will be by Eve.'[5] Adam, too, was large of heart but uxorious; and he reproaches Eve for beguiling him:

> with the Serpent meeting
> Fool'd and beguil'd, by him thou, I be thee.   (x. 879–80)

And Eve is a fair idolatress; after her fall,

> from the Tree her step she turnd,
> But first low Reverence don, as to the power
> That dwelt within.   (ix. 834–36)

If the allusion to Solomon in Book i does not reflect on Adam, then there are a strange number of coincidences. That the allusion in Book ix is linked with the earlier one is suggested by the fact that a reference to Adonis follows 'that uxorious King' just as it precedes 'the Sapient King'.

4. [Richard Bentley, ed., *Paradise Lost* (1732),] p. 115 (misnumbered 215).   5. [John] Peter, *A Critique of P.L.*, p. 37.

More support can be found in *Paradise Regain'd*. There Satan dismisses the idea of setting women in Christ's eye, not (as one might expect) because the second Adam is stronger than the first, but because he is stronger than Solomon. 'Women, when nothing else, beguil'd the heart/Of wisest Solomon'; but 'Solomon he liv'd at ease',[6] and 'he whom we attempt is wiser far/Then Solomon'.[6]

But the verbal points are crucial. 'The Sapient King held dalliance with his faire Egyptian Spouse': twice, Eve is 'his fair Spouse'.[7] Much more importantly, neither *Sapient* nor *dalliance* is a common word, and their recurrence together after the Fall (in this same Book) would be a most remarkable coincidence:

> in Lust they burne:
> Till Adam thus 'gan Eve to dalliance move.
> Eve, now I see thou art exact of taste,
> And elegant, of Sapience no small part ...   (IX. 1015–18)

At which Adam unfolds the importance of *taste* and *sapience*, combining as they do the two great themes of the poem, knowledge gained by tasting (the Latin *sapere*):

> of Sapience no small part,
> Since to each meaning savour we apply,
> And Palate call judicious ...

Indeed Eve herself had seen sapience as the great quality of the fruit she had just tasted:

> O Sovran, vertuous, precious of all Trees
> In Paradise, of operation blest
> To Sapience.   (IX. 795–97)

The allusion to Solomon, then, ominously and beautifully hints at the Fall. But in that case what of the single-line sentence which follows? It is apparently usually taken as returning us to the serpent watching Eve.[8] But it is also strangely and brilliantly apt *within* the allusion:

> where the Sapient King
> Held dalliance with his faire Egyptian Spouse.
> *Much hee the Place admir'd, the Person more.*
> As one who long in populous City pent ...

Is it merely a coincidence that the line is so apt to Solomon and to Adam? That indeed it provides so terse a summary of the whole poem? Adam was struck with wonder by Paradise, 'this happie place'. But he was even more struck by Eve. It is not until the

6. *P.R.*, II. 169–70, 201, 205–6.
7. IV. 742; V. 129.
8. Editors are silent, but James Paterson

in 1744 paraphrased it: '*He*, i.e. *Satan*, admired *Paradise*, but much more *Eve*' (*A Commentary on P.L.*, p. 393).

452 · *Christopher Ricks*

closing lines of the poem that we see the true balancing of person and place, in Eve's moving penitence:

> thou to mee
> Art all things under Heav'n, all places thou.   (xii. 617–18)

It is interesting, but no more, that Christopher Pitt's reminiscence of the line should concern Dido and Aeneas, and so be more apt to Solomon than to the serpent:

> Charm'd with his Presence, Dido gaz'd him o'er,
> Admir'd his Fortune much, his Person more.[9]

More relevant is the fact that Adam's sin is twice seen as a matter of too *much admiring* Eve. Raphael, in a very important speech, rebukes him for

> attributing overmuch to things
> Less excellent, as thou thy self perceav'st.
> For what admir'st thou, what transports thee so,
> An outside? fair no doubt . . .   (viii. 565–68)

The conjunction of *much* and *admire* is closer when after the Fall Adam admits that

> I also err'd in overmuch admiring
> What seemd in thee so perfet.   (ix. 1178–79)

But there is another way of getting at whether or not it is completely satisfactory to take 'Much hee the Place admir'd, the Person more' as going simply with the lines that follow it. Does Milton ever begin a new sequence of thought with a single-line sentence? Or, more strictly, does he ever use a single-line sentence entirely detached from what precedes it?

Such sentences are rare and emphatic in Milton, because they so obviously conflict with his basic principle of 'the sense variously drawn out from one Verse into another'. And, as far as I can see, he never uses such a sentence without some continuity with the previous lines.[1]

9. *An Essay on Virgil's Aeneid, Being a Translation of the First Book* (1728), p. 49.
1. Single-line questions, such as 'Who first seduc'd them to that fowl revolt?', are not relevant—in any case they come naturally in a current train of thought, rather than as the start of a new one. Nor are the single-line stage-directions relevant ('Whereto with speedy words th' Archfiend reply'd'). But they too never show a complete break with the previous lines. The continuity is always provided by words like 'whereto', 'to whom', or 'whom thus'. There remain, then, the comparable single-line sentences. Not counting the line under discussion, there seem to be thirteen in *Paradise Lost*. In no case is one of them completely de-tached from the previous lines. Seven of them, on the contrary, are used to end a speech: 'Awake, arise, or be for ever fall'n' (i. 330. Also iii. 735; ix. 566, 732; xi. 180, 633, 835). Three of them are embedded in the continuing argument: 'This was that caution giv'n thee; be advis'd' (v. 523. Also viii. 490; x. 526). Two show the reciprocation of dialogue— a very different thing from what would be postulated here Eve 'thus abasht repli'd. / The Serpent me beguil'd and I did eate' (x. 162). And: 'I yield it just, said Adam, and submit' (xi. 526). The remaining one of the thirteen sentences does, admittedly, begin a new narrative phase, but without snapping the continuity: 'So all was cleard, and to the Field they haste' (v. 136).

In other words, if we take this line as simply and solely returning us to the serpent, we are postulating not only a very harsh break (in the work of a poet who is a master of transitions), but also a unique usage of the single-line sentence. Not only is the line extremely apt within the allusion, but Milton's practice would suggest that it belongs there.

Does this mean that the line *cannot* refer to the serpent? It is certainly very apt there too; it fits exactly both with the following simile and narrative, and the fact that it is so often read as belonging to the serpent means that one should not lightly transfer it. In fact, the reasons for treating the line as *within* the allusion are powerful, and so are the more obvious reasons for treating it as outside.

But Milton is a master of syntactical fluidity. He achieves some of his finest effects precisely by leaving it possible for a word or a clause to look backward or forward. And what Mr. Prince says of the rhyme-scheme in *Lycidas* could well be applied to Miltonic syntax: 'The rhetoric of rhyme derived from the *canzone* has thus provided Milton with an invaluable instrument—a type of rhyme which looks both back and forward.' The six-syllable lines 'not only always rhyme with a previous longer line (thus looking back), but they give the impression of a contracted movement which must be compensated by a full movement in the next line (which is always of full length), and they thus look forward. This effect is most marked when, as in most cases, these short lines rhyme with the line immediately preceding them.'[2]

It is at any rate possible that this line is Milton's masterpiece of syntactical fluidity. It stands as a self-contained sentence between two sentences each ten lines long; and it acts as a hinge, with a hinge's property of belonging to both sides, to the preceding allusion and to the following narrative.

> Nature that hateth emptiness,
> Allows of penetration less.

But this would be a supreme feat of penetration, in which two sentences occupy exactly the same space. If this is so—and one should say no more, and no less, than that it may be—then the only way of unfolding the syntax would be to say the line twice:

> Or that, not Mystic, where the Sapient King
> Held dalliance with his faire Egyptian Spouse.
> (Much hee the Place admir'd, the Person more.)
> Much hee the Place admir'd, the Person more.
> As one who long in populous City pent . . .

*   *   *

2. *The Italian Element*, pp. 86–87.

454 · *Christopher Ricks*

Since the use of these cross-connexions has been well studied
recently, I want to comment on only one such image, in an attempt
to show that this kind of allusion can radically alter our attitude
even to passages usually thought of as laughably bad. Adam and
Eve's gardening has often been laughed at; Dr. Tillyard, who calls
their work 'ridiculous', has said that 'Adam and Eve are in the
hopeless position of Old Age Pensioners enjoying perpetual
youth'.[3] At the very least, the gardening is usually thought of as an
intractable corner of the myth that Milton could do no more than
tidy up.

Certainly he is bound to be involved in many difficulties when he
has to show the nature of labour before the Fall. I can think of
only one really successful treatment of the paradox, the closing
lines of Marvell's 'Bermudas'. The Bermudas were traditionally
thought of as Paradise—as Waller said,

> Heaven sure has kept this spot of earth uncursed,
> To show how all things were created first.[4]

Marvell's poem describes this Paradise, ending with a brilliantly
unobtrusive insight into labour before the Fall:

> Thus sung they, in the *English* boat,
> An holy and a chearful Note,
> And all the way, to guide their Chime,
> With falling Oars they kept the time.

In fact, the point is made so unobtrusively that some readers never
seem to notice it at all; without any nudge, Marvell tells us that
they *rowed* in order to keep time in their song—not, as we would
expect in this fallen world, that they sang in order to keep time in
their rowing. Before the Fall, man worked simply in order to praise
God with 'an holy and a chearful Note'—now life is the other way
round. It is a brilliant poetic summing-up of the paradox of pre-
lapsarian labour.

It would be foolish to argue that Milton achieves anything like
the same success with Adam and Eve's gardening; but he faces very
different problems from Marvell. Marvell could rely on a moment
of poetic intuition; but Milton is writing a long narrative poem, and
the problem cannot be seized once and for all. Yet to me the
gardening is far from ridiculous if we are fully aware of what
Milton is saying.

This is a case where it is essential to consider, not the separable
problem, but the actual words in which Milton presents it. And just
as in alluding to the field of Enna, the real focus of the allusion was
not on the beauty of the field but on the drama of Eve and Satan,

3. *Milton* (1930), p. 282.   Canto I.
4. *The Battle of the Summer Islands,*

so the gardening is not primarily a matter of horticulture, but is at every point enmeshed with the imminent tragedy.

Let me take Eve's first speech to Adam when she suggests going off on her own:

> Adam, well may we labour still to dress
> This Garden, still to tend Plant, Herb and Flour,
> Our pleasant task enjoy'nd, but till more hands
> Aid us, the work under our labour grows,
> Luxurious by restraint; what we by day
> Lop overgrown, or prune, or prop, or bind,
> One night or two with wanton growth derides
> Tending to wilde. Thou therefore now advise
> Or hear what to my mind first thoughts present,
> Let us divide our labours, thou where choice
> Leads thee, or where most needs, whether to wind
> The Woodbine round this Arbour, or direct
> The clasping Ivie where to climb, while I
> In yonder Spring of Roses intermixt
> With Myrtle, find what to redress till Noon:
> For while so near each other thus all day
> Our task we choose, what wonder if so near
> Looks intervene and smiles, or object new
> Casual discourse draw on, which intermits
> Our dayes work brought to little, though begun
> Early, and th' hour of Supper comes unearn'd. (IX. 205–25)

First, a brief mention of the psychological acuteness here. There is the grave presentation of Eve's self-will, still disguised by words about Adam's superior wisdom and authority (words that do not pause):

> Thou therefore now advise
> Or hear what to my mind first thoughts present . . .

And subtly making the same point is the contrast between the proliferation of choice for Adam and the direct decision for herself; she doesn't care what he does, and she knows very well what she will do. After all, there follow more than a hundred and fifty lines of argument between them; then she leaves; and when we, and the serpent, next see her, it is exactly where she had insisted she was going when she first mentioned the subject: in the thicket of roses tying up the flowers with myrtle.

But my present concern is not with deft psychology, but with the emblematic correspondences between the gardening and the Fall. The work, says Eve, 'under our labour grows,/Luxurious by restraint'. *Luxurious* is before the Fall a harmless horticultural word, but its fallen meaning jostles against it here; luxury is not only one of the most important results of the Fall, it is the first ('in Lust they burne'). And 'luxurious *by restraint*' is also grim with anticipation.

Milton at the very beginning of his poem had called on his muse to

> say first what cause
> Mov'd our Grand Parents in that happy State,
> Favour'd of Heav'n so highly, to fall off
> From their Creator, and transgress his Will
> *For one restraint*, Lords of the World besides? (I. 28–32)

Eve's obstinacy is to lead very soon to the Fall, since abandoning the one restraint means abandoning all restraints: 'Greedily she ingorg'd without restraint' (IX. 791).

So that we should be prepared for her words to Adam to tighten from detail to sombre generality:

> what we by day
> Lop overgrown, or prune, or prop, or bind,
> One night or two with wanton growth derides
> Tending to wilde.

'Wanton' begins etymologically as 'undisciplined, disobedient', and ends as 'lustful', so that it compresses the reason for the Fall and the immediate effects of it. Then to describe the garden as 'tending to wilde' finely thrusts home the point. Not that Eve can shuffle off her responsibility, and claim that sin was a natural tendency.[5] But with Eve in it, the garden will certainly tend to wild; so that Adam cries out when he hears that she has fallen—her sin and the thought of losing her shatter the leaves:

> How can I live without thee, how forgoe
> Thy sweet Converse and Love so dearly joyn'd,
> To live again in these wilde Woods forlorn? (IX. 908–10)

There is a similarly subtle hint in the word *redress*: 'find what to redress till Noon'. This is a technical application, to horticulture, of the ancient meaning: 'To set a person or thing upright again; to raise again to an erect position.'[6] But it seems improbable that Milton is unaware of the moral resonance in the word—its moral meaning is also ancient, and found in Chaucer. Eve may believe that she is going to set the plants upright and erect. In fact, she 'her self, though fairest unsupported Flour', will be 'drooping unsustained'. It is a bitter irony that seizes on the word 'redress'.

The poet turns the notes to tragic, too, when Eve says that if she stays near Adam, some *object new* may

> Casual discourse draw on, which intermits
> Our dayes work brought to little.

---

5. Mrs. I. G. MacCaffrey: 'the wilderness is there, waiting to encroach at the slightest neglect' (*P.L. as 'Myth'*, p. 154).

6. *O.E.D.* I, from Chaucer on. Examples include the horticultural application—one from Sylvester's Du Bartas.

What in fact is the 'object new' on this fatal day? What but the snake? For as Adam says,

> Reason not impossibly may meet
> Some specious object by the Foe subornd.   (IX. 360–61)

And the snake draws on, not casual discourse, but the most pregnant conversation in the history of mankind. There is grim irony, almost parody even, in the echo of God's instructions to Raphael to warn Adam:

> such discourse bring on,
> As may advise him of his happie state,
> Happiness in his power left free to will . . .   (V. 233–35)

Casual, moreover, means not only 'which befalls', but also 'which falls', as Milton shows elsewhere in the poem.[7] And the discourse certainly will have *brought* their *day's work to little*.

What is essential, then, is to insist on the huge web of anticipation and echo. So that when Adam in his reply says

> for nothing lovelier can be found
> In woman, then to studie houshold good,
> And good workes in her Husband to promote,

the appropriate comment is not biographical, that Milton is showing his usual 'Turkish contempt of females', but critical—that Adam speaks unwittingly to an Eve who is not exactly going to study household *good*, and who is about to promote in her husband not good works, but the first act of evil.

Milton's demands are very great, and the most important of all is that we should know his poem well enough to be able to see when a phrase, a line, or a moment is touched by tinctures or reflections. His sublimities are superbly direct, but his subtleties depend on our receiving not only the delicacies of simile and allusion, but also those of allusion within the poem itself.

As Milton's earliest commentators saw, his Grand Style is as remarkable for its accurate delicacy as for its power. Miltonic criticism since then, whether hostile or friendly, has tended to dwell most on its power; so that the case for the other virtues has often gone by default. One of the main points to make is that there is more than one 'traditional' way of reading Milton, and that Mr. Empson's choice of the eighteenth-century editors was not capricious or peripheral. Not that the Victorian tradition is wrong. It points to something very important in Milton, but with a dangerously exclusive gesture. His earliest editors were open to more various powers.

7. XI. 562, where 'casual fire' is lightning.

But isn't there also something dangerously exclusive in concentrating on Milton's *style* alone? Surely there can be no satisfactory divorce of style from content? In general terms one might reply that for any critical argument to get off the ground, one must reluctantly select from the poem. But certainly the points about the Grand Style ought now to be related briefly to the poem itself.

It seems to me that there is a very close analogy between the successes of the style and the wider successes of the poem. The more closely one looks at the style, the clearer it seems that Milton writes at his very best only when something prevents him from writing with total directness. And the same is true of what is good or bad in *Paradise Lost* in other terms.

Milton's Grand Style is delicately suggestive, very much more flexible or supple than is sometimes thought. To Milton, a man of great conviction, great energy, and great emotion, the danger was of being too direct, of stunning or bludgeoning us. But as Richardson insisted, Milton's felicities 'when they Awaken the Mind do it not with a Sudden Crash, but as with Musick; if they Surprize, they don't Startle Us'.[8] Naturally we are in favour of a poet's words having 'masculine persuasive force'—but masculinity is not enough. At its very best, Milton's style is remarkable for its simultaneous combination of what is energetically strong with what is winning soft and amiably mild. It is this which undoes Mr. Eliot's comparison of Milton's style with Henry James's, since indirectness is to James the congenial excess which directness is to Milton. How often we wish that Milton would not affirm too directly and powerfully. And how often we long for an affirmation of some kind from James.

This is not to say that either in style or in content Milton is never successful in directness. But as a rule it seems that his greatest effects are produced when he is compelled to be oblique as well as direct. The analogy with the wider successes of the poem is clear. For example, it seems to me that there are two descriptions of Paradise which soar above all Milton's other accounts of it; and what they have in common is that neither directly confronts Paradise. The first begins:

> Not that faire field
> Of Enna, where Proserpin gathring flours
> Her self a fairer Floure by gloomie Dis
> Was gatherd . . .   (IV. 268–71)

It is, I believe, the very fact that Milton's gaze is *not* directly on Paradise which makes these lines among the most haunting he ever wrote. And the *not* of 'Not that faire field . . .' is itself an opportunity for Milton to release his full feelings while still gaining all the advantages of the oblique. It seems to me similarly remarkable that if asked to point to the most moving account of Eve in the poem, it is once again these lines that I would quote. Eve is never more powerfully and tragically herself than when Milton glimpses her as Proserpin. Mr. Empson, in the notes to one of his poems, points out that 'a star just too faint to be seen directly can still be seen out of the corners of your eyes'; and his poem itself emphasizes the limited reach of 'the stoutest heart's best direct yell', while at the same time wryly defining the right kind of indirection:

> the spry arts
> Can keep a steady hold on the controls
> By seeming to evade.

The other outstanding description of Paradise seems to me this:

> then shall this Mount
> Of Paradise by might of Waves be moovd
> Out of his place, pushd by the horned floud,
> With all his verdure spoil'd, and Trees adrift
> Down the great River to the op'ning Gulf,
> And there take root an Iland salt and bare,
> The haunt of Seales and Orcs, and Sea-mews clang.
> (XI. 825–31)

Nowhere else in the poem, not even at the magnificent moments when Milton lavishes his full luxuriance on the Garden, do we so yearn for Paradise. And of all Milton's touching oxymorons, perhaps the greatest is the title of his epic.

The finest successes of the poem in larger terms all seem to me to have been created when total directness was impossible. Hell is more memorable than Heaven, because Hell resists directness. Not that it gets out of hand, or that Milton is lax with it; merely that, at any rate in the first two books, its inhabitants are irreducible. Pandæmonium is both beautiful and desperate. In the content of the poem, as well as in its style, Milton is at his best when his directness is at one with indirections. The vibrant understanding which we occasionally feel when we see Satan or Adam and Eve is due to the fact that here Milton is grappling with things that strength alone will not be able to open, things that need delicacy too. A balance that is not precarious and is the result of a strength manifesting itself in innumerable tiny, significant, internal movements— this is the balance of Milton's Grand Style.

J. B. BROADBENT

Satan†

> The character of Satan engenders in the mind a pernicious casuistry which leads us to weigh his faults with his wrongs, and to excuse the former because the latter exceed all measure. In the minds of those who consider that magnificent fiction with a religious feeling it engenders something worse.
>
> SHELLEY

Satan's mobility, his articulacy, and muscularity ("Forthwith upright he rears from off the Pool His mighty stature") make him the most vital character in *Paradise Lost*. So far as we value vitality, and so far as the characters symbolise ideal states of existence, we must then accept Blake's inversion of the values the myth assigns to them. Satan's response to environment is more progressive than the aristocratic theorising of the Father, the phantastic omnipotence of the Son and the passivity of Adam. This is not a Nietzchean perversity but so much a matter of common experience that Blake could properly call his aphorisms "proverbs" of Hell: "The tygers of wrath are wiser than the horses of instruction", "Damn braces. Bless relaxes", "Exuberance is beauty". But it is perverse to read so ethico-symbolically, as if all literature were directly propagandist, and the characters in *Paradise Lost* as flatly symbolic as the figures in Blake's etchings and prophetic books; or as if all that were "life-enhancing" were absolutely good.

Hell and Satan in it are Milton's vision of human powers corrupted by ὕβρις. In this they simply extend the invocations subversion of all that had previously been regarded as sublime. We should be happier if the powers which are corrupted in Satan were to be found pure in some opponent of his. But Satan succeeds as a symbol of human corruption because, like us, his own best self is foil to his worst. This duality has worried critics: is Satan hero or fool? The question may be argued in psychological terms[1] but the literary symptoms are obvious enough. Books I and II are full of paradoxical expressions—antithesis, antimetabole, oxymoron, etc. —Of which "darkness visible" is only the most familiar. These are facets of the total paradox: Satan is an angel in Hell and as such an exaggerated version of fallen man: "infinite in faculties! in form and moving, how express and admirable! in action, how like an

---

† From *Some Graver Subject: An Essay on Paradise Lost*, (London, Chatto & Windus, 1960), pp. 70–80. Reprinted by permission of the author and Chatto & Windus Ltd. Additions by the editor appear in brackets.
1. See Ernest Jones, *On the Nightmare* (1931), and J. C. Flugel, *Man, Morals and Society* (1945), Chap. XVII. The reaction against psychology as an element in literary criticism has reached the stage of dishonesty, as if a late 19th-century clergyman had pretended Darwin was a lunatic and the Higher Criticism an undergraduate joke, so as to preserve his own universe of discourse inviolate.

angel! in apprehension, how like a god! the beauty of the world! the paragon of animals! . . . quintessence of dust".[2] So his feats of energy derive from a power not his own: his elevation from "Prone on the Flood" like a whale through the stages of reared upright, "incumbent on the dusky Air", moving towards the shore and standing like a tower, to enthronement at the beginning of Book II, is mechanical, seen by the reader to be done rather than done by Satan as a living person. This frankensteinian quality is most apparent when Satan returns to his throne after the Fall, incognito, and without volition, dubiously,

> as from a Cloud his fulgent head
> And shape Starr-bright appeer'd, or brighter, clad
> With what permissive glory since his fall
> Was left him, or false glitter:
>
> (X. 449)

Milton's frank casuistry about the permissive existence of evil (I. 211) is supported by Satan's poetic nature. Even at the beginning, before his angelic accoutrements drop off as he persists in unheroic behaviour, Satan's glory is derivative, inhering in the ikons that clutter him as much as in personality. Sun, moon, star, cloud, storm, vulture, wolf lend him vitality and virility, but any admiration we have for Satan on their account must rely more on our own symbolic valuation of them than Milton's. When Satan strides to the edge of the lake to call his legions,

> his ponderous shield
> Ethereal temper, massy, large and round,
> Behind him cast; the broad circumference
> Hung on his shoulders like the Moon, whose Orb
> Through Optic Glass the *Tuscan* Artist views
> At Ev'ning from the top of *Fesole*,
> Or in *Valdarno*, to descry new Lands,
> Rivers or Mountains in her spotty Globe.
> His Spear, to equal which the tallest Pine
> Hewn on *Norwegian* hills, to be the Mast
> Of some great Ammiral, were but a wand,
> He walkt with to support uneasie steps
> Over the burning Marle, not like those steps
> On Heavens Azure, and the torrid Clime
> Smote on him sore besides, vaulted with Fire;
> Nathless he so endur'd . . .
>
> (I. 284)

With the shield, Satan outdoes Goliath and Achilles as epic hero. But while he is left king of that castle, the verse drifts into an area where Galileo represents a culture quite different from, and implic-

2. *Complete Works of Shakespeare* ed. Alexander (1951).

itly superior to, the military heroism and phallicism of the moon's blank orb and the flagship's mast, fixing the gaze of 17th-century rationality on the heroic shield. We are brought back to Hell by the sudden change of scale—"were but a wand"—and the realistic description of Satan's gait; just as in the earlier volcanic simile we are brought back by "Such resting found the sole of unblest feet". These physical details are strong, but not enough to withstand the evacuating force of the great similes. Thus again, when the devils parade before Satan,

> he above the rest
> In shape and gesture proudly eminent
> Stood like a Towr; his form had yet not lost
> All her Original brightness, nor appear'd
> Less then Arch Angel ruind, and th' excess
> Of Glory obscur'd: As when the Sun new ris'n
> Looks through the Horizontal misty Air
> Shorn of his Beams, or from behind the Moon
> In dim Eclips disastrous twilight sheds
> On half the Nations, and with fear of change
> Perplexes Monarchs. Dark'n'd so, yet shon
> Above them all th' Arch Angel: but his face
> Deep scars of Thunder had intrencht, and care
> Sat on his fading cheek, but under Browes
> Of dauntless courage, and considerate Pride
> Waiting revenge:
>
> (I. 589)

The tower is left merely towering; the sun, rising with the rhythm, is unexpectedly strained through fog, its strength lost like Samson's. So each chink of spendour is shuttered, each surge of vitality arrested before reaching the fulness traditionally endowing an epic hero—a fulness seen as uninhibited lustre in the poem's Son. Yet the repression is not external: it is a natural change of state in the phenomenal ikons.

Of course Satan is much more "real" than the hellish ogres of earlier epics and contemporary romances. He is related to Virgil's Cyclops, and other primitives such as the club-wielding giant Ascapard in *Bevis of Southampton*,[3] but only as distantly as his wand is related to "trunca manu pinus regit et vestigia firmat" (*Aen*. III. 659). The physiognomy of Tasso's Pluto, who had eyes like beacons, "feltred locks, that on his bosom fell" and whose yawning mouth "fomed clotted blood", "Gapte like a whirle-poole wide in Stygian flood" and "as mount Etna vomits sulphur out" (iv. 7–8), is reserved to the landscape of Milton's Hell.

Satan's prototype is not the villain but the epic hero. But because

---

3. One of the most popular romances in 16th and 17th Centuries. See [L. B.] Wright, *Middle-Class Culture in Elizabethan England* (1934).

he starts where Tamburlaine ends, raging against fate, he is fitfully more human, tragical, than he would have been if presented first in the flush of heroic success. On these occasions his role is reversed, he appears as a tragic hero[4] caught in an epic plot. Thus the last-quoted description of him as epic hero *manqué* is followed by one of his most dramatic moments—he weeps: "Thrice he assayd, and thrice in spite of scorn, Tears such as Angels weep, burst forth". All these suppler moments, as when he is rendered stupidly good by the beauty of Paradise and of Eve (IV. 373; IX. 469), are spontaneous acknowledgments of tragic weakness, the emotions negative—fear, doubt, misery. In each case he wilfully indures himself again with cries, much less convincing, of positive, epical determination—"evil be thou my good". So here it is the tears, not Satan, which govern their own "burst forth"; stored in his eyes before sin dried them, they transpire through his heroic shell of thunder-scarred responsibility like the other permissive glories, like the shuttered sun. But at once he draws them in, reverting in the peroration of his first public speech to extraordinary epical crudity —"Warr then, Warr/Open or understood must be resolv'd", as if he were the rebel general of some Middle Eastern state (ikons suggest that he is). The devils respond appropriately with brazen sound-effects: "Clashd on their sounding shields the din of war". This fluctuation is a model of an historical shift in sensibility: as the Renaissance matured, to conscious guilt at its own temerity and rottenness, and as the revival of learning turned inwards to the learning soul, the heroic mood of *I Tamburlaine* altered to tragedy of the Jacobean sort with flat characters caught in a rigid plot, though shooting occasional gleams of still-alive despair and pride. The whole movement was adumbrated by Marlowe: Faustus cries, "ah my God, I woulde weepe, but the diuel drawes in my teares" (1386). Shakespeare enjoyed a middle phase between the extremes of saga and melodrama, *Ur-Hamlet* and the *Revenger's Tragedy*. He moved in *Hamlet* from the primitive epical "overcoming of external difficulties and dangers by a singlehearted hero" to "the fateful unrolling of the consequences that result from an internal conflict in the hero's soul",[5] without declining into the guilty cynicism of the Jacobeans. Milton, though not skilled at dramatic expression, was intuitive of dramatic feeling; sometimes Satan fluctuates through a Shakespearean humanity. But these moments are always described, not dramatised. So Satan's nihilistic determina-

---

4. Satan's dramatic character also derives partly from the mutation of avenging furies into the heroes of revenge tragedy. Othello cries, "Arise, black vengeance, from the hollow hell" (III. iii. 451), and Hieronimo: "Hieronimo, 'tis time for thee to trudge: / Down by the dale that flows with purple gore, / Standeth a fiery tower; there sits a judge / Upon a seat of steel and molten brass, / And 'twixt his teeth he holds a fire-brand, / That leads unto the lake where hell doth stand." (III. xii. 7)

5. Ernest Jones, "Hamlet" in his *Essays in Applied Psychoanalysis* (2 vols. 1951).

464 · J. B. Broadbent

tions to be absolutely wicked in spite of his angelic self, supposed to
motivate the poem, are unconvincing, as verse, in relation to the
squirts of vitalised description they suppress:

> To do aught good never will be our task,
> But ever to do ill our sole delight.   (I. 157)

> Evil be thou my Good;   (IV. 108)

> Save what is in destroying, other joy
> To me is lost.   (IX. 473)

The difficulty is really that we do not see Satan's nihilism arising in
direct reciprocity between his will and God's, as we see Gloster's,
for instance, arising from the conflict between him and society:

>   . . .
> I, that have neither pity, love, nor fear.
> Indeed, 'tis true that Henry told me of;
> For I have often heard my mother say
> I came into the world with my legs forward.
> Had I not reason, think ye, to make haste,
> And seek their ruin that usurp'd our right?
> The midwife wonder'd; and the women cried
> "O, Jesus bless us, he is born with teeth!"
> And so I was, which plainly signified
> That I should snarl, and bite, and play the dog.
> Then, since the heavens have shap'd my body so,
> Let hell make crook'd my mind to answer it.
> I have no brother, I am like no brother;
> And this word "love", which greybeards call divine,
> Be resident in men like one another,
> And not in me! I am myself alone.
>   (III Henry VI, V. vi. 68)

We are convinced not by the content of the speech so much as its
air of familiar actuality—Gloster had a mother. His histrionic
manifesto as villain, "I am myself alone", is reached through the
quizzical smile, as good fellow, "And so I was".[6] It is noticeable,
though, that the provocation of Satan's nihilism is always "human"
—his troops' steadfastness, the sun's glory, Eve's beauty. In this
way Satan is made essentially the enemy of man, yet shown to be
essentially a demon: "The demoniacal becomes thoroughly evident
only when it is touched by the good, which now comes to its
confines from the outside . . . The demoniacal is dread of the

6. Such breeding of motive was unusual
though, outside Shakespeare, especially
for villains. D'Amville labours to explain
his motives intellectually, as an atheist,
but he comes and goes pat like a morality
Vice all the same: "Let all men lose, so
I increase my gain, I have no feeling of
another's pain" (I. ii. Tourneur's *Plays*
ed. Symonds [1948, no line numbers,
Mermaid]). This is like Chaos at *P.L.*
II. 1009. All the same, D'Amville sins
actually for personal gain; Satan, for all
his imperialistic ambitions, is sinner *tout
court.*

good".[7] We can also see that Milton is dealing with a theological process, hardening of the heart, which has a special significance in *Paradise Lost*. Whatever the technical causes, Satan is presented as undergoing a series of reactions which progressively extinguish his own gleams of self-knowledge and other-pity and block the angelic impulses that might have saved him; so that by Book IV and Book IX he embodies irredeemable despair more than absolute evil. Hardening is an awkward doctrine. Milton's exposition of it in *De Doctrina*, that God's "hardening of the heart, therefore, is usually the last punishment inflicted on inveterate wickedness and unbelief in this life" (iv. 207), is supported by dozens of texts; but none of them turns out to refer to permanent hardening as a punishment, and editors refrain from citing them at their parallel in *Paradise Lost*:

> This my long sufferance and my day of grace
> They who neglect and scorn shall never taste;
> But hard be hard'nd, blind be blinded more,
> That they may stumble on, and deeper fall;
> And none but such from mercy I exclude.
>
> (III. 198)

Yet the doctrine is entirely orthodox. *Faustus* is built on it: "My hearts so hardened I cannot repent"[8] he says, and plunges away from faith into scholastic dispute again—"Tell me, are there many heauens aboue the Moone?" Later, "I do repent, and yet I do dispaire" (1301)—negative repentance can do nothing without positive love of God. At the end the febrility of his intellect drags his heart away from Christ's saving blood in the firmament—Latin tags, the nature of time, quotations from the Bible, astrology, meteorology, metempsychosis, how many drops of water in the ocean. With Bunyan's man in the iron cage it is a simpler lack of saving faith. The cage symbolises the despair he is shut up in because he "left off to watch, and be sober; I laid the reins upon the neck of my lusts; I sinned against the light of the Word, and the goodness of God: I have grieved the Spirit, and he is gone; I tempted the Devil, and he is come to me; I have provoked God to anger, and he has left me: I have so hardened my heart, that I *cannot* repent."[9] When Christian is told that there is no hope at all for this man, he expostulates, "Why? The Son of the Blessed is very pitiful"; but the man lists the unforgivable spiritual sins he has committed, and says he cannot repent because "God hath denied me repentance; his Word gives me no encouragement to believe; yea, himself hath shut me up in this Iron Cage: nor can all the men

7. Kierkegaard, *The Concept of Dread*, trans. W. Lowrie (1944), pp. 106, 113, etc.
8. Line 629. *Works* ed. Tucker Brooke (Oxford, 1910).
9. *Pilgrim's Progress* ed. Wharey (Oxford, 1928), p. 37.

in the world let me out". This allegory is immediately followed by
the dream of Judgment Day; but it is implied in the weakness of
character displayed by the man in the iron cage that hope and
hardening are both reciprocal actions: the sinner's original harden-
ing provokes a reaction from God which, if it does not soften him,
hardens him still more; so that the state of despair grows like a
stalactite-stalagmite formation. Satan's despair only seems to be
inhuman because it is, properly, what Kierkegaard called demoniac.
Kierkegaard distinguishes between the introvert's despair at his own
weakness, and defiance. This—Satan's first and public mood—is

> despair by the aid of the eternal, the despairing abuse of the
> eternal in the self to the point of being despairingly determined
> to be oneself . . . one might call it Stoicism—yet without think-
> ing only of this philosophic sect. . . . It acknowledges no power
> over it, hence in the last resort it lacks seriousness and is able
> only to conjure up a show of seriousness when the self bestows
> upon its experiments the utmost attention . . . the self in its
> despairing effort to will to be itself labors itself into the direct
> opposite, it becomes really no self. . . .

The final stage is demoniac despair, which

> with hatred of existence wills to be itself, to be itself in terms of
> its misery; it does not even in defiance or defiantly will to be
> itself, but to be itself in spite; it does not even will in defiance to
> tear itself free from the Power which posited it, it wills to ob-
> trude upon this Power in spite, to hold on to it out of malice.
> And that is natural, a malignant objection must above all take
> care to hold on to that against which it is an objection. Revolting
> against the whole of existence, it thinks it has hold of a proof
> against it, against its goodness. This proof the despairer thinks he
> himself is, and that is what he wills to be, therefore he wills to be
> himself, himself with his torment, in order with this torment to
> protest against the whole of existence.[1]

Publicly, such despair is most apparent in the peculiarly epical
situation of total warfare waged to unconditional defeat; and it is in
this milieu that Satan holds office in Books I and II. Hell's totali-
tarianism is most obvious in the devils; but Satan, though in the
created world he occasionally turns humane, in Hell is predomi-
nantly a *führer*. Hell is of his own ordering and he carries its
essence about with him. The device is familiar; but what Satan
cannot escape is self-domination. It is his reputation as avenging
demagogue that in his lonely subsequent soliloquies inhibits finer,
personal feeling—"Thoughts, whither have ye led me, with what
sweet Compulsion thus transported to forget What hither brought
us [the royal and schizophrenic "we"], hate, not love" [IX. 473].
Satan's essential duality constitutes a grave satire on corruption of

1. *The Sickness unto Death* trans. Lowrie (1941), pp. 108ff.

the condition Milton valued above all others, rational sovereignty of the soul. When sin

> Lets in defilement to the inward parts,
> The soul grows clotted by contagion,
> Imbodies, and imbrutes, till she quite loose
> The divine property of her first being.
> [*Comus*, ll. 466–69]

This happens to Satan, body and soul. But also:

> he that hides a dark soul, and foul thoughts
> Benighted walks under the mid-day Sun;
> Himself is his own dungeon.
> [*Comus*, l. 383–85]

It is when Satan addresses the sun that he first confesses, "Which way I flie is Hell; my self am Hell" (IV. 75). He cannot relent, though:

> *Disdain* forbids me, and my dread of shame
> Among the spirits beneath, whom I seduc'd
> With other promises and other vaunts
> Then to submit, boasting I could subdue
> Th' Omnipotent.

Typically, Milton leaves it at the remote public level; how intimately we apply it will depend on our experience. Satan is archetype of all those we know who will not "come to the place where the word 'insult' has no meaning", who fearfully barricade their souls against the possibility of having been wrong, whose heroism fathers unnatural vices, and who die in the hell of deluded self-respect. Milton himself was in danger of it; the problem of whose side he was on is more complicated than Blake thought.

It is finally through Satan's bondage to himself that Milton escapes the limitations of a merely physical Hell:

> To banish for ever into a local hell, whether in air or in the centre, or in that uttermost and bottomless gulf of chaos, deeper from holy bliss than the world's diameter multiplied; they [classical poets and philosophers] thought not a punishing so proper and proportionate for God to inflict, as to punish sin with sin.
> [*The Doctrine and Discipline of Divorce*, Bk. II, Ch. iii]

And through the very dramatic inwardness of Satan Milton marks him as sinful:

> the wicked and profane . . . think that they were out of danger, if God would forbear a positive infliction; and that hell is only an incommodious place, that God by his power throws them into. This is the grand mistake. Hell is not only a positive inflicton . . . the fewel of *Tophet* burning is the guiltiness of man's con-

science, malignity, and a naughty disposition against goodness and holiness; and God's withdrawing because the person is incapable of His communication. Sin is an act of violence in itself: the sinner doth force himself, and stirs up strife within himself; and in a sinner there is that *within* which doth reluctate, and condemn him in the inward court of his own conscience.[2]

We may feel that Milton, being a Puritan, was foolishly antagonistic to the dramatic attitude to life. But the kind of dramatics he condemns in Satan is the romantic villain's autocentricity, or the possessed's despairing egoism, not the interchange of personality that fruits to action and sympathy. The characters of *Paradise Lost* do not soliloquise until they have fallen; unfallen speech and gesture are directed always to another person, on the supreme model of light inter-reflected by Father and Son.

IRENE SAMUEL

The Dialogue in Heaven: A Reconsideration of *Paradise Lost*, III, 1–417†

When Douglas Bush and C. S. Lewis—not to name readers as disparate in time and temperament as Pope, Blake, and Shaw—find the God of *Paradise Lost* unattractive, it may be ill-advised to attempt the justification of Milton's ways with Heaven. Even the excellent refutation of the Satanist position in John S. Diekhoff's book on *Paradise Lost* ignores rather than answers, perhaps quite properly, those who have objected to Milton's God as not so much a tyrant as a wooden bore.[1] My paper is addressed to such readers and to any others who are willing to start from the assumption that Milton may have known what he was about in the first half of Book III as surely as in Books I and IX. I put it thus because objections have generally turned on the first episode in Heaven and have rather consistently echoed Pope's quip that "God the Father turns a school-divine." I wish to argue that we have mistakenly read the scene as a mere presentation of doctrinal assertions conveniently divided between the Father and the Son, and that to take it thus is to forget both how highly Milton prized poetic economy[2]

---

2. Benjamin Whichcote, quoted in [F. J.] Powicke, *The Cambridge Platonists* (1926), pp. 75–76.

† From *PMLA*, LXXII (1957), 601–11. Reprinted by permission of the Modern Language Association of America. The author's footnotes have been renumbered.

1. Cf. *English Literature in the Earlier Seventeenth Century* (London, 1946), p. 381, and *A Preface to Paradise Lost* (London, 1942), p. 126; and see *Milton's Paradise Lost* (New York, 1946), Chs. v and vi.

2. The popular word now is "strategy,"

though one may still prefer the metaphor of the productive household to the metaphor of the destructive battlefield. Milton, at any rate, used the term "economy," explaining it in the Preface to *Samson Agonistes* as "such . . . disposition of the fable as may stand best with verisimilitude and decorum." For what he meant by "decorum," "verisimilitude," and "economy" the reader should consult Ida Langdon, *Milton's Theory of Poetry and Fine Art*, Cornell Stud. in Eng., No. 8 (New Haven, 1924).

and how central he made this episode to the action of his whole poem. For may not the trouble be that we have incautiously mis-construed as dogma what Milton intended as drama? In short, the failure may be not in the scene but in our reading of it.

Milton, we know, thought mere presentation of testimony of "very little power for proof" even in logical argument: "testimony affirms or denies that a thing is so and brings about that I believe; it does not prove, it does not teach, it does not cause me to know or understand why things are so, unless it also brings forward reasons."[3] How unlikely then that he would have rested the poetic argument of *Paradise Lost*, turning as it must on this very scene in Heaven, on the mere testimony of theological statement or on his own mere assertion that these statements are made by personages named God and the Son. Surely we do more wisely to assume that Milton intended the statements in the scene to demonstrate that the persons involved are recognizably God, the creator of the universe, and the Son, his "word, wisdom, and effectual might."

The meaning of the council in Heaven starts before either person speaks, since it depends in large part on the continuity of the poetic fabric: the obvious contrasts with Hell indicate how we are to regard Heaven.[4] Thus, for example, the invocation of light in the opening lines of Book III at once helps to establish Milton's God as the cosmic principle, the source of ordered nature, partly because we have seen Hell's darkness filled with unnatural perversions and monstrosities. We are impelled by the lines to mark such contrasts, though we ought also to note the near-absurdity of the word "contrast"; it suits Satan's pretensions well enough, but hardly suggests that what he opposes is the entire universe. We have to bear in mind from the first that we could predict nothing of Milton's God and Heaven by simply inverting his Satan and Hell, though we are expected to learn much by observing their differences.

What we learn, to begin with, is that, unfortunately for Satan, the God of *Paradise Lost* is not merely another being on whose pattern he can model his rebel state, but Total Being, *the* Primal

3. *Logic*, I, 32, trans. A. H. Gilbert, *The Works of John Milton*, Columbia ed., XI, 283. My references to Milton's prose are to the volume and page numbers of this edition. For *Paradise Lost* I have used the edition by Merritt Y. Hughes (New York, 1935), but have normalized some spellings for the quotations incorporated into my own prose.
4. Ernest Schanzer has collected a number of such parallels in "Milton's Hell Revisited," *UTQ*, XXIV (1955), 136–145. My notion of these contrasts is that Milton used his augmented treatment of Hell to make possible an abbreviated treatment of Heaven. Thus, for example, because Hell is finally summed up as "a universe of death" where "all life dies, death lives," and Death in fact is king (as he

claims [II.698–699] and his crown proves [II.673]), we recognize more immediately that Heaven is the realm of vitality and indeed of nature, without any hammering at the point. And thus in turn the list of the beauties of nature from which blindness has cut the poet off (III.40–50) can suggest to us that Milton's God is the God of Nature long before we meet the phrase "God and Nature bid the same" (VI.176). Or again, because we have noted the incestuous monstrosities, ugly contention, and even uglier agreement between Satan, his perfect image Sin, and their only begotten son Death, the whole dialogue in Heaven between the Father and *his* only begotten Son, who is his perfect image, takes on added meaning.

Energy, *the* Voice of Reason, *the* Moral Law that makes possible a moral cosmos as surely as the laws of physics make possible a physical cosmos. He is *the* Creator who by intention brings into being others who act of themselves, and consequently *the* Intelligence that comprehends the universe. Significantly enough, his first act in the poem is to bend "down his [omniscient] eye,/His own works and their works at once to view." To try to read the dialogue that follows without allowing the first speaker his full nature would indeed make nonsense of the scene.[5] But as soon as we take Milton's God as Being, infinitely beyond all created beings, the scene has dramatic point. The near tonelessness of his first speech at once proves itself the right tone. It has offended readers because they assume that the "I" who speaks is or should be a person like other persons. The flat statement of fact, past, present, and future, the calm analysis and judgment of deeds and principles—these naturally strike the ear that has heard Satan's ringing utterance as cold and impersonal. They should. For the omniscient voice of the omnipotent moral law speaks simply what is. Here is no orator using rhetoric to persuade, but the nature of things expounding itself in order to present fact and principle unadorned.[6]

Clearly Milton uses that toneless voice of the moral law to destroy immediately the straw figure of a gloating, tyrannical victor that Satan and his followers had conjured up in Books i and ii. More important, he uses it to afford the Son opportunity for his impassioned reply. And this we must mark emphatically before turning to what either says: the Father in dialogue with the Son is not listening to an echo, but encouraging the distinctive tones of a quite different voice. To take the difference as showing the amiability of the Son at the expense of the cold, rigorous Father is to mistake Milton's point. The compassion, love, and grace we are asked to observe in the Son (ll. 140–142) are emphatically equated with the substantial expression of the invisible Godhead (ll. 138–140): the Son's compassionate tone is made possible by the passionless logic of the Father.[7]

5. Lewis shows that Milton keeps to "the great central tradition" of Christian doctrine throughout *P.L.* (pp. 81–91). But Lewis, it occurs to me, makes heavier theological demands on the reader than Milton ever suggests in the poem.
6. Milton, of course, knew the ancient distinction between what is appropriate in persuasion and in exposition. Cf. Aristotle, *Rhetoric*, trans. Lane Cooper, iii, 1404a: "Strict justice, of course, would lead us, in speaking, to seek no more than that we should avoid paining the hearer without alluring him; the case should, in justice, be fought on the strength of the facts alone, so that all else besides demonstration of fact is superfluous. . . . No one uses them [the devices of style] in teaching mathematics." And see Plato, *Phaedrus*, especially 263.
7. It will be evident that I fully agree with Maurice Kelley that "no indecision is present in *Paradise Lost*, iii" (*This Great Argument*, Princeton, 1941, p. 34) and even that nothing Milton says in *P.L.* conflicts with his *Christian Doctrine*. But is there any evidence that Milton wanted his reader to adopt, or so much as recognize, the Arianism implicit in Bk. iii? Any reduction of the drama of the council-scene to exposition of doctrine surely distorts Milton's intent.

We may now turn to what is said, noting briefly that it is said in the presence of the assembled angels, for all to hear, though the opening words are directed to the Son. God states that man will fall, expounds the doctrine of free will, observes a difference between the rebellion of Satan's crew and the disobedience of man, uses past, present, and future tenses interchangeably, announces his intention of mercy to man, and ends as though the final word had been spoken. The Son, unbidden, answers; and what he answers, though put most respectfully, sounds remarkably unlike mere assent:

> O Father, gracious was that word which clos'd
> Thy sovran sentence, that Man should find grace. . . .
> For should Man finally be lost, should Man
> Thy creature late so lov'd, thy youngest Son
> Fall circumvented thus by fraud, though join'd
> With his own folly? . . .
> Or shall the Adversary thus obtain
> His end, and frustrate thine, shall he fulfil
> His malice, and thy goodness bring to naught . . .
> . . . or wilt thou thyself
> Abolish thy Creation, and unmake,
> For him, what for thy glory thou hast made?
> So should thy goodness and thy greatness both
> Be question'd and blasphem'd without defence.

Put any such figure as Satan feigned to rebel against in the place of the Godhead here, and what the Son says would surely win him the most crushing reply. Unlike the "yes man" Satan had made of Beelzebub by the time he dared to make his second speech in Hell, the Son *argues*: "That be from thee far,/That far be from thee, Father." In Milton's Heaven the independent being speaks his own mind, not what he thinks another would like to hear.[8]

And that independent voice turns out to be precisely what this other does like to hear. When the voice of the moral law resumes to congratulate its interlocutor, it briefly adopts a tone of praise:

> O Son, in whom my Soul hath chief delight . . .
> All hast thou spok'n as my thoughts are, all

8. Milton clearly knew the traditional treatment of the dispute in Heaven on this very theme of man's condemnation or salvation, so that he would feel no suggestion of impiety in attributing vigorous argument for opposing views to the participants in such a celestial *débat*. See Hope Travers, *The Four Daughters of God*, Bryn Mawr Coll. Monographs, No. 6 (Bryn Mawr, 1907), for the history of this popular mediaeval theme from the Hebrew *Midrash* to the Renaissance. Miss Travers observes that Milton "knew a number of the versions of the allegory" (p. 146) and that it "would have reached crowning expression in English drama" if he had carried out the plan of the Cambridge Manuscript (p. 143). I am indebted to Professor Merritt Y. Hughes for calling my attention to the relevance of Miss Travers' work to my thesis. Milton with his true epic touch reassigns the old arguments of mercy and justice, along with some decidedly new arguments, to the Son and God, transmutes the *débat* into a dialogue, uses what he had assimilated from Homeric scenes on high Olympos, and creates an episode central to *P.L.*

> As my Eternal purpose hath decreed:
> Man shall not quite be lost. . . .

Now the eternal purpose, though the same as in the first speech, can reveal another aspect that the Son's answer has brought into prominence. The new statement of the moral law proceeds, again with the cold logic of "thus it is and thus must be," to redefine the future of man:

> But yet all is not done . . .
> Die hee or Justice must; unless for him
> Some other able, and as willing, pay
> The rigid satisfaction, death for death.

Thus the question is raised,

> Say, Heav'nly Powers, where shall we find such love,
> Which of ye shall be mortal to redeem
> Man's mortal crime, and just th' unjust to save,
> Dwells in all Heaven charity so dear?

These are the first words directly addressed to the angels, a synthesis that combines with the immutable moral law the Son's opposing love. But to the angelic ear it apparently sounds no less harsh than the original statement and no less final: "all the Heav'nly Quire stood mute." The question and the moment of silence inevitably remind us of the council in Hell when Beelzebub proposed the voyage to Earth and asked who dared go (II.402–426). But the resemblance underscores the difference.

In Hell the stage was in every way set. All the ceremonious preliminaries, the trumpet proclaiming a solemn council, the call summoning the worthiest of each band, the signal dividing nobility from commoners, all served to prepare those admitted to the inner chamber for the lofty tone in which Satan asked their advice. In marked contrast, the council in Heaven starts without fanfare, in every possible way in the open. It takes place outdoors and in the presence of "all the Sanctities of Heaven." Though no one's presence has been commanded, any one who wishes may hear. (Uriel, Gabriel, and Gabriel's troop are notably absent for reasons of dramatic necessity.) Without a word of preface, presumably on the spur of the occasion, God speaks, and as if with the utmost finality. He does not pretend to seek advice, but calls attention to Satan loose in the world, and announces what will follow.

In Hell, after Satan's explicit request, three of his followers offer two distinct plans. But just as the second is about to win unanimous approval (II.284–298), Beelzebub intervenes to propose as his own, and win acceptance for, what is in fact Satan's plan, stated piecemeal in Book I (ll. 120–122, 162–165, 650–656). The proposal calls for the selection of a spy; and Beelzebub makes it, evidently as Satan planned, stressing the risk involved with the clear purpose of frightening off every one but Satan (ii.378–385). When Satan then offers to go, he is the actor taking his cue in a scene he had written for himself. It is a magnificent moment designed to show his magnificent courage. And if he almost spoils it for his deluded audience with his final words, "This enterprise/None shall partake with me," he saves his pose by at once moving offstage.

What of the monarch Satan thought to emulate?[9] God makes no pretense of willingness to collect opinions on an open question. Yet he immediately sanctions and adopts the view presented by the Son, incorporating it into his new statement and modifying his first so that a task emerges. Without urgency or emphasis, he names the task. And it needs only to be named, for it involves not risk or danger but what to angelic ears must sound like annihilation. The grand opportunity—"Which of ye will be mortal to redeem/Man's mortal crime?"—presumably means utter abolition of being. But this is a prospect that even in Hell only the brutal Moloch could regard with equanimity; this is the very penalty that the Son could not bear to think the Father intended for fallen man.

Little wonder that "none appeared/. . . that durst upon his own head draw/The deadly forfeiture." Yet these are no cowardly puppets dependent on constant approval and reassurance from God. Every angel we later meet acts on his own responsibility without running to the Godhead for advice: thus Uriel counsels what seems a young angel (iii.681–735), then copes with what has proved an escaped devil (iv.124–130 and 555 ff.); the lesser Ithuriel and Zephon meet Satan's taunts (iv.820–856); Gabriel confronts him (iv.877 ff.); Abdiel stands against him and all his forces (v.804 ff.); and the loyal angels wage their war against the rebels, all on their own momentum. That is indeed the most striking characteristic of Milton's angels, the independence with which they demonstrate the lie of Satan's talk about their harp-playing servility (iv.942–945; vi.166–170).

But what is now involved is presumably a certainty. The speaker is omniscient; none of his hearers is. Milton thought the point worth making at some length in his *Christian Doctrine.* "The good angels do not look into all the secret things of God," he asserted (i, ix; Columbia ed., XV, 107) after arguing that "Even the Son . . . knows not all things absolutely" (i, v; xiv, 317), since "the attributes of divinity belong to the Father alone" (xiv, 227), and the first

9. Need we cite evidence of Satan's attempts at "Godlike imitated state?" Perhaps the most interesting are the echoes in v.772, and throughout Bks. i and ii of God's words in v.600–601; the most obvious, the palace on the mount in v.756–766, and the throne in ii.1–5, to be compared with God's in iii.58; the most significant the sudden self-revelation in x.444–450, with its almost ludicrous effort to duplicate the effect of God described in iii.375–382.

of the divine attributes listed is omniscience.[1] Here too omniscience is God's alone. His hearers are confident of his goodness, but they cannot fully know what is in his mind. That is what gives the Son's offer its great dramatic value. The Son cannot know any more than others at the council that the task named does not mean annihilation. The moment of silence includes his silence to underscore the clear enormity of the solution. When after that moment's hesitation he offers to die for man, he does not know that the death he undertakes will not be final; he *trusts* that the omnipotence whose goodness he does know will not permit injustice.

Again he answers what he has heard: "Father, thy word is past, man shall find grace;/And shall not grace find means?" But his answer is far more than the offer of his life for man's. Again he responds to the unalterable law out of his own nature, now out of his boundless trust:

> I shall not long
> Lie vanquisht; thou hast giv'n me to possess
> Life in myself for ever, by thee I live,
> Though now to Death I yield, and am his due
> All that of me can die, yet that debt paid,
> Thou wilt not leave me in the loathsome grave
> His prey . . .
> But I shall rise Victorious.

What the Son speaks is no assurance privately communicated nor any prescience bestowed uniquely on him. To read his speech so would destroy its meaning, the point of the scene in Heaven, and much of the system of values on which the whole poem rests. All that the Son says of his eventual triumph over death comes from nothing but a perfect confidence in the nature of the Godhead. He does not foreknow any part of his resurrection, the harrowing of Hell, or the reunion of Heaven and Earth at Doomsday. His lines can only mean that, knowing the omnipotence and perfect benevolence of the Father, he can not believe that his sacrifice of himself will have a different kind of issue. And in fact he does not name the details of his victory as God, again approving and adopting all that he has said, will presently name them.

For the moment his words hang unconfirmed as he "attends the will/Of his great Father." He has not pronounced that will. And the angels too attend, "what this might mean, and whither tend/ Wond'ring." If they still wonder so should the reader; the outcome of the dialogue is as yet uncertain, the last word not yet spoken.

The final speech of God, reconciling the immutable moral law

1. Note that when Michael is to give Adam knowledge of the future Milton makes clear twice over that Michael's prophecy has to be allowed him by Omniscience: "reveal / To Adam what shall come in future days, / As I shall thee enlighten" (xi.113–115); and "So both ascend / In the visions of God," where "of God" must mean "provided by God" (xi.376–377).

and the Son's trusting offer, the proposed vicarious atonement and the Son's hope of victory, does indeed transcend both. For one thing, we immediately note that the Father's voice, so cold and logically formal in stating fact and principle, can adopt a tone more warm and loving even than the Son's when a deed is to be praised, a reassurance given. The warmth in God's tone began, we noted, in the first five lines of his second speech where he applauded the Son's answer (ll. 168–172), but was at once lost in the severe abstractions that followed. Now in the third and last of God's speeches the warmth is unmistakably dominant, a warmth toward the Son that embraces the humanity he will share. For the Son there is rapturous delight and praise, and by no cosmic pathetic fallacy, but because Milton evidently thinks rapturous praise in the nature of the moral law when it sanctions what is praiseworthy. Even more important, each of the Son's hopeful phrases is caught up into a detailed affirmation: as he trusted it would be thus it shall be, and each time with something affirmed beyond what he had hoped.

He had said "Account me man" as the equivalent of "on me let thine anger fall." Now God promises that it shall be so—and more: "Their nature also to thy nature join/And be thyself man among men on earth,/. . . Be thou in Adam's room/The head of all mankind." He had said, "I for his sake will leave/Thy bosom, and this glory next to thee/Freely put off." Now God promises: "Nor shalt thou by descending to assume/Man's nature, lessen or degrade thine own. . . ./Thy humiliation shall exalt/With thee thy manhood also to this throne." He had said, "By thee raised I [shall] ruin all my foes . . . and return,/Father, to see thy face." Now God promises: "Here shalt thou sit incarnate, here shalt reign/Both God and Man . . ./Anointed universal king; all power/I give thee, reign for ever." He had hoped, "Wrath shall be no more/Thenceforth, but in thy presence joy entire." Now God assures him: "The world shall burn, and from her ashes spring/New Heaven and Earth, wherein the just shall dwell/And . . ./See golden days . . ./With Joy and Love triumphing and fair Truth."[2]

But the climactic element in God's final utterance is that it shifts the emphasis of the discussion from the subject initially proposed, the redemption of man, which now becomes secondary, to a new theme, the exaltation of the Son. That this is finally the major theme we know both from the expansion given it in God's final speech with its emphatic ending,

2. The phrase "joy and love," emphatically repeated in the first reference to Eden (III.67–68), recurs here to make us doubly sure that the atonement will reestablish true Paradise; for the phrase is virtually the leitmotiv of Eden. See IV.519, VI.94, VIII.621; and cf. the anticipations in *Comus*, ll. 1010–11, and *Lycidas*, l. 177. The excellent collection of Milton's repeated phrases by Edward S. Le Comte, *Yet Once More* (New York, 1953), to my mind, offers no adequate explanation of Milton's intended repetitions.

> But all ye Gods,
> Adore him, who to compass all this dies,
> Adore the Son, and *honour him as me;*

and from the hymn of praise with which the angels at once, rightly grasping all they have heard, meet the command.

The dialogue, for all its brevity, for all its use of the familiar and expected, has moved from its presumably fixed beginning to an unforeseen end. Where the corresponding scene in Hell made a stately progress to a foregone conclusion, proceeding with all possible solemnity from Satan's plan to Satan's plan, though it had to run a course more tortuous even than Belial's speech, the quick, terse, unplanned scene in Heaven arrives by tremendous leaps at a resolution unimaginable except to Omniscience at the outset. The "high decree unchangeable" has been radically altered, not of course in its unalterable essence, but in its application to man's destiny. The cold logic of the moral law has confirmed the Son's compassion, incorporated that compassion into the administration of the decree, and exalted it into the virtue most to be honored in the universe. What has made possible the changed application of the law has been raised by the law itself to an importance equal to its own. The role of the Son in the dialogue has elicited a resolution worlds removed from the initial prediction. And beyond working out a plan for man's redemption, the dialogue of the council in Heaven has shown in dramatic process the Son's growth to what the Father himself calls virtual equality.

And again we mark the contrasts of Hell. Before the council there Satan had been supreme, and through the council he affirmed his supremacy, establishing his power and prestige beyond the need of such arguments as he had opened the session with. Before the scene in Heaven the Son had already had a notable career: as first born and "only begotten"—the one creature produced directly by the creator; then as the instrument of the creation of the angels—the point Satan disputed with Abdiel (v.835–837 and 853–863); then as appointed head of all the angels, his second "begetting"[3]—the occasion of Satan's offended pride. Next he had the power of God transferred to him for the purpose of ending the war in Heaven (vi.710 ff.) and yet again for the creation of the new universe (vii.163–166 and 192–196). The first two of these steps are alluded to, the rest we hear of later in Raphael's account to Adam. The whole career is neatly summed up in the angels' song of praise (iii.372 ff.) with which the scene here ends.

We witness directly only the final elevation of the Son, and for the meaning of *Paradise Lost* it is of moment that we should

---

3. For the dual meaning of "beget" in the Son's career see *Christian Doctrine*, i, v (Columbia ed., xiv, 181–191), and the expositions of John S. Diekhoff and Maurice Kelley.

directly witness it, since it is the great contrast to the process by which Satan—and Eve and Adam after him—fell. In his opening pronouncement God had said:

> Freely they stood who stood, and fell who fell.
> Not free, what proof could they have giv'n sincere
> Of true allegiance, constant Faith or Love,
> Where only what they needs must do, appear'd,
> Not what they would? what praise could they receive?
> What pleasure I from such obedience paid,
> When Will and Reason (Reason also is choice)
> Useless and vain, of freedom both despoil'd,
> Made passive both, had serv'd necessity,
> Not mee.

There the doctrine as major premise of a syllogism condemning the fallen sounded harsh. Here we see its obverse. Freely the Son makes his choice of word and deed; and if the choice has been foreknown, foreknowledge had no influence on his virtue. What praise is given to the right choice freely made, what pleasure taken in it by the moral law, we again see in Book VI in the reception of Abdiel. But we must know the happy meaning of the law of free will at the very time that we first hear it expounded in its unhappy significance for man.

Without the freedom which permits rebel angel and man to err the full wisdom and compassion of the Son would be impossible. This is not to argue for a "fortunate fall" any more than for explicit Arian doctrine as essential to the meaning of *Paradise Lost*. Doubtless Milton's Arianism made it possible for him to handle the council in Heaven as a dramatic dialogue between distinct speakers more easily, with less conflict between what he saw as dramatically desirable and what he felt as doctrinally correct,[4] than a Trinitarian might. Doubtless too his conviction of man's ultimate redemption permitted him to think that man's *culpa* proves ultimately *felix* despite the cost of that dearly bought felicity. But the doctrinal heart of the scene is neither Arianism nor the *felix culpa*, but free will, central to Milton's thought everywhere, not in *Areopagitica* alone, nor only where it makes for tragedy in *Paradise Lost*. Here in the first scene in Heaven the same principle makes for all that we consider desirable in a universe.

Moreover what happens in the dialogue in Book III is analogous to what might have happened in Book IX. If Eve had her moment when she might, like Abdiel, have caught the liar in his lie, Adam had his when he might, like the Son, have risked himself to redeem Eve. He himself recounts to Raphael in Book VIII what independent

---

4. I am indebted for my phrasing here to Professor Hoxie N. Fairchild, whose critical comments on my argument have, I trust, helped me to avoid theological pitfalls.

assertion of his mind and will to his maker had won for him. What his making a like assertion in like confidence might have won for fallen Eve we cannot know since he does not make it. But it is worth observing that tragedies stem from alternatives ignored as well as choices made. A trust comparable to—on however lower a level than—the Son's and a self-abnegation willing to risk whatever was to be risked demanded only Adam's faith that the benevolence he had always known would remain benevolent, and the whole application of the moral law might have changed as the Son's choice changes it. What Adam, perfect and therefore "able," could have done for Eve remains unfortunately outside the action. But Eve was not irredeemably lost, as Adam at once concluded in his immediate assumption of a hostile universe. So much is clear from what follows for fallen Eve and Adam both. It is specifically clarified in advance by the dialogue of the Son with the Father. The trust that confronts and by confronting changes "Die hee or justice must" into "Thy humilitation shall exalt/With thee thy manhood also to this throne" is a possibility at some level for every being in the universe Milton established in *Paradise Lost*. His success in establishing it is no less remarkable in the swift dialogue in Heaven than in the poem that hinges on that brief scene.

WILLIAM EMPSON

Milton's God†

* * * The motive of the Father in crucifying the Son is of course left in even deeper obscurity.

Milton did however I think mean to adumbrate a kind of motive by his picture of the Last Things. Professor C. S. Lewis[1] once kindly came to a lecture I was giving on the half-finished material of this book; and at question time, after a sentence of charitable compunction, recognizing that the speaker wasn't responsible for this bit, he said "Does Phelps Morand[2] think God is going to abdicate, then?" I tried to explain that M. Morand regarded this as the way Milton's dramatic imagination worked, after it had been corrupted by his patriotic labours, not as part of his theological system. The answer felt weak, and soon afterwards another difficulty drove me back to the book of M. Saurat,[3] which I had

† From *Milton's God* (Norfolk, Conn., New Directions, 1961), pp. 130–37, 140, 142–43, 144–46, 204–10. Reprinted by permission of New Directions Publishing Corporation, the author, and Chatto & Windus Ltd. The footnotes for this selection are by the editor.

1. Author of *A Preface to Paradise Lost* (London, 1942).
2. Author of *De Comus à Satan* (Paris, 1939).
3. Denis Saurat, *Milton: Man and Thinker* (London, 1925).

probably not read since I was an undergraduate; I thus suddenly realized, what M. Saurat was not intending to prove, that Milton did expect God to abdicate. At least, that is the most direct way to express the idea; you may also say that he is an emergent or evolutionary deity, as has been believed at times by many other thinkers, for example Aeschylus and H. G. Wells.

There has been such a campaign to prove that only the coarsely worldly Victorians would even want the world to get better that I had better digress about that, or I may be thought to be jeering at Milton. We are often told that *In Memoriam* is bad because Tennyson tries to palm off progress in this world as a substitute for Heaven. But he says in the poem that he would stop being good, or would kill himself, if he stopped believing he would go to Heaven; it is wilful to argue that he treats the progress of the human race as an adequate alternative. Indeed, he seems rather too petulant about his demand for Heaven, considering that *Tithonus*, written about the same time (according to Stopford Brooke) though kept from publication till later, appreciates so nobly the hunger of mankind for the peace of oblivion. But the underlying logic of *In Memoriam* is firm. The signs that God is working out a vast plan of evolution are treated as evidence that he is good, and therefore that he will provide Heaven for Tennyson. To believe that God's Providence can be seen at work in the world, and that this is evidence for his existence and goodness, is what is called Natural Theology; it is very traditional, and the inability of neo-Christians to understand it casts an odd light on their pretensions. Tennyson has also been accused of insincerity about progress because in another poem he expressed alarm at the prospect of war in the air; but he realized the time-scale very clearly; while maintaining that the process of the suns will eventually reach a good end, it is only sensible to warn mankind that we are likely to go through some very bad periods beforehand. Now, when mankind seems almost certain to destroy itself quite soon, we cannot help wincing at a belief that progress is inevitable; but this qualification seems all that is needed. I think that reverence *ought* to be aroused by the thought that so long and large a process has recently produced ourselves who can describe it, and other-worldly persons who boast of not feeling that seem to me merely to have cauterized themselves against genuine religious feeling. The seventeenth century too would have thought that so much contempt for Providence verged upon the Manichean. Milton claimed to get his conception of progress from the Bible; but he would have found corroboration, one would think, in the *Prometheus*, which was well known. There is only one reference to the myth in the epic, and it is twisted into a complaint against women (IV. 720); but Mr. R. J. Z. Werblowsky, in his broad and philosophical *Lucifer and Prometheus* (1952), may well be right to think that Milton tried to avoid direct comparsion between Prometheus and his Satan.

At the point which seemed to me illuminating, M. Saurat was calling Milton 'the old incorrigible dreamer' (p. 165, 1944 edition), apparently just for believing in the Millennium on earth, though that only requires literal acceptance of Revelation xx; but he was quoting part of Milton's commentary in Chapter XXXIII of the *De Doctrina*, "Of Perfect Glorification", and no doubt recognized that Milton was somehow going rather further. Milton says:

> It may be asked, if Christ is to deliver up the kingdom to God and the Father, what becomes of the declarations [quotations from Heb. i. 8, Dan. vii. 14, and Luke i. 33] "of his kingdom there shall be no end". I reply, there shall be no end of his kingdom . . . till time itself shall be no longer, Rev. x. 6, until everything which his kingdom was intended to effect shall be accomplished . . . it will not be destroyed, nor will its period be a period of dissolution, but rather of perfection and consummation, like the end of the law, Matt. v. 18.

The last clause seems to recall the precedent of an earlier evolutionary step, whereby the New Dispensation of Jesus made the Mosaic Law unnecessary; it is clear that the final one, which makes even the Millennium unnecessary, must be of an extremely radical character. The Father, I submit, has to turn into the God of the Cambridge Platonists and suchlike mystical characters; at present he is still the very disagreeable God of the Old Testament, but eventually he will dissolve into the landscape and become immanent only. The difficulty of fitting in this extremely grand climax was perhaps what made Milton uncertain about the controverted time-scheme of the Millennium. The doctrine of the end of time, if one takes it seriously, is already enough to make anything but Total Union (or else Total Separateness from God) hard to conceive.

The question which Milton answers here is at least one which he makes extremely prominent in the speech of rejoicing by the Father after the speech of sacrifice by the Son (III. 320). The Father first says he *will* give the Son all power, then in the present tense "I give thee"; yet he had given it already, or at least enough to cause Satan and his followers to revolt. Without so much as a full stop, the Father next says that the time when he will give it is the Day of Judgement, and the climax of the whole speech is to say that immediately after that "God shall be All in All". The eternal gift of the Father is thus to be received only on the Last Day, and handed back the day after. This has not been found disturbing, because the paradox is so clear that we assume it to be deliberate; nor are interpretations of it hard to come by. But Mlton would see it in the light of the passage in the *De Doctrina*; there "God shall be All in

All" ends the Biblical quotation which comes just before Milton's mystical "reply":

> Then cometh the end . . . but when he saith, all things are put under him, it is manifest that he is excepted which did put all things under him; and when all things are subdued unto him, then shall the Son himself also be subject unto him that put all things under him, that God may be all in all. (I Corinthians xv. 24–28)

St Paul is grappling with earlier texts here in much the same scholarly way that Milton did, which would give Milton a certain confidence about re-interpreting his results even though they were inspired because Biblical. After hearing so much from M. Morand about the political corruption of Milton's mind, one is pleased to find it less corrupt than St Paul's; Milton decided that God was telling the truth, and that he would keep his promise literally. At the end of the speech of the Father, Milton turns into poetry the decision he had reached in prose:

> The World shall burn, and from her ashes spring
> New Heav'n and Earth, wherein the just shall dwell . . .
> Then thou thy regal Sceptre shalt lay by,
> For regal Sceptre then no more shall need,
> God shall be All in All. But all ye Gods
> Adore him, who to compass all this dies,
> Adore the Son, and honour him as me.   (III. 340)

I grant that the language is obscure, as is fitting because it is oracular; and, besides, Milton wanted the poem to be universal, so did not want to thrust a special doctrine upon the reader. But the doctrine is implied decisively if the language is examined with care. St Paul presumably had in mind a literal autocracy, but Milton contrives to make the text imply pantheism. The O.E.D. records that the intransitive use of the verb *need* had become slightly archaic except for a few set phrases; the general intransitive use needed here belongs to the previous century—e.g. "stopping of heads with lead shall not need now" 1545. But a reader who noticed the change of grammar from *shalt* to *shall* could only impute the old construction: "Authority will then no longer be needed"— not, therefore, from the Father, any more than from the Son. There is much more point in the last two lines quoted if the Father has just proposed, though in an even more remote sense than the Son, that he too shall die. *All* is rather a pet word in Milton's poetry but I think he never gives it a capital letter anywhere else, and one would expect that by writing "All in All" he meant to imply a special doctrine, as we do by writing "the Absolute". Then again, this is the only time God calls the angels Gods, with or without a capital letter. He does it here meaning that they will in effect become so after he has abdicated. The reference has justly been used as a partial defence of Satan for calling his rebels Gods, but we are meant to understand that his claim for them is a subtle misuse of the deeper truth adumbrated here. Taking all the details together, I think it is clear that Milton wanted to suggest a high mystery at this culminating point.

There was a more urgent and practical angle to the question; it was not only one of the status of the Son, but of mankind. You cannot think it merely whimsical of M. Morand to call God dynastic if you look up the words *heir* and *inherit* in the concordance usually given at the end of a Bible. Milton was of course merely quoting the text when he made the Father call the Son his heir (as in VI. 705); but the blessed among mankind are also regularly called 'heirs of God's kingdom' and suchlike. The word *heir* specifically means one who will inherit; it would be comical to talk as if M. Morand was the first to wonder what the Bible might mean by it. The blessed among mankind are heirs of God through their union with Christ; Milton's Chapter XXIV is 'Of Union and Fellowship with Christ and the Saints, wherein is considered the Mystical or Invisible Church', and he says it is 'not confined to place or time, inasmuch as it is composed of individuals of widely separated countries, and of all ages from the foundation of the world'. He would regard this as a blow at all priesthoods, but also regard the invisible union as a prefiguring of the far distant real one. We can now see that it is already offered in the otherwise harsh words by which the Father appointed the Son:

> Under his great Vice-regent reign abide
> United as one individual Soul
> For ever happy   (V. 610)

As a means of achieving such unity the speech is a remarkable failure; but God already knew that men would be needed as well as angels before the alchemy could be done. When the unity is complete, neither the loyal angels nor the blessed among mankind will require even the vice-regency of the Son, still less the rule of the Father; and only so can they become 'heirs and inheritors of God's Kingdom'.

The texts prove, I submit, that Milton envisaged the idea, as indeed so informed a man could hardly help doing; but the poetry must decide whether it meant a great deal to him, and the bits so far quoted are not very good. Milton however also ascribes it to God in the one really splendid passage allotted to him. This is merely an earlier part of the same speech, but the sequence III. 80–345 is full of startling changes of tone. The end of the speech happens to let us see Milton's mind at work, because we can relate it to the *De Doctrina,* but the main feeling there is just immense pride; Milton could never let the Father appear soft, and his deepest yielding must be almost hidden by a blaze of glory. Just before advancing upon thirty lines of glory, he has rejoiced that his Son:

> though thron'd in highest bliss,
> Equal to God, and equally enjoying
> God-like fruition, quitted all to save
> A world from utter loss, and hast been found
> By Merit more than Birthright Son of God,
> Found worthiest to be so by being Good,
> Far more than Great or High; because in thee
> Love hath abounded more than Glory abounds,
> Therefore thy Humiliation shall exalt
> With thee thy Manhood also to this Throne;
> Here shalt thou sit incarnate, here shalt Reign
> Both God and Man, Son both of God and Man,
> Anointed universal King; all Power
> I give thee, reign for ever, and assume
> Thy Merits; under thee as Head Supreme
> Thrones, Princedoms, Powers, Dominions I reduce: (III. 305)

It is a tremendous moral cleansing for Milton's God, after the greed for power which can be felt in him everywhere else, to say that he will give his throne to Incarnate Man, and the rhythm around the word *humiliation* is like taking off in an aeroplane. I had long felt that this is much the best moment of God in the poem, morally as well as poetically, without having any idea why it came there. It comes there because he is envisaging his abdication, and the democratic appeal of the prophecy of God is what makes the whole picture of him just tolerable.

*   *   *

Thus, by combining the views of M. Saurat and M. Morand, the one attributing to Milton thoughts beyond the reaches of our souls and the other a harsh worldliness, we can I think partly solve the central problem about the poem, which is how Milton can have thought it to justify God. I think the 'internal' evidence of Milton's own writing enough to decide that he meant what I have tried to describe, because it makes our impression of the poem and indeed of the author much more satisfactory; but, even so, external evidence is needed to answer the objection that Milton could not have meant that, or could not have thought of it. I had best begin by saying what I learned from M. Saurat and where I thought his view inadequate. His main interest, as I understand, was to show that the European Renaissance could not have occurred without an underground influence from Jewish mystics beginning two or three centuries before Milton; the main reason for supposing that Milton had read the *Zohar*, even after textual evidence had been found, was that he was a man who habitually went to the sources of the ideas which he had already found floating about. The doctrine that matter was not created from nothing but was part of God M. Saurat considered fundamental to the Renaissance, because it allowed enough trust in the flesh, the sciences, the arts, the future before man in this world. Milton undoubtedly does express this doctrine, but it does not strike me as prominent in other poets of the time, except for the paradoxes of Donne's love-poerty.

*   *   *

The trouble with M. Saurat's position, I think, is that he welcomes the liquefaction of God the father, making him wholly immanent in his creation, and argues that Milton intended that in his epic, without realizing that Milton and his learned contemporaries would think the liquefaction of all the rest of us a prior condition. The idea of the re-absorption of the soul into the Absolute does get hinted at a good deal in the literature, if only in the form of complete self-abandonment to God; whereas the idea that God himself is wholly immanent in his creation belonged mainly to the high specialized output of the Cambridge Platonists. Marlowe's Faustus, in his final speech, desires to return his soul like a rain-drop to the sea rather than remain eternally as an individual in Hell, and this is a crucial image for grasping the Far-Eastern position; the same idea is quite noisy in the supposedly orthodox peroration of *Urn-Burial*: "if any have been so happy as truly to understand Christian annihilation . . . liquefaction . . . ingression into the divine shadow". When Lovewit at the end of *The Alchemist* rebuffs a superstitious fool by saying "Away, you Harry Nicholas" (the founder of the mystical Family of Love which maintained that any man can become Christ), the now remote figure is presumed to be familiar to a popular audience. The ideas which Milton hinted at in the bits of his epic which I have picked out were therefore not nearly so learned and unusual as they seem now; indeed, he probably treated them with caution because they might suggest a more Levelling, more economic-revolutionary, political stand than he in fact took. But the Cambridge Platonists were not dangerous for property-owners in this way; they were a strand of recent advanced thought which deserved recognition in his epic; also they allowed of a welcome contrast to the picture of God which the Bible forced him to present, and gave a bit more body to the mysterious climax of the Fortunate Fall. The abdication of the Father was thus quite an important part of his delicately balanced structure, and not at all a secret heresy; and of course not 'unconscious' if it needed tact. At bottom, indeed, a quaintly political mind is what we find engaged on the enormous synthesis. Milton knows by experience that God is at present the grindingly harsh figure described in the Old Testament; after all, Milton had long been printing the conviction that his political side had been proved right because God had made it win, so its eventual defeat was a difficult thing to justify God for. But it was essential to retain the faith that God has a good eventual plan; well then, the Cambridge Platonists can be allowed to be right about God, but only as he will become in the remote future. It seems to me one of the likeable sides of Milton that he would regard this as a practical and statesmanlike proposal.

*   *   *

The well-argued view of M. Morand, that the purblind Milton described God from his experience of Cromwell, also allows of an unexpectedly sublime conclusion. Milton's own political record, as I understand, cannot be found contemptible; he backed Cromwell and his Independents in the army against the Presbyterians in Parliament because he wanted religious freedom, but always remained capable of saying where he thought Cromwell had gone wrong; for example, in refusing to disestablish the Church. However, on one point Cromwell was impeccable, and appears to be unique among dictators; his admitted and genuine bother, for a number of years, was to find some way of establishing a Parliament under which he could feel himself justified in stopping being dictator. When Milton made God the Father plan for his eventual abdication, he ascribed to him in the high tradition of Plutarch the noblest sentiment that could be found in an absolute ruler; and could reflect with pride that he had himself seen it in operation, though with a tragic end. Milton's God is thus to be regarded as like King Lear and Prospero, turbulent and masterful characters who are struggling to become able to renounce their power and enter peace; the story makes him behave much worse than they do, but the author allows him the same purifying aspiration. Even the lie of God "Die he or Justice must", we may now charitably reflect, is partly covered when Milton says that Satan

<blockquote>
with necessity
The Tyrant's plea, excused his devilish deeds.   (IV. 395)
</blockquote>

It must be added at once that we cannot find enough necessity; the poem, to be completely four-square, ought to explain why God had to procure all these falls for his eventual high purpose. Such is the basic question as it stood long before Milton handled it; but he puts the mystery in a place evidently beyond human knowledge, and he makes tolerably decent, though salty and rough, what is within our reach.

This I think answers the fundamental objection of Yvor Winters, with which it seemed right to begin the chapter;[4] Milton's poetical formula for God is not simply to copy Zeus in Homer but, much more dramatically, to cut out everything between the two ends of the large body of Western thought about God, and stick to Moses except at the high points which anticipate Spinoza. The procedure is bound to make God interesting; take the case of his announcing to the loyal angels that he will create mankind to spite the devil. God must be supposed to intend his words to suggest to the angels what they do to us, but any angel instructed in theology must realize that God has intended throughout all eternity to spite Satan, so that when he presents this plan as new he is telling a lie, which he has also intended to tell throughout all eternity. No wonder it will be 'far happier days' after he has abdicated (xii. 465). Milton was well able to understand these contradictions, and naturally he would want to leave room for an eventual solution of them.

Perhaps I find him like Kafka merely because both seem to have had a kind of foreknowledge of the Totalitarian State, whether or not this was what C. S. Lewis praised as his beautiful sense of the idea of social order. The picture of God in the poem, including perhaps even the high moments when he speaks of the end, is astonishingly like Uncle Joe Stalin; the same patience under an appearance of roughness, the same flashes of joviality, the same thorough unscrupulousness, the same real bad temper. It seems little use to puzzle ourselves whether Milton realized he was producing this effect, because it would follow in any case from what he had set himself to do.

* * *

I hope these extracts[5] will be enough to make clear that Milton genuinely considered God in need of defence, and indeed that, when Milton said at the beginning of his epic he intended to justify God, he was so far from expecting a reader to think the phrase poetical rhetoric that he was not even stepping out of the usual procedure of his prose. A curious trick has been played on modern readers here; they are told: 'Why, but of course you must read the poem taking for granted that Milton's God is good; not to do that would be absurdly unhistorical. Why, the first business of a literary critic is to sink his mind wholly into the mental world of the

4. "It requires more than a willing suspension of disbelief to read Milton; it requires a willing suspension of intelligence. A good many years ago I found Milton's procedure more nearly defensible than I find it now; I find that I grow extremely tired of the meaningless inflation, the tedious falsification of the materials by way of excessive emotion. . . . [Comparison to the gods in Homer] . . . Milton, however, is concerned with a deity and with additional supernatural agents who are conceived in extremely intellectual terms; our conceptions of them are the result of more than 2000 years of the most profound and complex intellectual activity in the history of the human race. Milton's form is such that he must first reduce these beings to something much nearer the form of the Homeric gods than their proper form, and then must treat his ridiculously degraded beings in heroic language." *Hudson Review* (1956).

5. From Milton's *De Doctrina Christiana*.

author, and in a case like this you must accept what they all thought way back in early times.' I think this literary doctrine is all nonsense anyhow; a critic ought to use his own moral judgement, for what it is worth, as well as try to understand the author's, and that is the only way he can arrive at a 'total reaction'. But in a case like this the argument is also grossly unhistorical. No doubt Milton would only have snorted if a Victorian had come up and praised him for making Satan good, but anyone who told him he had made God wicked would find his mind surprisingly at home; there would be some severe cross-questioning (is this a Jesuit or merely an Arminian?), but if that passed off all right he would ask the visitor to sit down and discuss the point at length. Nor was it only the later Milton, after the disillusion of the Fall of the Commonwealth, who felt God to need defence; he can be shown feeling it both before and after a major change in this theology. In *The Doctrine and Discipline of Divorce* (1643), writing as a believer in predestination, he remarks of Jesuits and Arminians that, if they could only understand the argument he has just propounded, 'they might, methinks, be persuaded to absolve both God and us' (*us* meaning the Calvinists). Near the end of Chapter III of the *De Doctrina* we find he has abandoned predestination, and his reason for it is still that he is anxious to absolve God:

> free causes are not impeded by any law of necessity arising from the decrees or prescience of God. There are some who, in their zeal to oppose this doctrine, do not hesitate even to assert that God himself is the cause and origin of evil. Such men, if they are not to be looked upon as misguided rather than mischievous, should be ranked among the most abandoned of all blasphemers. An attempt to refute them would be nothing more than an argument to prove that God was not the evil spirit.

This exasperation against his opponents, this extreme readiness to see that they are making God into the Devil, while the point of distinction he wants to insist upon is really so very slight, makes evident that Milton himself was sensitive and anxious about the danger of finding that he too was worshipping the Devil. When Milton gets round to his own pronouncement on this point, in Chapter VIII, after listing the crucial texts, he is hardly able to do more than issue a rule of decorum:

> But though in these, as well as in many other passages of the Old and New Testaments, God distinctly declares that it is himself who impels the sinner to sin, who binds his understanding, and leads him into error; yet, on account of the infinite holiness of the Deity, it is not allowable to consider him as in the smallest instance the author of sin.

What first struck me, when I began to nose about in the English translation of the *De Doctrina*, rather belatedly, was that its tone is very unlike what the learned critics who summarize it had led me to expect. But maybe, I thought, having no judgement of Latin style, this is only a result of translation; the work was done by Sumner, later an Anglican bishop, who must have been working fairly rapidly; it was printed (and reviewed by Macaulay) in 1825, two years after the Latin text had been discovered. One can imagine a translator making it sound like Gibbon, partly because that was an easy formula but also through feeling a certain impatience with this heretic. But the following passage, frovm Chapter VII, 'Of the Creation', another discussion of the effects of the Fall, seemed to me enough to refute the suspicion; it rises above the variations of tone available to a translator:

> But, it is contended, God does not create souls impure, but only impaired in their nature, and destitute of original righteousness; I answer that to create pure souls, destitute of original righteousness,—to send them into contaminated and corrupt bodies,—to deliver them up in their innocence and helplessness to the prison house of the body, as to an enemy, with understanding blinded and with will enslaved,—in other words, wholly deprived of sufficient strength for resisting the vicious propensities of the body—to create souls thus circumstanced, would argue as much injustice, as to have created them impure would have argued impurity; it would have argued as much injustice, as to have created the first man Adam himself impaired in his nature, and destitute of original righteousness.

Surely, in the face of this burning sense of the injustice of God, which Milton only just manages to drag into line, it was rather absurd of C. S. Lewis to say that nobody had ever doubted Milton's account of the Fall until the Romantics made rebellion fashionable. A sympathetic reader of Milton's prose is accustomed to feel that he writes like a lawyer or a politician, concerned to convince his reader by any argument which would serve, though really more humane or enlightened arguments are what have made Milton himself choose the side he is arguing on. But in discussing the justice of God Milton admits that the conscience of every decent man is against what he has to maintain; there is an 'outcry' against it; but what he has found in the Bible is the horrible truth about the justice of God, and men had much better learn to face it.

I shall end these quotations from the *De Doctrina* with an example which seems to me coldly hair-raising, though Sewell does not appear to find it so, and perhaps Milton did not either. In Chapter XVI, 'Of the Ministry of Redemption', the section *By Payment of the Required Price* consisted of a list of texts and then one sentence claiming that they refute any Socinian view, that is, any theory that

Christ died not to pay for us but merely to set us an example to follow. The idea of payment is indeed deeply embedded in the system, as we too are paying all the time for Adam; what Satan reaches as rock-bottom, after abandoning his suspicion that God is a usurper, is that he could not in any case submit to a God who is a usurer. Some while after writing this section, Milton must have told his secretary to read it out to him, and then he dictated one further Latin sentence:

> At the time I confess myself unable to perceive how those who consider the Son of the same essence with the Father can explain either his incarnation or his satisfaction.

Maybe the shock comes partly from putting the sentence into English; the English word *satisfaction* has its own suggestions beside the central achievement of the Christ, 'a full oblation, remission and satisfaction for the sins of the whole world'. But these seem to me to act as a just satire. What Milton is thinking has to be: 'God couldn't have been satisfied by torturing himself to death, not if I know God; you could never have bought him off with that money; he could only have been satisfied by torturing somebody else to death.' Until I tried to follow the mind of Milton, I did not realize why the doctrine of the Trinity had been considered so important. Surely, if you regard God the Father as Milton had come to do here, he cannot possibly be justified. Milton when he embarked upon his epic was exactly in the position of the Satan he presents, overwhelmingly stubborn and gallant but defending a cause inherently hopeless from the start.

It is a difficult matter to try to sum up. The quotations I think make clear that Milton only just managed, after spiritual wrestling and the introduction of a certain amount of heresy, to reconcile his conscience or keep his temper with his God. When he says that the Holy Spirit dictated the poem to him, we can readily believe that, as the problems at issue had been gone over so long and anxiously, it was by a fairly direct process that the blind man at once invented and learned by heart a whole paragraph, commonly at night, and then waited as he said to be 'milked' of it; what is surprising is that the parts of the narrative fit together as well as they do. Even so, it is clear that he could have recognized the more alarming aspects of the narrative, merely by switching his attention; and his character makes him unlikely not to have recognized them. I should think that, with his usual nerve, he just refused to be rattled. Perhaps the main point is that when composing he felt like a defending counsel; such a man is positively wanted to realize at what points his client's case is weak, and he does not feel personally disgraced if his client still loses after he has gone as far as he can. Adding a little human interest to the admittedly tricky client God, by emphasizing his care to recover the reputation of his son, and giving a glimpse of the deeper side of his nature which makes him prepare for his latter end, is about all that can be done to swing the jury when the facts of the case are so little in dispute. On the other hand, when he made the case as strong as he could for Satan, Eve and Adam, he somehow did not mind driving home the injustice of God, because God was not at the moment his client. This picture is very inadequate because the problems about God are never out of sight in the poem; but still, being such a good advocate was what made the poetry so dramatic and in a way so broad. He understood how all contemporary sects would react to the words and situations he arranged for God, or the contradictions with which he had himself wrestled; it seems fair to add, he knew what he could get away with in the poem, even when it was necessarily very dickey. Though apparently isolated, he thus became an echoing-chamber for the whole mind of his period. The fact that he went on to make out a strong case for Delilah, even though in a narrower and fiercer frame of mind, proves I think that the moral generosity of *Paradise Lost* is not due to accident, muddle-headedness or split personality.

* * *

FRANK KERMODE

Adam Unparadised†

* * *

We may conclude that there is reason to suppose that we shall miss the force of Milton's poem if we assume that he was strictly limited by the *naïveté* of his theme or the inerrancy of its biblical expression. His method is to affect the senses of his audience and not its reason directly. He could not have hoped for total control over the affective power of the poem, for that is not consistent with the nature of poetry; and in this particular poem the material is common property, so that there must be many aspects of it which interest other people and not Milton, yet cannot be excluded. The original myth is a myth of total explanation, and therefore infinitely explicable; the poet can only say some of the things about it but the rest of it is still in men's minds, or indeed below them—Joyce's umbilical telephone line to Edenville. It is not of course doubted that Milton does offer interpretations, that he gets at the reader in many ways; the theology of Book iii, for example, is made to sound very

† From *The Living Milton: Essays by Various Hands*, collected and edited by Frank Kermode (London, Routledge & Kegan Paul Ltd., 1960), pp. 98–106, 109–23. Reprinted by permission of the publisher. The author's footnotes have been renumbered.

dogmatic, though only to prevent irrelevant speculation; and we are always being told the proper way to think about Satan. As well as presenting the human predicament the poet suggests ways of understanding and accepting it. It should even be admitted that the general design of the poem is governed by this double purpose of presentation and interpretation; and that not only in the strategic theologizing of the third book and the loaded education of Adam between Books iv and ix. For although it is commonly said that Milton, on the ancient epic pattern, proceeds *in medias res*, he in fact strikes into his subject nothing like so near the middle as Virgil and Homer; he starts not in the Garden but with the fall of the angels, which is why some schoolchildren, having read Books i and ii, go through life thinking it was Satan who lost paradise. The reason for this, one guesses, is that Milton wanted us to think of events in this order: the Fall from heaven, the Fall from Paradise, and finally the effect of the Fall in the life of humanity in general, just in the manner of Ignatian meditation on these subjects.[1] But it is important that we should not allow considerations of this sort to lead to a conviction that there is at all times a design upon us. So deceived, we can easily miss something far more obvious and important to the structure of the poem: namely, that it is based on a series of massive antitheses, or if you like huge structural pseudo-rhymes, and the central pseudo-rhyme is *delight/woe*. The delight and woe are here and now, which is the real point of all the squeezing together of the time-sequence that Milton carries on in his similes, in upsetting allusions to clerical corruption, in using expressions like 'never since created man' or 'since mute'; in a hundred other ways, some of which I shall discuss later. The poem is absolutely contemporary, and its subject is human experience symbolized in this basic myth, and here made relevant in a manner not so different from that to which our own century has accustomed us.

The Themes

Miss Rosemond Tuve, in her magnificent and too brief book, has persuasively expounded Milton's treatment in the minor poems of certain great central themes. They lie at the heart of each poem and govern its secondary characteristics of imagery and diction; given the theme, the poet thinks in the figures appropriate to it, and in every case the theme and the figures have a long and rich history. 'The subject of *L'Allegro* is every man's Mirth, our Mirth, the very Grace herself with all she can include';[2] the *Hymn on the Morning of Christ's Nativity* proliferates images of harmony because

1. See for example *The Sermons and Devotional Writings of Gerard Manley Hopkins*, ed. C. Devlin (1959), pp. 131 ff.

2. *Images and Themes in Five Poems by Milton* (1957), p. 20.

its theme is the Incarnation. I now take a step of which Miss Tuve would probably not approve, and add that beneath these figures and themes there is Milton's profound and personal devotion to an even more radical topic, potentially coextensive with all human experience: the loss of Eden. In the *Hymn* there is a moment of peace and harmony in history—the 'Augustan peace', which looks back to human wholeness and incorruption, as well as forward to a time when, after generations of human anguish, the original harmony will be restored. The same moment of stillness, poised between past and future, is there in 'At a Solemn Musick', for music remembers as well as prefigures. In *Comus* too there is presented that moment of harmony, of reunion and restitution, that prefigures the final end, and in *Comus* as in the others there is an emphasis on the long continuance of grief and suffering; for in the much misunderstood Epilogue Adonis is still not cured of his wound and Venus 'sadly sits.' Only in the future will Cupid be united with Psyche and the twins of Paradise, Youth and Joy, be born. *Lycidas* tells of disorder, corruption, false glory as incident to life here and now, with order, health, and the perfect witness of God to come. All of them speak of something that is gone.

Paradise Lost deals most directly with this basic theme, the recognition of lost possibilities of joy, order, health, the contrast between what we can imagine as human and what is so here and now; the sensuous import of the myth of the lost Eden. To embody this theme is the main business of *Paradise Lost*; thus will life be displayed in some great symbolic attitude and not by the poet's explanations of the how and the why. His first task is to get clear the human experience of the potency of delight, and its necessary frustration, and if he cannot do that the poem will fail no matter what is added of morality, theology or history.

My difficulty in establishing this point is that some will think it too obvious to be thus laboured, and others will think it in need of much more elaborate defence. What is rare is to find people who read *Paradise Lost* as if it were true that the power of joy and its loss is its theme; and though it is true that for certain well-known and important reasons Milton's poem is not accessible to the same methods of reading as Romantic literature, it is also true that this is the theme of *The Prelude*, and that we can do some harm by insisting too strongly upon differences at the expense of profound similarities. Anyway, I think I can make my point in a somewhat different way by a reference to Bentley,[3] and in particular to his observations on the last lines of *Paradise Lost*, stale as this subject may seem.

Adam, hearing Michael's promise of a time when 'Earth/Shall all be Paradise, far happier place/Than this of *Eden*' xii. 463–65 is

---

3. Richard Bentley, whose edition of *Paradise Lost* was published in 1732 [*Editor*].

'replete with joy and wonder' (468) and replies with the famous
cry of *felix culpa*:

> full of doubt I stand,
> Whether I should repent me now of sin
> By mee done and occasiond, or rejoice
> Much more, that much more good thereof shall spring . . .
>
> (473–76)

Michael says that the Comforter will watch over and arm the faith-
ful; Adam, benefiting by Michael's foretelling of the future (in
which 'time stands fixt' as it does in the poem) has now all possible
wisdom (575–76); and Eve is well content with her lot. And thus
matters stand when Eden is closed, and Adam and Eve move away

> The World was all before them, where to choose
> Thir place of rest, and Providence thir guide:
> They hand in hand with wandring steps and slow,
> Through *Eden* took thir solitarie way.
>
> (xii. 646–49)

'Why' asks Bentley, 'does this distich dismiss our first parents in
anguish, and the reader in melancholy? And how can the expres-
sion be justified, *with wandring steps and slow? Why wandring?*
Erratick steps? Very improper, when, in the line before, they were
guided by Providence. And why slow? even when Eve has professed
her readiness and alacrity for the journey:

> but now lead on;
> In me is no delay.

And why their *solitarie way?* All words to represent a sorrowful
parting? when even their former walks in Paradise were as solitary
as their way now; there being nobody besides them two both here
and there. Shall I therefore, after so many prior presumptions,
presume at last to offer a distich, as close as may be to the author's
words, and *entirely agreeable to his scheme?*

> Then hand in hand with *social* steps their way
> Through Eden took, *with heavenly comfort cheer'd.'*

Bentley assumes that he has exact knowledge of Milton's 'scheme',
and quarrels with the text for not fitting it. He seems to be forget-
ting God's instructions to Michael—'so send them forth, though
sorrowing, yet in peace' (xi. 117), and also Adam's knowledge of
the events leading up to the happy consummation; yet it remains
true that if Milton's 'scheme' was simply to show that everything
would come out right in the end, and that this should keenly please
both Adam and ourselves, Bentley is not at all silly here; or if he is,
so are more modern commentators who, supported by all that is
now known about the topic *felix culpa*, tend to read the poem in a

rather similar way though without actually rewriting it, by concentrating on Milton's intention, somewhat neglected in the past, to present this belated joy of Adam's as central to the whole poem. There is, of course, such an intention or 'scheme'; the mistake is to suppose that it is paramount. It is in fact subsidiary, *Paradise Lost* being a poem, to the less explicable theme of joy and woe, which has to be expressed in terms of the myth, as a contrast between the original justice of Paradise and the mess of history: between Paradise and Paradise Lost. The poem is tragic. If we regard it as a document in the history of ideas, ignoring what it does to our senses, we shall of course find ideas, as Bentley did, and conceivably the closing lines will seem out of true. But our disrespect for Bentley's Milton, and in this place particularly, is proof that the poem itself will prevent our doing this unless we are very stubborn or not very susceptible to poetry. The last lines of the poem are, we *feel*, exactly right, for all that Adam has cried out for pleasure; death denounced, he has lost his Original Joy. The tragedy is a matter of *fact*, of life as we feel it; the hope of restoration is a matter of faith, and faith is 'the substance of things hoped for, the evidence of things unseen'—a matter altogether less simple, sensuous, and passionate, altogether less primitive. We are reminded that 'the conception that man is mortal, by his nature and essence, seems to be entirely alien to mythical and primitive religious thought'.[4] In the poem we deplore the accidental loss of native immortality more than we can applaud its gracious restoration.

Adam Imparadised

One of the effects of mixing up Milton with the Authorized Version, and of intruding mistaken ideas of Puritanism into his verse, is that it can become very hard to see what is made absolutely plain: that for Milton the joy of Paradise is very much a matter of the senses. The Authorized Version says that 'the Lord God planted a garden' (Gen. ii. 8) and that he 'took the man and put him into the garden of Eden to dress it and keep it' (i. 15). But even in Gen. ii. 8 the Latin texts usually have *in paradisum voluptatis* 'into a paradise of pleasure'—this is the reading of the Vulgate currently in use. And the Latin version of ii. 15 gives in *paradiso deliciarum*. Milton's Paradise is that of the Latin version; in it, humanity without guilt is 'to all delight of human sense expos'd' (iv. 206), and he insists on this throughout. Studying the exegetical tradition on this point, Sister Mary Corcoran makes it plain that Milton pushes this sensuous pleasure much harder than his

4. E. Cassirer, *An Essay on Man* (1944), pp. 83–84.

'scheme' as Bentley and others might conceive it, required. For example, he rejected the strong tradition that the first marriage was not consummated until after the Fall, choosing to ignore the difficulty about children conceived before but born after it. For this there may be an historical explanation in the Puritan cult of married love; but it could not account for what has been called Milton's 'almost Dionysiac treatment'[5] of sexuality before the Fall; Sister Corcoran is sorry that she can't even quite believe the assertion that 'in those hearts/Love unlibidinous reignd (v. 449–50).[6]

In fact Milton went to great trouble to get this point firmly made; had he failed no amount of finesse in other places could have held the poem together; and it is therefore just as well that nothing in the poem is more beautifully achieved.

Why was innocent sexuality so important to Milton's poem? Why did he take on the task of presenting an Adam and an Eve unimaginably privileged in the matter of sensual gratification 'to all delight of human sense expos'd'? There is a hint of the answer in what I have written earlier about his view of the function of poetry. Believing as he did in the inseparability of matter and form, except by an act of intellectual abstraction, Milton could not allow a difference of kind between soul and body; God

> created all
> Such to perfection, one first matter all,
> Indu'd with various forms, various degrees
> Of substance, and in things that live, of life;
> But more refin'd, more spiritous and pure,
> As nearer to him plac't or nearer tending
> Each in thir several active Sphears assignd,
> Till body up to spirit work, in bounds
> Proportiond to each kind. So from the root
> Springs lighter the green stalk, from thence the leaves
> More aerie, last the bright consummat flowre
> Spirits odorous breathes: flowrs and thir fruit
> Mans mourishment, by gradual scale sublim'd
> To vital Spirits aspire, to animal,
> To intellectual, give both life and sense,
> Fancie and understanding, whence the Soule
> Reason receives, and reason is her being,
> Discursive or Intuitive; discourse
> Is Oftest yours, the latter most is ours . . .
>
> (v. 471–89)

An acceptance of Raphael's position involves, given the cosmic scale of the poem, a number of corollaries which Milton does not shirk. Matter, the medium of the senses, is continuous with spirit;

5. Harris Fletcher, *Milton's Rabbinical Readings* (1930), p. 185.   6. *Paradise Lost with reference to the Hexameral Background* (1945), pp. 76 ff.

or 'spirit, being the more excellent substance, virtually and essentially contains within itself the inferior one; as the spiritual and rational faculty contains the corporeal, that is, the sentient and vegetative faculty' (*De Doctrina Christiana* I. vii). It follows that the first matter is of God, and contains the potentiality of form;[7] so the body is not to be thought of in disjunction from the soul, of which 'rational', 'sensitive and 'vegetative' are merely aspects. Raphael accordingly goes out of his way to explain that the intuitive reason of the angels differs only in degree from the discursive reason of men; and Milton that there is materiality in angelic spirit. It is a consequence of this that part of Satan's sufferings lie in a deprivation of sensual pleasure. Milton's thought is penetrated by this doctrine, which, among other things, accounts for his view of the potency of poetry for good or ill; for poetry works through pleasure, by sensuous delight; it can help 'body up to spirit work' or it can create dangerous physiological disturbance. Obviously there could be no more extreme challenge to the power and virtue of his art than this: to require of it a representation of ecstatic sensual pleasure, a *voluptas* here and only here not associated with the possibility of evil: 'delight to Reason join'd' (ix. 243). The loves of Paradise must be an unimaginable joy to the senses, yet remain 'unlibidinous.'

If we were speaking of Milton rather than of his poem we might use this emphasis on materiality, on the dignity as well as the danger of sense, to support a conclusion similar to that of De Quincey in his account of Wordsworth: 'his intellectual passions were fervent and strong; but they rested upon a basis of preternatural animal sensibility diffused through *all* the animal passions (or appetites); and something of that will be found to hold of all poets who have been great by original force and power . . .' (De Quincey was thinking about Wordsworth's facial resemblance to Milton). And it would be consistent with such an account that Milton also had, like Wordsworth, a constant awareness of the dangers entailed by a powerful sensibility. This gives us the short reason why, when Milton is representing the enormous bliss of innocent sense, he does not do so by isolating it and presenting it straightforwardly. He sees that we must grasp it at best deviously; we understand joy as men partially deprived of it, with a strong eense of the woeful gap between the possible and the actual in physical pleasure. And Milton's prime device for ensuring that we should thus experience his Eden is a very sophisticated, perhaps a 'novelistic' one: we see all delight through the eyes of Satan.

* * *

7. See W. B. Hunter, Jr., 'Milton's Power of Matter', *Journal of the History of*   *Ideas*, xiii (1952), 551–62.

The Garden of Love

The degree of literary sophistication in Milton's treatment of the biblical account of Adam and Eve in Paradise is a reasonably accurate index of his whole attitude to what I have called the myth. I have already mentioned the incorporation of other literary and mythological gardens in this Eden; they are significant shadows of it. But the full exploration of the literary context of Milton's Paradise would be a very large inquiry, and here there is occasion only for a brief and tentative sketch of it, touching only upon what affects the present argument.

When Milton comes to treat of the inhabitants of the garden he plunges us at once into a dense literary context. The Bible says: 'And they were both naked, the man and his wife, and were not ashamed' (Genesis ii. 25). According to Milton, however, they were 'with native Honour clad/In naked Majestie' (289–90); and a little later he moralizes this:

> Nor those mysterious parts were then conceal'd,
> Then was not guiltie shame, dishonest shame
> Of Natures works: honor dishonorable,
> Sin-bred, how have ye troubl'd all mankind
> With shews instead, mere shows of seeming pure . . .
> (312–15)

This is in open allusion to a literary topic so often treated in Renaissance and seventeenth-century writing as to be unwieldy in its complexity. First one needs to understand the general primitivistic position which held that custom and honour were shabby modern expedients unnecessary in a Golden Age society, with all its corollaries in Renaissance 'naturalism'. Then one has to consider the extremely complex subject of literary gardens and their connection with the Earthly Paradise and the Golden Age, not only in Renaissance, but also in classical and mediaeval literature. Of the first of these I now say nothing. The easy way to approach the second is through the *locus classicus*, the chorus *O bella età de l'oro* in Tasso's *Aminta*. In the Golden Age, as in Eden, the earth bore fruit and flowers without the aid of man; the air was calm and there was eternal spring. Best of all, there was continual happiness because—in the translation of Henry Reynolds—

> Because that vain and ydle name,
> That couz'ning Idoll of unrest,
> Whom the madd vulgar first did raize,
> And call'd it Honour, whence it came
> To tyrannize o're ev'ry brest,

> Was not then suffred to molest
> Poore lovers hearts with new debate. . . .
> The Nymphes sate by their Paramours,
> Whispring love-sports, and dalliance. . . .

It was Honour that ruined Pleasure,

> And lewdly did instruct faire eyes
> They should be nyce, and scrupulous . . .
> (*Torquato Tassos Aminta Englisht*, 1628)

This is the Honour, a tyrant bred of custom and ignorant opinion, which inevitably intrudes into Milton's argument when he uses the word in forcible oxymoron, 'honor dishonorable.' But he is not using the idea as it came sometimes to be used in poetry Milton would have called dishonest; his Honour is 'sin-bred,' a pathetic subterfuge of the fallen, and not, as it is in libertine poems, an obstacle to sexual conquest that must yield to primitivist argument.[1] Of these ambiguities Milton must have been fully aware, since the poetry of his time contains many libertine attacks on Honour which imply that reason and 'native Honour' will be satisfied only by an absolute surrender to pleasure. Furthermore, many of these poems are set in gardens, and we should not overlook the difficulties Milton had to overcome before he could be reasonably satisfied that his garden of love was the right kind. The garden of love has a long history, and the topic nowadays called the *locus amoenus*[2] is as old as the garden of Alcinous in the *Odyssey*; the expression *locus amoenus* meant to Servius 'a place for lovemaking', and *amoenus* was derived by a false etymology from *amor*. This tradition, mingling with the continuous traditions of the Earthly Paradise, and modified by the allegorical skills of the Middle Ages, sometimes conformed and sometimes conflicted with the garden of Genesis; gardens could be the setting for all kinds of love, just as Venus herself could preside over all kinds of love and all kinds of gardens. Milton needed a *paradisus voluptatis*, but it must not be the same as a 'naturalist' or libertine garden, and it must not be connected with 'courtly love'—hence the disclaimers in II. 7 ff. and II. 769–70. Whatever the dishonest and sophisticate, or for that matter the falsely philosophical, might do with imaginary Edens, he was dealing with the thing itself, and must get innocent delight into it. So he uses these conventions, including the usual attack upon Honour, with his customary boldness, as if his treatment, though late, were the central one, and all the others mere shadows of his truth; the same method, in fact, as that used for pagan mythology. In Book ix, having risked all the difficulties

1. I have said part of my say about this in 'The Argument of Marvell's Garden', *Essays in Criticism*, ii (1952), 225–41.
2. See E. R. Curtius, *European Literature in the Latin Middle Ages* (1952), Cap.

10, especially pp. 195 ff. And among the growing literature on this theme, E. G. Kern, "The Gardens of the Decameron Cornice," *PMLA*, LXVI (1951), 505–23.

of his contrast between love unlibidinous and love libidinous by showing them both in the experience of Adam and Eve, he is able to enlarge upon the oxymoron 'honor dishonorable,' saying that

> innocence, that as a veil
> Had shaddowd them from knowing ill, was gon,
> Just confidence and native righteousness,
> And honour from about them. . . .
> (ix. 1054–57)

And Adam sees that the fruit of knowledge was bad, 'if this be to know,/Which leaves us naked thus, of Honour void' (1073–74); here the fig-leaves are assimilated to the literary tradition. As for *locus amoenus*, Milton also contrives to give two versions of it: in Book iv it is worked into the account of 'unreprov'd' lovemaking (see especially ii. 1034 ff.) as the scene of the first fallen act of love. Pope first saw another link between these two passages, and Douglas Bush has recently written upon this link a brilliant page of commentary:[3] each derives a good deal, and the manner of derivation is ironical, from a single episode in the *Iliad*, the lovemaking of Zeus and Hera in Book xiv.

So, erudite and delicate, yet so characteristic a device might find, among fit audience, someone to value it for itself; but Milton's object was to exploit, with what force all the literature in the world could lend, the contrast between the true delight of love and the fallacious delight which is a mere prelude to woe; between possible and actual human pleasure. And however complex the means, the end is simply to show Adam and Eve as actually enjoying what to us is a mere imagination, and then explain how they lost it, and what was then left. In this sense their simple experience contains the whole of ours, including that which we feel we might but know we cannot have; and in this sense they include us, they are what we are and what we imagine we might be. This inclusiveness is given remarkably concrete demonstration in lines so famous for their unidiomatic English that the reason for the distorted word-order has been overlooked:

> the lovliest pair
> That ever since in loves imbraces met,
> *Adam* the goodliest man of men since born
> His Sons, the fairest of her Daughters *Eve*.
> (iv. 321–24)

The syntax may be Greek, but the sense is English, and inclusiveness could hardly be more completely presented; Adam and Eve here literally include us all. The illogic of the expression serves the same end as the illogic of those mythological parallels inserted only to be

3. *Paradise Lost in our Time* (1948), pp. 105–6.

denied, or of those continuous reminders that the whole of history 'since created man' is somehow being enacted here and now in the garden. What must never be underestimated is the sheer absorbency of Milton's theme; everything will go into it, and find itself for the first time properly placed, completely explained. Todd[4] has a note on the passage (iv. 458 ff.) in which Milton adapts to the awakening of Eve Ovid's account of Narcissus first seeing himself in the pool: he cites one commentator who enlarges upon Milton's enormous improvement of Ovid's lines, and another who adds that 'we may apply to Milton on this occasion what Aristotle says of Homer, that he taught poets how to lie properly'. Lying properly about everything is a reasonable way of describing the poet's achievement in *Paradise Lost*, if a proper lie is one that includes the *terra incognita* of human desires, actual love and possible purity.

That is why we see Adam and Eve in the garden of love not directly, but through many glasses; and the darkest of these is the mind of Satan. He looks at his victims with passionate envy and even regret:

> Ah gentle pair, ye little think how nigh
> Your change approaches, when all these delights
> Will vanish and deliver ye to woe,
> More woe, the more your taste is now of joy;
> Happie, but for so happie ill secur'd
> Long to continue, and this high seat your Heav'n
> Ill fenc't for Heav'n to keep out such a foe
> As now is enterd.
>
> (iv. 366–73)

He is reluctant to harm them; he pleads necessity (Milton calls this 'The Tyrants plea' (394) and neatly gives it to Adam in x. 131 ff.). But what he must take away from them is *delight*, physical pleasure in innocence; his dwelling in Hell 'haply may not please/Like this fair Paradise, your sense' (iv. 378–79). They are to 'taste' something other than Joy; and one remembers how frequently, at critical moments, the word 'taste' occurs in *Paradise Lost*, from the second line on. The shadow of Satan falls most strikingly over the pleasures of the garden when he watches Adam and Eve making love. It is not merely that the absolutely innocent and joyous act is observed as through a peep-hole, as if the lovers had been tricked into a bawdy-house; Satan himself acquires some of the pathos of an old *voyeur*. Pursuing his equation of delight with innocence, Milton boldly hints that the fallen angel is sexually deprived. He has forfeited the unfallen delights of sense. There is, we are to learn, lovemaking in heaven, but not in hell; the price of warring against omnipotence is impotence.

4. H. J. Todd, whose edition of *The Poetical Works of John Milton* first ap- peared in 1801 [*Editor*].

> Sight hateful, sight tormenting! thus these two
> Imparadis't in one anothers arms
> The happier *Eden*, shall enjoy thir fill
> Of bliss on bliss, while I to Hell am thrust,
> Where neither joy nor love, but fierce desire,
> Among our other torments not the least,
> Still unfulfilld with pain of longing pines . . .
>
> (iv. 505–11)

Satan is so sure of their sexual joy that he anticipates later love poetry in making the body of the beloved a paradise in itself—his 'happier Eden' is not the same as that promised later to Adam (xii. 587)—and he uses a word, 'imparadis't' which was to have its place in the vocabulary of fallen love. But at this moment only Satan can feel desire without fulfilment, and Milton reminds us that he resembles in this fallen men; thus he actualizes the human contrast between innocence and experience, and between love and its counterfeits—the whole 'monstruosity of love', as Troilus calls it.

Milton, in short, provides an illogical blend of purity and impurity in the first delightful lovemaking. He does not present an isolated purity and then its contamination, as the narrative might seem to require, but interferes with this order just as he does with word-order, and for similar reasons. Not only does he show us the unfallen Adam and Eve in such a way that we can never think of their delight without thinking of its enemies; he also establishes such links between the fourth and ninth books that we can never think of his account of unfallen love without remembering the parallel passages on lust. It is here relevant to emphasize the unpraised brilliance of one of the linking devices, Milton's use of the theme of physiological perturbation. At the opening of Book iv Uriel observes that Satan is affected by unregulated passions, as the unfallen Adam and Eve cannot be; he is the first person on earth to experience this. But by the end of the Book he has established by an act of demonic possession that Eve is physiologically capable of such a disturbance (iv. 799 ff.; v. 9–11); and the effect of the Fall in Book ix can be measured by the degree to which the humours of the lovers are distempered by the fruit:

> Soon as the force of that fallacious Fruit,
> That with exhilerating vapour bland
> About thir spirits had playd, and inmost powers
> Made err, was now exhal'd, and grosser sleep
> Bred of unkindly fumes, with conscious dreams
> Encumberd, now had left them, up they rose
> As from unrest. . . .
>
> (ix. 1046–52)

We happen to know what Milton, as theologian, believed to be the significance of the eating of the fruit. He regarded the tree of the knowledge of good and evil as merely 'a pledge, as it were, and memorial of obedience.' The tasting of its fruit was an act that included all sins: 'it comprehended at once distrust in the divine veracity, and a proportionate credulity in the assurances of Satan; unbelief, ingratitude; disobedience; gluttony; in the man excessive uxoriousness, in the woman a want of proper regard for her husband, in both an insensibility to the welfare of their offspring, and that offspring the whole human race; parricide, theft, invasion of the rights of others, sacrilege, deceit, presumption in aspiring to divine attributes, fraud in the means employed to attain the object, pride, and arrogance' (*De Doctrina Christiana* I. xi, Sumner's translation). But none of this stemmed from the intoxicating power of the fruit; God was testing fidelity by forbidding 'an act of its own nature indifferent.' In other words Milton the poet establishes the theme of perturbation as a structural element in the poem, using it as an index of fallen nature, of the disaster brought upon Joy by Woe, by means which must have earned the disapproval of Milton the theologian, namely the attribution of intoxicating powers to the forbidden fruit. Joy and Woe in the poem take precedence over theological niceties; Milton's theology is in the *De Doctrina*, not in *Paradise Lost*.

Adam Unparadised

Joy and Woe, the shadow of one over the other, the passage from one to the other, are the basic topic of the poem. We turn now to Adam unparadised, to Joy permanently overshadowed by Woe, light by dark, nature by chaos, love by lust, fecundity by sterility. Death casts these shadows. It is not difficult to understand why a very intelligent Italian, reading *Paradise Lost* for the first time, should have complained to me that he had been curiously misled about its subject; for, he said, 'it is a poem about Death'.

> For who would lose
> Though full of pain, this intellectual being?
> (ii. 146–47)

Belial asks the question, as Claudio had done; it is a human reaction, and most of the time we do not relish the thought of being without 'sense and motion' (ii. 151); nor can we help it if this is to be called 'ignoble' (ii. 227). In the same book, Milton gives Death allegorical substance, if 'substance might be calld that shaddow seemd' (669); for it is all darkness and shapelessness, a 'Fantasm' (743), all lust and anger, its very name hideous (788). The only thing it resembles is Chaos, fully described in the same book; and it stands in relation to the order and delight of the human body as Chaos stands to Nature. So, when Satan moved out of Chaos into

Nature, he not only 'into Nature brought/Miserie' (vi. 267), but into Life brought Death, and into Light (which is always associated with order and organic growth) darkness. At the end of Book ii he at last, 'in a cursed hour' (1055), approaches the pendant world, having moved towards it from Hell through Chaos; and the whole movement of what might be called the *sensuous* logic of the poem so far—the fall into darkness and disorder, the return to light and order—is triumphantly halted at the great invocation to Light which opens Book iii. But the return is of course made with destructive intent. We see the happiness of a man acquainted with the notion of Death but having no real knowledge of it—'So neer grows Death to Life, what e're Death is,/Som dreadful thing no doubt' (iv. 425–26); and then, after the long interruption of Books v–viii, which represent the everything which stretched between life and death, we witness the crucial act from which the real knowledge of Death will spring, when Eve took the fruit, 'and knew not eating Death' (ix. 792). The syntax, once again, is Greek; but we fill it with our different and complementary English senses: 'she knew not that she was eating death'; 'she knew not Death even as she ate it'; 'although she was so bold as to eat Death for the sake of knowledge, she still did not know—indeed she did not even know what she had known before, namely that this was a sin'. Above all she *eats* Death, makes it a part of her formerly incorruptible body, and so explains the human sense of the possibility of incorruption, so tragically belied by fact. The function of Death in the poem is simple enough; it is 'to destroy, or unimmortal make/All kinds' (x. 611–12). There is, of course, the theological explanation to be considered, that the success of Death in this attempt is permissive; but in terms of the poem this is really no more than a piece of dogmatic cheering-up, and Milton, as usual, allows God himself to do the explaining (x. 616 ff.). From the human point of view, the intimation of unimmortality takes priority over the intellectual comfort of God's own theodicy, simply because a man can feel, and can feel the possibility of immortality blighted.

Milton saw the chance, in Book ix, of presenting very concretely the impact of Death on Life; and it would be hard to think of a fiction more completely achieved. The moment is of Eve's return to Adam, enormously ignorant and foolishly cunning, 'with Countnance blithe. . . . But in her Cheek distemper flushing glowd' (ix. 886–87). This flush is a token of unimmortality; and then, since 'all kinds' are to be affected, the roses fade and droop in Adam's welcoming garland. He sees that Eve is lost, 'Defac't, deflowrd, and now to Death devote' (901). He retreats into Eve's self-deception; but all is lost.

The emphasis here is on *all*; from the moment of eating the fruit to that of the descent of 'prevenient grace' (end of Book x and beginning of xi) Adam and Eve have lost everything, and are, without mitigation, to death devote. If one bears this steadily in mind the tenth book is a lot easier to understand; it seems often to be misread. Adam, 'in a troubl'd Sea of passion tost' (718) cries out 'O miserable of happie!' (720) and laments the end of the 'new glorious World' (721). He feels particularly the corruption of love:

> O voice once heard
> Delightfully, *Encrease and multiply*,
> Now death to hear!
>
> (729–31)

and sums up in a couplet using the familiar pseudo-rhyme: 'O fleeting joyes/Of Paradise, deare bought with lasting woes!' (741–42). He has knowledge of the contrast between then and now, but of nothing else. Deprived of Original Justice, he is now merely natural; hence the importance of remembering that he is here simply a human being in a situation that is also simple, and capable of being felt naturally, upon our pulses. Deprived as he is, Adam finds life 'inexplicable' (754); knowing nothing of the great official plan by which good will come of all this, his speculations are by the mere light of nature. Rajan made something of this in his explanation of how Milton got his heterodox theology into the poem— mortalism, for example, is not very tendentious if proffered as the opinion of a totally corrupt man.[5] But, much more important, Adam is here for the first time true kindred to the reader. The primary appeal of poetry is to the natural man; that is why it is called simple, sensuous and passionate. When Eve proposes that they should practise a difficult abstinence in order not to produce more candidates for unimmortality, or Adam considers suicide (x. 966 ff.) we should be less conscious of their errors than of their typicality. Whatever the mind may make of it, the sensitive body continues to feel the threat of unimmortality as an outrage:

> Why is life giv'n
> To be thus wrested from us? rather why
> Obtruded on us thus? who, if we knew
> What we receive, would either not accept
> Life offerd, or soon beg to lay it down,
> Glad to be so dismisst in peace.
>
> (xi. 502–7)

Michael's treatment of the same topic that the Duke inflicts upon Claudio in *Measure for Measure* can only strengthen such sentiments:

> thou must outlive
> Thy youth, thy strength, thy beauty, which will change

5. B. Rajan, *Paradise Lost and the Seventeenth Century Reader* (1947), Cap. ii.

To witherd weak and gray; thy Senses then
Obtuse, all taste of pleasure must forgo,
To what thou hast, and for the Air of youth
Hopeful and cheerful, in thy blood will reign
A melancholly damp of cold and dry
To weigh thy spirits down, and last consume
The Balm of Life.

(xi. 538–46)

Whatever the consolation offered by Death—no one would wish to
'eternize' a life so subject to distempers of every kind—it is not
pretended that this makes up for the loss of the 'two fair gifts . . .
Happiness/And Immortalitie' (xi. 56–8). Most criticism of the
verse of Book x and xi amounts to a complaint that it is lacking in
sensuousness; but this is founded on a misunderstanding of the
poem. *Paradise Lost* must be seen as a whole and whoever tries to
do this will see the propriety of this change of tone, this diminution
of *sense* in the texture of the verse.

A striking example of this propriety is the second of the formal
salutations to Eve, Adam's in xi. 158 ff. * * * Here Adam sees
that Eve is responsible not only for death but for the victory over
it; as she herself says, 'I who first brought Death on all, am grac't/
The source of life' (xi. 168–9). This paradox, considered as part of
the whole complex in which Milton places it, seems to me much
more central to the mood of the poem than the famous *felix culpa*,
because it is rooted in nature, and related to our habit of rejoicing
that life continues, in spite of death, from generation to generation.
Yet Adam is still under the shadow of death, and his restatement of
the theme Venus-Eve-Mary is very properly deprived of the sensu-
ous context provided for Raphael's salutation; and since the second
passage cannot but recall the first, we may be sure that this effect
was intended.

There is, indeed, another passage which strongly supports this
view of the centrality of the paradox of Eve as destroyer and giver
of life, and it has the same muted quality, casts the same shadow
over the power and delight of love. This is the curious vision of the
union between the sons of Seth and the daughters of Cain (xi.
556–636). The Scriptural warrant for this passage is extremely
slight, though there were precedents for Milton's version. Adam
rejoices to see these godly men united in love with fair women:

Such happy interview and fair event
Of love and youth not lost, Songs, Garlands, Flowrs
And charming Symphonies attachd the heart
Of *Adam*, soon enclin'd to admit delight,
The bent of Nature. . . .

(593–97)

And he thanks the angel, remarking that 'Here Nature seems ful-
filld in all her ends' (602). He is at once coldly corrected; these
women, against the evidence of Adam's own senses, are 'empty of all
good' (616), and nothing but ill comes from the 'Sons of God'
(622) yielding up all their virtue to them. Milton remembered how
much of Pandora there was in Eve. From women Adam is taught
to expect woe; but, more important, this change in the divine
arrangements means that the evidence of the senses, the testimony
of pleasure, is no longer a reliable guide:

> Judge not what is best
> By pleasure, though to Nature seeming meet . . .
> (603–4)

Paradise Lost is a poem about death, and about pleasure and its
impairment. It is not very surprising that generations of readers
failed to see the importance to Milton's 'scheme' of Adam's ex-
clamation upon a paradox which depends not upon the senses but
upon revelation; I mean the assurance that out of all this evil good
will come as testimony of a benevolent plan

> more wonderful
> Than that which by creation first brought forth
> Light out of darkness.
> (xii. 471–73)

The senses will not recognize that out of their own destruction will
come forth 'Joy and eternal Bliss' (xii. 551). In that line Milton
echoes the *Comus* Epilogue—Joy will come from the great wound
the senses have suffered, but it is a joy measured by what we have
had and lost. And the sense of loss is keener by far than the
apprehension of things unseen, the remote promise of restoration.
The old Eden we know, we can describe it, inlay it with a thousand
known flowers and compare it with a hundred other paradises;
throughout the whole history of loss and deprivation the poets have
reconstructed it with love. The new one may be called 'happier
farr', but poetry cannot say much more about it because the senses
do not know it. The paradise of Milton's poem is the lost, the only
true, paradise; we confuse ourselves, and with the same subtlety
confuse the 'simple' poem, if we believe otherwise.

Shelley spoke of Milton's 'bold neglect of a direct moral pur-
pose', and held this to be 'the most decisive proof of the supremacy
of Milton's genius'. 'He mingled, as it were', Shelley added, 'the
elements of human nature as colours upon a single pallet, and
arranged them in the composition of his great picture according to
the laws of epic truth; that is, according to the laws of that princi-
ple by which a series of actions of the external universe and of

intelligent and ethical beings is calculated to excite the sympathy of succeeding generations of mankind.'[6] This passage follows upon the famous observations on Satan, and is itself succeeded by and involved with a Shelleyan attack on Cristianity; and perhaps in consequence of this it has not been thought worth much attention except by those specialized opponents who contend for and against Satan in the hero-ass controversy. Theirs is an interesting quarrel, but its ground ought to be shifted; and in any case this is not the occasion to reopen it. But the remarks of Shelley I have quoted seem to be substantially true; so, rightly understood, do the much-anathematized remarks of Blake. I say 'substantially' because Milton himself would perhaps have argued that he accepted what responsibility he could for the moral effect of his poem, and that in any case he specifically desiderated a 'fit' audience, capable of making its own distinctions between moral good and evil. Yet in so far as poetry works through the pleasure it provides—a point upon which Milton and Shelley would agree—it must neglect 'a direct moral purpose'; and in so far as it deals with the passions of fallen man it has to do with Blake's hellish energies. And however much one may feel that they exaggerated the truth in applying it to Milton, one ought to be clear that Shelley and Blake were not simply proposing naughty Romantic paradoxes because they did not know enough. Indeed they show us a truth about *Paradise Lost* which later commentary, however learned, has made less and less accessible.

With these thoughts in my mind, I sometimes feel that the shift of attention necessary to make friends out of some of Milton's most potent modern enemies is in reality a very small one. However this may be, I want to end by citing Mr. Robert Graves; not because I have any hope of persuading him from his evidently and irrationally powerful distaste for Milton, but to give myself the pleasure of quoting one of his poems. It is called 'Pure Death', and in it Mr. Graves speculates on a theme that he might have found, superbly extended, in Milton's epic:

> We looked, we loved, and therewith instantly
> Death became terrible to you and me.
> By love we disenthralled our natural terror
> From every comfortable philosopher
> Or tall grey doctor of divinity:
> Death stood at last in his true rank and order.[7]

Milton gives us this perception, but 'according to the laws of epic truth'; which is to say, he exhibits life in a great symbolic attitude.

6. *A Defence of Poetry*, in *Shelley's Literary and Philosophical Criticism*, ed.   J. Shawcross (1909), p. 146.
7. *Collected Poems* (1959), p. 71.

ISABEL GAMBLE MAC CAFFREY

Paradise Lost as Myth†

To describe the meaning of a work of art completely is impossible, since the meaning is articulated only in the finished work itself. The best summary of a critical analysis is a re-reading of the work analyzed, so that the coarse discriminations of criticism may be replaced by the finer ones of art. Our first experience in reading a poem or a novel is a unified one; our final experience should be the same. The complexity of *Paradise Lost* is visible to anyone who has penetrated even slightly beneath the surface. What should be just as visible, but often is not, is its enormous simplicity. A myth seeks to circumscribe, depict, explain basic realities of human experience; and, in the end, the facts that we can call basic are few. Only they are hard to disinter from the welter of irrelevance and triviality that surrounds each of our lives. Milton's poem is, perhaps, most truly mythological in its comprehensiveness, in the boldness and breadth of its outlines, the relevance of its design to the fundamental issues of the soul's life. The images of *Paradise Lost* knit us, even in an urban and scientific age, to the world around us and to each other. They are the polar elements that go to compose our mixed unity and the systole and diastole that we observe in nature. Joined to the rhythmic alternation of opposites in *Paradise Lost*, as we have seen, is another pattern, almost as ancient: the threefold mythical scheme of loss, quest, and return.

The themes contained in these images—vast, resonant, living at the roots of human life—were perfectly congenial to Milton's genius. "No theme and no setting, other than that which he chose in *Paradise Lost*, could have given him such scope for the kind of imagery in which he excelled";[1] And, conversely, no other imagery could have expressed so completely the themes that had always compelled his imagination. If any poet ever *thought* in terms of myth, Milton did. Having said this, however, one must move on to qualifications. The myth, in the poem, has been assimilated into a larger design, which cannot be called mythical in any sense acceptable to modern theory; it becomes part of a moral pattern that is actually anti-mythical. In the course of this transformation, it has moved away from its early development in "primitive" or pre-Christian minds. It is to be ordered into a scale of values; to be turned into a religion, made to accommodate a theology.

---

† From *"Paradise Lost" as Myth* (Cambridge, Mass., Harvard University Press, 1959), pp. 207–14. Reprinted by permission of the publisher. The author's footnotes have been renumbered.
1. Eliot, "Milton," *Sewanee Review*, LVI (1948), 198.

One of the essential qualities of myth, in its original state, is its shiftiness. The personages and images of mythology are fluid, their meaning often ambiguous. The unity of the mythical world enforced a basic instability.

> The limits between the different spheres are not insurmountable barriers; they are fluent and fluctuating. There is no specific difference between the various realms of life. Nothing has a definite, invariable, static shape. By a sudden metamorphosis everything may be turned into everything. If there is any characteristic and outstanding feature of the mythical world, any law by which it is governed—it is this law of metamorphosis.[2]

It is hard to think of a paragraph that would be less pertinent to Milton's world in *Paradise Lost*. For, as Blake said, "In Eternity one Thing never Changes into another Thing. Each Identity is Eternal."[3] The myth of Milton's eternity is the product of a sensibility civilized, rational, and above all, moral. Held in the perspective of good and evil, these eternal identities take on clearer outlines; they have a definite, bounded quality unknown to their earliest incarnations. Milton's life was ruled by the conviction that moral choice, and the distinctions on which it is based, are not only possible but necessary. Freud has said that dreams—"the myths of the individual"—are characterized by "an absence of either-or."[4] The fluid boundaries of primitive myth do not lend themselves to the clear presentation of moral issues, where either-or is demanded, and they must therefore be fixed by a stiffening process either moral or aesthetic, or both.

From this it follows that myth, for Milton, was what we have seen it to be in examining *Paradise Lost:* a structural and epistemological principle, reflecting accurately, as he thought, the real nature of our first world. It was never, in itself, a moral principle, so that in the process of accommodating Milton's moral intuitions, it loses some of the qualities technically belonging to myth, in particular its magical, shape-shifting versatility. Milton was willing to admit that ambiguity exists; he would have agreed that good and evil may spring from the same root, that right and wrong are two directions confronting one force in the soul. The intimate union of opposed qualities in a single organism is necessary for life, as the Garden of *Paradise Lost* attests. Even in Hell, we see the distorted outlines of something heavenly, and Satan the ruined leader was "brighter once amidst the Host Of Angels" than the brightest star (vii. 132–33). Milton's picture of Chaos is the best evidence that he recognized genuine ambiguity when he saw it, and did not flinch

2. Cassirer, *Essay on Man*, p. 81.
3. *Vision of the Last Judgment, Poetry and Prose*, p. 640.
4. *Wit and Its Relation to the Uncon-* scious, *The Basic Writings of Sigmund Freud*, ed. A. A. Brill, The Modern Library (New York, 1938), p. 780.

from it. Chaos is tormented by real ambivalence, because it is still potential; "*Chance* governs all" because no end has been appointed to any of the warring elements. With the emergence of actuality striving toward an end, chance ceases to operate, and fulfilment in the ordained shape, or deviation from it, ensues. All things come of Chaos, perhaps; but once they have come, they are no longer the same. Milton never committed the genetic fallacy which claims that good and evil are rendered indistinguishable when they are seen to have a common source. They are often hard to distinguish, but it is our duty to do so.

In reading *Paradise Lost*, then, we have a sense at once of completeness and of limitation, and this is as Milton would have wished. The completeness comes from the poem's capacity to surround human life, so that every point on the circumference of our days is touched—even though, as Virginia Woolf thought, the private selfhood at the center may remain untouched, darkly unregarded. The limitation comes from Milton's insistence on portraying his mythical images as embodiments of definite moral qualities. The spirit that sees the denial of limit as the only path to full humanity will condemn the fixed boundaries of *Paradise Lost* as a crippling fault. Limit can also be regarded, however, as the condition of any complete individuality, in man or poem. "Nothing is complete which has no end," Aristotle observed; "and the end is a limit."[5] Whether *end* is taken as a physical boundary or as *telos*,[6] the implication is the same: completeness, by its very nature, involves limitation; to be *thus* is *not* to be otherwise. A systematic view of life is complete only when it has imposed certain defining boundaries. Belief in system and limit is part of a major strain in European thought, though it is a view alien to our own anarchic, confused society, where every creature is rootless or incomplete, by definition or desire. Milton's classicism is not a mere matter of allusions and similes; in the assertion of limit, he is most deeply classical. At the same time, he is most truly Christian, for human limitation is a corollary to the belief in a single infinity, God.

It is one of the axioms of modern "psychological" mythology that myths exist to show the way, through the example of the hero, to a full integration of the personality. Jung insists on the necessity of including opposites in any complete view of life, of exploring all four compass points, recognizing all four "faculties" in the psyche. The persistent theme of the night journey indicates that if we are to be whole, we must descend into the darkest places of the soul; completeness is hard-won.

5. *Physics*, 207a, trans. R. P. Hardie and R. K. Gaye, *The Basic Works of Aristotle*, ed. Richard McKeon (New York, 1951), p. 267.
6. I.e., the end proposed, or the purpose fulfilled [*Editor*].

Before he can cope with the multiplicity of life's forces, he must be introduced to the universal law of coexisting opposites. . . . For he does not yet understand that the pattern of existence is woven of antagonistic co-operation, alternations of ascendancy and decline, that it is built of bright *and* dark, day *and* night. . . . He must come to grips with the forces of evil, hence the necessity to follow the hidden road of the dolorous quest. His myth . . . is an allegory of self-completion through the mastery and assimilation of conflicting opposites.[7]

Milton would not have found this view wholly uncongenial or strange; he had formulated something like it himself, when he spoke of fallen man.

And perhaps this is that doom which Adam fell into of knowing good and evil; that is to say, of knowing good by evil. And therefore as the state of man now is; what wisdom can there be to choose, what continence to forbear, without the knowledge of evil? He that can apprehend and consider vice with all her baits and seeming pleasures, and yet abstain, and yet distinguish, and yet prefer that which is truly better, he is the true warfaring Christian. . . . Assuredly, we bring not innocence into the world, we bring impurity much rather; that which purifies us is trial, and trial is by what is contrary. That virtue therefore which is but a youngling in the contemplation of evil, . . . and rejects it, is but a blank virtue, not a pure; her whiteness is but an excremental whiteness. . . . Therefore the knowledge and survey of vice is in this world so necessary to the constituting of human virtue, and the scanning of error to the confirmation of truth.[8]

The myth, and the very composition of *Paradise Lost* itself, expresses a recognition, a "coming to grips with" evil. To follow the road of trials, to look on the face of darkness as well as the bright countenance of truth—this was part of Milton's creed. Divergence, as always, arises in the definition of the goal which this process is to achieve. Milton's end is "the constituting of human virtue," and the value of the dark journey hinges on the will, the power "to see and know, and yet abstain." Devoted to the goodness of knowledge as one of his first principles, Milton would have agreed that total self-knowledge is necessary; but necessary for self-discipline. And, since we are by nature impure, a full searching of the dark places was as essential for him as for any modern theorist. He insisted, however, that the descent should be voluntary and deliberate: Satan's knowledge of Hell is not a virtue in itself, though he tries to make it one by inventing the cult of "experience": he taunts Gabriel, as one who "knowst only good, But evil hast not tri'd" (iv.895–96). Any excursion into the depths must, moreover, be followed by a reascent into the celestial light. Man is not properly defined unless he stands partly in the light, because self-knowledge includes knowledge of our relation to God, which is positive as well as negative. For that, we must ascend as high as the reach of human reason will permit.

Though he included in *Paradise Lost*, therefore, the images of darkness, of underground caves, of hybrid monsters, and of Chaos, Milton arranged them in a pattern that was not their own, being orderly and moral. The mountain-shaped structure alone is evidence of his insistence on the reality of good and evil; in it, moral directions are given physical locations, and the physical itself becomes ethically meaningful. If we fail to see the moral structure of *Paradise Lost*, toward which the myth contributes as the most important of Milton's tools, then we have failed to understand the poem, precisely because moral issues are imbedded in its very texture. Neither images, nor structure, nor dramatic action can be accurately located and described unless they are placed within the ethical frame. If they are so placed, our experience in reading *Paradise Lost* can run parallel to Milton's experience in writing it, which he charted in the prologues to its various books. With him, we can explore the depths and heights, and feel that we have seen and known the span of human experience.

> Thee I re-visit now with bolder wing,
> Escap't the *Stygian* Pool, though long detain'd
> In that obscure sojourn, while in my flight
> Through utter and through middle darkness borne
> With other notes then to th' *Orphean* Lyre
> I sung of *Chaos* and *Eternal Night*,
> Taught by the Heav'nly Muse to venture down
> The dark descent, and up to reascend,
> Though hard and rare: thee I revisit safe,
> And feel thy sovran vital Lamp.   (iii. 13–21)

Milton did not pretend that understanding is anything but hard and rare; but as one of his contemporaries wrote, we cannot have the glory without the hardship. "For all noble things are as difficult as they are rare."

Earlier Criticism

VOLTAIRE

[Milton]†

Milton is the last in Europe who wrote an epic poem; for I waive all those whose attempts have been unsuccessful, my intention being not to descant on the many who have contended for the prize, but to speak only of the very few who have gained it in their respective countries.

* * *

If the difference of genius between nation and nation ever appeared in its full light, 'tis in Milton's *Paradise Lost*.

The French answer with a scornful smile when they are told there is in England an epic poem the subject whereof is the Devil fighting against God, and Adam and Eve eating an apple at the persuasion of a snake. As that topic hath afforded nothing among them but some lively lampoons, for which that nation is so famous, they cannot imagine it possible to build an epic poem upon the subject of their ballads. And indeed such an error ought to be excused, for if we consider with what freedom the politest part of mankind throughout all Europe, both Catholics and Protestants, are wont to ridicule in conversation those consecrated histories; nay, if those who have the highest respect for the mysteries of the Christian religion, and who are struck with awe at some parts of it, yet cannot forbear now and then making free with the Devil, the Serpent, the frailty of our first parents, the rib which Adam was robbed of, and the like; it seems a very hard task for a profane poet to endeavour to remove those shadows of ridicule, to reconcile together what is divine, and what looks absurd, and to command a respect that the sacred writers could hardly obtain from our frivolous minds.

What Milton so boldly undertook he performed with a superior strength of judgment, and with an imagination productive of beauties not dreamt of before him. The meanness (if there is any) of some parts of the subject is lost in the immensity of the poetical invention. There is something above the reach of human forces to

† From *An Essay Upon the Civil Wars of France. . . . And also Upon the Epick Poetry of the European Nations From Homer to Milton* (London, 1727), pp. 70–88.

have attempted the creation without bombast; to have described the gluttony and curiosity of a woman without flatness; to have brought probability and reason amidst the hurry of imaginary things belonging to another world, and as far remote from the limits of our notions as they are from our earth; in short, to force the reader to say, "If God, if the Angels, if Satan would speak, I believe they would speak as they do in Milton."

I have often admired how barren the subject appears, and how fruitful it grows under his hands.

The *Paradise Lost* is the only poem wherein are to be found in a perfect degree, that uniformity which satisfies the mind, and that variety which pleases the imagination—all its episodes being necessary lines which aim at the center of a perfect circle. Where is the nation who would not be pleased with the interview of Adam and the Angel? With the Mountain of Vision, with the bold strokes which make up the relentless, undaunted and sly character of Satan? But above all, with that sublime wisdom which Milton exerts whenever he dares to describe God and to make him speak? He seems indeed to draw the picture of the Almighty as like as human nature can reach to through the mortal dust in which we are clouded.

The heathens always, the Jews often, and our Christian priests sometimes, represent God as a tyrant infinitely powerful. But the God of Milton is always a creator, a father, and a judge; nor is his vengeance jarring with his mercy, nor his predeterminations repugnant to the liberty of man. These are the pictures which lift up indeed the soul of the reader. Milton in that point, as well as in many others, is as far above the ancient poets as the Christian religion is above the heathen fables.

But he hath especially an undisputable claim to the unanimous admiration of mankind when he descends from those high flights to the natural description of human things. It is observable that in all other poems love is represented as a vice; in Milton only 'tis a virtue. The pictures he draws of it are naked as the persons he speaks of, and as venerable. He removes with a chaste hand the veil which covers everywhere else the enjoyments of that passion. There is softness, tenderness, and warmth without lasciviousness; the poet transports himself and us into that state of innocent happiness in which Adam and Eve continued for a short time. He soars not above human, but above corrupt, nature; and as there is no instance of such love, there is none of such poetry.

* * *

To come to more essential points, and more liable to be debated: I dare affirm that the contrivance of the Pandemonium would have been entirely disapproved of by critics like Boileau, Racine, etc.

That seat built for the parliament of the devils seems very preposterous, since Satan has summoned them all together and harangued them just before in an ample field. The council was necessary, but where it was to be held 'twas very indifferent. The poet seems to delight in building his Pandemonium in Doric order, with frieze and cornice, and a roof of gold. Such a contrivance favors more of the wild fancy of our father Le Moine, than of the serious spirit of Milton.

But when afterwards the devils turn dwarfs to fill their places in the house, as if it was impracticable to build a room large enough to contain them in their natural size, it is an idle story, which would match the most extravagant tales. And to crown all, Satan and the chief lords preserving their own monstrous forms, while the rabble of the devils shrink into pigmies, heightens the ridicule of the whole contrivance to an inexpressible degree. Methinks the true criterion for discerning what is really ridiculous in an epic poem is to examine if the same thing would not fit exactly the mock-heroic. Then I dare say that nothing is so adapted to that ludicrous way of writing as the metamorphosis of the devils into dwarfs.

The fiction of Death and Sin seems to have in it some great beauties and many gross defects. In order to canvass this matter with order, we must first lay down that such shadowy beings as Death, Sin, Chaos are intolerable when they are not allegorical, for fiction is nothing but truth in disguise. It must be granted too that an allegory must be short, decent, and noble. For an allegory carried too far or too low is like a beautiful woman who wears always a mask. An allegory is a long metaphor, and to speak too long in metaphors must be tiresome because unnatural. This being premised, I must say that in general those fictions, those imaginary beings, are more aggreeable to the nature of Milton's poem than to any other, because he has but two natural persons for his actors, I mean Adam and Eve. A great part of the action lies in imaginary worlds, and must of course admit of imaginary beings.

Then, Sin springing out of the head of Satan seems a beautiful allegory of pride, which is looked upon as the first offense committed against God. But I question if Satan getting his daughter with child is an invention to be approved of. I am afraid that fiction is but a mere quibble; for if sin was of a masculine gender in English, as it is in all the other languages, that whole affair drops, and the fiction vanishes away. But suppose we are not so nice, and we allow Satan to be in love with Sin, because this word is made feminine in English (as death passes also for masculine), what a horrid and loathsome idea does Milton present to the mind in this fiction? Sin brings forth Death; this monster, inflamed with lust and rage, lies with his mother, as she had done with her father. From that new commerce, springs a swarm of serpents, which creep in and out of their mother's womb, and gnaw and tear the bowels they are born from.

Let such a picture be ever so beautifully drawn, let the allegory be ever so obvious, and so clear, still it will be intolerable on the account of its foulness. That complication of horrors, that mixture of incest, that heap of monsters, that loathsomeness so far fetched, cannot but shock a reader of delicate taste.

But what is more intolerable, there are parts in that fiction which, bearing no allegory at all, have no manner of excuse. There is no meaning in the communication between Death and Sin, 'tis distasteful without any purpose; or if any allegory lies under it, the filthy abomination of the thing is certainly more obvious than the allegory.

I see with admiration Sin, the portress of Hell, opening the gates of the Abyss, but unable to shut them again: that is really beautiful, because 'tis true. But what signifies Satan and Death quarrelling together, grinning at one another, and ready to fight?

* * *

Now the sublimest of all the fictions calls me to examine it. I mean the war in heaven. The Earl of Roscommon, and Mr. Addison (whose judgment seems either to guide, or to justify the opinion of his countrymen) admire chiefly that part of the poem. They bestow all the skill of their criticism, and the strength of their eloquence, to set off that favorite part. I may affirm that the very things they admire would not be tolerated by the French critics. The reader will perhaps see with pleasure in what consists so strange a difference and what may be the ground of it.

First, they would assert that a war in heaven, being an imaginary thing which lies out of the reach of our nature, should be contracted in two or three pages, rather than lengthened out into two books, because we are naturally impatient of removing from us the objects which are not adapted to our senses.

According to that rule they would maintain that 'tis an idle task to give the reader the full character of the leaders of that war, and to describe Raphael, Michael, Abdiel, Moloch, and Nisroch as Homer paints Ajax, Diomede, and Hector.

For what avails it to draw at length the picture of these beings, so utterly strangers to the reader, that he cannot be affected any way towards them? By the same reason, the long speeches of these imaginary warriors, either before the battle or in the middle of the action, their mutual insults, seem an injudicious imitation of Homer.

The aforesaid critics would not bear with the angels plucking up the mountains with their woods, their waters, and their rocks, and flinging them on the heads of their enemies. Such a contrivance (they would say) is the more puerile, the more it aims at greatness. Angels armed with mountains in heaven resemble too much the

Dipsodes in Rabelais, who wore an armour of Portland stone six foot thick.

The artillery seems of the same kind, yet more trifling, because more useless.

To what purpose are these engines brought in? Since they cannot wound the enemies, but only remove them from their places, and make them tumble down. Indeed (if the expression may be forgiven) 'tis to play at nine-pins. And the very thing which is so dreadfully great on earth, becomes very low and ridiculous in heaven.

* * *

I leave it to the readers to pronounce if these observations are right, or ill-grounded, and if they are carried too far. But in case these exceptions are just, the severest critic must however confess there are perfections enough in Milton to atone for all his defects.

I must beg leave to conclude this article on Milton with two observations. His hero (I mean Adam, his first personage) is unhappy. That demonstrates against all the critics that a very good poem may end unfortunately, in spite of all their pretended rules. Secondly, *Paradise Lost* ends completely. The thread of the fable is spun out to the last. Milton and Tasso have been careful of not stopping short and abruptly. The one does not abandon Adam and Eve till they are driven out of Eden. The other does not conclude before Jerusalem is taken. Homer and Virgil took a contrary way: the *Iliad* ends with the death of Hector, the *Aeneid* with that of Turnus. The tribe of commentators have upon that enacted a law that a house ought never to be finished, because Homer and Virgil did not complete their own; but if Homer had taken Troy, and Virgil married Lavinia to Aeneas, the critics would have laid down a rule just the contrary.

JONATHAN RICHARDSON

[Remarks on *Paradise Lost*]†

There is music in all language; the meanest peasant varies the sound as he speaks, though in that he is easily known from a gentleman. Sound is abundantly more expressive of the sense than is commonly imagined; animals who have not the use of words, that we understand at least, express their minds by sounds as well as by gestures, looks and actions; and we know their meaning as we know that of a man whose language we are absolute strangers to.

† From *Explanatory Notes and Remarks on Milton's 'Paradise Lost.'* "by Jonathan Richardson, Father and Son; with a Life of the Author and a Discourse on the Poem by Jonathan Richardson senior" (London, 1734), pp. cxxxix–clx.

Verse and prose have each their peculiar music, and whether one or the other, 'tis different according to the subject. All kinds of verse have sounds of their own; blank verse comes nearest to prose, and as the prose of some writers approaches verse, Milton's blank verse, that of *Paradise Lost*, has the beauty of both; it has the sweetness of measure, without stopping the voice at the end of the line, or anywhere else but as the sense requires; one verse runs into another, and the period concludes in any part of a line indifferently, and as if 'twas his choice 'tis very often not at the end of one or of a couplet, as is too frequent with those who write in rhyme. He has frequently eleven syllables in a verse, but 'tis rarely so unless those are no more in quantity than the ten of another.

> Fall'n Cherube, to be Weak is Miserable
> Doing or Suffering: but of This be Sure,

the *e* in the middle of the word *Suff'ring* must be melted in the pronunciation, as if written without it as here; and the two syllables made by that vowel, and the *a* that follows in *Miserable* are so short as to be equal to but one in any part of the line. So

> Assur'd me and still Assure: though what thou tell'st

here *me* and *and* are both so short as to be no more in quantity than if they were but one syllable. To read right requires some judgment, and some experience in Milton's manner who abounds more with these instances than most English poets; but, well read, the music of his verse is exceeding delicate and noble, though somewhat peculiar to himself; for he (as in his language) has profited himself of the Greeks and Latins; his ictus, or cadence, or music bears towards them, as he has formed himself upon their examples into something of his own, by his own ear, and which was a very musical, experienced, and judicious one.

* * *

Milton's language is English, but 'tis Milton's English; 'tis Latin, 'tis Greek English; not only the words, the phraseology, the transpositions, but the ancient idiom is seen in all he writes, so that a learned foreigner will think Milton the easiest to be understood of all the English writers. This peculiar English is most conspicuously seen in *Paradise Lost*, for this is the work which he long before intended should enrich and adorn his native tongue.

* * *

As his mind was rich in ideas, and in words of various languages to clothe them with, and as he had a vast fire, vigor and zeal of imagination, his style must necessarily distinguish itself; it did so; and even in his younger days, his juvenile poems, English, Latin, and Italian, have a brilliance not easily found elsewhere; nor is it not seen in his controversial prose works; *Paradise Lost* wants it not, in which there are specimens of all his kinds of styles, the tender, the fierce, the narrative, the reasoning, the lofty, &c. . . . There is something in every man's style whereby he is known, as by his voice, face, gait, &c. In Milton there is a certain vigor, whether versing or prosing, which will awaken attention be she never so drowsy, and then persuade her to be thankful though she was disturbed.

A reader of Milton must be always upon duty; he is surrounded with sense, it rises in every line, every word is to the purpose; there are no lazy intervals, all has been considered, and demands, and merits observation. Even in the best writers you sometimes find words and sentences which hang on so loosely you may blow 'em off; Milton's are all substance and weight; fewer would not have served the turn, and more would have been superfluous.

His silence has the same effect, not only that he leaves work for the imagination when he has entertained it, and furnished it with noble materials; but he expresses himself so concisely, employs words so sparingly, that whoever will possess his ideas must dig for them, and oftentimes pretty far below the surface. If this is called obscurity, let it be remembered 'tis such a one as is complaisant to the reader, not mistrusting his ability, care, diligence, or the candidness of his temper; not that vicious obscurity which proceeds from a muddled inaccurate head, not accustomed to clear, well separated and regularly ordered ideas, or from want of words and method and skill to convey them to another, from whence always arises uncertainty, ambiguity, and a sort of a moon-light prospect over a landscape at best not beautiful. Whereas, if a good writer is not understood, 'tis because his reader is unacquainted with or incapable of the subject, or will not submit to do the duty of a reader, which is to attend carefully to what he reads.

What Macrobius says of Virgil is applicable to Milton. "He keeps his eye fixed and intent upon Homer and emulates alike his greatness and simplicity, his readiness of speech and silent majesty." By *silent majesty* he seems to mean, with Longinus, "his leaving more to the imagination than is expressed."

And now 'tis of no great importance whether this be called an heroic or a divine poem, or only, as the author himself has called it in his title-page, a poem. What if it were a composition entirely new, and not reducible under any known denomination? But 'tis properly and strictly heroic, and such Milton intended it, as he has intimated in his short discourse concerning the kind of verse, and which is prefixed to it, as also in his entrance on the ninth book. And 'tis not his fault if there have been those who have not found a hero, or who he is. 'Tis Adam, Adam, the first, the representative of human race. He is the hero in this poem, though as in other heroic poems, superior beings are introduced. The business of it is to conduct man through variety of conditions of happiness and distress, all terminating in the utmost good: from a state of precarious innocence, through temptation, sin, repentance, and finally a secure recumbency upon and interest in the Supreme Good by the mediation of His Son. He is not such a hero as Achilles, Ulysses, Aeneas, Orlando, Godfrey, &c., all romantic worthies and incredible performers of fortunate, savage cruelties; he is one of a nobler kind, such as Milton chose to write of, and found he had a genius for the purpose. He is not such a conqueror as subdued armies or nations, or enemies in single combat, but his conquest was what justly gave heroic name to person and to poem. His hero was more than a conqueror through Him that loved us (as Rom. viii. 37).

This was declared to be the subject of the poem at the entrance on it, man's first disobedience and misery till our restoration to a more happy state. The design of it is also declared: 'twas to justify providence, all which is done. The moral we are also directed to, and this the poet has put into the mouth of an angel. Many moral reflections are excited throughout the whole work, but the great one is marked strongly (XII. 581 ff.): PIETY AND VIRTUE, ALL COMPRISED IN ONE WORD CHARITY, IS THE ONLY WAY TO HAPPINESS.

* * *

Poetry pleases by a peculiarity and majesty of style and language. Its numbers, its rhyme (if used, and skilfully) pleases as music does, and as painting, the imagery of things not only real but fictitious. For poetry is a sort of new creation, not only as it produces to the imagination what is unknown to nature (such as Harpies, Sphinxes, Gorgons, Hydras, Centaurs &c. or a sort of men as Shakespeare's Caliban, or the people of romances, men better or worse than ever were), but as it raises and embellishes (where 'tis possible) what is seen in nature, or related in history, and by so doing shows things otherwise than they really are, or ever were. And this not only agreeably entertains the mind ('tis a sort of new acquisition), but it helps us ofttimes to see real beauties, and which would else have passed unregarded and perhaps makes us fancy we see what in truth we do not.

There is another pleasure in poetry, oftener felt perhaps than placed to its account. 'Tis this. Much of art is essential to this kind of writing, and to observe the address and capacity of the poet is vastly pleasing. 'Tis so for example when we meet with a true poetical word, phrase or expression, an apt simile, a beautiful allusion, a noble sentiment, a sublime image, &c.

Besides the pleasure we have in these particulars, 'tis some addition to it when we reflect (as self-love will teach us) on our own ability to discover, and lift up ourselves to the perception of the brilliance of these beauties. And thus, as it were, become sharers in the honor of them. There is yet a further pleasure in thinking this is the work of our friend, our countryman, at least of one of our species. 'Tis true this kind of pleasure is to be had from prose, but not the degree.

* * *

If ever any book was truly poetical, if ever any abounded with poetry, 'tis *Paradise Lost*. What an expansion of facts from a small seed of history! What worlds are invented, what embellishments of nature upon what our senses present us with? Divine things are more nobly, more divinely represented to the imagination than by any other poem; a more beautiful idea is given of nature than any poet has pretended to: nature as just come out of the hand of God, in its virgin loveliness, glory, and purity. And the human race is shown, not as Homer's, more gigantic, more robust, more valiant, but without comparison more truly amiable, more so than by the pictures and statues of the greatest masters. And all these sublime ideas are conveyed to us in the most effectual and engaging manner. The mind of the reader is tempered and prepared by pleasure, 'tis drawn and allured, 'tis awakened and invigorated to receive such impressions as the poet intended to give it. It opens the fountains of knowledge, piety and virtue, and pours along full streams of peace, comfort, and joy to such as can penetrate the true sense of the writer and obediently listen to his song.

* * *

SAMUEL JOHNSON

[*Paradise Lost*]†

I am now to examine *Paradise Lost*; a poem, which, considered with respect to design, may claim the first place, and with respect to performance the second, among the productions of the human mind.

By the general consent of critics, the first praise of genius is due to the writer of an epic poem, as it requires an assemblage of all the powers which are singly sufficient for other compositions. Poetry is the art of uniting pleasure with truth, by calling imagination to the help of reason. Epic poetry undertakes to teach the most important truths by the most pleasing precepts, and therefore relates some great event in the most affecting manner. History must supply the writer with the rudiments of narration, which he must improve and exalt by a nobler art, animate by dramatic energy, and diversify by

† From "Milton," in *The Lives of the Most Eminent English Poets*, revised ed. (London, 1783). The footnotes for this selection are by the editor.

retrospection and anticipation; morality must teach him the exact bounds, and different shades, of vice and virtue: from policy, and the practice of life, he has to learn the discriminations of character, and the tendency of the passions, either single or combined; and physiology must supply him with illustrations and images. To put these materials to poetical use, is required an imagination capable of painting nature, and realizing fiction. Nor is he yet a poet till he has attained the whole extension of his language, distinguished all the delicacies of phrase, and all the colors of words, and learned to adjust their different sounds to all the varieties of metrical modulation.

Bossu[1] is of opinion that the poet's first work is to find a *moral*, which his fable is afterwards to illustrate and establish. This seems to have been the process only of Milton; the moral of other poems is incidental and consequent; in Milton's only it is essential and intrinsic. His purpose was the most useful and the most arduous; *to vindicate the ways of God to man*;[2] to shew the reasonableness of religion, and the necessity of obedience to the Divine Law.

To convey this moral there must be a *fable*, a narration artfully constructed, so as to excite curiosity, and surprise expectation. In this part of his work, Milton must be confessed to have equalled every other poet. He has involved in his account of the Fall of Man the events which preceded, and those that were to follow it: he has interwoven the whole system of theology with such propriety, that every part appears to be necessary; and scarcely any recital is wished shorter for the sake of quickening the progress of the main action.

The subject of an epic poem is naturally an event of great importance. That of Milton is not the destruction of a city, the conduct of a colony, or the foundation of an empire. His subject is the fate of worlds, the revolutions of heaven and of earth; rebellion against the Supreme King, raised by the highest order of created beings; the overthrow of their host, and the punishment of their crime; the creation of a new race of reasonable creatures; their original happiness and innocence, their forfeiture of immortality, and their restoration to hope and peace.

Great events can be hastened or retarded only by persons of elevated dignity. Before the greatness displayed in Milton's poem, all other greatness shrinks away. The weakest of his agents are the highest and noblest of human beings, the original parents of mankind; with whose actions the elements consented; on whose rectitude, or deviation of will, depended the state of terrestrial nature, and the condition of all the future inhabitants of the globe.

Of the other agents in the poem, the chief are such as it is

1. René le Bossu, author of *Traité du Poème Epique* (1675). 2. Johnson confuses Milton's line with Pope's, in *Essay on Man*, I.16.

irreverence to name on slight occasions. The rest were lower powers;

> ——of which the least could wield
> Those elements, and arm him with the force
> Of all their regions.

powers, which only the control of Omnipotence restrains from laying creation waste, and filling the vast expanse of space with ruin and confusion. To display the motives and actions of beings thus superior, so far as human reason can examine them, or human imagination represent them, is the task which this mighty poet has undertaken and performed.

In the examination of epic poems much speculation is commonly employed upon the *characters*. The characters in the *Paradise Lost*, which admit of examination, are those of angels and of man; of angels good and evil; of man in his innocent and sinful state.

Among the angels, the virtue of Raphael is mild and placid, of easy condescension and free communication; that of Michael is regal and lofty, and, as may seem, attentive to the dignity of his own nature. Abdiel and Gabriel appear occasionally, and act as every incident requires; the solitary fidelity of Abdiel is very amiably painted.

Of the evil angels the characters are more diversified. To Satan, as Addison observes,[3] such sentiments are given as suit *the most exalted and most depraved being*. Milton has been censured, by Clark,[4] for the impiety which sometimes breaks from Satan's mouth. For there are thoughts, as he justly remarks, which no observation of character can justify, because no good man would willingly permit them to pass, however transiently, through his own mind. To make Satan speak as a rebel, without any such expressions as might taint the reader's imagination, was indeed one of the great difficulties in Milton's undertaking, and I cannot but think that he has extricated himself with great happiness. There is in Satan's speeches little that can give pain to a pious ear. The language of rebellion cannot be the same with that of obedience. The malignity of Satan foams in haughtiness and obstinacy; but his expressions are commonly general, and no otherwise offensive than as they are wicked.

The other chiefs of the celestial rebellion are very judiciously discriminated in the first and second books; and the ferocious character of Moloch appears, both in the battle and the council, with exact consistency.

To Adam and to Eve are given, during their innocence, such sentiments as innocence can generate and utter. Their love is pure

3. Joseph Addison's essays on *PL* appeared weekly in the *Spectator* from Jan. 5 to May 3, 1712. Johnson's reference here is to the essay of Feb. 16, 1712.
4. John Clarke, author of *An Essay upon Study* (1731).

benevolence and mutual veneration; their repasts are without luxury, and their diligence without toil. Their addresses to their Maker have little more than the voice of admiration and gratitude. Fruition left them nothing to ask, and Innocence left them nothing to fear.

But with guilt enter distrust and discord, mutual accusation, and stubborn self-defense; they regard each other with alienated minds, and dread their Creator as the avenger of their transgression. At last they seek shelter in his mercy, soften to repentance, and melt in supplication. Both before and after the Fall, the superiority of Adam is diligently sustained.

Of the *probable* and the *marvellous*, two parts of a vulgar epic poem, which immerge the critic in deep consideration, the *Paradise Lost* requires little to be said. It contains the history of a miracle, of Creation and Redemption; it displays the power and the mercy of the Supreme Being; the probable therefore is marvellous, and the marvellous is probable. The substance of the narrative is truth; and as truth allows no choice, it is, like necessity, superior to rule. To the accidental or adventitious parts, as to everything human, some slight exceptions may be made. But the main fabric is immovably supported.

It is justly remarked by Addison, that this poem has, by the nature of its subject, the advantage above all others, that it is universally and perpetually interesting. All mankind will, through all ages, bear the same relation to Adam and to Eve, and must partake of that good and evil which extend to themselves.

Of the *machinery*, so called from θεὸς ἀπὸ μηχανῆς,[5] by which is meant the occasional interposition of supernatural power, another fertile topic of critical remarks, here is no room to speak, because everything is done under the immediate and visible direction of Heaven; but the rule is so far observed, that no part of the action could have been accomplished by any other means.

Of *episodes*, I think there are only two, contained in Raphael's relation of the war in heaven, and Michael's prophetic account of the changes to happen in this world. Both are closely connected with the great action; one was necessary to Adam as a warning, the other as a consolation.

To the completeness or *integrity* of the design nothing can be objected; it has distinctly and clearly what Aristotle requires,[6] a beginning, a middle, and an end. There is perhaps no poem, of the same length, from which so little can be taken without apparent mutilation. Here are no funeral games, nor is there any long description of a shield. The short digressions at the beginning of the

5. *Deus ex machina*, or a god lowered onto the stage by means of a theatrical machine.

6. Like Addison before him, Johnson referred to Aristotle's *Poetics* for topics of criticism.

third, seventh, and ninth books, might doubtless be spared; but superfluities so beautiful, who would take away? or who does not wish that the author of the *Iliad* had gratified succeeding ages with a little knowledge of himself? Perhaps no passages are more frequently or more attentively read than those extrinsic paragraphs; and since the end of poetry is pleasure, that cannot be unpoetical with which all are pleased.

The questions, whether the action of the poem be strictly *one*, whether the poem can be properly termed *heroic*, and who is the hero, are raised by such readers as draw their principles of judgment rather from books than from reason. Milton, though he intituled *Paradise Lost* only a *poem*, yet calls it himself *heroic song*. Dryden,[7] petulantly and indecently, denies the heroism of Adam, because he was overcome; but there is no reason why the hero should not be unfortunate, except established practice, since success and virtue do not go necessarily together. Cato is the hero of Lucan;[8] but Lucan's authority will not be suffered by Quintilian to decide.[9] However, if success be necessary, Adam's deceiver was at last crushed; Adam was restored to his Maker's favor, and therefore may securely resume his human rank.

After the scheme and fabric of the poem, must be considered its component parts, the sentiments and the diction.

The *sentiments*, as expressive of manners, or appropriated to characters, are, for the greater part, unexceptionably just.

Splendid passages, containing lessons of morality, or precepts of prudence, occur seldom. Such is the original formation of this poem that, as it admits no human manners till the Fall, it can give little assistance to human conduct. Its end is to raise the thoughts above sublunary cares or pleasures. Yet the praise of that fortitude, with which Abdiel maintained his singularity of virtue against the scorn of multitudes, may be accommodated to all times; and Raphael's reproof of Adam's curiosity after the planetary motions, with the answer returned by Adam, may be confidently opposed to any rule of life which any poet has delivered.

The thoughts which are occasionally called forth in the progress, are such as could only be produced by an imagination in the highest degree fervid and active, to which materials were supplied by incessant study and unlimited curiosity. The heat of Milton's mind might be said to sublimate his learning, to throw off into his work the spirit of science, unmingled with its grosser parts.

He had considered creation in its whole extent, and his descriptions are therefore learned. He had accustomed his imagination to

---

7. John Dryden, in "A Discourse Concerning the Original and Progress of Satire" (1693).
8. I.e., of Lucan's epic *Pharsalia* (1st century A.D.).

9. A contemporary of Lucan, whose work on rhetoric and literary criticism was well known by Milton as well as Johnson and later English critics.

unrestrained indulgence, and his conceptions therefore were extensive. The characteristic quality of his poem is sublimity. He sometimes descends to the elegant, but his element is the great. He can occasionally invest himself with grace; but his natural port is gigantic loftiness. He can please when pleasure is required; but it is his peculiar power to astonish.

He seems to have been well acquainted with his own genius, and to know what it was that nature had bestowed upon him more bountifully than upon others; the power of displaying the vast, illuminating the splendid, enforcing the awful, darkening the gloomy, and aggravating the dreadful: he therefore chose a subject on which too much could not be said, on which he might tire his fancy without the censure of extravagance.

The appearances of nature, and the occurrences of life, did not satiate his appetite of greatness. To paint things as they are, requires a minute attention, and employs the memory rather than the fancy. Milton's delight was to sport in the wide regions of possibility; reality was a scene too narrow for his mind. He sent his faculties out upon discovery, into worlds where only imagination can travel, and delighted to form new modes of existence, and furnish sentiment and action to superior beings, to trace the counsels of hell, or accompany the choirs of heaven.

But he could not be always in other worlds: he must sometimes revisit earth, and tell of things visible and known. When he cannot raise wonder by the sublimity of his mind, he gives delight by its fertility.

Whatever be his subject, he never fails to fill the imagination. But his images and descriptions of the scenes or operations of nature do not seem to be always copied from original form, nor to have the freshness, raciness, and energy of immediate observation. He saw nature, as Dryden expresses it, *through the spectacles of books;*[1] and on most occasions calls learning to his assistance. The garden of Eden brings to his mind the vale of *Enna*, where Proserpine was gathering flowers. Satan makes his way through fighting elements, like *Argo* between the *Cyanean* rocks, or *Ulysses* between the two *Sicilian* whirlpools, when he shunned *Charybdis* on the *larboard*. The mythological allusions have been justly censured, as not being always used with notice of their vanity; but they contribute variety to the narration, and produce an alternate exercise of the memory and the fancy.

His similies are less numerous, and more various, than those of his predecessors. But he does not confine himself within the limits of rigorous comparison: his great excellence is amplitude, and he expands the adventitious image beyond the dimensions which the

1. *An Essay of Dramatic Poetry* (1668):   of books to read nature."
Shakespeare "needed not the spectacles

occasion required. Thus, comparing the shield of Satan to the orb of the moon, he crowds the imagination with the discovery of the telescope, and all the wonders which the telescope discovers.

Of his moral sentiments it is hardly praise to affirm that they excel those of all other poets; for this superiority he was indebted to his acquaintance with the sacred writings. The ancient epic poets, wanting the light of Revelation, were very unskilful teachers of virtue: their principal characters may be great, but they are not amiable. The reader may rise from their works with a greater degree of active or passive fortitude, and sometimes of prudence; but he will be able to carry away few precepts of justice, and none of mercy.

From the Italian writers it appears, that the advantages of even Christian knowledge may be possessed in vain. Ariosto's pravity is generally known; and though the *Deliverance of Jerusalem* may be considered as a sacred subject, the poet has been very sparing of moral instruction.

In Milton every line breathes sanctity of thought, and purity of manners, except when the train of the narration requires the introduction of the rebellious spirits; and even they are compelled to acknowledge their subjection to God, in such a manner as excites reverence and confirms piety.

Of human beings there are but two; but those two are the parents of mankind, venerable before their fall for dignity and innocence, and amiable after it for repentance and submission. In their first state their affection is tender without weakness, and their piety sublime without presumption. When they have sinned, they show how discord begins in natural frailty, and how it ought to cease in mutual forbearance; how confidence of the divine favor is forfeited by sin, and how hope of pardon may be obtained by penitence and prayer. A state of innocence we can only conceive, if indeed, in our present misery, it be possible to conceive it; but the sentiments and worship proper to a fallen and offending being, we have all to learn, as we have all to practice.

The poet, whatever be done, is always great. Our progenitors, in their first state, conversed with angels; even when folly and sin had degraded them, they had not in their humiliation *the port of mean suitors*; and they rise again to reverential regard, when we find that their prayers were heard.

As human passions did not enter the world before the Fall, there is in the *Paradise Lost* little opportunity for the pathetic; but what little there is has not been lost. That passion which is peculiar to rational nature, the anguish arising from the consciousness of transgression, and the horrors attending the sense of the Divine displeasure, are very justly described and forcibly impressed. But the passions are moved only on one occasion; sublimity is the general and prevailing quality in this poem; sublimity variously modified, sometimes descriptive, sometimes argumentative.

The defects and faults of *Paradise Lost,* for faults and defects every work of man must have, it is the business of impartial criticism to discover. As, in displaying the excellence of Milton, I have not made long quotations, because of selecting beauties there had been no end, I shall in the same general manner mention that which seems to deserve censure; for what Englishman can take delight in transcribing passages, which, if they lessen the reputation of Milton, diminish in some degree the honor of our country?

The generality of my scheme does not admit the frequent notice of verbal inaccuracies; which Bentley,[2] perhaps better skilled in grammar than in poetry, has often found, though he sometimes made them, and which he imputed to the obtrusions of a reviser whom the author's blindness obliged him to employ. A supposition rash and groundless, if he thought it true; and vile and pernicious if, as is said, he in private allowed it to be false.

The plan of *Paradise Lost* has this inconvenience, that it comprises neither human actions nor human manners. The man and woman who act and suffer, are in a state which no other man or woman can ever know. The reader finds no transaction in which he can be engaged; beholds no condition in which he can by any effort of imagination place himself; he has, therefore, little natural curiosity or sympathy.

We all, indeed, feel the effects of Adam's disobedience; we all sin like Adam, and like him must all bewail our offences; we have restless and insidious enemies in the fallen angels, and in the blessed spirits we have guardians and friends; in the redemption of mankind we hope to be included; and in the description of heaven and hell we are surely interested, as we are all to reside hereafter either in the regions of horror or of bliss.

But these truths are too important to be new; they have been taught to our infancy; they have mingled with our solitary thoughts and familiar conversation, and are habitually interwoven with the whole texture of life. Being therefore not new, they raise no unaccustomed emotion in the mind; what we knew before we cannot learn; what is not unexpected cannot surprise.

Of the ideas suggested by these awful scenes, from some we recede with reverence, except when stated hours require their association; and from others we shrink with horror, or admit them only as salutary inflictions, as counterpoises to our interests and passions. Such images rather obstruct the career of fancy than incite it.

Pleasure and terror are indeed the genuine sources of poetry; but poetical pleasure must be such as human imagination can at least

2. Richard Bentley's edition of *PL* was published in 1732.

conceive, and poetical terror such as human strength and fortitude may combat. The good and evil of eternity are too ponderous for the wings of wit; the mind sinks under them in passive helplessness, content with calm belief and humble adoration.

Known truths, however, may take a different appearance, and be conveyed to the mind by a new train of intermediate images. This Milton has undertaken, and performed with pregnancy and vigor of mind peculiar to himself. Whoever considers the few radical positions which the Scriptures afforded him, will wonder by what energetic operation he expanded them to such extent, and ramified them to so much variety, restrained as he was by religious reverence from licentiousness of fiction.

Here is a full display of the united force of study and genius; of a great accumulation of materials, with judgment to digest, and fancy to combine them: Milton was able to select from nature, or from story, from ancient fable, or from modern science, whatever could illustrate or adorn his thoughts. An accumulation of knowledge impregnated his mind, fermented by study, and exalted by imagination.

It has been therefore said, without an indecent hyperbole, by one of his encomiasts, that in reading *Paradise Lost* we read a book of universal knowledge.[3]

But original deficience cannot be supplied. The want of human interest is always felt. *Paradise Lost* is one of the books which the reader admires and lays down, and forgets to take up again. None ever wished it longer than it is. Its perusal is a duty rather than a pleasure. We read Milton for instruction, retire harassed and overburdened, and look elsewhere for recreation; we desert our master, and seek for companions.

Another inconvenience of Milton's design is, that it requires the description of what cannot be described, the agency of spirits. He saw that immateriality supplied no images, and that he could not show angels acting but by instruments of action; he therefore invested them with form and matter. This, being necessary, was therefore defensible; and he should have secured the consistency of his system, by keeping immateriality out of sight, and enticing his reader to drop it from his thoughts. But he has unhappily perplexed his poetry with his philosophy. His infernal and celestial powers are sometimes pure spirit, and sometimes animated body. When Satan walks with his lance upon the *burning marle*, he has a body; when, in his passage between hell and the new world, he is in danger of sinking in the vacuity, and is supported by a gust of rising vapors, he has a body; when he animates the toad, he seems to be mere spirit, that can penetrate matter at pleasure; when he *starts up in his own shape*, he has at least a determined form; and when he is

3. See second paragraph of Northrop Frye's essay, above.

brought before Gabriel, he has a *spear and shield*, which he had the power of hiding in the toad, though the arms of the contending angels are evidently material.

The vulgar inhabitants of Pandaemonium, being *incorporeal spirits*, are *at large, though without number*, in a limited space; yet in the battle, when they were overwhelmed by mountains, their armor hurt them, *crushed in upon their substance, now grown gross by sinning*. This likewise happened to the uncorrupted angels, who were overthrown *the sooner for their arms*, for *unarmed they might easily as spirits have evaded by contraction, or remove*. Even as spirits they are hardly spiritual; for *contraction* and *remove* are images of matter; but if they could have escaped without their armor, they might have escaped from it, and left only the empty cover to be battered. Uriel, when he rides on a sun-beam, is material: Satan is material when he is afraid of the prowess of Adam.

The confusion of spirit and matter which pervades the whole narration of the war of heaven fills it with incongruity; and the book, in which it is related, is, I believe, the favorite of children, and gradually neglected as knowledge is increased.

After the operation of immaterial agents, which cannot be explained, may be considered that of allegorical persons, which have no real existence. To exalt causes into agents, to invest abstract ideas with form, and animate them with activity, has always been the right of poetry. But such airy beings are, for the most part, suffered only to do their natural office, and retire. Thus Fame tells a tale, and Victory hovers over a general, or perches on a standard; but Fame and Victory can do no more. To give them any real employment, or ascribe to them any material agency, is to make them allegorical no longer, but to shock the mind by ascribing effects to nonentity. In the *Prometheus of Aesechylus*, we see *Violence* and *Strength*, and in the *Alcestis* of Euripides, we see *Death* brought upon the stage, all as active persons of the drama; but no precedents can justify absurdity.

Milton's allegory of Sin and Death is undoubtedly faulty. Sin is indeed the mother of Death, and may be allowed to be the portress of hell; but when they stop the journey of Satan, a journey described as real, and when Death offers him battle, the allegory is broken. That Sin and Death should have shown the way to hell might have been allowed; but they cannot facilitate the passage by building a bridge, because the difficulty of Satan's passage is described as real and sensible, and the bridge ought to be only figurative. The hell assigned to the rebellious spirits is described as not less local than the residence of man. It is placed in some distant part of space, separated from the regions of harmony and order by a chaotic waste and an unoccupied vacuity; but Sin and Death worked up a *mole* of *aggregated soil,* cemented with *asphaltus;* a work too bulky for ideal architects.

This unskilful allegory appears to me one of the greatest faults of the poem; and to this there was no temptation, but the author's opinion of its beauty.

To the conduct of the narrative some objections may be made. Satan is with great expectation brought before Gabriel in Paradise, and is suffered to go away unmolested. The creation of man is represented as the consequence of the vacuity left in heaven by the expulsion of the rebels, yet Satan mentions it as a report *rife in heaven* before his departure.

To find sentiments for the state of innocence, was very difficult; and something of anticipation perhaps is now and then discovered. Adam's discourse of dreams seems not to be the speculation of a new-created being. I know not whether his answer to the angel's reproof for curiosity does not want something of propriety: it is the speech of a man acquainted with many other men. Some philosophical notions, especially when the philosophy is false, might have been better omitted. The angel, in a comparison, speaks of *timorous deer,* before deer were yet timorous, and before Adam could understand the comparison.

Dryden remarks, that Milton has some flats among his elevations.[4] This is only to say that all the parts are not equal. In every work, one part must be for the sake of others; a palace must have passages; a poem must have transitions. It is no more to be required that wit should always be blazing, than that the sun should always stand at noon. In a great work there is a vicissitude of luminous and opaque parts, as there is in the world a succession of day and night. Milton, when he has expatiated in the sky, may be allowed sometimes to revisit earth; for what other author ever soared so high, or sustained his flight so long?

Milton, being well versed in the Italian poets, appears to have borrowed often from them; and, as every man learns something from his companions, his desire of imitating Ariosto's levity has disgraced his work with the *Paradise of Fools;* a fiction not in itself ill-imagined, but too ludicrous for its place.

His play on words, in which he delights too often; his equivocations which Bentley endeavors to defend by the example of the ancients; his uncessary and ungraceful use of terms of art; it is not necessary to mention, because they are easily remarked, and generally censured, and at last bear so little proportion to the whole, that they scarcely deserve the attention of a critic.

Such are the faults of that wonderful performance *Paradise Lost;* which he who can put in balance with its beauties must be consid-

4. In Preface to *Sylvae* (1685).

ered not as nice but as dull, as less to be censured for want of candor than pitied for want of sensibility.

* * *

Through all his greater works there prevails an uniform peculiarity of *diction*, a mode and cast of expression which bears little resemblance to that of any former writer, and which is so far removed from common use, that an unlearned reader, when he first opens his book, finds himself surprised by a new language.

This novelty has been, by those who can find nothing wrong in Milton, imputed to his laborious endeavors after words suitable to the grandeur of his ideas. *Our language*, says Addison, *sunk under him*. But the truth is, that, both in prose and verse, he had formed his style by a perverse and pedantic principle. He was desirous to use English words with a foreign idiom. This in all his prose is discovered and condemned; for there judgment operates freely, neither softened by the beauty nor awed by the dignity of his thoughts; but such is the power of his poetry, that his call is obeyed without resistance, the reader feels himself in captivity to a higher and a nobler mind, and criticism sinks in admiration.

Milton's style was not modified by his subject: what is shown with greater extent in *Paradise Lost*, may be found in *Comus*. One source of his peculiarity was his familiarity with the Tuscan poets: the disposition of his words is, I think, frequently Italian; perhaps sometimes combined with other tongues. Of him, at last, may be said what Jonson says of Spenser, that *he wrote no language*, but has formed what Butler calls a *Babylonish dialect*,[5] in itself harsh and barbarous, but made by exalted genius, and extensive learning, the vehicle of so much instruction and so much pleasure, that, like other lovers, we find grace in its deformity.

Whatever be the faults of his diction, he cannot want the praise of copiousness and variety: he was master of his language in its full extent; and has selected the melodious words with such diligence, that from his book alone the Art of English Poetry might be learned.

After his diction, something must be said of his *versification. The measure*, he says, *is the English heroic verse without rhyme*. Of this mode he had many examples among the Italians, and some in his own country. The Earl of Surry is said to have translated one of Virgil's books without rhyme; and, besides our tragedies, a few short poems had appeared in blank verse; particularly one tending to reconcile the nation to Raleigh's wild attempt upon Guiana, and probably written by Raleigh himself. These petty performances cannot be supposed to have much influenced Milton, who more probably took his hint from Trisino's *Italia Liberata*; and, finding

5. Ben Jonson in *Timber, or Discoveries*   (1662–78).
(1641) and Samuel Butler in *Hudibras*

blank verse easier than rhyme, was desirous of persuading himself that it is better.

Rhyme, he says, and says truly, *is no necessary adjunct of true poetry*. But perhaps, of poetry as a mental operation, meter or music is no necessary adjunct: it is however by the music of meter that poetry has been discriminated in all languages; and in languages melodiously constructed, by a due proportion of long and short syllables, meter is sufficient. But one language cannot communicate its rules to another: where meter is scanty and imperfect, some help is necessary. The music of the English heroic line strikes the ear so faintly that it is easily lost, unless all the syllables of every line cooperate together: this cooperation can be only obtained by the preservation of every verse unmingled with another, as a distinct system of sounds; and this distinctness is obtained and preserved by the artifice of rhyme. The variety of pauses, so much boasted by the lovers of blank verse, changes the measures of an English poet to the periods of a declaimer; and there are only a few skilful and happy readers of Milton, who enable their audience to perceive where the lines end or begin. *Blank verse*, said an ingenious critic, *seems to be verse only to the eye*.

Poetry may subsist without rhyme, but English poetry will not often please; nor can rhyme ever be safely spared but where the subject is able to support itself. Blank verse makes some approach to that which is called the *lapidary stile*; has neither the easiness of prose, nor the melody of numbers, and therefore tires by long continuance. Of the Italian writers without rhyme, whom Milton alleges as precedents, not one is popular; what reason could urge in its defence, has been confuted by the ear.

But, whatever be the advantage of rhyme, I cannot prevail on myself to wish that Milton had been a rhymer; for I cannot wish his work to be other than it is; yet, like other heroes, he is to be admired rather than imitated. He that thinks himself capable of astonishing, may write blank verse; but those that hope only to please, must condescend to rhyme.

The highest praise of genius is original invention. Milton cannot be said to have contrived the structure of an epic poem, and therefore owes reverence to that vigor and amplitude of mind to which all generations must be indebted for the art of poetical narration, for the texture of the fable, the variation of incidents, the interposition of dialogue, and all the stratagems that surprise and enchain attention. But, of all the borrowers from Homer, Milton is perhaps the least indebted. He was naturally a thinker for himself, confident of his own abilities, and disdainful of help or hindrance: he did not refuse admission to the thoughts or images of his predecessors, but he did not seek them. From his contemporaries he neither courted nor received support; there is in his writings nothing by which the pride of other authors might be gratified, or favor gained; no exchange of praise, nor solicitation of support. His great works were performed under discountenance, and in blindness, but difficulties vanished at his touch; he was born for whatever is arduous, and his work is not the greatest of heroic poems, only because it is not the first.

SAMUEL TAYLOR COLERIDGE

[Milton] †

Born in London, 1608.—Died, 1674.

If we divide the period from the accession of Elizabeth to the Protectorate of Cromwell into two unequal portions, the first ending with the death of James I. the other comprehending the reign of Charles and the brief glories of the Republic, we are forcibly struck with a difference in the character of the illustrious actors, by whom each period is rendered severally memorable. Or rather, the difference in the characters of the great men in each period, leads us to make this division. Eminent as the intellectual powers were that were displayed in both; yet in the number of great men, in the various sorts of excellence, and not merely in the variety but almost diversity of talents united in the same individual, the age of Charles falls short of its predecessor; and the stars of the Parliament, keen as their radiance was, in fulness and richness of lustre, yield to the constellation at the court of Elizabeth;—which can only be paralleled by Greece in her brightest moment, when the titles of the poet, the philosopher, the historian, the statesman and the general not seldom formed a garland round the same head, as in the instances of our Sidneys and Raleighs. But then, on the other hand, there was a vehemence of will, an enthusiasm of principle, a depth and an earnestness of spirit, which the charms of individual fame and personal aggrandisement could not pacify,—an aspiration after reality, permanence, and general good,—in short, a moral grandeur in the latter period, with which the low intrigues, Machiavellic maxims, and selfish and servile ambition of the former, stand in painful contrast.[1]

The causes of this it belongs not to the present occasion to detail at length; but a mere allusion to the quick succession of revolutions in religion, breeding a political indifference in the mass of men to

† "Lecture X," in Lectures of 1818, from *Coleridge's Miscellaneous Criticism*, edited by Thomas Middleton Raysor (Cambridge, Mass., Harvard University Press, 1936), pp. 157–65. Some of Raysor's notes to this essay have been deleted. The editor's additions appear in brackets.
1. Cf. Coleridge's *Shakespearean Criticism*, [ed. T. M. Raysor,] ii. 115–16, for another treatment of this subject.

religion itself, the enormous increase of the royal power in consequence of the humiliation of the nobility and the clergy—the transference of the papal authority to the crown,—the unfixed state of Elizabeth's own opinions, whose inclinations were as popish as her interests were protestant—the controversial extravagance and practical imbecility of her successor—will help to explain the former period; and the persecutions that had given a life and soul-interest to the disputes so imprudently fostered by James,—the ardour of a conscious increase of power in the commons, and the greater austerity of manners and maxims, the natural product and most formidable weapon of religious disputation, not merely in conjunction, but in closest combination, with newly awakened political and republican zeal, these perhaps account for the character of the latter aera.

In the close of the former period, and during the bloom of the latter, the poet Milton was educated and formed; and he survived the latter, and all the fond hopes and aspirations which had been its life; and so in evil days, standing as the representative of the combined excellence of both periods, he produced the Paradise Lost as by an after-throe of nature. "There are some persons (observes a divine, a contemporary of Milton's) of whom the grace of God takes early hold, and the good spirit inhabiting them, carries them on in an even constancy through innocence into virtue, their Christianity bearing equal date with their manhood, and reason and religion, like warp and woof, running together, make up one web of a wise and exemplary life. This (he adds) is a most happy case, wherever it happens; for, besides that there is no sweeter or more lovely thing on earth than the early buds of piety, which drew from our Saviour signal affection to the beloved disciple, it is better to have no wound than to experience the most sovereign balsam, which, if it work a cure, yet usually leaves a scar behind." Although it was and is my intention to defer the consideration of Milton's own character to the conclusion of this Lecture, yet I could not prevail on myself to approach the Paradise Lost without impressing on your minds the conditions under which such a work was in fact producible at all, the original genius having been assumed as the immediate agent and efficient cause; and these conditions I find in the character of the times and in his own character. The age in which the foundations of his mind were laid, was congenial to it as one golden aera of profound erudition and individual genius;—that in which the superstructure was carried up, was no less favourable to it by a sternness of discipline and a show of self-control, highly flattering to the imaginative dignity of an heir of fame, and which won Milton over from the dear-loved delights of academic groves and cathedral aisles to the anti-prelatic party. It acted on him, too, no doubt, and modified his studies by a charac-

teristic controversial spirit, (his presentation of God is tinted wit'
it)—a spirit not less busy indeed in political than in theological an
ecclesiastical dispute, but carrying on the former almost alway;
more or less, in the guise of the latter. And so far as Pope's censui
of our poet,—that he makes God the Father a school divine[2]—
just, we must attribute it to the character of his age, from which th
men of genius, who escaped, escaped by a worse disease, the licen
tious indifference of a Frenchified court.

Such was the *nidus* or soil, which constituted, in the strict sens
of the word, the circumstances of Milton's mind. In his mind itsel
there were purity and piety absolute; an imagination to which nei
ther the past nor the present were interesting, except as far as the
called forth and enlivened the great ideal, in which and for whic
he lived; a keen love of truth, which, after many weary pursuit
found a harbour in a sublime listening to the still voice in his ow
spirit, and as keen a love of his country, which, after a disappoin
ment still more depressive, expanded and soared into a love of ma
as a probationer of immortality. These were, these alone could be
the conditions under which such a work as the Paradise Lost coul
be conceived and accomplished. By a life-long study Milton ha
known—

> What was of use to know,
> What best to say could say, to do had done.
> His actions to his words agreed, his words
> To his large heart gave utterance due, his heart
> Contain'd of good, wise, fair, the perfect shape;
> [Cf. *PR*, III. 7–11]

and he left the imperishable total, as a bequest to the ages coming
in the Paradise Lost.

Difficult as I shall find it to turn over these leaves without catch
ing some passage, which would tempt me to stop, I propose t
consider, 1st, the general plan and arrangement of the work;—
2ndly, the subject with its difficulties and advantages; 3rdly, th
poet's object, the spirit in the letter, the ἐνθύμιον ἐν μύθῳ, the tru
school-divinity; and lastly, the characteristic excellencies of th
poem, in what they consist, and by what means they were pro
duced.

1. As to the plan and ordonnance of the Poem.

Compare it with the Iliad, many of the books of which migh
change places without any injury to the thread of the story. Indee
I doubt the original existence of the Iliad as one poem; it seem
more probable that it was put together about the time of the Pisi
tratidae. The Iliad—and, more or less, all epic poems, the subjec

---

2. "And God the Father turns a school   Epistle of the Second Book, 1. 102.
divine." *Imitations of Horace, First*

of which are taken from history—have no rounded conclusion; they remain, after all, but single chapters from the volume of history, although they are ornamental chapters. Consider the exquisite simplicity of the Paradise Lost. It and it alone really possesses a beginning, a middle, and an end; it has the totality of the poem as distinguished from the *ab ovo* birth and parentage, or straight line, of history.

2. As to the subject.

In Homer, the supposed importance of the subject, as the first effort of confederated Greece, is an after-thought of the critics; and the interest, such as it is, derived from the events themselves, as distinguished from the manner of representing them, is very languid to all but Greeks. It is a Greek poem. The superiority of the Paradise Lost is obvious in this respect, that the interest transcends the limits of a nation. But we do not generally dwell on this excellence of the Paradise Lost, because it seems attributable to Christianity itself;—yet in fact the interest is wider than Christendom, and comprehends the Jewish and Mohammedan worlds;—nay, still further, inasmuch as it represents the origin of evil, and the combat of evil and good, it contains matter of deep interest to all mankind, as forming the basis of all religion, and the true occasion of all philosophy whatsoever.

The Fall of Man is the subject; Satan is the cause; man's blissful state the immediate object of his enmity and attack; man is warned by an angel who gives him an account of all that was requisite to be known, to make the warning at once intelligible and awful; then the temptation ensues, and the Fall; then the immediate sensible consequence; then the consolation, wherein an angel presents a vision of the history of men with the ultimate triumph of the Redeemer. Nothing is touched in this vision but what is of general interest in religion; anything else would have been improper.

* * *

But notwithstanding the advantages in Milton's subject, there were concomitant insuperable difficulties, and Milton has exhibited marvellous skill in keeping most of them out of sight. High poetry is the translation of reality into the ideal under the predicament of succession of time only. The poet is an historian, upon condition of moral power being the only force in the universe. The very grandeur of his subject ministered a difficulty to Milton. The statement of a being of high intellect, warring against the supreme Being, seems to contradict the idea of a supreme Being. Milton precludes our feeling this, as much as possible, by keeping the peculiar attributes of divinity less in sight, making them to a certain extent allegorical only. Again, poetry implies the language of excitement; yet how to reconcile such language with God? Hence Milton confines the poetic passion in God's speeches to the language of scripture; and once only allows the *passio vera,* or *quasihumana* to appear, in the passage, where the Father contemplates his own likeness in the Son before the battle:—

> Go then, thou Mightiest, in thy Father's might,
> Ascend my chariot, guide the rapid wheels
> That shake Heaven's basis, bring forth all my war,
> My bow and thunder; my almighty arms
> Gird on, and sword upon thy puissant thigh;
> Pursue these sons of darkness, drive them out
> From all Heaven's bounds into the utter deep:
> There let them learn, as likes them, to despise
> God and Messiah his anointed king.
>
> [*PL,* VI. 710–18]

3. As to Milton's object:—

It was to justify the ways of God to man! The controversial spirit observable in many parts of the poem, especially in God's speeches, is immediately attributable to the great controversy of that age, the origination of evil. The Arminians considered it a mere calamity. The Calvinists took away all human will. Milton asserted the will, but declared for the enslavement of the will out of an act of the will itself. There are three powers in us, which distinguish us from the beasts that perish;—1, reason; 2, the power of viewing universal truth; and 3, the power of contracting universal truth into particulars. Religion is the will in the reason, and love in the will.

The character of Satan is pride and sensual indulgence, finding in self the sole motive of action. It is the character so often seen *in little* on the political stage. It exhibits all the restlessness, temerity, and cunning which have marked the mighty hunters of mankind from Nimrod to Napoleon. The common fascination of men is, that these great men, as they are called, must act from some great motive. Milton has carefully marked in his Satan the intense selfishness, the alcohol of egotism, which would rather reign in hell than serve in heaven. To place this lust of self in opposition to denial of self or duty, and to show what exertions it would make, and what pains endure to accomplish its end, is Milton's particular object in the character of Satan. But around this character he has thrown a singularity of daring, a grandeur of sufferance, and a ruined splendour, which constitute the very height of poetic sublimity.

Lastly, as to the execution:—

The language and versification of the Paradise Lost are peculiar in being so much more necessarily correspondent to each than those in any other poem or poet. The connexion of the sentences and the position of the words are exquisitely artificial; but the position is rather according to the logic of passion or universal logic, than to the logic of grammar. Milton attempted to make the

English language obey the logic of passion as perfectly as the Greek and Latin. Hence the occasional harshness in the construction.

Sublimity is the pre-eminent characteristic of the Paradise Lost. * * * There is a greatness arising from images of effort and daring, and also from those of moral endurance; in Milton both are united. The fallen angels are human passions, invested with a dramatic reality.

The apostrophe to light at the commencement of the third book is particularly beautiful as an intermediate link between Hell and Heaven; and observe, how the second and third book support the subjective character of the poem. In all modern poetry in Christendom there is an under consciousness of a sinful nature, a fleeting away of external things, the mind or subject greater than the object, the reflective character predominant. In the Paradise Lost the sublimest parts are the revelations of Milton's own mind, producing itself and evolving its own greatness; and this is so truly so, that when that which is merely entertaining for its objective beauty is introduced, it at first seems a discord.

In the description of Paradise itself you have Milton's sunny side as a man; here his descriptive powers are exercised to the utmost, and he draws deep upon his Italian resources. In the description of Eve, and throughout this part of the poem, the poet is predominant over the theologian. Dress is the symbol of the Fall, but the mark of intellect; and the metaphysics of dress are, the hiding what is not symbolic and displaying by discrimination what is. The love of Adam and Eve in Paradise is of the highest merit—not phantomatic, and yet removed from every thing degrading. It is the sentiment of one rational being towards another made tender by a specific difference in that which is essentially the same in both; it is a union of opposites, a giving and receiving mutually of the permanent in either, a completion of each in the other.

Milton is not a picturesque, but a musical, poet; although he has this merit that the object chosen by him for any particular foreground always remains prominent to the end, enriched, but not incumbered, by the opulence of descriptive details furnished by an exhaustless imagination. I wish the Paradise Lost were more carefully read and studied than I can see any ground for believing it is, especially those parts which, from the habit of always looking for a story in poetry, are scarecely read at all,—as for example, Adam's vision of future events in the 11th and 12th books. No one can rise from the perusal of this immortal poem without a deep sense of the grandeur and the purity of Milton's soul, or without feeling how susceptible of domestic enjoyments he really was, notwithstanding the discomforts which actually resulted from an apparently unhappy choice in marriage. He was, as every truly great poet has ever been, a good man; but finding it impossible to realize his own aspirations, either in religion, or politics, or society, he gave up his heart to the living spirit and light within him, and avenged himself on the world by enriching it with this record of his own transcendant ideal.

The reader of Milton must be always on his duty: he is surrounded with sense; it rises in every line; every word is to the purpose. There are no lazy intervals: all has been considered, and demands and merits observation. If this be called obscurity, let it be remembered 'tis such a one as is complaisant to the reader: not that vicious obscurity, which proceeds from a muddled head.[3]

I dare not pronounce such passages as these [from *Romeo and Juliet*] to be absolutely unnatural, not merely because I consider the author a much better judge than I can be, but because I can understand and allow for an effort of the mind, when it would describe what it cannot satisfy itself with the description of, to reconcile opposites and qualify contradictions, leaving a middle state of mind more strictly appropriate to the imagination than any other, when it is, as it were, hovering between images. As soon as it is fixed on one image, its becomes understanding; but while it is unfixed and wavering between them, attaching itself permanently to none, it is imagination. Such is the fine description of Death in Milton:—[II.666–73]

The grandest efforts of poetry are where the imagination is called forth, not to produce a distinct form, but a strong working of the mind, still offering what is still repelled, and again creating what is again rejected; the result being what the poet wishes to impress, namely, the substitution of a sublime feeling of the unimaginable for a mere image. I have sometimes thought that the passage just read might be quoted as exhibiting the narrow limit of painting, as compared with the boundless power of poetry: painting cannot go beyond a certain point; poetry rejects all control, all confinement. Yet we know that sundry painters have attempted pictures of the meeting between Satan and Death at the gates of Hell; and how was Death represented? Not as Milton has described him, but by the most defined thing that can be imagined—a skeleton, the dryest and hardest image that it is possible to discover; which, instead of keeping the mind in a state of activity, reduces it to the merest passivity,—an image, compared with which a square, a triangle, or any other mathematical figure, is a luxuriant fancy.[4]

---

3. An entry of about 1796 in a notebook of Coleridge's; from Raysor, op. cit., pp. 169–70. [*Editor.*]
4. From Coleridge's *Seven Lectures on Shakespeare and Milton*, delivered in 1811–12, and first published in 1856. The text is from *Coleridge's Shakespearean Criticism*, edited by Thomas Middleton Raysor (Cambridge, Mass., Harvard University Press, 1930), Vol. II, pp. 138–139. [*Editor.*]

But neither can reason or religion exist or co-exist as reason and religion, except as far as they are actuated by the will (the Platonic *υμὸς,*) which is the sustaining, coercive and ministerial power, the functions of which in the individual correspond to the officers of war and police in the ideal Republic of Plato. In its state of immanence or indwelling in reason and religion, the will appears indifferently as wisdom or as love: two names of the same power, the former more intelligential, the latter more spiritual, the former more frequent in the Old, the latter in the New Testament. But in its utmost abstraction and consequent state of reprobation, the will becomes Satanic pride and rebellious self-idolatry in the relations of the spirit to itself, and remorseless despotism relatively to others; the more hopeless as the more obdurate by its subjugation of sensual impulses, by its superiority to toil and pain and pleasure; in short, by the fearful resolve to find in itself alone the one absolute motive of action, under which all other motives from within and from without must be either subordinated or crushed.

This is the character which Milton has so philosophically as well as sublimely embodied in the Satan of his Paradise Lost.[5]

In my judgment, an epic poem must either be national or mundane. As to Arthur, you could not by any means make a poem on him national to Englishmen. What have *we* to do with him? Milton saw this, and with a judgment at least equal to his genius, took a mundane theme—one common to all mankind. His Adam and Eve are all men and women inclusively. Pope satirises Milton for making God the Father talk like a school divine. Pope was hardly the man to criticise Milton. The truth is, the judgment of Milton in the conduct of the celestial part of his story is very exquisite. Wherever God is represented as directly acting as Creator, without any exhibition of his own essence, Milton adopts the simplest and sternest language of the Scriptures. He ventures upon no poetic diction, no amplification, no pathos, no affection. It is truly the Voice or the Word of the Lord coming to, and acting on, the subject Chaos. But, as some personal interest was demanded for the purposes of poetry, Milton takes advantage of the dramatic representation of God's address to the Son, the Filial Alterity, and in *those addresses* slips in, as it were by stealth, language of affection, or thought, or sentiment. Indeed, although Milton was undoubtedly a high Arian in his mature life, he does in the necessity of poetry give a greater objectivity to the Father and the Son, than he would have justified in argument. He was very wise in adopting the strong anthropomorphism of the Hebrew Scriptures at once.[6]

From Appendix B, to Coleridge's *The Statesman's Manual* (1816), in *Lay Sermons* (3rd ed., London, 1852), pp. 68–9. [*Editor*.]

6. Entry for September 4, 1833, in Coleridge's *Table Talk* (1835), from Raysor, *Coleridge's Miscellaneous Criticism*, pp. 429–30. [*Editor*.]

Selected Bibliography

I. EDITIONS

Patterson, Frank Allen, gen. ed. [The Columbia edition of] *The Works of John Milton.* 18 vols. New York, 1931–38.
Wolfe, Don M., gen. ed. [The Yale edition of] *The Complete Prose Works of John Milton.* Vols. I–VI. New Haven, 1953–.

Bush, Douglas, ed. *The Complete Poetical Works of John Milton.* Boston, 1965.
Darbishire, Helen, ed. *The Poetical Works of John Milton.* 2 vols. Oxford, 1952–1955.
Fowler, Alastair, ed. *Paradise Lost.* London, 1971.
Hughes, Merritt Y., ed. *John Milton. Complete Poems and Major Prose.* New York, 1957.
Madsen, William G., ed. *Paradise Lost.* New York, 1964.
Shawcross, John T., ed. *The Complete Poetry of John Milton.* Rev. ed. Garden City, 1971.

II. BIBLIOGRAPHIES, REFERENCE BOOKS, GUIDES

Broadbent, John. *"Paradise Lost." Introduction.* Cambridge, 1972.
———. ed. *John Milton: Introductions.* Cambridge, 1973.
Gilbert, Allan H. *A Geographical Dictionary of Milton.* New Haven, 1919.
Hanford, James Holly. *Milton* (one of the "Goldentree Bibliographies"). New York, 1966.
Hanford, James Holly, and James G. Taaffe. *A Milton Handbook: Fifth Edition.* New York, 1970.
Huckabay, Calvin. *John Milton: A Bibliographical Supplement, 1929–1957.* Rev. ed. Pittsburgh, 1960.
Ingram, William, and Kathleen Swaim. *A Concordance to Milton's English Poems.* Oxford, 1972.
Le Comte, Edward S. *A Milton Dictionary.* New York, 1961.
Lockwood, Laura E. *Lexicon to the English Poetical Works of John Milton.* New York, 1907.
MLA International Bibliography, Vol. I. "English Literature VII." (Published annually by the Modern Language Association of America.)
Nicolson, Marjorie Hope. *John Milton: A Reader's Guide to His Poetry.* New York, 1963.
Patrides, C. A. "An Annotated Reading List." In his *Milton's Epic Poetry.* Harmondsworth, 1967.
Patterson, Frank Allen, and French R. Fogel. *An Index to the Columbia Edition of the Works of John Milton.* 2 vols. New York, 1940. (A useful subject index.)
Potter, Lois. *A Preface to Milton.* London, 1971.
Stevens, David H. *A Reference Guide to Milton from 1800 to the Present Day.* Chicago, 1930.
Studies in Philology, annual bibliography. "Recent Literature of the English Renaissance."

III. BIOGRAPHIES

Diekhoff, John S., ed. *Milton on Himself: Milton's Utterances upon Himself and His Works.* 2nd ed. London, 1965.
Darbishire, Helen, ed. *The Early Lives of Milton.* New York, 1965.
Masson, David. *The Life of John Milton: Narrated in Connexion with the Political, Ecclesiastical, and Literary History of His Time.* 7 vols. London 1895–94. (Reprinted New York, 1946.)

Parker, William Riley. *Milton: A Biography.* 2 vols. Oxford, 1968.

Bush, Douglas. *John Milton: A Sketch of his Life and Works.* New York, 1964.
Daiches, David. *Milton.* London, 1957.

Fletcher, Harris Francis. *The Intellectual Development of John Milton*. 2 vols. Urbana, 1956.
Hanford, James Holly. *John Milton, Englishman*. New York, 1949.
Tillyard, E. M. W. *Milton*. London, 1930.
Wolfe, Don M. *Milton in the Puritan Revolution*. New York, 1941.

IV. BACKGROUNDS

Barker, Arthur E. *Milton and the Puritan Dilemma, 1641–1660*. Toronto, 1956.
Bush, Douglas. *Mythology and the Renaissance Tradition in English Poetry*. Rev. ed. Minneapolis, 1963.
Clark, Donald L. *John Milton at St. Paul's School, A Study of Ancient Rhetoric in English Renaissance Education*. New York, 1948.
Fletcher, Harris. *The Use of the Bible in Milton's Prose*. Urbana, 1929.
Greene, Thomas M. *The Descent from Heaven: a Study in Epic Continuity*. New Haven, 1963.
Haller, William. *The Rise of Puritanism; or The Way to the New Jerusalem as Set Forth in Pulpit and Press from Thomas Carwright to John Wilburne and John Milton, 1570–1643*. New York, 1938.
———. *Liberty and Reformation in the Puritan Revolution*. New York, 1955.
Hill, Christopher. *The Century of Revolution 1603–1714*. Edinburgh, 1961.
Hoopes, Robert. *Right Reason in the English Renaissance*. Cambridge, Mass., 1962.
Kristeller, Paul O. *Renaissance Thought: the Classic, Scholastic and Humanistic Strains*. New York, 1961.
Kuhn, Thomas S. *The Copernican Revolution: Planetary Astronomy in the Development of Western Thought*. Cambridge, Mass., 1957.
Kurth, Burton O. *Milton and Christian Heroism: Biblical Epic Themes and Forms in Seventeenth-Century England*. Berkeley, 1959.
Lovejoy, Arthur O. *The Great Chain of Being. A Study of the History of an Idea*. Cambridge, Mass., 1936.
Mahood, M. M. *Poetry and Humanism*. New Haven, 1950.
Nicolson, Marjorie Hope. *The Breaking of the Circle: Studies in the Effect of the "New Science" upon Seventeenth-Century Poetry*. Rev. ed. New York, 1960.
Williams, Arnold. *The Common Expositer: An Account of the Commentaries on Genesis, 1527–1633*. Chapel Hill, 1948.
Wolfe, Don M. *Milton and his England*. Princeton, 1971.
Yates, Frances A. *The French Academies of the Sixteenth Century*. London, 1947.
———. *Giordano Bruno and the Hermetic Tradition*. London, 1964.
———. *The Rosicrucian Enlightenment*. London, 1972.

V. COLLECTIONS OF CRITICAL ESSAYS

Barker, Arthur E., ed. *Milton: Modern Essays in Criticism*. New York, 1965.
Critical Essays on Milton from "ELH." Baltimore, 1968.
Dyson, A. E., and Julian Lovelock. *Milton "Paradise Lost": A Casebook*. London, 1973.
Emma, Ronald David, and John T. Shawcross, eds. *Language and Style in Milton*. New York, 1967.
Kermode, Frank, ed. *The Living Milton: Essays by Various Hands*. London, 1960.
Kranidas, Thomas, ed. *New Essays on "Paradise Lost."* Berkeley, 1969.
Martz, Louis L., ed. *Milton: A Collection of Critical Essays*. Englewood Cliffs, 1966.
Patrides, C. A., ed. *Approaches to "Paradise Lost,"* London, 1968.
Patrides, C. A., ed. *Milton's Epic Poetry: Essays on "Paradise Lost" and "Paradise Regained."* Harmondsworth, 1967.
Rudrum, Alan, ed. *Milton: Modern Judgments*. London, 1968.
Shawcross, John T., ed. *Milton: The Critical Heritage*. New York, 1970.
Thorpe, James Ernest, ed. *Milton Criticism*, New York, 1950.

VI. STUDIES OF *PARADISE LOST*

Adams, Robert M. *Ikon: Milton and the Modern Critics*. Ithaca, 1955.
Armstrong, John. *The Paradise Myth*. London, 1969.
Arthos, John. *Dante, Michelangelo and Milton*. London, 1963.

Babb, Lawrence. *The Moral Cosmos of "Paradise Lost."* East Lansing, 1970.

Banks, Theodore H., Jr. *Milton's Imagery.* New York, 1950.

Barker, Arthur E. "Structural Pattern in *Paradise Lost.*" *Philological Quarterly,* 23 (1949), 17–30.

Bridges, Robert. *Milton's Prosody, with a Chapter on Accentual Verse and Notes.* Oxford, 1921.

Brisman, Leslie. *Milton's Poetry of Choice and Its Romantic Heirs.* Ithaca, 1973.

Broadbent, J. B. *Some Graver Subject: An Essay on "Paradise Lost."* London, 1960.

Burden, Dennis H. *The Logical Epic.* Cambridge, Mass., 1967.

Bush, Douglas. *"Paradise Lost" in Our Time: Some Comments.* Ithaca, 1945.

Colie, Rosalie L. "Time and Eternity: Paradox and Structure in *Paradise Lost.*" *Journal of the Warburg and Courtauld Institutes,* 23 (1960), 127–138.

Cope, Jackson I. *The Metaphoric Structure of "Paradise Lost."* Baltimore, 1962.

Corcoran, Mary Irma. *Milton's Paradise with Reference to the Hexameral Background.* Washington, 1945.

Curry, Walter Clyde. *Milton's Ontology, Cosmology and Physics.* Lexington, 1957.

Daniells, Roy. *Milton, Mannerism and Baroque.* Toronto, 1963.

Davie, Donald. "Syntax and Music in *Paradise Lost.*" *The Living Milton,* ed. Frank Kermode. London, 1960.

Diekhoff, John S. *Milton's "Paradise Lost": A Commentary on the Argument.* New York, 1946.

Duncan, Joseph E. *Milton's Earthly Paradise.* Minneapolis, 1972.

Eliot, T. S. "Milton," and "A Note on the Verse of John Milton." In his *On Poetry and Poets.* London, 1957.

Emma, Ronald David. *Milton's Grammar.* The Hague, 1964.

Empson, William. *Milton's God.* Rev. ed. London, 1965.

Evans, John Martin. *"Paradise Lost" and the Genesis Tradition.* Oxford, 1968.

Ferry, Ann Davidson. *Milton's Epic Voice.* Cambridge, Mass., 1963.

Fish, Stanley Eugene. *Surprised By Sin: The Reader in "Paradise Lost."* London, 1967.

Fixler, Michael. *Milton and the Kingdoms of God.* London, 1964.

Frye, Northrop. *The Return of Eden: Five Essays on Milton's Epics.* Toronto, 1965.

Frye, Roland Mushat. *God, Man, and Satan: Patterns of Christian Thought and Life in "Paradise Lost," "Pilgrim's Progress," and the Great Theologians.* Princeton, 1960.

Gardner, Dame Helen Louise. *A Reading of Paradise Lost.* Oxford, 1965.

———. "Milton's 'Satan' and the Theme of Damnation in Elizabethan Tragedy." *Essays and Studies* by Members of the English Association, n.s.1 (1948), 46–66.

Giamatti, A. Bartlett. *The Earthly Paradise and the Renaissance Epic.* Princeton, 1966.

Gierson, Sir Herbert J. C *Milton and Wordsworth, Poets and Prophets.* London, 1956.

Halkett, John. *Milton and the Idea of Matrimony.* New Haven, 1970.

Hanford, James Holley. *John Milton, Poet and Humanist.* Cleveland, 1966.

Harding, David P. *The Club of Hercules: Studies in the Classical Background of "Paradise Lost."* Urbana, 1962.

Hartman, Geoffrey. "Milton's Counterplot." *ELH: A Journal of English Literary History,* 25 (1958), 1–12.

Hertz, Neil, "Wordsworth and the Tears of Adam." *Studies in Romanticism,* 7 (1967), 15–33. Reprinted with revisions in M. H. Abrams, ed., *Wordsworth: A Collection of Critical Essays.* Englewood Cliffs, 1972.

Hughes, Merritt Y. *Ten Perspectives on Milton.* New Haven, 1965.

Hunter, William B. Jr., et al. *Bright Essence: Studies in Milton's Theology.* Salt Lake City, 1971.

Kelley, Maurice. *This Great Argument: A Study of Milton's "De Doctrina Christiana" as a Gloss upon "Paradise Lost."* Princeton, 1941.

Kermode, Frank. "Milton's Hero." *Review of English Studies,* n.s. 4 (1953), 317–330.

Kirkconnell, Watson. *The Celestial Cycle: The Theme of "Paradise Lost" in World Literature, with Translations of the Major Analogues.* New York, 1952.

Knight, Douglas. "The Dramatic Center of Paradise Lost." *South Atlantic Quarterly,* 63 (1964), 44–59.

Knott, John Ray. *Milton's Pastoral Vision.* Chicago, 1971.

Kranidas, Thomas. *The Fierce Equation: A Study of Milton's Decorum.* The Hague, 1965.

Lawry, Jon S. *The Shadow of Heaven: Matter and Stance in Milton's Poetry.* Ithaca, 1968.
Lieb, Michael. *The Dialectics of Creation: Patterns of Birth and Regeneration in "Paradise Lost."* Amherst, 1970.
Leavis, F. R. "Milton's Verse." In his *Revaluation.* London, 1936.
———. "Mr. Eliot and Milton," and "In Defence of Milton." In his *The Common Pursuit.* London, 1952.
Lewalski, Barbara Kiefer. "Structure and the Symbolism of Vision in Michael's Prophecy, *PL*, XI–XII." *Philological Quarterly, 42* (1963), 25–35.
Lewis, C. S. *A Preface to "Paradise Lost."* London, 1942.
Lovejoy, Arthur O. "Milton and the Paradox of the Fortunate Fall." *ELH: A Journal of English Literary History, 4* (1937). Reprinted in his *Essays in the History of Ideas* (Baltimore, 1948) and in *Critical Essays on Milton from ELH* (Baltimore, 1969).
MacCaffrey, Isabel Gamble, *"Paradise Lost" as "Myth."* Cambridge, Mass., 1959.
McColley, Grant, "Milton's Dialogue on Astronomy: The Principal Immediate Sources." *PMLA, 52* (1937), 728–762.
———. *"Paradise Lost": An Account of Its Growth and Major Origins.* New York, 1963.
Madsen, William G. "The Idea of Nature in Milton's Poetry." In *Three Studies in the Renaissance.* New Haven, 1958.
———. "The Fortunate Fall in *Paradise Lost.*" *Modern Language Notes, 74* (1959), 103–105.
———. *From Shadowy Types to Truth.* New Haven, 1968.
Marshall, W. H. "*Paradise Lost*: Felix Culpa and the Problem of Structure." *Modern Language Notes, 76* (1961), 15–20.
Miriam Joseph, Sister. *Orthodoxy in Paradise Lost.* Quebec, 1954.
Murray, Patrick. *Milton: The Modern Phase. A Study of Twentieth-Century Criticism.* London, 1967.
Nicolson, Marjorie Hope. "The Spirit World of Milton and More." Studies in Philology, 22 (1925), 433–452.
———. "Milton and Hobbes." *Studies in Philology, 23* (1926), 405–433.
———. "The Telescope and Imagination." *Modern Philology, 32* (1935), 233–260.
Patrides, C. A. *Milton and the Christian Tradition.* Oxford, 1966.
Peter, John D. *A Critique of "Paradise Lost."* New York, 1960.
Pointon, Marcia R. *Milton and English Art.* Toronto, 1970.
Prince, F. T. *The Italian Element in Milton's Verse.* Oxford, 1954.
Quarnström, Gunnar. *The Enchanted Palace.* Stockholm, 1967. (On Milton and numerology see also Röstvig, below.)
Rajan, Balachandra. *"Paradise Lost" and the Seventeenth Century Reader.* London, 1962.
———. *The Lofty Rhyme: A Study of Milton's Major Poetry.* London, 1970.
Ricks, Christopher. *Milton's Grand Style.* Oxford, 1963.
Riggs, William G. *The Christian Poet in "Paradise Lost."* Berkeley, 1972.
Robins, Harry F. *If This Be Heresy: A Study of Milton and Origen.* Urbana, 1963.
Ross, Malcolm M. "Milton and the Protestant Aesthetic." In his *Poetry and Dogma.* New Brunswick, 1954.
———. *Milton's Royalism.* Ithaca, 1943.
Röstvig, Maren-Sofie. *The Hidden Sense.* New York, 1963.
Ryken, Leland. *The Apocalyptic Vision in "Paradise Lost."* Ithaca, 1970.
Samuel, Irene. *Plato and Milton.* Ithaca, 1947.
———. "Milton on Learning and Wisdom." *PMLA, 64* (1949), 708–723.
———. *Dante and Milton: The "Commedia" and "Paradise Lost."* Ithaca, 1966.
Schultz, Howard. *Milton and Forbidden Knowledge.* New York, 1955.
Sensabaugh, George F. *That Grand Whig, Milton.* Stanford, 1952.
Sewell, Arthur. *A Study in Milton's Christian Doctrine.* London, 1939.
Shawcross, John T. "The Balanced Structure of *Paradise Lost.*" *Studies in Philology, 62* (1965), 696–718.
Shumaker, Wayne. *Unpremeditated Verse: Feeling and Perception in "Paradise Lost."* Princeton, 1967.
Sims, James H. *The Bible in Milton's Epics.* Gainesville, 1962.
Spaeth, Sigmund G. *Milton's Knowledge of Music.* Ann Arbor, 1963.
Sprott, Ernest S. *Milton's Art of Prosody.* Oxford, 1958.
Steadman, John M. *Milton and the Renaissance Hero.* Oxford, 1967.
———. *Milton's Epic Characters.* Chapel Hill, 1968.
Stein, Arnold. *Answerable Style: Essays on "Paradise Lost."* Minneapolis, 1953.
Summers, Joseph H. *The Muse's Method: An Introduction to "Paradise Lost."* Cambridge, Mass., 1962.

Svendsen, Kester. *Milton and Science*. Cambridge, Mass., 1956.
Tillyard, E. M. W. *Studies in Milton*. London, 1951.
————. *The Miltonic Setting, Past and Present*. London, 1957.
Tuve, Rosemond. "Baroque and Mannerist Milton." *Journal of English and Germanic Philology*, 60 (1961), 817–833.
Waldock, A. J. *"Paradise Lost" and Its Critics*. Cambridge, 1947.
Watkins, W. B. C. *An Anatomy of Milton's Verse*. Baton Rouge, 1955.
Weber, Burton J. *The Construction of "Paradise Lost."* Carbondale, 1971.
West, Robert H. *Milton and the Angels*. Athens, Ga., 1955.
Whaler, James. "The Miltonic Simile." *PMLA*, 46 (1931), 1034–1074.
————. *Counterpoint and Symbol*. Copenhagen, 1956.
Whiting, G. W., and Ann Grossman. "Siloa's Brook, the Pool of Siloa, and Milton's Muse." *Studies in Philology*, 58 (1961), 193–205.
Williams, Charles. "Milton." In his *The English Poetic Mind*. Oxford, 1932.
Williamson, George. "The Education of Adam." *Modern Philology*, 61 (1963), 96–109.
Woodhouse, A. S. P. *The Heavenly Muse: A Preface to Milton*, ed. Hugh MacCallum. Toronto, 1972.
Wright, B. A. *Milton's "Paradise Lost."* London, 1962.